Supervision in Education

Supervision in Education

Problems and Practices

Daniel Tanner

Rutgers University

Laurel Tanner

Temple University

Macmillan Publishing Company
New York

Collier Macmillan Publishers
London

MACMILLAN PUBLISHING COMPANY
866 Third Avenue, New York, New York 10022

Collier Macmillan Canada, Inc.

Library of Congress Cataloging-in-Publication Data

Tanner, Daniel.
  Supervision in education.

  Includes bibliographies and index.
  1. School supervision—United States. I. Tanner,
Laurel N. II. Title.
LB2822.2.T36 1987   371.2   85-23932
ISBN 0-02-418950-2

Printing: 1 2 3 4 5 6 7   Year: 7 8 9 0 1 2 3

ISBN 0-02-418950-2

To: The American Teacher

Foreword

The importance of supervision, in its broadest sense, is well recognized as a crucial aspect of organized education. Thus, superintendents, principals, and others with specific titles as supervisors need insight and skill in helping teachers in their activities with children and youth. Yet, supervision as a theoretical and practical concern has received less consideration than it deserves. In *Supervision in Education* the Tanners have drawn upon basic and fundamental studies in a variety of disciplines and have reinterpreted these studies in their supervision context. The authors have contributed significantly to defining the field of supervision through a historical approach to the origins of supervision in relation to schooling and by giving continuing attention to the meaning of professionalism in the supervision field.

The authors have taken a historical stance and thus have presented a most useful perspective on the supervision field. This helps to bring together the theory and the methodology of supervision. While viewing supervision as being concerned with aiding teachers with both teaching and curriculum development, this textbook directs attention to the problems of teachers as the starting place for joint efforts of supervisors and teachers. The insistence on beginning with teacher problems rather than with an innovation, in improving curriculum and instruction, is a powerful idea. Teachers are viewed as capable independent professionals, and supervision is treated as a problem-solving approach to the related foci of teaching methodology and curriculum. The importance of the teacher having a vital role is stressed again and again. But, just as firmly, the position is taken that teachers must not be left on their own without professional help. While teachers are viewed as well-educated people, they need leadership in dealing with various problems they face.

Attention is given to the use and importance of research, yet there is no blind or doctrinaire acceptance of either past experience or research findings. Instead there is a continuing stress on a questioning attitude based on values of teachers, of supervisors, as well as of the schooling enterprise in which they are participants. In other words, careful interpretation of research findings, and sometimes a tryout locally of research findings, is necessary. Again the history of ideas, values, and practices is introduced to give perspective on many current issues.

Textbooks on supervision vary substantially in their focus and treatment of the field. Some are centered on the related literature in a range of supporting fields. Some texts have taken a work-book or cook-book approach with specific aids or routines for supervisors to use. This text is a comprehensive approach to the field, focused on the development of independent thinking on the part of supervisors as they continually face new conditions and changing circumstances. This book gives major attention to teachers and teaching as well as to curriculum development.

As has been noted, the concept of supervision is very broad. Many individuals in a school system may have supervisory leadership potential. Titles may vary, but the possibility for help to teachers is there. Thus, this book has value for superintendents, principals, and a host of others. Duties vary, but school systems today have a host of individuals who are assigned to working with teachers: helping teachers, department chairmen, special education supervisors, mainstreaming advisors, directors of education for the gifted, supervisors of bilingual programs, and others. This book is addressed to all of these and seeks to assist professionals in clarifying their leadership role.

Gordon N. Mackenzie
Professor Emeritus
Teachers College
Columbia University

Preface

The focus of this book is on educational supervision as a problem-solving process. The field of education has been vulnerable to shifting and conflicting tides for reform and counterreform in successive epochs, consequently the responses of professional educators have been largely reactive and defensive, rather than reconstructive. To demonstrate responsiveness, professional educators have been prone to seize upon segmental changes, improvisations, recipes, and innovations aimed at treating symptoms rather than the underlying causes of problems. The impression given is that of much movement in education, but movement is not necessarily indicative of progress. The key to progress lies in the problem-solving capacity of individuals and groups. The professionalization of a field derives from a cumulative tradition of knowledge and practice marshalled toward diagnosing and solving substantive problems. Obviously, such knowledgeable professional practice requires considerable autonomy and responsibility on the part of practitioners.

As discussed in Part I of this book, educational supervision has come a long way since its origins as the inspection of teaching. Nevertheless, in far too many school districts, supervision is regarded by teachers with aversion. Yet the attitude of teachers toward supervision is determined by the kind of supervision provided. If teachers see supervision as inspection for deficiencies or for conformance to externally imposed mandates, the professionalism of the teacher and the supervisor is diminished. In sharp contrast, when teachers see supervision as a developmental process of cooperative effort toward diagnosing and solving substantive problems in the classroom and school, they are more likely to seek supervisory assistance and their professionalism is enhanced enormously. The professionalization of supervision and of teaching hinges on the elimination of deficiency-oriented supervision in favor of a developmental approach.

Part II is focused on the administrative organization of supervision and supervisory roles and functions. The traditional confusion and conflict between administrative and supervisory roles and functions are resolved by seeing administration and supervision as vitally interdependent for the effective organizational functioning of the school and school system. The importance of a functional, organic form of organization is stressed as opposed to a mechanistic one. The former provides for open communication and flexibility in meeting emergent problems through a team approach, whereas the latter is hierarchical and segmental because it is geared to established or static conditions, and is characterized by a restrictive flow of communication. The hierarchical-segmental form of organization places teachers at the bottom. Yet teachers must perform the most crucial role in the educative function of the school since they are closest to the learners and are responsible for interpreting and implementing the curriculum. The problem of providing teachers with adequate material resources is examined along with the needed coordination of effort throughout the district for curricular and instructional improvement. The roles and functions of the superintendent, curriculum director, supervisor, and principal are examined to reveal their necessary interdependence in exercising democratic leadership responsibility. The traditional conflict between supervision as teacher inservice education and as teacher evaluation is addressed. The conflict is resolved when the key criteria for teacher evaluation include the teacher's readiness to expose problems, and to seek help with problem-solutions. Here the supervisor and the teacher see problems as opportunities, and not barriers, for educational improvement. An effective program of inservice education provides teachers with opportunities to overcome their isolation by sharing their problems and solutions as a total faculty, and to make a conjoint effort toward school-wide and district-wide educational improvement.

Part III examines in detail the theory and practice of educational supervision in terms of the ecology of the school and the climate for supervision, the various contrasting and conflicting models for supervision, research and practice on teacher effectiveness, and common classroom problems that must be addressed by teachers and supervisors. Principles from the body of research on teacher effectiveness are incorporated into a supervisor's checklist for educational problem-solving.

Also in Part III, the outmoded view of schooling as an established-convergent production process (like the factory) is contrasted against schooling as an emergent-developmental process. Four systems of supervisory organization are examined, namely (1) exploitive authoritative, (2) benevolent authoritative, (3) consultative, and (4) participative group (democratic). The authors see the participative-group system of organization as the appropriate environment for developmental supervision since it provides for the most open flow of communication, taps expertise at all levels in seeking problem-solutions, and allows for the widest possible sharing of professional responsibility and decision-making. Such a system cannot be said to exist unless the educative process is designed to provide students with the opportunity to develop the capability and commitment for intelligent self-direction and shared social responsibility.

The four models of supervision examined in Part III are (1) inspectional supervision, (2) production supervision, (3) clinical supervision, and (4) developmental supervision. The developmental approach to supervision was first proposed by the authors in *Curriculum Development: Theory Into Practice* (Macmillan 1975, 1980, 2nd edition). Of the four models of supervision, clinical supervision is most closely related to developmental supervision. Yet there are marked differences. Proponents of clinical supervision tend to see such supervision as appropriately delimited to instruction, while curriculum design, development, and evaluation are regarded as residing at higher levels of jurisdiction in the administrative structure. This obviously delimits and diminishes the professional role and responsibility of the supervisor and teacher. It also serves to segment curriculum from instruction when, in reality, problems in teaching cannot be treated effectively apart from the wider curricular and educational problems. In developmental supervision, educational improvement is treated as a holistic problem-solving process in which all elements of the educational situation are seen in their interdependence.

Although teacher effectiveness is addressed throughout this text, Chapter 7 in Part III is devoted to this topic and to the implications for supervision. The final chapter of Part III examines common classroom problems and the ways through which teachers and supervisors can work together in solving these problems.

Part IV examines the forces and sources for educational improvement, revealing how reform movements in education have been marshalled to a great extent as reactions to wider sociopolitical influences. The major national reports on educational policy and practice during the twentieth century are assessed to signify to the administrator, supervisor, and teacher why it is incumbent upon them to subject externally proposed remedies to systematic evaluation based on local school conditions and in the light of a sound philosophical outlook. It is shown in Part IV how too many schools function at an imitative-maintenance level of "knowledge/ability" or, at best, at the mediative-adaptive level of "knowledge/ability." In such schools, the orientation toward change is segmental, decision-making is not widely shared, and there is the tendency to be concerned with maintaining established practice or modifying established practice so as to conform to dominant external pressures or fashions. How schools can be transformed so as to function at the generative-creative level of "knowledge/ability" is one of the central concerns of this book. In such schools, administrators, supervisors, and teachers are devoted to optimizing conditions through problem-diagnosis and problem-solving. Decision-making on educational policy and practice is widely shared, and there is full and open communication. Changes in any part of the system are made with the fullest consideration of possible ramifications throughout the system. A paradigm for educational improvement is presented to show how administrators, supervisors, and teachers can utilize key criteria to guide their efforts in improving their schools. The use of the paradigm in assessing the worth of external proposals for educational reform is also demonstrated.

"What the supervisor should know about the curriculum" is the theme of Part V. Specific illustrations are provided to show how educational improvement cannot be effected on any significant scale without conscious attention to building a coherent curriculum design. Subject specialists must give concerted attention to how their fields relate to the total program of studies, and to the life of the learner in a free society. The various functions of the curriculum need to be treated in their complementarity rather than in opposition. Unfortunately, our schools have suffered from the tendency to embark on educational improvement on an *ad hoc* or piecemeal basis, and without due consideration as to how given measures relate to the entire curriculum. Decisions are made without any real conceptual basis for curriculum design and development. In Part V systematic attention is given to the several alternative curriculum designs in connection with the various functions of the curriculum.

Finally, Part VI is targeted on staff development and school improvement. Chapter 13 is devoted to inservice education. The culminating chapter of the book shows how a comprehensive and specific set of developmental criteria can be used for school evaluation and renewal. The criteria are organized according to (1) the climate for supervision, (2) supervisory roles and functions, (3) teacher effectiveness and classroom climate, (4) inservice education/staff development, (5) philosophy of the school, (6) administrative policy and practice, (7) innovations and reforms, (8) curriculum development, and (9) teaching-learning resources, facilities, and services.

Each chapter of the text concludes with a list of problems for study and discussion, designed to stimulate the student to examine the implications of central ideas and issues. The bibliography accompanying each chapter has been selected to guide the student to explore a wide range of references and resources in education and the behavioral sciences having significant bearings on educational supervision.

Our work on this book has been helped immeasurably through both formal and informal discussions with a number of individuals. We are indebted to Gordon N. Mackenzie, Professor Emeritus, Teachers College, Columbia University, and to Dean Gary A. Griffin of the University of Illinois at Chicago for their systematic reviews and suggestions, chapter by chapter, during the preparation of the book. At the time when the authors were conceptualizing the plan for this book, Arthur W. Foshay, Professor Emeritus, Teachers College, Columbia University, provided invaluable suggestions in identifying the major topics to be included. We are grateful to Ralph W. Tyler, Director Emeritus of the Center for Advanced Study in the Behavioral Sciences and N. L. Gage of the Center for Educational Research at Stanford University, who shared their ideas so generously with the authors. Professor E. Edmund Reutter, Jr. of Teachers College, Columbia University, deserves special thanks for providing the authors with valuable materials on personnel administration and school law. Informal discussions with Professor Leroy C. Olson of the College of Education, Temple University, have been most helpful in providing insights into some significant supervisory problems. Our appreciation is expressed to Marion Ann Keller for typing the manuscript.

D.T.
L.T.

Contents

Supervision in Education

Part I

The Emergent Field of Educational Supervision

Chapter 1

The Evolution of Supervision

"Once upon a time the classroom teacher was required to provide school buildings, pupils, books, materials and instruction," began the storyteller. "Since those primitive days there has developed a department of school activity called administration whose primary function is to provide everything which will improve classroom teaching." The storyteller went on to explain that supervision is a function of school administration for improving instruction and, further, that its potential is yet to be realized.[1]

The storyteller was W. W. Charters at the University of Illinois. The time was 1918, the viewpoint progressive. Although begun humorously in fairy-tale fashion, his thumbnail sketch of the marked change in the public schools in the course of almost 300 years is entirely accurate. More important for us as the year 2000 draws nearer is that although great educational gains have been made by the development of school systems, professional supervision continues to miss its opportunity for constructive leadership in educational problem solving. This book examines the supervisor's opportunity (and responsibility) for educational leadership.

All professions have associated with them certain functions. Education in the United States is an organized enterprise that expends billions of dollars annually. Supervision is needed to assure that this money is being used most effectively in the interests of children. In any given school system, it is necessary that there be unity of purpose. This is possible only through supervision. Teachers need to be kept alert to the best work that is being done in other school systems. This is a function of supervision. Supervisors and teachers must diagnose and solve problems of common concern. Supervisors have the leadership responsibility in dealing with problem situations.

3

THE IMPORTANCE OF EARLY IDEAS

The functions of supervision evolved with the development of the public school system, its problems and its opportunities. Moreover, the development of public education and the field of supervision are so completely intertwined that they defy separation, even for purposes of analysis. The story of totally supported public schools, for example, is one of educational leadership, and leadership is the underlying concept of supervision. Nevertheless, supervision is a professional field in its own right and, as such, has a history of its own. (The evolution of a profession is its history.) Supervisors need to see their professional task in vital relationship to the great achievements already made in the field and the problems and difficulties that still face them.

Early Ideas as Limitations

The evolution of a profession is continual. The concept of professionalism implies readiness to replace any theoretical idea or practice, no matter how time-honored, with one found to be more valid. Yet, this principle is often violated and inherited outlooks and practices continue to operate. This is one of supervision's great problems. If supervisors are to build on earlier practical and theoretical knowledge, they must understand the traditions that limit this development.

Early Ideas as Useful Knowledge

Not all of the early ideas in the field are outmoded outlooks. As J. D. Bernal, the late scientist and historian of science, pointed out about science, the opinions of men of the past have a greater relevance than is usually realized.[2] The idea of the atom, for example, runs through the course of development from the Greeks to the modern physicist. Bernal emphasized that the past still lives in physics and many of the old ideas are still useful. This is no less true of the field of supervision. The point is that the evolution of professional supervision is an integral part of the knowledge of the supervisor. This chapter attempts to show how present-day supervision emerged as a field of professional practice.

Lay Control: An Enduring Tradition

A characteristic of education in the United States is the delegation by the states of management and administration of public schools to local school districts. The public, through boards of education, sets policy; and the profession, through administrators and teachers, conducts the schools and determines the nature of instruction. Thus we speak of *public control* of the school and the *professional prerogative* to determine teaching practice. Yet, as anyone knows, public control extends into the realm of instruction. Consider the widespread concern of the 1970s and early 1980s over falling test scores, which were blamed on the educational innovations of the 1960s. In many school systems, judgments on the adequacy of the school's performance by parents and nonparent citizens led to an impoverished curriculum through "back-to-basics" and an emphasis on low-level cognitive processes (those most easily measured).

In a democratic society, the public must have a voice in the control of the schools, including what is taught and how it is taught. The high expectations of the public for education are a positive force for school improvement and one that professionals have yet to marshal effectively. One way that they can begin to do so is by communicating educational problems to the public along with possible solutions. Lay people expect this kind of leadership from professionals. Public concern can be translated into public support just as easily as into an attack on the schools.

Still, if professional workers are to understand the attitude toward public control and supervision that lives on in the American people as a tradition, and make better judgments about it in concrete situations, they need to know just how it began. We turn now to the patterns of public supervision established in the colonial period.

SUPERVISION IN THE COLONIAL PERIOD

Stories about the colonial schoolmaster—Washington Irving's "The Legend of Sleepy Hollow" is the quintessential example—tend to one conclusion: that the teacher of the colonial period was his own boss. In fact, however, even the first schoolmasters in seventeenth-century New York had to be licensed to teach. Dutch schoolmasters in New Amsterdam were given detailed instructions for their task, which were drawn up by the burgomasters and dealt with such matters as the opening of school, daily program, curriculum, and pupil discipline. The specificity of these directions certainly implies some kind of supervision, though probably not systematic, as it does not appear in the public records. We do know that public catechizing of school children by schoolmasters was required by law, as a check on the religious teaching of the school.[3]

The teacher of the town school in New England was chosen by the public through its town meeting or a committee and was subjected to supervision by the minister or special committees. Throughout the colonies, the purposes, policies, curriculum (including teaching methods), and standards of the public school (a school existing by government authority) were determined not by the teacher but by governing boards. They often expended a great deal of effort to see that the teacher lived up to expectations.

"Teachers in American schools financed partially or wholly at public expense have never been completely free from supervision and control," noted Elsbree in his classic book, *The American Teacher.*[4]

Public Supervision

Throughout the colonies, supervision was by lay assessment. The principle that government could control and supervise schools through management by public officials was enunciated in the famous Massachusetts law of 1647 requiring towns to establish schools. Quite naturally, the responsibility fell on the town selectmen. They were instructed by the town to visit the schools and make reports to the town. Thus the first purpose of supervision was to determine whether children were being given instruction as required by law. The means was school visitation. An entry in the selectmen's records at Billerica, Massachusetts, in 1668 states that they "appoint the next day to go the rounds to examine the teaching of children and youth according to law."[5]

Some towns did not leave the matter of supervision entirely to the selectmen or a committee. In Boston on March 29, 1734, it was voted "that the several Writing Masters in the Town, do present, at the next General Town Meeting, some of their own performances in writing for the Town's Inspection."[6]

Prominence of the Clergy. The most characteristic visiting committee in New England towns during the colonial period was one composed of selectmen, ministers, and prominent citizens. The clergy played a leading role in the supervision of schools. This is often attributed to the dominantly religious purpose and content of education, but perhaps it is well to emphasize that the minister was one of the few well-educated individuals in the colonies and, as such, was much in demand to evaluate the work of teachers. Moreover, although the civil government exercised authority over education from the beginning in the American colonies, the minister was a public official. (In the colonial period, church and state were closely allied, and the minister was supported by taxes.) The official duties of the minister did not end until the state-controlled school systems took root well within the nineteenth century. Separation of church and state had been a majority viewpoint since the end of the eighteenth century, but there are accounts of visitation by ministers in Connecticut at least as late as the 1840s.[7] The tradition died hard.

School Visiting in New England: Purposes and Practices

Cremin observes that in New England, parents and taxpayers had a voice in school policymaking that was less common in England.[8] It should be added that in the colonial period in New England, school systems, with their administrative and supervisory machinery, were unknown. Thus the public did more than determine policy; townsmen, through their school committees, also inspected and directed the schools. Public responsibility for management and supervision of schools is shown clearly in the Boston town records. Among the most interesting and illuminating are the accounts on school visiting. The purposes and procedures of school supervision were couched in these terms in 1710:

> We further propose and recommend, as of Great Service and Advantage for the promoting of Diligence and good literature, That the Town, Agreeably to the Usage in England, and (as we understand) in Some time past practiced here, Do nominate and Appoint a Certain Number of Gentlemen, of Liberal Education, Together with Some of Ye Rev[d] Ministers of the Town, to be Inspectors of the S[d] Schools. . . . To Visit y[e] School from time to time . . . to Enform themselves of the methods used in teaching of y[e] Schollars and to Inquire of their proficiency, and be present at the performance of Some of their Exercises, the Master being before Notified of their Comeing, And with him to consult and Advise of further Methods for x[e] Advancement of Learning and the Good Government of the Schools.[9]

Appraisal of Pupil Progress. As noted, the dominant purpose of school visitation was to determine whether children were being given an education as required by law. Then, as now, the principal means of determining whether teachers lived up to expectations was to appraise pupil progress. In the absence of achievement tests this was often done by what was called an "examination" on the last day of school; the master exhibited the oral and written accomplishments of the children and the visitation committee put questions of their own. However, some towns required more frequent inspection of the schools. The dates were fixed by the town (such as the last Wednesday in every quarter), and it seems clear that the practice of informing the master before the visit was common.

Improvement of Teaching and Learning. But another purpose of visitation, which persists to this day, was the improvement of teaching. Methods of teaching should move people away from conditions of ignorance and toward higher levels of civilization. Colonial intellectuals believed in human progress, particularly progress in the arts and sciences.[10] Schools were seen as the instrument of progress. A careful reading of the foregoing citation from the Boston records shows that the objective of supervision was qualitative and progressive: the advancement of learning. Similarly, in 1714 in Connecticut, school visitors were "required to give such directions as they find needful to render schools most serviceable to the increase of that *knowledge,* civility, and religion which is designed in the erecting of them. . . ."[11] (Interestingly, knowledge was listed as the first purpose of schooling—religion, last. Secularism was on the rise.)

Unhappily, some towns were negligent about school matters. Committee members were frequently derelict in their duty, paying little attention to the schools. Even in Boston, some extrinsic motivation was apparently needed to get the committee to perform their duty. In 1733, a dinner was provided by the town for the visitors of the schools (schoolmasters were also invited), and the dinner readily became established as a custom. Although discontinued during the Revolutionary War, the visitation dinners were resumed in 1781 with the surrender of Cornwallis and the approach of peace.[12]

Supervision in the Southern Colonies

The southern colonies followed the pattern in England, where the Church of England controlled and supervised schools; civil authorities paid less attention to educational matters than in New England. The chief educational involvement of the colonial assembly of Virginia (followed by the other southern colonies) was the apprenticeship act of 1642, which asserted the authority of the states to see to it that poor children were apprenticed and taught a trade. In Maryland, however, the state did take the initiative in founding a system of free schools for poor children. Such an effort was made by an act of 1723 which envisioned one free school for each county, which would be supervised by a county board of visitors and supported by public funds. Several schools were established, but the counties were less willing than the New England towns to continue their support in a colony where Protestants and Catholics were warring factions.[13] (Maryland had tried to bring about a truce through multiple establishment of religion. This did not bode well for public education; it was all but impossible to establish a public school system when each religious group could share in public funds.)

Supervision in Maryland: Minutes of the Visitors. How did the visitors of the county schools in Maryland view their supervisory role and responsibility? An excellent account of the supervision in the first free school in Queen Anne's County, Maryland, was provided by Brown from the minutes of the meetings of the visitors.[14] He reported that the visitors, who were the leading men of the county during the colonial period, "considered going to school a serious business and would allow nothing to interfere with it if they could possibly help. They required that the 'hours of teaching from the 1st of April to the last of September be from 7 o'clock to 11 in the morning and from 1 o'clock to 5 in the evening and from the last of September to the 1st of April from 8 o'clock to 11 in the morning and from 1 o'clock until 4 in the evening.' " Brown finds no mention of holidays or vacation for the first fifty years—from the time school was opened in 1724 until May 1775.[15]

The character of supervision is shown clearly in this incident related by Brown:

> Upon one occasion the "visitor observing the scholars shooting at marks with guns had them called together and admonished and ordered them not to bring guns to school again and also in their presence order the master to have strict attention to them in their playtime, and to punish any who shall be catched contrary to this order." At the same time "observing most of the scholars pronounce badly" they "order the master to be particularly attentive to make them express their words and syllables as distinct and clear as possible" and they "advise and admonish the scholars to use their utmost endeavors to break themselves of the bad habit which they have heretofore contracted in uttering their words in a thick confused manner."[16]

The Primacy of Instructional Improvement. The master in the incident above, Luther Martin, paid little attention to the school, was reprimanded in the presence of the pupils, and finally left the county. Martin came to fame as a lawyer—the one who defended Aaron Burr. In this period, teaching was often regarded as temporary employment (the same problem exists today but to a lesser degree). But the point of importance here is that the visitors viewed their chief supervisory function as the improvement of teaching and, furthermore, they considered themselves qualified both to make judgments about the worth of teaching and to improve the teacher's method. The incident reported by Brown also illustrates how ingrained in American thought is the belief that lay persons are able to render accurate judgments about good teaching.

Legacy from the Colonial Period

Building a new society with public responsibility for schooling was an experience without precedent in the world. Thus the nature of supervision of public schools had to be worked out by the colonists from their own experience. Granted that lay sponsorship and control of grammar schools was current in England at the time of American colonization, and the idea was not unknown to the colonists, and granted that schooling in England was becoming increasingly available.[17] But the English concept of lay supervision and control underwent significant adaptations on American soil. Present in America almost from the start was the requirement of compulsory education of children; whereas in England the Poor Law of 1601 authorized parishes to undertake responsibility for the apprenticeship of poor children, the Massachusetts General Court of 1647 went further, requiring the establishment of schools so that all children would be taught to read and write. Although the purpose of education for all may have been pragmatic—the survival of the state depended on good citizens with the basic essentials of education—the ultimate result was a shift away from the concept of education as an aristocratic privilege and toward a widely available education to be achieved by public control.

Americans are proud of their heritage of educational opportunity for all. From the beginning, supervisors were concerned with the responsibility of seeing to it that parents send their children to school. The responsibility of providing educational opportunities for all children in accord with the law was a marked departure from the responsibility of English governing boards; England did not promote education as a public and civil matter; education was private, entrepreneurial, and tied to social class. This is not to say that class differences were left behind by the colonists, but that they became less distinct by dint of the democracy present in New England towns (a liberal land policy meant that most men could become property owners and thus voters)—including the requirement that all children attend the town schools.

We have pointed out that one of the dominant traditions in American education, lay involvement in educational affairs, began in early colonial America. Although in England only citizens of note were likely to sit on school governing boards, in the colonies the matter of schools was often left to selectmen who could not write. Increasingly in the eighteenth century, school matters were delegated to special committees,[18] but it is important to understand clearly that the people have been concerned with the conduct of schools since the colonial period.

In addition to the traditions of providing children and youth with opportunities for a good education and public supervision and approval of schools, there is another important supervisory concept that has been inherited from colonial times: improvement of instruction as the goal of supervision. It is fascinating, indeed, that many supervisors in early colonial America defined their role in terms of improving the quality of education rather than narrowly, as that of establishing and maintaining the schools required by the laws. This indicates that supervisors did more than believe in the American dream; they believed that the future was amenable to human effort and set about to make the dream come true. (This is not to say that there was not indifference to the laws, or even defiance of them, but that concern for improving education for the sake of human progress was clearly evident among colonial supervisors.)

SUPERVISION IN THE EARLY YEARS OF THE REPUBLIC

The Revolutionary War sparked few, if any, immediate changes in the supervision of schools. For some decades after the founding of the new republic, school boards exercised supervision of teachers and pupils in much the same manner as before the war. This is not surprising, as the tradition of lay supervision had of course become well established by the time of the Revolution. A new and distinctively American system of educational thought and practice was in the making, but the quality of supervision would not improve appreciably between 1776 and 1865.

The Battle for Public Education: A Supervisory War

If one were to judge by supervisory methods alone, not much happened in the early years of the republic that is worthy of mention. But there were, nevertheless, important landmarks in the evolution of supervision in this period. The establishment of state control and supervision, achieved in the great battle for state schools, is an enormously important landmark. The methods of supervision, after all, depend on organization and a structure within which to work. In actuality, the question of supervision is reflected in the long and bitter fight to subordinate local systems, which had already developed, to oversight and control by the state. Education was neglected in many free schools after the Revolution (in Massachusetts, for example) and private establishments began to take the lead. State supervision saved the free schools from decline into a pauper system just in time.

The most important advances in the improvement of teachers in this period were made in the cities. Elsbree observed that "the tasks confronting city school boards were so time-consuming and so difficult that delegation of the instructional phase of school administration to professional educators seemed expedient."[19] Thus Buffalo and Louisville established the office of superintendent in 1837. St. Louis, Providence, Rochester, and New Orleans followed soon after. Superintendents did the work of supervision, devoting nearly all of their time to visiting schools. Their supervisory techniques, and those of the school principal, are considered later.

There were other innovations as well. The graded system of schools (which brought important changes in the teacher's scope of responsibility) and the organization of educators into local, state, and national associations for professional improvement took place in the decades before the Civil War. But most important of all was the realization that the teacher makes the school, which led to much discussion about teacher qualifications and stimulated the development of public normal schools. Supervision is intimately concerned with the movement to professionalize education, which is never-ending.

The Jeffersonian Ideal. Thomas Jefferson saw with remarkable clarity the central role of education in the preservation of a free society. "Above all things," he wrote from Paris in 1787 in a letter to James Madison, "I hope the education of the common people will be attended to; convinced that on their good sense we may rely with the most security for the preservation of a due degree of liberty."[20]

Each of the early presidents was deeply interested in universal education as a support for the republic, as shown in their writings. However, Jefferson's proposals for education actually forecast the future pattern of educational reform for the new nation. In 1779, Jefferson proposed a complete system of public education for the state of Virginia, from elementary school through the state university. But the state of Virginia was not ready to begin public education at either the higher or lower levels. Jefferson kept trying, and the University of Virginia eventually made its magnificent appearance. Jefferson truly fathered the university, selecting the site, planning the buildings, and deciding what should be taught.

But although our nation's leaders wrote and spoke memorably about the crucial role of education in the life of a republic, our systems of public schools were very slow in developing. A number of states included provisions for public education in their early constitutions, but it would be the middle of the nineteenth century before the ideal of the public school was widely in practice.

In Pennsylvania, for example, the constitution of 1776 included a provision for establishing a school system for all. But the provision was changed in the constitution of 1790 to establishing schools so "that the poor may be taught gratis." The law, providing instruction only for children who were too poor to pay for it, established a system of class education that was in violation of the republican ideal that opportunity must be equal. Not until 1834 was a general system of education established in Pennsylvania. And even then the new school law was fiercely attacked by people who opposed free schools. For months it seemed almost certain to be repealed. But public education had gained a foothold and would not be flung back.

There is often a lag of years, decades, and even centuries between the declaration of ideals by great men and women and their realization. Such was the case of public education being made truly available to all.

The Monitorial System of Instruction. As any teacher or supervisor knows, the field of education is vulnerable to fads. Suddenly, a new method of school organization or instruction is greeted with enthusiasm. And just as suddenly, the excitement dies down. The idea, eventually found defective, soon dies. The Gary Plan, the Dalton Plan, performance contracting and the open school were once viewed widely as educational panaceas, but went the way of all fads. Now they belong only to history. Imported from England, the monitorial, or Lancasterian system of instruction (originated by Joseph Lancaster) may be properly viewed as an educational fad of the early nineteenth century. The main features of the plan were a large number of youngsters (from 200 to 1,000 in one room) seated in rows, with each row of ten pupils assigned to a bright youngster, called a monitor. The teacher taught the monitor a reading or an arithmetic lesson, and then the monitors taught the lesson to their charges. This system of education wsa extremely popular from about 1815–1830. Then its defects became obvious, and by 1840 it was all but dead. (It continued in partial use in New York City until 1853.)

That it was a passing enthusiasm should not be taken to mean that monitorial instruction had no influence on the development of supervision. It was a minutely detailed system, complete with instruction manuals. Teachers were expected to follow instructions down to the last detail. The idea of a system of instruction was (and still is) attractive to many educators—teachers and supervisors alike. As Kaestle pointed out, "Lancaster popularized the idea of a uniform system of instruction and, in America, the broader concept of organized systems of schools."[21]

As noted, in Pennsylvania the constitution of 1790 provided for the establishment of pauper schools at public expense. The Lancasterian system of education made it possible to establish a better and less expensive system of elementary schools for poor children in Philadelphia than the one then in operation (charity and pay schools with a limited number of places for paupers). A law passed by the Pennsylvania legislature in 1818 established free schools in Philadelphia, in which the Lancasterian system of instruction was to be used. (Joseph Lancaster was invited to come over from England to help in implementing the law.) But the schools were open only to poor children, until after the law of 1818 was amended in 1836 so that all children were admitted without distinction. The monitorial pauper school was the predecessor of the public school in Philadelphia and New York City. Significantly, the Lancasterian system of education was abandoned in the Philadelphia schools the same year they were opened to all youngsters, rich and poor alike. As Cubberley observed about the monitorial system: "It was born in poverty, and poverty was ever its best excuse for being."[22]

Cubberley noted that the monitorial system awakened the interest of the public in free schools and hastened the adoption of free public school systems by accustoming people to the necessary taxation.[23] It also pointed to the need for teacher training. (Lancaster placed great emphasis on teacher training.) The Lancasterian Model Schools that were established in 1818, and provided pedagogical courses and supervised student teaching, were the forerunners of our normal schools. And finally, the monitorial system was a step toward total class instruction, instead of individual instruction. (Before the monitorial movement, the time-honored method of instruction was the master hearing individuals recite, one by one, which was a slow and expensive process.)

That the monitorial system did all these things should not obscure its great defect. It was mechanical, and suitable only for producing automatons, not for developing the self-directing citizens of a republic. Moreover, a new educational psychology was being born that stressed observation of natural objects and talking about what was seen instead of parrotlike repetitions of someone else's words. These ideas were largely the contribution of the Swiss reformer Johann Pestalozzi (1746–1827) and are dealt with in the next chapter. The monitorial system may be dead, but the bombardment of supervisors by machinelike plans of education (like the monitorial system, impressive because of their alleged efficiency) is a continuing problem in education.

Local Versus Centralized Control: The District System. As suggested earlier, in New England education actually declined greatly during the first half-century of the republic. The problem was the district system of school organization and control. In 1789, Massachusetts legally recognized the school district, which simply took account of the system that had evolved since people began moving out into the country a hundred years earlier. Since their needs could not be met by one town school, a way had to be found to establish and maintain local schools in different parts of the township. District schools were the way of meeting their needs. Under the law of 1789, the town school committee was recognized as the agency for control and supervision of schools. The committee had two main tasks: hiring teachers and visiting schools. In 1800 the districts were given the power to tax for schools, and by 1827 they were given power to select their textbooks and employ and certify their teachers. The New England states generally adopted the district system, and New Englanders carried it with them as they migrated to other parts of the country. It rapidly spread and became the prevailing form of school organization and control. As Cubberley quipped, "Starting as a social institution, the school district had now evolved into a political institution."[24]

It is not difficult to see why the district system was so popular. It met the needs of a sparse and rural population in an era when intercommunication was difficult and the question of school support by taxation was still unresolved. The power and control of the state were kept distant. A community that wanted a school could organize a district, vote to levy a tax on their property, build a schoolhouse, hire a teacher, and maintain the school. The major merit of the district system lay in its potential. Parents who placed a high value on education could give the school strength and life by their interest in the school and their direct control.

The problem was that localities (like individuals) differ in their interest in schools and in their ability to pay for them. Inequities were inevitable. In many Massachusetts districts, resistance to taxation resulted in economy as the main objective of school policy, and school standards rapidly deteriorated. One of the most persistent problems of educational administration and supervision had made its appearance: centralization versus decentralization.

A vicious circle was in operation in Massachusetts from 1789 to 1830, and it threatened the very existence of the free public schools. Parents had lost confidence in the free schools and were establishing academies and private schools. This, in turn, had led to further neglect of the schools. The problem was the district system of school administration, which was incapable of equalizing educational opportunity and seemed to be degenerating into a pauper school system. The alarm was sounded by a young teacher named James G. Carter, who in a series of published letters and essays recounted the history of legislation relating to free public schools in Massachusetts. Carter reminded the public of their proud educational heritage; in the colonial period the legislature had laid the basic foundations for a truly universal educational system. Later, under the district system, it had abdicated its educational leadership role. The schools had received almost no legislative attention for more than forty years, but the legislature had provided aid for the establishment of private schools. The result, said Carter, was an educational subsidy for the well-to-do rather than for the mass of people who needed it; probably not more than 2 percent of the people could afford the expense of tuition (if, indeed, they were admitted to academies and private schools). "Hence," wrote Carter:

> if any measures are to be taken, or any appropriations to be made by the legislature for the diffusion of knowledge generally, it should seem that the free schools demand their first attention. They are the foundation not only of our whole system of public instruction, but of all our free institutions.[25]

Carter's campaign had direct results. An act was passed in 1826 to strengthen town (opposed to district) control of education. Each town (township) was required to appoint annually a school committee (school board) of not fewer than five persons to supervise and manage all the district schools in the town. The school board, which was to be comprised of lay citizens rather than ministers or professional teachers, was to visit and certify all public school teachers. The law was bitterly opposed by many districts as being an infringement on their "rights."

STRENGTHENING THE ROLE OF THE STATE IN THE SUPERVISION OF SCHOOLS

The abuses of the district system were by no means eliminated by strengthening town control. Carter believed that unless the state regained the power and authority which it had lost years before by bad legislation (the law of 1789), supervision and the quality of instruction would not improve. Carter's approach to strengthening state authority for education was bold and effective. He got himself elected to the legislature. In 1837, as chairman of the Massachusetts House Committee on Education, Carter obtained passage of a bill creating the first state board of education in the United States. Among the multiple problems faced by Horace Mann, the new secretary, were the violations of the law of 1826. In two-thirds of the towns, persons were teaching without being certified by the school committee, and schools were not being visited as required by law. During his twelve years as secretary, Mann issued twelve annual reports to the state board of education, which are remarkably insightful (now, as then) discussions of the purposes and problems of public schools. His condemnation of the district system in his *Fourth Report* ultimately led to state control of education and the responsibility of the state to supervise and improve the quality of the schools.

Yet, as Cremin reminds us, "no one was more aware than Mann that in local public interest, the schools had their greatest strength," and that, for Mann, the answer to the neglect of schools by their communities "lay not in the *substitution* of state for local authority. It lay in the invigoration of local interest."[26] Much of Mann's time was spent on starting a school revival movement in Massachusetts. He was so successful in regenerating the schools and in designing a system of universal schooling there that he influenced the development of education in state after state.

Conditions in Connecticut schools were, if anything, worse than they were in Massachusetts. A survey, conducted in 1838, found that less than one-half of Connecticut's children were attending school. "From probably the best schools of any state at the end of the colonial period, the Connecticut schools had fallen to a very inferior position," noted Cubberley.[27] Connecticut's history of school support was somewhat different than that of Massachusetts. In 1795, Connecticut enriched its state school fund with an enormous grant from the sale of its "Western Reserve" (public lands in northeastern Ohio). Interest from this well-managed fund paid a sizable portion of the cost of maintaining schools. There was too much confidence in the fund and people became negligent about raising money for their schools from taxation. At the same time, the growing power of the district system led to a decline of interest in the schools. In 1821 the state tax was terminated, and for a third of a century schools in Connecticut were supported almost totally by income from the fund.

The effect of this arrangement on the schools was devastating. Most schools were in session only two or three months a year, teachers received paltry salaries (based on what the fund would pay for), buildings and equipment were inadequate (sometimes schools were closed for days for want of fuel), and the schools were rarely visited as the law required. Private schools were on the increase and a pauper-school system was being proposed. The great educational reformer Henry Barnard took a runaway bull by the horns and campaigned to reinstate local taxation and use the interest from the fund simply to develop and finance special programs. But the resistance to tax-supported schools from rural and property interests was long and bitter, and it was 1854 before state taxation was reinstated and the power of "school societies" (as districts were called in Connecticut) was curtailed.

State Aid and State Supervision

State aid was an important factor in the development of state systems of education. Communities had to meet state requirements to receive state funds. States required a local tax in proportion to the state aid received, and they had other requirements as well. One of the earliest was that a school term of a certain length must be provided. But however important school finance may have been, it was not the whole of school administration. Someone had to enforce the state's demands. This meant supervision.

"The want of a general supervisory power in some individual functionary, with qualifications adapted to the peculiar duty of improving the system and keeping every part of it in healthy exercise," was properly recognized in Connecticut in 1831.[28] (The case of Connecticut is not unique, but it is instructive.) The legislature was aware that the general condition of the schools was deplorable, but legislative action to improve the schools had to be based on information about the actual condition of the schools. Any question—whether about curriculum, or the books used, or the successes and failures of the schools—led again and again to incomplete answers and an unsafe basis for legislative action. Thus, to determine existing conditions, the legislature conducted a survey of local school boards, but it received responses (many of them incomplete or useless) from only two-thirds of the districts.

Legislators came away from this experience even more convinced of the importance of the inquiries, and the importance of "a legal provision for obtaining full and correct answers."[29] In 1839, Connecticut created a state board of education whose duties were to collect and diffuse school information and make recommendations to the legislature. Barnard was elected its first secretary. The office, under Barnard, grew in stature, as it had in Massachusetts under Mann.

It is important to understand clearly that one reason why educational reformers sought state supervision was the poor quality of supervision at the local level. In many districts, the visitors went through the motions of overseeing and directing the schools, simply to avoid being charged with neglect. A widely circulated pamphlet on the condition of Connecticut common (public) schools described the supervisory visits as follows:

> They merely enter the school, spend a short time in hearing brief recitations in the various branches, and just glancing at the writing books, slates and children; then, after making a few common-place remarks, they retire. . . . These visits seldom occupy more than one-fourth of a day, while it is impossible to form a just estimate of most schools in so short a time. In some instances, the visitors make it a point to visit three schools in half a day![30]

The Certification of Teachers

In general, the way teachers were examined and hired in Connecticut exemplified more or less what happened in other states. Not only did the licensing procedure fail to protect the public against incompetent teachers, but it was terribly demeaning for the teacher. A teacher's term of office lasted only one year. He or she had to be examined annually and receive a "bran new" certificate before going into the classroom again. At the NEA meeting in 1872, John Swett, who worked to establish free public schools in California, strongly attacked the system of lay certification. Swett described his personal experience with the method as a teacher in San Francisco in the 1850s. (Swett later became state superintendent of public instruction.)

> Fifteen of us, all in a row, like good little boys in school, were questioned "once round" in arithmetic, "once round" in grammar, "once round" in geography, "once round" in spelling, by the Superintendent and the Mayor—the former a Vermont Yankee, and the latter like unto him, except he hailed from a city nigh unto Boston, where they gibbeted witches instead of teachers.
>
> I was told I ranked first of the batch; and of course somebody else, who had "influence with the board" got the place. The successful somebody this time was a young doctor without patients. He soon resigned, and I was allowed the privilege, at $125 a month, of conquering a peace by subduing the young hoodlums, or of meeting the fate of my predecessor.
>
> This was how I became a schoolmaster, and how I won my way into the noblest profession. I think that is what they call it sometimes in educational conventions.
>
> For eight successive years I taught the same school, and—I am ashamed to own it, and would not tell it were it not necessary to illustrate what I intend to present—I had the cowardice, like other teachers with me, to submit to eight annual examinations, in order to determine my fitness, at each annual revolution of the sun, to teach the same school each succeeding school year. . . . Much as I honor the occupation of teaching, I am not in love with a system that tends to take all the manliness out of a man, and all the independence from a woman.[31]

Swett told the NEA how, under the strain of studying for the annual examination a *ninth* time, he contracted typhoid fever, from which he nearly died. While he was convalescing, Swett vowed to reform the examination system in California. His account of these reforms is fascinating, for it illustrates the pattern that was followed in the development of a state system of examinations managed by city, county, and township boards of examiners.

> So I left the school-room, went into political conventions, secured a nomination for the only office ever open to a schoolmaster, that of State Superintendent of Public Instruction, stumped the State, won two successive elections . . . framed a school law; established free schools; lobbied legislatures; secured legal recognition of professional teachers; abolished the New England annual-examination farce . . . placed the examination of teachers throughout the State exclusively in the hands of experienced teachers, thereby ruining the occupation and the glory of many a learned committeeman; secured life diplomas for experienced and capable teachers; gained a legal recognition of the normal school diplomas of all State normal schools in the United States; and, by law, made valid in California the life diplomas and State certificates granted to teachers by other States.[32]

At the time when Swett was addressing the NEA, no state except California legally recognized the normal-school diplomas of other states. Swett put forth a proposal for reform of state certification systems, modeled on the progressive lines of the California system. Today, a number of states offer reciprocity in the certification of teachers who are graduates of colleges and universities accredited by the National Commission on Accreditation of Colleges of Teacher Education (NCATE). As Swett clearly recognized, the key principle in licensure is professional self-regulation. NCATE is based on this principle, and has well over 500 member institutions. One would think that by now NCATE accreditation would be mandatory but, unfortunately, this is not the case.

Some of the larger school districts in the nation are utilizing a list of NCATE-accredited colleges and universities in the hiring of teachers.

THE BEGINNINGS OF TEACHER EDUCATION

Grudgingly in some quarters, willingly in others, universal public education was becoming a reality. The question was, would it be of high quality (such high quality that even those who could afford private schools would not use them)? Clearly, if this free school were not of high quality, it would shortly be labeled "pauper education" and rejected by everybody. Since the common school had been entrusted with the very survival of a free republic, it had to "be made fit to educate all."[33]

Good schools are impossible without good teachers. Nineteenth-century educational idealists recognized this well and acted upon their recognition. Teaching was professionalized by the middle of the nineteenth century through the efforts of Horace Mann and his contemporaries. This is not to say that professional preparation was universal after 1850, far from it. At the turn of the century, an overwhelming majority of teachers in the United States had no professional training at all. But there were important changes in the conception of teaching and the teacher held by the public. Before 1820, few people had any expectations where the professional preparation of teachers was concerned. It was believed that nearly anyone could "keep school." But Mann, Carter, and Barnard believed that *teaching school* was not the same as *keeping school,* and that competent teachers can be provided through a well-designed education. These reformers did a good job of putting their case before the public. As Cremin notes, the effect of Mann's belief in a strong teaching profession was prodigious.[34]

Teacher Education and Professionalization

The first public normal school in the United States was established at Lexington, Massachusetts, in 1839, with Mann playing an active role. The innovation of the professionalizing of teaching took hold, and there was no turning back. It is fascinating indeed that the period between 1839 and the Civil War was one of the most important in our entire history from the standpoint of the teaching profession. Public normal schools were established for the training of teachers and the teachers' institute developed as a means of improving those already engaged in teaching. The contemporary structure of preservice and inservice education was rapidly developing. (A second major advance for the profession was when teacher education became part of the university. This was mainly a post–Civil War development.)

The Normal School Idea. As we have noted, Massachusetts was the first state to establish normal schools. However, by 1900 all forty-five states in the Union had this new institution in one form or another. As for the origin of the idea, one often hears that it is of Prussian and French origin. The history of normal schools lives on in us and is worth examining. The term "normal school" is a translation of the French *école normale,* which was a derivative of the Latin word *norma,* meaning "a rule or authoritative standard; model type, pattern." The *École Normale Supérieure* (higher normal school) was founded under a reorganization of French higher education by Napoleon in 1809. More important, between 1831 and 1833, thirty normal schools were established by the new government in France, after the old restored monarchy had been overthrown. This was part of the development of a new state school system in France. (The *Écoles Normales Supérieures* eventually evolved into the most prestigious institutions of learning at the highest level.)

Why, one wonders, so many normal schools so suddenly? In designing their own educational system, enlightened French leaders decided to look elsewhere for ideas. They sent the noted philosopher, Victor Cousin, to Prussia to study what was at that time the outstanding state school system in Europe. Cousin's famous *Report on the Condition of Public Instruction in Germany, and Particularly Prussia* was made to the French government in 1831. Two key ideas were contained in this report: the importance of centralized state control of education, and teacher training in normal schools. The thirty new normal schools (and a new state school system in France) resulted from Cousin's enormously influential report.

The *Report* was published in New York in 1835 and quickened certain developments in Michigan and Massachusetts. Michigan was the first state to provide for the appointive office of State Superintendent of Public Instruction, which, according to Cubberley, was "a pure Prussian imitation."[35] In Massachusetts, the

Report came along just in time to support the efforts of Carter, Mann, and others who were attempting to establish the first normal schools of the state.

Clearly, however, the normal schools were already on the way as an American innovation. In the 1820s, Carter was campaigning insistently for the establishment of an institution for the preparation of teachers. The winter of 1824–25 saw publication of his article, "Outline of an Institution for the Education of Teachers," in the *Boston Patriot*.[36] Carter did more than campaign for normal schools. He showed his belief in teacher-training institutions by opening one himself in 1827, at Lancaster, Massachusetts, and requesting the state legislature for aid. "The normal school idea in America," as Cubberley noted, "was of native American growth, and had clearly taken form before Prussian normal schools were known of in this country."[37]

Carter's proposal for a teacher-education institution is strikingly contemporary. It must provide a general (academic) education for the prospective teacher as well as a grounding in pedagogical theory, with ample opportunity for practice under the supervision of an experienced and skillful professor. The practice school would be experimental, for teaching "must be made a science."[38] Today, the work of professional schools of education in universities across the length and breadth of our land is based on each of these principles. There is no denying that Carter anticipated the structure of today's school of education.

Returning to the first public normal school at Lexington, there were about forty students in the teacher-training program. Cyrus Peirce, the principal, left journals which show that he did the following: (1) taught ten subjects in a term and seventeen different subjects in a year, (2) supervised a model school of thirty youngsters, (3) served as a demonstration teacher, (4) developed the professional materials used in the normal school, and (5) acted as janitor of the building. It is of interest that Peirce taught a review of the "Common Branches"—spelling, reading, writing, grammar, and arithmetic—in addition to courses in child development and the methods of teaching each of the common branches. The point is that although admissions were selective for this school, it could not be assumed that the students were well versed in "the basics."

The idea that teachers ought to be professionally educated, while attracting growing interest, was by no means universally accepted. In fact, many people vehemently opposed the normal schools. As an observer pointed out to the NEA in 1872:

> Normal schools more than perhaps any other of our educational institutions, are liable to criticism and likely to incur hostility. . . . To set up as a teacher of teachers, to profess ability and intention to instruct mankind in a business that three-quarters of Yankee *man*kind and nine-tenths of Yankee *woman*kind have been considered competent to perform by mere force of natural instinct—is to put one's self into an invidious sort of attitude that sets all tongues agog.[39]

In 1840 the normal schools (there were three by then) came under sharp attack in the Massachusetts legislature, and the numerous opponents of normal schools (including some veteran teachers) recommended their abolition. But the new schools were sufficiently successful in the probationary three-year period to be finally adopted by the state in March 1842. A month later Peirce, worn out from the strain of the "period of experiment," not to mention the work itself, implored Mann to release him from the principalship.

Evolution into State Colleges. Normal schools were a definite advance, but they had glaring weaknesses. There were few admissions requirements, and what they were might seem startling to us. For example, to be admitted as a pupil in the normal school at Philadelphia in 1848, a candidate had to be at least 14 years of age and have been a pupil in the public grammar schools for at least one year.[40] Not surprisingly, the level of instruction was very similar to that given in high schools. Moreover, the course of instruction was only one or two years in length. Most graduates of normal schools taught in the elementary schools. After universal education became well established, there was a growing demand for high school teachers holding a bachelor's degree. Eventually, some normal schools evolved into teachers colleges offering curricula leading to the bachelor's degree. In Michigan, for instance, the normal school at Ypsilanti was designated the Michigan State Normal College by the Michigan legislature in 1897. Under legislative action in 1903, a college-level curriculum was organized and in 1905 the first B.A. degree was granted. Viewing normal schools in America, one might well accept that "the institutions generally were more important for what they were to become than for what they were."[41] Eventually, the state teachers colleges evolved into multipurpose state colleges, and teacher education became a strong function of the state universities.

Teachers' Institutes. About the same time Horace Mann was opening the first public normal school in Massachusetts, Henry Barnard was organizing another kind of agency for improving teaching in Connecticut—the teachers' institute. Barnard brought together twenty-six young men for a six-week session which included instruction in the methods of teaching and a review of the common branches. A number of well-known educators served as guest lecturers and the Hartford schools were made available for observation by the group. Obviously, the results were encouraging because the institute was offered again the next year, and a class was added for female teachers. The idea rapidly spread to other states in the late 1840s and 1850s.

Interestingly, as we look back on the origin of our own teachers' institutes, the terms "convention" and "institute" were often used interchangeably. The term "institute" was first used in connection with a two-week convention, consisting of twenty-eight teachers, held at Ithaca, New York, in 1843. The institute was conducted by the county superintendent of schools.

Institutes were intended both for those already engaged in teaching and for prospective teachers. Thus Rhode Island's law of 1845 made it the responsibility of the commissioners of public schools to establish institutes "where teachers and such as propose to teach may become acquainted with the most approved and successful methods of arranging the studies and conducting the discipline of instruction of public schools."[42]

According to Elsbree, the influence of institutes in stimulating professional development and solidarity "has frequently been underestimated."[43] The evidence, however, is mixed. Some institutes produced admirable results worthy of emulation today. The teachers' convention held in Hartford in the fall of 1846, for example, established a journal, the *Connecticut School Manual*. More important, perhaps, the convention was not seen by the teachers as a substitute for normal schools. A piece in the *Manual* made this clear: "Such conventions can be of but a few days continuance, and can never take the place, valuable as they are, of a school in which the philosophy of a child's mind, and the studies best adapted to develop it, are made the subjects of thorough investigation."[44]

Institutes were the forerunners of teachers associations, and as such, attempted certain reforms in the effort to make teaching a profession. In 1846, for example, an effort was made to obtain equal pay for men and women at an institute held in New York State. The resolution adopted was:

> Whereas, the education of a lady is obtained at no less expense than that of a gentleman, and as it is generally admitted that they can impart instruction with equal facility and success, therefore,
>
> Resolved, That ladies and gentlemen of equal qualifications, should receive equal compensation.[45]

The above resolution seems astonishingly contemporary. But the topics at institutes were not always the earmarks of a professional calling. "Should the rod be used in school?" and "Should the door be closed against pupils, who are not present at 9 o'clock in the morning?" were discussed at an institute held in Jamestown, Pennsylvania, in 1858.[46]

As the institute developed, the quality of the problems pondered in institute programs improved significantly. "What are the prominent causes of failure in teaching?," "Can teaching be reduced to a science?,"and "Does the pecuniary prosperity of a nation depend upon its intelligence?" were suggested by Bates, an influential institute worker, in his widely used handbook, published in 1864.[47]

There is no doubt that carefully planned institutes really served a useful purpose in providing "training" when it would not have been available otherwise. And in some institutes the teacher was clearly viewed as a professional, for the pedagogical problems studied were truly significant and demanded deep thought. Nevertheless, some institutes were almost counterproductive. They were intended for teacher training, but their management was left to local committees who were without experience in or knowledge of the work involved. These temporary schools met annually, but there was no consecutive plan from year to year. With no plan and limited time (and committees that were always changing), only little and superficial work was done. As Cubberley noted, "These Institutes were hailed as a quick and cheap means for giving some little training to those who desired to teach, and as offering a substitute, for a time at least, for the more expensive normal school then being developed."[48]

Today, however, there is no doubt that carefully designed institutes, conferences, or workshops can contribute much to the professional growth of those who are engaged in educational work.

THE EMERGENCE OF MODERN SUPERVISION

As we have indicated, educational leadership made its most rapid advances in the city. This was the direct outcome of demands by an education-conscious labor movement for more adequate educational opportunity for their children, which threw a huge load on the schools. The workers also demanded compulsory school attendance legislation which placed the responsibility of providing education for all the children of all the people squarely on the school system and increased the size and the complexity of the educational service. Thus the evolution of the city superintendency is, in one important respect, at least, an outcome of the Industrial Revolution.

A discussion of reasons for the improvement of educational services must not ignore the character of the city itself. In the city were concentrated people of wealth and talent, which won for it the lead in cultural development. This carried with it both the opportunity and the responsibility of providing a greater variety of educational service at increasingly higher levels. The challenge for educational leadership was enormous.

The Need for Professional Supervision

In the days when education was extremely limited, lay committees were able to administer the schools directly. But new improvements meant new duties that made boards of education increasingly helpless. For example, new subjects were being added to the curriculum, which were more difficult than spelling and arithmetic for untrained committeemen to supervise. And teachers were using new and different methods. There was no one to aid or advise any teacher who was pursuing, or who wished to pursue, a new instructional method. There was no one to recruit well-trained teachers in the first place. The most critical problems contributing to the establishment of the superintendency centered on the teacher and teaching.

The Superintendent as Supervisor. The organization of industry, with a board of directors and executives, was brought out in school committee reports to show the need for a superintendent. But, as Reller reported, the analogy between the two institutions, business and industry, quickly proved to be "false and deceptive" where supervision was concerned.[49] There was much uniformity in the work in a manufacturing establishment, making efficient supervision relatively easy, but as one school committee observed in 1857:

> A teacher, on the other hand, who deserves the name, is to some extent an original; that is to say, he views and explains subjects in a way peculiar to himself and the natural working of his own mind. . . . To require him to surrender his individuality, and to do his work after some favorite method of ours, is easy, and as preposterous as easy. To see that he does his work well, whatever be the mode, or if he does it ill, to show him where the defect is, and how to remedy it, and yet allow him the freedom so essential—requires more soundness of judgment, and delicacy of discrimination than are always at command.[50]

Thus, before the Civil War there was awareness of the complexity of educational supervision. This understanding (as stated above by a remarkably enlightened school committee) would ultimately be reflected in programs of preparation for supervisors (including internships in actual professional situations).

Victor Cousin's frequently quoted maxim, "As is the teacher, so is the school," was so commonly accepted that work with teachers was the most important part of the superintendent's job. The most commonly used supervisory techniques were classroom observation and teachers' meetings. Some superintendents were mere inspectors, flitting from one classroom to another without staying long enough to accomplish anything, and thus differing not at all (except by dint of title) from their lay predecessors. Others really served as advisors, regarding the teacher's problems as their problems.

Most superintendents devoted most of their time to visiting schools. This is not surprising since the superintendency was established to take over the work of supervision from lay committees, which had gotten out of hand. And in some cities, a required number of visits to schools per year was mandated by law. A question arises, of course, as to how effective this practice of school visitation was in improving teaching. Superintendents had virtually no professional preparation. Some superintendents had as many as 900 teachers to supervise, so their work could have had little effect. Taken on the whole, however, there were favorable effects for supervision. Elsbree offered this observation:

> With supervisors so poorly equipped by preparation for the task as were the superintendents, it seems highly improbable that the technique of teaching was vastly improved during this period. On the other hand, intelligent superintendents learned a great deal from their observations, which contributed to the ultimate improvement of instruction. Outstanding achievements of teachers were brought to the attention of those who were less successful and the whole problem of method became a subject of study and discussion.[51]

In some cities (New Haven and Wilmington, for example) teachers were given the opportunity to observe each other's methods of teaching and classroom management, under the guidance of the superintendent. We have tended to regard teacher intervisitation as a relatively recent innovation in supervision, yet there is clear evidence that it was practiced before the last quarter of the nineteenth century.

Efforts to improve teachers frequently took the form of meetings. General meetings were held in which teachers heard outside lecturers, and there were grade-level meetings and special subject meetings as well. At times the meetings were similar to regular course instruction, and at times they were devoted to a discussion of professional literature. (Emphasis was put on the use of the professional library which had been developed in many cities by the superintendent.) At other times, teachers participated very little, if at all. On the whole, teachers were not viewed as professionals and did not participate widely in the business of curriculum making until the early 1920s. In most cities, attendance at meetings was compulsory and absentees were reported to the board of education. When a city became large, the principals were often in charge of meetings. Nevertheless, setting up the meetings was generally a responsibility of the superintendent, required by board rules. Meetings were usually held on Saturday or after school.

Looming large among the superintendent's problems was that large numbers of teachers had no preservice preparation. As Superintendent Maxwell of Brooklyn declared, the damage being done by recruiting untrained teachers "was incalculable."[52] The problem could not be solved simply by requiring professional or university training for an appointment to a position in the public schools, because the supply of qualified teachers did not begin to meet the demands of mushrooming urban communities. This problem called for local initiative.

One solution was to establish city normal schools and hire teachers who had taken their training in the local training institution. The beginnings of a number of city normal schools can be traced to the urging of the superintendent, who often played a leading part in deciding what courses should be offered (and who even taught a course or two).

A few cities adopted the training-school idea so completely that no teachers were appointed who had not received their preparation in the city training institution. In some cities (Detroit, for example), the policy continued until mid-twentieth century, long after professionally prepared teachers were generally available.

The School Principal as Supervisor. In the first half of the nineteenth century, a position destined to be of tremendous importance in supervision rapidly developed—the principalship. As villages and cities grew and one- and two-room schools were enlarged to accommodate the enormous increases in pupils, "head teachers" were appointed to keep an eye on discipline and come to the aid of assistant teachers whenever the need arose. Before the establishment of the superintendency, the principal performed duties and had powers that were later assumed by the superintendent. The principal was frequently present at board meetings, reporting to the board on his school and advising them on organizational and instructional matters. But his time was occupied mainly in teaching, usually the upper grades.

In the larger cities, some principals even served as district superintendents (without the title, of course), administering a group of schools in addition to their own building. But this transition to complete freedom from teaching duties was a long one in many cities. Although principals were supposed to give advice to teachers in any grade in their schools, they evidently knew little about the work in the lower grades, as indicated by the superintendent's report on supervision by principals in Cincinnati in 1858:

> The most efficient agency in the improvement of the schools has been the constant and active supervision of the Principals over the labors of their assistants. *They were, till within the last two years, only teachers of the highest classes in their respective schools.* Though nominally the Principals, they were almost as ignorant of the classification and instruction administered in the lower grades of their own schools, as of the schools in the adjoining districts. By a regulation of your Board, which I had the honor of submitting for your consideration, the Principals are now, with one or two exceptions, relieved of the personal charge of any

one department, and almost all of them have small recitation rooms assigned to them, where they may keep the records, examine classes, and transact the general business of their schools.[53]

As might be expected, experience as a principal was (and is today) a major consideration in being selected for a school superintendency. In the 1880s the Brooklyn board of education elected a principal as superintendent. The *Daily Eagle* applauded the action, commenting that "the superintendency is a prize which ought to be held before the eyes of the principals as a stimulus to exertion in their calling."[54]

There is no doubt, however, that the most important gain from separating the principalship from teaching was the opportunity that it provided for the improvement of instruction. This opportunity is discussed in detail later. Particularly significant here is that in the early days of the principalship, when it was impossible to obtain trained teachers, the role of the principal was teacher training. Elsbree and Reutter probably did not exaggerate the situation when they wrote that "the principal was looked upon as a kind of foreman who through close supervision helped to compensate for ignorance and lack of skill of his subordinates." Elsbree and Reutter pointed out that until the 1920s, it was the responsibility of the principal "to take over classes on occasion, and to demonstrate to the teacher exactly how the job should be done."[55]

Today, teachers are as well prepared as principals, and in too many schools the principalship has turned into a purely managerial position. Yet it has been established by research that leadership from the school principal is a crucial factor in the improvement of teaching and learning.

Recently, the principal as educational leader has been the focus of growing interest. In fact, the educational literature of the late 1970s and of the 1980s is virtually crammed with the findings of studies on what effective principals do. It is fascinating that some of these studies lend support to the ideas about supervision from very early in our educational history. For example, research on school effectiveness finds that "the effective principal is less likely to prescribe specific methods than to offer continual assistance in response to the problems which teachers identify for themselves."[56] It will be recalled that this was the position taken by the school committee in Worcester (Massachusetts) back in 1857. And in 1891, Aaron Gove, superintendent of the Denver schools, wrote in the *Educational Review* that "a teacher, to be in the best way successful must not be subjected to dictation in details."[57] More credit is due to our predecessors (lay supervisors and professionals alike) than is generally accorded them.

SUMMARY

In any profession—whether medicine, law, dentistry, social work, or education—the development of the field itself is an important part of professional knowledge. This is especially true in the case of school supervision, which began as a lay function. Although supervision has long been professionalized, the tradition of public supervision lives on in us. The American public jealously guards the gate to equality and excellence, the public schools. One need only turn to the daily newspaper; the reports of committees on excellence in education are frontpage news. Supervisors have yet to marshal this public concern effectively for educational problem solving.

There is clear evidence that articulate lay supervisors in the colonial period were concerned with the improvement of teaching, not just the maintenance of schools in accord with the laws. Some school committees visited the schools regularly, knowing that without their attention and reflection education in their town would surely fail. Other committees neglected the schools and the results were deplorable. When the Founding Fathers declared that "all men are created equal," they meant that all persons should have an equal opportunity to develop their talents and not be held back by the inherited status of family, class, or property. But in the years immediately following the Revolution, educational inequities became more pronounced. The problem was the district system of control; with little state control, districts managed their schools in the interest of economy, often ignoring the barest educational standards. It is often a source of wonder to historians that the battle for state support of schools was won. If it were not for reformers of great intelligence and courage who cared passionately about what happened to the schools, the battle for the public schools would have been an unmitigated defeat. The development of professional supervision is inseparable from the development of public support for schools, which is a story of true educational leadership. The first professional supervisor was Horace Mann, secretary of the State Board of Education in Massachusetts.

Supervision evolved with the total American educational system, including teacher education and the professional administration of schools. Good teaching was at the very center of the ideal of public schools of such high quality that they would attract pupils of all social classes. Preservice teacher education had a beginning with the establishment of normal schools, which eventually evolved into state colleges, but the work of teacher education also went on in teachers' institutes and public schools. Cities led in the development of professional supervision with the establishment of the superintendency. They had to. As new subjects were added that were more difficult than spelling and arithmetic for the untrained laymen to supervise, and as teachers were using more advanced methods, school committees realized the hopelessness of their situation and saw the need for a superintendent. Since trained teachers were unavailable, teacher training was the major responsibility of supervisors well into the twentieth century. The situation had changed a great deal from the days when each teacher ran the school pretty much to suit himself.

PROBLEMS FOR STUDY AND DISCUSSION

1. What factors have caused the tradition of lay supervision of schools to live on in the present?

2. In your opinion, what are some of the ways that supervisors can translate the high expectations of the public for their schools into public support for educational problem solving?

3. In the colonial period, the usual view of the public was that teaching in the schools did not require special preparation beyond that of a liberal arts

education. It was believed that if teachers knew enough about their subject matter, they could pass their knowledge on to their pupils. This argument is still being voiced today by critics of teacher education. Is it a valid argument? Why or why not?

4. In your state, what are some of the requirements that communities must meet to receive state funds for education?

5. Horace Mann and his contemporaries set forth the ideal of the common school—a school common to all the people. It was to be a free school open to rich and poor alike, and of as high quality as any institution that could be established privately. To what extent has this ideal been accepted as an ideal of contemporary America? Explain.

6. What are the weaknesses of decentralized control of the schools that became apparent to Horace Mann's generation? Do you think that these arguments would apply today? Why or why not?

7. According to a reader of the *Pennsylvania School Journal* in 1856:

   Complaints of incompetency, against teachers, should be received with a great deal of allowance. If they are incompetent, let them be encouraged, rather than censured. This is the only just and politic course. *Charges of incompetency can never supply the great demand for good teachers.* Men and women of education and talents will not thus be induced to enter the profession. Neither will those who are already teachers, be thereby encouraged to make constant untiring exertions for improvement, without which even the best instructors may soon become incompetent.[58]

   Do you agree with this position? Why or why not? Does it help any to realize that the origins of "teacher competency" are at least as old as the public school system itself? Explain.

8. Nineteenth-century principals gave model lessons as a means of turning poor teachers into good teachers. Do you think that this method ought to be used by principals today? Support your position.

9. In this chapter, it was pointed out that the most commonly used supervisory techniques in the cities during the nineteenth century were classroom observation and teachers' meetings. Is this still the case? Support your answers.

10. In the nineteenth century, educational reformers worked to extend Victor Cousin's maxim, "As is the teacher, so is the school," by establishing normal schools and setting up teachers' institutes. Do you think that contemporary educators still subscribe to the position that the teacher makes the school? Explain.

NOTES

1. W. W. Charters, "The Administration of Methods of Teaching," *Educational Administration and Supervision*, Vol. 4 (May 1918), p. 237.

2. J. D. Bernal, *The Extension of Man* (Cambridge, Mass.: MIT Press, 1972).
3. William H. Kilpatrick, *The Dutch Schools of New Netherland and Colonial New York* (Washington, D.C.: U.S. Government Printing Office, 1912), p. 78.
4. Willard S. Elsbree, *The American Teacher* (New York: American Book, 1939), p. 71.
5. Cited in Walter H. Small, *Early New England Schools* (Boston: Ginn, 1914), p. 334.
6. "Boston Town Records," *Report of the [Boston] Record Commissioners,* Vol. 19, pp. 152–153.
7. "Letter from a Teacher," *Connecticut School Manual,* Vol. 1 (May 1, 1847), p. 107.
8. Lawrence A. Cremin, *Traditions of American Education* (New York: Basic Books, 1977), p. 18.
9. "Boston Town Records," *Report of the [Boston] Record Commissioners,* Vol. 8, p. 65.
10. Robert Nisbet, *History of the Idea of Progress* (New York: Basic Books, 1980), p. 7.
11. Small, op. cit., p. 335.
12. Ibid., p. 342.
13. R. Freeman Butts and Lawrence A. Cremin, *A History of Education in American Culture* (New York: Holt, Rinehart and Winston, 1953), pp. 106–107.
14. Edwin H. Brown, "First Free School in Queen Anne's County," *Maryland Historical Magazine,* Vol. 6 (March 1911), pp. 1–15.
15. Ibid., p. 4.
16. Ibid.
17. Lawrence A. Cremin, *American Education: The Colonial Experience 1607–1783* (New York: Harper & Row, 1970), pp. 167–176.
18. Ibid., p. 193; and Small, op. cit., pp. 325–333.
19. Elsbree, op. cit., p. 170.
20. Letter to James Madison, in Gordon C. Lee (ed.), *Crusade Against Ignorance: Thomas Jefferson on Education* (New York: Teachers College Press, 1961), p. 37.
21. Carl F. Kaestle, *Joseph Lancaster and the Monitorial School Movement* (New York: Teachers College Press, 1973), p. 47.
22. Ellwood P. Cubberley, *Public Education in the United States,* rev. ed. (Boston: Houghton Mifflin, 1947), p. 137.
23. Ibid., pp. 134–135.
24. Ibid., p. 219.
25. James G. Carter, *Essays upon Popular Education* (Boston: Bowles and Dearborn, 1826), p. 33.
26. Lawrence A. Cremin, *The Republic and the School: Horace Mann on the Education of Free Men* (New York: Teachers College Press, 1957), p. 20.
27. Cubberley, op. cit., p. 227.
28. Henry Barnard, "A History of Common Schools in Connecticut," *The American Journal of Education,* Vol. 5 (1858), p. 149.
29. Ibid.
30. Ibid., p. 142.
31. John Swett, *History of the Public School System of California* (San Francisco: A. L. Bancroft, 1876), p. 175.
32. Ibid., p. 176.
33. Orville Taylor, [New York] *Common School Assistant,* Vol. 2 (1837), p. 1.
34. Cremin, *The Republic and the School: Horace Mann on the Education of Free Men,* op. cit., p. 23.
35. Cubberley, op. cit., p. 358.
36. Carter, op. cit., pp. 42–60.
37. Cubberley, op. cit., p. 359.
38. Carter, op. cit., p. 44.

39. Richard Edwards, "The Duties and Dangers of Normal Schools," National Education Association *Proceedings* (Peoria, Ill.: The Association, 1872), p. 11.
40. James J. Barclay, *An Address Delivered at the Organization of the Normal School* (Philadelphia: First School District of Philadelphia, 1848), pp. 17–18.
41. Butts and Cremin, op. cit., p. 449.
42. Cited in Elsbree, op. cit., p. 156.
43. Ibid., p. 155.
44. "A Seminary for Teachers," *Connecticut School Manual*, Vol. 1 (April 1847), p. 81.
45. Samuel N. Sweet, *Teachers' Institutes* (Utica, NY: H. H. Hawley, 1848), p. 95.
46. *Pennsylvania School Journal*, Vol. 6 (1858), p. 268.
47. Samuel P. Bates, *Method of Teachers' Institutes and the Theory of Education* (New York: A. S. Barnes and Burr, 1864), pp. 53–55.
48. Cubberley, op. cit., pp. 324–325.
49. Theodore L. Reller, *The Development of the City Superintendency of Schools in the United States* (Philadelphia: The Author, 1935), p. 47.
50. Worcester, *Report, School Committee*, 1857, pp. 9–10.
51. Elsbree, op. cit., p. 173.
52. Quoted in Minneapolis, *Annual Report, Board of Education*, 1890, p. 50.
53. Cincinnati, *School Report*, 1858, p. 35.
54. Brooklyn, *Daily Eagle*, February 11, 1882.
55. Willard S. Elsbree and E. Edmund Reutter, Jr., *Staff Personnel in the Public Schools* (Englewood Cliffs, N.J.: Prentice-Hall, 1954), p. 231.
56. Donald E. Mackenzie, "Research for School Improvement: An Appraisal of Some Recent Trends," *Educational Researcher*, Vol. 12 (April 1983), p. 11.
57. Aaron Gove, "City School Supervision," *Educational Review*, Vol. 2 (October 1891), p. 260.
58. "Letter to the Editor," *Pennsylvania School Journal*, Vol. 5 (October 1856), p. 121.

SELECTED REFERENCES

Cremin, Lawrence A. *American Education: The Colonial Experience 1607–1783*. New York: Harper & Row, Publishers, Inc., 1970.

———. *American Education: The National Experience 1783–1876*. New York: Harper & Row, Publishers, Inc., 1980.

———. *The Republic and the School: Horace Mann on the Education of Free Men*. New York: Teachers College Press, 1957.

———. *Traditions of American Education*. New York: Basic Books, Inc., Publishers, 1977.

Elsbree, Willard S. *The American Teacher*. New York: American Book Company, 1939.

Goodlad, John I. *A Place Called School*. New York: McGraw-Hill Book Company, 1984.

Kaestle, Carl F. *Joseph Lancaster and the Monitorial School Movement*. New York: Teachers College Press, 1973.

Kilpatrick, William H. *The Dutch Schools of New Netherland and Colonial New York*. Washington, D.C.: U.S. Government Printing Office, 1912.

Lortie, Dan C. *Schoolteacher: A Sociological Study*. Chicago: The University of Chicago Press, 1975.

Small, Walter H. *Early New England Schools*. Boston: Ginn and Company, 1914.

Swett, John. *History of the Public School System in California*. San Francisco: A. L. Bancroft and Company, 1876.

Tanner, Daniel, and Laurel N. Tanner. *Curriculum Development: Theory Into Practice*, 2nd ed. New York: Macmillan Publishing Company, 1980.

Wickersham, James P. *A History of Education in Pennsylvania*. New York: Arno Press and The New York Times Company, 1969 (originally published by Inquirer Publishing Company in 1886).

Chapter 2

The Professionalization of Supervision

The framework for professional supervision was established in the nineteenth century in the form of superintendents, principals, and supervisors. Simply to create a new position, however, does not make it a profession worthy of the name. Those holding the position must think of themselves as a group having common professional concerns and problems. They must have professional organizations and standards of preparation. True professionalism requires scientific investigation of the practical problems of a profession in order to improve practice and provide a solid base for it.

When supervisors began to organize themselves for mutual discussion of their common problems, when preparation in the field of supervision came to be expected for entrance upon the job, and when the theory and practice and administration of education began to be studied in the universities, supervision gradually became a profession. Beginnings in these directions were made in the nineteenth century, but professionalization remains a difficult problem as we approach the twenty-first century. This chapter is concerned with the continuing evolution of supervision—the theoretical and practical base for supervision, the changing roles of supervisors, the serious problems facing the profession, and preparation for supervisory positions.

The purpose of supervision is to improve the education provided by schools for children. In order to improve education the prospective supervisor needs to understand what the prevailing methods of instruction in the past have been. This is useful knowledge because it can prevent supervisors from reinventing the wheel. The field of education keeps cycling back to old educational models and treating them as new. It fails to learn from the past and, consequently, it proceeds to repeat its failures.

For example, contingency contracting or "contracting" with pupils to do their work is a reinvention of the Dalton Plan, developed by Helen Parkhurst in 1913. As one might think, the division of the curriculum into contract jobs presents the same theoretical difficulties now as it did then. To mention just one, not all of the functions of the school can be met mechanically. This problem and others were aired in the educational literature of a half century ago.[1] Clearly, those who reinvented the Dalton Plan did not search the educational literature for previous experiences with contracts. There is a need to benefit from the vast store of thinking and experience in education—to build on what we already know. This is one of supervision's great problems.

Mention should be made of the fact that reinventing old educational models is less likely when supervision is problem focused. Curriculum (and instructional) improvement begins as an attempt to help a teacher solve a problem. The starting point is the problem, not the innovation. A problem-solving process is presented in Chapter 4. This text takes a problems approach to supervision.

THE DEVELOPMENT OF METHOD

As indicated in Chapter 1, Pestalozzi's ideas about the educational process began to cross the Atlantic early in the nineteenth century. According to Pestalozzi, people are born neither good nor evil, it is their environment which makes them into what they are. According to this philosophy, which was actually applied by Pestalozzi in Switzerland, education is an enjoyable process by which children develop naturally in a favorable environment. Pestalozzi believed that the child must be allowed much freedom in learning. "Sense impression" was his trademark and summed up his basic principle of instruction: Children acquire their ideas through the senses—seeing, hearing, smelling, tasting, feeling, and doing. Therefore, the study of natural objects and pictures must precede words and symbols, and class discussion and thinking must replace parrotlike recitations of the words of a book.

In the early part of the nineteenth century these ideas about the child and his education began to appear with increasing frequency in American educational thinking. They were important beginnings of progressivism in American education (although instructional methods based on cultivation of the senses were frequently as formal as those they were intended to replace).

The new educational methods were the inevitable outcome of the revolutionary influence of scientific evidence and scientific method. For hundreds of years, the traditional, and theologically sanctioned, method of arriving at truth and acquiring knowledge was Scholasticism, which, as Butts and Cremin put it, "was simply a playing with words and a refinement of language with little or no regard to actuality and present experience."[2] What Pestalozzi called "empty chattering of mere words" and "outward show"[3] in the schools was simply a reflection of the traditional system of arriving at truth which began with the generalization of some writer long gone. The scientific method caused the greatest intellectual revolution the world has ever known. The cause of the revolution was this: By using controlled methods of observation instead of preordained ideas, scientists were making fantastic progress in learning about the natural world. The old idea that knowledge came from traditional authorities was overthrown.

A crucially important outcome for education was the development of a philosophy of how people learn. The old view had been that man's faculty of reason or intellect was developed by vigorous exercise from the proper studies—the classical languages, mathematics, and philosophy. In striking contrast, the scientific method led thinkers about learning (including educational reformers) to realize that knowledge is developed through experience. Thus learning is best when teachers begin with observation of nature and cultivate the method of science. The point is that philosophies of learning and instructional methods are the results of methods of arriving at the truth and acquiring knowledge. A new method of thinking used by intelligent people in the world was bound to result in new proposals for reforming education.

Object Teaching

In 1859, Edward A. Sheldon, superintendent of schools in Oswego, New York, took a trip to Toronto, where he saw in the museum an exhibit on Pestalozzian methods of instruction. American education was never the same again. He returned to Oswego, full of enthusiasm about learning through real experiences with objects, and proposed to his teachers that they study this method of teaching. They became so intensely involved that they contributed to a fund (some as much as a half year's salary) to bring experts from abroad to assist them in their study. The ultimate result was the creation of a city normal school to train teachers in the new methods for the schools of Oswego.

Soon the work in the Oswego schools became the talk of the school world. Visitors came in droves to see the new methods and students came from all over to study at Oswego, which became known as "a mecca of American elementary education."[4] As might be expected, Oswego graduates were eagerly sought after by school systems and normal schools across the length and breadth of the United States. For at least three decades, oral instruction of a class using real objects was the accepted method in the elementary grades.

A Real "Technique of Instruction." Object teaching was nothing less than an instructional revolution. Until the middle of the nineteenth century in some schools (and much later in most schools), the prevailing instructional method was the recitation, in which the teacher or assistant heard the children recite what had been memorized from a book. Many of the early history and geography books were even written in the style of the Catechism, with nothing but questions and answers. The teacher's job was relatively simple, to see that pupils could recite the answers to the questions. The Pestalozzian type of instruction, based on careful observation and personal judgment, required a total change in teaching procedure. Getting children to use their senses and their minds and then be able to respond to questions because they had observed and reasoned carefully called for professional skill. The class had to be kept interested, the teacher had to know the subject and keep what was to be taught clearly in mind, encourage the use of all the senses, raise the right questions, and guide the class thinking along to the correct conclusions.

This conception of teaching was new, and it was the first time in history that a professional "technique of instruction" was required.[5] By "technique" is meant "method." For teachers were not technicians. They had to understand both the ends and means of instruction. And they had to think out their lessons ahead of time. The effect was to professionalize teaching as it had never been before. As Cubberley pointed out, "Able to stand before a class full of a subject and able to question freely, teachers became conscious of a new strength and a professional skill," and "it is not to be wondered that the teachers leaving Oswego went out feeling that teaching, by the Oswego methods, was the greatest thing in the world."[6]

A Force for Supervision. Pestalozzian methods figured prominently in the arguments for the establishment of the superintendency in city schools. Someone had to be able to help teachers who wished to use the pedagogy of the Swiss reformer. Clearly, this hastened the professionalization of supervision. It is important to note, in this connection, that the ideas of Pestalozzi had been brought to American attention well before the Oswego movement in the 1860's. Books were written about Pestalozzian procedures by American visitors to Europe in the 1820s. And in the 1830s and 1840s, school people and lay people were familiarized with what was happening on the continent of Europe instruction-wise through numerous magazine articles and articles in the new educational journals (Barnard's *American Journal of Education,* for example).

The most influential report on Pestalozzian methods in Europe was Horace Mann's *Seventh Report* (1843). "There are many things abroad which we at home should do well to imitate," wrote Mann.[7] Mann's report centered public attention on the need to improve American education through the adoption of a better (the Pestalozzian) form of instruction. As a result of Mann's report, Pestalozzian methods were introduced in some Massachusetts schools in the 1840s. The real point of importance is that public interest in the new European methods was a force that called the professional supervisor into being.

Criticisms of Object Teaching. Normal-school students prepared for the work of object teaching by studying model lessons. The teacher's manual used at Oswego emphasized that the sample lessons were "only designed as suggestions and models to guide teachers in working out their *own plans and methods.*"[8] But many of the model lessons in the guidebook included both questions and answers. The following lesson is illustrative.

A Piece of Bark

"What is this? A piece of bark. All look at it. Where do we find bark? On trees. On what part of trees? Look and see. (The teacher brings in a piece of the stem of a tree on which the bark still remains.) On the outside. Repeat together— 'Bark is the outer part of the stems of trees.'

"Look at the bark; what do you perceive? It is brown. Repeat—'Bark is *brown.*' Look again; is it like glass? No, we cannot see through it. What can you say of it then? We cannot see through bark. Compare it with glass. It does not shine. When anything does not shine at all, it is said to be *dull;* what is the bark? It is dull. Repeat—'The bark is dull.' Show me some things in the room that are dull. Now feel the bark. It is rough. And what more? It is dry. Now look: (the teacher separates the fibre) it has strings or hairs. These strings or hairs are called fibers, and we say the bark is fibrous. Repeat—'The bark is *fibrous.*' Some plants have very fibrous stems, and are very useful to us on this account; here are some of the fibers of hemp; and here are some of flax, which supplies much of our clothing. I think you can find out something more if you feel the bark again. Yes; it is hard.

"Now repeat all you have said. 'Bark is the *outside covering of the stems of trees;* it is brown; we cannot *see through it; it is rough, dull, dry, hard, and fibrous.*' "[9]

As the example shows clearly, the old catechetical approach to learning was still alive. Any teacher who followed the manual too closely was in danger of having her teaching degenerate into mechanism and deadly routine. The manual suggested that prospective teachers write outlines of prospective lessons but *not* detailed questions and answers. But then there were the model lessons that said something else, and were, willy-nilly, the old recitation method, adapted to a class group.

In some school systems object lessons were prepackaged for the teacher. It was reported to the NEA in 1874 that St. Louis had a course on "common objects" for young children, in which the child was expected to remember that the penny has on it the "impression, the image, the date, the superscription," the shell has "the body and the spire," and the spire its "whorls, sutures, and apex."[10] It was almost inevitable that even in the hands of gifted teachers, prepackaged object lessons would turn into something very flat and uninteresting. Undoubtedly, many object lessons were just that (and some were something very near nonsense). On the other hand, it is all too easy to overlook the contributions of object teaching and to fail to see it in the perspective of what went before and what came after.

Contributions of Object Teaching. The Oswego movement led to (1) a demand for supervisors, (2) interest in basing teaching and learning on principles and methods, (3) changes in the curriculum of the public schools, and (4) further attempts to apply and extend the ideas of Pestalozzi. The demand for professional (as opposed to lay) supervisors has been discussed. The second important effect of the work at Oswego was to awaken interest in putting teaching on a more scientific basis. Clearly, Oswego took the lead in the professionalization of teaching. For more than a quarter of a century, the normal school at Oswego was the source of supply for instructors in the new normal schools established elsewhere. The professional enthusiasm of Sheldon and his followers, who worked to apply Pestalozzi's ideas in teacher training and school practice, was important in securing our professional beginnings.

Object teaching profoundly influenced the curriculum. The work at Oswego showed clearly the importance of oral language in the instruction of children, and a new subject, oral language work, entered the primary grades. In the upper elementary grades, oral and written language work replaced to some extent the narrow stress on drill in English grammar. Object teaching did much to introduce science as a school subject. Geography, which formerly had been taught as facts (imports, exports, statistical data), was revolutionized by Pestalozzi's pedagogy. The new "home geography" began with study of the local terrain. This required observation outdoors. Physical and human geography were substituted for political and statistical data. Arithmetic, too, underwent changes—from words about numbers to concrete number ideas.

Pestalozzian ideas formed a basis on which other reformers would build. For example, Colonel Francis W. Parker introduced Pestalozzian methods on an experimental basis in an individual school system: Quincy, Massachusetts. In 1875, Parker was appointed superintendent of schools because school officials had found to their horror that children in the Quincy schools could not read from a strange book. They could only recite memorized passages from their textbooks, selected in advance by their teacher. Drastic changes were called for, and Parker had traveled abroad and observed firsthand the outgrowth of Pestalozzi's work. Functionalism became an important criterion for the work of the Quincy schools. Language was used as a tool of communication; the geography of the local area was more important than that of faraway lands. Science was introduced, as well as arts and crafts, and arithmetic was used to solve everyday problems. The Massachusetts Board of Education visited the Quincy schools and found that Quincy's children were ahead of the majority of Massachusetts pupils. Quincy was for a time the new mecca of American education.

Formal Steps of Instruction

In the 1890s there was a wave of pedagogical excitement that resembled the Pestalozzian enthusiasm of the 1860s. Classroom instruction had been organized into a formula that promised to be highly useful to teachers and supervisors—five steps to be followed in order. The instructional procedure grew out of the theories of the eminent German psychologist Johann Friedrich Herbart, who died in 1841 and whose ideas went almost unnoticed by anyone during his lifetime. Herbart was "discovered" in Germany in 1865, and a scientific society was founded for the study of his ideas. Herbart's ideas were introduced in America by Americans who had studied in Germany and founded the National Herbart Society, an imitation of the German society. (The National Herbart Society later grew into the National Society for the Study of Education.)

Herbart was the first educational writer to put emphasis on instruction as a process. According to Herbart, since consciousness consists of association of ideas, the teacher must present new ideas in a way that associates them with ideas that are already part of the pupil's experience. Of primary importance for good instruction was the learner's interest. If interest was given immediately, so much the better. If not, the teacher must develop interest through skill in instruction.

Herbart's followers formalized his emphasis on association and interest into the rather inflexible procedure that came to be known as the *five formal steps of teaching and learning.* The steps were (1) *preparation,* in which the old ideas useful in learning the new material are called to the pupil's mind; (2) *presentation,* or giving out the new information; (3) *association,* or showing relationships between the new facts or material and the old; (4) *generalization,* or making up rules, definitions, or general principles that express the meaning of the lesson; and (5) *application,* or giving the general principles meaning by using them in practical situations or applying them to specific examples. (Through the application of knowledge, the learning process was completed.) "Without question," wrote Elsbree, "these five simply stated steps exercised more influence on teaching practice between 1890 and 1905 than all other psychological and philosophical creations combined."[11]

The Advent of the Lesson Plan. But there were also effects on supervision that merit close examination. The formal lesson plan began with the formal steps. Although no longer based on the formal steps of instruction, lesson planning is still used by supervisors of student teachers and supervisors of teachers in service as a means of promoting good teaching. This is not to say that it is always well used. (Sometimes plans are used as a bureaucratic device, for example, requiring inservice teachers to turn in their lesson plans every week.)

The Facts of Lesson Planning. Teachers tend to resist making lesson plans because they see the plans as something mechanical rather than functional. Whether they know it or not, every teacher has *a* plan (even if it is simply to use the textbook or workbook). Our problem as supervisors is how to help teachers plan so that better instruction and learning may result. Careful planning means that more of the variables in a teaching situation are under the teacher's control, including the curriculum. Nevertheless, the degree of detail in a plan should depend on the needs of the individual teacher.

THE METHOD OF INTELLIGENCE

John Dewey was (and still is) the leading figure in the theory and practice of American education. One of Dewey's most influential ideas was his conception of thinking as a method of problem solving. For Dewey, thinking is applying the scientific method to all sorts of problems, from the simple everyday type of problem to complicated social problems and abstract intellectual problems. Dewey developed a problem-solving method for the school that corresponded to the method of experimental inquiry. Dewey's book *How We Think* (1910) was designed to help teachers understand what thinking (problem solving) is and how to develop habits of reflective thought in their pupils.

The Significance of the Teacher

Dewey's problem-solving method had a revolutionary impact on education, spawning a variety of innovations in methods that were ostensibly based on his ideas. (Some had a sound Deweyan base; others were, to say the least, off-base). Before describing the steps in Dewey's method and the ensuing proposals, it is important to understand just why Dewey wrote *How We Think.* (Not many great philosophers, it is safe to say, write methods books for teachers.)

Dewey believed that if the scientific method is the most effective way of thinking, then the schools are obliged to lay the groundwork for such thinking. In a free society, we have the chance to shape our destinies, he tells us, rather than submitting to a necessary destiny. In fact, there is really no limit to what we as individuals and our country might attain if we apply the scientific method to our problems. The key is to develop the capacity for using the method of intelligence (scientific method) in problem situations.

Attitudes and habits are best learned in the early years. Moreover, children are by nature curious and open-minded. In Dewey's own words, "The native and unspoiled attitude of childhood, marked by ardent curiosity, fertile imagination, and love of experimental inquiry, is near, very near, to the attitude of the scientific mind."[12] Dewey was by no means saying that the two minds are identical, but that childhood curiosity and imagination are ready resources for developing the powers of the child to grow in the ability to think scientifically.

The Dewey of 1910 plainly believed that teachers who understand the why and the how to develop scientific attitudes in their pupils will proceed to develop them. But two decades later, Dewey was clearly disappointed in the implementation (or lack of it) of his problem-solving method. "I venture to say," he wrote in 1931, "that for the most part the formation of intellectual habits in elementary education, in the home and school is hardly affected by the scientific method. Even in our so-called progressive schools, science is usually treated as a side line, an ornamental extra, not as the chief means of developing the right mental attitudes. It is treated generally as one more body of ready-made information to be acquired by traditional methods, or else as an occasional diversion. *That it is the method of all effective mental approach and attack in all subjects has not even gained a foothold.*"[13]

If Dewey were here, he would probably make the same statement today. Nevertheless, his idea is a main part of our educational theory—though unfulfilled in practice.

The Complete Act of Thought

Dewey's complete act of thought consists of five steps: (1) *Defining the problem* that is raised by a disturbing or perplexing situation. Setting the problem to be solved may be easy to do in a simple problem (such as how to get somewhere in a hurry to meet an appointment just remembered), or it may be a long, drawn-out sequence of procedures in the case of a complex scientific problem. (2) *Observing the conditions* that surround the problem, taking into account the entire situation and studying its origin and all the important factors that may be involved. This is a stage of gathering significant facts or evidence (data) pertinent to the problem. (3) *Formulating hypotheses* that may solve the problem. The hypotheses are ideas or alternative plans of action for possible solution to the problem. (4) *Tracing out the possible consequences* of acting on the various alternative hypotheses. (5) *Active testing* to determine which idea best solves the problem. The idea that solves the problem when tested by experimentation or observation is the true idea; it has been validated by its power to produce the desired consequences.

Dewey emphasized that the five steps do not have to follow one another in sequence. Moreover, in complicated cases, some of the five phases include subphases, and the parts could be identified as distinct phases. This is a matter of what suits one best. "There is nothing especially sacred about the number five," Dewey observed.[14]

Dewey contended that this conception of thinking should be at the center of the educative process. The job of the teacher should be to involve students in a situation in which they are truly interested—one that means something to them. A perplexity or difficulty will generate a real problem for them to solve. They will then make the needed observations that will lead to suggestions (hypotheses) for solving the problem. A good teacher will help the students obtain the relevant knowledge, formulate creative suggestions, and put them to the test to determine whether they are valid for solving the problem.

The Project Method

Dewey felt that students will learn to think as they work at solving problems of interest to them. "*But interest is not enough,*" warned Dewey sharply in the second edition of *How We Think* (1933).[15] For more than a decade activities known as "projects" had increasingly found their way into the school. The "project method," in which students are involved in activities that require thinking as well as doing, can be an effective way to learn. (Home projects, where the student tests new seed or a new method of farming, have long been used in agricultural education.) But doing is not thinking. Real thinking and real education should have the elements of the complete act of thought, warned Dewey.

The Project Method and Reflective Thinking. Dewey gave four conditions that must be met in order for projects to be educative: (1) the project must be of interest; (2) the project must involve thought, which excludes merely trivial activities that are of no worth beyond the immediate pleasure derived from engaging in them; (3) the project must awaken new curiosity and lead the students' minds into new fields; and (4) the project must involve a considerable span of time for its execution. The point here is that the plan and objective must be capable of development. It is the teacher's responsibility "to look ahead and see whether one stage of achievement will suggest something else to be looked into and done."[16] A curriculum is not a succession of unrelated projects and activities but a consecutive development.

Actually, the teaching method was the same as the steps in thinking. As Dewey put it, "The essentials of method are identical with the essentials of reflection."[17] Following the steps is both the teaching method and the learning method, and the method of thinking itself. It was in *Democracy and Education* (1916), which is the most important work on education of the twentieth century, that Dewey made his conception of thinking the primary goal of the school.

The Project Method Misconstrued. Despite the clarity with which Dewey set forth his idea of thinking as the scientific method applied to problems, it was misconstrued by many of his interpreters. Unbelievable though it may seem, one of these interpreters was none other than his student William H. Kilpatrick, of whom Dewey was reported to have said, "He's the best I ever had."[18] From 1918 until 1938, Kilpatrick occupied the senior chair of philosophy of education at Teachers College, Columbia University, and influenced large numbers of teachers, supervisors, and teacher educators. "More than any other," wrote Lawrence Cremin, "he has been acclaimed as the great interpreter and popularizer of Dewey's theories."[19]

In 1918, Kilpatrick published an article titled "The Project Method," which put "the purposeful act" (as opposed to the thinking process) at the center of the educational process. For Kilpatrick, a project was a "wholehearted purposeful activity proceeding in a social environment."[20] A project could be constructing something (for example, making a kite), an esthetic experience (listening to music or a story), solving a problem (using Dewey's method), or even drill (an example given by Kilpatrick is learning French irregular verbs). There was just one important condition for an activity to be labeled a project; "purposing" by the child. This was nothing other than child interest under another name.

The differences with Dewey were striking. For Dewey, interest was just one of the conditions that had to be met to make a project educational. A truly educative activity had to go beyond Kilpatrick's criterion, and thought had to be involved. For Kilpatrick, the term *project* could apply to virtually any activity as long as the child "purposed" to do it. Kilpatrick even proposed that the entire curriculum of the school be comprised of such projects. (Little wonder that Dewey included a section on the conditions to be met to make a project educational in the second edition of *How We Think*.)

Hence Kilpatrick's project method bore little resemblance to the project method in high school classes in vocational agriculture at that time, which required systematic investigation and knowledge applications. Projects continue to be a useful method in such classes as well as in other subjects to this day, but such projects require far more than "pupil purposing."

Kilpatrick's project method caught on like wildfire during the 1920s and 1930s. More than 60,000 reprints of his article on the project method were circulated. Moreover, Kilpatrick taught some 35,000 students at Teachers College, and had an engaging, compelling personality. Kilpatrick's influence manifested itself in thousands of classrooms in the form of Eskimo projects, dollhouse projects, Dutch projects, train projects, boat projects, and so on. For most teachers a project meant making something, and most projects were of this type. Only rarely were projects based on Dewey's conception of thinking as problem solving.[21] Kilpatrick's project method often involved mere doing without concerted thought and could not be expected to develop thinking power. As Cremin has observed, Kilpatrick, "in seeking to make Dewey's ideas manageable for mass consumption by the teaching profession, ended by transforming them into versions quite different from the originals."[22]

Responsibility of Supervisors. Supervisors were enthusiastic promoters of the project method. A study of the professional literature of the 1920s documents well this assertion. The first volume of *The Journal of Educational Method*, which was published in 1921 and devoted almost entirely to the project method, is an excellent case in point. The articles written by supervisors reflect a single-minded concern with how to get "wholehearted" (after Kilpatrick) adoption of the new method by teachers. This is not to say that there was no discussion about the specific problems with the method, but that it had mainly to do with implementation: the need to "prevent endless duplication (of projects) without throttling child initiative" and the need to help teachers "understand that projects in enjoyment, appreciation, problem solving, and development of skill, if they be purposeful, are as much projects as making a dress or building a sailboat."[23] There was no criticism of Kilpatrick's conception of the project method, although anyone working with teachers could not help but be aware that many of the projects were not educative.

In 1931, Dewey warned that projects were not the only alternative to the traditional curriculum and that many projects were already so trivial that they were miseducative.[24] Kilpatrick's version of progressive education had become the dominant image of progressive education. It would soon tarnish, for it had misconstrued the true nature of thought. Who was to blame for the trivial projects in schools? Were supervisors in any way responsible? These questions are of enormous importance, for it is not just the project method that concerns us but the entire problem of educational fads.

The stark truth which must be faced by supervisors is that they bear the responsibility for screening innovations. Supervisors should know the educational literature and not be beguiled by promotional rhetoric. One of the reasons why the project method spread is that it was promoted as an exemplification of Dewey's theories. Supervisors who accepted this had not read their Dewey. Dewey's conception of thinking as the scientific method applied to all kinds of problems was outlined in *How We Think* and *Democracy and Education*. It is not expecting too much for professionals, to whom the public has entrusted the responsibility of educational leadership, to know the basic ideas of the leading thinkers in the field.

Most of the literature on the project method in professional journals was promotional. This is all too typical in fads. What must be looked for are dissenting ideas from authoritative sources. Is there a dissenting view? (In the case of the project method, there were several.) What does it say? In screening educational innovations, supervisors must comb the literature. This takes time, but it can prevent the tragic waste of resources: energy, money—and time.

The adoption of innovations should be based on systematic evaluation of the innovation rather than on personal conviction. One supervisor exclaimed her "deep-seated conviction regarding the value of the project method in our schools" and then launched into a sea of rhetoric about her "gripping interest."[25] Faith and conviction are not substitutes for evidence that a new method meets the goals of the school more effectively than present procedure. Although we like to think of ourselves as more sophisticated than the supervisors of the 1920s, we keep making the same mistakes. The open classroom movement of the late 1960s and early 1970s, for example, was based largely on faith, and rhetoric, and the "bandwagon effect."

Finally, as mentioned earlier, innovations should spring from an attempt to solve a problem in the classroom or school rather than being imposed on the present situation. Kilpatrick's project method was spun out of his own imagination, and visited on the schools as the one true method. It went the way of all fads while Dewey's conception of thinking as problem solving prevailed as a key principle for educational and social progress.

In sum, the supervisor's responsibility is to create among teachers a desire to use those methods that have been shown to be most effective. Certainly, we want teachers to give up old methods—when the newer methods are better than the old ones. Supervisors can avoid fads by doing the following: (1) knowing the basic ideas in American education (e.g., thinking as an educational method of problem solving), (2) searching for dissenting ideas from authoritative sources when bombarded with propaganda about a new instructional innovation (computers, for instance), (3) basing the adoption of a new method on research that shows that the new method helps children learn more effectively, and (4) helping teachers to solve *their* classroom problems.

The Core Curriculum

Some schools did base their curriculums on Dewey's problem-solving method. The famed Lincoln School of Teachers College, Columbia University, is one example.[26] The core curriculum, an innovation at the secondary school level, was based on Dewey's idea of thinking as problem solving. Sometimes a core curriculum was devoted to certain preplanned themes or social issues which became the areas for problems for the students to solve. Materials needed to solve the problems were drawn from whatever fields of knowledge were appropriate. A more radical version of the core was the "open core," where part or much of the educational program was planned by the students and teachers cooperatively, on the basis of the problems and interests of the students. The objective was wider personal and social understanding and involvement.

The Eight-Year Study. When evaluations of such core programs were undertaken, improved achievement and attitudes were found to result. Of great importance for supervisors was one effort to improve education by putting into practice core curricula based on student needs and interests—the Progressive Education Association's Eight-Year Study. The study was instituted in 1933 and thirty progressive schools took part. It was found that the graduates of these schools did as well or better in college than the graduates of traditional high schools. Moreover, the students in schools judged to be the most experimental (departed most from tradition) did the best.[27]

Of great importance for supervisors were the findings of the Eight-Year Study on the effects of supervision. Curriculum consultants were available to assist each of the thirty schools in making changes in the curriculum. First they made an introductory visit, and then they were available on call. Those schools that took the most advantage of assistance from the consultants made the most significant curriculum changes.[28]

Origin of the Workshop

One of the most important approaches to inservice education is the workshop. The workshop is actually a contribution of the Eight-Year Study. The first workshop was organized in the summer of 1936 by Ralph W. Tyler, director of evaluation for the Eight-Year Study, in response to demands by teachers from the thirty schools. The teachers were feeling confused about how to approach the task of developing a curriculum. They came to the Tyler-led six-week institute at The Ohio State University with definite problems on which they wished to work, and then the term "workshop" was coined. The participants received assistance from various faculty members, and the results were so useful that more workshops were organized. The workshop quickly became recognized as an effective instrument for the inservice education of professionals. How to conduct a workshop is discussed in Chapter 13.

METHODS FOR INDIVIDUALIZED INSTRUCTION

As we have discussed, the coming of class instruction was a great advance. In addition to making it more economically possible to realize the ideal of universal educational opportunity in practice, class instruction permitted progressive methods of learning. Through class discussion and mutual study of public issues, for instance, schools could devote direct effort to helping youngsters develop the skills of participation in civic life required of citizens in a democracy. Moreover, there was an opportunity for a richer curriculum. Class organization made it possible to bring a wider range of experience into the school through dramatics, social studies, vocal and instrumental music, dance, recreation, physical education, and laboratory science.

Self-Paced Instruction

There is no doubt that enormous gains were made by class organization. But as we developed it into a standardized system of groupings and promotions, some debits were evident. Children varied tremendously in their rate of progress. Although class teaching and promotion of pupils in large numbers had administrative merits, it left much to be desired pedagogically. Children differed in the time required of the teacher. Some children, if allowed to work on their own without interruption, forged ahead quickly, but other children needed help. "Different amounts of time are required by the various pupils for the mastery of various topics," observed a school psychologist in 1925.[29] "Most students can attain a high level of learning capability . . . if they are given sufficient time to achieve mastery," wrote Bloom a half century later.[30] What were known as "individual instruction" in the 1920s and "mastery learning" in the 1970s and 1980s were based on the idea that the knowledge and skills needed by all children can be broken into unit tasks which children can master through the use of self-instructive, self-corrective materials. Mastery learning and programmed instruction have had a long (if not always distinguished) history.

It is of interest and importance that these plans were attempts to adjust schoolwork to the child *within* the traditional class organization. As early as 1888, however, an administrator (interestingly enough) had gone further to advocate completely individual progress. Preston Search, superintendent of schools in Pueblo, Colorado, held that each child should proceed at his or her own rate, and this was done in Pueblo during the years of Search's superintendency, 1888–94. When Search went to Los Angeles in 1894, he attempted to introduce his plan of individual instruction without gaining the support of the public. Within a few months the school board was dissatisfied and removed Search on the ground that he was not legally elected. According to the Los Angeles *Daily Times,* the real reason would read: "Dismissed for attempting to introduce improved methods in the Los Angeles public schools."[31]

Be that as it may, most plans for adapting the school program to individual differences retain the class and promotion system (perhaps because of the advantages mentioned earlier). Although "learning at one's own pace" may sound radical at first, it seems less so as one recognizes that children are still required to complete the course of study ("master" a set of objectives) for promotion. Some so-called systems of "individualized instruction" are less flexible in this regard than are systems that leave the decision of whether to promote to teachers.

The Burk Plan of Individual Instruction. In 1913 an innovation went forward at the San Francisco State Normal School that was destined to leave an ineradicable mark on education. Under the leadership of Frederic L. Burk, the faculty of the training school department had written self-instructive materials that would permit pupils to progress in their work with little or no assistance from their teacher. Class recitations were abandoned and no daily assignments were given. Known as the "Individual System," there can be little doubt that Burk's system was the forerunner of programmed instruction.

Under the San Francisco State Normal School Plan, the curriculum was organized into "fundamental subjects" and group work. The fundamental subjects were, of course, those subjects that lent themselves most readily to the individual system—arithmetic, reading, spelling, and grammar. The material for the individual system of instruction was simply drawn from state texts, and the promotion system was not done away with. When a youngster could pass a test on the work outlined for a grade, he or she received a promotion slip.

Burk wrote a monograph, *Remedy for Lock-Step Schooling,* on the "Individual System" at the normal school. He indicted the traditional class system for doing "permanent violence" to all kinds of pupils. "It does injury to the rapid and quick-thinking pupils, because these must shackle their stride to keep pace with the mythical average," he wrote, going on to point out that "the class system does a greater injury to the large number who make progress slower than the rate of the mythical average pupil . . . By setting the pace of a mathematical average, education for nearly one half the class is made impossible. *They are foredoomed to failure before they begin.* . . . This policy is, of course, as inhuman as it is stupid."[32] Burk's monograph was widely read and his plan of individual instruction attracted national attention.

The Winnetka Plan. In 1918, the school board in Winnetka, Illinois, decided that they wanted a superintendent who would administer the schools in the spirit of Burk's work at San Francisco. As might be expected, they went directly to Burk, who recommended a member of his faculty, Carleton W. Washburne. Thus began the educational program that came to be known as the Winnetka Plan.

At Winnetka Superintendent Washburne started with arithmetic; as at the San Francisco State Normal School, teachers developed self-instruction materials. "We did an intensive job of what is now called 'programming' instruction," recalled Washburne years later.[33] Whereas under Burk's plan teachers had corrected the children's daily work, Washburne and his staff introduced self-correction. When a pupil had completed a set of arithmetic exercises, he or she turned to the answer sheet and corrected his or her own work. If they made errors, they tried a second, similar group of exercises, and if they still made errors, they tried a third. They were free to ask other children or the teacher for help.

Following arithmetic, reading, spelling, and grammar were also programmed. Washburne had divided the curriculum into two parts. The first part consisted of "the common essentials—the 'three R's' and similar subject matter," and the second, self-expression and group activities. Washburne defined the "common essentials" as "those knowledges and skills needed by everyone."[34]

But how was it decided what everyone needed to know? Was it simply on the basis of what could be programmed? No one raised these questions more insightfully than William Kilpatrick. In a critique of the Winnetka Plan, he pointed out that attitudes, appreciations, and ideals had been omitted from Washburne's list of "common essentials," which was to "queer the list." They had been left out not because they were deemed unessential, contended Kilpatrick, but because they did not lend themselves to programming. In Kilpatrick's own words, "The content is chosen on one basis; a name that implies a better basis is the given. Not 'the common essentials' but 'some common essentials that lend themselves to self-teaching assignment'—these constitute the content of the first part of the Winnetka scheme."[35] More than a half century later, letting the mechanism itself determine what should be taught, and then rationalizing the choice as "what everyone needs to know," continue to be troublesome earmarks of schemes for "individualization of instruction."

Mastery Learning. According to Bloom[36] and many other psychologists, virtually all children can learn what schools have to teach with well-designed instruction, remedial help when needed, and the time they need to master the material. The idea is sound and constructive. What has come to be known as "mastery learning" is, ostensibly, an effort to put the idea into practice. But when we look at mastery learning as it is often applied, we see that it is nothing more or less than a system of programmed instruction. Mastery learning has all the problems of Washburne's system of individual instruction—and more.

What, actually, is the mastery learning approach? Essentially, it is a procedure in which pupils progress through sequences of hierarchically ordered learning tasks. They may take as much time as they need to "master" the material, but are not allowed to start a unit of material until they have "mastered" previous units. Whether a youngster has achieved "mastery" is determined by evaluation—usually by a score such as 85 percent on an end-of-unit test.

Mastery learning is based on the concept of "equality of outcomes" as a goal of education, rather than optimization of opportunity. According to Bloom, for 95 percent of students equality of outcomes is a realistic possibility with good teaching, remedial help and enough time to learn.[37] But "mastery" systems of instruction are ready-made and self-contained. As such they eliminate the need for the teacher's own plan and the opportunity for the teacher to vary the curriculum to meet individual needs. In addition, as Arlin points out, "relying upon competency testing to determine if an individual student has mastered the material gives little value and validity to teachers' professional judgment." As Arlin contends, "The tests should serve only as one source of information available to the professional staff who must then exercise judgment in making a decision."[38] And as far as remediation is concerned, it is built into the system of programmed instruction.

For Bloom, as for Washburne before him, the crucial learning variable is time. But Washburne probably would have been dismayed at the permutation of this idea in the convergent-group model of mastery learning. All youngsters must master a given unit before the class as a whole begins the next unit. This is the lockstep decried by Frederic Burk, only worse because it is under the guise of egalitarianism.

As any supervisor knows, the teacher's problem of dealing with learners who are first to finish assignments is major. Any plan of self-paced learning that expects pupils merely to sit and wait is self-defeating. Moreover, time is a finite resource in education as in any other domain of life. It is how time is used that counts, not time itself. The good teacher uses time in making his or her teaching more effective and in providing for individual differences.

Mastery learning is narrowly focused on specific skills and factual lessons. Arlin contends, as did Kilpatrick a half-century earlier, that "what is quantitatively measurable can drive out that which is not. Some of our most important school goals are not quantitatively measurable."[39] Moreover, mastery learning goals are stated as minimum competencies. Fast learners and slow learners are drawn to the lowest common denominator. This is absolutely untenable in a democratic society which seeks the optimal, not the minimal development of every individual.

There is no question that adapting the curriculum to individual differences is one of the teacher's major problems. The teacher must understand that programmed instruction is not synonymous with individualized instruction, whatever the name given the system of programmed instruction. (Such approaches are often misleadingly labeled "individual learning systems" or the like.) Devices for self-paced learning can be helpful in learning skills and factual knowledge, but this is not the whole curriculum. The supervisor can assist the teacher in accommodating individual differences by suggesting group activities where every youngster works at her or his level. Each student can work on a subdivision of a group project. If she has a special talent, she can be directed into an assignment that will develop it or, if she has a weakness, an assignment that will remedy it.

In a sixth-grade unit on Europe, some youngsters may be studying architectural epochs while others are making a papier-mâché model of the Leaning Tower of Pisa. A third group is planning a two-week trip to the British Isles. The first and third groups may need less creative skill than the second, but all will have to do library work to gain the needed information. Differentiated assignments are an excellent means of providing for individual differences. The point is that concern for the problems related to teaching children who are vastly (and gratifyingly) different individuals, rather than the imposition of mechanical devices, must characterize supervision.

TOWARD A THEORY OF SUPERVISION

The specialized body of knowledge in supervision (as in any profession) is in a continual state of development. This body of knowledge is enlarged and enriched as solutions are found to the practical problems of supervisors. Good supervision, in turn, requires that supervisory practices are based on this body of knowledge, or theoretical principles. Principles are guides to thinking and selecting practices. Put another way, methods or techniques are ways of doing things, and principles are the basis for doing them. The true professional always has a clear idea of why he or she selects certain procedures.

The historical development of supervisory principles is important professional knowledge. Some of the early concepts of supervision have evolved into fundamental principles of modern supervision. Similarly, some of the early problems of supervision are still unresolved today. They must be solved if supervision is to be fully professional.

Fundamental Principles

In this section we consider two early concepts of supervision that are so fundamental that we almost take them for granted.

The major emphasis of supervision should be on improving the quality of teaching and learning. A basic principle of supervision that goes back to our earliest educational leaders (persons such as Mann and Barnard) is that the emphasis of supervision should be on the improvement of instruction. As we have seen, improving the quality of teaching was uppermost in the minds of our first city superintendents, who appeared in the second quarter of the nineteenth century.

Even today, however, one still finds supervisors whose major concerns are with such matters as the punctuality of teachers and seeing to it that administrative edicts are obeyed.

Supervision and curriculum development are a complementary process. The idea that in proper educational practice, supervision of instruction and curriculum development will be found operating hand in hand dates from the 1920s. It was a basic concept in the famous program of curriculum revision that Superintendent Jesse Newlon introduced in Denver in 1922. (According to Cremin, Newlon's program was "probably the first in which classroom teachers participated significantly in a system-wide effort at reform."[40] The Denver concept of supervision and curriculum development as an interrelated process became a basic principle of school administration. As one writer put it in 1927, "In the instance of administrative practice, supervision of instruction and curriculum development should operate conjointly."[41]

Addressing the matter of the professionalization of supervisors, Cremin dates the training of curriculum specialists to the Denver program in 1922. "Once the

Denver program caught on," he explains, "it was obvious that specialists other than the superintendent would be needed to manage the process, and it was for the purpose of training such specialists that the curriculum field was created. Beginning initially as a subfield of educational administration in some universities, of elementary education in others, and of secondary education in still others, the study of curriculum gradually came into its own. . . . "[42]

In her classic book, *Curriculum Development: Theory and Practice* (1962), Taba also viewed supervision and curriculum development as an interrelated process, and this idea is also central in subsequent treatments of the curriculum field by other writers, including the present authors.[43] This principle has important implications for the professional preparation of supervisors. Preparatory programs should deal in depth with the problems of curriculum development and they should provide prospective supervisors with internships in school systems committed to curriculum improvement. At present, this necessary component (the internship) is not universally included in programs for preparing supervisors.

Fundamental Problems

One measure of a profession is the application of scientific methods to the problems encountered by practitioners in their day-to-day work. Problem solving leads to improved conditions and better ways of doing things and is a means of development in any field, be it medicine, engineering, or education. Unfortunately, the fundamental problems of professional supervisors on the job in the 1920s are still the fundamental problems of supervisors in the closing decades of the twentieth century. This is not to say that there has been no improvement in the knowledge base for educational supervision. Quite the contrary, in the past twenty years there has been a striking expansion in the body of knowledge and skill on which supervisory services rest (for example, in the skills and understandings needed for effective leadership). But the improvement in the knowledge base for educational supervision has, in the main, resulted from developments in other fields, such as organizational theory and psychology. Moreover, the best knowledge will remain only theoretical unless put to use on the job, and this depends on the solution of such mundane but critical problems as time for supervision.

This section will attempt to discuss very briefly three of the fundamental problems of supervision. They are dealt with in detail later in the text.

Time for Supervision. "The improvement of class instruction is a *function* of the superintendent, the supervisors and the principals. The *responsibility* for the improvement of instruction in a particular building or group of buildings belongs to the principal."[44] So wrote a member of the National Education Association's research division in the late 1920s, who went on to report that according to NEA's Department of Elementary Principals, at least half of the principal's time should be allotted to supervision (the rest being divided among administrative, clerical, teaching, and miscellaneous activities). He hastened to add, however, that "not until competent clerical help is provided, useless reports eliminated, and adequate office facilities supplied will it be possible for many principals to give half of their time to supervision."[45]

This proviso could have been written yesterday. The instructional leadership role of the principal has, if anything, become more firmly established in the literature on the principalship and is the focus of a new body of literature on school change. Moreover, principals (and superintendents) continue to view principals as instructional leaders.[46] But principals continue to be bogged down with paperwork and secretarial chores, and they continue to devote little time to educational leadership. A national survey, undertaken cooperatively by the Association for Supervision and Curriculum Development, the University of Tulsa, and both national elementary and secondary principals' associations, revealed that the majority of principals "were found most often in the office responding to communications and engaged in other forms of paper work."[47] The study, which involved a sample of 163 elementary, middle, junior high, and senior high principals, concluded that "as reported by the principals themselves, instructional leadership is generally being compromised in favor of office mandates."[48]

The problem of time for supervision may be old but it is not unsolvable. In fact, the first step toward solution, observational research on school principals, has already taken place, giving us some highly useful generalizations. The second step, putting what we know into action and overcoming the conditions that stand in the way of principals devoting time to educational leadership has yet to be taken. Interestingly, there is ample evidence that more is involved in the problem than a simple shortage of clerical help. Personal choice of activities is also a factor. If one observes the on-the-job behavior of principals, as Morris and his associates did (over a three-year period in Chicago), one finds that "like other workers, principals hold attitudes toward their own job; they like some parts and dislike others" and that "principals can shape the job to their own liking— *spending time on the things they are good at or enjoy doing.*"[49]

The importance of personal choice as a factor in how principals spend their energies is buttressed by the national survey cited above which found that the majority of principals had clerical assistance, but that instructional leadership was still a limited function. In fact, staff development, an important component of instructional leadership, was not shown as an activity engaged in by principals for even thirty minutes over a two-day period.[50]

Why do principals choose to spend their time on activities other than instructional leadership?

The answer, in many cases at least (and probably in most cases), is that they have not had the professional preparation for instructional leadership. If you are prepared to do it, you see it as your area of competence and responsibility, and consequently it becomes a professional obligation. As Morris and his fellow researchers conclude, "Improved understanding of the workaday life of the principal is casting doubts on the adequacy of university training programs for administrators."[51] Despite the fact that most preservice programs in educational administration do provide an internship or field experience, typically the experiences provided are with administration and management only. If we expect principals to exercise instructional leadership, preparation for the principalship must include observation of building principals involved in instructional leadership and a guided internship, similar to the student teaching experience, where real problems of curriculum improvement and staff development are turned over to the administration student.

Thus the problem of time for supervision is undergirded by the far deeper problem of preparation for the profession. As long as preservice programs for principals neglect the kind of preparation described above, the problem of time for supervision will remain. More important, principals will be unable to exert the leadership needed for educational improvement.

Attitude of Teachers Toward Supervision. "The success of America's great experiment in public education will be determined to a large extent by the attitude of the classroom teacher toward supervision." So remarked Jesse Newlon in 1923, in an address before the NEA. "No system of supervision will function," he continued, "unless the attitude of the classroom teacher is one of sympathetic cooperation. The attitude of the teacher will be determined by the kind of supervision that is attempted."[52]

Newlon observed that supervision was still, as it had been in the past, "inspectorial, fault-finding, and mechanical in character." If we were to expect a favorable attitude on the part of teachers, we would have to "get rid of the old idea that the chief function of the supervisor is to give directions and to hold the teacher responsible for a minute following of these directions. *I conceive of the supervisor as a leader charged with the responsibility of organizing a teaching force for the study of its professional problems,*" he said.[53]

Newlon's observations are still strikingly valid. The future of public education depends strongly on leadership for problem solving. Yet, as Leiter and Cooper have observed, supervision continues to follow "highly mechanical and structured rote models—education as received doctrine. . . . Staff development programs appear to regard adult learners as below average in intelligence, requiring that they be talked down to and that they be asked to handle only the most oversimplified, predigested, and flimsy ideas and concepts. They are thought to prefer 'hands on' activities, and the glossy or 'turn on' approach rather than the analytic and serious."[54] Supervision is lagging far behind the best theory, which conceives of teachers as professionals and supervisors as real leaders who help teachers face their professional problems and continually grow in the ability to relate theory to practice.

If authoritarian supervisory practices were unacceptable in the 1920s when elementary school teachers spent a year or two in a normal school to obtain professional preparation and did not receive a good general education, they are even less acceptable today when both elementary and secondary school teaching require a longer, broader, and deeper preparation in a college or university. In fact, teachers today are well-educated people. They simply need leadership in dealing with the basic problems they meet. As Leiter and Cooper point out, "Imposed inservice (education) is met with deserved cynicism. It is someone else's notion of what one needs."[55] Newlon's conception of the supervisor as a leader of other professionals remains fresh, valid—and untried. It must be implemented if teaching is to attract and hold the most able persons and make good its claim to professional status.

Influence of the Business and Industrial Ideology on Supervision. "Scientific Management finds the methods of procedure which are most efficient for actual conditions, and secures their use on the part of the workers." The writer was Franklin Bobbitt, a young professor of educational administration at the University of Chicago. The time was 1913 and a mania for "scientific management," a new system of industrial management, was sweeping the country. Bobbitt was connecting the operation of the schools (which were being accused by the public of gross inefficiency) with scientific management. The "workers" in the school-as-factory were, of course, teachers. Management (supervisors) was to measure the methods of teaching being used in terms of "productivity" (pupil outcomes), select the best ones, and see that workers use them. "The burden of finding the best methods is too large and too complicated to be laid on the shoulders of the teachers," said Bobbitt.[56]

Needless to say, this view of the teacher is diametrically opposed to the conception of the teacher as a professional. Under the latter conception, teachers act on their own on the basis of a body of professional knowledge and their own insight and ability. Unfortunately, the concept of education as an industry in which productivity is assessed in quantitative units of output has done much to retard the development of teaching as a profession. The "teacher-proof" curricula of the 1960s and the accountability movement of the 1970s, which viewed teachers as technicians rather than as responsible professionals, were based on the industrial model and did much to weaken the conception of education as a profession. Moreover, research favors the professional approach to school improvement over the managerial-efficiency approach. The Ford Foundation learned from its policy of excluding teachers from curriculum improvement that *"the people who are expected to put new programs into operation should participate in defining problems and developing solutions."*[57]

Yet despite what we know, Bobbitt's version of scientific management is alive and well in the field of supervision. One of the results is that supervisors stress time-on-task (an industrial term if ever there was one) and the mastery of narrow, mechanical skills in reading and arithmetic—those skills that can be most easily measured. As McNeil points out, "We do not know that the education of pupils is advanced by teachers who follow the newly prescribed processes, only that certain skills are attained."[58] In fact, as McNeil reminds us, not unexpectedly, since the "achievement tests demand low level responses," there are "low correlations between high level questions asked by teachers and achievement of pupils."[59] Thus the processes prescribed by supervisors are not validated for higher-level understandings such as critical thinking and application and, indeed, could work against the development of higher-level cognitive processes.

Educators learned before 1920 that teaching was not comparable with handling tons of pig iron; one could not develop the "science of the job" as easily. (Pig-iron handling was the example of the system of scientific management given by Frederick Taylor, who is credited with the origin of the system.[60]) In education the relation between teaching methods and "productivity" would have to be confined to outcomes that were measurable by achievement tests. This had the effect of reducing education to its lowest terms. The industrial shoe simply did not fit the educational foot. What is so unbelievable, however, is that educators are still walking around with pinched toes. The seduction of efficiency (for efficiency's sake, but outwardly for the sake of children) has been irresistible.

Like our other fundamental problems in supervision, this one is not insoluble. One key, as Raymond Callahan pointed out in his classic book *Education and the Cult of Efficiency,* is in the education of teachers and administrators. "We must require that our school administrators have an excellent education at the graduate level . . . in the social sciences and in the humanities as well as in their professional work. . . . The future of our free society requires that our schools be centers of learning and not factories or playgrounds. To make them so will require educators who are students and scholars, not accountants or public relations men."[61]

It is also important that supervisors on the job recognize the difference between science and scientism—the former being focused on problem solutions, whereas the latter is concerned with mechanistic approaches in the management of teaching and learning. The development of a science of education is the concern of every professional. But it will be recalled that science begins with a problem in the educational situation identified by practitioners.[62]

SUMMARY

The professionalization of supervision is inseparable from the professionalization of teaching, which actually began as a result of the influence of the scientific method on educational method. Ways of teaching reflect ways of knowledge getting. In earlier times, when the method of arriving at truth was closed and authoritarian, many of our geography and history books were written on the plan of the Catechism—on a question-and-answer basis. The child simply had to memorize the content and the teacher's role was simply to see that the pupil could recite the answers to the questions. Teaching skill was not required. But a new method of acquiring knowledge was formulated in the world, based on observation and experience rather than on given ideas. When educators began to apply the outlook of the scientific method to the learning process of children, pupils had to use their senses and their minds. Teaching skill was required. Public interest in the new Pestalozzian methods, which were based on the elements of the scientific method and the view of education as an enjoyable process, called the professional supervisor into being. Oddly, although the best educational theory for children has long moved away from received truths, supervision of adults is, on the whole, still authoritarian and traditional (despite the vast body of research supporting an approach to school improvement that involves teachers in problem diagnosis and problem solution).

We tend to think of supervision as an influence on teaching rather than the reverse. Yet innovations in teaching have profoundly influenced supervisory functions and practices. As a result of the object-teaching idea, a Pestalozzian form of instruction popularized at Oswego, new subject matter was introduced into the school (science, for instance), necessitating the writing of new courses of study. Supervisors became involved in curriculum development. The Herbartian five formal steps for organizing a lesson were, of course, intended for teachers, but the neat sequence of steps provided a ready tool for supervisors—

the lesson plan (one that has been used and misused ever since). The success of our educational system depends on teachers understanding the theories behind what they teach. And only then can they be true professionals. Thus supervisors as educational leaders must be cognizant of the basic ideas of the leading thinkers in education. Some of the earlier methods are important to this day. The problem-solving method set forth by Dewey early in this century remains a fresh and vital part of our educational theory. (Unfortunately, it remains far too seldom implemented.)

As professionals, supervisors also need to understand that many of our innovations are not new, but reinventions of old educational models that had deep and fundamental problems. Educators who developed programmed instruction in the early decades of this century quickly found that what is most easily measured quantitatively (mechanical skills in arithmetic and reading, for example) can drive out that which is not so easily quantified (higher-level abilities such as critical thinking and the application of knowledge in life-related situations, for instance). We are experiencing the same problem today with mastery learning and other systems of "individualized instruction." This is not progress. As professionals, those who are involved in the administration and supervision of school systems are responsible for preventing the terribly wasteful repetition of past mistakes. Innovations should develop from attempts to solve problems, and this is the best way to avoid fads and to make progress.

Supervision in education rests on two fundamental principles: the major emphasis of supervision is on improving the quality of teaching and learning, and supervision and curriculum development operate hand in hand. Personal choice and professional preparation for educational leadership are factors in the problem of time for supervision. The attitude of teachers toward supervision is determined by the kind of supervision received. The school-as-factory model, which sacrifices educational goals for "efficiency," has been very deleterious for the professionalization of teaching. Under this model, teachers are viewed as technicians who mechanically follow detailed instructions from supervisors. If competent people are to be attracted into the teaching profession, and if we are to provide an excellent education for our children, teachers must be treated as professionals. This is one of supervision's most crucial problems.

PROBLEMS FOR STUDY AND DISCUSSION

1. How adequately does the graduate program in educational administration and/or supervision in which you are involved prepare prospective principals and/or supervisors to exercise educational leadership? Explain.

2. Draw up a list of procedures used by schools and teachers to adapt instruction to individual differences. Which, in your opinion, are the most effective? Why?

3. In this chapter it was pointed out that the attitude of teachers toward supervision is determined by the kind of supervisory services provided. Interview a

number of teachers (in a private setting with one person at a time) and report on the following:

(a) The problems that they find most serious in classroom instruction and management.

(b) The comments that they make about staff development programs in which they are or have been involved.

(c) The means that you might select for developing the staff development program into a desirable and effective service for teachers.

4. As discussed in this chapter, supervisors have the professional responsibility for preventing educational fads. List three or four principles that supervisors can use as guidance in meeting this responsibility.

5. Do you think that object teaching has had a lasting influence on the methods of teaching in the elementary school? Explain.

6. For Dewey, thinking is not a matter of "disciplining the mind" but the application of the scientific method to all kinds of problems from a simple everyday kind of problem to complex social problems and abstract intellectual problems. Examine several curriculum guides in the social studies at the secondary level. What conclusions can you draw regarding the influence of Dewey's conception of thinking on objectives and methods in the social studies?

7. Do you agree with the authors of this text that the business and industrial ideology has undermined the professionalization of supervision? Explain.

8. What is your assessment of the following statement by Raymond E. Callahan?

Efficiency and economy—important as they are—must be considered in the light of the quality of education that is being provided. Equally important is the inefficiency and false economy of forcing educators to devote their time and energy to cost accounting. We must learn that saving money through imposing an impossible teaching load on teachers is, in terms of the future of our free society, a very costly practice.[63]

NOTES

1. Allison Comish, "The Contract Plan in Retrospect," *School and Society,* Vol. 34 (July 18, 1931), pp. 95–97. See also Clay J. Daggart and Florence A. Petersen, "A Survey of Popular Plans for Instruction," *Educational Administration and Supervision,* Vol. 18 (October 1932), pp. 499–522.
2. R. Freeman Butts and Lawrence A. Cremin, *A History of Education in American Culture* (New York: Holt, Rinehart and Winston, 1953), pp. 54–55.
3. Johann Pestalozzi, *How Gertrude Teaches Her Children* (Syracuse, N.Y.: 1894).
4. Ned H. Dearborn, *The Oswego Movement in American Education* (New York: Teachers College Press, 1925), p. 102.
5. Elwood P. Cubberley, *Public Education in the United States* (Boston: Houghton Mifflin, 1947), p. 390.
6. Ibid., p. 391.

7. Cited in Cubberley, op. cit., p. 362.
8. Elizabeth Mayo, *A Manual of Elementary Instruction, for Infant School and Private Tuition,* 1860; cited in Lois Coffey Mossman, *Changing Conceptions Relative to the Planning of Lessons* (New York: Teachers College Press, 1924), p. 4.
9. Ibid.
10. Mrs. A. C. Martin, "What Shall We Attempt in Elementary Schools?" National Education Association, *Proceedings* (The Association: 1874), p. 276.
11. Willard S. Elsbree, *The American Teacher* (New York: American Book, 1938), p. 407.
12. John Dewey, *How We Think* (Lexington, Mass.: D. C. Heath, 1933; originally published in 1910), Preface to the first edition.
13. John Dewey, *Philosophy and Civilization* (New York: Minton, Balch, 1931), p. 326.
14. Dewey, *How We Think,* op. cit., p. 116.
15. Ibid., p. 218.
16. Ibid., p. 219.
17. John Dewey, *Democracy and Education* (New York: Macmillan, 1916), p. 180.
18. Quoted in Lawrence A. Cremin, *The Transformation of the School* (New York: Alfred A. Knopf, 1961), p. 216.
19. Ibid., p. 215.
20. William H. Kilpatrick, "The Project Method," *Teachers College Record,* Vol. 19 (September 1918), p. 320.
21. William H. Kilpatrick, "Dangers and Difficulties of the Project Method and How to Overcome Them," *Teachers College Record,* Vol. 22 (September 1921), pp. 283–321.
22. Cremin, op. cit., p. 221.
23. Margaret E. Wells, "One Phase of the Technique of the Project Method of Teaching," *The Journal of Educational Method,* Vol. 1 (October 1921), p. 18; H. G. Masters et al., "The Supervisor and the Project Method," *The Journal of Educational Method,* Vol. 1 (March 1922), p. 268.
24. John Dewey, *The Way Out of the Educational Confusion* (Cambridge, Mass: Harvard University Press, 1931).
25. Rose Carrigan, "A Supervisor's Experience in Directing a Try-out of the Project Method," *The Journal of Educational Method,* Vol. 1 (October 1921), p. 2.
26. Cremin, op. cit., pp. 280–291; Daniel Tanner and Laurel N. Tanner, *Curriculum Development: Theory into Practice,* 2nd ed. (New York: Macmillan, 1980), pp. 313–320.
27. Dean Chamberlain et al., *Did They Succeed in College?* (New York: Harper & Row, 1942), p. 209.
28. Wilford M. Aikin, "The Eight-Year Study: If We Were to Do It Again," *Progressive Education,* Vol. 31 (October 1953), p. 12.
29. A. A. Sutherland, "Factors Causing Maladjustment of Schools to Individuals," Chapter 1 in *Adapting the Schools to Individual Differences,* Twenty-fourth Yearbook of the National Society for the Study of Education (Bloomington, Ill.: Public School Publishing Co., 1925), p. 16.
30. Benjamin S. Bloom, *Human Characteristics and School Learning* (New York: McGraw-Hill, 1976), p. 4.
31. [Los Angeles] *Daily Times,* June 19, 1895; as cited in Theodore L. Reller, *The Development of the City Superintendency of Schools in the United States* (Philadelphia: The Author, 1935), p. 92.
32. Frederic L. Burk, *Remedy for Lock-Step Schooling,* cited in Carleton W. Washburne and Sidney P. Marland, Jr. (eds.), *Winnetka: The History and Significance of an Educational Experiment* (Englewood Cliffs, N.J.: Prentice-Hall, 1963), p. 9.
33. Washburne and Marland, op. cit., p. 26.
34. Carleton W. Washburne, "Burk's Individual System as Developed at Winnetka,"

Chapter 2 in *Adapting the Schools to Individual Differences,* Twenty-fourth Yearbook of the National Society for the Study of Education (Bloomington, Ill.: Public School Publishing Co., 1925), p. 79.

35. William H. Kilpatrick, "An Effort at Appraisal," Chapter 6 in *Adapting the Schools to Individual Differences,* op. cit., p. 281.
36. Bloom, op. cit.
37. Ibid., pp. 215–216.
38. Marshall Arlin, "Teacher Responses to Student Time Differences in Mastery Learning," *American Journal of Education,* Vol. 90 (August 1982), p. 12.
39. Ibid., p. 11.
40. Lawrence A. Cremin, "Curriculum-Making in the United States," *Teachers College Record,* Vol. 73 (December 1971), p. 213.
41. J. A. Clement, "Supervision of Instruction and Curriculum Making in Secondary Schools as a Complementary Process," *Educational Administration and Supervision,* Vol. 13 (March 1927), p. 171.
42. Cremin, "Curriculum-Making in the United States," op. cit., p. 213.
43. Tanner and Tanner, op cit.
44. Frank W. Hubbard, "The Principal as a Supervisor," *The Journal of Educational Method,* Vol. 8 (June 1929), p. 497.
45. Ibid.
46. John Wedman, "Time Management and Instructional Supervision," *Clearing House,* Vol. 55 (March 1982), p. 297.
47. Bruce Howell, "Profile of the Principalship," *Educational Leadership,* Vol. 38 (January 1981), p. 334.
48. Ibid., p. 335.
49. Van Cleve Morris, "The Urban Principal: Middle Manager in the Educational Bureaucracy," *Phi Delta Kappan,* Vol. 63 (June 1982), p. 692.
50. Howell, op. cit., p. 335.
51. Morris, op. cit., p. 692.
52. Jesse H. Newlon, "Attitude of the Teacher Toward Supervision," National Education Association *Proceedings* (Chicago: University of Chicago, 1923), pp. 548–549.
53. Ibid.
54. Maurice Leiter and Myrna Cooper, "How Teacher Unionists View In-Service Education," in Ann Lieberman and Lynne Miller (eds.), *Staff Development: New Demands, New Realities, New Perspectives* (New York: Teachers College Press, 1978), p. 121.
55. Ibid., p. 119.
56. Franklin Bobbitt, *The Supervision of City Schools: Some General Principles of Management Applied to the Problems of City-School Systems,* Twelfth Yearbook of the National Society for the Study of Education, Part I (Bloomington, Ill.; Public School Publishing Co., 1913), pp. 51–52.
57. The Ford Foundation, *Annual Report* (New York: The Foundation, 1973), p. 3.
58. John D. McNeil, "A Scientific Approach to Supervision," Chapter 2 in *Supervision of Teaching,* 1982 Yearbook of the Association of Supervision and Curriculum Development (Alexandria, Va.: The Association, 1982), p. 29.
59. Ibid., pp. 29–30.
60. Frederick W. Taylor, *The Principles of Scientific Management* (New York: 1911).
61. Raymond E. Callahan, *Education and the Cult of Efficiency* (Chicago: University of Chicago Press, 1962), pp. 260–261.
62. John Dewey, *The Sources of a Science of Education* (New York: Liveright, 1929).
63. Callahan, op. cit., p. 263.

SELECTED REFERENCES

Association for Supervision and Curriculum Development. *Supervision of Teaching,* 1982 Yearbook. Alexandria, Va.: The Association, 1982.

Bloom, Benjamin S. *Human Characteristics and School Learning.* New York: McGraw-Hill Book Company, 1976.

Callahan, Raymond E. *Education and the Cult of Efficiency.* Chicago: The University of Chicago Press, 1962.

Cremin, Lawrence A. *The Transformation of the School.* New York: Alfred A. Knopf, Inc., 1961.

Dearborn, Ned H. *The Oswego Movement in the United States.* New York: Teachers College Press, 1925.

Dewey, John. *Democracy and Education.* New York: Macmillan Publishing Company, 1916.

———. *How We Think,* rev. ed. Lexington, Mass.: D. C. Heath and Company, 1933.

Lieberman, Ann, and Lynne Miller (eds.). *Staff Development: New Demands, New Realities, New Perspectives.* New York: Teachers College Press, 1978.

Monroe, Will S. *History of the Pestalozzian Movement in the United States.* Syracuse, N.Y.: C. W. Bardeen, 1907.

Mosher, Ralph L., and David E. Purpel. *Supervision: The Reluctant Profession.* Boston: Houghton Mifflin Company, 1972.

National Education Association, Department of Elementary School Principals. *Activities of the Principal,* Eighth Yearbook. Washington, D.C.: The Association, 1929.

National Society for the Study of Education. *Adapting the Schools to Individual Differences,* Twenty-fourth Yearbook, Part II. Bloomington, Ill.: Public School Publishing Co., 1925.

———. *The Supervision of City Schools: Some General Principles of Management Applied to Education,* Twelfth Yearbook, Part I. Bloomington, Ill.: Public School Publishing Co., 1913.

Reller, Theodore L. *The Development of the City Superintendency of Schools in the United States.* Philadelphia: The Author, 1935.

Sarason, Seymour B. *The Culture of the School and the Problem of Change,* 2nd ed. Boston: Allyn and Bacon, Inc., 1982.

Tanner, Daniel, and Laurel N. Tanner. *Curriculum Development: Theory Into Practice,* 2nd ed. New York: Macmillan Publishing Company, 1980.

Wolcott, Harry F. *The Man in the Principal's Office.* New York: Holt, Rinehart and Winston, 1973.

Wittrock, Merlin C. (ed.). *Handbook of Research on Teaching,* 3rd ed. New York: Macmillan Publishing Company, 1986.

Part II

Frameworks and Functions of Educational Supervision

Chapter 3

The Administrative Organization of Supervision

Like other professionals, supervisors work as individuals. But the supervisor is also a member of an organization—a team of individuals who accomplish objectives more efficiently together than these same persons would separately and individually. Recently, there has been much interest in how organizations behave. A vast body of literature has developed because many people want to understand how to make organizations better (to stop what seem to be faceless bureaucracies from controlling their lives). Still others are interested in high organizational performance, that is, how the organization's goals can be met more effectively. As Dewey suggested, educators should draw on knowledge from the behavioral sciences, as needed, to solve educational problems.[1]

The need to integrate the supervisory team into a coherent and effective whole is an important educational problem, and research on organizations can provide helpful insights. Our purpose in this chapter is to examine supervision in terms of the organizational milieu in which it takes place. The essential question with which we are concerned is how the organization of supervision can positively influence the achievement of supervisory goals.

THE RELATION BETWEEN ADMINISTRATION AND SUPERVISION

Azumi and Hage define organizations as "structured bodies designed to achieve *specific objectives* that are part of some larger institutional process." Schools, they go on to tell us, are part of our institution of education, as are colleges and universities.[2] The important point for us here is that organizations are designed to achieve specific goals. The reason we have schools is to provide education for children. Thus responsibility for curriculum and instruction is not merely one of the domains of administrative concern; it is the basic concern in school administration. This will come as no surprise to the reader, for in Chapters 1 and 2 we discussed the history of this central concern. The first superintendents spent much of their time offering suggestions to teachers when visiting schools and classrooms. Indeed, visiting and examining the schools and preparing courses of study for the schools were regarded by superintendents as their most important responsibilities. The establishment of the principalship was brought about because of the need for a principal teacher, a teacher who could provide educational leadership. As we have seen, this role continues to be given a top priority rating by principals.

Improving the Educational Program

From time to time the educational leadership role of the school superintendent has been reaffirmed by superintendents themselves. Thus in 1957, the American Association of School Administrators stated in their Thirty-fifth Yearbook, "The superintendent of schools knows his most important task is that of improving instruction."[3]

More recently, the superintendent of the Atlanta school system set goals in the area of curriculum and instruction as his top priority.[4] Interestingly, even if one happens to view the school executive as an educational "manager," the educational program is the prime concern. For as Monahan and Hengst point out in their textbook on educational administration, the "fundamental aim of school managers is to see that resources are applied to the maintenance and improvement of instruction."[5]

All of the other responsibilities in the day-to-day management and administration of public schools, such as staff personnel, pupil personnel, community relations, maintaining buildings and grounds, and business management, are engaged in for the purpose of providing the most effective educational program possible. Now, as in the early days of our school systems, there is an underlying theme that pervades all of these activities: the importance of excellence and the need to improve the schools continually. Excellence is defined in terms of the educational program (the specific reason for having schools), and the role of the school administrator is to improve the program. But responsibility for the educational program is not just the major area of administrative concern, it is the main concern of the entire organization, including, of course, the supervisors. The point is that it is impossible to separate administration from supervision in function. To do so is to regard the other administrative responsibilities (business management, for example) as ends in themselves and thus miss out on the opportunity for integrating the interests of the entire organization. Shared concerns lead to free communication throughout an organization and to a more effective organization.[6]

Although teaching and learning are the major functions of the school, the administrator is not a specialist in curriculum development, but works with and through all the persons involved in the instructional process. Because their responsibility is for the entire school district or school, superintendents and principals have an integrative and relational concern for the educational program. As Campbell and his associates emphasize, superintendents and principals are generalists, but generalists can be experts nonetheless. They point out that "the expert generalist has the ability to see the organization as a whole, to relate the organization to the larger society, and to give direction to the organization."[7]

Overlap Between Administrative and Supervisory Roles

In their classic book *Supervision: A Social Process* (1955), Burton and Brueckner discussed the overlap of administrative and supervisory duties. They concluded that it is more helpful for the educational program to view administration and supervision relatedly than to attempt to determine which duties each officer should perform (in contrast to those they do perform). "Intimate relationship and overlap," they wrote, "are inherent and inevitable."[8] They might have added "desirable," since teamwork (which inevitably involves overlap) can lead to more effective solutions for classroom problems because the ideas of three or more people [the teacher, principal, and supervisor(s)] have been integrated into the solution.

Overlap: Accentuating the Positive. In the view of the present authors, omission is a far more serious problem in supervision than the possibility of duplication through overlap. Many teachers rarely see a supervisor because there are not enough of them to do the job. If these teachers happen to be in schools where the principal does not devote time to educational leadership, they obviously will not receive the assistance they may need or want. Moreover, the principal is supposed to be the educational leader of her or his school. This alone creates a situation of "overlap" with other supervisors. But, as noted, the other side of the overlap subject is an opportunity for what Burton and Brueckner called "valuable cooperative relationships which are effective in furthering the work of education."[9]

Administrators and supervisors both have responsibility for curriculum improvement, and whether one is a "line" officer (administrator) or a "staff" officer (supervisor), that responsibility must be carried out in accord with the best recent theory. Radical changes have taken place in supervision. Authoritarian behavior and error-oriented supervision have given way to cooperative problem solving and mutual planning by teachers and supervisors. There is no such thing as "behaving in an administrative way" (bad) or "supervisory way" (good)—contrary to the viewpoint of Sergiovanni and Starratt in their textbook on supervision.[10] Research supports the importance of the administrators in improving the quality of education. There is nothing to be gained from an antiadministrator bias in the field of supervision, but there is plenty to be lost.

Nor is such a bias in tune with the latest developments in inservice education. Take, for example, staff development. The focus of staff development is on the individual school as a creative organization where the emphasis is on problem solving rather than on institutional maintenance or on "keeping things running smoothly." Oddly enough, staff development could be called "the administrative way" because, in the words of Goodlad, "the principal becomes central."[11] As

Rankin suggests, if staff development efforts are to result in educational improvement, administrators and supervisors must follow a developmental rather than a deficiency approach to changing staff behavior and increasing student learning.[12] However, this is not at issue when the emphasis is on improving the problem-solving capability of the staff. This approach is, in itself, developmental.

Overlap: Eliminating the Negative. To this point in our discussion of overlap in supervisory functions we may have inadvertently given the impression that there are always benefits to be obtained from overlap. Nothing could be less so. For example, many elementary schools have resource teachers who help other teachers with techniques and materials, and a number of high schools have an assistant principal for instruction. Certainly, a resource teacher, a team leader (in schools with a team-teaching program), or an assistant principal can provide a valuable addition to formal supervision. But the relationship between the principal's supervisory role and that of the helping teacher is not always clear. "As a result," Firth and Eiken point out, "teachers may consult the assistant principal or team leader on matters that the principal feels should have been referred to him or her. Conversely, they may bring to the principal matters that the principal feels should be handled by the subordinate."[13] The problem is, of course, that the principal has not defined clearly the limited supervisory role of the subordinate. Nevertheless, it should also be recognized that a whole new structural level has been created between the principal and the teachers. According to Firth and Eiken, "Whether the principal can appropriately function in such an organization remains a matter of conjecture."[14]

Principals are most likely to do so if they follow this guideline: *Resource teachers, even good ones, in whom principals have great confidence, are resources rather than a total program of supervision.* Properly engaged, they do not supplant the principal, whose first responsibility is to interact with and coordinate the total staff. This requires free-flowing and open communication between principal and staff. The importance of communication for an effective organization has been pointed out. Communication is not a problem when staff development is organized around problems identified by the staff.

Supervision is often included as a function of the state department of education. As Firth and Eiken observe, the result is often friction (with local supervisors), confusion, and waste. But their next observation is troublesome. "Some teachers are saturated with divergent, and perhaps contradictory views offered by supervisors representing several levels of organization. Other teachers receive little or no assistance from any organizational level."[15] Thus they seem to suggest that it is undesirable for teachers to have more than one supervisory viewpoint.

Divergent views should never be a problem in education. Although it is sometimes supposed that it is the supervisor's business to tell teachers what their viewpoint should be, teachers should not be blind followers of a single view. As already suggested, there is nothing wrong with divergent viewpoints—as long as these supervisors work as a team. As Dewey pointed out, the best help any supervisor can offer a teacher is to make that teacher "thoughtful about his work in the light of principles, rather than to induce in him a recognition that certain special methods are good and certain other special methods bad."[16]

The problem is not one of multiple viewpoints but is, rather, that services are being imposed rather than being developed in collaboration and participation. The practical solution is to provide services based on requests from school districts. Overlaps and omissions will then be dealt with as a matter of course. Moreover, the state's education department will be able to further the ongoing work of the school, to enrich the educational program rather than eroding it. (According to Firth and Eiken, the latter is all too often the case.) The support should be there from the state—but on a cooperative problem-solving basis.

Supervision: A Team Problem

Various dimensions of leadership must be provided by building principals and other administrators working with schools if teachers are to function effectively. In a word, administration must be supportive. Providing opportunities for inner-city teachers to have more "breathing time," so that they can deal with pedagogical problems in a more professional and less-harried manner, is one illustration of supportive administration. However, it is difficult, if not impossible, to separate such actions and policies from other dimensions of leadership, for example, efforts to help the faculty deal with the learning problems of low-achieving pupils. There is, willy-nilly, overlap in administrative and supervisory roles—in the same individual. This is to be expected, provided that the roles are not contradictory.

Nevertheless, we are dealing with an organization, not a one-man or a one-woman band. One may be able to play some of the instruments in the educational leadership combo, but probably not all, so more than one player is involved—at least for good effect. As Gersten and his coworkers point out, "On the whole, it makes more sense to consider a team approach in which critical support functions are carried out by those most able to perform them—not only the principal, but supervisors, teachers, curriculum specialists and other available personnel."[17] Support functions include providing concrete technical help for teachers. When principals are unable to perform such activities, they must see to it that teachers receive the assistance they need. Nor does the principal's responsibility end there. Support functions must be related to the overall program for school improvement and the principal's responsibility is to see it all whole. This requires cooperative interaction among principals, supervisors, and other leaders.

THE ORGANIC ORGANIZATION

What is called for is what Burns and Stalker have labeled an *organic*—as opposed to a *mechanistic*—form of organization. In a mechanistic system, the goals of the organization are broken down into individual tasks of an abstract nature which are pursued with purposes distinct from those of the organization as a whole. In an organic system, the members of the organization view themselves as working for a common goal, and their work is continually being adjusted and redefined through interaction with others.[18]

The difference becomes more critical as Burns and Stalker discuss potential for problem solving. Whereas the mechanistic form "is appropriate to stable conditions, the organic form is appropriate to changing conditions, which give rise constantly to fresh problems and unforeseen requirements for action which cannot be broken down or distributed automatically." They emphasize, however, that "the distinctive feature of the organic system is the pervasiveness of the working organization as an institution. In concrete terms, this makes itself felt in a preparedness to combine with others in serving the general aims." Thus, as they point out, the individual's job is no longer self-contained; it can be done only through continual participation with others in solving the problems facing the organization. In the words of Burns and Stalker, "Such methods of working put heavier demands on the individual."[19]

Applying this analysis to the school is fascinating, indeed. Conditions in education are always changing; there are new problems and new requirements for action. Clearly, there is an ever-present need to work with others in solving problems and in influencing the future. Although, as Burns and Stalker note, the two forms of organization represent polar extremes, there can be little doubt from the literature that effective schools operate under the organic form. For example, Rutter holds with supporting evidence that the ethos of an individual school can be altered in order to decrease the incidence of disciplinary problems and truancy, improve pupil–teacher relationships, and advance achievement.[20] Ethos is an organic rather than a mechanistic concept. In this regard, Goodlad has observed that school improvement does not mean improving the quality of administration, supervision, teaching, and the curriculum as though each were an abstract individual task, but means, rather, improving them all together.[21]

Needed Conditions

Educational leadership under the organic model emphasizes the contributive nature of the special knowledge represented by the foregoing areas to the common goal of the school—the improvement of teaching and learning. Supervisors and administrators are clearly members of a team who are professionally committed to this goal and whose activities are determined by the goal. The organic model is in accord with the requirements of the school as an institution. Yet as noted above, working as a team rather than individually puts great demands on individuals. If an instructional support team is to function effectively, the following conditions should be met: (1) administrators should stress the common goals and problems of the organization rather than the goals of specialized areas and subgroups, such as bilingual education and third-grade teachers; (2) communication should be kept open among those carrying out support functions; (3) team members should respect one another's individual expertise; and (4) team members should accept one another as persons as well as professionals. It is helpful to remember, as Griffin has observed in this context: "Educators are not all alike."[22] But this is what makes possible an effective team.

The Conflict Problem

In my job I associate constantly with uncooperative faculty members and indifferent principals.

I don't know what she really does. When she's in my school nothing happens.[23]

The first statement was made by a science supervisor, and the second, by a principal, about a reading specialist assigned to his school. Supervisors and principals both have crucial instructional support roles, but relations between them often contain the seeds of conflict. As Mangieri and McWilliams observe, "We might expect them to possess a natural allegiance to each other. Unfortunately, in many instances they are adversaries."[24]

The costs of conflict are enormous. Both persons are prevented from performing optimally. In a study of the effects of conflict, Kahn and his associates found "reason to doubt that constructive collaboration and coordination will be forthcoming in the face of strong role conflicts." Role conflicts cause people to like one another less and, as these researchers found, the problem goes beyond personal feelings into professional behavior. "People communicate less with their associates when under strong conflicts than when they are relatively free of them."[25]

Open communication, collaboration, and coordination are required for meeting organizational goals. Conflicts between supervisors and administrators impair the effectiveness of the school. Schools, and the public as a whole, cannot afford the curtailment of interaction between and among their instructional leaders. How can conflicts be dealt with or, better still, avoided?

Role Clarification. A favorite proposal of educators for eliminating role conflict is role clarification. This is based on the belief that a major source of conflict is lack of understanding of what it is that the other person does, and that making explicit the respective roles and responsibilities of administrators and supervisors is the surest means of avoiding conflict. (This is altogether logical since a role is, simply, what people do.) Moreover, it is felt that having distinct functions prevents conflict; if people do different things, they are less likely to step on one another's toes.

But "divided responsibility, rigidly adhered to" is a characteristic of mechanical systems, whereas "interdependencies and shared responsibility" is a characteristic of organic systems.[26] Principals and supervisors *share* the responsibility for curriculum improvement. This is a matter of necessity, not choice. In point of fact, few, if any, high school principals are prepared to help teachers in every area of the curriculum. As Babcock pointed out, "To assume competence in the content, materials and methods in all areas of our rapidly changing curriculum is completely unrealistic. . . . The principal's responsibility is to marshal all the resources of the curriculum staff to improve the quality of the curriculum in his school."[27]

The point is that one does not begin by emphasizing the division of labor; one begins with the problem to be solved, which is the improvement of teaching and learning. The division of labor is a result, not the cause, of a team effort.

Mention should be made of the fact that role conflict is a problem in industry. (Many of us tend to believe that industry has superior management strategies and is exempt from the problems that trouble education.) According to Rothlisberger, "As a result of the advance of science and technology, the acceleration of change, and the introduction of many new roles, modern industry seems to be riddled with role conflict and ambiguity."[28] More important, perhaps, as Wirth points out, attempts to solve such problems with procedures based on mechanistic forms of organization "inevitably break down." Thus, some companies, particularly in Scandinavia, have "decided to create a work process that would increase worker autonomy and collegial collaboration."[29] Clearly, this is a move toward an organic form of organization.

Taking a good lesson from industry, role clarification will not eliminate role conflict. As Rothlisberger suggests, "Role analysis, like any other method is a useful but limited tool. Applied to the diagnosis of a particular situation, it can reveal some of the factors that may be making for trouble. Applied as a general model for the analysis of organization behavior it may find only what it is looking for."[30] (Instead of consensus, there are conflicting or segmental expectations about what the supervisor is supposed to be doing.) Thus, when we attempt to use role clarification to eliminate role conflict, we may find ourselves walking in a circle. This is a manifestation of its mechanistic character.

Collaborative Educational Improvement

"Regardless of the specific complaints a supervisor and a principal, teacher, or a fellow supervisor may have about each other," write Mangieri and McWilliams, "the heart of the problem is invariably a breakdown in communication."[31] Mangieri and McWilliams have developed a process for facilitating communication that is based on the organic form of organization. The emphasis is on cooperative problem solving; two professionals lay out an action plan for dealing with a particular problem.

Building on the conception that communication is achieved through solving problems together, Mangieri and McWilliams state that the process consists of five steps: (1) The supervisor and the principal or other colleague *individually* identify factors or needs that they believe are creating the problem. This may be a general problem, such as how to use the supervisor's time most effectively, or it may be a specific problem, such as teachers' reluctance to ask the supervisor for help. (2) The two professionals compare their lists of factors and needs and *together* identify major needs. This list indicates what is to be done. (3) They develop a plan for action and list of responsibilities. The strategies and responsibilities must be clearly delineated so that each party understands how the other will meet the collaboratively established responsibilities. (4) They establish a timeline for each strategy or responsibility listed, with actual dates stated to determine when activities will be completed. (5) They schedule regular meetings (progress check sessions) with one another throughout the problem-solving sequence. Progress is assessed in terms of the "how" and "when" items established in the fourth stage.

An Illustration of Collaborative Participation. It will be helpful to consider an illustration of the application of this process by a reading supervisor (see Table 3–1) and an assistant superintendent for curriculum and instruction (see Table 3–2). The general problem was to determine how the supervisor's time could be used most profitably. In step 1, reasons contributing to the problem were identified by the assistant superintendent for instruction and the supervisor. The assistant superintendent listed the following: (1) most of the principals in

Table 3–1   Reading Supervisor's *How and When*

Strategies and Responsibilities	Timeline
Visit every designated school and discuss role with all teachers	By October 1
Visit with the principal of every designated school, outline supervisor's role, and seek support in performing duties	By September 15
Publish and distribute a monthly reading idea sheet for personnel in designated buildings	Ongoing; by last school day of each month
Chair reading committee to encourage inter- and intraschool activities in the designated schools	Ongoing; monthly
Review status in buildings with principal at least twice per semester	October, December, February, and April
Work with assistant superintendent for instruction to develop general visitation schedule	Prior to September 1

Source: John N. Mangieri and David R. McWilliams, "The What, How, and When of Instructional Improvement," *Educational Leadership,* Vol. 38 (April 1981), p. 536.

the schools served by the supervisor had limited knowledge about reading, thus did not know the precise services to be requested of the supervisor; (2) teachers were uncertain of the nature of the supervisor's role; and (3) the supervisor should use the time economically. Problems perceived by the reading supervisor were: (1) there were too many schools to be served in too wide a geographical area; (2) principals failed to make referrals; (3) there was insufficient time for follow-up work with teachers; and (4) teachers were reluctant to ask for help.

When the supervisor and the assistant superintendent had compared and discussed these factors, they agreed on what needed to be accomplished. The needs they collaboratively identified were (1) to help teachers and principals understand the reading supervisor's function, (2) to elicit the principals' support in carrying out responsibilities, (3) to establish an effective schedule for the

Table 3–2   Assistant Superintendent's *How and When*

Strategies and Responsibilities	Timeline
Meet with principals of designated schools to review job description and role of reading supervisor	August principals' meeting
Utilize reading supervisor for testing and/or consultation with teachers from designated schools who request or need technical assistance	Ongoing
Arrange for reading supervisor to have a leadership role in districtwide staff development endeavors	As per date
Assess the effectiveness with which the time and expertise of reading supervisor is being used by principals and teachers	November, January, March, and May
Meet with reading supervisor every two weeks	First and third Thursdays of each month

Source: John N. Mangieri and David R. McWilliams, "The What, How, and When of Instructional Improvement," *Educational Leadership,* Vol. 38 (April 1981), p. 536.

reading supervisor, and (4) to establish a procedure for collaborative follow-up work with teachers.

Table 3–1 presents steps 3 and 4, the "how" and "when," as they concern the reading supervisor's participation in the process. Table 3–2 shows steps 3 and 4 of the assistant superintendent. As shown, the parties agreed to meet every two weeks, both to discuss problems with "how" and "when" items and to assess progress (step 5).

As Mangieri and McWilliams point out, the process can serve many purposes. It can, for example, facilitate both planning and evaluation, and can serve as a means of documenting accomplishments. More important, it can solve the conflict problem by providing a vehicle for meaningful communication and collaboration between two professionals. What makes the dialogue meaningful, of course, is that it concerns a professional problem. An increment of collaborative problem solving is "helping each individual develop a better understanding of the other's position, educational beliefs, and expectations."[32]

SUPERVISION, SCHOOL SIZE, AND ORGANIZATIONAL PROBLEMS

The period from World War II to the closing decades of the twentieth century has seen a steep decline in the number of local public school systems in the United States. In the school year 1941–42, there were still 115,493 school systems in this country. The number has been steadily decreased, and in the 1984–85 school year there were only about 15,740 systems operating.[33]

The trend to fewer school systems represents the continuing attempt to provide greater educational opportunity to our nation's children. Consolidation of two or more small school systems makes it possible to attract (and pay for) competent teachers and meet the curriculum requirements for an adequate school. (A small high school in a small district, for example, cannot offer a comprehensive curriculum to meet the diversified needs of its youth, and this problem can be eliminated through district consolidation.) The 1954 *Brown I* decision, which found that separate educational facilities for white and black children were "inherently unequal," and the 1955 *Brown II* decision, which required that dual school systems be reorganized into single systems "with all deliberate speed" also resulted in a reduction in the number of school systems.[34] It is of interest that the rate of reduction was particularly rapid in the 1950s and 1960s when the number of systems was decreased by 51.6 percent and 52.7 percent, respectively.[35] This can be attributed to the aforementioned Supreme Court decisions and to the fact that the movement toward school district reorganization, which had started much earlier, was making headway. In sum, the decrease in the number of school systems points to gains that Americans have made in overcoming the inequality of educational opportunity of large groups of Americans, particularly minority groups and rural groups.

On the debit side of the ledger, despite the progress in school district reorganization, school districts of under 1,000 pupils still constitute the majority of districts in the United States (although pupils are concentrated heavily in large and middle-sized systems). This fact reveals the necessity of continued and even expanded effort to discontinue small school districts. Larger districts can provide administrators and educational specialists so that education can progress with modern society. As Neagley and Evans point out, "School district size affects the extent and quality of supervisory programs."[36]

What is the recommended size for a school district? As one looks back on the last half-century of educational development, one finds strikingly different answers to this question. Fifty years ago the popular view was that 3,000 to 5,000 pupils was ideal. In the 1960s it was 20,000 to 30,000 pupils. Some theorists prefer to answer the question in terms of minimums. For example, Stoops, Rafferty, and Johnson recommend that the ideal K–12 or K–14 district enrolls a minimum of 10,000 pupils. But Stoops, Rafferty, and Johnson are also responding to the question in terms of the form of district organization; they state that the district organization "that provides the most adequate educational program . . . includes kindergarten through the twelfth or fourteenth grades."[37]

In recent years, the emphasis has been to give greater attention to critical factors, such as articulation of the educational program, not just the number of pupils enrolled. Indeed, as Kimbrough and Nunnery point out, many theorists today believe "that the appropriate-size concept is a myth: other factors are more crucial."[38]

One of the most active groups concerning itself with the problem of criteria for judging school district adequacy is the American Association of School Administrators. The AASA Commission on School District Organization suggests nine areas to be examined in determining the adequacy of local school districts: educational program, pupil population, tax resources, provisions for educational leadership, instructional personnel, use of personnel, facilities, framework for operation, and provisions for community participation.[39] It is clear that the adequacy of a school district is determined in a great measure by the extent of quality of its supervisory program.

Supervisory Problems of Small School Districts

In our society, every school ought to have an adequate program of supervision and a rich and comprehensive curriculum to provide the education needed for the modern world. Like all ideals, however, this one is shattered by facts. In small districts that lack resources (and we know there are many), it is not possible to provide able administration and good school programs. Whatever the size, a school district should have the resources to provide the best possible education for its pupils. To meet this standard, many small districts have no recourse save reorganization with other districts to form a larger one. This idea often meets with strong local opposition, particularly in rural areas. The belief in local control (even if it results in poor quality), a fear of higher taxes, and the misidentification of small schools with educational superiority are some sources of opposition to larger districts. In many ways such opposition recalls the struggle for state control of the schools in the 1820s and 1830s. The problem of centralization versus decentralization comes down to the present.

School districts are judged in terms of the strength of the tax resources, but it should be remembered that pupils are also a resource—albeit a different kind.

(The AASA Commission on School District Organization recognized this very clearly when it included pupil population as a factor to be examined in assessing school district adequacy.) High school programs that meet the diverse needs of youth require a student population of sufficient size for maximum effectiveness and efficiency. A school district that cannot provide the requisite population cannot be defended.

Responsibility for Supervision. In small school systems, no single individual has full-time responsibility for the supervision of teachers. All administrators are responsible for the improvement of teaching and learning. An administrator must be well prepared professionally and able to work cooperatively and constructively with other administrators, teachers, and parents. These qualifications will make it possible to develop an effective program of supervision and curriculum development for the small district.

Good supervisory programs do not just happen in small school systems; they require time and effort on the part of the chief school administrator. This is true in large systems as well, but the difference is that the administrative organization in the large systems provides directors for the function of curriculum development. (The larger the school system, the more complex is its organization.) Thus the chief administrator of the small system (who may be a full-time superintendent or a principal) must also serve as coordinator of curriculum and instruction. If the individual does not do so, an effective supervisory program is an impossibility (except in individual schools where the principal happens to be a strong educational leader, but even then, the coordinated effort required for effective systemwide curriculum development will still be sorely lacking).

What does being a coordinator involve? Neagley and Evans see the responsibility this way:

> Whenever there is more than one school unit in a district, it is essential that all administrators be called to meet on a top-level, executive basis. Here is the opportunity to share ideas, to plan joint curriculum evaluation and development, and to work out common district policy on problems and issues that require thinking beyond the confines of one principal's building and staff. The chief school official would normally chair this administrative council, although this chairpersonship could rotate.[40]

An administrative council that meets on a regularly scheduled basis is an absolute necessity.

There is nothing new about classroom visitation, but as Neagley and Evans point out, it "is a basic supervisory technique." We would add that this time-honored method of supervision is the only means at the administrator's disposal for seeing the educational program in action and for finding out how teachers can be helped to deal with learning problems and to develop better materials and methods. Each teacher should be observed at least twice a year, and the classroom visits should be constructive. The aim is to improve teaching and give the teachers support so that they can use their talents, not merely to rate their performance. Developing a plan of visitation is the job of the administrative council.

There are many resources available that can help the administrator make strides forward with the supervisory program. Curriculum consultants, courses of study, directories of curriculum materials, and summaries of curriculum research are available, often free of charge, from the following sources:

1. The U.S. Department of Education.
2. State departments of education.
3. Association for Supervision and Curriculum Development, National Association of Elementary School Principals, National Association of Secondary School Principals, and the various national associations in the specialized curriculum areas.
4. Schools of education in state universities and university library collections.
5. Regional laboratories for educational research and development (such as the Far West Laboratory).
6. Curriculum guides and other materials from other school systems.

One of the main roads to a good school is the continuing inservice growth of professional workers. The chief administrator's own professional improvement through participation in conferences, continued graduate study, and teaching a college course occasionally (if possible) is important. By engaging in various forms of professional improvement, the chief administrator is also influential with the staff as a role model.

The chief school official has a basic responsibility for the professional development of the teaching staff, for this is carried over into the classroom. Schoolwide instructional improvement programs, teachers' continuing graduate work, and their attendance at conferences are greatly influenced by the executive's encouragement. In summary, then, there are four ways in which the head administrator of a small school district should assume supervisory leadership: creating an administrative council, getting into classrooms, drawing on the available resources for curriculum improvement, and fostering the professional development of the administrative and teaching staffs.

Need for a Full-Time Principal. If individual schools are to solve their problems and have quality education, they must have their own administrative head. This has been documented by research, yet many elementary schools in this country are still served by part-time principals (a foolish kind of "economy"). In a particularly interesting study, Brookover and his associates examined the relation between the school as a social system and school achievement. They found that differences between schools in student outcomes can be explained to a great extent by such factors as the nature of interaction among teachers, administrators, and students. In higher-achieving schools the principal devoted as much time, if not more, to activities relating to the educational program as to those relating to administration. This principal was engaged in educational-leadership activity. The message that the students could, and were, expected to achieve was thus communicated to teachers and students. In lower-achieving schools, the principal spent most of the time in administrative activities and did not demonstrate attitudes that were conducive to higher achievement. Particularly important here was the fact that the negative climate for achievement was especially evident when the administrator was a part-time principal.

> Because he served as the principal of two schools, he was in this building only on alternating mornings and afternoons. He could not be characterized as an educational or instructional leader. *Perhaps because of his dual responsibilities as a principal, there was little interaction between him and the teaching staff.*[41]

It appears that interaction between principal and teachers is an important element in school achievement. Obviously, this interaction is less likely when the principal's time (and allegiance) is divided between two staffs. We would concur with Neagley and Evans that "the first step toward effective supervision at the elementary level is organizing schools geographically into units that can be directed by full-time principals."[42]

Larger Districts: The Administrative Hierarchy

As school systems expand in size, adequate administration requires able professional assistance for the superintendent. Titles of the superintendent's assistants at the central office level are varied: assistant superintendent for curriculum and instruction (included more often than other functions), assistant superintendent (sometimes called administrative assistant or deputy superintendent), director of elementary education, director of secondary education, director of curriculum, director of research, primary supervisor, elementary supervisor, music supervisor, art supervisor, physical education supervisor, mathematics coordinator, science coordinator and foreign language coordinator. The list is not exhaustive.

Campbell and his associates point out that what is created with expansion is an administrative hierarchy.[43] Although it is now fashionable to speak negatively of "bureaucratic" elements of large organizations, such as a hierarchical authority structure, the division of labor in a school system makes it more possible to meet the needs of children and youth in a highly complex society. Not only has knowledge expanded and become more complex (particularly in the sciences and the social sciences) so that many high school youngsters can understand concepts that would have been beyond the comprehension of many eminent scholars of 200 years ago, but we know more about the learning process and the factors that affect learning. The job that schools are doing has become more complex and demanding. If schools are to do as good a job as they are capable of doing, school executives must depend on expert assistance to meet their leadership responsibilities.

Along with the responsibilities in large school systems there are what our mothers and grandmothers used to call certain "advantages." Specialists in music and art can assist in the development of programs in these areas, helping children gain full access to the fine arts. Increasing size of organizations generates differentiation of staff.[44] This can be an enormous advantage, particularly when the organization is a school system. The effectiveness of good teachers can be increased by specialist services (and it can be diluted without them).

Hierarchy or Team? An important problem for us here concerns the utility of the hierarchical model for educational supervision. An assistant superintendent for instruction, for example, has professional authority rooted in expert knowledge and assumes the responsibility and leadership for improving curriculum and teaching. A study of the organizational structure of school systems by the American Association of School Administrators described the assistant superintendent for instruction as "a member of the [administrative] team" and "representative of the superintendent."[45] While technically, the assistant superintendent for instruction (often called assistant superintendent for curriculum and instruction) is a second-echelon position, this administrator is a member of a team who see themselves as working for a common goal, namely that of providing the best possible educational program. As noted earlier, this (the team) perspective is characteristic of organic forms of organization which lend themselves more readily to problem solving than do mechanistic forms. It is hardly surprising, then, that the AASA utilized a team model rather than the hierarchy (a mechanistic form) when analyzing the organizational structure of school systems.

It must also be noted that a hierarchical view of the organization of schooling places teachers at the bottom of the hierarchy.[46] Yet teachers have the most crucial function in the organizational structure that is the school. Although they are not part of the administrative structure, teachers are essential members of any curriculum improvement team.

In the hierarchical-segmental structure, communication flow is largely top-down and jurisdictional. In contrast, the professional team model, shown in Figure 3-1, is focused holistically on the major function and responsibility of the school—the education of children. This is clearly more functional than is the hierarchical structure. (The organizational model should be focused on the curriculum and the learner, not on jobs or positions.)

School Systems as "Bureaucratic" Organizations. It was Max Weber who, in the late 1940s, put forward the list of organizational characteristics that constitute the bureaucratic form of organization.[47] These characteristics include a closely followed hierarchy of authority, intricate division of labor, extensive rules governing behavior on the job (an illustration would be strict regulation of coffee breaks), a well-developed, strict system of procedures for dealing with work situations, separation of administration from ownership, and hiring and promotion based on technical competence. From the time of Weber, the bureaucratic model has been used to conceptualize the system of interrelationships in organizations. Some of the research on the degree to which schools are bureaucratized has stated simply that schools are bureaucratic, without any attempt to examine all the bureaucratic dimensions.

Such studies do not help us understand (and improve) schools as organizations. Research has shown clearly that the characteristics of bureaucracy are not either all present or all absent in any single organization.[48] Schools are no exception. Although there is a "hierarchy" dimension (which seems to be the main characteristic in determining the bureaucratization in organizations), an intricate division of labor does not exist. Both supervisors and principals, for example, are concerned with the improvement of instruction. (So are assistant superintendents and superintendents, for that matter.)

Moreover, although they may be influenced by mechanisms such as consulta-

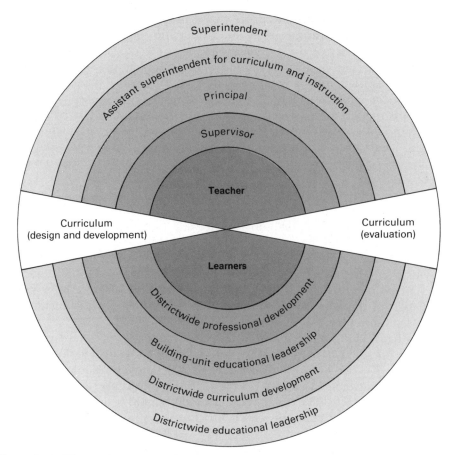

Figure 3–1. The professional team in the school system: an organic model.

tion with supervisors, teaching activities are controlled by the teacher in the classroom. This is as it should be, for teachers are professionals. (In this regard, Likert found that influence exercised by persons at all levels brought with it an increased sense of responsibility and motivation to achieve organizational goals.[49]) Nor are schools administered apart from their "owners." School board members who represent the "owners" (the public) employ and exercise control over the chief executive officer of the school district. The history of this position was discussed in Chapter 1.

The high level of education and ability of many educators goes beyond mere "technical competence." The point is that bureaucracy as a totality is a myth. The dimensions are not all present in educational organizations. Simply to label the large school system as a "bureaucratic" setting, and then to assert that school improvement is an impossibility until the bureaucracy is done away with (as many radical critics did in the 1960s and 1970s) is not very useful in helping schools achieve their objectives. A basic problem for supervisors is to determine the advantages and disadvantages of their organizational structure. Organizations can and should be reformed when they are not functioning effectively, but not before careful analysis.

School Systems as "Loosely Coupled" Organizations. In the bureaucratic model, described above, control and coordination are basic elements. By *control* is meant those devices that work within the organization to ensure that individuals perform their own special part of the main task. (Teachers, for instance, would follow one set of methods and procedures, and would have no autonomy in their classrooms.) Under the hierarchical-bureaucratic model, coordination means all the specialized functions of individuals fitting together through tightly-linked hierarchical levels to meet the organization's objectives. These assumptions of the bureaucratic model about control and the nature of connections between hierarchical levels do not explain organizational life in schools, as we have indicated (and as anyone knows who works in a school system).

The organic model, described earlier in this chapter, recognizes the necessary interdependence of individuals and their specialized functions through systematic collaboration in a comprehensive organizational framework to meet the organization's objectives. The organizational framework is organic, not hierarchically segmental. The organic model provides the framework for the democratic participative-group system of organization, discussed in detail in Chapter 5.

There is yet another, competing, theoretical model with different expectations about the character of connections in educational organizations. The loosely coupled model of organization views educational organizations as loosely articulated subsystems.[50] According to this model, teachers work autonomously in their classrooms, principals work autonomously in their offices, and local schools function without control of instructional activities by the school district central office.

The difficulty with this model is that it is (unlike the bureaucratic model) one-dimensional. The only dimension it provides for delineating the structure of an organization is the hierarchical dimension, that is, the degree to which hierarchical levels are linked. And as we pointed out in our discussion of the bureaucratic model, the hierarchical dimension is of limited utility in the study of educational organizations because the responsibility for educational improvement is not defined within a hierarchic structure; commitment to better education is spread throughout the organization. The loosely coupled model represents the mechanistic form of organization because each subsystem goes about its own work without regard for the total situation of the school system and, more important, without exploiting the resources of all for problem solving.

The idea that school districts operate as loosely coupled systems has been accepted by many as how they *should* work. For example, a study of thirty-four elementary school districts in the San Francisco area concluded that teachers' classroom methods "are virtually unaffected by organizational or administrative factors at the school or district levels."[51] Therefore, according to Deal and Celotti, who reported the findings, "administrators should not use action or strategies based on conventional images of schools and districts as tightly linked, cohesive organizations. . . . Instructional activities do not seem to be effectively coordinated through formal channels." They go on to suggest that "while organizational factors and administrative efforts do not appear to have an impact on classroom instruction, they may serve other important purposes. . . . *Meetings between district office specialists and teachers may provide opportunities for teachers to vent gripes or frustrations or to 'feel professional'.*"[52] Ignored here is that administrative and supervisory specialist positions were originally created to help teachers improve their effectiveness as professionals, not to patronize teachers and regard them as children.

Little interaction among the parts of an educational system should be viewed as evidence of a dysfunctional organization rather than as verification of the "loose coupling" theory. A study of the work activities of personnel in one school district found that central office supervisors were spending only a tiny portion of their time engaged in work (e.g., organizing curriculum materials) at the request of school principals.[53] This means that the principals were not drawing on the district resources that were available to help teachers. This study also found that district-level supervisors rarely initiated school-level curriculum development activities. When central office administrators and supervisors did initiate activities, they had mainly to do with district-required information (keeping track of materials, supplies, and paper) rather than with curriculum matters.[54] The main goal, instructional improvement, had become lost.

The concern of school district central-office supervisors is (or should be) with the educational program. Their professional preparation and talents are wasted if they merely requisition supplies and issue personnel forms. They are responsible for curriculum articulation and continuity, districtwide, and they must provide assistance for teachers. As Gersten, Carnine, and Green point out, support for teachers must be multilevel and comprehensive. It must come from several sources, principals, supervisors, administrators, and external consultants.[55]

The district in the foregoing study was not functioning according to the loosely coupled theory; it was failing to function as it was designed to—as a coherent, integrated whole.

Decentralization and the Problems of Urban Schools. The problems of schools in urban America are, by now, bleakly familiar: precarious funding, overcrowded classrooms, massive educational retardation, tremendous dropout rates, decaying buildings, dissatisfied teachers. The problems of urban education are the problems of our whole society—not just our schools. Joblessness, for example, is epidemic among inner-city young people. The problems of our urban school systems are economic and educational. They are not soluble by reorganization.

Yet on the basis that urban bigness was responsible for failure to bring the educational achievements of poor children up to par with children of the middle class, many big-city systems "decentralized." The Commission on School District Reorganization of the American Association of School Administrators defined decentralization as the delegation of administrative authority and responsibility on a geographic instead of a departmental basis.[56] Los Angeles, for example, decentralized in the early 1970s with a zone plan in which the huge geographic area of the district was broken into ten areas. Each area has relative autonomy in terms of administration but is under the curricular and financial jurisdiction of the central board. The number of decentralized units in a school system ranges from two areas in Portland and Oakland to thirty-two community school districts in New York City. There are a variety of decentralization plans, ranging from very limited to extensive community control. New York City and Detroit have decentralized school boards elected by the "communities."[57]

In New York City, the movement for decentralization began in the late 1960s. (Decentralization in some cities, for example, Philadelphia and St. Louis, took place much earlier.) The case of New York City is both interesting and instructive. The argument advanced for the establishment of autonomous school districts was that the schools in New York City were not educating minority-group children. It was contended that, by giving local communities control over their schools, educators would be made more accountable to the community they served, and achievement levels would be raised.

As Cohen pointed out at the time, however, there was "no evidence that the level of parent participation in schools is related to students' achievement" and further, there was "no relation whatsoever between the size of a school district (or whether its board is elected or appointed) and the achievement of the students in its schools." But there was "abundant evidence that parents who are involved in a direct way in their children's education tend to have children who achieve at higher levels. Involvement of this sort includes reading to children, taking them to libraries, talking to them, explaining things, and otherwise providing lots of cognitive stimulation and support for intellectual accomplishment. Thus, when poor parents are trained to behave toward their children in the way that middle-class parents do, the children's level of achievement rises. . . ." This, he concluded, argues "for the establishment of parent-education efforts . . . rather than programs aimed at eliminating bureaucracy in schools."[58]

There was also evidence supporting school desegregation as a means of improving the achievement of minority-group children. The Coleman Report, conducted in response to Section 402 of the Civil Rights Act of 1964, found that the social background of fellow students had the greatest effect on achievement, and that this effect was greater than that of school facilities, staffing, instructional resources, and other factors. It was therefore crucial for lower-class minority group pupils to have middle-class whites or Orientals as classmates.[59]

In New York, rather than drawing district lines to achieve maximum desegregation, the boundaries of the created districts were drawn along "community" lines, thus strengthening segregation. Acceptance of segregation was reflected in the decentralization proposal developed by an advisory committee to the mayor, chaired by McGeorge Bundy of the Ford Foundation. The report stated that the committee was "unanimous in its conclusion that integration in the New York City system is likely to come only after a drastic improvement in the general effectiveness of New York's schools."[60]

Integration never came, at least, in part, due to the abandoning of the ideal. The process of decentralization did not affect the curriculum or the relationships between teachers and principals. Reading scores and attendance figures continued to plummet. As foreseen by the central board of education, some districts today are "unable to attract a sufficient number of qualified teachers."[61] In the 1980s New York City's poorest neighborhoods experienced a severe teacher shortage. The problem was worsened by a rapid turnover of teachers, who accepted jobs and then quit shortly after assuming their responsibilities. Indeed, one out of four who accepted jobs in September 1983 quit within two weeks. Many told superintendents that they could not handle classroom pressures.[62] What is desperately needed in urban schools is support for teachers. The precise nature of this support is discussed in the following chapter. All that can be said here is that there is a lesson to be learned from the New York experience: No reorganization is a substitute for adequate resources, administrative support, team effort, individual commitment, and high morale.

Despite the dismaying problems, one may say with certainty that urban education (all of education, for that matter) is more than ever full of promise. We know far more than we did in the 1960s about how to improve the quality of teaching (and what we know has nothing to do with the bigness or smallness of school systems). The chapter on improving the teacher's role in this text indicates that certain methods do work in classrooms, and that effective teaching of all youngsters need not be a mystery. The best available knowledge can be replicated in schools and classrooms.

Communication Versus Isolation in Urban Schools. Arguments about bureaucratic dysfunction in the 1960s centered on the inability of the complex central administration of the school system to meet the needs of low-income residents in the central cities. The focus of the bureaucratic problem was on the psychological distance between clients (the parents) and the schools. Virtually ignored in the client-centered discussions was the equally important problem of communication within the organization itself. Lack of communication between parts of vast and complex school systems makes effective supervision impossible. Yet communication can be a problem in small systems as well as large ones.

Deficiencies in communication are often reflections of deficiencies in decision-making processes. When the power to make decisions is concentrated in the hands of a few, the opportunity for interaction decreases. But if power is shared throughout the organization, the volume of communication increases, and the flow across subsystems is also increased. The point of importance (really a principle) is that structure is inseparable from function. It is fruitless to try to improve communications in an organizational structure without something to communicate about.

Even the most cursory glance at school system flowcharts reveals the operation of this principle. In many urban systems only the deputy superintendent communicates with the superintendent. The central office administration is isolated from the teachers and principals of the various schools in the systems. The isolation (lack of communication) is in great measure, a result of the centralization of decision making. The problems of low morale and alienation among teachers (and, yes, principals) in some urban schools are the result of a structure that makes them powerless. But the structure shown on the flowchart is simply a reflection of where the decision-making power lies. By involving teachers in the decisions that affect them, the structure can be modified and integrated. As one inner-city teacher commented, "What I'm required to teach is predetermined. The equipment is predetermined. All the books are predetermined."[63] Needless to say, interaction with central office personnel about these decisions would considerably improve the flow of communication in this school system (and, in so doing, "reform" the organizational structure).

Opportunities for horizontal communication must also be provided. In the words of Stoops, Rafferty, and Johnson, "Teachers must talk with teachers, principals with principals, assistant superintendents with assistant superintendents, and simultaneously every effort must be made to give the chief administrative officer opportunities to communicate with people other than himself (or herself)." Otherwise, he or she is "condemned to a state of solitary confinement" in the "little cubicle at the top of the organization pyramid."[64] Horizontal communication is an important element of professionalism. It is common among physicians, lawyers, and engineers, but teachers tend to remain behind their own classroom doors. As one teacher in a large urban district put it: "Teaching is certainly an isolated kind of thing. It's true that we deal with children, but there is fairly limited contact professionally with our peers."[65]

Communication strategies must be worked out at each level of the school system that make it possible to exchange information with those at other levels. As pointed out by Stoops, Rafferty, and Johnson: "Face to face encounter after thoughtful preparation is the most effective method. . . . The more specific, brief, and personally delivered the presentation, the more effectively the message will be communicated."[66] In the event that time is short, thoughtfully composed letters and memoranda provide alternatives. Conferences and coffee hours are excellent strategies for bringing people together from various parts of the system. (This is as true in an affluent suburb as in a big city.)

It is well to remember that the "faceless bureaucracies" that we wrote about on the first page of this chapter are merely the creations of people. They will only be reformed by human beings through human encounters.

SUMMARY

Every organization has a purpose and schools exist to provide systematic education for the rising generation. Since the educational program is the central concern in school administration, it is impossible to separate administration from supervision in function. There is overlap in administrative and supervisory roles, but this is only a problem if the view of the school is a *mechanistic* system where the goals are broken down into fixed stable tasks (distinct from the purposes of the organization as a whole) and each person sees his (or her) job in isolation. Shared responsibility is a characteristic of the *organic* form of organization, which is appropriate to changing conditions and solving new problems. Under the organic form, the work of organization members is continually being redefined as they face fresh problems together, and through interaction with one another. If schools are to solve their problems, they must operate as organic systems and take a team approach to supervision. (Figure 3–1 presented an organic model of the professional team.) Role clarification will not eliminate role conflict. The best approach is collegial cooperation whereby individuals and groups (e.g., a supervisor and a principal, a principal and faculty members) together develop an action plan for dealing with a problem. This way of working together collaboratively is based on the organic form of organization.

Throughout the twentieth century there has been a movement to consolidate small and weak school districts and thus offer better education to larger numbers of pupils in fewer schools. There is also a trend to reorganize elementary school districts and secondary school districts into a single administrative unit with responsibility for the whole educational program. The unified school district provides greater opportunity to develop the needed articulation of the curricular offerings from kindergarten through high school or junior college. In a small school system, the chief school administrator must serve as coordinator of curriculum and instruction or there will be no supervisory program. In districts with more than one school, curriculum development and classroom visitation are planned by the administrative council.

As school systems grow in size they become more complex. School superintendents must depend on experts to help them meet their leadership responsibilities. Neither the bureaucratic model nor the loosely coupled model adequately describes educational organizations. An intricate division of labor—a dimension of bureaucracy—does not exist. (Both principals and supervisors are responsible for educational supervision.) Moreover, a school system that functions as isolated subsystems—the loosely coupled concept—is dysfunctional. (Central office personnel must interact with local school personnel.) Researchers who say that school systems should operate as disconnected parts have done the schools a monumental disservice.

No reorganization is a substitute for adequate funds and intelligent educational leadership. In many urban high schools, classes are overcrowded, the arrival of supplies is deemed worthy of a schoolwide announcement, and the physical facilities are outmoded. Disadvantaged children achieve when we use what we know about how children learn best. Decentralization cannot solve communication problems in large school systems when these problems stem from the centralization of decision-making power. Decentralization, taken by itself, can lead to isolation. When power is widely shared in an organization, the amount of communication increases and the quality of communication improves. Horizontal communication in a school system is as important as vertical communication: Teachers seldom have the opportunity to talk with teachers. Face-to-face encounters are the best means of communication in large school systems and can put a "face" on "faceless bureaucracies."

PROBLEMS FOR STUDY AND DISCUSSION

1. This book takes the view that it is impossible to separate administration from supervision in function. Do you agree? Why or why not?

2. In your opinion, does school district size affect the extent and potentialities of supervisory programs? Explain. Assuming that you are the chief administrator of a small school district, how would you proceed to develop a good supervisory program?

3. A large urban school system is having communication problems within the organization. As discussed in this chapter, what variables should be examined in attempting to improve the flow of communication?

4. How might such problems be expected to relate to the organizational structure itself? Construct administrative flowcharts (diagrams of the organizational structure) to illustrate your response.

5. Why is the unified school district recommended as the type of school district that provides the most adequate educational program?

6. What is the best means to eliminate role conflict in a school system? Why?

7. The following are two contrasting statements on administrative power and authority. In your opinion, which position is more promising for educational improvement? Why?

> The educational system best serves its varied clientele and performs its diverse functions if there is substantial power, wisely administered, at the local school level and if this is balanced with substantial power and authority, wisely administered, at a central place in the school system. This one place is the central office.[67]

> My picture of decentralization is not, then, one of schools cut loose, but rather of schools linked both to a hub—the district office—and to each other in a network. The ship is not alone on an uncharted sea, cut off from supplies and communication. But neither are decisions for the welfare of those on the ship the prerogative of persons in the hub or in charge of other ships. The principal is the captain with full authority and responsibility for the ship.[68]

8. Would you label your school system an organic form of organization, or would the mechanistic label be more appropriate? Explain.

9. A classroom teacher in a western state wrote:

> Merging three small districts into one larger entity was a delicate matter in 1971. Each district was afraid of losing its identity, its unique responses to local community needs. Only when "autonomy" was guaranteed to each school did the three districts agree to the merger that created South Counties School District. . . .
>
> Under the concept of building autonomy each school in the newly formed district had its own budget and developed an educational plan suited to its own specific needs. . . . Committees of teachers evaluated new textbooks and made recommendations to the entire faculty, who then collectively chose texts that they believed would best meet the needs of teachers and the school community. . . .
>
> As a teacher, I appreciated the recognition of my professional competence to make these choices, and I took the responsibility seriously. . . . Two years ago, unilateral decisions from the central office began to replace school autonomy in South Counties District. Today, faculties of the elementary and junior high schools are allowed to choose between only two series (compared to eight in 1980), two spelling programs, and two K–12 language arts series. . . . When the staff at my school was informed that our building-level reading committee would be looking at just two series, a ripple of anger ran through the room.[69]

In your opinion does the curtailment of teachers' power to decide on professional materials necessarily result from consolidation of local school districts? Explain.

10. A recent large-scale study, headed by John Goodlad, asked teachers about the availability of resource personnel. Although more than 80 percent of the teachers indicated that district-level resource persons are available, only about half said that they had actually used them.[70] As an assistant superintendent for curriculum and instruction, how would you increase the use of district-level resource people by teachers?

NOTES

1. John Dewey, *The Sources of a Science of Education* (New York: Liveright, 1929), pp. 48–50.
2. Koya Azumi and Jerald Hage, "Organizational Perspectives and Programs," in Koya Azumi and Jerald Hage (eds.), *Organizational Systems* (Lexington, Mass.: D. C. Heath, 1972), p. 7.
3. American Association of School Administrators, *The Superintendent as Instructional Leader,* Thirty-fifth Yearbook of the American Association of School Administrators (Washington, D.C.: The Association, 1957), p. 18.
4. See Jacqueline P. Danzberger and Michael D. Usdan, "Building Partnerships: The Atlanta Experience," *Phi Delta Kappan,* Vol. 65 (February 1984), pp. 393–396.
5. William G. Monahan and Herbert R. Hengst, *Contemporary Educational Administration* (New York: Macmillan, 1982), pp. 5–6.
6. Clagett Smith and Oguz Ari, "Organizational Control Structure and Member Consensus," in Azumi and Hage, op. cit., pp. 492–504; and Paul Hersey and Kenneth H. Blanchard, *Management of Organizational Behavior,* 4th ed. (Englewood Cliffs, N.J.: Prentice-Hall, 1982), p. 295.
7. Roald F. Campbell et al., *The Organization and Control of American Schools,* 4th ed. (Columbus, Ohio: Charles E. Merrill, 1980), p. 254.
8. William H. Burton and Leo J. Brueckner, *Supervision: A Social Process* (New York: Appleton-Century-Crofts, 1955), p. 98.
9. Ibid., p. 99.
10. Thomas J. Sergiovanni and Robert J. Starratt, *Supervision: Human Perspectives,* 3rd ed. (New York: McGraw-Hill, 1983), pp. 12–13.
11. John I. Goodlad, "The School as a Workplace," Chapter 3 in *Staff Development,* Eighty-second Yearbook of the National Society for the Study of Education, Part II (Chicago: University of Chicago Press, 1983), p. 40.
12. Stuart C. Rankin, "A View from the Schools," Chapter 11 in *Staff Development,* op. cit., p. 253.
13. Gerald R. Firth and Keith P. Eiken, "Impact of the Schools' Bureaucratic Structure on Supervision," Chapter 11 in *Supervision of Teaching,* 1982 Yearbook of the Association for Supervision and Curriculum Development (Alexandria, Va.: The Association, 1982), p. 164.
14. Ibid.
15. Ibid., p. 168.
16. John Dewey, "Relation of Theory to Practice," in Reginald D. Archambault (ed.), *John Dewey on Education* (New York: Random House, 1964), p. 325; originally published in National Society for the Scientific Study of Education, *Third Yearbook,* Part I, 1904.
17. Russell Gersten, Douglas Carnine, and Susan Green, "The Principal as Instructional Leader: A Second Look," *Educational Leadership,* Vol. 40 (December 1982), p. 48.
18. Tom Burns and G. M. Stalker, "Models of Mechanistic and Organic Structure," in Azumi and Hage, op. cit., pp. 251–252.

19. Ibid., pp. 250–251, 255.
20. Michael Rutter et al., *Fifteen Thousand Hours: Secondary Schools and Their Effects on Children* (Cambridge, Mass.: Harvard University Press, 1979).
21. Goodlad, op. cit., p. 39.
22. Gary A. Griffin, "Toward a Conceptual Framework for Staff Development," Chapter 10 in *Staff Development,* Eighty-second Yearbook of the National Society for the Study of Education, op. cit., p. 232.
23. Quoted in John N. Mangieri and David R. McWilliams, "The What, How and When of Professional Improvement," *Educational Leadership,* Vol. 38 (April 1981), p. 535.
24. Ibid.
25. Robert L. Kahn et al., "Role Conflict in Organizations," in Azumi and Hage, op. cit., p. 395.
26. Warren G. Bennis, *Changing Organizations* (New York: McGraw-Hill, 1966), p. 118.
27. Chester D. Babcock, "The Emerging Role of the Curriculum Leader," Chapter 3 in *Role of Supervisor and Curriculum Director in a Climate of Change,* 1965 Yearbook of the Association for Supervision and Curriculum Development (Washington, D.C.: The Association, 1965), p. 59.
28. F. J. Rothlisberger, *Man-in-Organization* (Cambridge, Mass.: Harvard University Press–Belknap Press, 1968), p. 57.
29. Arthur G. Wirth, "Alternative Philosophies of Work: Some Questions for Educators," *Phi Delta Kappan,* Vol. 63 (June 1982), p. 678.
30. Rothlisberger, op. cit., p. 57.
31. Mangieri and McWilliams, op. cit., p. 535.
32. Ibid., p. 537.
33. U.S. Department of Education, National Center for Education Statistics, *Digest of Educational Statistics 1983–84.* (Washington, D.C.: U.S. Government Printing Office, 1983.)
34. See E. Edmund Reutter, Jr., *The Supreme Court's Impact on Public Education* (Phi Delta Kappa and National Organization on Legal Problems in Education, 1982), pp. 54–89.
35. W. Vance Grant, "Trend to Fewer School Systems," *American Education,* Vol. 19 (October 1983), p. 29.
36. Ross L. Neagley and N. Dean Evans, *Handbook for Effective Supervision of Instruction,* 3rd ed. (Englewood Cliffs, N.J.: Prentice-Hall, 1980), p. 58.
37. Emery Stoops, Max Rafferty, and Russell E. Johnson, *Handbook of Educational Administration: A Guide for the Practitioner* (Boston: Allyn and Bacon, 1975), p. 135.
38. Ralph B. Kimbrough and Michael Y. Nunnery, *Educational Administration: An Introduction* (New York: Macmillan, 1983), p. 158.
39. American Association of School Administrators, *School District Organization,* Report of the AASA Commission for School District Reorganization (Washington, D.C.: The Association, 1958), p. 122.
40. Neagley and Evans, op. cit., p. 63.
41. Wilbur Brookover et al., *School Social Systems and Student Achievement* (New York: Praeger, 1979), p. 107.
42. Neagley and Evans, op. cit., p. 62.
43. Campbell et al., op. cit., pp. 251–274.
44. Peter M. Blau, "A Formal Theory of Differentiation in Organizations," in Azumi and Hage, op. cit., pp. 178–193.
45. American Association of School Administrators, *Profiles of the Administrative Team* (Washington, D.C.: The Association, 1971), pp. 50, 52.
46. James G. March, "American Public School Administration: A Short Analysis," *School Review,* Vol. 86 (February 1978), p. 219.

47. Max Weber, *The Theory of Social and Economic Organization*, A. M. Henderson and T. Parsons, eds. (Glencoe, Ill.: Free Press, 1947).
48. Richard H. Hall, "The Concept of Bureaucracy: An Empirical Assessment," in Azumi and Hage, op. cit., pp. 256–264.
49. Rensis Likert, "Influence and National Sovereignty," in John G. Pealman and Eugene L. Hartly (eds.), *Festschrift for Gardner Murphy*, (New York: Harper & Row, 1960), pp. 214–227.
50. Karl E. Weick, "Educational Organizations as Loosely Coupled Systems," *Administrative Science Quarterly*, Vol. 21 (March 1976), pp. 1–19.
51. Terrance E. Deal and Lynn D. Celotti, "How Much Influence Can (and Do) Educational Administrators Have on Classrooms?" *Phi Delta Kappan*, Vol. 61 (March 1980), p. 471.
52. Ibid., p. 473.
53. Jane Hannaway and Lee S. Sproull, "Who's Running the Show? Coordination and Control in Educational Organizations," *Administrator's Notebook*, Vols. 27, No. 9 (1978–79).
54. Ibid.
55. Gersten, Carnine, and Green, op. cit., p. 49.
56. American Association of School Administrators, *School District Organization*, op. cit., p. 300.
57. Allan C. Ornstein, "Decentralization and Community Participation Policy of Big School Systems," *Phi Delta Kappan*, Vol. 62 (December 1980), p. 257.
58. David K. Cohen, "The Price of Community Control," *Commentary*, Vol. 48 (July 1969), pp. 26–27.
59. James S. Coleman et al., *Equality of Educational Opportunity* (Washington, D.C.: Office of Education, U.S. Department of Health, Education, and Welfare, 1966).
60. McGeorge Bundy et al., *Reconnection for Learning: A Community School System for New York City* (New York: Office of the Mayor, 1967), p. 75.
61. *The New York Times*, November 10, 1967, pp. 1, 40.
62. *The New York Times*, February 29, 1964, pp. 1, 6.
63. Fred M. Hechinger, "Teachers Tell of Powerlessness and Frustration," *The New York Times*, February 14, 1984, p. C8.
64. Stoops, Rafferty, and Johnson, op. cit., p. 153.
65. Hechinger, op. cit., p. C8.
66. Stoops, Rafferty, and Johnson, op. cit., p. 153.
67. Robert J. Havighurst, "The Reorganization of Education in Metropolitan Areas," *Phi Delta Kappan*, Vol. 52 (February 1971), p. 354.
68. John I. Goodlad, *A Place Called School* (New York: McGraw-Hill, 1983), p. 277.
69. N. J. Phipps, "Autonomy or Uniformity?" *Phi Delta Kappan*, Vol. 65 (February 1984), pp. 416–417.
70. Kenneth A. Tye and Barbara Benham Tye, "Teacher Isolation and School Reform," *Phi Delta Kappan*, Vol. 65 (January 1984), p. 30.

SELECTED REFERENCES

American Association of School Administrators. *Profiles of the Administrative Team*. Washington, D.C.: The Association, 1971.
———. *School District Organization*, Report of the AASA Commission for School District Reorganization. Washington, D.C.: The Association, 1958.
Association for Supervision and Curriculum Development. *Supervision of Teaching*, 1982 Yearbook. Alexandria, Va.: The Association, 1982.

Azumi, Koya, and Jerald Hage (eds.). *Organizational Systems.* Lexington, Mass.: D. C. Heath and Company, 1972.

Bennis, Warren G. *Changing Organizations.* New York: McGraw-Hill Book Company, 1966.

Brookover, Wilbur, et al. *School Social Systems and Student Achievement.* New York: Praeger Publishers, 1979.

Burton, William H., and Leo J. Brueckner. *Supervision: A Social Process.* New York: Appleton-Century-Crofts, 1955.

Campbell, Roald F., et al. *The Organization and Control of American Schools,* 4th ed. Columbus, Ohio: Charles E. Merrill Publishing Company, 1980.

Goodlad, John I. *A Place Called School.* New York: McGraw-Hill Book Company, 1983.

Hersey, Paul, and Ken Blanchard. *Management of Organizational Behavior,* 4th ed. Englewood Cliffs, N.J.: Prentice-Hall, Inc., 1982.

Monahan, William G., and Herbert R. Hengst. *Contemporary Educational Administration.* New York: Macmillan Publishing Company, 1982.

National Society for the Study of Education. *Staff Development,* Eighty-second Yearbook, Part II. Chicago: The University of Chicago Press, 1983.

Neagley, Ross L., and N. Dean Evans. *Handbook for Effective Supervision of Instruction,* 3rd ed. Englewood Cliffs, N.J.: Prentice-Hall, Inc., 1980.

Rothlisberger, F. J. *Man-in-Organization.* Cambridge, Mass.: Harvard University Press—Belknap Press, 1968.

Reutter, E. Edmund, Jr. *The Supreme Court's Impact on Public Education.* Phi Delta Kappa and National Organization on Legal Problems in Education, 1982.

Rutter, Michael, et al. *Fifteen Thousand Hours: Secondary Schools and Their Effects on Children.* Cambridge, Mass.: Harvard University Press, 1979.

Stoops, Emery, Max Rafferty, and Russell E. Johnson. *Handbook of Educational Administration: A Guide for the Practitioner.* Boston: Allyn and Bacon, Inc., 1975.

Weber, Max. *The Theory of Social and Economic Organization,* A. M. Henderson and T. Parsons (eds.). Glencoe, Ill.: The Free Press, 1947.

Chapter 4

Supervisory Roles

In the preceding chapter, it was pointed out that effective educational programs require both moral support and practical advice for teachers—provided not only by the principal but supervisors and curriculum specialists. A school system best serves the children if there is substantial responsibility for curriculum improvement at the local school level and if this is balanced with substantial responsibility and support at the central office level. But, as Cohen points out, in recent years, the trend has been for central administrators to "pass on much problem solving responsibility (and authority) to teachers and principals."[1] This is, in part, because state and federal policymaking has added to the work that central offices must do (such as implementing new programs for disadvantaged or handicapped children). Typically, central offices establish subunits to handle some of the administrative work and delegate most of the difficult problems to principals and teachers (such as how to relate teachers' regular work to the new program).

But there is a second reason why the responsibility for educational leadership has been passed on to principals (and even to teachers, via "peer supervision"). The emphasis in the field of supervision has been on the individual school, and the principal's role is seen as the key to educational improvement.[2] Thus many superintendents believe, erroneously, that their educational leadership role is simply to promote educational leadership among their principals.[3] The responsibility and specialized knowledge of central office personnel is all but ignored. It is a dangerous strategy to bypass the central office because no building principal, no matter how talented and extraordinary he or she may be, can supply concrete assistance for teachers in every subject field and in every problem area. Moreover, there are problems of curriculum planning and articulation which must be dealt with on a districtwide level. This chapter discusses the roles and functions of districtwide supervisory personnel as well as those at the individual school level. The focus throughout will be on a coordinated program of educational leadership, based on the organic form of organization discussed in the preceding chapter.

AUTHORITY FOR SUPERVISION

The American public school system is characterized by a unique relationship between local, state, and federal units of control. As Reutter points out, "The legislature has complete control over the public schools within the state."[4] (The struggle for state control was discussed in Chapter 1.) Legislative authority to carry out the education function on a statewide basis is delegated to a state education department, a state board of education (in all but one state), and a chief state school officer. Citations of court decisions point to the "general statutory authority" of state commissioners of education to supervise educational activities of local schools in the state.[5] Thus chief state school officers have the leading supervisory role in public education. As discussed in Chapter 1, Horace Mann and Henry Barnard provided dynamic models for this post (although it must be observed that they are all too infrequently emulated).

Although legal authority and responsibility for education is vested in the state, the day-to-day administration and supervision of local schools are mainly decentralized and delegated to local units. According to Reutter, despite the fact that all states have "certain statutory prescriptions related to the curriculum of the public schools," covering "certain things that must be taught in the schools and in some instances directions as to how they should be taught," the implied powers of local units to introduce new educational practices have been broadly interpreted by the courts. Reutter points out that "In the overwhelming number of instances of legal challenge to a new educational practice, the local school district has been upheld. The usual legal basis offered is that the activity in question is a desirable educational method of achieving broad educational goals enunciated in general legislation."[6] The point of importance here is that supervisors have a great deal of freedom to improve the school curriculum. Indeed, it is a legal fact that they are actually *encouraged* to do so. Curriculum improvement is a power (and a responsibility) of school systems that enables them to carry out the state function of providing educational opportunity for children. This responsibility points to the crucial importance of districtwide educational leadership. School systems cannot engage in experimentation and a search for better methods without effective organization at the central office level. And unless they do, they are not meeting their responsibility to the public, the parents, and the children.

The Problem of Coordination

In recent years, the federal government has played a larger and larger role in American education. Actually, the national government has always pulled an oar in education. Starting with the land-grant acts of the Continental Congress in

1785 and 1787, which enunciated a policy of federal aid, and continuing until the present session of Congress, various provisions for schools have been enacted—a number of which have impacted on the school curriculum. In 1917, vocational education began on a large scale under the Smith–Hughes Act, in which federal funds were disbursed to promote instruction in agriculture, home economics, and the trades in secondary schools and to aid in the preparation of teachers of these fields. Subsequent acts increased the funds and expanded the programs for vocational education, particularly the Vocational Education Act of 1963 and its subsequent revisions. Every state long ago established a state board of vocational education to supervise the use of federal funds. Thus there is certainly nothing new in the concept of aid granted by the Congress for the support of certain programs and projects in the schools and universities.

Increase in the Federal Role in Education.   However, there has been an enormous boom of federal activity since the Cold War era of the 1950s. All three branches of the federal government have been involved. The U.S. Supreme Court, for example, told the states that as a condition for receiving federal funds, special instruction must be provided for students who do not understand the English language.[7] And in the mid-1980s, the executive branch established a policy of reform in science and mathematics education, based on the report of a national commission it had formed. Said President Reagan, in a radio address to the nation: "You may have heard the disturbing report by the National Commission on Excellence in Education that I created shortly after taking office. Their study reveals that our education system, once the finest in the world, is in a sorry state of disrepair. . . . The Commission . . . recommends requiring three solid years each of math and science."[8]

Shortly after the report of the National Commission on Excellence in Education was published, governors and state legislatures were enacting programs for "excellence in education," based on the Commission's recommendations.[9] In several states the "excellence" programs involved reducing the number of units that high school students were permitted to take in elective courses and programs, including vocational education, and instituting new requirements in science and mathematics for graduation. This was striking evidence of a lack of coordination in federal policies. The policy messages received by local schools about the place of vocational education in the curriculum were contradictory.

As Cohen notes, "The unusual fragmentation of U.S. government makes coordination at higher levels difficult and unusual."[10] It is of interest that the Department of Education was established as a means of coordinating federal activities in education. Thus far this has not happened, nor is it likely to, given the structure of our government and the fact that the Department of Education has been generally ineffective. It should not be assumed, however, that lack of coordination is merely a problem at the federal level. There is a lack of coordination among federal, state, and local levels of education.

Implications for Supervision.   Cohen observes that the schools that are the target for federal and state educational programs have been left with the, not inconsiderable, responsibility of coordinating these programs. Coordination, according to Cohen, has two meanings. First, school districts must relate state and federal programs and policies to existing operations, for example, how to work with handicapped youngsters in regular classes so that all of the children benefit. Although federal authorities provide guidelines for meeting the requirements of Public Law 94-142, the Education of All Handicapped Children Act, they are procedural, concerning how to make decisions about handicapped children. How pupils should be taught is left to the local educator.[11] This is where teachers could profit greatly from the practical advice of supervisors—general supervisors as well as special education supervisors. Typically, supervision of the education of handicapped children in regular classrooms is left to special education supervisors. This is inadequate because the specific procedures that special education supervisors suggest usually concern handicapped children, not the class as a whole, and the teacher may still be unable to connect his or her work with the program. Thus the purpose of the program, to provide handicapped children with a regular educational environment, is defeated. The base of consultation should be widened to include general supervisors as well as special subject supervisors.

The second kind of coordination is concerned with relating state and federal programs and policies to each other. Federal and state agencies have given scant attention to the local effects of adding a new policy to the existing policies. Often the agencies compete with or are unaware of the other policies or programs. As Hill observes, "No program provides resources to support its integration with other programs; consequently school districts must choose between letting the programs operate independently or using local resources to integrate and adjust the different program activities."[12]

In studying the interactions among federal programs, Hill found that the task of coordinating programs was often left to the classroom teacher, and in some schools with many federal programs teachers were simply unable to manage the unbelievable flow of youngsters in and out of their classes. In these schools fragmentation within government was leading to a fragmented educational program. As McLaughlin points out, some states initiated coordination efforts in the 1970s but funding reductions in the 1980s eroded such efforts.[13]

Central offices and local schools have the responsibility of creating integrated educational programs. The fact that state and federal governments seldom establish priorities and relationships among the numerous programs directed at local schools is actually advantageous for local curriculum development. Schools are liberated to improve their programs under fewer restrictions. With enlightened supervision, for example, teachers can adopt better classroom practices that combine some mandated responsibilities.

Harrassed though they may be by the multiple demands of federal programs, many educators have come to realize that the trend toward expansion of federal educational activities is on the whole a gain for education. There is no doubt that social problem-solving activities (education to combat youth unemployment, meet the needs of the handicapped, and so on) were undertaken by the federal government because of the unwillingness or inability of state and local agencies to do so. (The policies of a few states, most notably New York and California, reflect the social problem-solving goals of the federal government.[14]) Such activities are well in accord with the supervisory goal of providing improved opportunities for all children and youth.

On the other hand, a long list of problems is often handed down to principals and teachers, without sufficient resources for doing the job. This is partly due to budget cuts but, as mentioned earlier, many central administrators have been influenced by the movement toward the individual school as a capsulated entity for problem solving. Of course, not all central administrators have a carefully thought out rationale for delegating problems to local schools. According to Cohen, "Delegation is such a familiar approach to local school district management that in many cases administrators are probably quite unaware of what they are doing."[15]

Delegation has had costly consequences because it has increased teachers' work loads, often unrealistically. "Whatever they do," writes Cohen, "teachers must cope with an important change in their practice: the addition of impossible tasks. . . . (and) there are limits on the number of dilemmas that teachers can handle well."[16] Although some teachers seem to thrive on conflict and increased pressure, others feel angry and defeated because they are held "responsible alone to correct complex societal and institutional dilemmas."[17] Needless to say, teachers in a defeated mood cannot function effectively.

Professionals who are being presented with more problems in their work need more, not less, aid and support. Yet, as Costa and Guditus report, "During the last decade the number of districtwide instructional supervisors has slowly but steadily declined," and "the loss of positions suggests that lower priority is being given to districtwide instructional leadership."[18] Clearly, the districts that have lost their supervisory staff are not in a position to help weak teachers who are getting through teacher education programs and getting jobs. (Unfortunately, during periods of education retrenchment, budgetary cuts take their toll on supervisory staff.)

But more bright people are also coming into education due to the publicity created by the national reports on education, which, as Lawrence A. Cremin points out, "have done a great service in moving education back on the national agenda. They have emphasized the need for good teaching and for high public expectations and that's all to the good."[19] It can be safely said, however, that what Cremin calls "the sense that teaching is an important career" is not enough to keep men and women of ability in teaching. They must also have the resources they need to function effectively. These include mundane but necessary supplies and materials, but they also include consultants to improve student learning. The availability of resources districtwide is a condition for which the superintendent of schools, through the board of education, bears responsibility.

Supervision: A Field in Transition

In a very real sense, the title of this section is a misnomer, because every field is a field in transition—be it law, engineering, or medicine. The very essence of professionalism is new knowledge and new methods which develop as solutions are found to problems in the field. (Problem solutions in any field are the foundations for practice.) The difficulty is that many educators see problems in the field as a threat rather than as a promise or opportunity for improvement. Actually, however, problems are more than just opportunities. If they go ignored, the field is in danger of extinction. (Adapt and regenerate or die is a professional as well as a biological principle.) This, unfortunately, is the condition of the field of supervision; central office supervisors are becoming an endangered species.

Do Districtwide Supervisors Make a Difference? Costa and Guditus observe that the decline in central office supervisory personnel "seems to be inconsistent with mounting demands for increased effectiveness." Noting that "objective data on the role and importance of districtwide supervisors are largely unavailable," they propose that, "If it can be shown that central office supervisors do make a difference in the quality of curriculum and instruction, then school boards will need to reexamine their staffing patterns." They believe that there is a need to answer questions such as: "What are the consequences for curriculum and instructional effectiveness when these [supervisory] functions are not performed or are shifted to others?" They also call for a comparison of "effective" versus "ineffective" schools and school systems in relationship to staffing patterns.[20]

The observation that the declining number of districtwide supervisors is inconsistent with demands for quality is not arguable. But there are problems with using research on "effective" schools as a means of determining whether supervisors "make a difference," because effective schools research has serious shortcomings. According to three researchers at the Far West Laboratory for Educational Research and Development:

> An initial problem is that research on effective schools has focused on a single dimension of school effectiveness: basic skills outcomes. This narrow focus is neither new to education . . . nor is it unimportant. But it has led to the development of indicators of school effectiveness that do not correspond to practitioners' subjective assessments of this construct. For example, recent research demonstrates that school personnel and their constituencies assess school effectiveness in a variety of domains, including the attainment of administrative, social and emotional objectives.[21]

Supervisors are concerned with a variety of educational goals, and since research on effective schools has defined school effectiveness in terms of just one goal—basic skills achievement—it is invalid as a means of determining whether central office supervisors "make a difference."

Moreover, we already know what happens when teachers have inadequate resources for problem solving. In many school systems the supervisory function of helping teachers to solve their problems is not performed and those teachers who can get out are leaving. In these school systems the supervisory programs are a failure.

Asking whether "supervisors make a difference" is about as unproductive as asking whether "schools make a difference"—a popular question in the antischool movement of the 1970s. (Such questions have built-in negative valuations.) It is the wrong approach to reversing the decline in central office supervision. The evidence is that a more useful question would be: What can supervisors do to solve educational problems?

Requirements for Educational Leadership. One of the most persuasive arguments for supervision is that all schools have problems that require fresh approaches to solve them. Solving chronic and acute problems demands leadership. What is leadership? How does it raise the quality of education? There are no more important questions for educators to ask, yet we have not asked them well in recent years. The insights of Ralph Tyler are extremely helpful for us here.

> Leadership, whether epitomized in an individual or emanating from a group, requires, among other things, identification and clarification of a goal that can be perceived as important and attainable, the development of a plan of action that appears likely to carry forward to the goal, and the assignment and acceptance of particular responsibilities for each individual in carrying out the plan of action. *All too often these essential characteristics are overlooked or not implemented in programs of college and school improvement.*[22]

Tyler observes that there is considerable talk about innovation and change, but far less discussion of the particular problems faced by a given school, problems that require new approaches to solve them. *"The general goal of improving the school or college is too vague to allow effective focusing of limited resources. . . . It is necessary to identify a problem on which to concentrate the attack."*[23]

Examples of serious problems that schools face are, unfortunately, not difficult to find. In some school districts, many of the students who enter the ninth grade fail to graduate from high school. If a high dropout rate is a problem in a particular school system, it could (should) be the focus for an improvement program. And as Tyler points out, although the results of the National Assessment of Educational Progress (NAEP) show no evidence of a serious decline in educational achievement nationally, they do point to problems that are opportunities for improvement—if they exist locally.

School superintendents can best use national assessment data by conducting similar assessments in their own schools. In Tyler's own words:

> If a superintendent can relate a local problem to a national problem, he doesn't have to be ashamed that it's there; others have it, too. If the facts can be faced frankly, it really helps. Facts are not things to be ignored or brushed under the table. A good administrator has to face them and say, "What does it mean? Could we do something about it? Should we apologize for the lack? Shouldn't we say frankly that it's consistent with the national picture, that it is something American schools haven't learned to do, but that we're going to start working on it immediately?"[24]

As an illustration, the recent assessment reported that more than 90 percent of 17-year-olds could add, subtract, multiply, and divide accurately with whole numbers, but only 45 percent of them could use their computations in figuring taxes, making purchases, or estimating materials required for simple constructions.[25] If this were true locally, the problem of more effective mathematics instruction could become the focus of efforts for improvement. Although the reading comprehension of 19-year-olds and 17-year-olds has increased, there has been a slight decrease for 13-year-olds.[26] If this were the case locally, the problem of improving the effectiveness of reading instruction in the middle grades could be the focus of a systemwide improvement effort.

The point of importance is that a difficult problem faced by the schools offers an opportunity for leadership, but that the broad goal of rebuilding the educational program is just too nebulous to permit the effective concentration of resources. (Moreover, as Tyler points out, "most schools are by no means altogether ineffective."[27]) And while each step taken may seem to be modest, there can be no denying that out of the collective problem solutions emerges an educational program of improved quality. Like supervision itself, educational improvement is a developmental process.

Need for a Monitoring System. In the minds of many educators, a good program will remain that way. According to Tyler, this is a dangerous assumption. "Because external conditions change and because the internal operations of the school are affected by human problems, a program that has been highly effective may become mediocre or worse." A school system should have a way of monitoring its educational efforts, for, as Tyler observed, "unless problems are identified, they are likely to continue; others also may develop." Means of monitoring may include survey testing, teacher self-reports, principals' observations, supervisors' observations, follow-up studies of students, and evaluation by standing committees. The objective is to identify problems that can be referred to study groups for careful investigation. Once again, state and national data (such as the NAEP results) are good guides to local studies.

Tyler warns that "an effective attack on a serious problem often requires concentrated efforts over several years. The dynamic organization must be prepared to mobilize the personnel and other resources if it is to reach its project goals."[28] Thus we are reminded once again of the need for organization at the central office level. An educational program, like the preservation of health, is something that must be worked at constantly. The ideal is the best possible program for children and youth.

Yet in many instances supervisors' time is not being used to provide educational leadership. A study by the Association for Supervision and Curriculum Development on the use of districtwide supervisory personnel reported: "Superintendents ask them to deal with tedious paperwork, to generate data to justify and support central office causes, and to help maintain their positive image in the view of the board and the public."[29] In such instances, the superintendents are engaging in unprofessional and unethical conduct. More important, the effectiveness of school systems is impaired when the legitimate role of the professional staff is subverted. More than three decades ago, Elsbree and Reutter wrote: "Anyone who has given thought to the leadership tasks inherent in a sound program of curriculum improvement can scarcely fail to realize that there are prodigious tasks confronting our supervisory and administrative personnel."[30] The observation is, if anything, more valid today.

THE ROLE OF THE SUPERINTENDENT

It will be recalled from Chapter 1 that in earlier days, superintendents of city school systems personally supervised teachers and carried out the curriculum development responsibilities. Today, we tend to think of curriculum development as a delegated responsibility, associating it with curriculum directors, supervisors, and principals. Actually, no matter how large the school system, the superintendent is still responsible for good teaching and a curriculum tailored to meet each learner's needs (although the superintendent does not have sufficient time to do everything personally). In a small school system, the responsibilities carried out in larger systems by the director of curriculum (sometimes called the assistant superintendent for instruction) must be performed personally by the superintendent. Whatever the size of the school system, the superintendent is the one person who can assure the districtwide conditions necessary for improving the educational program.

Educational Leadership Responsibilities

As shown in Table 4–1, the superintendency involves many functions that bear directly on the quality of the educational program. When analyzed by functions, it becomes clear that the heavy administrative responsibility of the superintendent is nothing more or less than an attempt to provide an educational program that is ever more effective in meeting the needs of children. Moreover, the leadership responsibilities of the superintendent should dispel any doubts that the reader may have to this point that supervision is an administrative function as well as a service function.

This is not to say that all the functions in Table 4–1 are being performed well (or even performed at all), only that they should be. Curriculum development and curriculum articulation are not being done at all by many supervisors and principals. These two critical functions are among the most neglected of the leadership responsibilities. The situation is much better with respect to providing educational support services (for education of the handicapped, for example), due to state and federal interventions.[31]

The superintendent is also responsible for creating a climate of professionalism in which teachers can function most effectively. As Lucio tells us, this official must make certain that the following conditions prevail throughout the school system: (1) an atmosphere where teachers feel free to experiment, (2) released time for teachers for curriculum development work, and (3) provision of outside consultant help when necessary.[32]

As shown in Table 4–1, the superintendent must also be committed to problem solving as a way of improving education. He or she will make certain that there is an atmosphere where problems are openly faced, by selecting subordinate staff who are committed to identifying and dealing with problems and who see problems as opportunities for improvement. Figure 4–1 presents a process for solving problems.

As has been indicated, in recent years the idea that educational improvement is the responsibility of the individual school has been very seductive for superin-

Table 4–1 Supervisory Functions

Position	Leadership Responsibilities (Examples)
Superintendent	Planning and deployment of physical facilities; amalgamating the best available faculties for the schools; selecting administrators and supervisors who see problems as opportunities for improvement; budgeting for the total educational program; encouraging continuous curriculum development and evaluation; providing for professional development; providing for a coordinated program for solving districtwide and local-school problems; promoting a balanced curriculum; providing for continuous evaluation of the functions of the schools; providing for educational-support services (counseling, special education, etc.); communicating with the board concerning implementation policies and programs, and how problems are being solved
Assistant superintendent for curriculum and instruction (or curriculum director)	Planning and conducting programs for inservice teacher education; assisting teachers in solving classroom problems; assisting principals in evaluating teachers; working with the assistant superintendent and principals on curriculum development and evaluation; promoting horizontal and vertical curriculum articulation; providing learning resources; interpreting the professional research literature for application to local conditions; working with other supervisors on the total educational program
Supervisor	Providing for a continuous program of curriculum development and evaluation; promoting horizontal and vertical curriculum articulation; providing for a balanced curriculum; ascertaining and developing the capabilities of principals and supervisors; providing for professional development; providing for learning resources; coordinating the efforts of principals and supervisors in solving problems; extending successful programs throughout the district; developing the program of inservice teacher education in cooperation with supervisors, principals, and teachers—along with colleges and universities; recommending supervisory and other staff appointments; preparing grant proposals to state and federal agencies; coordinating school-accreditation processes; interpreting the professional and research literature for application to local conditions
Principal	Maintaining a constructive school climate; assisting teachers in solving problems; planning utilization of school plant facilities; allocating educational resources; recruiting, selecting, and evaluating faculty; providing for a continuous program of curriculum development and evaluation; promoting horizontal and vertical curriculum articulation; providing for professional development; working with the assistant superintendent (curriculum director), supervisors, and other principals on problems of common concern; providing for educational-support services; interpreting the professional and research literature for application to local conditions
Department head (secondary school)	Working with principal, supervisors, and teachers on curriculum development in the subject fields; working with supervisors, other department heads, and teachers on horizontal and vertical curriculum articulation; assisting teachers with professional improvement; selecting curricular resources with supervisors and teachers; scheduling course offerings and teaching assignments; coordinating other departmental activities (examinations, etc.); interpreting the professional and research literature for application to local conditions

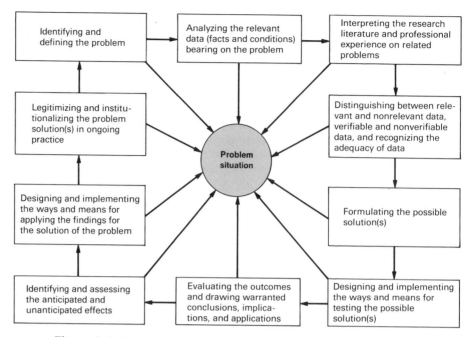

Figure 4–1. Developmental supervision: a problem-solving process.

tendents. There are at least two serious weaknesses in a highly *decentralized approach:* first, problems of the entire school system are not faced, and, second, stimulation, encouragement, and help from the central office are lacking.

Nor is a *centralized approach* the answer, for it focuses on systemwide problems, not on the problems of individual schools or individual teachers. When the central office determines the goals to be met and the methodologies to be used by individual teachers, teachers are not viewed as professionals who have the ability to identify, analyze, and solve problems. It has been shown time and time again that teacher participation is essential for the improvement of education.

The superintendent must provide for an *organic-coordinated approach* to problem solving which faces problems of concern to an individual school and problems of concern to the whole system, working on some on a local school basis and some on a districtwide basis. The problem-solving efforts of individual teachers, individual schools, and the central office must be viewed by the superintendent as essential and in organic interrelation. The teachers in individual schools are encouraged to identify and solve classroom problems with the help of supervisors, principals, and others. In this way they can better serve their own students. Simultaneously, staff members in several or all schools, together with supervisors and consultants, may combine their efforts to attack a problem common to some or all schools. For example, several schools may be interested in providing opportunities for secondary school youngsters to engage in socially useful activities (to help them learn to take on adult community responsibilities). Simultaneously, a committee of English teachers from all schools and the central office may be attacking the problem of developing effective means for helping students to improve their ability to express ideas in writing, which is of concern throughout the entire school system.

The organic-coordinated approach is based on the organic form of organization discussed in the preceding chapter, whereas the centralized approach is based on the mechanistic-hierarchical concept. A school system that is organized for educational improvement in the local school only is representative of neither a mechanistic nor an organic form of organization. It is simply dysfunctional; the executive administrator has abdicated responsibility.

Influence of the Superintendent

In a good deal of the literature there is recognition that the superintendent's control over material resources (books, supplies, and equipment) can affect the quality of the educational program. Superintendents frequently determine which buildings and departments will receive more resources. As Campbell and others point out, "The superintendent can by the allocation of resources, determine which areas of the curriculum and which student activities will be promoted and which deemphasized."[33] During the back-to-basics retrenchment era of the 1970s and early 1980s many superintendents deemphasized music and art. The results of the recent National Assessment of Education Progress show a marked decrease in achievement in both music and art.[34] This should come as no surprise to anyone. Granted that superintendents are under great pressures to jump on national bandwagons, they must have a clear vision of a balanced educational program and their own responsibility for keeping it in balance. As Cremin observes, however, "They have too often been managers, facilitators, politicians in the narrowest sense."[35] The hope for the future is improved pre-service preparation and recruitment of the superintendent.

Professional Leader of the School Board. A good school board is a prerequisite for improved education. As professional leader of the board of education, the superintendent must communicate with the board in detail about the needs of the district, how programs are being implemented, and how problems are being solved. He or she must convey to the board why changes in the educational program are being contemplated and why they should be supported. The wise superintendent keeps board members supplied with a constant stream of data concerning schools which they can keep on hand for ready reference. Briefs on budgets, enrollment trends, class size, standardized test results, and the educational program make it possible for board members to speak with authority on various issues to audiences that professional educators cannot reach. The point of importance is that boards look to the superintendent for leadership in improving their schools' educational programs, and a unified and enthusiastic board can be a nucleus for school–community relations that promote improved education.

Countering Educational Cycles and Fashions. A serious problem in education is the adoption of "new" ideas that have been tried and discarded. The child-centered school that enjoyed its heyday in the early decades of this century, but was abandoned by teachers as unworkable in the 1930s, is an example. It was recycled in the late 1960s and treated as new, only to be abandoned for the second time. (Recall the open-education movement.) Such failures are expensive and prevent education from moving ahead in desirable directions. *Schools have the primary responsibility for countering cycles and fashions in education.* School administrators have to deal with board and community pressure to adopt a "new" educational model that failed in the past. Superintendents can deal with the problem by following two principles.

> First any discussion of a "new" educational model or program should take advocates beyond the "we want it" stage to a consideration of the problem it was meant to solve. *Every* innovation was originally developed to solve a problem, which may not be your school's problem at all. In fact, by adopting someone else's solution, you may create new problems of your own. If this happens you can be certain that the next era of reform in your district will be an attempt to undo the excesses of this one. . . .
>
> Second, curriculum reform efforts should not be mere reactions to the excesses of a preceding era of reform, but should begin as an attempt to solve a problem. One starts with the problem, not the innovation or model. In working on a problem we must see what happened before. (Most problems, like most proposals are not new.)[36]

By discussing with board members the problem an innovation is intended to solve, they may decide that it is not for their schools. For example, the open classroom (imported from Great Britain) was created as a means of providing greater freedom for children who come from highly structured working-class homes. Under this model, learning was supposed to be largely self-directed. If transplanted to schools where children have a great deal of freedom outside the school and need a sense of direction, the results could be disastrous. (This is just what happened in American inner-city schools, whose board members were unaware of where the movement came from and were disarmed by its rhetoric.)

THE ROLE OF THE ASSISTANT SUPERINTENDENT FOR CURRICULUM AND INSTRUCTION

An individual may hold the title of assistant, associate, or deputy superintendent, or may even be called director of curriculum. Whatever the title, this person is the member of the superintendent's team who is concerned with the function of improving curriculum and teaching. An important (but, as noted, terribly neglected) responsibility of the assistant superintendent is articulation of the educational program from kindergarten through twelfth grade. In carrying this out, the assistant superintendent serves in a line relationship to the directors of elementary and secondary education (who may be called coordinators). The effectiveness of the assistant superintendent depends on the ability to work well as a team with many people and to utilize their talents in developing ever-improving school programs.

Major Responsibilities

Does curriculum development involve staff development? Is staff development important for the effective use of instructional resources? Does the way resources are used depend on the staff's vision of curriculum?

To all three questions, yes. As Taba told us, curriculum development and the inservice education of teachers in the skills of curriculum development are an integral process.[37] Instructional resources are ineffective unless teachers have a way to gain and update competencies and knowledge. And how resources are used reflects whether teachers view teaching as routine management or have an imaginative vision of curriculum.[38]

Importance of Viewing Functions Interrelatedly. As shown in Table 4–1, the assistant superintendent for curriculum and instruction has the responsibility and provides the leadership for improving the educational program. The development of a desirable educational program depends on implementing a strong program of professional development in which teachers learn to use instructional resources and services and understand the theories behind what they are doing. The assistant superintendent is effective only to the extent that he or she views the basic job responsibilities of curriculum development, teachers' professional development, and instructional services interrelatedly (see Figure 4–2).

Yet the major responsibilities of the assistant superintendent are often presented in the literature as if they were unrelated. For example, they are classified by the American Association of School Administrators into three categories: (1) instructional services, (2) curriculum development, and (3) staff development.[39] Similarly, they are grouped by Neagley and Evans as (1) those related to the educational program, (2) those connected with staff development and professional growth, and (3) those related to providing instructional materials and special services.[40]

Actually, curriculum development is impossible if these major functions are treated in isolation rather than in organic interrelationship. For example, if books and other media are selected apart from ongoing efforts to bring about an improved educational program, the latter will never happen. The organization is kept moving in its customary direction. The assistant superintendent for curriculum and instruction has the administrative responsibility to see that programs are conceived, developed, and carried out conjointly. To carry out the role, he or she must not think in compartments.

Extending Successful Programs

Successful programs in one or more schools should be extended throughout the district, and it is the responsibility of the assistant superintendent for curriculum and instruction to provide the necessary leadership. The following excerpt from an item in *The New York Times* is illustrative.

> The second graders in Room 210 at Public School 11 in the Highbridge section of the Bronx knew something special was happening one morning last week when several authors showed up in person to read from their works.

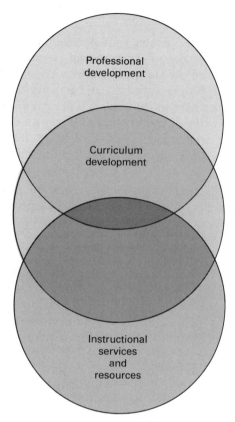

Figure 4–2. Interdependent functions of the assistant superintendent for curriculum and instruction.

The authors, books in hand, stood anxiously at the front of the room and took turns reading aloud, occasionally stumbling over a multisyllable word. Never mind that the authors were Stephanie Raphael, Rosalind Burgess, Glenn Kenney and Marie Rolling, whose own second grade class meets in Room 208, just down the hall.

This was Author's Day at P.S. 11, and though all the authors were first and second graders it was a celebration of books and of the energies that go into creating them. The bound, laminated pages of the "books" the students had written were the culmination of a serious attempt to enhance their reading and writing skills.

The program that led to Author's Day is part of an effort that reaches into several elementary schools in Community School District 9 in the Bronx and parts of some of the city's other districts. It has been so successful that *Charlotte Frank, head of curriculum for the Board of Education, is trying to get $500,000 for the teacher training needed to extend the program throughout the city.*[41]

A Problem-Solving Effort. The program described above was the result of a problem-solving process (see Figure 4–1). The problem situation was to develop effective procedures for helping children learn to write. As shown in Figure

4–1, an important part of the process is to interpret the research literature bearing on the problem. The program was developed for the participating schools in collaboration with a nearby university (Columbia's Teachers College) and was based on the theories of an authority on the teaching of writing from the University of New Hampshire. The basic principle is that children should learn to write the same way that they learned to talk—without having to worry about mistakes.

"Thus, in the early stages of the writing, very little is said to the students about errors of spelling, punctuation and grammar, penmanship, margin widths and other mechanics. The corrections are dispensed in small doses after the children have thought of something to say and gained confidence in their ability to say it."

Each child comes up with his or her own topic and develops a story line with the teacher and other children "before putting a word on paper. Once a child starts writing, the teacher and fellow students offer advice, but the only one who ever puts a mark on the paper or changes anything in the revising or editing is the student."

As authors have always done, these children have tended to write about familiar things. Generally of fewer than ten pages, the books are bound between covers designed by the youngsters. Some are placed in the school library as part of the permanent collection.

" 'This is my first book ever published and it feels real good,' said Darnella Beale, author of 'The Missing Money,' a mystery. 'I guess it's not that difficult to get a book published when you're in the first or second grade because your teacher can help you do it.' "

Observed the director of early childhood education in District 9: "A result of what they are doing is an awakening that behind every book there is a human being and that books are not just produced by machines."[42]

The program development process involved teacher education and the use of resources (outside consultants). Thus it exemplifies the interaction of the major functions shown in Figure 4–2.

Appropriate for Other Levels. It is also worth noting that the method (for learning to write) is appropriate at any level, as illustrated by the *Foxfire* series. In the 1960s, students in a rural Georgia high school began a project to capture the folkways, legends, and traditions of the region through cameras, tape recorders, and typewriters; they proceeded to publish the material in magazine form. Eventually, eight volumes of the "Foxfire" material were published commercially in book form with national sales approaching 7 million copies by the mid 1980s—attesting to the universal appeal of the subject matter.

Developing an Outstanding School System

The quality of the educational program depends on the quality of the teachers in the school system. There are two principal means of improving the quality of the teaching staff: selecting the best available teachers, and providing for teachers' continuous professional development. The latter is a responsibility of the assistant superintendent for curriculum and instruction. However, it should be borne in mind that this person does not work alone in carrying it out. He or she works with the superintendent, supervisors, principals, and teachers (see Table 4–1).

Employment and Assignment of Teachers. Improving the educational program depends heavily on additions and replacements to the teaching staff, and thus the assistant superintendent must make recommendations to the superintendent or personnel administrator. According to the American Association of School Administrators, the assistant superintendent "should have knowledge of individual schools and be able to recommend the kinds of teaching staff needed to carry out a defined program."[43] Although the assistant superintendent usually does not recommend the employment of a particular person for a key position (this is the responsibility of the personnel administrator), he or she may be asked to develop the job description and qualifications. The size of the school district is a major consideration in determining the responsibility of the assistant superintendent in working with principals in the recruitment, selection, and assignment of the teaching personnel. In a small district, he or she may be the only immediate member of the superintendent's team and may assume joint responsibility for staff personnel.

Professional Development of Teachers. Teachers bring professional knowledge to their work, but much of it is soon outdated. Yet they are responsible for using the best available knowledge of the present day. The welfare of children and youth, and of our society, demands no less of teachers. Inservice education programs were severely reduced through budget cutbacks in supervisory staffs during the 1970s and 1980s. Reconceptualizing and regenerating these programs depends on the leadership of the assistant superintendent for curriculum and instruction.

An effective inservice education program for teachers should have two dimensions. The first is a *school-related* dimension and involves inservice work with supervisors. Classroom supervision and workshops conducted by supervisors are examples. As noted, these approaches to professional improvement are absolutely essential for curriculum improvement.

The second is a *university-related* dimension. To keep abreast of the developments in their profession, teachers should be required to take university courses. Every profession requires its practitioners to keep abreast of the field. In the absence of advanced university study, physicians may rely on the "detail men" from the pharmaceutical companies to keep them up to date, and teachers may rely on the salespeople from the various concerns that market educational materials, including computers, programmed instructional materials, textbooks, workbooks, and the like. In too many school districts curriculum development is listening to the salespeople and deciding what to adopt.

The university is a very different learning environment for inservice education. The university is interested in generalizable knowledge rather than the particular. The university makes the school district look beyond itself rather than only at its own particular situation. The resources of the university (library and people) are more comprehensive than the school district in the sense of advancing knowledge in the field of education. Finally, the university is a more cosmopolitan environment because it brings teachers from a given district into contact with teachers, supervisors, and school administrators from other school districts in the state, region, and nation.

The outstanding school system looks outward rather than inward. As Tyler points out, "Part of the role of a good administrator is somehow to get outside influences to come in."[44] Good administrators, for example, want teachers to visit schools where things are going on.

But some of the larger school systems have attempted to perform the university function themselves, by offering school district courses for credit. School district workshops (which is what these courses really are) should be conducted as part of professional inservice education, *not* for "academic" credit. Otherwise, they are a sham; supervisors teaching the "courses" often try to ingratiate themselves with teachers, so that the credits are meaningless. The point of importance is that in no way can the school-related dimension of professional development substitute for the university-related dimension. (The reverse is also true, of course.)

THE ROLE OF THE SUPERVISOR

A very small school district may have only one person working in the area of supervision and curriculum improvement, and that person may be called a supervisor. In a somewhat larger school district the supervisor may be called the deputy superintendent of curriculum and instruction, with essentially the same functions as the supervisor in the first district. Is the use of different titles cause for concern?

According to one writer, there is a problem of communication in the field because even those persons who are known by identical titles may be found to perform different functions. "There are supervisors who are generalists and supervisors of specific subjects; there are supervisors of services and supervisors of instructional media. However, all are usually known simply as supervisors or consultants."[45]

But there are doctors who are internists and doctors who are obstetricians; there are doctors who are oncologists and doctors who are ophthalmologists. But all are usually known as doctors and this seems to trouble no one. The same would seem applicable to supervisors. As Harris observes, *supervision* and *supervisor*, as terms, are well understood in the field of education. "An extensive literature, dating back . . . to the classic work of Barr, Burton and Brueckner, is surprisingly consistent in its use of these terms by most of the writers in the field," and the concept of school supervision as a specialization with the purpose of improving teaching and learning "is clear and persistent in nearly all major writings. The concept of the supervisor . . . as a broad class of specialized personnel with various titles and primary responsibility for leadership in supervision is well established also."[46]

Thus the concept of supervision as a means of improving the educational program is well understood (its history was discussed in the first two chapters of this text) and the titles of supervisory personnel are not nearly as important as the function itself. The size of the school district as well as its financial resources affect supervisory staffing. For example, a small school district may be able to afford only one supervisor, and it is almost a certainty that he or she would have to be a generalist.

Determining Supervisory Needs

The overriding principle for determining staffing for supervisory services is to begin with the curriculum; one begins with a view of the curriculum, and the supervisory needs of the district should stem from that view. At the secondary school level the total curriculum may be classified in accord with four broad functions: (1) general education or those learnings that all members of a free society should share in common, (2) exploratory education, (3) enrichment education, and (4) specialized education—including college-preparatory, prevocational, and vocational studies. The exploratory and enrichment education include not only formal studies, usually provided through controlled and free electives, but also student activities such as band, orchestra, publications, clubs, intramural and varsity athletics, and so on.

At the elementary level, the curriculum may be conceptualized as encompassing the function of general education and the functions of exploratory and enrichment education. Although the fundamental skills are essential to general education, the traditional elementary school focuses on these skills as though they were ends in themselves rather than as tools for further and richer learning. An important role of the supervisor, both generalist and specialist, is to help teachers understand that skills, concepts, and patterns of thinking are developed as children attempt to enlarge and deepen their understanding of the environment.

We turn now to the roles of the general supervisors, elementary and secondary.

Supervisors of Elementary and Secondary Education

In small school systems these supervisors are responsible directly to the superintendent and, in middle-sized and large school systems, to the assistant superintendent for curriculum and instruction. In some school systems supervisors are known as coordinators (or even as directors of elementary and secondary education). In systems with no assistant superintendent for curriculum and instruction, the supervisors assume the responsibilities of this post. Table 4–1 presents the functions of the supervisor.

The supervisor of elementary education and the supervisor of secondary education are generalists in the sense that they are not specialists in a subject field. However, they have a specialization—the total program of education at a given level of schooling. They bear the responsibility for aiding the assistant superintendent in developing balanced and coherent programs of elementary and secondary education. When policies directed at the schools conflict (as noted, this is a growing problem in education), they must make recommendations to the assistant superintendent based on the principle of developing the best possible total program for the education of individual children and youth. This responsibility should not be left to the individual schools operating in isolation.

The role of the generalist is enormously important because someone in the school system must take a comprehensive view of the curriculum. In the words of Lawrence A. Cremin, "Someone must look at the curriculum whole and raise insistent questions of priority and relationship. Education is more than a succession of units, courses and programs, however excellent; and to refuse to look at curricula in their entirety is to relegate to intraschool politics a series of decisions that ought to call into play the most fundamental philosophical principles."[47] Cremin adds that no one person should (or can) be entirely responsible for this matter, but that it should be the "leading business" of the generalist. It should be added that keeping the curriculum articulated and in balance is no easy business, given the enormous pressures of special interests on the school. What is demanded is strong leadership combined with professional expertise and commitment.

Inservice Education Versus Evaluation: A Basic Conflict. Like all professions, supervision is continually evolving. As we have discussed, in the early days of public school systems, supervision was strictly a teacher training function. Supervision has evolved from faultfinding-inspectional supervision to developmental supervision (see Chapter 6). The objective of supervision, however, has not changed—to improve teaching and learning and thereby improve the educational opportunities of children and youth.

Supervisors are effective only to the extent that they can assist teachers in solving classroom problems. The literature of supervision has long emphasized that supervision "involves a definite process for helping teachers to locate their problems" and "skill in helping them to solve their problems."[48] In this way, supervisors help teachers to do better the professional work in which they are engaged. This is inservice education.

But supervisors are also engaged in evaluation. First, the very process of problem solving involves evaluation—determining whether the problem has indeed been solved. Second, as shown in Table 4–1, one of the supervisor's responsibilities is to "assist the principals in a staff capacity in evaluating the quality of teaching and learning."[49] As Costa and Guditus observe, "Principals often use them (supervisors) to evaluate and assist in dismissing incompetent teachers. These circumstances tend to interfere with the helping relationship needed to work productively with other staff members."[50] As mentioned, the findings of research indicate that although district-level supervisors are usually available to bring their expertise to bear on teacher's problems, most teachers do not take the initiative in drawing upon supervisors for help. No doubt, many teachers are afraid to ask for help from supervisors because they believe that by exposing a problem with their teaching, they are inviting a low evaluation of their work from the principal; good teachers do not have problems, or so the myth goes, and any help that might be forthcoming is viewed as not being worth the risk.

As for the research reporting that teachers who "used" supervisors tended to find them not helpful, one wonders whether the teachers themselves requested help or the principal made the request (for whatever reason). This is not clear in the major study reported by Tye and Tye, but it makes all the difference.[51] The teacher's perception of a classroom problem may not be the same as the principal's perception. Yet it is the principal who states the nature of the problem when making a request that the teacher be supervised. One quickly recognizes the difficulty: It is the principal, not the teacher who is asking for help. Little wonder, then, that teachers tend to find supervisory personnel of little or no help in solving *their* problems.

As professionals, *teachers must be able to request aid from supervisors directly, without having to go through the principal.* Yet, astonishingly, one finds statements such as the following in supervision textbooks: "All requests for coordinators (supervisors) to work in individual schools should be made through the principal."[52] It is no wonder that teachers often view supervisors as adversaries. But the real problem is that supervisors are being underutilized as improvers of teaching and learning.

Resolving the Conflict. The involvement of supervisors in both inservice education and evaluation is inevitable. The basic conflict between these functions is probably the most serious and, up until now, unresolved problem in the field of supervision. The present authors propose a solution that is well in keeping with the purposes of supervision. Among the key criteria for evaluating their work, teachers should be evaluated on whether they seek help in identifying and solving problems (they must be willing to expose problems). When the supervisor (or principal) asks, "How can I help you get the job done?" and, "What problems do we have together to work on?," the teacher should indicate some areas for assistance. (Not to have problems—for improving the curriculum, for example—means that one is no longer seeking better methods and has stopped growing.) Possible solutions for problems should be formulated by the teacher and supervisor together. The problem-solving procedure shown in Figure 4–1 illustrates how problems may be attacked systematically and collaboratively.

Supervisors (including principals) must, themselves, view problem situations that arise in the classroom as beginning points for professional growth (not to mention improving the quality of education).

Specific Subject Supervisors

The special supervisor is a specialist in a knowledge field such as mathematics, or in a fine and performing art such as music, or in a skill area such as reading. Specific needs of the school district and the current developments in the curriculum affect supervisory staffing. One of the results of federal aid to meet the special needs of educationally deprived youngsters was a saturation of supervisory services for teachers in disadvantaged areas. Many urban school districts gave supervisory assistance in reading the top staffing priority, believing that a specific need in some schools was more important than having balanced supervisory staffing (generalists and specialists in various curriculum areas) for all schools in the district. Certainly, federal financial assistance for the special purpose of reading instruction was a key factor. Unfortunately, in focusing on "basic skills development," many large school districts severely retrenched their supervisory programs in other curriculum areas, such as music and art.

Similarly, the national importance given science and mathematics in the 1980s led school districts to provide more supervisory assistance to teachers in those fields. National concerns have a way of appearing on local agendas.

The Subject Specialist and General Education. The special supervisor is a specialist in the content, methods, and materials of a particular curriculum field. Nevertheless, it is of crucial importance that the specialist understands how it relates to border fields, for example, how mathematics relates to science. How should mathematics meet the general education function of the curriculum? It is the responsibility of the mathematics supervisor to seek continually to answer this question.

At the elementary level, children need to use mathematics in social studies, where they are using graphs and charts. And mathematics (statistics) must be utilized effectively in the social studies and business courses at the secondary level. Mathematics is being offered here as an illustration, but the same need to relate the special field to its general education function also exists in science. Every school district should have a curriculum council, consisting of special supervisors, general supervisors, and teachers, which deals with this problem of curriculum articulation and other curriculum problems on a continuing basis.

The Subject-Field Specialist and Type of School District. Ideally, the subject-field specialist should serve in grades K–12, thus providing for continuity in the curriculum from elementary through secondary school. However, not all school districts have the unified form of organization. In those that do not, the subject-field specialist must function on the elementary or the secondary level. So much of curriculum development depends on the type of school district organization.

THE ROLE OF THE PRINCIPAL

> All of a sudden there stood Grissum, looking in as he had said he would. He stood there in the door, erect, unsmiling, while the readers faltered and stopped. He took a quick look around the room and then, when everything was silent, glared straight into the room. Glared; there was no question that he didn't like very much what he saw. We all knew it; we suddenly all felt pretty guilty. We wished we had been sitting up straight in our desks, all in rows, silent, diagramming sentences or writing out our spelling words. After perhaps 20 seconds he stepped back, closed the door, and was gone without saying a word.[53]

The principal described above seemed intent on creating a climate of terror. Although the vivid picture was portrayed by a child, this kind of principal often appears in teachers' accounts of their lives in school.[54] But the principal's role is to provide moral support for teachers. Research indicates that a "positive climate and overall atmosphere" is essential for the improvement of teaching and learning.[55]

Principals must also create a climate in which teachers are encouraged to have an imaginative vision of curriculum. Actually, studies show that "principals consider creating a climate which encourages experimentation and sharing [ideas] as their most effective contribution to improving instruction."[56] (The principal above was creating a repressive climate.)

Similarities and Differences with Central Office Supervisors

As Table 4–1 shows, if principals are working effectively, they should perform on the building level many of the same functions of the central office supervisor on a district-wide basis. Both are engaged in supervision and the improvement of education. The extent and quality of the supervisory program at the central-office level profoundly affects the principal's responsibility; where there is little or no help for teachers from the central office, principals must assume the primary responsibility for assisting teachers.

However, there are differences as well. In addition to working in the area of curriculum improvement, the principal necessarily is concerned with personnel administration and must be able to answer the question: Does this teacher meet the district's standards? An affirmative answer at the time of appointment is not only common sense but absolutely essential; the principal should participate in teacher selection as well as teacher evaluation. As Elsbree and Reutter pointed out, "A principal who shares in the responsibility of selecting the members of his (or her) staff (as vacancies arise) has a greater interest in the success of the candidates chosen than the principal who is not consulted or who, if consulted, had little real part in the final choice."[57]

Day-to-Day Supervision. It is the principal, not the supervisor, who provides day-to-day supervision and who knows (or ought to know) the teacher's needs. The principal must get inside the classroom, keeping in mind at all times that teachers need all the support they can get. The attitude, in itself, is helpful. Teachers must bring enthusiasm and excitement to their teaching. They are more likely to do so when the principal is optimistic and enthusiastic—and really comes through with concrete assistance. This assistance may be in the form of people; an effective principal can identify supervisory personnel to assist the teacher. But it may well be in the form of materials; the lack of curriculum materials has been consistently viewed by teachers as a leading curriculum problem. One of the principal's most important responsibilities is allocating resources to facilitate the work of the teacher.

Resourcefulness. It is interesting to note that in England, the principal has much more leeway budgetarily than in American schools. Be that as it may, it is the principal's job to make it clear through the central office when resources are needed. As Cawelti points out, "Effective principals do not stop with the limited resources provided them through normal channels," but "demonstrate ingenuity in convincing central office personnel, parent groups . . . and others of the school's needs."[58] As educational facilitator, the principal must make sure that the resources are made available as needed.

Good Teachers and School Tone. The point is that the principal is really there to facilitate teaching and learning. The principal establishes the climate where teachers use (or lose) their talents. A British study on why some schools succeed in promoting the academic and social success of their pupils found that "it was much easier to be a good teacher in some schools than in others."[59] What matters most, the researchers found, was what they called the ethos of a school—the general tone of the place—which seemed to have a greater effect on pupil performance than such factors as how strictly the children were disciplined. The principal sets the tone of the school. There was group planning in successful schools rather than policies being dictated from above.

School Leadership

What It Is Not. No doubt, "Mr. Grissom," the principal in the child's vivid picture portrayed earlier, viewed himself as carrying out his curriculum improvement role. That role, as he saw it, was to get teachers to use in their classrooms methods of drill and skill that *he* considered to be most effective. (He seemed to rely on practices that stemmed from the mental discipline doctrine of the nineteenth century.) Educational leadership does not mean prescribing methods. The teacher is a professional and must be treated as a professional. Principals can depress pupil achievement by treating teachers as student teachers. As discussed in Chapter 1, research on successful schools indicates that effective principals do not prescribe actual methods but offer continuing assistance to teachers in solving teacher-identified problems. Inservice education is often directed at providing specific methods of teaching, with the idea that they are the key to school improvement. "But the narrow specifics *are less important than the process of focusing attention on teaching and learning and on problems of decision-making in the classroom.*"[60] The idea is not to "program" the teacher as one would a machine, but to enhance the teacher's capacity as a student of teaching, so that he or she can grow as a teacher.

What It Is. School leadership is working cooperatively with the faculty and supervisors on educational problems. If education is a profession, decisions are made in a democratic-participatory mode. All decisions should be made on the best available evidence (see Figure 4–1). This requires that the principal have a strong commitment to the scientific method of solving practical problems. Add to this good interpersonal skills; effective principals not only have strong feelings but the ability to evoke consensus and commitment in others.[61]

Take, for example, the problem of pupil grouping. The conclusion from research is that interaction of children with their more accomplished peers is an important factor in learning. Yet teachers tend to favor segregation of pupils by ability. If the grouping policy is discussed and worked out together by the principal and teachers, and the decision is based on the best evidence, teachers will be more likely to support the decision. The principal will find that it is helpful to engage the faculty in identifying teachers to serve on the school's curriculum council, and it is important that the faculty representatives and the principal share the view that decisions are based on the best available knowledge. If, despite the evidence, there is still opposition to heterogeneously grouped classes, the principal has the right and duty to make the decision based on the evidence, making the reasons direct and clear to the faculty. Nevertheless, the principal should provide teachers with special assistance to ensure that the transition is successful, and to demonstrate his or her commitment to helping the faculty. (It is important to note in this connection that successful principals use a variety of strategies to make certain that teachers assigned to their schools share their professional commitments and vision of a school.[62])

Involving the faculty in making the major decisions that affect what they are doing together may seem like risk taking, but leaving them out is an even greater risk. The greater their participation in the policy decisions that affect their work, the more likely they are to implement the decisions. (There is no way in the world that principals can control what goes on in teachers' classrooms through authoritarian means.) Thus, while involving the faculty in making decisions may seem like risk taking, leaving them out will invite problems. Successful principals are able to communicate their confidence in teachers and convey the feeling that they are part of a team.[63]

Objections to curriculum materials from the community and evaluating pupil progress are other examples of educational problems that should be dealt with on the best evidence in the educational literature. In connection with community problems, like successful superintendents, successful principals develop networks of supporters in their communities who support their schools against capricious attack at school board meetings. According to Dwyer, "These principals also displayed political savvy as they used their community work to build commitments that buffered their schools against capricious shifts in district policies."[64]

But probably the most important characteristic of principals who were nominated by fellow administrators as successful educational leaders was that they "were able to find opportunity where others might see only problems."[65] This lends support to Tyler's concept of educational leadership, discussed earlier. The reader will recall that according to Tyler, leadership is the ability to turn an educational problem into an opportunity for improvement.

Coordination of Department Heads

According to Glatthorn and Newberg, because secondary schools are organized departmentally and the curriculum is specialized, secondary principals should "decentralize" leadership, that is, delegate the function of curriculum improvement to department heads.[66] They label the delegation of responsibility "a team approach to instructional leadership."[67] In effect, what they are suggesting is that the principal's extremely important responsibility for coordinating isolated (and insulated) subjects be dealt with by doing away with it. Obviously, secondary schools are organized according to subject fields, but that is not enough. Without a coordinated effort to interrelate the various fields, there is a specialized-segmental arrangement for curriculum development which is dictated by subject fields. The parts do not add up to the whole. The department head has jurisdiction over a specialized subject field. The curriculum director and principal must together get the work coordinated.

Table 4–1 presents the functions of the department head. There is no question that principals should use their department heads more effectively. The curriculum improvement role of many department heads is confined to textbook adoption and scheduling classes. As Turner has suggested, the department head should encourage and assist individual teachers in improving their teaching effectiveness and should recognize departmental meetings "as opportunities for problem solving rather than merely treating routine administrative details."[68]

But they should work with other departments to coordinate their fields as a total curriculum. Principals must see to it that department heads work together because the students do not make the integration between and among the isolated subjects. For example, students should write themes in social studies and science courses, not just in English courses. All departments should be concerned with the total development of the learner, and this requires that the curriculum be seen and treated in its totality.

SUMMARY

School systems are legally responsible for curriculum improvement in order to achieve state educational goals. Although this requires organization at the central office level, many school systems have been cutting back their central office staffs because the idea of the individual school as a unit for educational improvement has been misconstrued to mean a totally decentralized approach to curriculum improvement. Problems of concern to the whole system are being passed on to teachers (and thus going unsolved), such as a fragmented educational program caused by a multiplicity of uncoordinated federal and state programs. Curriculum articulation is a districtwide as well as a local school problem and requires the best combined efforts of supervisors and principals, who must see the curriculum whole. Teachers are being presented with more problems in their work, and need more, not less, assistance from supervisors. Teachers must be able to request supervisory assistance on their own, without having to go through the principal.

Whatever the size of the school system, the superintendent is the one who can assure the districtwide conditions necessary for curriculum improvement. As one looks at the responsibilities of the post, one sees why. The superintendent is responsible for selecting competent teachers, budgeting for the educational program, providing for supervision (and consultant help when necessary), and providing for educational evaluation and research. The best superintendents are committed to problem solving as a way of improving education, and select subordinate staff who are committed to identifying and dealing with problems, and who see problems as opportunities for improvement. This chapter presented the process of problem solving. Schools have the responsibility for countering educational cycles and fashions and can do so by using problems (their own, *not* someone else's) as the starting point for innovation.

The assistant superintendent for curriculum and instruction (who may have the title of curriculum director or even director of instruction) has the responsibility for continuously improving the school program, which embraces the functions of curriculum development, teachers' professional development, and providing instructional resources. His or her effectiveness depends on viewing these functions interrelatedly. An effective inservice education program is both school related and university related. Classroom supervision and workshops conducted by supervisors and outside consultants are essential for curriculum improvement, but teachers should also be required to take university courses to keep up with developments in their field. In no way can school districts provide the university function themselves.

One begins with the curriculum in determining supervisory needs. Although they are not specialists in a subject field, supervisors of elementary education and supervisors of secondary education (sometimes known as coordinators) have a specialization—the total program of education at a given level of schooling, and aiding the assistant superintendent in developing balanced programs of education. When there is a conflict in policies (a growing problem in education) they must make recommendations based on the best possible entire program for children and youth. This responsibility cannot be left to teachers alone.

There is a basic conflict between the inservice and evaluation functions of the supervisor, but it can be resolved by evaluating teachers on their awareness of problems (and willingness to expose them) and on whether they seek help in solving problems. Teachers and supervisors together should formulate possible solutions for problems using the problem-solving process. The special supervisor should understand how his or her particular field or discipline relates to border fields or disciplines (such as mathematics to science), and should continually seek to relate his or her special field to its general education function. Balanced supervisory staffing (generalists and specialists in various curriculum areas) is not only a reflection of a balanced view of the whole curriculum but tends to keep the curriculum in balance. A balanced curriculum is like health; it must be worked on continuously to be maintained. If an area is deemphasized, one should not be surprised when achievement declines in that area; music and art are recent examples, as reflected by national assessment data. (Achievement underwent declines in both areas.)

It is easier to be a good teacher in some schools than in others. Pupils do better in schools where the principal is encouraging, enthusiastic, and provides concrete assistance for teachers, and where decisions are made in a democratic-participatory mode on the basis of the best available evidence. Effective principals perform many of the same functions as central office supervisors, but there are important differences. The principal is in the same building with the teacher and can provide day-to-day supervision, and the principal is the prime evaluator of the teacher's work. But the ultimate difference, where educational improvement is concerned, is the principal's role of facilitator of teaching and learning. Principals must make sure that the teacher's needs for resources are met. (Effective principals are resourceful.) Effective principals do not attempt to impose specific classroom methods on the teacher but offer continual assistance in solving the problems that teachers identify for themselves. Principals nominated as successful by their fellow administrators are able to find opportunity for improvement where others see only insurmountable problems. The principal and curriculum director (or assistant superintendent) must get the work of the secondary school coordinated. This function cannot be delegated to department heads. (The parts of the curriculum do not add up to the whole.)

PROBLEMS FOR STUDY AND DISCUSSION

1. Do you believe that the function of promoting a balanced and coherent curriculum is being performed by school superintendents? Explain.

2. Identify a problem in your school district, school unit, or classroom that requires new approaches for its solution. Using Figure 4–1, formulate the possible solutions.

3. Do you agree with the following statement? Why or why not?

One of the unwritten laws of supervision is that the supervisor gets only what he insists upon: If you don't get it the first time, you insist again and again and again. It doesn't take teachers very long to smell out which item the supervisor must get and which item can be overlooked because the supervisor will have forgotten about it. In order to achieve standards of performance from teachers the supervisor must learn to practice the art of insistence.[69]

4. Do you agree with the authors of this book that teachers should be required to take university courses to keep up with the developments in their field? Why or why not?

5. John Goodlad made the following statement:

For all schools, the priority item always to be on the agenda is the quality of life in the workplace—its assessment and subsequent continuing improvement. Creating a satisfying place of work for the individuals who inhabit schools is good in its own right but it appears also to be necessary to maintaining a productive educational environment.[70]

Would you accept this as a premise for school improvement? Explain. Which of the principal's functions in Table 4–1 are important for making schools satisfying places of work? Why?

6. According to the American Association of School Administrators, the position of assistant superintendent for curriculum and instruction "is probably the most effective preparation for the superintendency."[71] Using Table 4–1, does a comparison of the functions of the assistant superintendent with those of the superintendent support this viewpoint? Explain.

7. As discussed in this chapter, there is a basic conflict between the inservice function and the evaluation function of the supervisor. What is your assessment of the solution proposed by the authors for resolving the conflict?

8. Do you agree that teachers should be able to request help from supervisors directly, without having to go through the principal? Explain.

9. Is curriculum development and supervision in your school district organized on a K–12 basis? If not, what ways can you suggest for developing continuity in the educational program from level to level?

NOTES

1. David K. Cohen, "Policy and Organization: The Impact of State and Federal Educational Policy on School Governance," *Harvard Educational Review*, Vol. 52 (November 1982), p. 487.
2. See, for example, Ronald R. Edmonds, "Programs of School Improvement: An Overview," *Educational Leadership*, Vol. 40 (December 1982), pp. 4–11. See also, John I. Goodlad, "The School as a Workplace," Chapter 3 in *Staff Development*, Eighty-second Yearbook of the National Society for the Study of Education, Part II (Chicago: University of Chicago Press, 1983), pp. 36–61.
3. Philip Hallinger and Joseph Murphy, "The Superintendent's Role in Promoting Instructional Leadership," *Administrator's Notebook*, Vol. 30, No. 6 (1982).
4. E. Edmund Reutter, Jr., *The Law of Public Education*, 3rd ed. (Mineola, N.Y.: Foundation Press, 1985), p. 86.
5. Ibid., pp. 104–106.
6. Ibid., pp. 139, 147.
7. *Lau* v. *Nichols*, 414 U.S. 563, 94 S.Ct. 786 (1974).
8. Ronald Reagan, "The President's Radio Address to the Nation on Education," *American Education*, Vol. 19 (June 1983), p. 4.
9. National Commission on Excellence in Education, *A Nation at Risk: The Imperative for Educational Reform* (Washington, D.C.: U.S. Government Printing Office, April 1983).
10. Cohen, op. cit., p. 487.
11. Ibid.
12. Paul Hill, *Do Federal Programs Interfere with One Another?* (Santa Monica, Calif.: Rand Corporation, 1979), p. 11.
13. Milbrey W. McLaughlin, "States and the New Federalism," *Harvard Educational Review*, Vol. 52 (November 1982), pp. 464–483.
14. Ibid.
15. Cohen, op. cit., p. 489.
16. Ibid., p. 494.
17. Fred M. Hechinger, "Teachers Tell of Powerlessness and Frustration," *The New York Times*, February 14, 1984, p. C 8.
18. Arthur Costa and Charles Guditus, "Do Districtwide Supervisors Make a Difference?" *Educational Leadership*, Vol. 41 (February 1984), p. 84.
19. Edward B. Fiske, "Noted Educator Sees Resurgence in Teaching," *The New York Times*, June 5, 1984, pp. C 1, C 11.
20. Costa and Guditus, op. cit., pp. 84–85.
21. Brian Rowan, Steven T. Bossert, and David C. Dwyer, "Research on Effective Schools: A Cautionary Note," *Educational Researcher*, Vol. 12 (April 1983), p. 25.
22. Ralph W. Tyler, "Dynamic Response in a Time of Decline," *Phi Delta Kappan*, Vol. 63 (June 1982), p. 656.
23. Ibid.
24. Kevin Ryan, John Johnston, and Katherine Newman, "An Interview with Ralph Tyler," *Phi Delta Kappan*, Vol. 58 (March 1977), pp. 544–545.
25. National Assessment of Educational Progress, *Mathematics Technical Report: Summary Volume* (Denver, Colo.: Education Commission of the States, 1980).
26. National Assessment of Educational Progress, *Three National Assessments of Reading:*

Changes in Performance, 1970–1980 (Denver, Colo.: Education Commission of the States, 1981).

27. Tyler, op. cit., p. 656.
28. Ibid., p. 657.
29. Costa and Guditus, op. cit., p. 84.
30. Willard S. Elsbree and E. Edmund Reutter, Jr., *Staff Personnel in the Public Schools* (Englewood Cliffs, N.J.: Prentice-Hall, 1954), p. 242.
31. Cohen, op. cit., p. 490.
32. William H. Lucio (ed.), *Supervision: Perspectives and Propositions* (Washington, D.C.: Association for Supervision and Curriculum Development, 1967), p. 51.
33. Roald F. Campbell et al., *The Organization and Control of American Schools*, 4th ed. (Columbus, Ohio: Charles E. Merrill, 1980), p. 242.
34. National Assessment of Educational Progress, *Art and Young Americans, 1974–79; Results from the Second National Art Assessment* (Denver, Colo.: Education Commission of the States, 1981); and National Assessment of Educational Progress, *Music 1971–79; Results from the National Music Assessment* (Denver, Colo.: Education Commission of the States, 1981).
35. Lawrence A. Cremin, *The Genius of American Education* (New York: Vintage Books, 1965), p. 111.
36. Laurel N. Tanner, "Curriculum History and Educational Leadership," *Educational Leadership*, Vol. 41 (November 1983), p. 42.
37. Hilda Taba, *Curriculum Development: Theory and Practice* (New York: Harcourt, Brace Jovanovich, 1962), p. 460.
38. Daniel Tanner and Laurel N. Tanner, *Curriculum Development: Theory into Practice*, 2nd ed. (New York: Macmillan, 1980), pp. 636–639.
39. American Association of School Administrators, *Profiles of the Administrative Team* (Washington, D.C.: The Association, 1971), p. 50.
40. Ross L. Neagley and N. Dean Evans, *Handbook for Effective Supervision of Instruction*, 3rd ed. (Englewood Cliffs, N.J.: Prentice-Hall, 1980), p. 95.
41. Gene I. Maeroff, "Author's Day at P.S. 11: A Celebration of Books," *The New York Times*, June 19, 1984, p. C 1.
42. Ibid.
43. American Association of School Administrators, *Profiles of the Administrative Team*, op. cit., p. 53.
44. Ryan, Johnson, and Newman, op. cit., p. 546.
45. Evelyn F. Carlson, "Introduction," *Role of Supervisor and Curriculum Director in a Climate of Change*, 1965 Yearbook of the Association for Supervision and Curriculum Development (Washington, D.C.: The Association, 1965), p. 2.
46. Ben M. Harris, "Altering the Thrust of Supervision Through Creative Leadership," *Educational Leadership*, Vol. 34 (May 1977), pp. 567–568.
47. Cremin, op. cit., p. 58.
48. William S. Briscoe, "Recent Development of Supervision in the Oakland Public Schools," in Department of Elementary School Principals, *Activities of the Principal*, Eighth Yearbook (Washington, D.C.: National Education Association, 1929), p. 143.
49. Neagley and Evans, op. cit., p. 99.
50. Costa and Guditus, op. cit., p. 84.
51. Kenneth A. Tye and Barbara Benham Tye, "Teacher Isolation and School Reform," *Phi Delta Kappan*, Vol. 65 (January 1984), p. 320.
52. Neagley and Evans, op. cit., p. 100.
53. James Herndon, *The Way It 'Spozed' to Be* (New York: Simon and Schuster, 1968), p. 168.

54. Hechinger, op. cit., p. C 8.
55. Donald E. Mackenzie, "Research for School Improvement: An Appraisal of Some Recent Trends," *Educational Researcher*, Vol. 12 (April 1983), p. 8.
56. Neagley and Evans, op. cit., pp. 130–131.
57. Elsbree and Reutter, op. cit., p. 71.
58. Gordon Cawelti, "Behavior Patterns of Effective Principals," *Educational Leadership*, Vol. 41 (February 1984), p. 3.
59. Michael Rutter et al., *Fifteen Thousand Hours: Secondary Schools and Their Effects on Children* (Cambridge, Mass.: Harvard University Press, 1979), p. 139.
60. Mackenzie, op. cit., p. 11.
61. A. Lorri Manasse, "Principals as Leaders of High-Performing Systems," *Educational Leadership*, Vol. 41 (February 1984), p. 44.
62. David C. Dwyer, "The Search for Instructional Leadership: Routines and Subtleties in the Principal's Role," *Educational Leadership*, Vol. 41 (February 1984), pp. 32–37.
63. Ibid.
64. Ibid., p. 34.
65. Ibid.
66. Allan A. Glatthorn and Norman A. Newberg, "A Team Approach to Instructional Leadership," *Educational Leadership*, Vol. 41 (February 1984), pp. 60–63.
67. Ibid., p. 62.
68. Harold E. Turner, "The Department Head—An Untapped Source of Instructional Leadership," *NASSP Bulletin*, Vol. 67 (September 1983), p. 28.
69. Richard Lonoff, "Supervisory Practices That Promote Academic Achievement in a New York City School," *Phi Delta Kappan*, Vol. 52 (February 1971), p. 340.
70. Goodlad, op. cit., p. 59.
71. American Association of School Administrators, *Profiles of the Administrative Team* (Washington, D.C.: American Association of School Administrators, 1971), pp. 54–55.

SELECTED REFERENCES

American Association of School Administrators. *Profiles of the Administrative Team.* Washington, D.C.: The Association, 1971.

Callahan, Raymond E. *Education and the Cult of Efficiency.* Chicago: The University of Chicago Press, 1962.

Campbell, Roald F., et al. *The Organization and Control of American Schools*, 4th ed. Columbus, Ohio: Charles E. Merrill Publishing Company, 1980.

Cremin, Lawrence A. *The Genius of American Education.* New York: Vintage Books, 1965.

Dwyer, David C., et al. *Five Principals in Action: Perspectives on Instructional Management.* San Francisco: Far West Laboratory for Educational Research and Development, 1983.

Goodlad, John I. *A Place Called School.* New York: McGraw-Hill Book Company, 1983.

Harris, Ben M. *Supervisory Behavior in Education*, 3rd ed. Englewood Cliffs, N.J.: Prentice-Hall, Inc., 1985.

National Society for the Study of Education. *The Courts and Education*, Seventy-seventh Yearbook, Part I. Chicago: The University of Chicago Press, 1978.

———. *Policy Making in Education*, Eighty-first Yearbook, Part I. Chicago: The University of Chicago Press, 1982.

———. *Staff Development*, Eighty-second Yearbook, Part II. Chicago: The University of Chicago Press, 1983.

Neagley, Ross L., and N. Dean Evans. *Handbook for Effective Supervision of Instruction,* 3rd ed. Englewood Cliffs, N.J.: Prentice-Hall, Inc., 1980.

Reutter, E. Edmund, Jr. *The Law of Public Education,* 3rd ed. Mineola, N.Y.: The Foundation Press, Inc., 1985.

Rutter, Michael, et al. *Fifteen Thousand Hours: Secondary Schools and Their Effects on Children.* Cambridge, Mass.: Harvard University Press, 1979.

Sarason, Seymour B. *The Culture of the School and the Problem of Change,* 2nd ed. Boston: Allyn and Bacon, Inc., 1982.

Tanner, Daniel, and Laurel N. Tanner. *Curriculum Development: Theory into Practice,* 2nd ed. New York: Macmillan Publishing Company, 1980.

Task Force on Increased High School Graduation Requirements. *With Consequences for ALL.* Alexandria, Va.: Association for Supervision and Curriculum Development, 1985.

Part III

The Theory and Practice
of Educational Supervision

Chapter 5

The Ecology of the School and the Climate for Supervision

Members of any highly structured organization must make special efforts not to get so caught up in the day-to-day routines and demands that they fail to gain the sense of perspective that comes from being an observer. Complex organizations, such as schools or school systems, are composed of interdependent units. Because problems of any significance tend to have ramifications throughout the organization, they cannot be treated segmentally. The structural and social interdependence of the complex organization, especially one that is committed to a democratic-participatory system of operation, requires that the participants also be observers. This is especially important when an unanticipated problem arises, requiring the participants to look into and beyond their immediate situation if they are to locate possible causes of the problem, and if they are to share in devising and evaluating possible strategies for solution of the problem.

As long as situations are routine and segmental, the participant need not stand back as an observer. Nevertheless, improvement does not come from such routine or established situations. When an unforeseen problem arises, the routine or established situation becomes an emergent one—a situation requiring a new perspective. The new perspective makes problem solutions possible.

The emergent situation in a democratic-participatory system is an educative situation because it requires new insights and powers on the part of the participants. Because the role and function of the school and school system are uniquely educative, the system of organization and operation must be so construed that the educative function is paramount, not only for the pupils, but for all participants—teachers, supervisors, and administrators. School administrators must perceive themselves as educators and educational leaders, not as business managers. Unfortunately, this has not always been the case.

ESTABLISHED AND EMERGENT SITUATIONS

The story is told of Woodrow Wilson, when he was president of Princeton, being confronted in his office by a mother of a newly enrolled freshman. Despite Wilson's repeated assurances, the mother continued to raise endless questions regarding the university's concern and responsibility for her son's welfare. Finally, in exasperation, Wilson stoood up at his desk and said, "Madam, we guarantee the results or we cheerfully return your boy."

In various periods during the twentieth century, our school administrators and supervisors have been urged to adopt the managerial-efficiency methods of the business–industrial enterprise. The influences of these efforts and the damage inflicted on the schools over a period spanning the first six decades of this century is well documented.[1]

The Production-Efficiency Approach

The demand to model the schools along the lines of the efficient industrial enterprise has been relentless, despite the dismal record of failure to produce the promised results through such efforts during the first half of this century. For example, a 1958 *Fortune* magazine cover story pointed to the low production efficiency of the schools in comparison to the American automobile and steel industries. These industries were portrayed as models of production efficiency as measured by the maximization of output and the minimization of input of labor hours and capital. "In this respect," contended the author of the article, "the schools are no different from General Motors," as he went on to show how our school expenditures and staffing had increased over the years in relation to student output.[2] Ironically, the author and editors of *Fortune* failed to see the looming Japanese and German industrial gains that were then in clear evidence in the American and world markets for automobiles and other products. Instead, American industrial efficiency was portrayed as the paragon for the "education industry."

The New Technology. One of the major premises underlying the passage of the National Defense Education Act (NDEA) of 1958, in the wake of *Sputnik I,* was that by providing funds to bring the new educational technology to our schools, a vast increase in production efficiency would result. However, the electronic language laboratories, television, teaching machines, and other technological devices failed to bring about the promised revolution. The technological legacy of NDEA was the increase in the use of the overhead projector by the lecturing classroom teacher.

In a special publication commemorating the centennial of the U.S. Office of Education, issued in 1967, it was envisioned that before the end of this century, the schools would be replaced by computer workstations in the home in which Johnny is hooked up to a central monitoring system.[3] Such visions of the future fail to recognize the unique attributes of education as a social process and the need to differentiate this process from the automated processes of the new technology.

Performance Contracting and Accountability. The 1970s were marked by federal efforts to support performance contracting and accountability in education by adopting the methods utilized in business, industry, and the military. The education profession was admonished for its inefficiency and the public was promised that by adopting the methods of business, industry, and the military, the enterprise of education should be able to guarantee results. A former U.S. Deputy Commissioner of Education declared that our schools had a mandate "to develop a 'zero reject system' which would guarantee quality in skill acquisition just as a similar system now guarantees the quality of industrial production." He went on to advocate that business be called on to formulate a redevelopment plan for education and actually manage the education enterprise.[4]

When the U.S. Office of Economic Opportunity launched its performance-contracting program for the schools in 1970, the head of that agency described it as "a new process to bring to the improvement of education the same ingenuity, craft, and realism that got us to the moon" and as "an example of engineering . . . a method of management that uses engineering insights on which leading firms rely—but which our schools have largely ignored." And he went on to predict that it would revolutionize our educational system.[5]

Not only did independent evaluations of performance contracting reveal that it had failed even to measure up to conventional teaching approaches, but that it had produced a host of unanticipated problems—such as reducing the curriculum to skill-drill subjects and repertoires, and teaching-to-the-test.[6]

Oddly, in promoting performance contracting and in portraying the industrial-production methodology as the archetype of efficiency to be emulated by our schools, the proponents made no mention of the enormous cost overruns and the widespread failure to meet performance specifications in the industrial–military enterprise.

By the early 1980s the schools were being blamed by various national commissions for our nation's loss of world industrial markets to the Japanese. Instead of placing the blame on the corporate sector, the schools were attacked once again.[7] These attacks came after a decade and a half of educational retrenchment, statewide minimum-competency testing, and teaching by narrow-minded behavioristic objectives.

Inexplicably, despite the unmitigated failure of performance contracting, some of the national reports on educational reform issued during the 1980s were calling for a partnership between business and schools to bring about the needed managerial efficiency in our schools.[8]

In various time periods throughout the twentieth century, the concern for efficiency in education has been so overriding that school administrators, politicians, corporate leaders, and the general public have sought simplistic panaceas for public education not unlike the simplistic diet books and other "how-to" manuals that dominate our best-seller lists. In so doing, they fail to recognize that the educative process has certain unique qualities that must be taken into account if problems are to be solved and progress is to be made. Education cannot be likened to an industrial-production process, for it occurs primarily in an *emergent* situation, whereas the industrial-production process is conducted largely in what might be termed an *established-convergent* situation. School administrators and supervisors are not mere managers of a production enterprise. They must be educators.

Established-Convergent Situations

An established situation, according to Boguslaw, a systems-design engineer, "is one in which all action-relevant environmental conditions are specifiable and predictable; all action-relevant states of the system are specifiable and predictable; available research technology or records are adequate to provide statements about the probable consequences of alternative actions."[9] Hence the efficiency of the factory production line can be measured in terms of the ratio of outputs to unit costs of inputs. The situation becomes an emergent one when, for example, the workers walk off the job or the machinery breaks down as the result of an unanticipated malfunction. The situation becomes an emergent one when people problems arise. In essence, the established situation, which might also be termed the established-convergent situation, is one in which we are dealing with products or services under the most reliable and predictable conditions. The garage mechanic using the manufacturer's repair manual is in an established-convergent situation. If he encounters a defect unanticipated by the manufacturer, he finds himself in an emergent situation.

Even the most simple situations that might appear to be established-convergent on the surface have a way of becoming emergent situations because of the human element. A factory bakery producing Wonder Bread allows for little variation in the product. In fact, the plant manager must see to it that the product is as uniform as possible and the machinery is designed to ensure such uniformity. Now we might think of a task like following a cookbook recipe as an established-convergent situation. But different homemakers following a given recipe for baking bread or coq au vin, for example, will produce quite different results. The reason is that each of them has brought different experiences, taste preferences, and levels of imagination to what on the surface appears to be the simple task of following a recipe from a cookbook. Such variation not only is expected but is valued, because it allows for individual differences and makes improvement possible.

Behaviorism. The psychology of behaviorism conceives of the teaching–learning transaction as an established-convergent situation. According to Skinner, teaching is merely a matter of administering the conditions for the reinforcement of behaviors and "once we have arranged the particular type of consequence called a reinforcement, our techniques permit us to shape the behavior of the organism almost at will."[10] Consequently, teaching is successful to the degree to which the behavior of the learner is controlled and made predictable. "What is needed is more control, not less, and this is itself an engineering problem of the first importance," contends Skinner.[11]

Behaviorists see the environment as unambiguously reducible to specifiable stimuli which serve as reinforcers to elicit predictable responses or behaviors. Learning is regarded as a process through which behavior (responses) is modified through classes of stimuli that serve as reinforcers.

Behaviorism emerged as a dominant school of psychology during the first half of this century based on stimulus–response (S-R) theories deriving from laboratory work with lower animals. Dewey criticized this psychology for failing to distinguish training from education, for ignoring the importance of the social environment in learning, and for neglecting the higher-ordered thinking abilities that enable human beings to develop their intelligence so as to exercise control over conditions rather than being brought under the control of conditions. Although the actions of humans beings, as with lower animals, can be modified through stimulus–response training, such overt behavior fails to account for other dispositions of human behavior and is not educative, contended Dewey. Moreover, Dewey argued, even the behavior of lower animals is not as mechanistic as some psychologists would have us believe.[12]

The S-R psychology which was dominant during the first half of this century has been described as "a positivistic–mechanistic–reductionistic approach which can be epitomized as the robot model of man."[13] In his view of teaching as a technological process of stimulus–response reinforcement conditioning, Skinner regards the problem of human control as an "engineering problem." Boguslaw observes that Skinner's rationale corresponds to the treatment and use of human beings as operating units in an engineering-design system, but he cautions that where such operating unit designs are fixed in their functions, human beings are not so reliable and are capable of behaving intelligently and independently of the system. Hardware engineering involves operating units comprised of metal, electricity, chemicals, and so on—whereas "human engineering" requires all sorts of special considerations because human behavior is not so controllable.[14] Even under established conditions, human beings will tend to resist externally and arbitrarily imposed controls and will even exercise considerable cunning to foul up the system when they regard the controls as unreasonable. In the emergent situation, human intelligence gets its best chance, for such a situation requires the solving of unforeseen problems.

Behaviorism has been of demonstrable use in aiding children with abnormal behavior, such as autism and retardation, where highly specific reinforcements are applied in modifying highly specific behaviors. However, as already noted, emergent situations require the engagement of the higher cognitive processes of critical and independent thinking for problem solving, and the engagement of the imagination. Here behaviorism collapses not only on philosophical grounds, but on functional grounds. Glaser points out that although modern cognitive psychology has been the dominant force in the field since midcentury, much of the psychological applications currently used in the schools continue to follow the behavioristic approach—as evidenced by the emphasis given to behavioral (behavioristic) objectives in the curriculum, to skill-drill exercises, as well as to behavior modification in special education.[15]

The use of behavior modification has been tried with inmates in federal prisons. But in 1974, in response to prisoner protest and prisoner lawsuits in federal courts, wherein the inmates objected to the projects as "Pavlovian" and "Clockwork Orange," the Federal Bureau of Prisons dismantled its behavior-modification program, and the Law Enforcement Assistance Administration banned any further use of federal funds for behavior-modification projects involving adult prisoners and juvenile offenders. The American Psychological Association has taken the position that although some of the behavior-modification techniques are clearly abhorrent, others are humane and, therefore, not all of these techniques should be banned.[16]

Emergent Situations

The emergent situation is one in which action-relevant environmental conditions are not entirely specifiable and predictable, and where available research technology is insufficient to provide hard data on the consequences of alternative actions. The emergent situation is infinitely more variable and complex than the established-convergent situation. The school cannot be likened to a factory because a factory is geared to a production process in which the conditions are highly specifiable and predictable. Unlike the factory, the school is not dealing with machine products.

The implications for the school administrator, supervisor and teacher are clear. For example, the teacher working with twenty-five youngsters in a classroom—each with a distinctively different personality, home and family background, level of interest, level of physical development, and so on—is in an emergent situation. Some of the most elementary and mechanical processes, such as teaching the multiplication table, might be regarded as an established-convergent situation. But even here the experienced teacher knows that if the youngsters are to be able to utilize the processes in other subjects and in life situations, a great deal of ingenuity must be used beyond the lesson plan. Moreover, a given lesson cannot guarantee uniformity of results because of individual differences in the learner, the teacher, and so on.

The situation becomes so much more complex when teaching is idea oriented rather than being limited to facts and skills. When students must utilize facts, skills, and concepts to analyze and evaluate data, to assess issues, to weigh evidence, to solve idea-focused problems in new situations, they are engaged in emergent situations. Even high school teachers who have successive class sections in the same course will find that the two classes react very differently to the same lesson and that the lesson has to be adjusted in no small measure in view of the different and unanticipated student reactions and interactions. Even the use of an identical lesson, such as that presented in an instructional television program, will produce vastly different reactions and results among the learners in a given classroom.

Computer-assisted instruction is regarded by some proponents as the solution to the problem of making the action-relevant environmental conditions in the teaching-learning process almost entirely specifiable and predictable. B. F. Skinner has contended that machine instruction will assure "mastery at every stage" so that every student can earn an "A"—the only variable being the rate of learning.[17] However, the teaching machine has not lived up to any such expectations, despite the fact that the program can be likened to teaching-to-the-test. Nor has computer-assisted instruction lived up to the wondrous claims made by its proponents. This is not to hold that the computer is not a useful learning tool, but that the problem of education is not to transform it from being primarily an emergent process to becoming largely an established-convergent process. For life experience is mainly an emergent process, and to reduce education to an established-convergent process would remove education from life. The case is not one of sentimentality, but of reality. As Boguslaw points out, "To the extent that we increase predictability and performance reliability by selecting predictable and reliable components, to that extent we reduce the system's freedom and its capacity to deal with emergent situations effectively."[18] If the schools are to enable the rising generation to deal more effectively with emergent situations, the curriculum must be idea oriented rather than error oriented. It must encompass problems and issues that require the applications of skills and ideas in a wide range of contexts and even encourage divergent, though constructive, thinking.

Efforts to organize schooling as an established-convergent process cannot be successful because education is an emergent process. But even in an established-convergent process such as in a factory, when human beings are treated as mere components in an engineering frame of reference, when the human element is disregarded, workers will not fit the expected performance specifications of the system. They can find ways to convert the established-convergent situation to an emergent situation through disruptive ingenuity. (A comic example is the theater play and motion picture, *The Pajama Game*.) Youngsters in school are no less ingenious when required by the circumstances. The same applies to the relationships between supervisors and teachers.

Moreover, the very nature of the learner as a growing and developing organism in a complex environment constitutes an emergent situation. The learner's powers are not fixed but developing. The professional staff of the school is responsible for creating the best possible learning environment for the child's fullest possible cognitive and social development. Such development has no fixed end points, as in the case of the established situation. Like life itself, the development of the learner is never ending as long as there is lifelong learning. In Dewey's words concerning the wise teacher: "But save as the teacher knows, knows wisely and thoroughly, the race-expression which is embodied in that thing we call the Curriculum, the teacher knows neither what the present power, capacity, or attitude is, nor yet how it is to be asserted, exercized, and realized."[19]

The Managerial Ideology

Although the fields of educational administration and supervision have made increasing use of the advances in the behavioral sciences since midcentury, the industrial-management ideology continues to exert considerable influence. Whereas the school principal was conceived as an educator in the progressivist literature early in this century, we find frequent reference to the principal in the contemporary literature as a "school manager."[20] The concept of "school manager" is derived from the concept of "manager" in the business–industrial sector. At the height of the accountability movement during the late 1960s, an officer of the Ford Foundation addressed the annual convention of the National Association of Secondary School Principals in these words:

> Similar to the plant manager in a large industrial corporation, the principal is the key person responsible for the productivity of the organization. The school, like an industrial plant, represents a process. Raw material goes in and a product

comes out. The change that occurs between input, that is the entering pupil, and output, the departing pupil, will be determined by the ways in which you apply and coordinate the available resources of your school.[21]

The foregoing description of the principal as a plant manager, schooling as a factory-production process, and the learner as a product presents a picture of the process of education not unlike that of a sausage factory. Education is reduced to an established-convergent process of perfectly specifiable inputs and outputs, raw materials, and products—a model of engineering efficiency.

The conception of the school principal as a plant manager is reflected clearly in the following excerpt from the recommendations of the report of the Task Force on Education for Economic Growth, a group composed of fourteen chief executive officers of leading American corporations, thirteen governors, six organizational leaders, five educational administrators, and three state legislators:

> We recommend that the school principal in each school be acknowledged as the school's leader and as the manager of its instructional program. . . .
>
> We recommend that the states establish higher standards for recruiting, training, and monitoring the performance of school principals. Specifically, we urge that each state examine and improve its programs for training school principals and aspiring principals, and that effective new programs be established to train principals in effective educational management.
>
> We recommend that school systems expand and improve, at every level of administration, their use of *effective management techniques.* Business can help here, with exchange programs and other collaborative efforts to train school managers and to keep school officials abreast of the latest techniques in fiscal and personnel management.[22]

Educational Engineering. In reporting on his study of high schools, sponsored by the National Association of Secondary School Principals and the National Association of Independent Schools, Theodore Sizer sees the need for reform of our high schools as primarily a problem of "engineering." Referring to the answers he seeks to the problem of reforming the high schools, he states: "They all point in the same direction: high school reform will start as an effort in exploratory *engineering,* designing and testing new structures appropriate to the adolescents, the teachers, and the culture of the 1980s." He goes on to give the following advice to a young assistant professor of social studies education who is struggling to gain tenure: "Use your skills as an educational engineer to design a better structure, and try to find a school system that needs you and your design and that wants you to try it out."[23]

The managerial–engineering–production model of schooling, patterned after the industrial enterprise, is based on the premise that people problems in education stem mainly from the lack of processing efficiency, and that the solution is simply one of organizational and managerial redesign. The advocates of such approaches appear to have the matter in reverse. As Boguslaw tells us, the beginning point must be "a perspective that views human beings as human beings." Instead of starting with this perspective, the engineering frame of reference sees efficiency stemming from the reduction of human error and responsibility by fitting human beings into the production design, with the consequence that the resulting "people problems are left to the after-the-fact efforts of social scientists."[24]

The Concept of Organization

Efforts are commonly made to represent the organization through elaborate charts and manuals of job descriptions. However, such schema may have little bearing on how the organization actually functions. Yet many people conceive of an organization as represented in the stereotype of neatly charted departmental cubicles with interconnecting lines of hierarchy and communication. Because organizations are run by and for people, emergent situations constantly arise even under ordinary day-to-day operations. As Herbert Simon points out, "The term *organization* refers to the complex pattern of communication and relationships in a group of human beings."[25]

In seeking to understand the organization, we need to give attention to the people involved—their identifications and loyalties, authority and responsibility, communications and influence, motivations, shared beliefs and commitments, and other factors bearing on human behavior, along with the material resources and the physical environment—all of which comprise the ecology of the organization. Segmental approaches to organizational problems are bound to fail because in the final analysis the success of the organization derives from the interdependence of the membership in their functions and roles.

ECOLOGY OF THE SCHOOL

Anyone entering a school for the first time gains an immediate impression of the general atmosphere, culture, or ethos in which the pupils, teachers, and administrators work. This sense of atmosphere, or psychosocial context, cannot be separated from the physical environment—the buildings, classrooms, shops, laboratories, studios, offices, grounds, and so on. The initial impressions gained will of course undergo considerable modification as the visitor observes the school in operation and as subsequent visits are made. The observer will discern both the formal and informal organizational arrangements and interactions, and may begin to find specific patterns of behavior in evidence. Moreover, the school cannot be understood apart from the community and the wider culture in which it functions.

The Teaching Environment and Organizational Climate

At the turn of the century, progressive educators were giving concentrated attention to the school as a learning environment.[26] The research on group dynamics during the late 1930s and early 1940s included studies on social climates resulting from different leadership styles in learning groups. Although some of the proponents of group process during 1940s and 1950s tended to overlook the antidemocratic dangers of group social pressure[27] and consensual decision making, the research on group dynamics gave powerful evidence in support of the progressive educational literature favoring democratic school and classroom climates.[28] The concept of "climate" was later utilized in an instrument (*Climate Index*) to classify and measure the verbal behavior of teachers in classrooms in terms of learner-supportive behavior as contrasted against teacher-supportive behavior. This, in turn, led to a variety of studies and instruments to assess the nature of teacher–pupil interactions in the classroom.[29] Nevertheless, when we think of "climate" or "environment," whether in the classroom or school, we are usually conceptualizing a far more encompassing idea than teacher–pupil interactions.

Dimensions of Organizational Climate. During the early 1960s the term *organizational climate* was being used in a questionnaire (*Organizational Climate Description Questionnaire*) designed to elicit teacher perceptions of their relationships as members of a working group, including their perceptions of the principal's role and behaviors in the work setting. The questionnaire identified a number of climate factors, such as social cohesiveness among teachers, extent of teacher involvement in and commitment to the attainment of school goals, teacher morale, obstacles to teacher work fulfillment, consideration provided by the principal, the principal's social distance, production emphasis, and so on. As a result of this research, different types of school climates were identified, ranging from open to closed. The open environment is characterized by such factors as relatively unencumbered communication, constructive working relationships with strong incentives to solve problems, a relatively high degree of teacher autonomy and administrative trust, and high morale. The closed climate is characterized by very much the opposite conditions.[30]

Brookover et al. identified dimensions of school climate derived from perceptions of students, teachers, and principals concerning both their own and each others' characteristics and functions—such as expectations, commitment and efforts to improve academic norms, and so on.[31] The construct of "Quality of School Life" was developed in terms of student satisfaction with school in general, commitment to school work, and student–teacher relationships.[32]

Other efforts have been made to measure organizational climate in schools and college settings through questionnaires designed to index factors contrasting high development press (emphasis on intellectual and social–emotional needs, openness to initiative, sense of responsibility, etc.) against control press (emphasis on rules and restrictions, little opportunity for initiative, limited responsibility by students and faculty, etc.).[33] Yet other researchers have developed a technique for assessing the college environment (Environmental Assessment Technique) through measures of the characteristics of students and the institutional setting—for example, "intellectual" as contrasted with "social" orientation.[34]

As mentioned earlier, such concepts as "climate" and "environment" denote a far richer and more complex web of variables than those identified in questionnaires, scales, checklists, or other instruments designed to gain quantitative measures from qualitative factors. This does not mean that such instruments are not useful or are not valid, but rather that they each represent a piece of a much larger picture. As a consequence, the research literature on school climate often presents inconsistent findings as each study is focused on diverse elements of a highly complex phenomenon. Moreover, the orientation of the researcher will obviously influence the design and focus of the research. For example, the researcher adhering to a production model of inputs and outputs will perceive school climate very differently from one whose work is sociologically based or one whose work is ecologically based.[35]

Hence it is important to utilize and compare a wide range of instruments and techniques, including perhaps the case method, in attempting to assess the school or college climate or environment. As Trent and Rose point out in their analysis of the research literature on teaching environments: "Differences in methods and measurement used in assessing the environment of the teaching–learning function can be critical. This is true since quite different conclusions can be drawn about the environment depending upon the method or measurement employed."[36]

In reviewing the research on school climate, Anderson notes the many gaps and the unclear evidence concerning the interaction of variables to create positive pupil outcomes. Nevertheless, she concludes on a positive note that

> Despite the often confusing array of findings and methods in the search for school climate, the picture that emerges is beginning to take on distinct features. Certain characteristics of life within schools are recurring in the research in association with both climate and outcomes. . . .
>
> In addition to a few clear findings concerning important variables, the school climate research effect to date has explored the value of many research methods.[37]

The Ecological Approach

Jackson's *Life in Classrooms* represents an effort to bring together a range of different kinds of studies with the author's own observations, generalizations, and speculations on the ground that classroom life is too complex to be viewed from any single perspective.[38] More recently, a large-scale study by Goodlad ("A Study of Schooling") involved schools in thirteen communities in seven geographic regions, in which systematic observations were made of students and teachers in over 1,000 classrooms, along with thousands of interviews, in an effort to draw some generalizations concerning the functioning of the school and to find avenues for improvement.[39] The study confirmed much of the research literature showing teacher dominance of the elementary and secondary classroom environment, with only a very small proportion of the learning activity requiring student participation or initiation. Goodlad also found a general lack of concerted curriculum planning with virtually no attention to the concept and function of general education, and he found the widespread practice of student ability grouping to have a negative influence on the atmosphere for learning. The work of Goodlad, Jackson, Eggleston, Sarason, and Rutter et al. represent an ecological approach in that they are concerned with the fullest possible range of interactions bearing on the functioning of entire systems.[40]

Obviously, the researcher is on safer ground to the extent that a study is narrowly delineated and the variables are easily amenable to statistical treatment. But the data will represent only a segment of reality. Although strictly experimental designs can provide strong insights into causal relationships between treatments and outcomes, one cannot manipulate a total school environment and compare the results of the treatment with a control environment. One can manipulate only certain limited elements in the school environment. Similarly, instruments designed to assess the perceptions of the participants in any organizational setting cannot be expected to measure fully the organizational climate. Observations of the behaviors of the participants under both routine and problem situations can provide another set of useful data. Consequently, in attempting to understand and to solve significant problems connected with such a complex phenomenon as school climate, one must draw on a full range of knowledge, research designs, and instruments.

Need for Interdisciplinary Approaches. Drawing from his own research experiences in examining significant social problems, Myrdal expresses his "growing disrespect for the traditional rigid boundary lines between separate disciplines of social science" as a result of his "growing recognition of the fact that *in reality there are not economic, sociological, or psychological problems, but simply problems, and that as a rule they are complex.*"[41]

In the same sense, a complex educational problem requires interdisciplinary approaches, for such a problem is not purely psychological, sociological, economic, political, or anthropological. And to the extent that it involves the curriculum, it is concerned not with the boundaries of codified knowledge as represented by the cocoons of academic specialism, but in the function and application of knowledge as related to the life of the learner, both as an individual and a group member. Moreover, the curriculum must take into account the needs and demands of the wider society.

Environmental Dimensions. In a review of the research literature on school climate, Anderson utilized Taguiri's dimensions of the environmental quality of an organization.[42] Taguiri viewed climate as a broad concept virtually synonymous with environment, and he described the environment as including four dimensions: its ecology (physical and material aspects), its milieu (characteristics of persons and groups), its social system (organizational structure), and its culture (belief systems, cognitive structures, norms, etc.).[43] A problem with Taguiri's dimensions is that his use of the term *ecology* merely to denote physical and material aspects of an environment is not consonant with the general use of the term in either the social sciences or in the biological sciences from where it was borrowed. In biology, the term *ecology* represents the complex web of interrelationships that tie a population to other populations, and organisms to the environment. These interrelationships involve both the biotic and abiotic or physical environment.

Drawing on the work of Barker and Gump,[44] Sarason makes the case for an ecological approach to the school culture, noting that there are different "positions" from which the school can be studied and that each is focused on only partial elements of complex and interdependent sets of relationships. He sees the ecological approach as the most promising for studying the school in efforts to improve education.[45]

A Definition. Using an ecological perspective, organizational climate may be thought of as *the conditions under which an organization and its members function in relation to its structure, expectations, goals, roles, policies, materials, practices, and accomplishments—encompassing not only the influence of the environing conditions (designed and otherwise) on the participants, but the influence of the participants on the designed conditions.*

SYSTEMIC MODELS OF ORGANIZATION

In this chapter, essential differences are drawn between the school and the business and industrial enterprise. Nevertheless, the model of democratic supervision in education, which emerged during the progressive educational reforms before World War II, had a counterpart in the industrial-management literature. Particularly since World War II, the traditional mechanistic, autocratic, and exploitive pattern of industrial operations has come under increasing criticism as studies revealed that it produced adversarial relationships between workers and management, along with organizational malfunctions and low productivity.[46] The point is that even in an established-convergent situation, such as an industrial plant, human relationships must be recognized and developed in ways that are congruent with the values of the wider culture. If this is the case even for the established situation of the factory, it is even more paramount for the emergent situation of the school and classroom where the teacher is expected to exercise professional judgment continually.

From Autocratic to Participative Systems

From his work at the University of Michigan's Institute of Social Research over a period spanning more than thirty years, Rensis Likert identified sets of properties portraying four types of management systems in a continuum from the most autocratic to the most participative. Although Likert's research was originally focused on industrial organizations, he later conducted research on settings in schools, universities, and other public agencies. Likert found that the system that functioned most effectively, whether in industry or in education, is the participative system which "encourages an open sharing of information and the involved influence by members over events and decisions affecting their lives."[47] These findings appear to be consistent with the literature on democratic educational administration and supervision,[48] and with the pioneering research of Kurt Lewin and his associates on the relationship of social climate to group behavior and productivity in a wide range of settings.[49] Unfortunately, many adherents of group dynamics and human relations failed to recognize that concentrating on group process as a means of treating people better suffers from superficiality. Unless the level of responsibility and the opportunity for initiative are enhanced for the purpose of solving substantive problems, little improvement can be expected in commitment and productivity. Moreover, group process, taken superficially, sometimes exerts its own tyranny of group pressure, whereby individuals are made to feel compelled to yield to consensus when they actually have a valid basis for constructive disagreement. Participative-democratic approaches

Table 5–1   Systems of Organization

System	Motivational Forces	Communication Pattern
1. Exploitive-authoritative	Fear, status, rank in hierarchy; feeling of responsibility at high levels only	Mainly downward; little upward and lateral communication
2. Benevolent-authoritative	Status, rank, power; need for money; sometimes fear; feeling of responsibility at managerial levels only	Little upward and lateral communication, much downward
3. Consultative	Status, rank, power; feeling of responsibility	Upward and downward good, with moderate to good lateral communication
4. Participative-group	Taps all major motives except fear, including motives from group processes; motives mutually reinforcing; trust prevalent; feeling of responsibility quite prevalent at all levels	Open and accurate flow

Source: Adapted from David G. Bowers, *Systems of Organization* (Ann Arbor, Mich.: University of Michigan Press, 1976), pp. 104–105.

not only allow for initiative and constructive disagreement, but provide the climate for their fullest expression and the opportunity for corrective and creative action.

Contrasting Types of Organizational Systems. Before focusing on participative-democratic organization, an examination of the contrasting systems of organizations will reveal vivid differences on the continuum of orientations and functions—from autocratic to democratic. Table 5–1 contrasts the following four types or models of organizational systems identified by Lickert: System 1: exploitive-authoritative; System 2: benevolent-authoritative; System 3: consultative; and System 4: participative-group.

Interaction-Influence Process	*Decision-Making Process*	*Goal-Setting Process*	*Control Process*
Little cooperative teamwork or mutual influence; influence mainly downward	Top-down, person-to-person or unit-to-unit basis by hierarchy; problems approached authoritatively	Orders issued and accepted overtly, but covertly resisted	Top-down only
Little cooperative teamwork; moderate downward influences; little upward influence except informally	Top-down, with some implementation decisions at lower levels on person-to-person basis; problems approached authoritatively	Orders issued, perhaps with some chance to comment; overt acceptance, but often covert resistance	Top-down mainly
Moderate cooperative teamwork and upward influence; moderate to substantial downward influence	Broad policy decided at top; specific decisions at lower levels; some group-based decision making; problems approached with some consultation	Goals set or orders issued after discussion with subordinates; occasional covert resistance	Primary at top, with some delegation at lower levels
High cooperative teamwork; substantial influence upward, downward, and laterally	Throughout organization, linked by overlapping groups; emphasis on problem solutions, tapping expertise at all levels and utilizing group processes	Established by group participation except in emergencies; full acceptance and commitment	Widespread real and felt responsibility for control

The typology of different systems of organization has been characterized by different authors in various ways, but there is a general correspondence with Lickert's schema. From his studies of industrial and business organization, McGregor characterizes organizational systems according to two types: Theory X and Theory Y.[50] Theory X is based on the assumption that human beings have an inherent dislike for work, seek to avoid responsibility, prefer to be directed, and tend to resist change. Consequently, they must be directed and controlled by management in a top-down hierarchical structure to meet the needs of the organization. Argyris describes two types of behavior patterns by administrators or leaders under Theory X: Pattern A (hard), characterized by authoritarian, directive, and tightly controlled leadership; and Pattern B (soft), characterized by benevolent paternalism and persuasion to "buy" compliance from subordinates.[51] The correspondence of Theory X (and Patterns A and B of administrative or supervisory leadership) with Lickert's Systems 1 and 2, exploitive-authoritative and benevolent-authoritative (Table 5–1), is obvious.

Theory Y, as postulated by McGregor, regards human motivation in a very different light. Under Theory Y, human beings will exercise self-direction, will seek responsibility, and will work toward an organization's goals when the goals and climate of the organization are congruent with their motivational needs. The capacity for productive effort, creativity, and responsibility are seen as widespread among people. Consequently, under Theory Y, there is a commitment on the part of the administration and staff to collaboration and participatory decision making. Theory Y clearly corresponds to Lickert's System 4: participative-group (Table 5–1).

Because Lickert has developed and applied his schema in connection with schools and other educational institutions, as well as with industrial organizations and governmental agencies, we shall use Lickert's constructs in this chapter in examining the contrasting models of organization and the implications for administration and supervision in the school and school system.

The Exploitive-Authoritative System

In the most autocratic system (exploitive-authoritative), decision making is concentrated at the very top with orders being issued downward. The top-down direction of communication may appear on the surface to be efficient because orders are simply expected to be carried out as issued. However, because there is little communication upward and laterally, deficiencies in a decision are not readily discernible at the top, with the consequence that errors are compounded as subordinates seek to protect themselves by covering up for the deficiencies.

The Engineering Frame of Reference and the Human Factor. Boguslaw likens the authority-control system to a physical-control system having an "engineering frame of reference" in which human beings are regarded as mere components with more or less specifiable performance characteristics. He goes on to point out that such a system often breaks down because consideration of the human element is lacking and because it lacks the flexibility and openness of communication necessary whenever unanticipated or emergent situations arise:

> The customary consequence of adhering to this frame of reference is to conclude that human components are exasperatingly unreliable, limited, and inefficient. Furthermore, they are difficult to control. The most obvious analogy to the physical-control system involves the use of formal authority and its delegation as the energy or power source necessary to insure that the desired signals pass through the entire system. This, of course, is the basis for the insistence upon unquestioning obedience to orders traditionally found not only in military organizations but in all bureaucracies of both private industry and government organizations. Human groups unfortunately (or fortunately) have devised many mechanisms for disrupting systems that exercise control exclusively or even primarily through the use of authority.

What happens when authority control systems run amuck is an endless source of case material for management seminars. The case of the employees who do · *everything* they are ordered to do by their supervisor—neither more nor less—is .a classic. They ignore obvious emergent situations and engage in assigned repetitive tasks beyond reasonable termination points. . . . The case of the industrial work group ordered to use a new, unwanted piece of equipment is perennially effective slapstick comedy material; the ingenious steps taken by members of the group to prove the existence of unsuspected faults in the new equipment provide universally understandable material for comedy writers. . . . The point to be made is simply this: The idea of control results in highly unreliable performance when applied to human components of a system.[52]

As shown in Table 5–1, the exploitive-authoritative system taps such motives as fear, status, and rank in the hierarchy. Decision making and responsibility are concentrated at the top and there is little cooperative teamwork.

Top-Down Climate Flow. Table 5–2 shows a hypothetical flow of climate and group events down the hierarchy in a school system that is exploitive-authoritative. On the surface, the organizational structure may appear to be highly efficient, for it is characterized by clearly segmental lines of authority, jurisdiction, and operation. Goals and decisions are derived readily, for they emanate from the top. The emphasis is on "running a tight ship."

However, because the flow of communication is downward, the messages are conceived and executed mainly as orders or mandates and there is little upward or lateral communication unless specifically called for. The consequence is poor coordination between and among subordinate groups. Because problems are addressed authoritatively, subordinate groups are not deemed to possess the knowledge/ability to diagnose and solve problems. There is a tendency to seek directives when problems arise, and directives may be followed even when the evidence may run counter to the orders from above. The concealment of emergent problems may occur as subordinate groups and individuals seek to protect their self-interests.

Unprofessional Climate. Other characteristic effects of the exploitive-authoritative system are poor motivation, with attitudes that are hostile upward and contemptuous downward; low feeling of responsibility except at highest levels; dissatisfaction with work, peers, administrators, supervisors, and the system in general; and low initiative and considerable conflict. The entire climate can be characterized as unprofessional and often adversarial. Quite typically, an informal organization emerges to undermine the formal organization of the exploitive-authoritative system. Consequently, the real control from the top is effectively reduced and organizational ends and means become discontinuous.

Although virtually no school system would characterize itself as operating strictly as System 1: exploitive-authoritative, the reader will perhaps recognize that various elements of this system are prevalent in schools and school districts of which he or she has acquaintance. Because the teacher can exercise a certain amount of autonomy in the isolation of the classroom, directives and mandates from above may be followed only nominally under the exploitive-authoritative

Table 5–2   Hypothetical Flow of Climate and Group Events down the Hierarchy in the Exploitive-Authoritative School System

Administrative Level	Organizational Conditions	Operational Effects
Superintendent Associate superintendents Assistant superintendents	Top-down flow of communication Messages mainly executed as orders Segmental lines of jurisdiction	Poor coordination between and among subordinate groups in areas of responsibility Low knowledge/ability by subordinate groups Problems addressed authoritatively with little recognition of and opportunity for expertise at lower levels Emphasis on "running a tight ship"
Principals Assistant principals	Coordination problem in climate Focus on established conditions	Problems in coordinating ends and means, and in facilitating cooperation of staff Lack of commitment and capability for diagnosing and solving emergent problems Concealment of emergent problems Emphasis on maintenance of operations except for mandated changes from above
Directors Supervisors Coordinators Department heads	Decision-making problem in climate	Tendency to seek and follow directives from above even when evidence runs counter Little responsibility and initiative Lack of commitment and capability for diagnosing and solving emergent problems Concealment of emergent problems
Teachers Guidance counselors	Motivational problem in climate Unprofessional climate	Little initiative (indifference, apathy, resentment, conflict) Concealment of emergent problems Poor performance Lack of commitment and capability for diagnosing and solving emergent problems

system. But this, in turn, creates other problems, such as the lack of cooperative faculty teamwork in developing curriculum articulation horizontally (between and among the fields of study) and vertically (from grade level to grade level). A nominal goal of the school may be the fostering of democratic citizenship. Yet the teachers are not treated by administrators and supervisors as members of a democratic organization, and the opportunity for student involvement in decision making is strictly limited to minor matters. The teaching tends to be focused on drill work in facts and skills and is primarily error oriented rather than idea oriented. Considerable emphasis is given to keeping order and maintaining discipline through externally imposed controls as self-discipline is largely lacking. There is little opportunity for pupil-initiated class discussion and little solicitation of pupils for ideas on school policy and classroom activity. Although pupils are allowed few initiatives, they exercise a great deal of initiative and ingenuity in undermining the system.

The Benevolent-Authoritative System

As shown in Table 5–1, although the communication pattern is mainly downward in the benevolent-authoritative system, and although policy decisions are made at the top, some implementation decisions and specific operational decisions are made at lower levels. In setting goals and deciding on orders, some opportunity is provided for comments by subordinates. There is limited communication upward and laterally except by informal means. The feeling of responsibility is manifest at the higher levels primarily and, consequently, initiative is lacking at lower levels, and upward communication becomes distorted and filtered to a considerable extent. Attitudes are mixed, but there is a tendency for them to be condescending downward and subservient upward. Attitudes toward work, peers, supervisors, administrators, and the organization in general range from dissatisfaction to moderate satisfaction. Relatively little cooperative teamwork is present. As directives are issued downward, there is overt acceptance, but a tendency toward covert resistance or distortion.

An informal organization is usually present, working counter to the formal in many respects. Motives for status, rank, and power are tapped at the higher levels, while untapped motives may cancel out the tapped motives.

Problems are addressed authoritatively from the top down, and there is a lack of commitment and knowledge/ability for diagnosing and solving emergent problems at the lower levels. The climate is paternalistic rather than professional.

In the setting of the school, discretionary measures by the teacher are confined mainly to the individual classroom, where such measures may or may not run counter to administrative policy or preference. The teacher is regarded as knowing *what* is expected of him or her, but may be given considerable leeway as to *how* the work is to be carried out. Consequently, ends and means may be discontinuous and even conflicting. As far as the pupils are concerned, many of the characteristics and shortcomings of the exploitive-authoritative system are present, and pupils will exercise considerable initiative and ingenuity in undermining the system. The problem of limited upward and lateral communication and of limited cooperative teamwork among supervisors and teachers is reflected in the curriculum where there is little evidence of horizontal and vertical articulation.

The Consultative System

The consultative system is a marked improvement over the exploitive-authoritative and the benevolent-authoritative systems with regard to organizational climate and function. As presented in Table 5–1, broad policy decisions are made at the top of the hierarchy, but more specific decisions concerning implementation and day-to-day operations are made at lower levels. Goals are formulated and orders are made after consultation with subordinates. As a result, attitudes are generally favorable and there is a feeling of responsibility on the part of individuals at subordinate levels. Although constructive motivational forces are tapped in the individual, such forces characteristic of group process are not adequately tapped. Consequently, cooperative teamwork, together with upward and lateral influence of groups, is only moderate. The control process remains mainly at the top, but there is some delegation below. Although there is generally little resistance to directives, an informal organization may exist which dilutes somewhat the formal control processes.

Most school administrators utilize at least some elements of the consultative system if only because practical considerations so demand. Unlike ordinary employees at the ground levels of fairly large industrial organizations, teachers can and do exercise considerable autonomy in their own immediate work setting (the classroom) if only by virtue of their classroom isolation. In recognition of this condition, along with some degree of acknowledgment of the professionalization of teaching, administrators are becoming increasingly aware of the need to utilize consultative mechanisms. Other administrators may employ the consultative approach mainly in realization that the classroom isolation reduces the control processes of the organization, and they find that the consultative system helps enhance the control processes.

The classroom autonomy of the teacher is desirable when it provides the individual with a sense of responsibility for diagnosing and solving emergent problems and for exercising professional initiative and individual creativity in the teaching–learning process. However, the relative autonomy of the individual teacher in the classroom may also create problems of lateral and upward communication. Moreover, less competent teachers may utilize the comparative isolation of the classroom as insulation against change. Routine busywork may characterize the classroom activity in such a situation, with the teacher's major efforts being directed at dealing with symptoms rather than the underlying causes of problems.

The consultative system improves the upward and lateral flow of communication over the authoritative system, although the flow is moderate. This, in turn, enhances somewhat the opportunity for addressing such systemwide problems as horizontal and vertical curriculum articulation, systemwide changes in the curriculum, and the identification and treatment of emergent problems. Yet serious difficulties arise when teachers, department heads, supervisors and curriculum coordinators, or principals are not in agreement with the policy decisions mandated from above. Having no say in the formulation of broad policy decisions—and under circumstances where they regard such decisions as arbitrary, coercive, or dysfunctional—the implementation of such decisions may be made reluctantly and with some modification and distortion. Thus an informal organization may appear, operating counter to certain directives of the formal organization.

The Participative-Group System

Of the four systems, System 4: participative-group is the most democratic. As portrayed in Table 5–3, the decision-making process extends organically throughout the organization, and there is consultation on broad policy decisions with goal setting through democratic group participation. Cooperative teamwork is high along with real and felt responsibility at all levels. Communication is open and accurate, and there is substantial influence upward, downward, and laterally. All constructive motives of individuals and groups are tapped, and there is a high degree of mutual trust. Considerable emphasis is given to the involvement of all pertinent groups in the diagnosis and solving of problems, with the leadership conveying a strong sense of confidence in the knowledge/ability of the staff. Hence there is little or no concealment of problems. Because of the openness of this system, there is no need for an informal organization operating counter to the formal organization.

Enhancement of Professionalization. As far as the school and the school system are concerned, the participative-group system results in the enhancement of professionalization from the superintendency to the classroom teacher. For example, should a problem arise such as a complaint from a community group or individual concerning the use of certain curriculum materials, along with pressures being exerted to remove such materials, the matter is referred to the curriculum committee (comprised of faculty, the curriculum coordinator or director, and representative students who may serve on the committee in a consulting or advisory capacity). The policy position of the administration and the school board is that the appropriateness of curriculum materials is determined by the faculty and the curriculum director because they have the professional expertise. The decision of the curriculum committee is supported fully by the administration and board.

Under the consultative system (System 3), the administration will consult with the teacher(s) involved along with the members of the curriculum committee, but the decision on whether or not to remove the allegedly offensive or inappropriate curriculum materials resides with the administrator. Under System 2: benevolent-authoritative, the attitude conveyed is that the administration is acting to protect the best interests of the teacher(s), students, and the school system. Under System 4: participative-group, the attitude conveyed throughout the

Table 5–3 Hypothetical Flow of Climate and Group Events in the Participative-Group System

Administrative Level	Organizational Level	Operational Effects
Superintendents Associate superintendents Assistant superintendents	Full flow of communication—upward and laterally as well as ⟷ downward Messages supported by reasons and evidence with focus on problem solutions Flexible lines of communication	Fullest coordination within, between, and among groups at all levels of responsibility Problems addressed hypothetically with involvement of expertise at other levels
Principals Assistant principals	Climate of interdependence among groups at all levels ⟷ Focus on emergent conditions and the improvement of established conditions	High knowledge/ability at all levels High levels of cooperation Ends and means clearly interconnected Emergent problems openly exposed and attacked
Directors Supervisors Coordinators Department heads	Cooperative decision making based on identification and ⟷ diagnosis of problems Climate of interdependence	Great flexibility in adjusting to and changing conditions as needed High responsibility and initiative by individuals and groups in identifying, diagnosing, and solving emergent problems
Teachers Guidance counselors	High motivation Professional climate	High knowledge/ability and initiative High performance Continuous improvement through problem solutions

school, school district, and community is that the faculty possess the professional expertise and responsibility for curriculum development and the selection and utilization of curriculum materials.

Under Systems 1 and 2 especially, but also under System 3, there is considerable self-censorship by teachers who fear that any complaints regarding the selection or use of certain curriculum materials will be viewed negatively by the administration. The attitude conveyed by the administration under Systems 1 and 2 is that problems emanating from the classroom reflect on the teacher's inability to prevent problems. Consequently, a great deal of effort is made to avoid the possibility of problem situations even at the expense of effective teaching and learning. Where problems do arise, much effort is expended to conceal them.

Cooperative Schoolwide Decision Making. In the participative-group system, teachers are engaged cooperatively with each other and with administrators, supervisors, and curriculum directors in addressing schoolwide problems and in making schoolwide decisions. In his "Study of Schooling," Goodlad found that the most satisfying school climates, as seen by teachers, are those where teachers are engaged in schoolwide decisions and problem solving, yet he found that teachers "rarely worked together on some school-based issue or problem" and that most principals lack the abilities required for problem solving to effect schoolwide improvement.[53]

Goodlad's findings indicate that our schools are a long way from proximating the participative-group system of organization and the professionalization of teaching. Although he found that teachers do perceive themselves as having considerable autonomy of decision making within the confines of their own classrooms, this autonomy is derived at the expense of teacher isolation. The consequence is that teachers are not deeply engaged with principals, supervisors, and curriculum directors in working to solve schoolwide problems.[54] Under such conditions, changes in school practices tend to be derived from external influences and pressures rather than from the problem-solving strategies of a professional staff. Hence change or reform, divorced from problem solving, fails to result in educational improvement.

Classroom Life. Turning to the classroom, Goodlad observed that although many teachers verbalize the importance of students becoming independent thinkers, inside classrooms the teachers initiated almost everything and students rarely shared in decision making concerning their own education. In Goodlad's words,

> There is little or nothing about classroom life as it is conducted, so far as I am able to determine, that suggests the existence of or need for norms of group cohesion and cooperation of a shared purpose.
>
> The most successful classrooms may be those in which teachers succeed in creating commonly shared goals and individuals cooperate in ensuring each person's success in achieving them.[55]

Goodlad also found that the mode of classroom activity was mainly that of passive pupil recitation, focused on factual information and narrow skills, and that the teacher-made tests were similarly geared to such a narrow-minded emphasis.[56] Under such conditions, youngsters are denied the opportunity to develop any real capability and commitment for responsible self-direction and shared social responsibility. The motive for learning, then, is derived not from a genuine interest in the curriculum, but mainly from the desire to get a good grade. Where the learners feel that they cannot succeed, they tend to regard the teacher and the school as adversaries. The consequence is an environment of externally imposed autocratic controls by the teachers and principal.

Goodlad's "Study of Schooling" clearly reveals the need for our schools to move toward the participative-group system of operation if they are to be more productive and and true to the ideals of a democratic society.

The Ad Hoc Approach

Bowers emphasizes that the various aspects of an organizational system must be mutually consistent. Merely grafting certain elements of the participative-group system to an essentially autocratic system will not work effectively because "the various behavioral, attitudinal, and structural parts of the organizational whole have a fundamental interdependence, and they must be mutually consistent."[57] If they are not consistent, conflicts will arise and eventually the more powerful elements will prevail. "Where an attempt is made artificially to implant intervening or lower echelon processes of a participative nature in an organization in which causal or upper echelon processes are more autocratic, it is likely that the whole system will shift, or revert, toward autocracy," cautions Bowers.[58]

Nevertheless, it should be recalled that the four systems represent a continuum, with organizations ranging in the degree to which they function as an exploitive-authoritative system at one end of the continuum to a participative-group system on the other end. It is possible for an organization to have no commitment to any particular system, although it will fall somewhere on the continuum. The overriding attitude of the ad hoc approach is to respond in whichever ways appear to be most expedient at a particular time.

At first glance the ad hoc approach may appear to be eminently flexible and practical. However, its conceptual deficiencies result in a lack of any clearly defined longer-range ends and means. As Boguslaw observes, under the ad hoc approach there is no clearly perceived view of the future system or its requirements; there is the tendency to rely on currently available techniques with the result that innovative ideas or solutions may be overlooked or even stifled, since ad hoc arrangements or temporary "solutions" have a way of becoming embedded simply because they "worked" in the past.[59] The operations tend to be reactive rather than proactive. The concern with perceived immediate needs often is at the expense of future vision. There is also the danger that insufficient consideration is given to the need for consistency, as segmental or piecemeal adaptations and adjustments are made to fit particular situations at a given time.

The Ad Hoc Approach in Schools. Aspects of the ad hoc approach are found in many schools and school systems. At one point in time a secondary school may be adding all kinds of electives and curricular options under the banner of curricular "relevance," only to be followed by a tightening up of "standards" by designating a selected list of "academic" courses and course credits for graduation, increasing homework assignments, and instituting more rigid grading practices. An elementary school may shift its classroom organization from the self-contained classroom to a modified departmental structure, from a modified departmental structure to an open classroom, and from an open classroom back again to a modified departmental structure. Or emphasis at one point in time might be on curriculum correlation and synthesis, to be followed by disciplinary studies or "back-to-basics." The painstaking process of designing a coherent curriculum in general education in the secondary school, requiring considerable faculty–administrative cooperation and philosophical commitment, is commonly avoided by simply prescribing a list of distribution requirements whereby students select courses from given categories—as in a Chinese menu.

The ad hoc approach is characteristic of organizations that are focused on meeting the demands of whatever external forces are perceived to be most influential at a given time. The schools are particularly vulnerable to external pressures. Yet the resources are so lacking and the relative autonomy of the teacher is such that the ad hoc changes, fortunately or unfortunately, may be relatively superficial. Teachers may respond to the external pressures for higher pupil achievement on statewide minimum-competency tests by teaching-to-the-test. When such statewide tests neglect writing, teachers give less emphasis to student themes. When such tests neglect the arts, less emphasis is given to the arts in the curriculum. As another example, the external pressure for higher SAT scores during the past decade has resulted in many high schools providing special courses to prepare students for the SAT. Such efforts may produce measurable "evidence" of improvement in pupil achievement through higher scores on external tests, but may have no effect, or even a negative effect, on intellectual curiosity, motivation for self-impelled learning, or attitudes toward learning.

School administrators and supervisors may believe that they are being "responsive" to societal needs when they follow the ad hoc approach, but in reality they are merely reacting to external influences rather than addressing problem solutions for educational improvement. The ad hoc approach is characteristic of school systems that lack a concerted philosophy and lack operational commitment to curricular coherence, faculty interdependence, and professionalism.

The Laissez-faire Approach

On the surface, the laissez-faire approach resembles the ad hoc approach, since neither has a commitment to a particular system. Both are characterized by conceptual deficiencies, particularly in the failure to link ends and means in any systematic way and in their absence of long-range prediction or planning. However, where the ad hoc approach might call for mandated changes in specific operations or practices that are deemed expedient at any particular time, the laissez-faire approach will allow these changes to occur through "natural selection" or adaptation in the normal course of events.

In the economic sphere, Adam Smith is the name associated with laissez-faire theory, and such theory was embraced by many of those who sought to protect their own advantageous position in the marketplace. As far as actual business or industrial organizations are concerned, it is inconceivable that any could survive under conditions of complete freedom in decision making and actions by each individual employee. In a given situation, an administrator may simply wait and see what happens when subordinates and operating units encounter an emergent situation or problem. But the organization will not function as an organization when each person is allowed to "do his own thing."

Administrative Decentralization. The laissez-faire prescription often arises as a reaction against the excesses of bureaucracy and is accompanied by a call for decentralization and local freedom of action. However, in large and complex organizations the arrangements for decentralization require systematic reorganization of administrative and operational units. If the channels of communication, coordination, and responsibility are not to become weakened and blurred as the result of granting the constituent units greater autonomy, new bureaucratic arrangements must be developed to ensure that the channels are open and functional. The paradox (and contradiction) in the laissez-faire prescription is that it requires systematic reorganization if disorganization is not to result.

In public administration, the laissez-faire prescription has suffered from a naive utopianism. For example, in the plan for decentralizing the New York City schools into some thirty autonomous "community" school districts, as proposed by the Mayor's Advisory Panel in 1967, it was claimed that "any Community School District could create within New York City a school system that in imagination, flexibility, and innovation could match or surpass the most dynamic suburban or small-city school district in the country," and that the proposed plan for decentralization "combines the advantages of big-city education with the opportunities of the finest small-city and suburban educational systems," and that it would "reflect the rich blend of unity and diversity that once made the city a gateway to opportunity for the millions who came to its streets."[60] Since 1969, when the school decentralization law for New York City was enacted to provide for greater "community control" in the elementary and intermediate schools, the local "community boards" have been marked by factional disputes and administrative irregularities necessitating the imposition of new administrative checks and controls by the central board of education. The utopian vision of wide community participation failed to materialize, as only a minute fraction of eligible voters (from 8 to 15 percent) turned out to elect their community school boards.[61] The disadvantaged and advantaged neighborhood schools remained isolated from each other, and the socioeconomic problems that had beset the schools before decentralization continued to plague the schools after decentralization. The utopian vision of creativity and excellence embodied in the plan for decentralization quickly evaporated in the face of opportunism and factionalism. The democratic concept of "community," which was supposed to engender a sense of unity through diversity, was reduced to narrow and competing interests as cosmopolitanism gave way to parochialism.

Romanticism. At the level of the individual school and classroom, the laissez-faire approach has been associated with a wing of the progressivist movement known as "romantic naturalism." In reaction against traditional authoritarian educational practices, romantic naturalists at the turn of the century were advocating that child life in the classroom be centered on the natural interests and spontaneous activities of the learner. Dewey, an experimentalist, repeatedly warned of the emptiness of such practices. "It is as if the child were forever tasting and never eating; always having his palate tickled upon the emotional side, but never getting the organic satisfaction that comes only with the digestion of food and transformation of it into working power," wrote Dewey.[63]

The laissez-faire pedagogy of romantic naturalism is promoted under the banner of "freedom." But to Dewey, the absence of a planned curriculum in favor of spontaneous pupil activity mitigates against freedom because genuine freedom requires thought directed by the power of intelligence. "To cultivate unhindered unreflective external activity is to foster enslavement," he warned, "for it leaves the person at the mercy of appetite, sense, and circumstance."[64]

Over a period of half a century, Dewey leveled criticisms at romantic progressivists and laissez-faire pedagogues who sought to do away with the formal curriculum in favor of learning experiences centered on children's spontaneous interests and felt needs. He called such approaches "really stupid" because they misconceive the conditions for independent thinking and lack intelligently directed thought.[65]

The 1960s witnessed a revival of radical-romantic prescriptions for educational reform. The writings of the psychologist Carl Rogers gained considerable popularity with college students and educators who favored education as a kind of individual-centered therapy in a relatively unstructured school and classroom environment.[66] A rash of best-selling books during the 1960s proposed that the schools be radically reformed by making them totally learner-centered and that the formal curriculum along with supervisory services should be discarded. "The idea of the curriculum would not be valid even if we could agree what ought to be in it. For knowledge changes," wrote Holt, and "learning is not everything, and certainly one piece of learning is as good as another."[67] A favorite radical prescription of the times was to "eliminate all full-time administrators and administrations," and that "most of the 'administration' at the school should be a student responsibility."[66] Paul Goodman, a radical critic popular with the college generation of that day, advised that "the effort to channel the process of growing up according to a preconceived curriculum and method discourages and wastes many of the best human powers to learn and cope." And in attacking the school as an organization, he proceeded to advocate that "incidental education, taking part in the ongoing activities of society, must again be made the chief means of learning and teaching."[68] Such sentiments were reflected in many of the alternative schools that were established during the 1960s. One such was described in detail by its founder in a best-selling book, relating how lesson plans and the formal curriculum were abolished in favor of learning activities centered on children's felt needs.[69] Another school, described as "existentialist," was featured in an education journal as having abolished all administrative structures, supervisory services, and required courses; basing all learning activities on the expressed interests of pupils and through spontaneous learning groups; providing children with voting rights equal to the faculty at general school meetings; and determining teacher retention according to student demand.[70]

Most of these schools, as was the case in the earlier efforts to embrace the laissez-faire pedagogy of romantic naturalism through alternative protest schools, eventually faced a crisis of administrative reality. The average life of alternative schools of every kind has been less than two years.[71]

Followed to its logical conclusion, under laissez-faire any formal system of administration and supervision is regarded as an intrusion upon the artistic freedom of the teacher, and any effort to build upon scientific knowledge is disparaged on the ground that teaching is an art form.

If history provides any lessons, one lesson is that the laissez-faire pedagogy of romantic naturalism will appear again without any cognizance on the part of the romanticists as to the historical record of such movements. Then, in short order, it will face a crisis of reality coupled with the renewed demand for externally imposed administrative controls and "standards."

TOWARD THE PARTICIPATIVE-GROUP SYSTEM: AN EDUCATIVE PROCESS

The research by Lickert points to a pattern of superior performance results in a wide variety of institutional settings—industry, education, government, and so on—as the organizational structure and function gravitate toward System 4: participative-group.[72] Lickert acknowledges that although some studies of the literature do not support such a favorable pattern,[73] he points out that such studies have focused on results in terms of short-term productivity, without taking adequate account of the changes effected in the productive capability of the human organization, and that such changes in capability must be measured in the long term. For example, the imposition of certain authoritative measures, such as production-quota pressures, budget cuts, and personnel cuts, will likely yield immediate measurable "improvements" in efficiency, but will eventually reveal adverse results in the long range as the effects of poor morale become manifest in negative attitudes, excessive grievances, and covert efforts to defeat the imposed changes. It takes time and education to develop the human conditions and capabilities characteristic of System 4.

It has been contended by some that there is no general administrative model that is superior in results to other models, as far as industrial organizations are concerned, since different kinds of work and work settings require different kinds of organizational systems; consequently, it is held that a contingency approach is necessary in which the management system is adapted to fit particular requirements of the organization, its work, and its people.[74] Although Lickert's own findings do not dispute this contingency orientation, he points out that moving an organization toward System 4 requires time and consideration of the capabilities and expectations of all members of the organization who will be involved and affected by the changes. Any effort to restructure an organization toward System 4 requires education. Democratic structures and processes cannot be imposed. Lickert cites a number of studies showing that the more productive organization is closer to System 4, whereas the less productive organization is closer to System 1, and this pattern applies to all kinds of organizations— whether business, industry, government, school, or university.[75]

Decision-Making Autonomy in Functional Supervision

Because human beings do not behave in perfectly predictable and specifiable ways, especially where the wider culture expresses democratic values, control by sheer authority in the school or work setting is bound to have unproductive consequences. Herbert Simon points out that negative consequences of such control efforts are likely even in quite ordinary decision-making work settings. According to Simon,

> Administrators have increasingly recognized in recent years that authority, unless buttressed by other forms of influence, is relatively impotent to control

decision in any but a negative way. The elements entering into all but the most routine decisions are so numerous and so complex that it is impossible to control positively more than a few. Unless the subordinate is himself able to supply most of the premises of decision, and to synthesize them adequately, the task of supervision becomes hopelessly burdensome.[76]

In the setting of the school, the statement above applies not only to the supervision of teachers but to the supervision of students. Moreover, aside from the fact that a vital requirement of any profession is that the practitioner must exercise considerable autonomy in decision making, the fact is that when the classroom door is closed the teaching–learning situation is so emergent that the teacher cannot possibly function effectively without such autonomy. Effective school administrators and supervisors are well aware of this. "Functional supervision necessarily takes the form of advice rather than authority," notes Simon, and the supervisory process is educative rather than coercive.[77] At the same time, the effective teacher knows that sheer control over students by authority not only is nonfunctional but is miseducative, since education requires the development of productive self-control and self-direction.

Moreover, autonomy is not synonymous with isolation. Decision making in the isolated compartment of the classroom will not add up to the decision making required for schoolwide problem solving. The latter requires a great deal of cooperation on the part of principals, supervisors, curriculum coordinators, teachers, and counselors—for their work is highly interdependent. Autonomy and interdependence must not be regarded as antithetical conditions.

Relevance to the Culture

Because organizations operate in a wider cultural context, they must take account of the norms and values of the wider culture if they are to function effectively. An autocratic organization in a society that places a high value on democratic processes will find its members resentful and resistant to the organization's goals and leadership. Moreover, democratic nations differ from each other in terms of their degree of population homogeneity, cultural traditions, economic orientations, and so on. Consequently, given a particular enterprise, a Systems 4 organization in Japan or Sweden, for example, will develop certain attributes that differ noticeably from a System 4 organization in the United States. Nations can and do learn from one another, but adaptations are required to allow for the unique cultural differences.

Lessons from Abroad: Transformation Rather than Transplantation. From the late 1970s and extending into the 1980s, the interest in the Japanese "economic miracle" prompted business schools, business journals, and the popular press to examine the conditions and methods underlying Japanese industrial productivity. From Harvard University to the University of Hawaii, business schools were offering courses on Japanese industrial management, and MIT was creating a Japan Science and Technology Program in which a joint undergraduate–graduate degree program in engineering or science included up to a year's working internship in Japanese industries.[78] At the same time, some of our largest industrial corporations were seeking to identify certain attributes of Japanese industrial organization and practice for adoption or adaptation on this side of the Pacific.

Through these efforts, it was discovered that leading Japanese industries were utilizing many attributes of a System 4 organization in combination with a kind of benevolent administrative leadership consonant with that nation's group-oriented cultural traditions. The Japanese system came to be described in the U.S. business schools as Theory Z, which essentially represented the values of McGregor's Theory Y being applied to the organizational system, as discussed earlier in this chapter.[79]

Japanese workers in leading corporations have permanent employment status or tenure. Employees meet regularly in quality circles to discuss ways and means of improving work conditions and productivity. Emphasis is given to problem solving.

During 1982 and 1983 a leading Japanese automaker ran double-page advertisements in leading American business and news magazines describing the emphasis given to worker involvement and responsibility through voluntary participation in quality circles. The advertisements described how the focus of the quality circles is on improving quality through problem solving. A graph in the advertisement showed that during the previous year, workers submitted more than 2.5 million suggestions and that most of the suggestions were adopted by management.[80]

Until recent years, most Japanese workers were not claiming overtime pay to which they were entitled. Managerial perquisites in Japan are limited, even to the extent of providing no special executive parking privileges or executive dining rooms. A typical practice is for managers to undergo job rotation at intervals of two to seven years to develop broad-gauged generalists who have working experience in all phases of manufacturing and operations. Job rotation is also intended to develop a closer working relationship with workers in all areas, enhancing communication and mutual understanding of the company's goals and problems. Moreover, it serves to enhance interest and motivation through new responsibilities and activities, stimulating fresh insights through new perspectives.

A rash of books were appearing in the United States during the 1980s advocating that American industry move toward a more consensual model of labor–management, and away from authoritarian management which issues orders to be carried down the hierarchy to segmented specialists and, finally, to bored and hostile workers. Leading graduate schools of business were being criticized for a curriculum focused on one-upmanship game theory, advertising and marketing ploys, taxation strategies, and various techniques of corporate manipulation—while neglecting the motivation of people, the significance of research and development, and problems in industrial operations at the ground level.[81]

During the early 1980s a number of leading American corporations, including automobile manufacturers, began establishing worker circles and were adopting some features of participative management to reduce the traditional apartheid and conflict between white collar and blue collar. To the extent that such adjustments represented a shift away from the old-style authoritarian and adversarial relationships, and toward a System 4 organization, there was cause for optimism that morale and productivity would be enhanced. However, to assume that the "Japanese way" could simply be transplanted to America is naive because that nation's cultural tradition places such powerful emphasis on cooperative group relationships and company loyalty. For example, it is not too much of an exaggeration to compare the company spirit at a leading Japanese industrial corporation with the "school spirit" at an American college or university noted for avid student and alumni loyalty. Nevertheless, the democratic tradition in the Western world places a high value on individual autonomy in a setting of social responsibility. This is one of the chief characteristic differences between the two cultures, and any effort to transfer elements from one culture to another must take such differences into account.

Ironically, many of the concepts of modern democratic management were brought to Japan by American theorists during the post–World War II period of reconstruction, including the idea of the quality circle.[82] However, the Japanese clearly adapted these concepts to their own cultural conditions.

In recent years, there has been increasing evidence from leading democratic nations in Europe, most notably Sweden and West Germany, linking improved productivity to the shift away from the traditional autocratic and mechanistic model of management and toward a more democratic-participative system. In *People at Work*, the president of Volvo chronicles such a shift in his corporation in recognition that "people don't want to be subservient to machines and systems. They react to inhuman working conditions in very human ways: by job-hopping, absenteeism, apathetic attitudes, antagonism. . . ."[83] He goes on to describe how solutions were devised to combine technological systems with increased human choice and describes the resulting improvement in morale and productivity by utilizing human initiative and intelligence at all levels of operation. Such changes, he points out, are necessary in a democratic society where increased levels of formal education are extended to each rising generation.[84]

It should be recognized that the cooperative tradition is far stronger in Sweden than in the United States and, obviously, a concerted shift toward a System 4 organization will require considerably more time and effort in this country. Moreover, although Sweden and Japan are very different cultures, they both are characterized as having relatively homogeneous populations, whereas the United States is highly heterogeneous. Obviously, a far greater investment in education is necessary in a nation such as ours to develop greater intercultural understanding and cooperation without sacrificing the benefits of cultural diversity.

Although cultural differences must be taken into account in adopting ideas and practices from other nations, a clear trend toward the participative-group system of organization has emerged in the industrial sectors of democratic nations throughout the world. Furthermore, as discussed in the next section of this chapter, many behavioral scientists believe that there are certain motivational needs, such as appreciation, recognition, accomplishment, worth, and so on, that are universal. Autocratic systems tend to play on these needs in subordinating the individual to the superior interests of the group or state. Democratic systems regard self-realization (enabling each person to become all that he or she is capable of being) as consonant with the interests of the group and the wider society.

The Quality Circle and the American School. The demonstrated success of the quality circle in Japanese industry has led some educators to propose that American school systems adopt the quality-circle concept to improve educational productivity.[85] However, in establishing such quality circles in our schools and school systems along the lines of the industrial enterprise, there is the danger that yet another organizational mechanism or operational layer is created in the administrative hierarchy, while existing avenues for effective problem solving through democratic participation are neglected. All of the desirable attributes of the quality circle can be incorporated in the work of the faculty curriculum committee and other faculty–student–administrator committees of the school and school system. The quality circle is an effective approach to enhancing communication and morale to improve worker productivity in a complex and greatly hierarchical system such as that characteristic of the industrial enterprise. But the educative enterprise need not and should not be so hierarchical. Moreover, if teachers are professionals, they must share in the responsibility for decision making and problem solving throughout the school unit and school district. Their work should not be confined only to the classroom in a manner corresponding to the immediate production unit in industry.

Finally, it cannot be overemphasized that educational productivity and industrial productivity do not share the same means and ends. Industry produces products. Education has no end beyond itself but is a process of continual growth and development. Yet it is all too common to find in the literature on education references being made to students as "products" in ways analogous to the products of industry.[86]

The Challenge for Our Schools

The United States has a long tradition of commitment to democratic ideals and practice. However, there has been a considerable lag in applying this commitment to the workplace and the school—despite the fact that some of the leading research on democratic-participative approaches to industrial organizations was conducted in this country, and despite the fact that American pedagogical theory led all other nations in forging democratic ideals for educational practice.[87]

Wirth observes that whereas American industry is beginning to recognize the need to shift away from technocratic management and toward more participative-democratic systems, our schools have continued to suffer from an outmoded production-efficiency model of management as manifested in the emphasis given to competency-based education, accountability, management by objectives, behavior modification, and so on.[88] It is ironic that at a time when American business and industry were coming to recognize the benefits in productivity of the democratic-participative system of organization, our schools continued to be buffeted by criticism and pressure favorable to the old-style, authoritarian, factory mode of production.

Teacher and Student Governance. In pointing to the success of the newly emerging democratic-participative approaches in industry, some educators have advocated that our schools adopt these "new" approaches[89] without taking cognizance of the rich body of literature on American education, stemming back over several decades, in support of democratic-participative schools. Dewey's *Democracry and Education,* published in 1916, laid the theoretical groundwork for such schools and for a vast body of professional literature in education calling for the reorganization of the schools in line with democratic-participative principles for both teachers and students. Dewey had pointed out how our schools suffered from the absence of a social motive for learning while offering little opportunity for individual variation. To Dewey, the antithesis between the social factor and individuality disappears under the conditions of democracy because democracy relies on and fosters independent thinking, initiative, and judicious invention in a context of social responsibility.[90]

In 1942, Caswell noted that while the schools give lip service to democratic ideals, they fail to practice such ideals, and even violate these ideals in connection with organizational arrangements, administrator–teacher relationships, and teacher–pupil relationships. In Caswell's words,

> There can be little doubt that many plans of school government violate elementary principles of democratic procedure. Not infrequently teachers are dominated by principals, and children by teachers. Many plans of grouping and regulating progress violate the principle of equalization of educational opportunity, a fundamental American concept. Often such plans persist in schools in which the curriculum gives great emphasis to democratic ideals and procedures. . . .
>
> Democratic procedures cannot be applied on a mechanical basis but must take into account the ability of various persons to assume responsibility. In the elementary school, children should be guided into participation and decision as rapidly as they are able to assume responsibility for their decisions. . . .
>
> The effort should be to develop types of organization which recognize the principles of democratic action and which foster democratic values. Participation of all members of the school staff should be recognized as essential in the formulation of educational policies, and the individual school should be made the operational unit in program development.[91]

In 1944, Myrdal observed that although no nation compares with the United States in its faith in and support of public education, and in "making real the old democratic principle that the complete educational ladder should be held open," the teacher is not accorded the recognition, status, and rewards comparable to that provided them in other advanced nations.[92] Myrdal went on to point out that "teachers in America have not even been allowed to have as much power over the government of their own schools as they have in comparable countries. Their status as employees is stressed."[93]

Despite the improvement of the conditions for the teacher since the time when Myrdal made his study, one commonly finds in the contemporary literature in educational administration references to the school administrator as representing "management." Caswell's recommendation that teachers, along with administrators, be involved in the formulation of educational policy is yet to gain common acceptance by school boards and administrators.

Shared Participation for Effective Schools. The rediscovery of the great potential for improving organizational effectiveness through democratic-participative environments has led to research studies in recent years similar to those undertaken during the period extending from the 1930s to midcentury, with similar findings.[94] For example, in a recent review of the research on school effectiveness, Mackenzie found that effective schools are characterized by shared consensus on values and goals, cooperative activity in the classroom, total staff involvement with school improvement, and teacher empathy, rapport, and personal interaction with students—along with other factors relating to the creation of a rich and stimulating environment for learning.[95] In reviewing the research on the effects of different goal structures on academic achievement, Johnson and others concluded that "cooperation is superior to interpersonal competition and individualistic efforts in promoting achievement and productivity."[96]

In his study of the American high school, Boyer observed that it is possible for American teenagers to complete their high school education without having engaged in responsible participation in the political life of the school and in social service.[97] Goodlad's study of our elementary and secondary schools, cited earlier, drew similar findings regarding the lack of pupil and teacher involvement in decisions affecting schoolwide policies and practices, and the lack of pupil-initiated learning activities in the classroom. Obviously, if youngsters are to develop the capability of and commitment to democractic social responsibility, a fundamental transformation will be required to make the school and classroom into a more constructive environment for learning and living.

MOTIVATIONAL NEEDS

It has been noted how the conception and function of the human being differ markedly according to the particular system of organization. Under the authoritarian system, motivational needs of the rank-and-file members of the organization may be deemed important if only to manipulate the membership toward the desired behavior. Human imperfections, individuality, and dissent are to be eliminated as much as possible for the sake of efficiency. If these imperfections in human components in the system cannot be corrected or eliminated, people-substitutes are devised wherever practicable.

In sharp contrast, the democratic participative-group system regards motivational needs as necessarily consonant with the success of the system. Constructive dissent and individuality are regarded as necessary to the improvement of conditions. Destructive dissent and individuality are regarded as symptomatic of problems to be diagnosed and solved cooperatively. Where people-substitutes are devised, they are devised to free people to do what people do best. The ideas and suggestions of the organizational membership at all levels are highly valued, constantly elicited, and continuously implemented wherever practicable. From the workers' quality circle in the factory to the faculty curriculum committee in the school district, the implicit message to all members of the relevant groups is that they are regarded as key sources for problem solutions.

Systems of Needs

The motivational needs of the individual are inextricably tied to the social context in which the individual lives and works. This social context encompasses membership in an immediate reference group and extends beyond, informally and formally, to the wider organization and to the society at large. Figure 5–1 is a schematic representation of this extended membership. The democratic group, organization, or social system places a high value on the uniqueness of the individual member because it finds in this uniqueness the source for continual renewal and improvement. At the same time the individual does not function in a vacuum. The individual's motivational needs are developed and exercised in a social context. Hence one cannot exercise individuality without reference to the social context in which it is exercised. In other words, a person's individuality is expressed not in isolation but in how the individual stands out in relation to others.

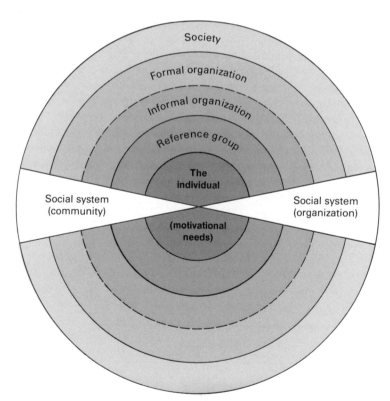

Figure 5–1. The individual as a group member in the organization and society.

Survival and Growth. Many psychologists have sought to shed light on the sources of motivation through the identification of human needs. Over the years, various lists of human needs have been formulated. The late Abraham Maslow proposed that motivation can be explained as a process of seeking to fulfill needs and that these needs, common to all healthy individuals, are in a hierarchical order.

As shown in Figure 5–2, the basic needs in the hierarchy are physiological—the need for food, shelter, and other elements necessary for physical health. Obviously, the need for safety and security are closely related to these physiological needs. The principle underlying Maslow's hierarchical needs system is that the more basic needs remain of greatest potency before the individual can progress to a higher-ordered set of motivational needs.

When the basic survival needs (physiological, safety, and security) are reasonably met, the individual is motivated by the need for love and belonging—affectionate and constructive relationships with other individuals and group membership. The next higher-ordered needs are self-esteem needs—needs that find expression through a sense of adequacy, usefulness, self-confidence, competence, worth, significance, recognition, and prestige. As these needs are met, the individual can be impelled to meet the need for self-actualization—the desire for self-fulfillment, to accomplish all that one is capable of accomplishing, whether as a homemaker, teacher, scientist, artist, athlete, or mechanic. In meeting the need for self-actualization, the individual may proceed toward the need for enlightenment and, eventually, toward meeting aesthetic and creative needs.

Maslow viewed the lower-ordered survival needs as *deficiency* needs, in that at these levels the individual must avoid or remove deficiencies so as to ensure survival. In contrast, self-actualization, enlightenment, and aesthetic-creative

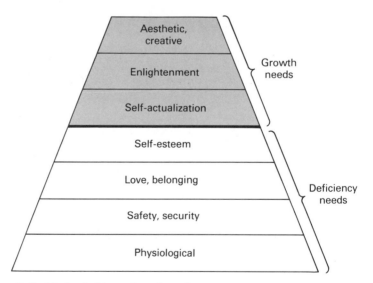

Figure 5–2. Maslow's hierarchy of needs.
[From Abraham Maslow, *Motivation and Personality*, 2nd ed. (New York: Harper & Row, 1970), pp. 35–51.]

needs are regarded as *growth* needs in that they are centered on life problems for which there are no perfect end results or solutions. Maslow held that only a small minority of the population is engaged in seeking to meet *growth* needs. However, this premise is subject to question in view of the evidence, for example, that the cave man engaged in aesthetic activity through the drawing of wildlife forms, or that the child's need to know and understand cannot be sharply demarcated from the quest toward enlightenment. In this sense, beyond the meeting of basic biological needs, Maslow's hierarchy of growth needs might be better portrayed as an upward spiral in which the various growth needs are interactive at ever-widening and deepening levels. Hence an individual may engage in creative activity as a means of gaining recognition and developing a stronger sense of worth and prestige in the human group or in society.

Cronbach sees the sources of motivation important for educational purposes as stemming from the need for affection, for secure relations with authority, for peer approval, for autonomy, and for competence and self-respect.[98] Assuming that the basic physiological and safety needs are met, the higher-ordered needs as identified by Cronbach bear a considerable resemblance to Maslow's list of needs.

Cronbach's List	*Maslow's List*
Affection	Love and belonging
Secure relations with authority	Security, belonging
Peer approval	Belonging, esteem
Autonomy	Self-actualization
Competence and self-respect	Self-esteem, enlightenment

Nevertheless, although Cronbach's list of needs bears a close relationship to the needs identified by Maslow, Cronbach goes beyond Maslow's humanistic psychology in favor of cognitive-developmental psychology. Although both are holistic psychologies, the latter focuses strongly on the active intellectual functioning of human beings in their capacity to utilize intelligence for illuminating and controlling experience and solving pervading problems.[99] This does not mean that cognitive-developmental psychology neglects the affective processes (attitudes, emotions, etc.), for any experience involving intelligence also engages the affective processes. Cognitive-developmental psychology also gives central importance to cognitive functioning in relation to biological development. The tradition on which cognitive-developmental psychology is based goes back to Dewey.[100]

Other cognitive psychologists have examined the various motivational needs in connection with educational settings and under the rubric of *achievement motivation*. In this connection, *achievement motivation* is seen as a process of seeking to meet three clusters of needs: (1) the need to know and understand, to formulate and solve problems; (2) the need for ego enhancement, status, self-esteem, and prestige; and (3) the need for affiliation and approval.[101] These three constellations of needs are clearly related to Maslow's and Cronbach's need categories.

Administrators, supervisors, and teachers must recognize that a school based upon the participatory-group system of organization not only must minister to the higher motivational needs of the faculty, but to those of the students. This problem is discussed further in the next section of this chapter.

Motivational Needs and Democratic Social Responsibility

Although one could go on almost indefinitely in comparing and evaluating the lists and classificatory schema of motivational needs as construed by different psychologists, and although there is no agreement on a common classification, the basis for some general agreement on certain major motivational needs is in evidence. The significance of these motivational needs has been addressed by many leading thinkers who are not psychologists. For example, after cautioning that his views on education were being offered from the vantage point of a "partial layman," Einstein pointed to the vital role of the school in taking into account the various motivational needs of learners; but he also cautioned that such needs must be met in the context of democratic social responsibility rather than selfish ambition.

> The aiming of recognition and consideration lies firmly fixed in human nature. With absence of mental stimulus of this kind, human cooperation would be entirely impossible; the desire for the approval of one's fellowman certainly is one of the most important binding powers of society. In this complex of feelings, constructive and destructive forces lie closely together. Desire for approval and recognition is a healthy motive; but the desire to be acknowledged as better, stronger or more intelligent than a fellow being or fellow scholar easily leads to an excessively egoistic psychological adjustment, which may become injurious for the individual and for the community. Therefore the school and the teacher must guard against employing the easy method of creating individual ambition, in order to induce pupils to diligent work.[102]

In seeking to promote academic excellence and high standards, teachers and school administrators, wittingly or unwittingly, may be giving undue emphasis to pitting students against one another. Under such circumstances, the worth of an individual student is raised in the degree to which the worth of his or her fellow students is diminished. The result is that the most productive psychological forces leading to the love of learning and artistlike workmanship are neglected, contended Einstein. The consequence is that society is denied the quality of workmanship that can derive from the enhancement of these productive psychological forces. In the words of Einstein,

> The most important motive for work in the school and in life is the pleasure in work, pleasure in its result and the knowledge of the value of the result to the community. In the awakening and strengthening of these psychological forces in the young man, I see the most important task given by the school. Such a psychological foundation alone leads to a joyous desire for the highest possessions of men, knowledge and artistlike workmanship.
>
> The awakening of these productive psychological powers is certainly less easy than the practice of force or the awakening of individual ambition but is the more valuable for it. The point is to develop the childlike inclination for play and the childlike desire for recognition and to guide the child over to important fields for society; it is that education which in the main is founded upon the

desire for successful activity and acknowledgment. If the school succeeds in working successfully from such points of view, it will be highly honored by the rising generation and the tasks given by the school will be submitted to as a sort of gift. I have known children who preferred schooltime to vacation.[103]

To unleash such powers in the immature learner would require a school climate or environment that is democratic-participative and rich in learning resources. Before the turn of the century, Dewey pointed to the ethical problem in which the school is charged with the preparation of the rising generation for membership in a democratic social order in a medium in which the conditions for such a spirit are lacking. He observed that school success was determined by the learner's capacity to exceed others in the accumulation of a maximum of information and narrow skills. "So thoroughly is this the prevailing atmosphere that for one child to help another in his task has become a school crime," Dewey noted.[104]

Although the schools have changed greatly, such cooperative activities as pupil–pupil tutoring, group projects, panel discussions, and administrative–faculty–pupil consultation on curricular problems and issues of significance to the pupils are not commonly in evidence in the schools of today. Educators who see society in the stereotype of "dog-eat-dog" competition, and who seek to justify coercion and competition as desirable in the school, fail to recognize that our society and its institutions could not exist without the cooperative motive being dominant. In a similar vein, teachers have resisted certain reward mechanisms such as merit pay not only on the ground of possible political favoritism, but because they see the deleterious consequences to morale when the members of a faculty are pitted against one another.

Independent Thinking in a Context of Democratic Social Responsibility. From the above it should not be concluded that the cooperative motive is necessarily realized at the expense of individuality. In a democratic society the two are not antithetical, but complementary. Einstein pointed out that as the productive motivational needs are given expression, the uniqueness of the individual is realized through the highest quality of workmanship and artistry while such work serves one's fellow beings. Accordingly, the aim of the school should be the development of "independently acting and thinking individuals, who, however, see in the service of the community their highest life problem."[105]

Einstein held that the climate of the school in a democracy must be consonant with the principles and ideals of a democracy. Moreover, he recognized that the climate of the school both determines and is determined by the ways in which the motivational needs of pupils and teachers are met; and that it is one thing to exploit these needs through authoritarian and coercive measures, and quite another to seek their realization through means that are consonant with democratic ends. A democracy requires schools that are committed to the development of student abilities to think critically and independently in examining pervasive social problems and issues. However, school administrators and supervisors tend to prefer that the curriculum avoid treatment of controversial questions. And teachers are reluctant to broach such questions in the curriculum because they are likely to be troublesome. The consequence is that many schools not only yield to externally imposed censorship, but to self-censorship on the part of teachers.[106]

The "efficiency" of teaching is more easily demonstrable when the curriculum and teacher-made tests are geared to narrow-minded facts and lower-ordered skills. The memorization–recitation process is safe ground. Administrators seeking to "run a tight ship" will favor such a curriculum.

But a democracy requires citizens who are capable of and committed to open and reflective inquiry into the profound social questions. No thinker gave more attention to this matter than John Dewey, as expressed early in this century in his orchestral work, *Democracy and Education*. To this day, this problem remains of central concern to those who see in the schools the means whereby our society's constant renewal is made possible.

SUMMARY

The school administrator often is portrayed in the literature on school administration as a "manager" or a "school executive" whose role can be likened to that of a manager or executive in business or industry. Various proposals for the reform of public education have been patterned after the production-efficiency model of the corporate sector. Reference is made to students as "products" and school resources and expenditures as "inputs." Gains in efficiency are to be derived from minimizing "inputs" relative to "outputs" as measured by standardized achievement tests. Adventures with performance contracting and statewide minimum-competency testing have failed to produce the promised results because the production-efficiency model is inappropriate to the school and the process of education. Results might be demonstrated by teaching-to-the-test, but such a procedure is miseducative rather than educative. Unlike the industrial enterprise, where success is measured by profits from receiving the most, the schools are expected to give the most. Schools and the process of education are centered on young human beings whose behavior is manifested through motivational needs in complex social situations. Unlike the end product of the industrial enterprise, there is really no end product of education because education must be focused on growth and development—intellectual, affective, and social. The teacher's goal to develop the pupil's continuing interest in learning—the desire to go on learning outside school and after formal schooling is completed—cannot be treated as an end product. Hence central office administrators, principals and those who have the title of supervisor must perceive themselves as educators and educational leaders rather than managers and overseers of a production enterprise. And they must share the wider educational goals of the school system.

Unlike the industrial plant where the properly functioning production line is an established-convergent situation, the educative process must be seen as an emergent situation. But even in the most routine established situations in industry, the human factor often gives rise to unforeseen problems, with the result that established situations become transformed into emergent situations. Human beings tend to resist being treated as mere operating units in a production system. As a consequence, business and industry have tended to move away from the traditional authoritarian system of management and toward the consultative or participative-group system.

When teachers regard supervisors (and administrators) as adversaries, the school and school system become malfunctional. To adopt the machinery of business and industry to schooling by treating teachers as employees and students as raw material is to defeat the educative process, for education is not akin to the manufacture of products or the delivery of services that can be gauged monetarily. But business and industry can benefit from utilizing the educative process as the means for effecting their progressive redirection and renewal.

The unique function of education, whereby the focus is on the growth and development of the learner, requires that teachers be concerned about enlarging the possibilities for the learner's development of the ability and desire for responsible self-direction. Whereas the factory setting requires that operating units function in the most specifiable, predictable, and reliable ways, the educative situation requires that teachers and learners develop the ability to deal intelligently with emergent situations. Unfortunately, many school administrators, supervisors, and teachers tend to construe the classroom situation as an established-convergent situation, as though the success of the educative process is to be determined by the extent to which the learning outcomes can be made perfectly specifiable and predictable. The consequence is that the focus is on facts and narrow skills to be treated as ends rather than as tools for intelligent thought and action in utilizing knowledge for solving emergent problems. Under these circumstances, students are denied the kinds of learning experiences required for responsible self-direction, and external disciplinary controls must constantly be imposed on the students. In the coercive climate, children and adolescents will exercise great ingenuity in devising ways of undermining the system. Wise school administrators, supervisors, and teachers know that they must work with each other and with students along consultative and participative-group lines. They know that their success as educators cannot be measured in short-term results as measured by the learner's demonstrated retention of factual information and narrow skills. They know that education is successful to the extent to which youngsters develop the ability to deal intelligently with emergent-learning situations so as to control the course of experience and develop a continuing interest in and commitment for self-impelled, lifelong learning.

PROBLEMS FOR STUDY AND DISCUSSION

1. In his study of schooling, Goodlad found that teachers "rarely worked together on some school-based issue or problem."[107] Is Goodlad's finding consistent with your own experiences and observations concerning teachers? Students? To what extent, if any, are the teachers in your school cooperatively and systematically engaged in the development and evaluation of the curriculum in general education? In allocating budgetary resources for curriculum improvement? In seeking to improve schoolwide curricular balance and articulation? To what extent, if any, are the supervisors and curriculum directors so engaged?

2. In the same study, Goodlad also found that the most satisfying school climates, as seen by teachers, are those where teachers are engaged in school-wide decisions and problem-solving processes. On the other hand, he found that although many teachers verbalize the importance of students increasingly becoming independent thinkers, inside classrooms the teachers initiated almost everything and students rarely shared in decision making concerning their own education.[108] How do you account for this contradiction? To what extent do the students in your school share in the decision making for curriculum development? What choices do the students have in initiating projects for investigation? Is independent thinking a major focus of the curriculum in your school? To what extent is this in evidence on the teacher-made tests and examinations?

3. Which system of organization is best attuned to the kind of satisfying school climate described above? How would you classify the system of organization as it operates in your school? What are the prevailing conditions that give evidence for such a classification?

4. How are motivational needs of vital significance in seeking to move toward a participative-group system of organization? Why is this transformation necessarily an *educative* process rather than a *training* process?

5. Albert Einstein was quoted in this chapter as having condemned the coercive or authoritarian classroom/school climate. Is it possible to have a participative-group organizational climate for teachers and administrators and an authoritarian climate for students? Explain.

6. How do you account for the fact that whereas corporal punishment has been ruled unconstitutional by the courts in connection with prisoners and the military, the U.S. Supreme Court has ruled that it may be inflicted on school-children?

7. How do you account for the action taken by the Law Enforcement Assistance Administration in banning the use of federal funds for behavior-modification projects in federal prisons, whereas federal funds were continued for behavior-modification projects in schools?

8. It has been pointed out that school administrators tend to regard themselves as school executives, along the lines of the business executive, rather than as educators or educational statesmen. A report issued by the Education Commission of the States refers to the school principal as "the manager of its instructional program" and recommends that business be enlisted to help school systems in training administrators in utilizing effective management techniques.[109] How do you account for this perception of the school administrator? What limitations and problems, if any, do you see resulting from such a perception of the role and function of the school administrator?

9. In 1944, Gunnar Myrdal observed that "teachers in America have not even been allowed to have as much power over the government of their own schools as they have in comparable countries. Their status as employees is stressed."[110] From your own experience, would you conclude that the status of teachers as employees continues to be stressed to this day? Explain.

10. "Of all the recent changes in the landscape of American education, none has been more dramatic and swift than the reappearance of the business sector" writes a college administrator in referring to our public schools. He goes on to observe that "no convention of educators fails to feature speeches and workshops on expanding and strengthening the 'partnership' between business and education," and he concludes that "education's best alternative seems to be to accept and work with business zestfully."[111] From the history of the influence of the business sector on public education, what precautions need to be raised concerning the " 'partnership' between business and education" in matters ranging from educational policymaking to educational administration and practice?

11. Why did performance contracting fail to produce the promised results in our schools?

12. From your own experiences, reconstruct some cases which you would describe as *emergent* situations in contrast to *established* situations in your school. Describe two hypothetical classrooms in which one teacher regards the teaching–learning process as primarily an *emergent* situation, whereas the other teacher regards it as primarily an *established* situation. What are the differences in the treatment of the subject matter? Which situation would you regard as more productive? Why?

13. A leading educator contends that the key road to school improvement is through "educational engineering" by means of which new schooling structures would be designed and tested.[112] Do you see any limitations and dangers in treating education as an "engineering" problem? Explain.

NOTES

1. Raymond E. Callahan, *Education and the Cult of Efficiency* (Chicago: University of Chicago Press, 1962).
2. Daniel Seligman, "The Low Productivity of the Education Industry," *Fortune*, Vol. 58 (October 1958), p. 136.
3. U.S. Office of Education, *OE 100—Highlighting the Process of American Education* (Washington, D.C.: U.S. Government Printing Office, 1967).
4. Leon Lessinger, "Accountability for Results," in Leon M. Lessinger and Ralph W. Tyler (eds.), *Accountability in Education* (Worthington, Ohio: Charles R. Jones, 1971), pp. 8, 10.
5. *The New York Times*, May 15, 1970, p. 9.
6. *The Office of Economic Opportunity Experiment in Educational Performance Contracting,*

Research Report (Columbus, Ohio: Battelle Memorial Institute, 1972); P. Carpenter, *Case Studies in Educational Performance Contracting*, Vol. 2 (Santa Monica, Calif.: Rand Corporation, 1971).

7. See National Commission on Excellence in Education, *A Nation at Risk: The Imperative for Educational Reform* (Washington, D.C.: U.S. Department of Education, 1983); Task Force on Education for Economic Growth, *Action for Excellence* (Denver, Colo.: Education Commission of the States, 1983); National Science Board, *Educating Americans for the 21st Century* (Washington, D.C.: National Science Foundation, 1983).

8. Task Force on Education for Economic Growth, op. cit., pp. 10, 40; Committee for Economic Development, *Investing in Our Children: Business and the Public Schools* (New York: The Committee, 1985).

9. Robert Boguslaw, *The New Utopians: A Study of System Design and Social Change* (Englewood Cliffs, N.J.: Prentice-Hall, 1965), p. 7.

10. B. F. Skinner, *The Technology of Teaching* (New York: Appleton-Century-Crofts, 1968), pp. 5, 10.

11. B. F. Skinner, *Beyond Freedom and Dignity* (New York: Alfred A. Knopf, 1971), p. 177.

12. John Dewey, *Democracy and Education* (New York: Macmillan, 1916), pp. 14–17; *Human Nature and Conduct* (New York: Henry Holt, 1922), pp. 106–107.

13. Ludwig von Bertalanffy, *Robots, Men and Minds: Psychology in the Modern World* (New York: George Braziller, 1967), p. 7.

14. Boguslaw, op. cit., pp. 112–121.

15. Robert Glaser, "Trends and Research Questions in Psychological Research on Learning and Schooling," *Educational Researcher*, Vol. 8, No. 10 (November 1979), p. 12.

16. *The New York Times*, February 7, 1974, p. 12; February 15, 1974, p. 66.

17. Skinner, *Technology of Teaching*, op. cit., p. 56.

18. Boguslaw, op. cit., p. 21.

19. John Dewey, *The Child and the Curriculum* (Chicago: University of Chicago Press, 1902), p. 31.

20. Norman J. Boyan, "Administration of Educational Institutions," in Harold S. Mitzel (ed.), *Encyclopedia of Educational Research*, 5th ed., Vol. 1 (New York: Free Press, 1982), p. 40.

21. Edward J. Meade, Jr., *Accountability and Governance in Public Education* (New York: Ford Foundation, 1968), pp. 6–7.

22. Task Force on Education for Economic Growth, op. cit., p. 40.

23. Theodore F. Sizer, "High School Reform: The Need for Engineering," *Phi Delta Kappan*, Vol. 64 (June 1983), p. 683.

24. Boguslaw, op. cit., pp. 3–4.

25. Herbert A. Simon, *Administrative Behavior*, 3rd ed. (New York: Free Press, 1976), p. xvi.

26. John Dewey, *The School and Society* (Chicago: University of Chicago Press, 1943; originally published 1899).

27. Solomon E. Asch, "Opinions and Social Pressure," *Scientific American*, Vol. 193 (November 1955), pp. 31–35.

28. Ralph K. White and Ronald Lippitt, *Autocracy and Democracy: An Experimental Inquiry* (New York: Harper & Row, 1960).

29. See John Withall and W. W. Lewis, "Social Interaction in the Classroom," in N. L. Gage (ed.), *Handbook of Research on Teaching* (Chicago: Rand McNally, 1963), pp. 696–703.

30. Andrew W. Halpin and Don B. Croft, *The Organizational Climate of Schools* (Washington, D.C.: Cooperative Research Report, U.S. Office of Education, 1962).

31. Wilbur B. Brookover et al., *School Social Systems and Student Achievement* (New York: Praeger, 1979).

32. Joyce L. Epstein and James M. McPartland, "The Concept and Measurement of the Quality of School Life," *American Educational Research Journal*, Vol. 13, No. 1 (1976), pp. 15–30.

33. George G. Stern, "Characteristics of Intellectual Climate in College Environments," *Harvard Educational Review*, Vol. 31 (Winter 1963), pp. 5–41; Robert G. Owens and Carl R. Steinhoff, "Strategies for Improving Inner-City Schools," *Phi Delta Kappan*, Vol. 50 (January 1969), pp. 259–263.

34. Alexander W. Astin and J. L. Holland, "The Environmental Assessment Technique: A Way to Measure College Environments," *Journal of Educational Psychology*, Vol. 52 (1961), pp. 308–316.

35. Carolyn S. Anderson, "The Search for School Climate: A Review of Research," *Review of Educational Research*, Vol. 52 (Fall 1982), pp. 381–382.

36. James W. Trent and Clare Rose, "Teaching Environments" in Robert M. W. Travers (ed.), *Second Handbook of Research on Teaching* (Chicago: Rand McNally, 1973), p. 999.

37. Anderson, op. cit., p. 411.

38. Philip W. Jackson, *Life in Classrooms* (New York: Holt, Rinehart and Winston, 1968), p. vii.

39. John I. Goodlad, *A Place Called School* (New York: McGraw-Hill, 1984).

40. J. F. Eggleston, *The Ecology of the School* (London: Methuen, 1977); Seymour B. Sarason, *The Culture of the School and the Problem of Change*, 2nd ed. (Boston: Allyn and Bacon, 1982); Michael Rutter et al., *Fifteen Thousand Hours: Secondary Schools and Their Effects on Children* (Cambridge, Mass.: Harvard University Press, 1979).

41. Gunnar Myrdal, *Objectivity in Social Research* (New York: Pantheon Books, 1969), p. 10.

42. Anderson, op. cit., pp. 369–370, 379–406.

43. Renato Taguiri, "The Concept of Organizational Climate," in Renato Taguiri and George H. Litwin (eds.), *Organizational Climate: Exploration of a Concept* (Boston: Harvard University, Graduate School of Business Administration, 1968).

44. Roger G. Barker and Paul V. Gump, *High School Size and Student Behavior* (Palo Alto, Calif.: Stanford University Press, 1964).

45. Sarason, op. cit., pp. 103–108.

46. Rensis Likert, *Past and Future Perspectives on System 4* (Ann Arbor, Mich.: Rensis Likert Associates, 1977).

47. David G. Bowers, *Systems of Organization: Management of the Human Resource* (Ann Arbor, Mich.: University of Michigan, 1976), p. 4.

48. See, for example, Clyde M. Campbell (ed.), *Practical Application of Democratic Administration* (New York: Harper & Row, 1952); B. Swan, "A Study of Faculty Staff Reactions to Three Types of Leadership," *Journal of Educational Administration*, Vol. 18 (1980), pp. 283–287.

49. Kurt Lewin and Ronald Lippitt, "Patterns of Aggressive Behavior," in E. E. Maccoby, Thodore M. Newcomb, and E. E. Hartley (eds.), *Readings in Social Psychology* (New York: Holt, Rinehart and Winston, 1958), pp. 496–511.

50. Douglas M. McGregor, *The Human Side of Enterprise* (New York: McGraw-Hill, 1960), pp. 37–57.

51. Chris Argyris, *Management and Organizational Development* (New York: McGraw-Hill, 1971), pp. 1–26.

52. Boguslaw, op. cit., pp. 33–34.
53. *A Place Called School,* op. cit., pp. 259, 279, 306.
54. Ibid., pp. 186–191.
55. Ibid., p. 108.
56. Ibid., pp. 217, 243.
57. Bowers, op. cit., p. 100.
58. Ibid., p. 101.
59. Boguslaw, op. cit., pp. 22–23.
60. McGeorge Bundy, Chairman, Mayor's Advisory Panel on Decentralization of the New York City Schools, *Reconnection for Learning* (New York: Office of the Mayor, 1967), pp. iii, 22.
61. *The New York Times,* April 30, 1983, p. 23.
62. Dewey, op. cit., p. 16.
63. John Dewey, *How We Think,* rev. ed. (Lexington, Mass.: D. C. Heath, 1933), p. 90.
64. John Dewey, "Individuality and Experience," in *Art and Education,* 2nd ed. (Merion, Pa.: Barnes Foundation, 1946), pp. 37–38.
65. Carl Rogers, *Freedom to Learn* (Columbus, Ohio: Charles E. Merrill, 1969).
66. Neil Postman and Charles Weingartner, *Teaching as a Subversive Activity* (New York: Delacorte Press, 1969), pp. 151, 153.
67. John Holt, *How Children Fail* (New York: Dell, 1964), pp. 176–177.
68. Paul Goodman, *New Reformation* (New York: Random House, 1970), pp. 85–86.
69. George Dennison, *The Lives of Children* (New York: Random House, 1969).
70. Arnold J. Rosenberg, "Educational Existentialism and the Sudbury Valley School," *Educational Leadership,* Vol. 30 (February 1973), pp. 479–480.
71. Panel of Youth of the President's Science Advisory Committee, *Youth: Transition to Adulthood* (Chicago: University of Chicago Press, 1974), p. 86.
72. Lickert, op. cit.
73. Joan Woodward, *Industrial Organization* (London: Oxford University Press, 1965); Paul R. Lawrence and Jay W. Lorsch, *Organizations and Environment* (Cambridge, Mass.: Harvard University Press, 1967).
74. Ibid.
75. Lickert, op. cit., pp. 16–72.
76. Simon, op. cit., p. 227.
77. Ibid., p. 226.
78. *The New York Times Survey of Education,* April 25, 1982, p. 51.
79. William Ouchi, *Theory Z: How American Business Can Meet the Japanese Challenge* (Reading, Mass.: Addison-Wesley, 1981).
80. *Forbes,* Vol. 131 (February 28, 1983), pp. 64–65.
81. Robert B. Reich, *The Next American Frontier* (New York: Times Books, 1983); John Simmons and William Mares, *Working Together* (New York: Alfred A. Knopf, 1983); Paul Solman and Thomas Friedman, *Life and Death on the Corporate Battlefield* (New York: Simon & Schuster, 1983).
82. Ouchi, op. cit., p. 264.
83. Pehr G. Gyllenhammar, *People at Work* (Reading, Mass.: Addison-Wesley, 1977), p. 4.
84. Ibid., pp. 21, 68, 159.
85. Larry Chase, "Quality Circles in Education," *Educational Leadership,* Vol. 40 (February 1983), pp. 18–26.
86. Ibid., p. 18.
87. Gunnar Myrdal, *An American Dilemma* (New York: Harper & Row, 1962; originally published in 1944), p. 883.

88. Arthur G. Wirth, "Socio-technical Theory: An Alternative Paradigm for Schools as 'Good Work' Places," *Teachers College Record*, Vol. 82 (Fall 1980), p. 1. See also Arthur G. Wirth, *Productive Work—In Industry and Schools* (Lanham, Md.: University Press of America, 1983).

89. Frank C. Pratzner, "Quality of School Life: Foundations for Improvement," *Educational Researcher*, Vol. 13 (March 1984), p. 24.

90. *Democracy and Education*, op. cit., p. 352.

91. Hollis L. Caswell, *Education in the Elementary School* (New York: American Book, 1942), pp. 65, 308.

92. Gunnar Myrdal, *An American Dilemma*, op. cit., pp. 883, 885.

93. Ibid., p. 885.

94. White and Lippitt, op. cit.

95. Donald E. Mackenzie, "Research for School Improvement: An Appraisal of Some Recent Trends," *Educational Researcher*, Vol. 12 (April 1983), p. 8.

96. Donald W. Johnson, Geoffry Maruyama, Roger Johnson, and Linda Skon, "Effects of Cooperative, Competitive, and Individualistic Goal Structures on Achievement: A Meta-analysis," *Psychological Bulletin*, Vol. 59 (January 1981), p. 56.

97. Ernest L. Boyer, *High School: A Report on Secondary Education in America* (New York: Harper & Row, 1983), p. 209.

98. Lee J. Cronbach, *Educational Psychology*, 3rd ed. (New York: Harcourt Brace Jovanovich, 1977), pp. 185–201.

99. Ibid., p. 31.

100. Dewey, *How We Think*, op. cit.

101. David P. Ausubel and Floyd G. Robinson, *School Learning* (New York: Holt, Rinehart and Winston, 1969), pp. 357–358.

102. Albert Einstein, *Out of My Later Years* (New York: Philosophical Library, 1950), p. 34.

103. Ibid., p. 35. The term *man* (or *men*) as used by Einstein in this passage translated from the German is not in reference to gender, but is derived from the German word *mann*, which means a "human being" or "person." The word *man* in English is derived from the German.

104. *School and Society*, op. cit., pp. 15–16.

105. Einstein, op. cit., p. 32.

106. See various issues of the *Newsletter on Intellectual Freedom*, American Library Association.

107. Goodlad, op. cit., p. 279.

108. Ibid., pp. 109, 259.

109. Task Force on Education for Economic Growth, *Action for Excellence* (Denver, Colo.: Education Commission of the States, 1983), p. 40.

110. Myrdal, *An American Dilemma*, op. cit., p. 885.

111. Michael Timpane, "Business Has Rediscovered the Public Schools," *Phi Delta Kappan*, Vol. 65 (February 1984), pp. 389, 392.

112. Sizer, op. cit.

SELECTED REFERENCES

Boguslaw, Robert. *The New Utopians: A Study of System Design and Social Change.* Englewood Cliffs, N.J.: Prentice-Hall, Inc., 1965.

Bowers, David G. *Systems of Organization.* Ann Arbor, Mich.: The University of Michigan Press, 1976.

Brookover, Wilbur B., et al. *School Social Systems and Student Achievement.* New York: Praeger Publishers, 1979.

Callahan, Raymond E. *Education and the Cult of Efficiency.* Chicago: The University of Chicago Press, 1962.

Committee for Economic Development. *Investing in Our Children: Business and the Public Schools.* New York: The Committee, 1985.

Dewey, John. *The School and Society.* Chicago: The University of Chicago Press, 1899.

———. *Democracy and Education.* New York: Macmillan Publishing Company, 1916.

———. *How We Think,* rev. ed. Lexington, Mass.: D. C. Heath and Company, 1933.

Eggleston, J. F. *The Ecology of the School.* London: Methuen & Company Ltd., 1977.

Gage, N. L. *The Scientific Basis of the Art of Teaching.* New York: Teachers College Press, 1978.

Goodlad, John I. *A Place Called School.* New York: McGraw-Hill Book Company, 1984.

Gyllenhammar, Pehr G. *People at Work.* Reading, Mass.: Addison-Wesley Publishing Company, Inc., 1977.

Herbert, Theodore T. *Dimensions of Organizational Behavior.* New York: Macmillan Publishing Company, 1976.

Jackson, Philip W. *Life in Classrooms.* New York: Holt, Rinehart and Winston, 1968.

Koestler, Arthur. *The Ghost in the Machine.* New York: Macmillan Publishing Company, 1967.

Likert, Rensis. *The Human Organization: Its Management and Value.* New York: McGraw-Hill Book Company, 1967.

Likert, Rensis, and Jane G. Likert. *New Ways of Managing Conflict.* New York: McGraw-Hill Book Company, 1976.

Lindgren, Henry C. *Leadership, Authority, and Power Sharing.* Malabar, Fla.: Robert E. Krieger Publishing Company, 1982.

Martin, Don T., George E. Overholt, and Wayne J. Urban. *Accountability in Education: A Critique.* Princeton, N.J.: Princeton Book Co., Publishers, 1976.

Maslow, Abraham. *Motivation and Personality,* 2nd ed. New York: Harper & Row, Publishers, Inc., 1970.

Myrdal, Gunnar. *An American Dilemma.* New York: Harper & Row, Publishers, Inc., 1962.

National Commission on Excellence in Education. *A Nation at Risk: The Imperative for Educational Reform.* Washington, D.C.: U.S. Department of Education, 1983.

National Science Board. *Educating Americans for the 21st Century.* Washington, D.C.: National Science Foundation, 1983.

National Society for the Study of Education. *Classroom Management,* Seventy-eighth Yearbook, Part II. Chicago: The University of Chicago Press, 1979.

———. *The Psychology of Teaching Methods,* Seventy-fifth Yearbook, Part I. Chicago: The University of Chicago Press, 1976.

Oettinger, Anthony G. *Run Computer, Run: The Mythology of Educational Innovation.* Cambridge, Mass.: Harvard University Press, 1969.

Owens, Robert G. *Organizational Behavior in Education,* 2nd ed. Englewood Cliffs, N.J.: Prentice-Hall, Inc., 1981.

Report of a Special Task Force to the U.S. Secretary of Health, Education, and Welfare. *Work in America.* Cambridge, Mass.: The MIT Press, 1973.

Rutter, Michael, et al. *Fifteen Thousand Hours: Secondary Schools and Their Effects on Children.* Cambridge, Mass.: Harvard University Press, 1979.

Sarason, Seymour B. *The Culture of the School and the Problem of Change,* 2nd ed. Boston: Allyn and Bacon, Inc., 1982.

Simon, Herbert M. *Administrative Behavior,* 3rd ed. New York: The Free Press, 1976.

Simmons, John, and William Mares. *Working Together*. New York: Alfred A. Knopf, Inc., 1983.

Skinner, B. F. *Beyond Freedom and Dignity*. New York: Alfred A. Knopf, Inc., 1971.

———. *The Technology of Teaching*. New York: Appleton-Century-Crofts, 1968.

Stogdill, Ralph M. *Handbook of Leadership: A Survey of Theory and Research*. New York: The Free Press, 1974.

Task Force on Education for Economic Growth. *Action for Excellence*. Denver, Colo.: Education Commission of the States, 1983.

Travers, Robert M. W. (ed.). *Second Handbook of Research on Teaching*. Chicago: Rand McNally & Company, 1973.

von Bertalanffy, Ludwig. *Robots, Men and Minds: Psychology in the Modern World*. New York: George Braziller, Inc., 1967.

White, Ralph K., and Ronald Lippitt. *Autocracy and Democracy: An Experimental Inquiry*. New York: Harper & Row, Publishers, Inc., 1960.

Wirth, Arthur G. *Productive Work—In Industry and Schools*. Lanham, Md.: University Press of America, Inc., 1983.

Wittrock, Merlin C. (ed.). *Handbook of Research on Teaching*, 3rd ed. New York: Macmillan Publishing Company, 1986.

Chapter 6

Models of Supervision

Supervision as inspection is treated in the general literature as an artifact of the past—a function that is no longer tenable or prevalent in the contemporary educational scene. The twentieth century has witnessed notable breakthroughs in understanding human motivation and behavior in various organizational settings, along with efforts to make supervisory practice consonant with democratic ideals. As a result, supervision as inspection justifiably came to be regarded in the professional literature as negativistic and deleterious to effective working relationships.

Yet in viewing the inspection function of supervision as merely an artifact of the past, there is the danger that educators will fail to recognize that many aspects of this allegedly outmoded and discredited function continue to reappear in contemporary times. As discussed in this chapter, the legacy of supervision as inspection is found in the *production* function of supervision, in which the school climate is permeated by an air of authoritative managerial efficiency. In sharp contrast are the other evolving models of supervision, namely clinical supervision and developmental supervision.

SUPERVISION AS PRODUCTION

In the preceding chapter, considerable emphasis was given to the persistent efforts to model the school along the lines of an industrial plant and to treat teachers as employees, with productivity and managerial efficiency being assessed by outputs (i.e., minimum-competency testing, standardized achievement-test scores) in relation to inputs (school expenditures). Some of the misadventures with the production-efficiency approach in schooling were discussed,

170

such as in performance contracting and accountability. It was pointed out that the factory-production model is inapplicable to schooling for the principal reason that this model is designed to function primarily as an established-convergent process, whereas education is primarily an emergent-developmental process. Human beings cannot be likened to raw materials and finished products. Nevertheless, the reductionist production-efficiency model continues to have its advocates who exert considerable influence on the schools, particularly in times of educational retrenchment.

As discussed in the preceding chapter, periodic breakthroughs in the new technology have been accompanied by sweeping claims for making the educative process more efficient by treating it as primarily a technological production problem. Under such circumstances, reductionist prescriptions have been conjured up, particularly by the behaviorists, in demonstrating how to utilize the new technology to manipulate rather than to understand the learner. Unfortunately, many of these efforts have been couched as "scientific" when, in fact, they are based on a narrow empiricism.

Science Misconstrued

Some authors have described scientific supervision as having originated in the scientific-management movement in industry. In this connection, they have linked scientific supervision with faith in the possibility of explaining supervisory, administrative, and teaching behavior through objective, quantitative measures—thereby providing for increased control and regulation of organizational behavior for optimal efficiency.[1] However, they neglect to point out that scientific management turned out to be unscientific in that it was concerned with quantitative measurement to promote production efficiency under established conditions, whereas science is concerned with problem solutions as developed through the formulation and the testing of hypotheses in problem situations (under emergent conditions). In essence, scientific management was scientism in operation and not science.

Teacher Evaluation. Sergiovanni and Starratt contrast two oppositional modes governing the assumptions underlying the teacher-evaluation process, namely the scientific mode and the artistic mode. They proceed to identify the scientific mode with the "technical-rational approach," in which various scales, tests, and other instruments are devised and utilized so as to gain quantitative measures of teacher effectiveness.[2] They portray the scientific mode as being concerned with measuring the extent to which predetermined objectives are being met by the teacher, with the teacher assuming a subordinate role in the process. And they see the scientific mode as being concerned with specifications from a "blueprint" with the focus on quantitative measurement. In contrast, they portray the artistic mode as being concerned with intuition, understanding, and discovering—with the teacher assuming a key role in the process. However, Sergiovanni and Starratt conclude that the present technology of classroom observation and evaluation suffers from a sense of scientism rather than of science, and that our technology of teacher evaluation may be ill-suited to the nature of the educational process. But unfortunately, their analytical scheme for contrasting the "scientific" mode against the "artistic" mode makes a caricature of the former by describing it in terms of scientism, while also setting the two modes in sharp opposition. Moreover, there is nothing inherent in the scientific mode that calls for a subordinate role on the part of the teacher.

Contrary to the view advanced by Sergiovanni and Starratt that the scientific mode is concerned with predetermined outcomes, whereas the artistic mode is open to such phenomena as the hidden curriculum and unanticipated outcomes, the fact is that scientific inquiry involves multiple working hypotheses so as to improve the possibilities for being open to unanticipated events. Moreover, the ability to formulate hypotheses for possible problem solutions requires considerable intuition in a situation in which the outcome is very much in doubt.

Progress Through Problem Solutions. Effective teaching requires artistry. At the same time, if educational progress is to be made, problems must be solved. The effective teacher must be aware of problems and, like the competent practicing physician, must be a good diagnostician of problems. Neither practitioner regards the problems encountered as idiosyncratic or as deriving from sheer happenstance, but draws from the best available knowledge in the profession—the body of research and the body of ethical principles that govern the profession. The practicing physician is not engaged in advancing the science of medicine, but is expected to keep abreast of the pertinent medical research in his or her field and to be an effective diagnostician. As such, the physician is engaged in utilizing the outcomes of scientific inquiry and applying the principles of scientific practice in the diagnosis of medical problems in his or her patients. The fact that the practicing physician is not engaged in advancing medical science per se does not make medical practice unscientific. Although effective teaching depends more on artistry than, say, the practice of medicine, the extent to which teaching is a profession depends on the degree to which practice is based on a systematic body of scientific research—with advances in practice derived from advances in research—coupled with a commitment to a system of ethical principles to guide practice (i.e., the principle of academic freedom).

To reduce teaching merely to artistry and intuition relinquishes the idea that there is a basis for developing a cumulative tradition of research through which the field can advance in knowledge and practice. As Dewey commented, under such conditions the successes of the gifted teacher would extend only to those students who are in personal contact with that individual, and that the knowledge of such a teacher would tend to be born and to die with that person.[3]

Education as a Production Enterprise

Callahan chronicles how school administrators early in this century sought to emulate the mechanisms of scientific management in industry under the assumption that the production-efficiency model for the factory plant is appropriate to the school.[4] The burgeoning testing movement of that era gave credence to the idea that increasing the production efficiency of education was simply a matter of establishing standards and devising the quantitative mechanisms for measuring the extent to which pupils and teachers met these standards.

The emphasis given to such quantitative measurement placed the focus on segmental and microcurricular assessments of learning outcomes. Thus in the Twelfth Yearbook of the National Society for the Study of Education, Franklin Bobbitt could point out how educators "had come to see that it is possible to set up definite standards for the various educational products. The ability to add at a speed of 65 combinations per minute, with an accuracy of 94 percent is as definite a specification as can be set up for any aspect of the work of the steel plant."[5]

The modern legacy of the production model of schooling and scientific management is found in such mechanisms as performance contracting,[6] behavioristic objectives and management by objectives, minimum-competency testing, time-on-task, process-product research, systems analysis, instructional technology, and so on.

Unfortunately, efforts to pattern education in accordance with the scientific-management movement in industry early in this century are often referred to in the literature as the "scientific movement."[7] The consequence is that the term "scientific" has been associated erroneously with the production-efficiency model of schooling and with a narrow empiricism. Accordingly, the ethos of the school as a workplace finds the administrator and supervisor serving hierarchically in a managerial and overseeing capacity, with the teacher serving as a production-line employee.

Behavioristic Objectives and Minimum-Competency Testing

Virtually identical efforts to what Franklin Bobbitt had been promoting early in this century, but on a wider and more intensive scale, were implemented during the 1970s under the banner of accountability as assessed through behavioral (behavioristic) objectives- and statewide minimum-competency testing—which accompanied the back-to-basics movement. For example, a publication of the Michigan Educational Assessment Program listed thousands of behavioristic objectives in mathematics for which students were to be tested, such as the following typical example offered for children in grades 4 to 6:

> Given a division exercise with a single-digit divisor and a two-digit dividend, the learner will:
>
> 1. Make a table of multiples of the divisor with at least 3 entries, and including the multiples just above and below the dividend.
> 2. Choose the largest entry in the table that has a product less than or equal to the dividend.
> 3. Tell which number in the chosen multiplication equation is the quotient.[8]

The schema for such competency testing is based on the assumption that educational outputs can be assessed in terms of discrete, reductionist elements. The educational problem, then, is merely a technological one, and the job of the supervisor and teacher is vastly simplified since they are seen as operating units in an established-convergent production process. However, such "competencies," mechanically expressed, are devoid of meaning beyond the mechanical expression. Consequently, what should be a simple operation to be employed when solving a meaningful problem becomes a mechanical end rather than a means. The numbers do not stand for anything and, consequently, the learner is less likely to utilize the skills conceptually when encountering a real problem in which the skills are required. The same difficulties arise when students are required to memorize the rules of grammar, definitions, and factual information without meaningful application.

Not until the late 1970s and early 1980s was it recognized that such reductionist mechanisms had failed to produce the promised results. In fact, reports from the National Assessment of Educational Progress were revealing that the emphasis given to narrow quantitative skills had resulted in the neglect of the applications and understandings necessary to solve problems. In other words, the focus on lower-level and more easily measured skills appeared to have been made at the expense of reasoning and problem-solving abilities, not to mention the neglect of abilities that are not amenable to quantifiable assessment—such as theme writing.[9] Nevertheless, in each era of education retrenchment, the clarion call is for "back-to-basics" and "efficiency" as determined through simplified quantitative measures of minimal standards.

Teaching as a Technological Process

The notion that teaching is a technological process continues to be promoted in influential quarters. The foremost proponent of this view over several decades has been the behaviorist B. F. Skinner, who maintains that "teaching is simply the arrangement of contingencies of reinforcement" and that "a teaching machine is simply any device which arranges contingencies of reinforcement."[10] By such definition, the teacher is indistinguishable from the teaching machine. For the supervisor, the "people problem" (teachers and pupils) is solved, for the educational process is reduced to mechanism.

The New Media Technology. During the 1950s and 1960s sweeping claims were made for an impending revolutionary breakthrough in educational productivity by means of the new technology and media—a breakthrough comparable to the impact of modern technology on industrial productivity.[11] Initially promoted by the private foundations (particularly Ford, Carnegie, and Kettering), the new media technology came to be financed largely through federal funds with the passage of the National Defense Education Act (NDEA) in 1958 and the Elementary and Secondary Education Act (ESEA) of 1965. However, the promised technological revolution anticipated for the 1960s and 1970s never materialized. The technological legacy of NDEA and ESEA turned out to be the language laboratory, which failed to produce a bilingual generation as promised, and the overhead projector.

Despite the failure of the new technology to live up to its promises, the 1980s witnessed revivified visions of a revolution in educational productivity through the newest technology, namely the microcomputer. Some educators have gone so far as to contend that the electronic revolution will be replacing print media.[12]

Exactly the same prediction had been made by some leading educators during the 1960s and 1970s.[13]

Doubts as to whether such prospects are likely to materialize can be raised not only from past experience, but principally from the questionable premise that teaching and learning are essentially a production process to be solved technologically in a manner similar to the technological production-efficiency model of the industrial enterprise.

Research Reveals Unwarranted Claims. In reviewing the research on learning via the new media, including the computer, Clark concludes that "one might reasonably wonder why media are still advocated for their ability to increase learning when research clearly indicates that such benefits are not forthcoming."[14] A seemingly puzzling aspect of such a finding is that computer-assisted instruction is programmed to provide students with the right answers to questions and problems on which they will be tested later, whereas conventional instruction is not so explicitly directed. In other words, although computer-assisted instruction can be likened to "teaching-to-the-test," the test results do not reveal that this repertoire produces superior results. A possible explanation is that the greater the specification of the material to be learned, the less likely the learner is to utilize the highly specified convergent material in a new or varied situation. Specification has been bought at the expense of variation for interpretation and application. In other words, when encountering situations calling for flexibility in making different applications of skills, concepts, and problem-solving processes, the great emphasis given to specificity may well impede the generality necessary for the transfer of learning. This may also explain the dim results, not to mention the student boredom, in the repetitive and mechanical skill-drill workbook exercises that are so popular with many administrators, supervisors, and teachers because such materials appear to keep students "busy" and "on task."

Pupil Preferences. A research finding that may confound many educators relates to the contrasting media preferences of students of higher and lower ability. Clark points out that higher-ability students prefer more structured and directive methods and media if only because they believe that such approaches will allow them to achieve success with less effort. On the other hand, lower-ability students appear to prefer methods and media that are less structured and more discovery oriented.[15]

There are several possible explanations for this phenomenon. High-ability students often appear satisfied when they know what is explicitly expected of them on the test. In this way they can use their time more easily and "efficiently" in order to get an "A." For example, it is possible for the high-ability student to complete three or four years of a foreign language with an "A" average without having developed any degree of functional fluency in the language. If the teacher-made tests are geared explicitly to mechanical skills and exercises, rather than to developing and assessing functional fluency, the high-ability student more easily knows what is expected and proceeds to demonstrate "mastery" over the explicit mechanical skills and exercises on the test.

Teachers may strive to make their classes more interesting by employing discussion techniques in broaching problems and issues, or by engaging students in knowledge applications and individual and group projects. But if the tests through which grades are largely determined are confined mainly to highly explicit factual information and skills, the higher-ability students understandably may prefer being taught-to-the-test.

On the other hand, lower-achieving students, whose experience has been largely unsuccessful, see little or no "payoff" in such meaningless repertoires. Hence, given the choice, they would prefer the meaningful material.

The key point is that high-ability students would much prefer the more meaningful discovery-oriented methods and media provided that their tests were geared to developing and assessing such learning outcomes. But as long as the tests are focused explicitly on the lower-cognitive skills, they will be satisfied to demonstrate the "mastery" required of the explicit target material because they know what is explicitly required in order to "make an A."

Production Versus Growth

The emerging technical jargon connected with the new instructional technology has impressed lay citizens with the notion that an educational revolution has arrived. And indeed, many professional educators have promoted this notion, particularly those who regard education as primarily a technological-production process. Such terms as *delivery system* (to denote the kinds of instructional modes employed)[16] and *educational engineering* are commonly used in the contemporary educational literature. Theodore Sizer, who regards himself as a humanist, inexplicably sees the needed reforms in secondary education being derived through educational "engineering."[17] A number of studies seeking correlations between teacher classroom behavior and student achievement have been referred to as "process-product studies," as though achievement is merely a "product" of a process known as "instruction."[18]

Such terminology may be suited to factory production or engineering processes in industry, whereas education is concerned not with the manufacture of finished products but with developing the fullest potentials of people so that they are capable of dealing intelligently with unforeseen problems throughout life. Hence education is a process of development, having no end beyond itself.[19] The growth conception of education is anathema to those who regard teaching as a technological process guided by "terminal objectives." In sharp contrast to the technologists, those who see education as growth recognize that the value of education is marked by the extent to which it reveals turning points in the life of the learner and not in the extent to which it leads to end points. Education as growth requires a developmental rather than a production model of supervision. We shall return to this issue later in this chapter.

Time-on-Task

Since the 1970s research studies have been increasingly directed at studying pupil time-on-task. Such endeavors have an uncanny parallel with the time-and-motion studies of American factory workers early in this century in an attempt to raise production efficiency through a system called "scientific management." Despite the worker indignation and hostility resulting from such management, many school administrators of that day were taken by the idea of scientific management for improving educational efficiency through a system of tests and standards for schooling operations.[20]

The recent efforts to study and promote time-on-task in our classrooms ignore the factors that made "scientific management" through time-and-motion studies obsolete in industry, namely that overt physical motions are not central to the principal role of the worker in modern industry, and as a human being who is a member of a social group. The human factor and the quality of the activity are of even more critical significance in the educative process, for reasons discussed in the preceding chapter and in this chapter. Supervisors and teachers need to work together developmentally, because the educative process itself is developmental (concerned with growth).

Quality of Learning Activity. Anyone familiar with classroom activity knows that different teachers vary widely in the proportion of time devoted to instructional activity in contrast to the time taken for miscellaneous routines, organizational details, pupil control, and so on. Nevertheless, the allocated time for instructional activity may not be significantly related to higher achievement simply because the key factor is the *quality* of the learning activity rather than the amount of time devoted to a given lesson.[21] Time-on-task studies have been directed at measuring the amount of time in which students are engaged in specific kinds of instructional activities.

However, as anyone can recollect from his or her own student days, one can be appearing to attend to a lesson while thinking about something else, or one can be looking out the window while thinking about the lesson. Consequently, observed time-on-task may not necessarily relate to achievement.

Academic-Learning Time. Some researchers have developed a measure termed academic-learning time—the amount of time in which the student is engaged in academic activity while exhibiting correct responses—with the finding that this measure is significantly related to higher achievement.[22]

One should not be surprised to find that students who exhibit a high rate of correct responses while devoting a high proportion of classroom time to academic learning will attain higher achievement scores in the specific subject matter than students who spend less time and exhibit a lower rate of correct responses while engaged in the given learning activity. The problem is that researchers engaged in such studies tend to focus on classroom activity and learning outcomes that are most amenable to quantification, while neglecting other important learning processes and outcomes—including collateral learning (i.e., the learner's interest and curiosity for continued self-impelled learning beyond what is required in the classroom). The danger is that practitioners will apply such research in an excessively task-oriented and mechanical way, and at the expense of such human factors as student choice, student exploratory investigation, and student self-direction.

Indeed, the misadventures with the back-to-basics retrenchment of the 1970s, along with the narrow behavioristic objectives formulated for minimum-competency testing, should offer educators a powerful lesson for regarding easy panaceas with skepticism and critical examination. It is all too easy for administrators and supervisors to seize on time-on-task or academic-learning time as an easy panacea for achievement production. The parallel with time-and-motion study ("the first element in the mechanism of scientific management"), which pervaded American industry early in this century, is probably not overdrawn when one considers how vulnerable and gullible educational administrators have been in seizing on simplistic production-efficiency mechanisms for education.[23]

Systematic interviews with students following the observation of their classroom behavior have led researchers to the conclusion that "it is virtually impossible to tell what students are thinking from their behavior" and that "observers' ratings of student engagement (on-task) behavior and off-task behavior were unrelated to students' reports of how much they were paying attention." Yet it has also been pointed out that although the higher-level thinking abilities can be developed through problem-solving approaches in teaching, teachers rarely engage students in the higher-thinking processes.[24] In short, neither time-on-task nor academic-learning time provides any measure of the extent to which teachers and students are engaged in the higher-cognitive processes.

Time on Instruction and Quality of Instruction

In his comprehensive study of schooling, Goodlad acknowledges that he had assumed "in line with recent research, that time alone is an important factor in learning," but he cautions that "we cannot equate time on instruction with quality of instruction."[25] He reported that only a very limited amount of classroom time was devoted to engaging students in writing and reading; and when students were engaged in writing, much of this was confined to workbook exercises, filling in blank spaces, and so on. Moreover, the students' time devoted to writing and reading decreased as they moved from the upper elementary grades to the high school.[26]

After more than a decade of minimum-competency testing and behavioristic objectives, Goodlad's findings should not be so surprising. Extended theme writing on ideas and issues, and the reading of biographies, essays, and other works of nonfiction and fiction, do not readily yield results on minimum-competency tests. Nor do such learning activities comply with the drill-skill repertoire of the back-to-basics mandates to which the schools were subjected during the latest era of educational retrenchment.

The production model of schooling requires easily and readily demonstrable measures (quantitative) of results. Unfortunately, the research on time-on-task and academic-learning time has tended to follow a production model of schooling (process–product) if only because this model is most amenable to quantitative measurement. This is not to imply that quantitative measures for evaluating educational outcomes are of negligible value, but rather that there has been a marked tendency to focus research and practice in recent years on those elements of classroom activity and learning outcomes that are most easily subjected to quantitative assessment, and that this has been done at the expense of higher cognitive learning and affective learning, not to mention teaching and learning as a social process.

SUPERVISION AS PRODUCTION: FURTHER PROBLEMS

Delimited Role of the Teacher

The production model of schooling and supervision, being based on measures that are most easily quantified for demonstrable assessment, tends to yield disappointing results in the long run. Teachers will "teach-to-the-test" if external tests are employed as the main criterion of productivity, and the short-run results may appear to be positive on the surface. But when students are required to make meaningful applications of the material in new situations, they are often at a loss. The equation for solving two unknowns in the algebra problem does not transfer to the chemistry problem. The mechanical skill-drill exercises in grammar and vocabulary do not transfer to the act of writing a report or theme on a critical topic. The factual aspects of the U.S. Constitution have no relationship in the eyes of the student to the application of constitutional principles to contemporary social life.[27]

Teacher as Technician. The production model of schooling and supervision conceives of the teacher as more of a production unit or technician than as a professional enjoying a high degree of autonomy. The options available for the teacher's exercise of judgment and artistry are clearly delimited. The same may apply to the supervisor. Under the circumstances, the teacher tends to regard the supervisor as an inspector whose principal functions are to see to it that the teacher is on task and to evaluate the teacher accordingly.

And as discussed earlier, the role and responsibility of the teacher under the production model of supervision are focused on established-convergent situations. Strategies for dealing with emergent situations are determined by higher authorities, such as the administrator. The production model places a premium on specificity of objectives, means, and outcomes. However, not only is human behavior far from being fully amenable to quantitative specification, but the educated person is one who is capable of coping intelligently with emergent conditions and problems. If the process of education is focused on established-convergent conditions and outcomes, to the neglect of the emergent, and if our conception of the educated person is valid, the process of "education" becomes miseducative. Such a process is more properly described as training rather than education.

Curriculum and Instruction as Separate Realms

In regarding the teacher as a production unit or technician under the rubric of production supervision, the focus is on the improvement of instruction, while the determination and development of the curriculum are left largely to the educational policymakers and subject-matter specialists. State boards of education and local school boards are, of course, empowered to set policy guidelines regarding the studies and credits required of all students, along with the guidelines and standards for various programs—such as vocational education, special education, and so on. These agencies are influenced greatly on matters of curriculum policy by various national commissions on education. However, these agencies do not and cannot assume the responsibility for curricular implementation and articulation. Traditionally, teachers have had a voice in the adoption of textbooks and curriculum packages. However, under the production-supervision model, they have been largely bypassed in connection with the matter of curriculum design, development, and evaluation—not to mention their having a voice concerning curriculum policy. Their role and responsibility have been delimited primarily to the delivery of instruction.

Under these circumstances, a great void is created in that insufficient attention is given to horizontal curriculum articulation (relationships between and among the various studies) and vertical curriculum articulation (relationships within a field of study from grade level to grade level and from the elementary school through the senior high school).

School administrators and directors of curriculum who recognize the need for curriculum articulation find that this cannot be accomplished without the direct involvement of teachers at every level and phase of the process. Production supervision mitigates against this as a result of the delimitation and segmentation of the teacher's professional role and responsibility. The consequence is curricular segmentation and fragmentation.

CLINICAL SUPERVISION

The concept of clinical supervision emerged from Harvard University's Master of Arts in Teaching (M.A.T.) program in conjunction with the Newton, Massachusetts, public schools during the late 1950s. M.A.T. programs were initiated by the Ford Foundation's Fund for the Advancement of Education during the early 1950s. Colleges and universities in various sections of the United States administered the M.A.T. programs in cooperation with school districts, enabling graduates in the liberal arts and sciences to attain certification for teaching by combining graduate studies in teacher education with a paid internship in the schools. The idea for such a program had its origins under the leadership of President Conant at Harvard in 1936, but failed to catch on during a period of economic depression and an oversupply of teachers. Fifth-year programs for certification of secondary school teachers were pioneered after World War II in California, where various colleges and universities organized a graduate year of professional study, combined with supervised teaching or a paid internship in cooperation with local school districts.

The move to bring preservice teacher education to the graduate level has had positive implications for the professionalization of teaching, inasmuch as one of the key criteria which marks a profession from other occupations is that entry to practice entails advanced graduate/professional study that provides a coherent theoretical-research base as a guide for intelligent practice. This is far different from a program designed to meet a teacher shortage by recruiting liberal arts graduates into a fifth-year program to meet existing certification requirements that apply to baccalaureate programs, and when such graduates find that their education in the liberal arts is otherwise inadequate for gainful employment.

In any case, the concept of clinical supervision is no longer confined to the practice-teaching or internship phase of preservice teacher preparation, but has been extended to inservice teacher education. As a relatively recent development, a considerable body of professional literature has been generated on clinical supervision.

The Clinical Professor

In his study on the education of teachers, Conant proposed that the supervision of students in the practice-teaching phase of their preparation be conducted under the direction of the clinical professor whose status would be "analogous to that of a clinical professor in certain medical schools."[28] The clinical professor of education, according to Conant, would be an outstanding teacher who is abreast of all significant developments in the field and who would keep the various disciplinary departments of the university informed of what is required of the practicing teacher. The clinical professor of education would not be expected to conduct research or to publish. He or she might hold a joint appointment with the university and a cooperating school district.

Conant held that this would go far to raise the prestige of the classroom teacher, as well as to improve an essential but poorly supported phase of preservice teacher preparation. He explicitly made the case for the study and practice of education as being analogous to the field of medicine. From his study, Conant reached these two conclusions:

> The first conclusion is that there are certain educational sciences bearing the same relation to the training of teachers that the medical sciences bear to the training of doctors; these sciences are not yet as well developed as their counterparts in a school of medicine, but nevertheless there is a function to be fulfilled by those who may be regarded as intermediaries between the basic social sciences and the future practitioner. The second conclusion is that the induction of the teacher into a classroom through practice teaching should be under the supervision of an experienced school teacher who holds high rank as a university professor. Such a clinical professor, maintaining or renewing his classroom experience, should also be in close touch with the new developments in the educational sciences. . . .[29]

Very few universities and school districts adopted these aspects of Conant's proposals, partly because of the required investment in staff and resources, and partly because the reward system of the university places the supervision of student teachers at a level of low priority.

Perspectives on Teacher Education

Conant called for a team approach in preservice teacher education so that it would be an all-university responsibility. Such approaches had been in operation at a number of colleges and universities, such as in California, more than a decade before Conant undertook his study. For example, during the 1950s at some of the California State Colleges, student teachers and interns were supervised by a general supervisor who held professorial rank in the School of Education and who worked as a team leader with special supervisors who, in turn, held joint rank as professors in the various departments in the arts and sciences and in the School of Education. Included in the team membership was the cooperative supervising teacher in the classroom. However, such programs were sharply curtailed after legislation was passed in California following *Sputnik I* to raise the requirements for academic specialization at the expense of professional education.[30] Professional teacher education had become a scapegoat of the Cold War and space race throughout the nation.

Similar conditions prevailed during the early 1980s, when our schools and programs in teacher education were criticized for the alleged decline of U.S. preeminence in world industrial markets.[31] One of the great contradictions of our time is the penchant of many politicians and academicians to criticize our schools and colleges of education in reaction to alleged crises in national life, while failing to give credit to these same institutions whenever our nation's ventures are successful.

The Emerging Concept and Function of Clinical Supervision

Like the concept of "internship," the term *clinical* is derived from the field of medicine, where it refers to practice based on the actual treatment and observation of patients as distinguished from experimental or laboratory study. However, where clinical medicine is focused on the treatment of ailments within a controlled environment, clinical supervision is conducted in the normal setting of the classroom and school, and involves the gathering of data from direct observation of actual teaching–learning events and conditions with the goal of improving classroom instruction.

Clinical Supervision Defined. Sergiovanni and Starratt define clinical supervision as "an in-class support system designed to deliver [sic] assistance directly to the teacher . . . to bring about changes in classroom operation and teacher behavior."[32] Mosher and Purpel define clinical supervision as "planning for, observation, analysis and treatment of the teacher's classroom performance."[33]

The late Robert Goldhammer, one of the earliest advocates of clinical supervision, regarded it as a process in which the supervisor's foci for analysis are the observational data on classroom teacher behavior, with such data being used as a basis for working with teachers on instructional improvement in a face-to-face relationship. Goldhammer viewed clinical supervision as an analogue of ego counseling rather than of medical treatment. He also contrasted it against supervision conducted from a distance, using supervision in curriculum development as an example.[34] Clinical supervision has also been defined as "that phase of instructional supervision which draws its data from first-hand observation of actual teaching events, and involves face-to-face (and other associated) interaction between the supervisor and the teacher in the analysis of teaching behaviors and activities for instructional improvement."[35]

Morris Cogan, another early advocate of clinical supervision, defines the term as "the rationale and practice designed to improve the teacher's classroom performance," with the principal data being derived "from events of the classroom" for the purpose of improving students' learning "by improving the teacher's classroom behavior." In contrast, he sees general supervision as occurring outside the classroom in connection with such functions as curriculum development and evaluation. Cogan holds that clinical supervision is neither counseling nor therapy, but functions as a professional "colleagueship" between supervisor and teacher.[36]

The Process of Clinical Supervision

Clinical supervision has been variously described as a process or cycle encompassing a number of stages, such as (1) establishing the teacher–supervisor relationship; (2) planning with the teacher (a lesson, series of lessons, or a unit—commonly including specification of outcomes, anticipated instructional problems, materials and methods, learning processes, and provisions for feedback and evaluation); (3) planning the strategy for observation; (4) observing instruction; (5) analyzing the teaching–learning processes; (6) planning the strategy of the supervisor–teacher conference; (7) conducting the supervisor–teacher conference; and (8) renewed planning (for the subsequent lesson or unit, encompassing the changes agreed on in the instructional procedures).[37]

The process described above is systematic but not rigid. In his review of the research on clinical supervision, Cooper noted that the research literature is sparse and that there is no single "style" of clinical supervision, but a variety of approaches which tend to be more democratic than the traditional supervisory process. Cooper also concluded that although the tenets of clinical supervision have gained wide acceptance in the professional literature, clinical supervision is not widely employed.[38]

Clinical Supervision: An Assessment

A number of appealing features obtain to clinical supervision over inspectional supervision and production supervision for those who seek to promote the professional role and responsibility of the classroom teacher—most notably the emphasis given to cooperative planning and collegial working relationships between supervisor and teacher. The focus on actual classroom practice ensures that the process is of practical significance to the teacher.

Nevertheless, the relationship between supervisor and teacher in clinical supervision tends to be more along the lines of a personalized-consultative approach rather than the participative-group system in which schoolwide and districtwide problems are addressed cooperatively and systematically by teachers, supervisors, and administrators. Although aspects of clinical supervision can be conducted in the group setting, the focus is on classroom instruction, while problems and concerns relating to curriculum design, development, and evaluation—along with other problems and concerns of schoolwide import—tend to be relegated to other (higher) levels of supervision and administration. Under such circumstances, clinical supervision becomes another specialized mode or tier of supervision in the supervisory structure and process.

Limitations to the Study of Overt Classroom Behavior. In focusing on the analysis of instructional methodology, clinical supervision relies heavily on observational instruments or schedules for the descriptive classification or categorization of verbal and nonverbal teacher–pupil interaction in the classroom. There has been a great proliferation of instruments for classifying classroom events in quantitative forms.[39] The assumption in clinical supervision is that all significant elements in classroom activity can be identified, described, classified, and analyzed—and that such approaches are sufficient for the improvement of the teaching–learning process.

However, the systematic collection and categorization of readily observable behavior leaves many highly significant aspects of the teaching–learning process undetected, such as inferential approaches. The act of teaching is not so easily divisible. As discussed earlier in this chapter, it is not possible to ascertain what students are thinking from studying their overt behavior in the classroom, and that although the higher-level thinking abilities can be taught, teachers seldom engage students in activities for enhancing such abilities. Consequently, it cannot be assumed that the analysis of teacher–student classroom behavior will lead to desired learning outcomes—such as the enhancement of intellectual curiosity, development of critical thinking, improvement in problem-solving abilities, enhancement of democratic values and processes, and so on.

Relatively few of the instruments for the direct observation of teaching have been developed and employed for research on the higher cognitive outcomes, and it is very rare to find such uses made of these instruments in clinical supervision. Yet if such outcomes are sought, they must become the focus of study on the part of supervisors and teachers, rather than the focus being the study of teacher–student interactions in the classroom. Teaching styles and behaviors in the classroom are not ends but integral means to larger purposes.

Curriculum and Instruction as Separate Realms. The focus given to the analysis of instruction in clinical supervision presupposes that matters pertaining to curriculum design, development, and evaluation are preordained at higher levels. The classroom teacher's main locus of responsibility is on instructional style and the specification of objectives and outcomes in connection with planning and conducting the lesson(s) or unit of teaching. Macrocurricular problems that extend throughout the school or district tend to be regarded as beyond the purview of clinical supervision.

The analysis of teaching via direct observation has become a field of specialized research and scholarship to the extent that it is most often studied apart from learning outcomes and subject matter, with the consequence that some researchers have criticized this field of specialization as "self-serving."[40]

Although clinical supervision may include the assessment of learning outcomes, particularly when such supervision is employed in connection with the process–product model of education, the focus is on the micro level [i.e., specification of objectives and outcomes in connection with the lesson(s) or teaching unit]. Hence the professional role and responsibility of the teacher are de-limited. Macrocurricular problems—such as the design, development, and evaluation of the program in general education—are rarely addressed.

Educational problems cannot be solved by focusing on instruction apart from curriculum. Yet this faulty premise of dualism between curriculum and instruction has been promulgated in inspectional supervision, production supervision, and most recently, in clinical supervision. As a consequence, the responsibility of the teacher under these models of supervision is primarily the delivery of instruction in connection with a curriculum that is predetermined at a higher jurisdictional level.

The need for an aggregate or holistic problem-solving model of supervision, as opposed to a segmental model which divides instruction from curriculum, is discussed later in this chapter in connection with developmental supervision.

A Consultative Approach. In sharp contrast to inspectional supervision and production supervision, which tend to be employed in the more authoritative systems of organization, clinical supervision embraces the consultative approach. Some leading advocates may see clinical supervision as more of a democratic-participative relationship between supervisor and teacher than a consultative relationship. However, as discussed earlier, in clinical supervision the larger curriculum questions are predetermined at higher levels and the locus of responsibility is delimited mainly to classroom instruction. Although clinical supervision can be conducted with groups, the main focus is on the individual teacher in the individual classroom. The mechanisms for the analysis of teacher–student interaction are pretty well predetermined by the supervisor, although they may be modified considerably in consultation with teachers.

An underlying assumption of clinical supervision is that the most effective path to educational improvement is by working with individual teachers on the improvement of classroom instruction. (Inspectional supervision and production supervision also share this premise, though the means employed tend to be authoritative rather than consultative.) However, problems of instruction cannot be solved apart from the wider curriculum and educational problems—such as those relating to the philosophy of the faculty, the kind of psychology to be employed (i.e., cognitive-field psychology versus behaviorism), curriculum articulation, development of a coherent program of general education (along with exploratory, enrichment, and special-interest education), determining and evaluating the longer-term and life-related outcomes of the curriculum, and so on. This would appear to be the most significant shortcoming in clinical supervision as it is described in the literature. Moreover, when the problems, such as those mentioned above, are determined at higher levels of administration and supervision, the function of clinical supervision becomes sharply delimited along with the professional role and responsibility of the classroom teacher.

Some advocates of clinical supervision have described it as an analogue of ego counseling,[41] whereas others see it being concerned with the teacher's classroom behavior, not with the teacher as a person.[42] Although the latter concern cannot be ignored when working with individuals and groups in any educative setting, those who regard clinical supervision as an analogue of ego counseling ignore the fact that it is possible to be successful in such counseling without actually solving the substantive problems that teachers (and students) face.

DEVELOPMENTAL SUPERVISION

The march of improvement is not inevitable, but depends on the capacity and commitment of human beings to engage consciously in self-renewal by solving problems. Progress derives from intelligent action on the environing conditions so as to control and shape these conditions rather than merely conforming to them. The school, as Dewey noted, is a specially designed environment "to insure the continuance of education by organizing the powers that insure growth."[43] In conceiving of education as development, Dewey stressed that the educational process is one of continual reorganization, reconstruction, and transformation of experience in order to add to the meaning of experience so as to increase the ability to direct the course of subsequent experience.[44] The conditions for enhancing such development cannot apply to the student without also applying to the teacher.

Developmental Supervision: A Cooperative Problem-Solving Process

The developmental concept of supervision as a problem-solving process for curriculum improvement was explicated in some detail by the present authors in earlier writings.[45] In a markedly different vein, Glickman has used the developmental concept in supervision to denote different styles of supervisory leadership for the improvement of instruction. He sees the supervisor appropriately employing different leadership styles with different teachers and according to different circumstances.[46] In this contingency approach, supervisors would employ any of three leadership orientations with teachers: namely, directive, collaborative, and nondirective. The directive approach would be used with teachers whose commitment and abstract-thinking ability are low. Conversely, the nondirective approach would be employed when these teacher qualities are high. The collaborative approach would be used under circumstances where these teacher qualities tend to be mixed.

Aside from the questionable assumptions underlying such a contingency approach, there is the developmental question as to how teachers can become independent thinkers with a high level of commitment to their work under the directive (top-down) orientation. Moreover, the nondirective orientation leaves each teacher to work out his or her own style or approach to problems, raising serious doubts as to how common problems are to be addressed. Curricular and other problems extend beyond the individual teacher's classroom, with the result that concerted collaboration is required continuously. A school faculty is more than the sum of individual teachers working in isolation. To function effectively, a faculty must have a joint commitment philosophically and operationally along with an open climate for individual creativity.

An additional difficulty with the contingency approach relates to how the supervisor is to shift from a directive approach with some teachers, to a nondirective approach with others, and a collaborative approach with yet another group, without creating a morale problem with the faculty. Each of the three approaches—directive, nondirective, or collaborative—represents a marked difference in philosophy, work style, and personality orientation. How does the supervisor reconcile these differences in working with a faculty on schoolwide and districtwide problems?

Finally, as discussed in the preceding chapter, in addition to the philosophical consideration that the professionalization of teaching in a free society requires a participatory-group or collaborative approach in administration and supervision, the body of research tends to support such an approach over directive (top-down) and nondirective (laissez-faire) orientations. If teachers are to grow in their professional commitment and capability for solving problems, a growth or developmental model of supervision is required.

Developmental Supervision: A Holistic Model

As depicted in Table 6–1, traditional models of supervision, namely inspectional supervision and production supervision, have treated the teacher as a mere agent or technician for carrying out the preordained goals of a curriculum that has been established by an external authoritative source. The environing conditions for carrying out the externally developed curriculum and mandates for education are regarded as established-convergent rather than emergent. The effectiveness of the teacher is determined by the extent to which the teacher conforms to the established conditions and mandates, along with the extent to which he or she is able to elicit learning outcomes that conform to the externally determined objectives. The consequence is a conception of the learning environment and the learning process as established-convergent rather than emergent.

In developmental supervision, the learning environment of the school and the learning process are regarded as emergent—in recognition that the environing conditions in life are emergent rather than static or established. In the same vein, the curriculum is regarded as emergent, requiring continuous development. Teachers are engaged continuously in curriculum development, working cooperatively with curricularists, supervisors, administrators, and students. Teacher effectiveness is based on the development of the capacity and commitment to solve educational problems and to enhance the growth of the learner as an autonomously thinking, socially responsible member of a free society.

Curriculum and Teaching: The Needed Unity

The notion that teaching or instruction can be improved apart from the curriculum is anathema to developmental supervision. Codified knowledge (subject matter) derives through the processes or methods of inquiry. Consequently, science cannot be studied apart from the modes of scientific inquiry, and art cannot be studied apart from the methods of artistic inquiry and expression.

As discussed in greater detail in Chapter 11, the concept of curriculum has come to be regarded as encompassing much more than the subject matter(s) in the course of study. It includes all of the learning experiences, designed for the learner's growth, under the auspices of the school.

Table 6–1 Contrasting Models of Supervision

Model of Supervision	Controlling Function	Controlling Milieu	Curriculum	Method
Inspection	Monitoring for accountability; improvement of efficiency; maintenance of "standards"; conformance to preordained segmental goals	Established-convergent; segmental; managerial	Established by external authoritative source; neglect of socialization goals; segmental studies; (focus on basic education, fundamental academic subjects, facts, and skills)	Time-on-task; mental discipline; "mastery" of academic subject matter; skill and drill
Production	Accountability; improvement of efficiency (minimal inputs; maximal outputs); raising "standards" as indicated by test scores; performance by segmental objectives and goals	Established-convergent; segmental; process–product; managerial	Established by external authoritative source; neglect of socialization goals; segmental studies; (focus on basic education, fundamental academic studies, facts, and skills)	Behavioristic objectives; time-on-task; academic-learning time; "mastery" of academic subject matter; skill and drill
Clinical	Instructional improvement; enhancement of teacher–pupil interaction in classroom; enhancement of teacher's insight and competence in instructional methodology	Eclectic; observable classroom behavior; segmental; consultative-cooperative	Eclectic; established by external authoritative source; focus on instruction; consideration of socialization goals	Consultative; analysis of teaching (observable classroom behavior)
Developmental	Educational improvement; curriculum improvement; enhancement of teacher's insight and competence in the teaching–learning process; growth in reflective thinking through personal–social problem solving; democratic citizenship; interdependence of goals	Emergent; holistic-interdependent; growth, ecological; cooperative	Developed cooperatively and continuously with teachers, curricularists, supervisors, administrators, and students; interdependence of academic and socialization goals; (comprehensive, interdisciplinary studies focused on ideas, issues, problems, generalizations,	Democratic-participative; problem solving; use of subject matter as means for adding meaning to experience

Because clinical supervision is focused on the improvement of instruction, while leaving the determination and development of the curriculum to other (higher) levels of supervision and/or administration, an artificial divide is created between the "how," the "what," and the "why" of the material to be learned. Dewey put the issue in these words:

> If the how and the what, the psychological and the social, method and subject matter, must interact cooperatively in order to secure good results, a hard and fast distinction between them is fraught with danger. We want a method that will select subject matter that aids psychological development, and we want a subject matter that will secure the use of methods psychologically correct. We cannot begin by dividing the field between the psychology of individual activity and growth and studies of subject matters that are socially desirable, and then expect that at the end in practical operation the two things will balance each other. . . .
>
> When we make a sharp distinction between *what* is learned and *how* we learn it, and assign the determination of the process of learning to psychology and of subject matter to social science, the inevitable outcome is that the reaction of what is studied and learned upon the development of the person learning, upon the tastes, interests, and habits that control his future mental attitudes and responses is overlooked. In that degree the psychological account of the process of personal learning and growth is deficient and distorted. It then deals with a short segment of the learning process instead of with its continuities.[47]

The Educative Process Fragmented. Much of the modern research on instruction has been conducted by educational researchers who have made a specialty of studying instruction apart from subject matter, and even apart from cognitive and affective learning outcomes. As a result, a means–ends dualism has been perpetuated in which subject matter is separated artificially from the processes through which it is generated.

At the same time, the teacher's professional role is diminished. The question of what knowledge is of most worth, and how such knowledge should be transformed into a living curriculum, is to be determined by others at higher levels of the educational enterprise.

The Teacher Must Be an Inquirer. As discussed in greater detail in Chapter 11, one of the great contradictions of the national, discipline-centered, curriculum-reform movement of the 1950s and 1960s was that the curriculum packages were to be "teacher-proof" while the inquiry–discovery mode was to permeate the teaching–learning process. The learner was to become an inquirer, while the teacher was to carry out the instructional task without tampering with the curriculum package.[48] How the learner was to become an inquirer when the teacher was to be regarded as a mere technician simply defied common sense. Yet this contradiction did not appear to bother the scholar-specialists who developed and promoted the new curriculum packages. Eventually, research revealed that teachers differ in their teaching styles and personalities to such an extent that the course content cannot be construed apart from these influences.[49] If teachers are not engaged as inquirers in the process of developing and implementing a curriculum, they cannot be expected to employ the inquiry mode in their teaching.

Moreover, there can be no such thing as a tamperproof curriculum because the teaching–learning process is necessarily emergent. Yet there is a critical difference between misconstruing an externally designed curriculum and deliberately modifying it to suit particular conditions, taking into account the teacher's professional preferences and philosophical outlook.

From the outset, the scholar-specialists who had developed and promoted the new curricula recognized that method (inquiry) is integral to the subject matter. But one of their fatal errors was the failure to recognize the obvious: If students are to become inquirers, teachers must also be inquirers. Other shortcomings, discussed in Chapter 11, were the failure to recognize the need for horizontal curriculum articulation through interdisciplinary approaches, the failure to recognize that the immature learner differs qualitatively from the mature scholar in cognitive style, the failure to relate the subject matter to the life of the learner and to social conditions, and the failure to recognize the importance of linking theoretical knowledge to practical applications.[50]

Continuity and Interdependence. Developmental supervision gives recognition to the necessary and vital continuity and interdependence of all the foregoing factors. It requires an ecological approach to the school and classroom as a learning environment.

Emphasis is given to the interdependence of studies and learning activities that comprise the curriculum. In taking cognizance of our highest social ideals, the central methods are democratic-participative in the processes of problem solving through reflective inquiry. This is in sharp contrast to the segmental approaches characteristic of other models of supervision.

Science Versus Scientism

At the beginning of this chapter it was pointed out how "scientific supervision" has been inaccurately characterized as scientific when it is concerned principally, if not solely, with narrow quantitative measurements of teacher effectiveness by assessing the extent to which teachers and learners meet predetermined objectives or specifications.

The penchant for quantification which has pervaded educational research, and indeed social-science research, since midcentury has left many people with the notion that such endeavors are in the scientific mode. However, galloping empiricism is not science; it is scientism. Systematic knowledge and generalizations having wide applicability in explaining human behavior do not derive simply from amassing statistical data.

Unmasking Valuations. The researcher must be governed by a quest to find solutions to significant problems through the testing of multiple working hypotheses. The researcher must expose the valuations underlying the research, must design the investigation so as to examine the different sides of the problem, must assess the findings in relation to the existing body of knowledge and practice in the field, and must hold the findings as tentative until they can be verified in the research community and in practical application.

As Myrdal has observed, statistical data are often used to mask the researcher's valuations, to convey the impression of scientific objectivity, with the consequence being systematic bias in the research—not to mention the concealment of the poverty of ideas governing the research. In educational research, as in social-science research, elaborate attempts are often made to employ statistical treatments so as to "objectify" what in reality cannot simply be objective.[51]

This does not mean that statistical treatment is of little value in seeking to understand human behavior and the teaching–learning process. Indeed, one cannot conduct an experiment, or make a wide-scale survey of prevailing conditions or of public opinion, without resorting to statistical treatments. The point is that statistical measures do not necessarily make a given investigation "objective" or "scientific." A scientific outlook is required, and this entails an abiding quest for solutions to problems of significance in the real world of education, the protection against bias in research by exposing valuations underlying the research, and the testing of different sides of the problem through multiple working hypotheses.

Scientific Outlook. Developmental supervision requires such a scientific outlook. It requires that practice be based on the best available evidence—and that when such evidence is not complete, it is held tentative pending further investigation and validation. It requires that the research from a single value-laden perspective, such as behaviorism, must be contrasted against the value premises and research undergirding other schools of psychology so that the practitioner (supervisor, teacher, counselor, and administrator) can exercise intelligent choices in linking theory and research to the improvement of practice. Otherwise, educators will tend to move as a flock in adopting and discarding given practices according to whatever happens to be the dominant vogue at a particular time. Moreover, the choices made require a philosophical outlook. The educator taking the scientific outlook will make very different choices than the one who simply seeks to follow the tide or the one who is wedded to some narrow and intractable school of thought. If supervisors are seeking guidance from the research literature in finding possible solutions to substantive problems, they will be more apt to select discriminately from the research literature.

DEVELOPMENTAL SUPERVISION: TEACHING AS A SCIENTIFICALLY BASED ART

The scientific outlook in developmental supervision does not negate the artistic aspect of teaching. As discussed earlier, it recognizes that the act of teaching (and learning) is a highly emergent and personal one. It recognizes the limits of quantitative measurement as well as the conditions under which such measurement is appropriate and even indispensable for solving problems. It recognizes that many aspects of the teaching–learning process cannot be objectified, though they can be described and portrayed under naturalistic or ecological conditions. To hold that the artistic side of teaching is beyond the pale of study and description would mean that such teaching dies with the individual teacher.

Fortunately, the artistry in teaching, like the creative act in science, is passed on both implicitly and explicitly, in spirit and substance, to those who are affected by it and to those who seek to understand and benefit from it. Moreover, it is not something that is simply to be copied, but must undergo transformation if it is to transform the existing problem condition and, thereby, to bring about greater understanding and improvement of present practices.

Like Conant, Gage draws an analogy between the practice of medicine and teaching. "In medicine," Gage comments, "where the scientific basis is unquestionable, the artistic elements also abound. In teaching, where the artistic elements are unquestionable, a scientific base can also be developed."[52] Neither Conant nor Gage sees medicine or teaching as sciences per se, but both regard these professions as necessarily scientifically based.[53]

Social Aspect of Teaching

Of course, the complexity of teaching is vastly compounded because it is conducted mainly in a social or group setting and, as such, has powerful social bearings. From the time the child enters kindergarten, the child experiences the give-and-take of political education and socialization. The child is brought into contact with a more cosmopolitan social group of peers than otherwise possible in the home, family, or neighborhood. This is one of the reasons why every civilized society requires systematic education of its young through schooling.

The task of the school is not merely acculturation of the young in conforming to established conditions, or merely the transmission of knowledge, but to provide the kind of education that will enable the rising generation to make the future better than the present. This requires the transformation of knowledge into working power. Teachers are expected to be key figures in this transformation, which requires that they make the best possible use of scientific knowledge in the practice of their artistry. As Gage observes, "using the science to achieve practical ends requires artistry."[54]

The Qualitative–Quantitative Dualism in Educational Research: An Untenable Conflict

The excessive concern for analyzing the act of teaching through quantitative measures has impelled some scholars to make the case for qualitative research in contrast to quantitative research. In presenting art as an archetype of qualitative expression, Eisner holds that the processes of connoisseurship and criticism utilized in the evaluation of art forms be applied to the evaluation of teaching, and that the artistic and scientific approaches to research are so essentially different that they have no common bases in the criteria for appraisal, points of focus, sources of data, basis of knowing, forms of representation, and so on. Each mode lives by its own sets of ground rules.[55]

This proposition has provoked considerable debate. Phillips raises this objection to the conception of a dualistic belief system for educational research:

> Eisner suggests that so long as members of a group of believers maintain their agreement, and so long as they can point (to their own satisfaction) to things that

they would count as instantiating their theories, the views they hold are true, for them. This is an extremely tolerant position: Nazis, flat-earthers, astrologers, paranoiacs, Freudians, Skinnerians, and anyone else who ever believed in a theory, in principle, could satisfy Eisner's criteria. But belief systems that can be accredited so cheaply are worth very little.[56]

Miles and Huberman observe that although it is contended that the two perspectives are irreconcilable, few working researchers are not actually blending the two perspectives.[57]

Need for a Coherent Outlook

The problem of setting up two totally separated and insulated perspectives for educational research (qualitative/quantitative) is that this mitigates against an intellectually and operationally coherent system or outlook. There is no question that much educational research has neglected many of the most significant problems because they do not easily lend themselves to quantitative treatment. The consequence is that the focus of research tends to move toward measuring the less important by-products of education. This also applies to the supervisor in evaluating the work of the teacher.

Early in this century, Dewey warned educators against focusing their energies on measuring those by-products of education that are most amenable to quantitative measurement, in the absence of an intellectually coherent system or outlook. "If he [the educator] can organize his qualitative processes and results into some connected intellectual form," wrote Dewey in 1928, "he is really advancing scientific method much more than if, ignoring what is actually most important, he devotes his energies to such unimportant by-products as may now be measured."[58]

Here Dewey was not setting up a dualism between qualitative and quantitative research; between artistic and scientific modes of inquiry. Nor was he holding that any one mode is superior to the other. His contention was that educational research must be conceived from a coherent and systematic framework of guiding ideas if it is to be scientifically based. In Dewey's words,

> the lack of an intellectually coherent and inclusive system is a positive warning against attributing scientific value to results merely because they are reached by means of recognized techniques borrowed from sciences already established and are being stated in quantitative formulae. Quantity is not even the fundamental idea of mathematics.[59]

Dewey illustrated this problem in criticizing the psychological research conducted "in the name of science," which focuses on the quantitative mechanisms of skill acquisition, such as in the teaching of reading, apart from the social conditions and needs bearing on the application of such skills. The consequence is that the ideas, attitudes, and interests that govern how such skills are used in life are ignored.[60] One does not necessarily develop an inquiring attitude and commitment to reading for enlightenment merely through acquisition of mechanical skills in reading. The teaching of reading, or any other subject, must be conducted not merely as skill acquisition, but in terms of developing social power and insight. Similarly, the supervisor must work collaboratively with the teacher in developing insight into problems so that solutions may be developed. Merely to concentrate the supervisory process on the teacher's skill acquisition and the imposition of instructional techniques is to treat the teacher as a technician.

Uniform Recipes Versus Problem Solving. Dewey pointed out that education was still in transition from an empirical to a scientific status, and that there is great danger of taking the empirical form as scientific. The former is concerned with uniformity and the identification of teaching ability with immediately demonstrated results—success being determined by correctness of responses to assigned lessons, test scores, workbook exercises, and so on. Under such circumstances, teachers seek recipes and school administrators seek to demonstrate that they are responsive to whatever external pressures happen to be dominant at a given time.[61] In contradistinction to such a narrow empiricism, "command of scientific methods," wrote Dewey, "liberates individuals; it enables them to see new problems, devise new procedures, and, in general, makes for diversification rather than for set uniformity."[62]

The Necessary Complementarity. The danger of attributing quantitative measures to science and qualitative measures to art is to make antagonists of science and art, of quantitative research and qualitative research. The necessary interdependence between the technical and the artistic may find expression in the widest range of human endeavors—from preparing an outstanding meal, to exhibiting pride in workmanship in the various crafts and trades; from designing a bridge, to designing a machine tool; from designing a park, to designing a house; from planning a garden, to cultivating vineyards and producing wine; from diagnosing and treating a medical ailment, to nursing a patient back to good health; and so on. As Bronowski commented, "It has been one of the most destructive modern prejudices that art and science are different and somehow incompatible interests."[63]

When the artistic is divorced from the scientific and technical, from the wider bearings of life, then art becomes pure aestheticism—something to be appreciated by the connoisseur and to be collected in museums. The danger of a self-serving aestheticism applies to all fields of knowledge. A great mathematician, the late John von Neumann, warned of the "danger of degeneration" of puristic mathematics as it becomes further and further removed from reality as the source of ideas that "it becomes more and more pure aestheticizing, more and more purely *l'art pour l'art.*"[64] At the same time, when the technical is regarded as merely technical or mechanical, it becomes imitative and routine; it loses the possibilities for creative change, for creative problem solutions.

In holding that "the paradigmatic use of qualitative inquiry is found in the arts," Eisner proposes that the act of teaching be studied by describing and interpreting it holistically through the methods of connoisseurship and criticism in the arts.[65] But his examples of such study are not far different from the case study, except that they allow the observer considerable license in imposing his or her own views on the situation under observation.

In medicine, the case history is not regarded as qualitative or artistic method apart from scientific method. In the same vein, it is unproductive to divide educational research into two distinctively different and competing realms, namely quantitative research and qualitative or interpretive [sic] research, as some would advocate.[66]

Statistical research is not merely quantitative, but is based on the testing of qualitative ideas (i.e., guiding hypotheses, the search for trends, etc.), and the results must be interpreted if they are to draw any meaning in connection with the existing body of research and practical application. Taken together with other kinds of research, such as the case study, insights into problems can be gained in fuller dimensions. The various approaches should be treated in their interdependence rather than in their separation and antagonism. Thus the case study is not merely criticism or connoisseurship; it is not esoteric. It is scientifically based. The case method is a most promising but underutilized technique in educational supervision. It provides for a dimension of study which, taken together with other methods of study, reveals a more holistic understanding of the educational situation or problem. Taken together, the prospects for a coherent intellectual and operational system or outlook become realized, bringing about significant progress in education.

LEADERSHIP IN EDUCATIONAL SUPERVISION

"Despite the democratic organization of American society with its emphasis upon liberty, equality of opportunity (with a strong leaning in favor of the underdog), and individualism, the idea of leadership pervades American thought and collective action," observed Gunnar Myrdal in 1944. Myrdal went on to characterize the American Creed as encompassing two fundamental attributes: the belief in education and the belief in the significance of "leadership" in waging an attack on problems.[67] He also noted that whereas the belief in education is a conscious ideological principle in the American culture, the demand for leadership is not so consciously recognized, for "Americans in general are quite unaware that the leadership idea is a particular characteristic of their culture."[68]

The idea and function of leadership are not widely reflected on by the general public, and although social scientists in the United States have given considerable attention to the study of leadership behavior in various organizational settings, they have tended to neglect why it is that Americans have such an implicit faith in leadership in the absence of a conscious interest in leadership ideology and practice.

The Concept of Leadership

The concept of leadership differs markedly according to the culture; hence it will be defined very differently in an autocratic setting as compared with a democratic one. Burns describes the two opposing concepts of leadership as follows:

> Some describe leadership as leaders making followers do what the leaders want them to do; I define leadership as leaders inducing followers to act for certain goals that represent the values and the motivations—the wants and needs, the

aspirations and expectations—of both *leaders* and *followers*. . . . Leadership, unlike naked power wielding, is thus inseparable from the followers' needs and goals. The essence of the leader-follower relation is the interaction of persons with different levels of motives and of power potential, including skill, in pursuit of a common or at least a joint purpose.[69]

Disraeli put the matter far more succinctly while reversing the leader–follower mindset when he said, "I must follow the people. Am I not their leader?"

Democratic leadership places great faith in the inherent potential of the wider population, the organizational membership, the working group, and the individual member for insight, ingenuity, flexibility, and educability for problem solving. It derives its legitimacy from the consent of the populace, constituency, or membership. Consequently, the relationship is not one of traditional leadership–followership, but is cooperative and participatory. It is incumbent on leadership to ascertain and to represent the best interests of the group, through the consent of the group, in ways that are consonant with the purposes of the wider organizational entity. Obviously, if the culture of the wider organizational entity is largely autocratic, democratic-participatory approaches in any subunit will be disruptive or malfunctional. In the same vein, if the values of the wider cultural entity are democratic, autocratic approaches in any subunit will be disruptive and malfunctional.

The Rise, Decline, and Rediscovery of the Democratic Outlook

The research by Lewin and his associates, established before midcentury what appeared to be the groundwork for democratic educational leadership and administration.[70] By the 1960s, writers in the field of educational leadership and administration had turned away from democratic theory as the major guiding principle and sought to borrow ideas and techniques from sources outside the educational situation, namely from the various behavioral sciences. In making the case in support of this shift, Griffiths and others implied that the theme of democratic administration in the 1946 yearbook of the National Society for the Study of Education was misguided and naive.[71]

There is no question that the behavioral sciences are potentially fertile ground for advancing educational research and improving educational practice. But this requires that the problems under study derive from the educational situation rather than from outside the educational situation, and that the value premises underlying the research be clearly identified.[72] It also requires that the field of inquiry be guided by a breadth of philosophical outlook to serve a regulative function in evaluating the wider implications and consequences of the research. Otherwise, problem solutions and techniques are artificially and externally imposed on our schools in segmental ways, while educational policy and practice are made to shift in accord with the dominant tide of the times.[73]

Undoubtedly, the concept of democratic educational leadership and administration, which reached its height by midcentury, often was applied superficially, or misapplied as laissez-faire leadership, while serving more as a slogan than a guiding principle. Compounding the problem was the failure of investigators in educational leadership and administration to relate the findings to the cultural milieu of the organization. As mentioned earlier, one cannot expect that democratic-participative approaches will work when introduced segmentally in a wider organizational milieu that is predominantly autocratic. Yet such efforts have led investigators to the erroneous conclusion that democratic-participative approaches are not consistently effective.[74]

As long as the basic values of American society as a whole are democratic, the concern for democratic-participative leadership in education will be recurrent. Indeed, it should be continuous. In reviewing the research on the quality of school life in relation to changing demands affecting the quality of work life, Pratzner sees these concerns as integral to a broader movement in society—"a set of individual and social transformations moving toward greater democratization of all of our institutions and greater responsibility and participation of individuals in decisions affecting their lives."[75] Such an observation may be overly optimistic or overdrawn, but the point is that democratic values cannot be held in the society at large without affecting the schools. The interest in democratic-participative leadership may have gone out of fashion in the field of educational administration and supervision over an extended time period, but it cannot be ignored indefinitely as long as the democratic ideal remains alive in the society at large.

Leadership Behavior

During the 1930s and 1940s, hundreds of studies were undertaken unsuccessfully to identify a common pattern of leadership traits.[76] The work of Lewin and his associates turned the study of leadership to styles of behavior, rather than to traits. During the 1950s, leadership behavior was described according to two factors: consideration behavior (interpersonal trust, respect, warmth, and participative communication) and initiation-of-structure behavior (organizing and delineating the work group, channels of communication, and procedures).[77] However, these two dimensions did not reveal consistent relationships with organizational outcomes (productivity, satisfaction, etc.).

Various contingency approaches have been proposed on the ground that no single style is best, and that the particular leadership style to be employed should be determined by the specific situation or environment in which the leadership is to be exercised.[78] Although the contingency approach may appear to be eminently sensible, the implication is that there are educational situations in which the autocratic style of leadership works best. However, this creates an inescapable contradiction, in that any truly *educative* situation in a society that is based on democratic values cannot be true to its mission under autocratic leadership. Autocratic leadership also violates the professional autonomy of the teacher. Consequently, it is incumbent on the educational leader to work with his or her faculty and students toward the creation of the needed environing conditions rather than to adopt a particular leadership style according to the existing environing conditions. Finally, personality factors are such that it is doubtful that an individual would be able to shift from authoritarian to democratic-participative styles of leadership and back again, according to the situational conditions. Also, the educative process implies that the organizational membership and its leaders together have the power and insight to transform rather than to conform to existing conditions when the conditions are found wanting.

SUMMARY

The traditional mode of supervision as inspection came to be rejected as dysfunctional during the early decades of the twentieth century in the light of advances in understanding human motivation and behavior in participatory-work settings, coupled with the growing professionalization of teaching. Nevertheless, the burgeoning interest in the technology of teaching and managerial efficiency since midcentury resulted in powerful efforts from many quarters to recast inspectional supervision into production supervision.

Indicative of the recent thrust toward production supervision is the language used in some of the professional literature which refers to students as "raw material," to school principals as "managers," to educational resources as "inputs," to teaching as an instructional "delivery system," to measures on achievement tests as "outputs," to school graduates as "products," and so on.

Sweeping claims have been and continue to be made for bringing about a revolutionary transformation of education by utilizing the new technology along with the production-efficiency techniques borrowed from the corporate sector. However, efforts to improve educational efficiency by treating schooling as primarily a technological production process have met with disappointing results, principally because the human equation is the key factor in the teaching–learning process. A free society values individual autonomy in the context of democratic social responsibility. The necessary condition for this is the exercise of intelligent choices by teachers and learners under emergent conditions, in contrast to the established-convergent conditions of the factory assembly line.

Production supervision erroneously has been referred to as "scientific" supervision, principally because many of the tenets underlying production supervision are drawn from the scientific-management movement in American industry early in this century. In both cases the term "scientific" was used to denote methods of explaining administrative, supervisory, and worker (teacher) behavior through objective-quantitative measures so as to bring about increased control and productive efficiency of the organization. But science is concerned with finding solutions to problems under emergent conditions, and this requires investigation through guiding hypotheses. The mode is hypothetical inquiry, not narrow empiricism. Both scientific management and production supervision are better described as scientism because they embrace a narrow empiricism and conceive of the human organization as primarily a production unit in an established-convergent process.

The emergence of clinical supervision since midcentury provided for systematic work on instructional improvement in the classroom through a face-to-face working relationship beween the supervisor and the teacher. The chief data base in clinical supervision is the analysis of the act of teaching through any one of several systems, or combination of systems, of direct observation. The supervisor–teacher relationship in clinical supervision is mainly consultative rather than democratic-group participative.

A serious problem in clinical supervision arises from the premise that all significant elements in the act of teaching can be identified, classified, and analyzed—and that such study of overt teacher–pupil classroom behavior is sufficient for the improvement of the teaching–learning process. This assumption is questionable because the teaching–learning process is not so easily divisible, and many of the most significant aspects of this process may go undetected. Most of the instruments employed in the analysis of teaching are not concerned with learning outcomes, particularly higher cognitive learning and collateral learning (i.e., attitudes toward learning, intellectual curiosity, and critical thinking).

Another serious shortcoming of clinical supervision is its focus on instructional improvement while leaving curriculum development and improvement to a higher level of the administrative–supervisory structure and process. Inspectional supervision and production supervision also share in this shortcoming. The effect is a diminished professional role of the teacher, with the relegation of curriculum determination to the higher policymaking bodies of the school district. The teacher is to deliver instruction in the classroom, while the curriculum is to be determined, designed, developed, and evaluated from above. This segmental and hierarchical arrangement also derives from the dualistic assumption that curriculum and instruction are separate realms of activity. The separation of what is to be learned from how it is to be learned, and why it is to be learned, is dysfunctional. Subject matter is not merely an assemblage of factual information and skills embodied in a textbook or course of study, but represents the ways through which a field of knowledge is developed, understood, and utilized. Moreover, if the curriculum is to be functional—such as in serving such functions as general education, exploratory education, enrichment education, and even specialized education—the interrelationships of the various subjects must be revealed to the learner and related to life experience. This requires a holistic model of curriculum and supervision.

Academicians have been debating the relative merits of quantitative versus qualitative research on teaching. In some quarters, the former is described as scientific and the latter as artistic. What is overlooked by both sides is that quantitative data in science are derived from and represent qualitative ideas. Teaching requires artistry. But if teaching is strictly an individual-artistic matter, the individual artistry will die with the retirement or death of the individual teacher.

The process of inquiry into significant problems with a view toward effecting needed solutions requires cumulative use of the best available evidence. It requires hypothetical thinking so as to shed light on the unknown. Problem solving in science requires artistry as well as technical competence. By regarding teaching as a scientifically based art, our knowledge of teaching can be advanced and communicated. The dualism between art and science is resolved.

Developmental supervision gives recognition to the teacher as a problem solver. It gives recognition to the need for the teacher to be an inquirer if the learner is to become an inquirer. It rejects the conception of the teacher as merely an agent for the delivery of instruction in carrying out the preordained goals of a curriculum established by an external source of authority. The teacher as a professional educator works continually with curricularists, supervisors, and administrators on curriculum improvement (which encompasses the improvement of teaching). The working relationships are democratic-participatory. Developmental supervision resolves the dualism between curriculum and instruction, between the quantitative and qualitative study of teaching, between the activity of teaching and the activity of learning.

A fundamental premise of developmental supervision is that education is a process of growth rather than a process leading to end products. In a free society, education must be regarded as a process through which the learner grows in the capacity to add meaning to experience and thereby to direct the course of ensuing experience with intelligence. In this sense, the individual gains in power and insight in controlling his or her own destiny. This applies not only to the student, but to the teacher as a learner.

Developmental supervision requires the recognition of the necessary interdependence between curriculum and teaching, subject matter and method, the theoretical and practical, the cognitive and affective, skills and ideas, the qualitative and the quantitative. Problems in the real world of education do not exist in isolation and cannot be solved when theoretical dualisms are allowed to become operational antagonisms. The case is not, for example, subject-centeredness versus child-centeredness, but a reconstruction of the situation in which the curriculum is consonant with the nature of the learner, taking account of the social situation in the light of the highest ideals of a free society.

PROBLEMS FOR STUDY AND DISCUSSION

1. Drawing from the contrasting models of supervision presented in Table 6–1, how would you describe the approach followed in your own school or school system—taking into account such factors as controlling function and milieu, curriculum development, and methods employed? Explain. In your view, what changes are required to provide for a more effective program of supervision in your school or school system?

2. Do you see any limitations and dangers in treating teaching as a technological process? Education as a production process? Explain. How do you account for the great emphasis given to education as a production process and to process–product research in teaching and learning? How does this conflict with the conception of education as *growth* in terms of theory and practice?

3. In reviewing the research on learning through various media, a researcher concludes that higher-ability students tend to prefer more directive methods and media of instruction, whereas lower-ability students tend to prefer methods and media that are more discovery oriented.[79] How do you account for such findings? What are the implications, as you see them, for the needed teaching approaches with learners of different levels of ability and achievement?

4. In 1929, Dewey leveled the following criticism at educators who would seek to reduce teaching to those techniques and outcomes that are most easily and uniformly subjected to demonstrable assessment:

In this situation there is a strong tendency to identify teaching ability with the use of procedures that yield immediately successful results . . . correct recitations by pupils in assigned lessons, passing of examinations, etc.

For the most part, these are the standards by which a community judges the worth of a teacher. Prospective teachers come to colleges with such ideas implicit in their minds. They want very largely to find out *how to do* things with the maximum of success. Put baldly, they want recipes.[80]

Do you believe that Dewey's criticism is relevant to the contemporary scene? Does this criticism apply to the mass media, school administrators, and supervisors? Explain. Why is the process of education not amenable to instant recipes?

5. How would a problem-solving approach, under the rubric of developmental supervision, serve to overcome the penchant for teachers, supervisors, and administrators to seek instant recipes and to follow the tides of fad, fashion, and external pressures?

6. Advocates of clinical supervision regard it as being focused on the improvement of classroom instruction, whereas curriculum development is a matter to be dealt with at higher levels of the administrative and supervisory structure of the school system. Is this hierarchical and operational division between curriculum and instruction tenable? Why or why not? How do you account for the tendency in the professional literature to treat curriculum and instruction as separate domains of specialization? Do you agree with Dewey's warning that "if the how and the what, the psychological and the social, method and subject matter, must interact cooperatively in order to secure good results, a hard and fast distinction between them is fraught with danger"?[81]

7. Comprise a list of what you consider to be the most significant problems faced by teachers in classrooms and schools—problems that teachers and supervisors must work on together for solution. As a teacher, on what problems, if any, have you sought the assistance of your supervisor and/or principal? What were the results? Would you say that teachers generally are reluctant to take the initiative in calling on supervisors and principals for help with problems? Explain. If you are a supervisor or administrator, on what problems, if any, have teachers taken the initiative in seeking your assistance? What actions were taken and what were the results?

8. What limitations do you see in the study of overt classroom behavior? What kinds of significant learning outcomes and problems may be overlooked under such study?

9. Why is "scientific supervision," as described in the professional literature, a misnomer?

10. Do you agree with the view that instead of setting the artistic side of teaching in opposition to efforts to develop a scientific basis for teaching, we need to work on a scientific basis for the art of teaching? Explain.

NOTES

1. Ralph L. Mosher and David E. Purpel, *Supervision: The Reluctant Profession* (Boston: Houghton Mifflin, 1972), p. 15; William H. Lucio and John D. McNeil, *Supervision in Thought and Action,* 3rd ed. (New York: McGraw-Hill, 1979), pp. 7–10.

2. Thomas J. Sergiovanni and Robert J. Starratt, *Supervision: Human Perspectives,* 3rd ed. (New York: McGraw-Hill, 1983), pp. 296–298.

3. John Dewey, *The Sources of a Science of Education* (New York: Liveright, 1929), p. 10.

4. Raymond E. Callahan, *Education and the Cult of Efficiency* (Chicago: University of Chicago Press, 1962).

5. Franklin Bobbitt, "Some General Principles of Management Applied to the Problems of City-School Systems," in National Society for the Study of Education, *The Supervision of City Schools,* Twelfth Yearbook, Part I (Bloomington, Ill.: Public School Publishing Co., 1913), p. 15.

6. Daniel Tanner, "Performance Contracting: Contrivance of the Industrial–Governmental–Educational Complex," *Intellect,* Vol. 101 (March 1973), pp. 361–365.

7. Lucio and McNeil, op. cit., p. 9.

8. Michigan Department of Education, *Minimal Performance Objectives for Mathematics Education in Michigan* (Lansing, Mich.: The Department, 1973), p. 34.

9. National Assessment of Educational Progress, *NAEP Newsletter,* Vol. 12 (October 1979), pp. 1–2; Vol. 16 (Winter 1983), pp. 1–5.

10. B. F. Skinner, *The Technology of Teaching* (New York: Appleton-Century-Crofts, 1968), pp. 5, 64.

11. Charles E. Silberman, "Technology Is Knocking on the Schoolhouse Door," *Fortune,* Vol. 74 (August 1966), pp. 120–128.

12. *TC Today,* Vol. 10 (Fall 1981), p. 4.

13. John I. Goodlad, *The Future of Learning and Teaching* (Washington, D.C.: National Education Association, 1968), pp. 22–23; Neil Postman and Charles Weingartner, *The School Book* (New York: Delacorte Press, 1973), pp. 88–89.

14. Richard E. Clark, "Reconsidering Research on Learning from Media," *Review of Educational Research,* Vol. 53 (Winter 1983), p. 456.

15. Ibid., p. 455.

16. Leslie J. Briggs, "System Design in Instruction," in Harold E. Mitzel (ed.), *Encyclopedia of Educational Research,* Vol. 4, 5th ed. (New York: Free Press, 1982), p. 1852.

17. Theodore R. Sizer, "High School Reform: The Need for Engineering," *Phi Delta Kappan,* Vol. 64 (June 1983), pp. 679–688.

18. Jere Brophy and Thomas L. Good, "Teacher Behavior and Student Achievement," Chapter 12 in Merlin C. Wittrock (ed.), *Handbook of Research on Teaching,* 3rd ed. (New York: Macmillan, 1986), pp. 328–355.

19. John Dewey, *Democracy and Education* (New York: Macmillan, 1916), p. 59.

20. Callahan, op. cit., pp. 39–94.

21. Michael Rutter et al., *Fifteen Thousand Hours: Secondary Schools and Their Effects on Children* (Cambridge, Mass.: Harvard University Press, 1979), p. 116.

22. Charles Fisher et al., "Improving Teaching by Increasing 'Academic Learning Time,'" *Educational Leadership,* Vol. 37 (October 1979), p. 52; Jane Stallings, "Allocated Academic Learning Time Revisited, or Beyond Time on Task," *Educational Researcher,* Vol. 9 (December 1980), pp. 11–16.

23. Callahan, op. cit., p. 28.

24. "Use of Thinking Skills Is the Essence of Ability," *Communication Quarterly,* Vol. 6 (Winter–Spring 1984), p. 3.

25. John Goodlad, *A Place Called School* (New York: McGraw-Hill, 1984), pp. 99, 101.
26. Ibid., pp. 106–107.
27. See Stanley M. Elam, "Anti-democratic Attitudes of High School Seniors in the Orwell Year," *Phi Delta Kappan*, Vol. 65 (January 1984), pp. 327–332.
28. James B. Conant, *The Education of American Teachers* (New York: McGraw-Hill, 1963), p. 143.
29. Ibid., pp. 144–145.
30. Ibid., pp. 24–25.
31. National Commission on Excellence in Education, *A Nation at Risk: The Imperative for Educational Reform* (Washington, D.C.: U.S. Department of Education, 1983), p. 22.
32. Sergiovanni and Starratt, op. cit., pp. 299, 303.
33. Mosher and Purpel, op. cit., p. 78.
34. Robert Goldhammer, *Clinical Supervision* (New York: Holt, Rinehart and Winston, 1969), pp. 53–54.
35. Robert Goldhammer, Robert H. Anderson, and Robert J. Krajewski, *Clinical Supervision*, 2nd ed. (New York: Holt, Rinehart and Winston, 1980), pp. 19–20.
36. Morris L. Cogan, *Clinical Supervision* (Boston: Houghton Mifflin, 1973), pp. 9, 62, 67.
37. Ibid., pp. 10–12.
38. James M. Cooper, "Supervision of Teachers," in Mitzel, op. cit., p. 1828.
39. See Barak Rosenshine and Norma Furst, "The Use of Direct Observation to Study Teaching," Chapter 5 in Robert M. W. Travers (ed.), *Second Handbook of Research on Teaching* (Chicago: Rand McNally, 1973), pp. 122–183.
40. Ibid., p. 122.
41. Goldhammer, op. cit., p. 53.
42. Cogan, op. cit., p. 58.
43. Dewey, *Democracy and Education*, op. cit., pp. 22, 59, 60.
44. Ibid., pp. 89–90.
45. Daniel Tanner and Laurel N. Tanner, *Curriculum Development: Theory into Practice*, 2nd ed. (New York: Macmillan, 1980), pp. 623–685.
46. Carl D. Glickman, *Developmental Supervision* (Alexandria, Va.: Association for Supervision and Curriculum Development, 1981).
47. Dewey, *Sources of a Science of Education*, op. cit., pp. 61–62.
48. William D. Romey, "The Curriculum-Proof Teacher," *Phi Delta Kappan*, Vol. 54 (February 1973), p. 407.
49. James J. Gallagher, "Teacher Variation in Concept Presentation," *BSCS Newsletter*, No. 30 (January 1967), p. 17.
50. Daniel Tanner, "Curriculum History" in Mitzel, op. cit., p. 418.
51. Gunnar Myrdal, *Objectivity in Social Research* (New York: Pantheon Books, 1969), pp. 44, 57, 59.
52. N. L. Gage, *The Scientific Basis of the Art of Teaching* (New York: Teachers College Press, 1978), p. 18.
53. Conant, op. cit., pp. 117–120.
54. Gage, op. cit., p. 18.
55. Elliot W. Eisner, "On the Differences Between Scientific and Artistic Approaches to Qualitative Research," *Educational Researcher*, Vol. 10 (April 1981), pp. 5–9.
56. D. C. Phillips, "After the Wake: Postpositivistic Educational Thought," *Educational Researcher*, Vol. 12 (May 1983), p. 11. See also Kenneth R. Howe, "Two Dogmas of Educational Research," *Educational Researcher*, Vol. 14 (October, 1985), pp. 10–18.
57. Matthew B. Miles and A. Michael Huberman, "Drawing Valid Meaning from Qualitative Data: Toward a Shared Craft," *Educational Researcher*, Vol. 13 (May 1984), p. 20.

58. John Dewey, "Progressive Education and the Science of Education," *Progressive Education*, Vol. 5 (July–September 1928), p. 200.
59. Dewey, *Sources of a Science of Education*, op. cit., p. 27.
60. Ibid., pp. 62–63, 72.
61. Ibid., pp. 14–15.
62. Ibid., p. 12.
63. Jacob Bronowski, *The Common Sense of Science* (Cambridge, Mass.: Harvard University Press, 1978), p. 3.
64. John von Neumann, in R. B. Heywood (ed.), *The Works of the Mind* (Chicago: University of Chicago Press, 1947), p. 196.
65. Elliot Eisner, *The Educational Imagination*, 2nd ed. (New York: Macmillan, 1985), pp. 216–225.
66. John K. Smith, "Quantitative Versus Qualitative Research: An Attempt to Clarify the Issue," *Educational Researcher*, Vol. 12 (March 1983), pp. 6–13.
67. Gunnar Myrdal, *An American Dilemma* (New York: Harper & Row, 1962; originally published in 1944), p. 709.
68. Ibid.
69. James McGregor Burns, *Leadership* (New York: Harper & Row, 1978), p. 19.
70. See for example, National Society for the Study of Education, *Changing Conceptions in Educational Administration*, Forty-fifth Yearbook, Part II (Chicago: University of Chicago Press, 1946); G. Robert Koopman, Alice Miel, and Paul J. Misner, *Democracy in School Administration* (New York: Appleton-Century-Crofts, 1943).
71. Daniel E. Griffiths et al., in National Society for the Study of Education, *Behavioral Science and Educational Administration*, Sixty-third Yearbook, Part II (Chicago: University of Chicago Press, 1964), p. 1.
72. Myrdal, *Objectivity in Social Research*, op. cit., pp. 50–64.
73. A notorious example is Christopher Jencks, *Inequality* (New York: Basic Books, 1972); see Daniel Tanner, "The Retreat from Education—For Other People's Children," *Intellect*, Vol. 102 (January 1974), pp. 222–225.
74. Fred E. Fiedler and Martin M. Chemers, *Leadership and Effective Management* (Glenville, Ill.: Scott, Foresman, 1974), pp. 94–95.
75. Frank C. Pratzner, "Quality of School Life: Foundations for Improvement," *Educational Researcher*, Vol. 13 (March 1984), p. 23.
76. See Ralph M. Stogdill, *Handbook of Leadership: A Survey of Theory and Research* (New York: Free Press, 1974), pp. 35–71.
77. Andrew W. Halpin, *Theory and Research in Administration* (New York: Macmillan, 1966), p. 86.
78. Fred E. Fiedler, *A Theory of Leadership Effectiveness* (New York: McGraw-Hill, 1967).
79. Clark, op. cit., p. 455.
80. Dewey, *Sources of a Science of Education*, op. cit., p. 15.
81. Ibid., p. 61.

SELECTED REFERENCES

Acheson, Keith A., and Meredith Damien Gall. *Techniques in the Clinical Supervision of Teachers.* New York: Longman, Inc., 1980.
Alfonso, Robert J., Gerald R. Firth, and Richard F. Neville. *Instructional Supervision: A Behavior System*, 2nd ed. Boston: Allyn and Bacon, Inc., 1981.
Bronowski, Jacob. *Science and Human Values.* New York: Harper & Row, Publishers, Inc., 1956.

————. *The Common Sense of Science.* Cambridge, Mass.: Harvard University Press, 1978.

Callahan, Raymond E. *Education and the Cult of Efficiency.* Chicago: The University of Chicago Press, 1962.

Cogan, Morris L. *Clinical Supervision.* Boston: Houghton Mifflin Company, 1973.

Conant, James B. *The Education of American Teachers.* New York: McGraw-Hill Book Company, 1963.

Dewey, John. *Democracy and Education.* New York: Macmillan Publishing Company, 1916.

————. *The Sources of a Science of Education.* New York: Liveright, 1929.

Eisner, Elliot W. *The Educational Imagination,* 2nd ed. New York: Macmillan Publishing Company, 1985.

Gage, N. L. *The Scientific Basis of the Art of Teaching.* New York: Teachers College Press, 1978.

Glickman, Carl D. *Developmental Supervision.* Alexandria, Va.: Association for Supervision and Curriculum Development, 1981.

Goldhammer, Robert, Robert H. Anderson, and Robert J. Krajewski. *Clinical Supervision,* 2nd ed. New York: Holt, Rinehart and Winston, 1980.

Good, Thomas L., and Jere E. Brophy. *Looking in Classrooms,* 3rd ed. New York: Harper & Row, Publishers, Inc., 1984.

Goodlad, John. *A Place Called School.* New York: McGraw-Hill Book Company, 1984.

Harris, Ben M. *Supervisory Behavior in Education,* 3rd ed. Englewood Cliffs, N.J.: Prentice-Hall, Inc., 1985.

James, William. *Talks to Teachers.* New York: W. W. Norton & Company, Inc., 1958.

Kellerman, Barbara (ed.). *Leadership: Multidisciplinary Perspectives.* Englewood Cliffs, N.J.: Prentice-Hall, Inc., 1984.

Lovell, John T., and Kimball Wiles. *Supervision for Better Schools,* 5th ed. Englewood Cliffs, N.J.: Prentice-Hall, Inc., 1983.

Lucio, William H., and John D. McNeil. *Supervision in Thought and Action,* 3rd ed. New York: McGraw-Hill Book Company, 1979.

McNergney, Robert F., and Carol A. Carrier. *Teacher Development.* New York: Macmillan Publishing Company, 1981.

Mosher, Ralph L., and David E. Purpel. *Supervision: The Reluctant Profession.* Boston: Houghton Mifflin Company, 1972.

Myrdal, Gunnar. *Objectivity in Social Science Research.* New York: Pantheon Books, Inc., 1969.

National Commission on Excellence in Education. *A Nation at Risk: The Imperative for Educational Reform.* Washington, D.C.: U.S. Department of Education, 1983.

National Society for the Study of Education. *Behavioral Science and Educational Administration,* Sixty-third Yearbook, Part II. Chicago: The University of Chicago Press, 1964.

————. *Staff Development,* Eighty-second Yearbook, Part II. Chicago: The University of Chicago Press, 1983.

————. *The Supervision of City Schools,* Twelfth Yearbook, Part I. Bloomington, Ill.: Public School Publishing Co., 1913.

Oliva, Peter F. *Supervision for Today's Schools,* 2nd ed. New York: Longman, Inc., 1984.

Rutter, Michael, et al. *Fifteen Thousand Hours: Secondary Schools and Their Effects on Children.* Cambridge, Mass.: Harvard University Press, 1979.

Sergiovanni, Thomas J., and Robert J. Starratt. *Supervision: Human Perspectives,* 3rd ed. New York: McGraw-Hill Book Company, 1983.

Skinner, B. F. *The Technology of Teaching.* New York: Appleton-Century-Crofts, 1968.

Travers, Robert M. W. (ed.). *Second Handbook of Research on Teaching.* Chicago: Rand McNally & Company, 1973.

Wittrock, Merlin C. (ed.). *Handbook of Research on Teaching,* 3rd ed. New York: Macmillan Publishing Company, 1986.

Chapter 7

Supervision and Teacher Effectiveness

We have defined supervisory leadership as the process of helping teachers to find the best possible methods to improve teaching and learning. Perhaps it is well to reemphasize that this does not mean telling them what to do but means sharing with them the problem-solving responsibility. To deal effectively with problems, one must draw on a body of working principles in education. (The reader is referred back to the problem-solving process, presented in Chapter 4.)

Recent years have been vastly fruitful for educational knowledge. Educational research has greatly increased our understanding of the relationship between teacher behavior and student learning. One of the most useful of the new ideas is to view the classroom as an ecological system consisting of factors or variables that directly influence students' achievement in school. These variables are nothing more or less than learning conditions that are modifiable through the efforts of teachers. As Bloom points out, by focusing on alterable variables, teachers can improve student learning greatly.[1] This is one way to use variables (such as styles of interactions with students), and it lends itself well to inservice teacher education programs. The supervisor can organize a series of workshops around variables studied by researchers. The workshops can (but need not) be combined with observation of teachers in classrooms; teachers are provided with feedback about what they are (or are not) doing and what they can do to change. According to Bloom, "When these interactions of teachers with their students are altered, there are significant improvements in student learning."[2]

But as we have indicated, another way of using variables is to begin with a classroom problem, identify the variables involved, and then find out what the literature says about the variable(s) and the teacher's role. The problem-solving approach has one enormous advantage: teachers are more likely to use the variables when they need them to get out of some difficulty. It is generally agreed that changes in knowledge (theory) are far easier to make than changes in behavior (practice). The link between the two is attitudes; there must be a change in teachers' attitudes before their behavior changes. How much simpler (and surer) to begin with the attitude or need. This is not to say that workshops built around knowledge changes are inadvisable but that changes in teacher behavior in this way are more difficult. At all costs, supervisors must be sure that the teacher's most critical problems are not going unmet—always a danger when one begins with research developments, not teachers' problems. The point is that each way of using variables has a place in a program of inservice education. When the school follows each way, we will have the best guarantee of improvement of education.

This chapter presents principles that are based on studies of teaching and learning as they take place under certain conditions. The conditions are variables that can be altered by teachers to solve problems in the educational situation and to increase their effectiveness.

WAYS OF TEACHING

"There are many ways of teaching and no one way is superior."[3] So concluded Cooley and Leinhardt in a large-scale study to identify effective methods in teaching reading and mathematics to disadvantaged children in grades 1 through 3. This does not mean that any method is as good as any other. The principle to be derived is that the methods selected should be congruent with the objectives sought in the curriculum. But the supervisor should be forewarned that most of the literature on teaching does not follow this principle and promotes a "best method." Although research on teacher effectiveness is usually cited, the supervisor should ask at least two questions about the research: (1) Are there hidden valuations? and (2) Is the research *au courant?* (Put another way, does it merely follow a particular trend at a given time?) *It must be examined in terms of the entire body of research.* For instance, as Peterson observes, "Recent reviews of research on teaching strongly suggest that direct instruction is the most effective way of teaching," but "a closer and more exhaustive survey of the literature suggests that such a conclusion may be simplistic."[4]

Direct Instruction

The influence of the back-to-basics movement can clearly be seen in "direct instruction," a concept introduced in the late 1970s by Barak Rosenshine, a researcher on teacher effects. In fact, back-to-basics received an enormous boost from the classroom setting and teaching activities that he promoted as direct instruction. Rosenshine examined research on instruction in "basic skills" (reading and mathematics) in grades 1 through 5 and concluded that effective teachers "ask questions at a low cognitive level so that students can produce many correct responses," and work with pupils in large-group settings to keep them under surveillance and "on-task." (When pupils work alone, reading a book or writing a report, they spend more time "off-task" and "in transition between activities."[5])

A Questionable Model for Teachers' Questions. According to Rosenshine, everything teachers do in their classrooms should be aimed at one target: the achievement test. Teachers' verbal questions should be like the ones found in workbooks for basal readers because the questions in workbooks are similar to the ones on standardized achievement tests. "Teaching behavior not directly aimed at furthering academic achievement of the kind measured by standardized achievement tests does not result in much academic gain."[6] But academic gain, as Rosenshine defines it, means the ability to answer questions at a low cognitive level. How, then, do teachers help children to develop higher-level cognitive abilities? Rosenshine is not concerned with this problem, only with the achievement tests that ask questions at a low cognitive level. The teacher's (and pupil's) entire effort begins and ends with this level.

Direct instruction ignores the work of Piaget, which suggests that teachers must have in mind the entire course of development if they are to help children move to higher levels.[7] The teacher who is guided by developmental psychology will be working toward higher-level understandings, not the fixation of pupils at the lowest level. The teacher must, for example, create the kind of environment where inquiry can exist. (There is no place for autonomous inquiry or reasoning in direct instruction. It is as if we were living in another era when the contributions of psychology did not exist.)

Similarities with Monitorial Instruction. Direct instruction bears some marked (and uncomfortable) similarities to monitorial instruction (1815–30), a system for educating poor children. The monitorial system fell out of favor with the advent of state-supported public schools for all children. It will be recalled from the discussion in Chapter 2 that one of the purported advantages of monitorial instruction was that children were kept in perpetual recitation (what Rosenshine calls "on-task"). It was believed that children under 10 had not developed the faculty of reasoning, but had a well-developed faculty of memory and should learn by rote and recitation in a large-group setting. Individual work was not provided for because it was considered a waste of time. Monitors asked predetermined questions and followed a mechanical repertoire (as teachers often do in direct instruction).

Monitorial instruction was abandoned because good schools were necessary if the public schools were to be used by all. It is clear from the educational proposals of the 1840s that monitorial instruction was dropped almost overnight and without a backward glance; there was no thought of continuing the system for the children of lower classes and providing something better for the advantaged. This was simply unthinkable; the ideal was a school where the children of the rich and the children of the poor sat down together and the same type of education was provided for all.

It will be remembered that another extremely important reason why monitorial education met its demise was that a new psychology was being born that was based on the scientific method and faith in human reason. (Pestalozzian pedagogy was discussed in Chapter 2.)

As Kaestle points out, Americans who wrote about monitorial education in the late nineteenth and early twentieth century (long after its demise) "looked upon monitorial education as inferior and temporary . . . as an episode that was, happily, closed forever."[8] But it has been reinvented under a different label for a new generation of poor children. A century and a half ago, educators viewed the idea of one educational method for the poor and another for the well-to-do as destructive of democratic ends. It is no less true today.

Teacher Effectiveness and the Kind of Pupil Taught. Our predecessors probably would have read with approbation the statement by Wilbur Brookover that "equality of opportunity is not facilitated by highly differentiated educational programs based upon the presumed differences between lower-class and middle-class children."[9] Brookover points out that "the interaction between the goals identified for individuals and the social outcomes of educational programs has frequently been ignored."[10] Put another way, when children are allocated to educational programs where more "low-level" and fewer "high-level" questions are asked, on the basis that this is how they learn best, something else is happening: Their opportunities for social mobility are being reduced. This is elitism of the most abhorrent and dangerous kind because it travels under the name of egalitarianism.

Research on effective teaching of disadvantaged pupils has produced "teacher should" statements that are based on a different set of criteria. According to Medley, for example, "effective" teachers of disadvantaged pupils: (1) ask "low-level" questions; (2) tend not "to amplify, discuss or use pupil answers"; (3) do not encourage pupil-initiated questions; and (4) give little feedback on pupil questions.[11] This type of teacher would be deemed grossly ineffective by middle-class parents (in a university community, for example) and probably would not be tolerated for long. This calls to mind Dewey's famous guideline: "What the best and wisest parent wants for his own child, that must the community want for all of its children. Any other ideal for our schools is narrow and unlovely; acted upon, it destroys our democracy."[12]

Medley reported a study indicating that "most of the behaviors found to be effective with pupils of low socioeconomic status were found to be ineffective with pupils of high socioeconomic status, and vice versa." Medley went on to state that "the implication is disturbing," because a teacher in a class with both kinds of pupils "must do what is wrong for half the class while doing what is right for the other half."[13] However, as cited in the preceding chapter, a review of the research relevant to the same question found that lower-ability students prefer more discovery-oriented approaches, whereas higher-ability students often tend to be satisfied with direct methods if only because they can gain their "A's" with less effort.[14] The supervisor or teacher who harkens back to the Dewey citation above will have no difficulty in doing what is right for the whole class.

A "Trendy" Method. Direct instruction is an example of a "best method" that follows a particular trend, in this case the back-to-basics movement of 1970s and 1980s, which was a reaction against the extremes of the open-classroom movement of the 1960s. In many open classrooms all or nearly all classwork was done by children individually with very little adult guidance; children were loosed to do their own thing. Direct instruction is an attempt to undo the excesses of the previous movement by substituting a new excess. (Children never working alone is substituted for children always working alone, and pupils never selecting activities is substituted for pupil autonomy.) As noted, direct instruction is inconsistent with the entire body of research on teaching and learning, which is concerned with the continuing development of the individual toward independence and social responsibility. As an extreme, it takes us back into the educational dark ages. It is incumbent on the practitioner to compare research supporting an alleged "best method" with the entire body of research.

Explicit Instruction. In the study cited earlier, Rosenshine found that when pupils worked alone they were off-task more than when they were in a supervised situation and, on this ground, he suggested that there be little or no independent work in classrooms. But children need to learn to work independently as part of their development. Moreover, Rosenshine never asked the most important question: Why do some children not do well on their own, whereas others do very well? In this regard, supervisors find that many teachers (especially new teachers) have difficulty working with a small group of pupils while managing seatwork of the other pupils at the same time. Usually, the problem is that the children do not understand how to do their seatwork. Very often the problem can be solved (or prevented) if teachers explain the work more clearly. How explicit teachers are when they give explanations and directions is a quality of teaching that is alterable by inservice education.

Researchers have always agreed that the ability to explain well is a dimension of effective teaching and, indeed, of successful classroom management. In his research on teacher qualities associated with liking the teacher and motivation to learn, Kounin found that liked teachers were described by students as explaining things well and disliked teachers as explaining things poorly; moreover, youngsters who liked their teachers and were motivated to learn also felt more like behaving themselves in class than did those who disliked their teachers.[15] Teachers who explain so that students can understand are regarded as competent by pupils and are therefore invested with authority.

Yet the relation of the quality of teachers' explanations to how well or how poorly pupils do on assignments has been given surprisingly little attention. It is probably assumed that teachers' instruction is as explicit as learners need it to be, just as a matter of common sense. The assumption is not based on reality; in fact, it is mired in delusion. (This might be surmised from the frequency of guessing and copying in many classrooms, which are indicators of misunderstanding and confusion.) Researchers at Michigan State University analyzed first-grade teachers' explanations of seatwork assignments and found that only 1.5 percent of the explanations included specific descriptions of the cognitive strategy to be employed to do the assignment.[16]

A large-scale study directed by John Goodlad that consisted of classroom observation, as well as questionnaires and interviews, found that teachers were not using practices that enhanced pupils' understanding of what was expected of them (although teachers were aware of such practices and recognized them as desirable). As a result, a large proportion of pupils spent much of their time in school in a fog.

About 57% of the students in the early elementary grades answered "yes" when asked whether they understood what their teachers wanted them to do. Forty percent answered "sometimes." Over half of the upper elementary students reported that many students did not know what they were supposed to do in class. . . . A substantial minority of senior high school students (averaging about 20% across classes at each school) were having trouble understanding teachers' directions and comments.[17]

Based on this evidence, supervisors must be alert to the quality of teachers' explanations as a factor in classroom problems (discipline problems as well as learning problems).

Helping the "Cue-Blind" Student See. As Bloom points out, cues are an important part of all learning, and include both explanations of what is to be learned and directions of what students are to do in the learning process.[18] A study at Michigan State University found that able tenth and eleventh graders look for cues from teachers such as verbal emphasis, verbal summaries, and the level of detail on handouts to ascertain which material is important to study and learn. Other students were described as "cue blind." As the study concluded: "Teaching them the thinking skill of looking for and using cues might help them learn more from instruction."[19] Other studies on teaching have indeed found that students who have difficulty in learning do better when they learn to use cues provided by the teacher and/or the instructional material.

But although students must know how to look for cues, teachers have the responsibility of providing strong explanations and directions. Students should not have to look hard for cues; teaching is not a guessing game. Teachers can discern whether students understand by students' explanations. The best way to find out if pupils understand is to ask them how they got a particular answer regardless of whether the answer was right or wrong. This also indicates whether they are applying rules without understanding. Simply doing the work is not enough; what we are aiming for is not factory production but thinking, or the noting of connections.

Supervisors can help teachers to help children to learn more effectively by working with them to make their teaching more explicit. Although as Goodlad indicates, teachers recognize clarity in regard to direction as good pedagogy, teachers frequently need help in putting pedagogical principles into practice.

Curriculum: The Master Variable of Pedagogy

Ways of teaching are determined by what we want children to learn and by what we want them to become. (This is another educational principle.) To separate what is taught from how it is taught is impossible. It is not surprising, therefore, that research on the relationship between teacher behaviors and student learning in seventh- and eighth-grade English classes found "little support for the direct instruction model."[20] English, properly taught, requires attention to life situations and the play of imagination, rather than work that is mechanical.

All learning is social, even when "basic skill mastery" is the primary goal, for skills such as writing are not learned unless put to use in the expression of ideas. Communication of ideas is social. In the words of Dewey, "Not only is social life identical with communication, but all communication (and hence all genuine social life) is educative. To be a recipient of a communication is to have an enlarged and changed experience. . . . Nor is the one who communicates left unaffected. . . . The experience has to be formulated in order to be communicated."[21]

As soon as teachers discuss pupil ideas and encourage pupils to formulate experience (as good teachers do beginning in the primary grades), they are no longer using the direct instruction model. According to Brophy, the educational objectives pursued in junior high English studies, "such as poetry composition, oral dramatization, or literature appreciation, are not easily or even appropriately pursued with the direct instruction approach."[22] All too easily overlooked in such conclusions is that the pupils are simply putting their skills to use, something that they should have been doing all along.

Curriculum Objectives and Teacher Behavior. Evertson and her colleagues attempted to determine how successful junior high teachers taught and what their classes were like.[23] The study involved observation of sixty-eight teachers (thirty-nine in English and twenty-nine in mathematics) as well as the measurement of student attitudes toward their teacher and the class. They found that teachers whose students had higher achievement also tended to be liked better by their students, and that this was especially true in mathematics classes. Of interest and importance is that the teachers given high ratings by students were also considered best by observers.

The study provided support for the importance of receptivity to student ideas. Teachers who the observers rated as being more receptive to student ideas and contributions were also more academically effective; "the number of student-initiated questions and comments was correlated positively with student achievement in mathematics."[24] Thus the study obviously does not support the direct instruction model for mathematics teaching.

"In general," the study found, "teachers who tended to respond to student questions, comments, or answers by ignoring them, asking another student, repeating the question, or giving the answer often received lower ratings than did teachers who asked new academic questions, simplified the original question, or integrated the students' contributions into the class discussion."[25] Asking new questions or simplifying the original question are, of course, attempts to make visible the invisible mental processes involved in solving mathematics problems. (It is important to note here that much of the research on teaching relates student learning to the *variety* of the explanations given by the teacher.[26]) Students like teachers who are flexible and responsive to their needs and who treat their contributions with consideration. This is true whatever the grade level and whatever the subject field. (Although the study dealt only with English and mathematics, it is consistent with other studies.)

Yet the study found that while students gave high ratings to mathematics teachers who used lectures and discussions to explain concepts, in English there was a trend in the opposite direction. Students in English classes "tended to give lower ratings to teachers who used class discussion extensively and higher ratings to teachers who gave them more choice and variety in their assignments," and further, "English students liked teachers who used more self-paced work, but mathematics students did not."[27] Students liked teachers who taught different things differently. Even more interesting, the students are supported by the educational literature. Consider the ideas of Dewey on the relation between curriculum and method. As Dewey tells us, methods are not something ready-made apart from subject matter; they are the most effective ways of managing subject matter for the desired results. Dewey gives this example: "Every artist must have a method, a technique, in doing his work. Piano playing is not hitting the keys at random. It is an orderly way of using them. . . . Order is found in the disposition of the acts which use the piano and the hands and the brain to achieve the results intended. . . . It is the same with pedagogical method."[28] Method is determined by our purposes and the subject matter. If we want children to develop an appreciation for literature, our method is to let them read for—and with—pleasure. (We want children to read, but it is worth noting that Goodlad found that students spent little time reading.) "Exclusive of the common practice of students taking turns reading orally from a common text, reading occupied about 6 per cent of class time at the elementary level and then dropped off to 3 per cent and 2 per cent for junior and senior highs, respectively."[29]

If we want students to learn to function effectively as citizens in a democratic society, we involve them in problem-solving activities which require collaboration and group work. As Goodlad observed, "Prescriptions calling for just teacher-dominated forms of pedagogy can have negative effects on such learning."[30]

The point of importance is that the literature supports the use of different methods for different subject fields. "Never is the method something outside of the material," warns Dewey, who would not have been a bit surprised at the student ratings of teachers in the Evertson study.[31] The Deweyan concept is so natural and logical that it is puzzling indeed that Goodlad found "a great deal of telling, explaining, and questioning by teachers *in all subjects,* as well as a good deal of passive seatwork by students."[32] One cannot but be impressed with the way in which many of the problems that continue to plague education were delineated by Dewey and the progressives, and one is struck by the logic and common sense in their advocations. Above all, we know how to improve teaching and learning if we will but put our knowledge into effect.

PATTERNS OF TEACHER–STUDENT INTERACTION

"There is no need to search for talent," wrote Lester Ward in 1883. "It exists already, and everywhere. The thing that is rare is opportunity, not ability."[33] Ward, who was the father of social science and one of our first educational theorists, pointed out that the difference between success and failure is the possession of opportunities. "For every actual great name in history," he wrote, "there are a hundred potential great names. Without opportunity, however great the native powers, nothing can result."

The trouble was, said Ward, that the individual who had "germs of some sort of talent in a latent state" that could "be brought out by opportunity was usually unconscious of them. *Opportunity, therefore must not merely be offered and accepted; it must be actively thrust upon him.*"[34] The means, said Ward, was public education.

Ward's idea that opportunity to learn is the critical variable in success was an important contribution to educational theory. It was based on the outlook of evolution and modern science. Ward was also a renowned natural scientist, but instead of finding Darwin's survival of the fittest in animal life to be paralleled in human society, Ward found that human society used intelligence to achieve human improvement. More than a century ago, Ward enunciated the principle that success depends on opportunities to learn. What is particularly fascinating is that the findings of recent research on the relation of classroom interaction patterns to children's achievement have given powerful support to Ward's principle. In a very real sense, interactions with students to enhance the communication of ideas will facilitate opportunities for success.

Characteristics of Teaching

Teaching is impossible without interaction. Note the characteristics of teaching: In addition to providing clear explanations, the teacher must give students recognition for their work, inform them of their mistakes, and guide them in improving their performance. This requires that teachers interact with their students. There is no other way. This includes arrangements whereby students learn to help other students.

Group Learning. School learning usually takes place in a group situation. The teacher's problem is to provide clear explanations, recognition, and correction for thirty or more learners. When teaching takes place without sufficient learning on the part of many of the youngsters, the teacher's interactions with students must be altered. According to Bloom, the fundamental problem of group learning is to find ways of providing correction and guidance to each learner.[35] (On a one-to-one basis, in tutoring situations, for example, the interactive exchange takes place quite naturally.) Often, all that is required is for teachers to become more aware of the characteristics of teaching noted above. Patterns of interaction are directly alterable. Even the best teachers can improve their interactions with students.

Two Separate Worlds. The problem in many classrooms is that these interactions are simply not happening. Students wait in vain to have their work recognized, to be informed of their mistakes, and to be helped to improve their performance. In Goodlad's study of schooling about 20 percent of the students at all levels saw themselves as not being informed of their mistakes and corrected in their work.[36] This is, in Goodlad's words, a "substantial minority" of students. It becomes even more significant since, as noted above, many students do not understand what they are supposed to be doing in the first place.

The Goodlad study found teaching, on the whole, to be uninspired and flat. An important part of teaching—praise (recognition)—was rarely observed in classrooms. The finding that "teachers' praise of students' work dropped from about 2 per cent of the observed time in the early elementary classes to about 1 per cent in senior high classes" is evidence that teacher behaviors which are vital to learning are not taking place, except very infrequently.[37] Instruction takes place without regard for its effects on individuals, and teachers and students are living in separate worlds. Although much of the research on teaching has found that teachers give encouragement and attention to some students but not others in the same classroom, Goodlad's study finds *a lack of interaction generally.* This is important for supervisors who may have been led to believe erroneously that the problem of inadequate interaction between students and teachers is confined to schools serving poor and minority children. Opportunities to learn adequately are being denied many children whatever their race or social class. The solution is not to blame teachers but to help them improve their interactions.

Influence of Teachers' Expectations

Studies of teacher interaction with students in the classroom show that teachers often direct their explanations to some children but ignore others. They give much encouragement and positive support to some children but not others, and they encourage some children to participate actively in the learning but discourage participation from others. According to Bloom, "typically the students in the top third of the class are given the greatest attention by teachers, while the students in the bottom third receive the least attention and support. These differences in the interaction between teachers and students provide some students with much greater opportunity and encouragement for learning than is provided other students in the same classroom."[38]

As Lester Ward quipped, if we want "to find who the real geniuses of society are, this can never be learned by giving all the opportunities to a class of assumed geniuses, and denying them to all the rest. It can only be arrived at by extending every possible opportunity to every member of society."[39] This was (as he pointed out) using the scientific method; it was also in accord with the democratic ethic, which is concerned not only with providing equal opportunity for all but is based on a faith in the intelligence of the common man and woman.

Are teachers aware that they are providing a classroom climate for some students that is different in kind from that provided for others? According to Bloom, teachers are "frequently unconscious of the fact that they provide more favorable conditions of learning for some students than others. Generally, they are under the impression that all students are given equal opportunity for learning."[40] Of great importance for supervisors is that when teachers are helped to see more clearly their styles of interaction with students, they become more able to provide salutary learning conditions for most of the students rather than for only the top part of the class. Research indicates that teachers who have altered their interaction patterns have made marked improvements in their students' learning.

The Self-fulfilling Prophecy Model. Since Rosenthal and Jacobson's landmark study in 1968, which proposed that students live up or down to their teacher's expectations of them,[41] supervisors have heard a great deal about the effects that teacher expectations have on student performance. Rosenthal and Jacobson found that teachers express their assessments of pupils' ability consciously and unconsciously, verbally and nonverbally, and that teachers actually teach more to students of whom they expect more. *Pygmalion in the Classroom* was criticized on methodological grounds. Robert Thorndike, for example, found "basic defects in the data that make its conclusions (although they may possibly be true) in no sense adequately supported by the data."[42]

But the question raised in Thorndike's statement continued to fascinate researchers, leading to a proliferation of inquiries into expectation effects. In a review of these efforts, Good and Brophy concluded that the idea that teacher expectations operate as self-fulfilling prophecies seemed to be an established fact rather than a hypothesis.[43] The model of the self-fulfilling prophecy has been refined by these researchers and others, and is summarized by Proctor as follows:

1. From a variety of sources and influences, teachers form differential expectations regarding the behavior and achievement of students in their classrooms.
2. Because of these expectations, teachers behave in different ways toward various students.
3. The different treatment will communicate to students what teachers expect from them and will begin to affect their self-perception and motivation and to decrease their opportunities to learn.
4. If this (differential) treatment continues over time, and if neither teachers nor pupils are successful at changing it, it will shape students' achievement and behavior. High-expectation students will achieve at high levels, and the achievement of low-expectation students will decline.
5. Differential achievement on the part of high and low achievers will continue.[44]

It is generally accepted today that teacher expectations influence student achievement, but not all researchers have been content with this conclusion. Some researchers have investigated the problem of causal direction; that is, whether teacher expectation causes achievement or achievement causes expectation. In 1976, West and Anderson argued that the evidence was as supportive of the latter as it was of the former.[45] In a review of the research, Cooper concluded that "a cyclical process of mutual influence seems most supportable by the literature."[46] However, he also concluded that expectations sustain rather than alter performance; that is, high expectations sustain high achievement and low expectations lead to the maintenance of poor performance.

As Proctor points out, a number of studies provide evidence that teacher expectations do far more than just "sustain" prior achievement variations among students.[47] These studies found that teacher expectations accounted for a substantial amount (as much as 18 percent) of the variance in student achievement when the effects of previous achievement had been eliminated. Thus, as Proctor concludes, "teacher expectations can act to alter student performance."[48]

Implications for Supervision. The "expectancy phenomenon" appears to be an important factor in learning. Based on the findings of research, teachers who expect students to succeed communicate this expectation to students and affect their self-concepts of academic ability. Moreover, expectations influence the frequency and nature of teacher–student interactions. Thus teachers should expect students to perform well because this appears to create a warmer atmosphere and more academic contact between them. But this is easier said than done. Feelings (one's expectations) are terribly personal and cannot be prescribed. For example, in the Brookover study of school climate discussed in Chapter 3, it was found that a combination of climate variables, including teacher expectation, explained differences in school achievement.[49] The teachers in successful schools expected their students to do work at grade level and the teachers generally were not disappointed. On the other hand, in another school, teachers "without exception expressed to the observer that the students' academic capabilities were limited by their family background," and the principal "stressed the 'fact' that their students were not 'Birmingham kids' [Birmingham and Grosse Pointe, Michigan, are wealthy communities with presumably high-achievement students] and therefore should not be expected to read the same books as those students. In fact, one reading series was rejected because Birmingham and Grosse Pointe school districts used that series."[50]

If teachers believe that their students cannot perform well academically, what good does it do to tell them that they really *should* feel differently? The answer is, probably, not much. Telling people that they ought to feel one way when they feel the opposite way accomplishes little of value because attitudes are emotionally charged. Yet teachers are told by supervisors and in the literature to expect their students to succeed, as if attitudes can be changed by a simple "teacher should" statement. (One might as reasonably wave a wand over the teacher.)

What, then, can supervisors do to have a positive effect on teachers' expectations of their students? There are a number of ways (hopefully, in combination) that supervisors can influence teachers' attitudes and behavior. The first is by turning to the teacher's own experience. As Dewey reminds us, we all have had in our own lives experiences by which to illustrate theoretical principles. Each of us has data contained within the experience best known to us, our own.[51] Someone's faith in our ability helped our development. In their inservice programs supervisors may find it helpful to ask teachers to relate thinking about their own pupils to thinking about their own personal experience with the expectancy phenomenon. We know from our own experience that if someone expects good things of us, we usually produce. Why should children be any different? (We were not when we were children.) Supervisors can have an impact by helping teachers to draw on their own experience as human beings.

A second way to raise teachers' expectations is in the form of high expectations by principals and supervisors. Teachers are more likely to have high expectations if the principal's outlook is positive. If the principal's expectations of students in his school are low, as in the illustration above, his low expectations will be communicated to teachers. In fact, this principal "made clear to the teachers that the students, because of their social class background, could not be expected to achieve at high levels."[52] Even where the principal does not actually verbalize his or her expectations of students' ability, they will be communicated to the faculty, just as teachers' expectations are communicated to the students. Figure 7–1 shows the chain of expectations from principal to teacher to students.

There are other important ways. Teachers' expectations are improved if they

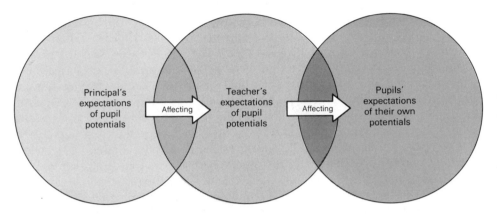

Figure 7–1. The chain of expectations of pupil potentials.

can work on a problem with the principal and other faculty of the school and see results.[53] And they are higher if the principal receives support from higher administrative levels.[54] Finally, teachers are more likely to have more satisfying interactions with their students when they have classes of reasonable size and are helped by supervisors to meet individual student needs. (Not only do teacher expectations influence interactions, but whether the interactions are pursued to a satisfactory conclusion influences expectations.)[55]

Time to Respond. Studies have found that students whom teachers perceive to be bright receive more smiles, more encouragement (including prompting), and more time to respond to questions, whereas students who are believed to be slow receive but fleeting moments of attention. Giving children time to respond has been significantly related to learning gains. Based on the findings of research on effective first-grade teachers, Brophy prescribed the following:

> After asking a question, the teacher should wait for the child to respond and also see that other children wait and do not call out answers. If the child does not respond within a reasonable length of time, the teacher should indicate that some response is expected by probing.[56]

What is meant by "probing" is not clear. (It sounds somewhat clinical and not too helpful.) As noted, other studies indicate that teachers should simplify the question or ask a new one. But the point of importance here is that in small-group instruction, it is important for the teacher to give the child enough time to respond. (The principle is equally applicable to large-group instruction.) How long the teacher should wait before simplifying the question or asking a different one is a matter of teacher judgment.

Even so, the evidence is that teachers do not give students time to think. It has been found that American teachers permit an average of only one second of thinking time before they repeat the question, ask a different question, or call on someone else.[57] As Gambrell points out: "While a fast pace in questioning may be appropriate for instruction in some situations, the evidence suggests that it does little to stimulate a student's depth of thought or quality of response."[58] Moreover, the problem may reflect the tendency for teachers to focus on questions limited to the recall of facts and the display of narrow skills, rather than the interpretation of ideas and the application of skills in new combinations.

Of major importance is the fact that teachers generally do not allow students time to integrate their thoughts and vocalize an answer. Much of the literature on teacher expectation has conveyed the erroneous impression that this is a problem only in schools composed of minority or poor-white students.

COOPERATIVE CLASSROOMS

Studies find that in classrooms where students achieve at high levels there is a cooperative-participative atmosphere. "Teachers and students show respect for one another. Students are at times allowed and even encouraged to work together."[59] The atmosphere of the classroom is a factor that can be greatly influenced by teachers.

If for no reason other than class control, teachers must have the students' respect. (If the class is in chaos and directions are ignored, students can learn very little.) But there is even another equally compelling reason to earn such respect. Students are more likely to value and enjoy learning. Teachers must also respect students if they are to communicate high expectations and students are to perform well. That there must be mutual respect between the teacher and the class if learning is to take place is not, of course, a new idea. It is an old educational principle that is, today, well supported by research.

Nor are cooperative-participative learning methods a new idea. The school as a microcosm of society with its members working together cooperatively on common problems is a concept that lies at the heart of Dewey's educational theory (see Chapter 2). Children learn democratic processes while applying scientific methods to social problems. As Joyce and Weil observe, such teaching approaches are "drawn from a conception of society" and "can be extremely useful for the classroom teacher because they provide him with ways of organizing classes into cohesive, productive groups."[60] Current research lends support to Dewey's emphasis on the social nature of learning. Cooperative methods have been found to have a strong effect on learning.[61]

Educational Troubleshooting

As Tyler reminds us, research on the factors that influence learning provides us with a guide for studying a particular classroom, teacher, or student in order to understand the situation more fully. We can more systematically "identify factors that may not be functioning and factors that can be strengthened in order to improve our instructional efforts. . . . What we need to do is determined by what we discover from this *trouble-shooting*."[62] (Tyler points out that this is true of anything in life; if it is malfunctioning, we check it out.) Be that as it may, supervisors and teachers need a guide for checking out these factors and it is with this in mind that Table 7–1 is offered. The list of variables is not meant to be definitive; those presented are the factors discussed in this chapter—factors on which researchers have focused, resulting in new understandings.

Table 7–1   Some Examples of Factors for Educational Troubleshooting: Supervisor's Checklist

Factors Influencing Learning	In Evidence	Not in Evidence/ Needs Attention
1. Quality of teacher's explanations		
(a) Teacher describes specific strategies to be employed	____	____
(b) Teacher asks students how they got a particular answer	____	____
(c) Teacher helps students make interconnections between and among the various subjects	____	____
(d) Subject matter is related to life experiences of students	____	____
2. Receptivity to students' ideas and contributions		
(a) Students initiate thought questions	____	____
(b) Teacher poses thought questions	____	____
(c) Teacher encourages students to ask questions, with emphasis on thought questions	____	____
(d) Teacher integrates students' questions and contributions into the class discussion	____	____
3. Quality of questioning procedure		
(a) Teacher poses thought-provoking questions	____	
(b) Teacher provides time for student to think and vocalize response	____	____
(c) Teacher poses new questions and/or clarifies original question when student is unable to respond effectively	____	____
(d) Emphasis is on ideas and problems	____	____
(e) Factual information and skills are applied to ideas and problems	____	
4. Selection of teaching methods		
(a) Method is determined by purposes and the subject matter	____	____
(b) Variety of methods used in illuminating ideas and problems (projects, themes, panel discussions, etc.)	____	____
(c) Emphasis given to student inquiry	____	____
(d) Cooperative-collaborative learning methods utilized	____	____
5. Quality of interactions with students		
(a) Teacher gives students recognition (including praise) for work	____	____
(b) Pupil mistakes regarded as fruitful opportunities for learning	____	____
(c) Teacher functions as a guide in helping students improve in their work	____	____
(d) Teacher provides encouragement and enlists attention of all (rather than some) students	____	____
(e) Teacher communicates high and realistic expectations to students	____	____
6. Atmosphere of the classroom		
(a) Climate is cooperative-collaborative	____	____
(b) Mutual respect between teacher and students	____	____
(c) Mutual respect among students	____	____
(d) Cooperative-collaborative learning methods (students encouraged to help one another)	____	____

Supervisor's Checklist

Factors Influencing Learning	In Evidence	Not in Evidence/ Needs Attention
7. Quality of student activity		
(a) Activity is purposeful	———	———
(b) Students are developing increased self-reliance and responsible self-direction	———	———
(c) Discipline is creative rather than restrictive/coercive	———	———
(d) Students exhibit responsibility for consequences of own actions	———	———
(e) Students exhibit a sense of controlling their own destiny	———	———
(f) Learning activities appropriate for student developmental levels	———	———
(g) Time allocation is flexible to allow continuation of exceptionally productive activities	———	———
(h) Resources and facilities appropriate for learning activity	———	———

The Problem of Respect. It is not difficult for an observer to tell when the teacher is well liked by the class. (Respect, after all, means to think well of.) Students show their approbation by paying attention and by emulating the teacher's behavior. If the teacher says "please" and "thank you," the students are likely to do so as a way to be more like him or her. When respect is a "trouble spot," this, too, is obvious. The class may be in a constant uproar with the teacher trying to shout above the din. (Nor is a quiet class necessarily indicative of mutual respect. The teacher may seem to be a good disciplinarian, but the classroom climate may be uneasy, as if trouble were brewing beneath the surface.)

Creative Versus Restrictive Discipline. The problem of discipline is discussed in Chapter 8. All that will be said here is that a positive atmosphere is most likely when the discipline is creative rather than restrictive; the emphasis is on the positive (what students can do) rather than on the negative (what they are not allowed to do). An example of creative discipline: "When you have finished this part of the assignment, you may go to the library to work on your reports." Restrictive discipline: "No one will be allowed to read magazines in the library without permission." Creative discipline generates constructive energy and activity. Restrictive discipline tells students what not to do. It creates a vacuum, behaviorally speaking, and nature abhors a vacuum. Schools where discipline is poor tend to have restrictive discipline. Respect for students is implied in creative discipline.

Gaining Respect. Mutual respect in the classroom is more likely when maintaining a positive school atmosphere is viewed as everyone's responsibility (teachers, students, administrators, and secretaries). Schoolwide (and some classroom) problems are dealt with cooperatively by the entire faculty.[63] It is also fostered when teachers model respect for individuals and insist on respect for others (forbid hostile criticism among students, for example). Respect is fostered by a way of speaking. According to Good and Brophy, "teachers should use a normal conversational tone in most situations. Their manner in giving explanations or asking questions in class should be the same as it would be if they were in the company of a group of friends."[64] If teachers want students' respect, they should not speak one way with students and a different way with adults.

It cannot be overemphasized that students are most likely to respect teachers who communicate high and realistic expectations to them (see Table 7–1) and whose interactions with them make a difference in their learning. (Students know when they are getting a good education.)

Cooperative-Collaborative Learning Methods

We tend to see dependence as a disadvantage. Yet as Dewey pointed out, dependence on others is important for human life; it is how we learn. Human infants are physically helpless but, as Dewey pointed out, through their social capacity they "enlist the cooperative attention of others." Children have remarkable social gifts and "vibrate sympathetically with the attitudes and doings of those about them." Few grown-ups retain this ability. Dewey's point is of enormous importance for educators:

> From a social standpoint, dependence denotes a power rather than a weakness; it involves interdependence. There is always a danger that increased personal independence will decrease the social capacity of an individual. In making him more self-reliant, it may make him more self-sufficient; it may lead to aloofness and indifference. It often makes an individual so insensitive in his relations to others as to develop an illusion of being really able to stand and act alone—an unnamed form of insanity which is responsible for a large part of the remediable suffering of the world.[65]

Even as adults, if we want to learn, we are dependent on others. Independent study may provide the illusion of learning alone but involves interaction with the ideas of others (the reader with authors of this book, for example).

Growth, a characteristic of education and life, depends on the need for others. As Dewey reminds us, this condition is at its peak in childhood and youth. Thus it is not at all surprising that studies find higher achievement in classrooms where collaborative-cooperative learning methods are used (see Table 7–1).

Kinds of Cooperative-Collaborative Learning. There are two principal approaches to cooperative learning. One involves simply encouraging children to help one another as the need arises. This practice dates back to the one-room district school, which was typically attended by several age groups, and teachers had to depend on students to help other students. The practice of cooperative-collaborative learning, as we have noted, was given its theoretical formulation much earlier by Dewey, and continues to this day because of its demonstrated effectiveness. Nor, it should be stressed, is this practice utilized only at the elementary school level. Suggesting that "students work together on difficult tasks" is today viewed as recommended educational practice for teachers in virtually all fields and at all grade levels, including those who teach high school mathematics and science courses.[66] The collaborative method, which developed in the progressive education era, involves children working together in small groups or in pairs.

Small-Group Learning. Many supervisors believe that the term *small-group learning* refers to a single approach to classroom organization and learning. But as Sharan and his associates warn, this is not at all the case. There are at least two very different conceptions of the term. "One approach conceives of small groups within the classroom as convenient units for promoting peer tutoring and pupil rehearsal of learning materials planned and provided by the teacher. The paradigm of school learning underlying this approach appears to be the traditional transmission model of teacher presentation and pupil rehearsal typical of whole-class instruction, except that peer tutoring is employed to generate motivation, peer relationships, and interaction." As they point out, experimenters who assess the effects of this model on student achievement tend to be concerned with learning at a low cognitive level: acquiring information and learning the basic skills or mechanics of language arts and mathematics.[67]

In the second conception of the term, children learn through collaborative-cooperative group inquiry. The learning paradigm underlying this method "is one of investigation and problem-solving, with pupils cooperating in seeking and interpreting relevant knowledge from a variety of fields and sources." Pupils are guided by the teacher in planning and carrying out their own work. As Sharan and others point out, experimenters who assess the effects of this approach "will evaluate higher-level functions" such as recognizing a problem, deciding what data will be needed, determining the accuracy of statements of fact, and so on. In other words, pupils will be evaluated on their use of the scientific method to solve a real problem. In addition to cognitive objectives, the development of social attitudes will be assessed and, of course, the contributions of individual members to the group's work.[68]

A study conducted in Israel by Sharan and his associates found that elementary school children who engaged in small-group learning through the use of inquiry methods (not peer tutoring) received better scores on high-level questions than did children from classrooms where teaching was in the traditional, whole-class mode. Pupils from small-group classrooms did *not* differ from peers in the traditional classrooms on measures of low-level cognitive functioning.[69] It is of interest and importance that in this experiment, the teachers selected the units for study; for example, second graders studied about the clinic (doctors and nurses, the nature of disease, and medical examinations). Children in the small-group classrooms planned their lessons in accord with subtopics, the division of labor (individual assignments of group members), and the conduct of their own investigation of resources and discussions. Teachers using the traditional whole-class approach presented the subject verbally, asked questions, and asked pupils to do identical assignments for homework. This was a small study involving the classrooms of pupils from two elementary schools. The findings are both interesting and encouraging, and more of such studies are certainly needed. (There has been a dearth of curriculum experimentation in the United States.)

Cooperative Problem Solving Versus Peer Tutoring. In recent years there has been considerable interest in peer tutoring in teams as a cooperative learning approach (Sharan's first model, above). For example, Aronson developed a jigsaw technique for creating interdependence among students. The material is divided among a five- or six-member team. Each pupil is given one item of information by the teacher and is responsible for "teaching" his part to the other members of the team. Pupils are tested individually for mastery of the material.[70] Studies on the jigsaw technique, as well as the other student team-learning methods, have found positive effects on race relations. In another team-learning method, a lesson is presented by the teacher, pupils work together in five- or six-member groups on a single worksheet on the lesson, and the students are quizzed individually on the material. The team's score is determined by the extent to which each student improved over his or her past average.

These cooperative approaches are learning games. As Slavin, who developed two of these techniques, observes: If students work together "toward a common goal, where each individual can contribute substantially to the mutually desired goal, the students will learn to like and respect one another."[71] There is every reason to believe that the same result would come out of students' working together to formulate a problem and pursue the solution. (In so doing, they would also better understand the role of a citizen in a democratic society.) Moreover, the problem would be real and the group situation would not be contrived.

The problem-solving method developed by Dewey is also a method of thinking (see Chapter 2). Children need to learn the intellectual processes of problem solving (thinking). Unfortunately, however, some present-day educators would discourage teachers from using group investigation on the ground that the method is too "complex."[72] It is, admittedly, more complex than worksheets.

Researchers have found positive effects of team-learning games on student achievement, but again, the learnings are at a low cognitive level. Returning to the point made by Sharan, in no way should such games or exercises be considered synonymous with the group model based on the principles of inquiry.

PURPOSEFUL ACTIVITY

In classrooms where children (and teachers) perform well, each individual has an image of his or her own of what is to be done, why it is to be done, and a sense of personal responsibility for the outcome.[73] If it is effective, developmental supervision should result in more purposive classroom behavior. At the heart of purposeful activity lies self-direction. Supervisors must help teachers to gain a feeling of personal power and control over what they do, and teachers must encourage this feeling in their students.

Purposeful Activity in the Learner

The supervisor will have no difficulty in distinguishing purposive from mechanical behavior on the part of pupils. The children have a clearly thought-out purpose in what they are doing and persist until it is done. Of striking importance is that discipline and purposeful activity are identical. This is a basic principle of education and goes back to Dewey's definition of discipline. "A person who is trained to consider his actions, to undertake them deliberately, is in so far forth disciplined. Add to this ability *a power to endure in an intelligently chosen course in the face of distraction, confusion and difficulty, and you have the essence of discipline.*"[74]

In mechanical behavior, on the other hand, there is a separation between the child and the task to be performed. An illustration is where children "work mindlessly like ants, routinely filling in the blanks on worksheets."[75]

Inner Versus Outer Attention: The Misleading Concept of Time-on-Task. "Children have an inner and an outer attention," wrote Dewey. "The inner attention is the giving of the mind without reserve or qualification to the subject at hand. . . . As such, it is a fundamental condition of mental growth." The "supreme mark and criterion of a teacher" is to be able to keep track of inner attention: to "recognize the signs of its presence or absence, to know how it is initiated and maintained, how to test it by results attained, and to test *apparent* results by it." This, Dewey said, "means insight into soul-action, ability to discriminate the genuine from the sham, and capacity to further one and discourage the other."

"External attention, on the other hand," continued Dewey, "is that given to the book or teacher as an independent object. It is manifested in certain conventional postures and physical attitudes rather than in movement of thought."[76]

Clearly, "engagement rate" and "time-on-task" do not denote purposeful activity. These are factory production concepts which have been superimposed on education, and thus no distinction is made between inner and outer attention.[77]

As has been indicated, the notion that teachers need only be concerned with external attention permeates much of the recent literature on teaching. Unfortunately, many supervisors have passed this misconception on to teachers. We have known better for a long time. As Dewey observed in 1904: "Children acquire great dexterity in exhibiting in conventional ways the *form* of attention to school work, while reserving the inner play of their own thoughts, images, and emotions for subjects that are more important to them, but quite irrelevant."[78]

Without advocating a return to the progressive education era, educational research is learning new respect for the principles of Dewey and the progressives. In their field observation study of second- and third-grade teachers, Brophy and Evertson report that "even students as young as those in the second and third grade have learned how to look like they are paying attention, whether they are or not. One implication of this is that apparent student attention is not a reliable index of anything."[79] Similarly, Taylor found that observers' ratings of students' attention to the teacher did not correlate with the students' own reports of their attention (or for that matter, with a recall of the lesson on a test given the next day).[80]

As Dewey pointed out in the citation above, the sign of an effective teacher is the ability to identify and foster inner attention in students. A study conducted by Peterson and Swing offers teachers some useful ideas. The subjects of the study were fifth- and sixth-graders who were videotaped during their mathematics classes. Observers also judged whether the students were on-task. After the youngsters had completed their seatwork, they were shown a segment of the videotape and asked what they were thinking of during that part of the lesson. Not surprisingly (given the findings of other researchers), "observers' judgments of off-task behavior were found to be unrelated to students' reports of attending as measured by the interview."[81]

For example, one student was judged to be attending all the time, but her responses in the interview indicated that she was not attending but was spending her time worrying about the possibility of failure. The study found that *"students' reports of their understanding of the lesson were positively and consistently related to their achievement on the seatwork problems and on the achievement test."*[82] Teachers can obtain important information about the quality of students' attention (and promote inner attention) by asking students what they are thinking at various times during a lesson. It is important to know whether youngsters are engaged in dysfunctional thinking (worry, for example).

The study found that some youngsters were unable to pinpoint what they did not understand and why. This suggests that teachers should do the following:

1. Determine which youngsters do not understand and try to get them to explain specifically what and why they do not understand. The teacher can then provide the needed help based on the students' reports. (Physicians have found that most correct diagnoses are made by talking with the patient.)

2. Provide additional aid for youngsters who cannot identify the reasons for their difficulty, beginning by assessing their understanding of the underlying concepts. [The study found that students' ability to relate what was being taught to prior knowledge was significantly related to their achievement.[83] This, of course, is an old teaching principle, dating back to Herbart's five formal steps of teaching.]

Inner attention is given when children become identified with learning activities, and when the goals seem important to them. The teacher should therefore continually attempt to relate the curriculum to the students' needs and interests and should provide opportunities for personal inquiry based on real problems. (Students should have opportunities to solve problems and make decisions by themselves.)

Promoting Persistence. Purposeful activity (or discipline) requires what Dewey called "executive persistence,"[84] the ability to stay with one's work until it is accomplished. As Dewey points out, interest is absolutely required for executive persistence. "Employers do not advertise for workmen who are not interested in what they are doing. If one were engaging a lawyer or a doctor, it would never occur to one to reason that the person engaged would stick to his work more conscientiously if it was so uncongenial to him that he did it merely from a sense of obligation."[85] Why should we assume any differently about children?

Interest is essential for persistence (it supplies the purpose in purposeful activity), but it is not the only factor. Time for completion of an educationally productive activity (see Table 7–1) is also of importance. Students who continually have to stop in the middle of an educationally productive activity and move on to something else may begin to see little point in persisting. (There seems to be little reason why this should have to happen in a self-contained classroom; it is, of course, more difficult to control at the secondary level.)

Teacher–student interactions have an effect on persistence. For example, an investigation of preschool children's persistence in their activities found that less persistence occurs in classrooms where teachers criticize frequently. The study also found that the use of suggestions was associated with high persistence, while the use of great numbers of directions was associated with low persistence.

> Directiveness may discourage the development of inner controls and autonomous behavior in children, of which persistent and independent work on a task is indicative. The use of suggestions on the other hand, implies some recognition of a child's autonomy and appears to foster independent, persistent behaviors. *These results imply that it is important for teachers to distinguish between the use of suggestions and directions.*[86]

Many teachers need supervisory help in understanding that there is a middle way between a series of formal directions and loosing children without guidance. Suggestions are natural and help bring to the child's consciousness what he or she is already trying to do in a vague (and ineffective) way, whereas a series of directions dictated by the teacher only makes the child more dependent on an external source. When a youngster is confused about using resources, the suggestion, "Why not use your own questions to organize the paper, instead of using the author's organization in the encyclopedia?" is better than a directive such as "Use your own words, please. Do not copy from the encyclopedia; that is plagiarism" or "Use your own questions as an outline for your paper, not the way it is organized in the encyclopedia article."

Teachers' questions also affect persistence (for better or for worse). According to Taba and her associates, the questions teachers ask "set limits within which students can operate." There are questions that "invite invention, discovery, the creative use of previous knowledge. Others control and limit both the content and nature of cognitive operations."[87] Questions that function as invitations for pupils to use their intelligence and creativity lead to executive persistence.

Locus of Control and Purposeful Activity. Another factor in whether a youngster persists at activities is whether he believes that he can, through his own efforts, achieve desired objectives. Dewey described this sense of self-responsibility as environmental control and, more recently, Rotter called it locus of control.[88] In Rotter's view, the perception by individuals that what happens to them is a result of forces outside themselves (fate, luck, or powerful others) is a belief in *external control.* If individuals perceive a causal relationship between what happens to them and their own behavior and characteristics, this is a belief in *inner control.*[89]

Persistence and purposeful activity are more likely when individuals are internally controlled rather than externally controlled. Moreover, there is a rapidly expanding research literature linking internal control with achievement. More important, perhaps, studies show that "an educational environment that encourages students to take responsibility for their learning can positively influence learning."[90]

Internal Control Can Be Taught. As emphasized above, teachers have the responsibility of teaching youngsters to take responsibility for their successes. (If a child believes that his or her marks are just a matter of luck, this is external control.) Teachers must also help children to understand that failures can be overcome by effort and persistence. (Marks get better when students do their homework carefully, for example.) These relationships must be pointed out explicitly; children cannot be depended on to make them by themselves. (Even adults cannot always do this.)

As we have discussed, many children wait in vain for feedback about their work. However, commenting on improved performance globally ("much better" scrawled across a student's paper, for instance) is not enough. According to Blumenfeld and others, teachers must "still be clear about aspects that are strong and weak." Increasing children's sense of control over outcomes (and their persistence) requires that they understand where they have done better and where they need to work harder.[91]

Education in a democratic society must be concerned with students' perceptions of control over events generally, not just in achievement situations. In this sense, Dewey's "environmental control" seems a better term than Rotter's "locus of control." A major (but unmet) goal of the curriculum is to help children become active participants in the process of improving themselves and their society; they must view themselves as actors rather than pawns. A useful method for increasing a student's sense of self-determination is cooperation with others in the pursuit of group goals. Deprived inner-city adolescents who were involved in conservation projects at a summer camp exhibited significant shifts toward internality after the camping experience.[92] They had coped successfully with challenge and had made a difference in their environment. Supervisors can help teachers plan group problem-solving activities for developing internal locus of control. (Chapter 8 offers suggestions.)

According to Lefcourt, internal control expectations (the idea that events are controllable) are "related to signs of vitality—affective and cognitive activity which indicates an active grappling with those self-defined important events."[93] One can easily make the connection with activity that is purposeful and vital rather than activity that is apathetic or fatalistic. Certainly, the vitality and enthusiasm of the teacher and the teacher's own expectancies of internal control are a good model for students.

Purposeful Activity in the Teacher

One of the great problems facing supervision today is that many teachers do not have a sense of inner control over events in their classrooms. In their research on the behavior and attitudes of effective teachers, Brophy and Evertson found that successful teachers felt that their problems (the range of pupil ability in their classrooms, for example) could be overcome and searched for ways to solve them, whereas unsuccessful teachers (faced with the same kinds of problems) felt that the problems were simply too difficult to solve and "usually attempted to shift responsibility to factors outside their control (administrative and structural restrictions, attitudes of the students or their families, etc.)."[94] Brophy and Evertson point out that the successful teachers did not always succeed but that their sense of personal causation and responsibility helped them to succeed more often than teachers who believed that problems were out of their control and did not even try to solve them.

Developmental Supervision and Locus of Control. Granted that successful teachers feel capable of handling problems and frequently succeed, there are some problems that are simply unsolvable without help (the problems of overcrowded facilities and of inadequate supplies, for example). Even those teachers who succeed more often because of their "can do" attitude will begin to shift toward externality when confronted with many situations that are out of their control. They may even leave the job, as we have discussed earlier. Two points that are overlooked by Brophy and Evertson are that locus of control can be altered in *either* direction by the person's experience, and that not all problems are solvable by the teacher alone. It is the supervisor's responsibility to help teachers identify the conditions or factors that need to be changed so that they can be more consistently successful. This is what is meant by developmental supervision.

"Stress Management" and Locus of Control. Many recent studies have addressed the problem of teacher stress. As Gibbons and Phillips observe: "Stress is caused by effort without success."[95] Teachers with high stress levels tend to be depressed; an aspect of depression is external control beliefs; outcomes seem independent of actions. Teachers feel that their classroom problems are beyond their own capability of control. One might assume that the best way to reduce stress is to help teachers deal with their very real problems and thus improve their sense of personal causation. Oddly enough, however, many stress reduction programs tend to ignore the problems and mask the symptoms.

For example, Friedman, Lehrer, and Stevens sought to reduce teachers' stress through relaxation exercises and having them "think more positively." The five-week treatment program called for meditation on a beach scene ("guided imagery") and deep breathing, as well as lessons to help the subjects "identify their personal self-talk patterns."[96] This was a course in problem ignoring rather than problem solving. The researchers concluded that locus of control is not an important factor in "stress management." But their approach was not cognitively oriented; it was to teach teachers to "manage" to live with their problems, not to develop a sense of personal causation and effectiveness.

"Stress management" is a fad, and a dangerous one at that. Teachers will still feel (and be) unable to accomplish their goals and they and their students will suffer. Behavior-modification techniques are no way to deal with feelings of depression, anxiety, hostility, and powerlessness that stem from real problems in the educational situation. The way to deal with problems is not to escape from the problems but to wage an intelligently guided attack on the problems (the method of intelligence).

SUMMARY

The classroom variables studied by researchers provide supervisors with a checklist for educational troubleshooting and a framework for organizing workshops for problem solving (for example, on the quality of teachers' explanations as a factor in classroom problems). These variables are best viewed as learning conditions that can be strengthened and improved. However, supervisors must beware of the quicksand of *au courant* "best methods." They must examine the research that is cited in terms of the entire body of research. A recent example is the advocacy of "direct instruction" at a low cognitive level for disadvantaged children whereas advantaged children are afforded more comprehensive learning experiences at higher cognitive levels. Aside from the undemocratic aspects (middle-class parents would not tolerate teachers for their own children who only asked questions at a low cognitive level and who refused to respond to pupils' thought questions and ideas), research finds that teachers who are receptive to student ideas and contributions are more academically effective with all kinds of students.

Yet one finds that in most classrooms, the instructional material and teaching methods seldom rise above the lowest category of the *Taxonomy of Educational Objectives*—recall of factual information. The emphasis is on specific content to be remembered, and teachers rarely give students opportunities to attack real problems in their environments and thus develop a sense of personal causation (important both for academic success and for solving the problems encountered in day-to-day living). Interactions with students are opportunities for success. Research has found a lack of teacher–student interaction generally, not just in schools serving disadvantaged students. For example, many students (regardless of race or social class) do not know how to do their work or even what they are supposed to be doing. "Time-on-task" and "engagement rate" (industrial production concepts that have been visited on education) are concerned only with students' external attention. Only by talking to students can we understand (and improve) their thought processes. Education can take a good lesson from medicine; doctors find that most correct diagnoses are made by talking with the patient.

The "Pygmalion effect" has been established by research; the teacher's expectations influence achievement. There is a chain of expectations of pupil potentials from principal to teacher to pupils. Teachers in successful schools expect their students to do well, but human expectations cannot be prescribed. Supervisors can have a positive effect on teachers' attitudes and behavior by encouraging teachers to think about their own experiences with the expectancy phenomenon. Supervisors must also communicate high expectations of pupils' potentials. It would seem almost like insubordination for a teacher whose principal had low expectations for student achievement to hold high expectations for the academic success of the students. Teachers behave differently in one school than they would in another school. Much of the difference can be explained by the expectations and role definitions that principals hold for them. Expectations tend to be schoolwide.

Cooperative learning and purposeful activity are old educational ideas (based on the principles of Dewey and the progressives) that have been found present in classrooms where children perform well. Learning games are a contrived means for achieving cooperation and respect among pupils and tend to deal with bits of remembered information. Higher mental processes (critical thinking, for example) can be taught when children work collaboratively in small groups on real problems of concern to them, and cooperation and mutual respect are developed naturally. Children should also be encouraged to help one another. (This, too, has been found to have a high relationship with achievement.)

Where there is purposeful activity, there is vitality and involvement rather than mechanical behavior and expectancies of external control. This is as true of teachers as it is of their students. Persistence in pupils is found in classrooms where teachers make suggestions rather than giving great numbers of directions, and where teachers pose questions that are not dead ends but invite further exploration. Teachers' feelings of powerlessness and depression will not be eliminated by "stress management" techniques designed to help them escape from their problems, a fact that should be understood by supervisors who must help teachers use the method of intelligence in attacking problems.

PROBLEMS FOR STUDY AND DISCUSSION

1. What role should supervisors play in reducing teacher stress? Justify your answer.

2. In this chapter it was pointed out that an external locus of control in teachers is an impediment to dealing with their classroom problems and is associated with negative feelings. Do you believe that effective supervision should shift a teacher's locus of control from an external to a more internal position? Explain.

3. Do you agree with the statement that "the difficulty of [teachers'] questions should be near the child's level of ability in classrooms with children of low socioeconomic status, whereas it is better to ask questions slightly above the child's level of ability in classrooms with children of high socioeconomic status."[97] Why or why not?

4. In view of the distinction between inner attention and outer attention made by Dewey in 1904, how do you account for contemporary educators' acceptance of time-on-task as evidence of learning?

5. An analysis of studies of time-on-task found that "time spent is not so consistently related to achievement as it may seem."[98] In light of your response to Problem 4, is this finding surprising? Explain.

6. The researcher in Problem 5 concluded that "trying to improve time-on-task is clearly a worthwhile objective that schools *should* pursue."[99] In your opinion, is this statement congruent with the findings of the researcher's study?

Why or why not? If your answer is negative, what recommendations would you see as indicated by the researcher's findings?

7. Using the list of factors in Table 7–1, study a classroom or teacher to identify factors that may not be functioning and factors that can be strengthened.

8. In your opinion, is the guide (Table 7–1) a useful tool for supervisors in improving teaching and learning? Explain.

9. Do you agree with the authors of this textbook that teacher–student interactions can be viewed as opportunities for students to learn? Give reasons for your answer.

10. According to Benjamin S. Bloom, author of the *Taxonomy of Educational Objectives—Cognitive Domain:*

> Although there is much of rote learning in schools through the world, in some of the national curriculum centers in different countries (e.g., Israel, Malaysia, South Korea) I find great emphasis on problem-solving, application of principles, analytical skills, and creativity. These abilities are stressed because they are retained and used long after the individual has forgotten the detailed specifics of the subject matter taught in schools. . . .
>
> In sharp contrast with some of these other countries, teachers in the United States typically make use of textbooks that rarely pose real problems. These textbooks emphasize content to be remembered and give students little opportunity to discover underlying concepts and principles and even less opportunity to attack real problems in the environment. . . . Our instructional material, our classroom teaching methods, and our teaching methods rarely rise above the lowest category of the Taxonomy—knowledge.[100]

As discussed in Chapter 2, Dewey believed, first and foremost, that schools in a democratic society must teach children how to use the method of intelligence in dealing with environmental problems. How, then, do you account for the fact that there is so little emphasis on problem solving in American educational practice? Do you see this as an important problem in the field of supervision? Why or why not?

11. Do you agree with the authors of this textbook that purposeful activity and discipline are one and the same? Explain.

NOTES

1. Benjamin S. Bloom, "The New Direction in Educational Research: Alterable Variables," *Phi Delta Kappan*, Vol. 61 (February 1980), p. 382.
2. Ibid.
3. William W. Cooley and Gacea Leinhardt, "The Instructional Dimensions Study," *Educational Evaluation and Policy Analysis*, Vol. 2 (January–February 1980), pp. 7–25.
4. Penelope L. Peterson, "Direct Instruction Reconsidered," Chapter 3 in *Research on Teaching* (Berkeley, Calif.: McCutchan, 1979), p. 58.

5. Barak Rosenshine, "Content, Time, and Direct Instruction," Chapter 2 in *Research on Teaching,* op. cit., pp. 38, 42, 47.
6. Ibid., p. 47.
7. Jean Piaget, *The Psychology of Intelligence* (New York: Harcourt Brace Jovanovich, 1950), pp. 87–158.
8. Carl F. Kaestle, *Joseph Lancaster and the Monitorial School Movement* (New York: Teachers College Press, 1973), p. 48.
9. Wilbur B. Brookover et al., "Quality of Educational Attainment, Standardized Testing, Assessment, and Accountability," Chapter 8 in *Uses of the Sociology of Education,* Seventy-third Yearbook, Part II, National Society for the Study of Education (Chicago: University of Chicago Press, 1974), p. 162.
10. Ibid.
11. Donald M. Medley, "The Effectiveness of Teachers," Chapter 1 in *Research on Teaching,* op. cit., p. 23.
12. John Dewey, *The School and Society* (Chicago: University of Chicago Press, 1899), p. 7.
13. Medley, op. cit., p. 22.
14. Richard E. Clark, "Reconsidering Research on Learning from Media," *Review of Educational Research,* Vol. 53 (Winter 1983), p. 456.
15. Jacob S. Kounin, *Discipline and Group Management in Classrooms* (New York: Holt, Rinehart and Winston, 1970), p. 45.
16. *Communication Quarterly,* Vol. 6 (Winter–Spring 1984), p. 3.
17. John I. Goodlad, *A Place Called School* (New York: McGraw-Hill, 1984), pp. 111–112.
18. Bloom, op. cit., p. 384.
19. *Communication Quarterly,* op. cit., p. 3.
20. Jere E. Brophy, "Teacher Behavior and Student Learning," *Educational Leadership,* Vol. 37 (October 1979), p. 35.
21. John Dewey, *Democracy and Education* (New York: Macmillan, 1916), p. 6.
22. Brophy, op. cit., p. 35.
23. Carolyn Evertson et al., "Relationships Between Classroom Behaviors and Student Outcomes in Junior High Mathematics and English Classes," *American Educational Research Journal,* Vol. 17 (Spring 1980), pp. 43–60.
24. Ibid., p. 57.
25. Ibid.
26. Bloom, op. cit.
27. Evertson et al., op. cit., pp. 55, 59.
28. Dewey, *Democracy and Education,* op. cit., p. 194.
29. Goodlad, op. cit., pp. 106–107.
30. Ibid., pp. 103–104.
31. Dewey, *Democracy and Education,* op. cit., p. 194.
32. Goodlad, op. cit., p. 115.
33. Lester F. Ward, "Broadening the Way to Success," *The Forum,* Vol. 2 (December 1886), p. 345.
34. Ibid., pp. 345, 347.
35. Bloom, op. cit., p. 384.
36. Goodlad, op. cit., p. 112.
37. Ibid.
38. Bloom, op. cit., p. 384.
39. Ward, op. cit., p. 344.
40. Bloom, op. cit., p. 385.
41. Robert Rosenthal and Lenore Jacobson, *Pygmalion in the Classroom* (New York: Holt, Rinehart and Winston, 1968).

42. Robert L. Thorndike, Review of *Pygmalion in the Classroom* by Robert Rosenthal and Lenore Jacobson, *American Educational Research Journal*, Vol. 5 (November 1968), p. 708.

43. Jere E. Brophy and Thomas L. Good, *Teacher–Student Relationships: Causes and Consequences* (New York: Holt, Rinehart and Winston, 1974).

44. Patrick Proctor, "Teacher Expectations: A Model for School Improvement," *The Elementary School Journal*, March 1984, p. 470.

45. Charles K. West and Thomas H. Anderson, "The Question of Preponderant Causation in Teacher Expectancy Research," *Review of Educational Research*, Vol. 46 (Spring 1976), pp. 185–213.

46. Harris M. Cooper, "Pygmalion Grows Up: A Model for Teacher Expectation Communication and Performance Influence," *Review of Educational Research*, Vol. 49 (Summer 1979), p. 392.

47. Proctor, op. cit., p. 474.

48. Ibid.

49. Wilbur Brookover et al., *School Social Systems and Student Achievement* (New York: Praeger, 1979).

50. Ibid., pp. 87, 104, 107.

51. John Dewey, "The Relation of Theory to Practice in Education," Chapter 1 in *The Relation of Theory to Practice in the Education of Teachers*, Third Yearbook of the National Society for the Scientific Study of Education, Part I (Bloomington, Ill.: Public School Publishing Co., 1904), p. 18.

52. Brookover et al., *School Social Systems and Student Achievement*, op. cit., p. 108.

53. Proctor, op. cit.

54. Harry Averch et al., *How Effective Is Schooling? A Critical Review and Synthesis of Research Findings* (Santa Monica, Calif.: Rand Corporation, 1972).

55. Cooper, op. cit., p. 399.

56. Brophy, op. cit., p. 37.

57. Mary Budd Rowe, "Wait-Time and Rewards as Instructional Variables, Their Influence on Language, Logic and Fate Control: Part One—Wait-time," *Journal of Research in Science Teaching*, Vol. 11 (March 1974), pp. 81–94.

58. Linda B. Gambrell, "The Occurrence of Think-Time During Reading Comprehension Instruction," *Journal of Educational Research*, Vol. 77 (November–December 1983), pp. 77–78.

59. Marjorie Powell, "New Evidence for Old Truths," *Educational Leadership*, Vol. 37 (October 1979), p. 51.

60. Bruce Joyce and Marsha Weil, *Models of Teaching*, 2nd ed. (Englewood Cliffs, N.J.: Prentice-Hall, 1980), p. 222.

61. See Donald E. Mackenzie, "Research for School Improvement: An Appraisal of Some Recent Trends," *Educational Researcher*, Vol. 12 (April 1983), p. 8; and Herbert J. Walberg, "Improving the Productivity of America's Schools," *Educational Leadership*, Vol. 41 (May 1984), p. 24.

62. Ralph W. Tyler, "A Guide to Educational Trouble-Shooting," *Educational Leadership*, Vol. 41 (May 1984), p. 29.

63. Thomas J. Lasley and William W. Wayson, "Characteristics of Schools with Good Discipline," *Educational Leadership*, Vol. 40 (December 1982), pp. 28–29; and Michael Rutter et al., *Fifteen Thousand Hours: Secondary Schools and Their Effects on Children* (Cambridge, Mass.: Harvard University Press, 1979).

64. Thomas L. Good and Jere E. Brophy, *Looking in Classrooms* (New York: Harper & Row, 3rd ed., 1984), p. 158.

65. Dewey, *Democracy and Education*, op. cit., pp. 51–52.

66. Grace M. Burton, "Revealing Images," *School Science and Mathematics,* Vol. 84 (March 1984), p. 205.
67. Schlomo Sharan, Rachel Hertz-Lazarowitz, and Zalman Ackerman, "Academic Achievement of Elementary School Children in Small-Group Versus Whole-Class Instruction," *Journal of Experimental Education,* Vol. 48 (Winter 1980), p. 125.
68. Ibid.
69. Ibid., p. 128.
70. Elliot Aronson, *The Jigsaw Classroom* (Beverly Hills, Calif.: Sage, 1978).
71. Robert E. Slavin, "Synthesis of Research on Cooperative Learning," *Educational Leadership,* Vol. 38 (May 1981), p. 657.
72. Ibid., pp. 656, 659.
73. Lasley and Wayson, op. cit.; Mackenzie, op. cit.; Powell, op. cit.
74. Dewey, *Democracy and Education,* op. cit., p. 151.
75. Celia S. Lavatelli, Walter J. Moore, and Theodore Kaltsounis, *Elementary School Curriculum* (New York: Holt, Rinehart and Winston, 1972), p. 76.
76. Dewey, *Relation of Theory to Practice,* op. cit., pp. 13–14.
77. See, for example, Rosenshine, op. cit.; see also D. John McIntyre et al., "A Survey of Engaged Student Behavior Within Classroom Activities During Mathematics Class," *Journal of Educational Research,* Vol. 77 (September–October 1983), pp. 55–59.
78. Dewey, *Relation of Theory to Practice,* op. cit., p. 14.
79. Jere E. Brophy and Carolyn M. Evertson, *Learning from Teaching: A Developmental Perspective* (Boston: Allyn and Bacon, 1976), p. 67.
80. M. Taylor, *Intercorrelations Among Three Methods of Estimating Students' Attention* (Stanford, Calif.: Stanford Center for Research on Teaching, 1968).
81. Penelope L. Peterson and Susan R. Swing, "Beyond Time on Task: Students' Reports of Their Thought Processes During Classroom Instruction," *The Elementary School Journal,* Vol. 82 (May 1982), pp. 481–491.
82. Ibid., p. 485.
83. Ibid., pp. 486–487.
84. Dewey, *Democracy and Education,* op. cit., p. 152.
85. Ibid.
86. Jane Hamilton and Donald A. Gordon, "Teacher–Child Interactions in Preschool and Task Persistence," *American Educational Research Journal,* Vol. 15 (Summer 1978), p. 465.
87. Hilda Taba et al., *Thinking in Elementary School Children* (Washington, D.C.: U.S. Office of Education, 1964), p. 177.
88. Dewey, *Democracy and Education,* op. cit., pp. 81–99; Julian B. Rotter, "Generalized Expectancies for Internal Versus External Control of Reinforcement," *Psychological Monographs,* Vol. 80, No. 1 (1966).
89. Rotter, op. cit., p. 1.
90. Deborah J. Stipek and John R. Weisz, "Perceived Personal Control and Academic Achievement," *Review of Educational Research,* Vol. 51 (Spring 1981), pp. 101–137.
91. Phyllis C. Blumenfeld et al., "The Formation and Role of Self Perceptions of Ability in Elementary Classrooms," *The Elementary School Journal,* Vol. 82 (May 1982), p. 417.
92. Steve Nowicki and Bonnie R. Strickland, "Effects of a Structured Summer Camp Experience on Locus of Control Orientation," *Journal of Genetic Psychology,* Vol. 122 (1972), pp. 247–252; Herbert M. Lefcourt, *Locus of Control: Current Trends in Theory and Research* (Hillsdale, N.J.: Lawrence Erlbaum, 1976), p. 125.
93. Lefcourt, op. cit., p. 152.
94. Brophy and Evertson, op. cit., p. 40.

95. Maurice Gibbons and Gary Phillips, "Joy or Misery in the Classroom," *Educational Leadership*, Vol. 38 (December 1980), p. 252.
96. Gail H. Friedman, Barry E. Lehrer, and James P. Stevens, "The Effectiveness of Self-directed and Lecture/Discussion Stress Management Approaches and the Locus of Control of Teachers," *American Educational Research Journal* (Winter 1983), pp. 568, 575.
97. Barak Rosenshine, "Classroom Instruction," Chapter 10 in National Society for the Study of Education, *The Psychology of Teaching Methods*, Seventy-fifth Yearbook, Part I (Chicago: University of Chicago Press, 1976), p. 361.
98. Nancy Karweit, "Time-on-Task Reconsidered: Synthesis of Research on Time and Learning," *Educational Leadership*, Vol. 41 (May 1984), p. 35.
99. Ibid.
100. Benjamin S. Bloom, "The 2 Sigma Problem: The Search for Methods of Group Instruction as Effective as One-to-One Tutoring," *Educational Researcher*, Vol. 13 (June–July 1984), p. 13.

SELECTED REFERENCES

Association for Supervision and Curriculum Development. *Improving Teaching*, 1986 Yearbook. Alexandria, Va.: The Association, 1986.

Brookover, Wilber B., et al. *School Social Systems and Student Achievement*. New York: Praeger Publishers, 1979.

Brophy, Jere E., and Carolyn M. Evertson. *Learning from Teaching: A Developmental Perspective*. Boston: Allyn and Bacon, Inc., 1976.

Dewey, John, *Democracy and Education*. New York: Macmillan Publishing Company, 1916.

———. *The School and Society*. Chicago: The University of Chicago Press, 1899.

Gage, N. L. *The Scientific Basis of the Art of Teaching*. New York: Teachers College Press, 1978.

Good, Thomas L., and Jere E. Brophy. *Looking in Classrooms*, 3rd ed. New York: Harper & Row, Publishers, Inc., 1984.

Goodlad, John I. *A Place Called School*. New York: McGraw-Hill Book Company, 1984.

Joyce, Bruce, and Marsha Weil. *Models of Teaching*, 2nd ed. Englewood Cliffs, N.J.: Prentice-Hall, Inc., 1980.

Lefcourt, Herbert M. *Locus of Control: Current Trends in Theory and Research*. Hillsdale, N.J.: Lawrence Erlbaum Associates, Inc., 1976.

National Society for the Study of Education. *The Psychology of Teaching Methods*, Seventy-fifth Yearbook, Part I. Chicago: The University of Chicago Press, 1976.

———. *Uses of the Sociology of Education*, Seventy-third Yearbook, Part II. Chicago: The University of Chicago Press, 1974.

Peterson, Penelope L., and Herbert J. Walberg (eds.). *Research on Teaching*. Berkeley, Calif.: McCutchan Publishing Corporation, 1979.

Piaget, Jean. *The Psychology of Intelligence*. New York: Harcourt Brace Jovanovich, Inc., 1950.

Rosenthal, Robert, and Lenore Jacobson. *Pygmalion in the Classroom*. New York: Holt, Rinehart and Winston, 1968.

Sharan, Schlomo, and Yael Sharan. *Small-Group Teaching*. Englewood Cliffs, N.J.: Educational Technology Publications, 1976.

Tanner, Laurel N. *Classroom Discipline for Effective Teaching and Learning*. New York: Holt, Rinehart and Winston, 1978.

Wittrock, Merlin C. (ed.). *Handbook of Research on Teaching*, 3rd ed. New York: Macmillan Publishing Company, 1986.

Chapter 8

Common Classroom Problems

According to Tyler, "Research gives us guidance—but we are responsible for finding and analyzing our problems, deciding on tentative solutions, testing them, and verifying or refuting our interpretations."[1] In the preceding chapter, we discussed the underlying factors or variables in school learning that can be altered by teachers and the school, and supervisors were provided with a guide for studying a given teaching situation.

Research has provided us with principles for analyzing problems and proposing possible solutions, but their application in the schools will depend on supervisory leadership. For example, a teacher may have difficulty controlling the class. Observation of the teacher (using the guide for troubleshooting, Table 7–1) reveals that providing clear explanations to students about what is to be learned is "not in evidence; needs attention." Good supervision does not stop with pointing out the deficiency as a possible cause of the problem, but involves stating the principle behind the judgment and indicating what the teacher needs to do to apply the principle. When teachers ask, "How would you do it differently and why?," they should receive a constructive and clear response. (In this case the supervisor would suggest that the teacher try the following: Be explicit about what students are to do, provide a variety of explanations, and find out what students are *thinking*. The "why" is that research relates both learning and pupil behavior to the quality of explanations.)

In this chapter we are concerned with diagnosing and solving common classroom and school problems—with putting theory into practice.

THE UNIVERSAL NATURE OF CLASSROOM PROBLEMS

There has been a remarkable consistency of teachers' classroom problems over time and space. The major problems faced by teachers a half century ago face teachers in our time. Moreover, there is a striking similarity in the problems of teachers in different countries. According to Veenman, who reviewed the international literature on the problems of teachers, classroom discipline is "by far" the most serious problem of beginning teachers everywhere.[2] Veenman rank ordered the most important problems in some 83 studies—55 from the United States, 7 from West Germany, 6 from Great Britain, 5 from the Netherlands, 4 from Australia, 2 from Canada, 2 from Austria, 1 from Switzerland, and 1 from Finland. Motivation of students was the second most frequently mentioned problem, and dealing with individual differences in students ranked third. "To vary curricular and instructional practices to accommodate differences among learners proved to be difficult."[3]

Assessing students' work and relationships with parents ranked fourth and fifth in the list of problems. (Teachers complained about lack of support from parents.) Organization of class work ranked sixth, and insufficient materials and supplies ranked seventh.

Discipline, as old as education, has always been a part of teaching, and is ranked as a leading problem by teachers and supervisors alike. Moreover, in a democratic society, discipline is inseparable from pedagogical aim and method. Discipline—that is, development toward self-direction—is part of everyone's education. Thus we can assume (and even hope) that the problem of discipline, like the problem of education, will always be with us. As emphasized throughout this book, the search for ways of improving teaching and learning is never-ending. Supervisors must help teachers to use the best available knowledge in dealing with classroom problems. This is the key to progress—and the path to professionalism. This principle was not foreign to our predecessors, as is shown clearly in these words from the Preface of a book on teachers' classroom problems that was published in 1922:

> Let nobody suppose that all of the problems in this book will be completely solved. Many of them will continue to be problems as long as there are children to be educated and human nature remains complex and variable. But they are all problems which teachers have to face. We shall have to do something about them. *If we learn to deal with them more wisely, regarding our own solutions not as final but as the most promising plans we can devise with our present knowledge—tentative steps to be tried and improved as we gain more light—we shall be making progress toward a real educational profession.*[4]

It is noteworthy that the book was written by a superintendent of schools, but of particular interest is the way in which he organized it, for the chapter sequence bears a marked similarity to the rank order of problems in Veenman's study. The first three chapters were on problems of discipline and motivation; and they were followed by chapters on problems of selecting instructional materials, problems "due to variations in ability of pupils," problems in the effective use of time, and problems of relationship with parents. The problems demanding supervisory attention in 1922 demand attention today: They are the persistent problems of classroom teaching.

As one examines the problems identified by teachers, however, it seems clear that some problems can be completely solved. No panacea is needed, for example, to solve the problem of insufficient materials and supplies, yet teachers regard this as one of their most serious problems. A study of elementary teachers' problems in Pittsburgh, Pennsylvania, found that inadequate resources was their leading problem—a startling finding, according to the researchers, "in view of the considerable amount of money budgeted for classroom supplies in the City of Pittsburgh."[5] But the amount of money notwithstanding, the supplies were not getting to the teachers. As discussed in Chapter 4, allocating educational resources is a supervisory function. The problem of inadequate resources is a problem of neglected leadership responsibilities. Another problem that is completely solvable is the teacher's need for evaluation of his or her teaching effectiveness and for supervisory assistance. One of the ten leading problems mentioned by teachers in the Pittsburgh study was obtaining a written evaluation of their teaching. Moreover, one of the ideas considered by teachers as valuable for alleviating, if not eliminating, their problems was the suggestion for individual conferences with supervisors to review the evaluation *and provide assistance with specific problems.*[6] As the researchers conclude, both the problem (need for a written evaluation) and the suggestion indicate that teachers are concerned about their effectiveness and want help in dealing with problems. (It was for precisely these purposes that the troubleshooting guide in Chapter 7 was developed.)

Reality Shock: The Misleading Label

New teachers emerge from their preparation programs filled with enthusiasm and professional ideals, both of which are doomed to destruction by school realities, or so the story goes. As Veenman reports, researchers have increasingly turned their attention to the transition from the preservice teacher education program to the first years of teaching. In the German and English literature on education this transition is frequently referred to as a "reality shock" and indicates the demolition of professional ideals formed during professional preparation "by the harsh and rude reality of everyday classroom life."[7] There are five symptoms (indications) of a reality shock: (1) perceptions of problems (examples given by Veenman are "inadequate staffing, a shortage of materials and supplies," and "loneliness in the work place"); (2) changes in teaching behavior in conflict with one's philosophy because of real or perceived external pressures; (3) changes of attitudes (for example, from progressive to conservative views with regard to teaching methods); (4) changes of personality (examples are a lowered self-concept of teaching ability and a shift toward externality in respect to locus of control); and (5) leaving the teaching position.[8] As Veenman observes, a number of studies have been done with regard to beginning teachers' perceptions of problems and attitude changes, but there is little evidence concerning the other manifestations of reality shock. Nevertheless, as pointed out in Chapter 3, some school districts are experiencing teacher shortages of acute proportions because new teachers leave after only a few weeks on the job—due to problems like those in the examples above—problems that are solvable.

To be sure, the problem of the transition from preservice education to professional teaching is of great importance for supervisors (as well as for teacher education faculties). The first months on the job determine whether promising people can be induced to develop optimally. But the fact is that global terms such as "reality shock" do little to help us understand or facilitate the transition. That there is a transition is undeniable; there is a fundamental difference between being a student and a teacher, and this is true no matter how excellent the student teaching program. The roles are just different. The beginning teacher may find himself saying, "No, I will not accept the excuse that your little brother destroyed your homework; you may not hand it in late," and that same evening may ask his professor at the university for an extension on an assignment in his graduate course. As a teacher he is unwilling to be lenient, but as a student he expects leniency for himself. Pointing this out may help the new teacher to deal with a perceived role conflict (and better understand the child's point of view).

Differing Realities. The term "reality shock" is misleading because it implies that the problems in a deleterious situation are present in all teaching situations. As any professional from the schools knows (and professionals from the university ought to know), this is simply not the case. Whereas in some schools, the reality may be "harsh and rude" and inhospitable in the development of teaching talents, in others quite the opposite is true. The reader will remember that a striking conclusion of the Rutter study was that some schools are far easier places than others in which to be a proficient teacher, and that in those schools that are pleasant workplaces achievement is higher.[9] The key, of course, is supervision that provides active support to teachers. To paraphrase the words of Dewey in a different context: "What the best and wisest supervisor provides for his (or her) teachers, so should all supervisors provide for their teachers. Any other ideal for supervision, if acted upon, will result in poor working conditions and poor schools."[10]

Moreover, a "reality shock" implies that there is something wrong in identifying problems in one's work. It would seem that just the opposite is the case. It would be difficult to find two things more opposed to each other than ignoring problems and problem solving. The position taken in this book is that teachers should be encouraged to identify their problems and should be evaluated on awareness of problems and willingness to seek help (see Chapter 4).

Finally, when bright and competent people leave their teaching positions because of classroom problems that could be solved with the help of supervisors, it is the public—not the teacher—that must face a crisis of reality. The great investment in teacher education is not producing a fair return. Unfortunately, however, the various reports on the state of American education have virtually ignored the importance of supervisory support for teachers in the schools.

It should be added that teacher education has an unmet responsibility to facilitate the successful transition from professional preparation to actual teaching. Teacher education should be restructured to include a one-year follow-up of teachers on the job, as is done in the field of agricultural education.

Changes in Attitude. A number of longitudinal studies have found that students become idealistic and progressive in their educational attitudes before student teaching and then move to more conservative views as they enter student teaching and the first years of teaching. As noted, this change has been identified by researchers as a symptom of a reality shock. Ignored in their studies, however, is the role factor, just discussed: A change of attitude is a necessary accompaniment of a new role. Moreover, this is by no means peculiar to education. As Veenman points out, "Revision of attitudes is a general phenomenon at the entry of a career and is not restricted to teachers."[11] Since the perception of problems in the educational situation is also normal and desirable, there are no conclusive symptoms of reality shock. The doctors may have invented an educational disease that does not exist.

Apart from reality shock, the question of whether teacher education ideals are washed out by the teaching situation has been of much interest to researchers. As Zeichner and Tabachnick tell us, "It now has become commonly accepted within the teacher education community that students become increasingly more progressive or liberal in their attitudes during their stay at the university and then shift to opposing and more traditional views as they move into student teaching and inservice experience."[12] The attitudinal change has been attributed by researchers to various factors—the bureaucratic structure of the school, cooperating teachers, teaching colleagues, the ecology of the classroom, and pupils.

The difficulty, once again, is that attitude change is treated in much of the literature as though it were the same for all new teachers in all schools. This is an unfounded, if not, dangerous, conclusion. Veenman notes that if one actually examines the research, "the change in attitudes does not follow a same pattern for all groups of teachers, but depends in part on personal variables, on the quality of teacher training, and on the situational characteristics of the work place (the variables that can be altered by supervisors). For instance, it appeared that depressive, introverted and uncommunicative young teachers changed their attitudes in a more conservative direction than young teachers who did not possess these qualities. *The more discrepancies the young teachers experienced between school reality and their teacher training ideals, the more their attitudes changed in a conservative direction, and the more they were inclined to use authoritarian behavior.*"[13] It is not difficult to see how in situations without supervisory support (and without leaders who communicate a sense of excitement and the possible) teachers could retreat into a shell of self-preservation.

Nor should it be assumed that preservice teacher education programs are always "liberal and progressive." This notion, report Zeichner and Tabachnick, has recently been called in question by researchers.[14] And well they might. The competency-based teacher education movement, which began as a well-intentioned attempt to connect teacher preparation with reality, degenerated into the old efficiency model; teaching was fragmented into tiny behaviors (in absence of evidence of their validity), and the goals of schooling in a democratic society (promoting an active commitment to justice, and teaching the skills of political participation, are examples) were allowed to fall by the wayside. Not only did this conservative model dominate teacher education for more than a decade (the 1970s extending into the early 1980s), but the validity problem has resulted in certification programs that may have been "rejecting as many competent teachers as incompetent ones—maybe more!"[15]

The point is that new teachers *should* be idealistic and they should be liberal and progressive because the objectives of education in a democratic society are liberal and progressive—individual opportunity, social mobility, and an improved society. As the research shows, new teachers are most likely to hold on to their progressive ideals (if they have them) and make them operational in progressive schools where supervisors are also concerned with these objectives.

More important, perhaps, attitudes of teachers can shift in a liberal as well as a conservative direction. The reader need only recall the teachers in Oswego, New York, who, with the leadership of Edward A. Sheldon (who was able to communicate his sense of vision to them), built an entire curriculum around object lessons (see Chapter 2). This was the start of the progressive education era and the liberal thinking that produced most of our educational principles: meeting individual differences, for instance. During the Great Depression, teachers were influenced by state curriculum programs that dealt with the critical problems of our society. (In Virginia, the program was developed through the participation of more than 18,000 teachers.) The curriculum development programs were enormously successful in Alabama, Florida, and Virginia, and were the result of constructive and competent supervision from the state level to the local school.[16]

The overwhelming reason why teachers in the late nineteenth and early twentieth centuries (most of whom had little, if any, professional preparation) began to give greater attention to the social, emotional, and physical as well as the intellectual development of the child was that they embraced higher ideals for education, buttressed through the advent of inservice education. Out of the ideals of supervisors and teachers emerged a new conception of the school. Ideals can and should be generated by dynamic leadership and a good inservice program. In schools where new teachers do not lose their ideals, democratic educational leadership is evident.

Problems of Teachers as Perceived by Principals

According to reports by principals, classroom discipline is the area in which beginning teachers (both elementary and secondary) have the most difficulty.[17] In addition to discipline, dealing with individual differences, motivation, teaching slow learners, organization of class work, and evaluation of students' work are given high priority. Not surprisingly, problems with class control are seen by principals as the leading cause of failure in their teachers. Thus there are marked similarities in the perceptions of teachers and principals about the areas in which teachers have problems. But as Veenman reports, some studies have found appreciable differences in the perceptions of problems between principals and beginning teachers. For example, in one observational study, beginning teachers saw principals as wanting them to use certain materials and methods rather than helping them to better make their own professional decisions.[18] In another study, principals were asked to identify the leading causes for the failure of beginning teachers and named the following problems: lack of control, personality clash, immaturity, lack of organization, and lack of confidence (control of class and personality were tied for first place as factors in failure).[19]

Teachers, with some justification, do not perceive their "personalities" or "maturity" as classroom problems. (These are global terms that do not indicate specifically what needs changing to improve teaching.) Obviously, if there are differences in the perceptions of principals and teachers generally, this is even more likely to be so in individual cases. The principal's perception of a problem being experienced by a teacher on his or her faculty may differ considerably from the teacher's perception. As discussed in Chapter 4, teachers must be able to request supervisory assistance without having to go through the principal— for precisely this reason.

It is important to emphasize, however, that, in most studies there are great similarities in the rankings given to teacher's problems by principals and teachers.[20]

Preventing Failure. As observed by Kurtz, principals who have major problems with beginning teachers often believe erroneously that colleges and universities should turn out "finished products." They do not understand that role development can take several years and that there are factors within their control that can lead to success or failure for the beginning teacher.[21] Some of the factors are so obvious that they are all too easily overlooked. In a study of beginning secondary school teachers, Kurtz identified five controllable causes of failure: (1) improper teaching assignment, (2) isolation of classroom from mainstream of school, (3) inadequate teaching facilities, (4) lack of understanding of the district expectations, and (5) inadequate supervision. In many schools, returning teachers choose all the "good" courses and leave the rest for the new teachers. Also, difficult students are passed on in the same way. Failure can be prevented by not permitting beginning teachers to end up with cast-off courses when planning the master schedule. "The proper mix of courses and students is critical to the success or failure of many beginning teachers."[22]

"Teachers who are isolated from the mainstream of the school tend to show lower success rates," found Kurtz, and "it appears that *the closer the classroom is to the central office, the better the chance for success.*"[23] The reasons seem clear. If help is unavailable from incidental contacts and if new teachers are isolated from master teachers, they are more likely to fail.

The choice of rooms and fixtures is usually a matter of seniority, and it is not unusual to find that rooms have been "literally stripped" in advance of the new teacher's arrival. According to Kurtz, "It is absolutely imperative that the necessary materials are available to the newcomer," and he suggests that someone be appointed to help the new teacher furnish and set up his or her room.

Since orientation programs for new teachers rarely extend beyond two or three months, an enormous communication gap is often created between administrators and new teachers about district expectations. "The administrator *intends* to provide explanations but for reasons undetected by him, the teachers do not understand them." This is, observes Kurtz, "a vivid example of the discrepancy between intent and impact." What is needed is *continuous* guidance as the teacher passes through the various stages of role development. This role development can take several years. A year-long inservice program should be planned with topics specifically addressed to beginning teachers.

According to Kurtz, "Most problems could be curtailed or eliminated through proper supervision," but, in most cases the interaction between beginning teacher and supervisor has been minimal. In fact, the study found that "contact only comes when serious problems occur." Based on the findings, Kurtz recommends regular contacts ("weekly at least") by administrators and supervisors "to open communication lines and to identify problems as soon as possible."[24]

Experienced and Inexperienced Teachers

Not only beginning teachers have difficulties. Studies reveal that a number of the problems of beginning teachers are also problems of experienced teachers. Veenman reports that the main problems of experienced teachers are motivating students, lack of motivational help from the school, finding time for remedial work with individual students, and adapting instruction to the needs of slow learners.[25] Discipline problems also trouble experienced teachers. A large study conducted by the Chicago Teachers Union reported that managing disruptive students ranked second to being involuntarily transferred as a cause of stress.[26] In another large study by Feitler and Tokar, 58 per cent of the teachers surveyed ranked "individual pupils who continually misbehave" as the leading cause of stress.[27] It is interesting to note that in this study a "difficult class" of students ranked fifth as a cause of stress. Feitler and Tokar explain: "It seems that teacher stress was produced more often by one or two students who chronically misbehave, rather than a general lack of discipline."[28] However, our interest here is in comparing experienced with inexperienced teachers. Experienced teachers seem to be less concerned than beginning teachers with controlling an entire class, but they do experience behavior problems with individual students.

We think of motivation and discipline as separate problems, but "they are related in the sense that a high level of motivation largely precludes disruptive behavior. Conversely, a low level of motivation produces a climate conducive to misbehavior."[29] Thus although motivation, not discipline, was found by Veenman to be the most serious problem of experienced teachers, the bass notes of discipline are heard in the designation of motivation as a problem. (Indeed, if an unmotivated student is not doing his work, he or she is behaving inappropriately.)

THE PROBLEM OF DISCIPLINE

When making a classroom visit, if there is no disruptive behavior and students obey the teacher, we tend to dismiss discipline as a problem. This teacher has control. There are other factors to check that may need strengthening (the quality of questioning procedure, for instance), so we turn our attention to the questions now being posed by the teacher. We have made a mistake. Discipline is more than the ability to keep children *under* control; in fact, this is only a rudimentary kind of discipline. We want children to be *in* control; that is, we want them to be self-directing. There is no evidence that children are developing toward self-direction when they are merely following the teacher's directions. This factor needs attention.

Actually, there are two aspects that supervisors must consider with regard to discipline. The first is the teacher's ability to control a class and deal with behavior problems, and the second is the students' development toward self-direction. Supervisors tend to focus almost exclusively on the first aspect, as though it were the whole of discipline. This is understandable, in view of the fact that most of the recent literature has treated discipline as a managerial problem. Discipline is also an educational problem. This section of the chapter will attempt to deal with both aspects of discipline: class control and the development of self-direction in pupils. (The two are, of course, not unrelated.)

Problems with Class Control

What does the teacher mean when she or he says "I need help?" If the request comes from a beginning teacher (one with less than three years of inservice experience), the problem may be lack of control, compounded by lack of confidence. Let it be said at once that beginning teachers can have other reasons for requesting supervisory assistance, for example, inadequate instructional materials for slow children. And experienced teachers may have the sense that they are losing control of their classrooms. But since discipline has been identified by new teachers as their major source of difficulty, it is not unreasonable to assume that this is what the teacher means, but often will not say so unless the barriers to communication with supervisors have been lowered. (Opening communication is a major purpose of the orientation program for new teachers.)

Teaching as Discipline: Removing the Mystique. Many colleges of education today deal with discipline in their methods courses. This is a great advance over an era when discipline was swept under the pedagogical carpet. Yet a surprising number of new teachers still believe that discipline and teaching are separate matters, and many of their problems of control can be traced to this misconception. Discipline focused only on orderly conduct and turning children's energy off is bound to fail—after the first day of school. (Almost everyone is "good" on the first day.) Effective discipline directs the flow of children's energy toward learning goals instead of trying to turn it off. The most promising principle for supervisors to impart to new (and experienced) teachers is that *discipline is inseparable from teaching.* There is nothing mystical or magical about discipline. Good teachers view discipline as part of the instructional–motivational process. Problem behavior can be handled (or prevented in the first place) by directions, questions, explanations, clarification, giving cues, and helping students to correct their mistakes. Methods of discipline relate not only to control but to learning. As pointed out elsewhere, "Successful discipline simply cannot be separated from what the disciplinarian does as a teacher."[30]

Behavior Modification: Answering the Hard Questions. Whenever there is clamor for the adoption in classrooms of a special technique for discipline, and behavior modification is an example, supervisors must consider its compatibility with district philosophy and its feasibility for use by teachers. There must also be evidence as to its effectiveness. Behavior modification is based on the viewpoint that learners are automatic and externally controlled. This philosophy is in conflict with the view that teachers are most likely to hold students' attention when students feel that they are learning how to do the things that they need to do in their lives. Moreover, as Brophy and Putnam point out, there are practical questions about feasibility. Behavior-modification systems attempt to control misbehavior by ignoring it, which is supposed to decrease its frequency, but "certain misbehaviors are too disruptive or dangerous to be ignored" and "some students interpret lack of overt disapproval as approval, assuming that anything not explicitly disapproved is acceptable."[31]

According to Brophy and Putnam, "Perhaps the greatest problem with behavioristic approaches is the lack of convincing evidence that short-term gains generalize to other settings and persist over time."[32] The philosophical and practical problems with behavior-modification systems, not to mention the lack of evidence about their effectiveness, give cause for caution by the classroom teacher. The point cannot be overstressed. The rise of behavioristic theory in the past two decades has led to the view, in some quarters (particularly in urban schools), that behavior modification is the sum and substance of discipline.

There are other approaches to class control and dealing with the problems of individual students, for example, the psychodynamic model of discipline, which is based on the idea that understanding the child is the key to solving behavioral problems. Space does not permit a discussion of the various models of discipline here. All that can be said is that these models serve as a source of ideals and methods in classroom discipline, and supervisors should emphasize that teachers can draw on a variety of approaches in preventing and dealing with discipline problems.[33]

But when all is said and done, the most effective approach to discipline is through the curriculum: what is taught and how it is taught. Work that is too difficult can cause discipline problems, as can work that is too easy. Class control can be improved with learning activities that are appropriate for student developmental levels and that provide a sense of growing power and accomplishment. Class control can also be increased by increasing the participation of more students in the learning activities.[34] This is not surprising. Classroom discipline must be connected with its purpose, the improvement of learning.

Troubleshooting for Class Control. Each of the factors influencing learning is also a factor in classroom control. Supervisors can help teachers to increase their effectiveness and decrease their problems of control by strengthening the factors that need attention. As shown in the troubleshooting guide in Chapter 7 (Table 7–1), some of these factors directly concern discipline. For example, discipline should be self-directing and students should exhibit responsibility for the consequences of their own actions. The supervisor observing the teacher needing help may find neither of these factors in evidence. How can students learn self-direction?

A number of strategies for use in classrooms proceed from the work of Piaget, and they are discussed shortly. However, lack of self-discipline and responsibility is a schoolwide problem as well as a classroom problem and should be viewed as an opportunity for school improvement. In this connection, a study conducted by the Phi Delta Kappa (PDK) Commission on Discipline identified two outstanding characteristics of schools that were especially effective in teaching students self-discipline. First, these schools had as the goal of their discipline program teaching students to behave appropriately without direct supervision. (Although this may seem patently obvious, stating goals clearly is absolutely essential if we are to evaluate our effectiveness in achieving them.) Second, the schools had developed a feeling of community. Punishments and formal rules, were seldom used in these schools and were found to "play only a small part in such communities." The emphasis was, rather, on trying to develop a positive climate, "one in which 'belongingness,' service, and learning are valued."[35] Based on the findings of the PDK study, schools can foster a sense of community in their students in the following ways: (1) Recognizing the importance of each individual in the school. For instance, teachers should know as many students' names as possible. (2) Involving as many students as possible in the life of the school. This may be done by seeing that there are enough extraclass activities to involve most of the students, by displaying students' work, and by giving students responsibility for maintaining the school and keeping it clean. (3) Developing a student leadership program. Students should be involved with teachers, administrators, and parents in identifying and solving school problems. (4) Modeling respect for others. Teachers and administrators who respect students are modeling the way that individuals are expected to treat one another; if modeled consistently enough, respect for others will become the norm of behavior in the school. (5) Setting up a system for recognizing students who demonstrate a willingness to work hard and learn (not necessarily those who achieve the highest grades). Teachers nominate students, and a joint letter from the principal and teacher goes to the parents. (6) Developing plan for dealing with students who are chronic behavior problems. In Charleston, South Carolina, for example, such youngsters are given tutorial assistance and psychological support services and they are "strongly encouraged to participate in extracurricular activities at school." By increasing their involvement and commitment, they are more likely to meet the behavioral norms and to feel better about themselves.[36]

Developing Responsible Self-direction

Teachers tend to live in the present where discipline is concerned. The absence of disciplinary problems in one's classroom is considered sufficient, if not cause for silent rejoicing, for many teachers. Yet teachers know that responsible self-direction is a central aim of education and discipline. Every educational psychology book includes a treatment of Piaget's theories of child development, and the central idea in books on the history of education and social studies methods is the democratic commitment to help the young become self-directing.

There are three major reasons why many teachers have neglected this all-important educational objective. First, they are afraid that in the course of teaching self-direction, which involves practice in choosing one's own actions intelligently, they will lose control of the class. Second, the idea of self-direction has been misconstrued by educators in the past; many educational reformers in the progressive education era, and in the open-education movement of the late 1960s and early 1970s, took the position that children are automatically ready for self-direction and need only to be left to themselves. When teachers tried to put this romantic and theoretically unsound idea into practice, the results were often disastrous. The third reason is that many teachers are not prepared to implement a developmental approach to self-direction. As Paul Hanna observes, "Few teachers have the necessary skills to set teaching–learning tasks that stimulate pupils to self-discipline."[37] Teacher education has been deficient in this area.

The Blueprint. What constitutes beginning competence in classroom behavior and what constitutes fully developed competence? How does one begin to build self-direction? Table 8–1 presents a three-stage sequence in discipline that is based on developmental theories, primarily the work of Piaget, and research on discipline and education.[38] The developmental stages are grounded on Piaget's idea that the direction of development is away from dependence on authority and toward autonomy. In Piaget's description of the development of moral judgment, young children see rules as rooted in adult authority and the world from their own perspective; they are incapable of true cooperation with others. But as their intellective capability undergoes qualitative developmental changes (which require appropriate environing conditions at home and at school), they should move away from obeying merely to please the authority figure and toward judging appropriate behavior by the situation. They should also be able to work with others to improve a situation. Finally, in late childhood or early adolescence they reflect on human relationships in general and can work out their own principles for dealing with them.

The idea of autonomy as an educational objective is often credited entirely to Piaget. For example, according to Kamii, Dewey "had ideas similar to Piaget's" but "based his objectives and methods on personal opinions rather than on scientific theories."[39] This is simply not the case; Dewey's ideas derived from his observations of children in his Laboratory School at the University of Chicago around the turn of the century. Moreover, Dewey's ideas contain the elements of a complete educational theory (see Chapter 2). Thus Dewey stressed the social as well as the psychological nature of learning. A classroom was a little society where the child learned to participate with others in realizing social goals. The emphasis on the social character of education is important for us here since much of the school's discipline problem involves appropriate membership in a society.

As shown in Table 8–1, the three stages of discipline are Stage I, the *basic* stage; Stage II, the *constructive* stage; and Stage III, the *generative* stage. Under this model, both pupils and teachers have specific responsibilities in each stage of discipline. The model is not intended to present an exhaustive list of pupil and teacher responsibilities for each stage but to provide examples. Thus pupils at the basic stage must be able to listen to their teacher, follow directions, and ask questions when they fail to understand concepts and procedures. They must also be able to share materials with others. Basic discipline is absolutely necessary for school learning. It is also necessary if teachers and students are to thrive together

Table 8–1 Disciplinary Stages

Stage	Pupil Responsibility (Examples)	Teacher Role
Stage I (basic disciplinary stage)	Listens to teacher and to other members of class; follows directions; asks questions when failing to understand concepts, procedures, etc.; knows how to share materials and resources.	Teaches effectively so that pupils understand concepts, procedures, etc.; encourages pupils to ask questions when they do not understand; helps pupils to judge behavior in terms of the work to be done; is a good role model.
Stage II (constructive stage)	Takes the role of the other person (reciprocity); recognizes the needs and rights of others; works cooperatively with others; understands the basis for all reasonable organizational rules and procedures; can select and develop procedures for accomplishing an objective; understands the concept of justice.	Explains bases for organizational rules and procedures; involves pupils in socially constructive activities; gives pupils opportunities to participate in planning and to work cooperatively together; uses incidents of daily life and the curriculum to develop the concept of justice; is a good role model.
Stage III (generative stage)	Autonomously behaving, socially responsible, leadership; upholds the concept of justice; conceptualizes a problem, generates and tests solutions; makes choices on his or her own responsibility in situations which have no rules.	Provides leadership opportunities; encourages the development of moral principles and values; helps students to conceptualize social problems and develop plans of action; provides students with the ego strength needed for autonomous, principled action; is a good role model.

Source: Laurel N. Tanner, *Classroom Discipline for Effective Teaching and Learning* p. 28. Copyright © 1978 by Holt, Rinehart and Winston, Reprinted by permission of CBS College Publishing.

in their classrooms, not just survive together. The teacher's job is to provide effective instruction so that students comprehend what is being taught and can actively engage in productive learning instead of doing something else. (That something else—chair pushing, teasing, or wandering aimlessly around the room—can make life miserable for the teacher and fellow students.) By teaching effectively the teacher is providing an environment where learning can take place. The teacher must encourage students to ask questions when they do not understand (see the troubleshooting guide, Table 7–1). Discipline is a stage, not an age. Some children come to school at the basic disciplinary stage (or beyond) as a result of home training, but others do not. The school must begin where the home leaves off in discipline. Pupils will be most likely to reach the basic stage (Stage I) if teachers utilize such suggestions as follow:

1. Pupils must be taught to raise their hands to speak and not to talk when someone else is talking. When youngsters are volatile, learning not to call out may take much practice (and much patience on the part of the teacher). Here we are using the training model of discipline which aims for control through force of habit.[40] But we aim for more than mechanical behavior; we hope to develop a sense of responsibility and consideration for others.

2. Children who have trouble listening should not be lectured to at length.

3. Learning should be broken up into small but interconnected and meaningful steps, and teachers should ask pupils what the steps are to make certain that directions and concepts are understood. To ensure growth in understanding, reasons underlying ideas and actions should be elicited from the pupils.

4. How pupils are to share materials should be made clear. Materials should be readily available because waiting for them can cause loss of control.

5. A definite place should be assigned for each material, and supply closets should be kept in good order to facilitate the distribution of materials and make sharing systematic.

A word must be said about the secondary school student who has not attained basic discipline, for this may be his last chance to learn to channel his energies and direct his powers constructively. Ultimately, his future rests on the ability to do so. The central problem of adolescence is the search for self-identity, which centers on the selection of an occupation or life goal. But no long-range purpose or integrated effort toward a life goal is possible until the youth is at least at the basic disciplinary stage. Helping him reach that state after so many years takes patience and hard work. An ever-present problem for the adolescent who has not attained basic discipline is motivation. Perhaps the best answer we have is individualizing—motivating him by developing goals for him as an individual and helping him to develop social responsibility. This is being done for mainstreamed handicapped youth. The 15-year-old who cannot listen and follow directions is handicapped, although the law may not recognize him as such. An individualized learning plan must be constructed for him and with him. Basic discipline is not an end point; it is a turning point. In our society it is not enough to listen and follow directions.

Pupils at Stage II, the constructive stage, can work cooperatively with others on a problem or project and can select and develop procedures for accomplishing an objective. As implied by the name, children in the constructive stage contribute to the social good of the classroom rather than simply abiding by the rules. An important feature of this stage is social responsibility. In the preceding chapter, collaborative-cooperative learning was discussed as a factor in achievement. Teachers are more likely to provide youngsters with opportunities to work cooperatively if they know that collaborative-cooperative learning influences not only development in discipline but also achievement and attitudes toward school. As Owens and Barnes summarize, "There is abundant data that leads to the claim that cooperative learning procedures in classrooms promote greater achievement and more positive attitudes toward schooling, teachers and peers."[41]

Teacher responsibilities at this stage are to involve pupils in socially constructive activities and to give pupils opportunities to help one another, to work cooperatively together on a problem or project, and to participate in planning. As an illustration of a socially constructive activity, a ninth-grade metal shop class in San Francisco designed and made adjustable wheelchair trays for handicapped persons to use at the local community recreation center. They personally delivered the trays and saw how their work brought pleasure to others. The point at which the activity conveyed to the students that their actions can have social value was when they saw the trays being put to use by handicapped persons. The impact of such activities is in their reality; they are ways of helping students meet real social problems. And they are discipline-developing activities.[42]

As noted, teachers are well aware that children should develop cooperative skills and attitudes by working together in small groups, but many teachers adhere to Stage I methods of control for fear of losing class control. Supervisors can suggest that possibly the best way to start with small-group work is to begin with one group. Teachers can work with the small group, training them in problem solving (see Chapter 2) and group discussion skills while the rest of the class is doing independent work. When this small group finishes its work it can be split and new members added to work on new problems or projects. There will then be some trained members in each group.

Individuals at Stage III, the generative stage, are self-directing; they have achieved the goal of discipline. The differences between responsibilities of pupils in the constructive and generative stages are in degree rather than in kind. Both engage in constructive action, but whereas an individual in the constructive stage recognizes the needs of others and is able to work cooperatively with others in solving problems, the individual at the generative stage is oriented to the improvement of conditions to the point of taking the initiative. Learners at this stage can conceptualize a problem and test solutions. They can make principled choices on their own responsibility in situations that have no externally imposed rules. Examples of teacher responsibilities are to put forward models of autonomous principled action from literature, science, and art; encourage the development of moral principles and values; and help students to conceptualize social problems. Of great importance, the teacher should be a good role model— socially optimistic and oriented to the improvement of society. As Havighurst's work conveys, children and youth are more likely to develop an active interest in social welfare if they are involved in projects that serve society.[43]

The idea, of course, is that we want children to make principled decisions for themselves—and to have the courage of their convictions. But as Kamii points out, children learn early not to trust their own thinking.

> When I visit first grade classrooms in which children are working on arithmetic worksheets, I often ask individual children how they arrived at particular answers. They typically react to my question by grabbing their erasers—even when their answers are perfectly correct. As early as first grade, many children have learned to distrust their own thinking.[44]

Autonomy is developed when children are encouraged to explain their reasoning. Most teachers do not do this; they simply mark an answer (such as $3 + 1 = 5$ incorrect on a worksheet) and the youngster is convinced that the truth comes out of the adult's head. Kamii's suggestions are most helpful here:

> A better reaction is to encourage two children who arrived at different answers to explain their thinking to one another. Alternatively, the teacher can ask the child, "How did you get 5?" Children often correct themselves autonomously as they try to explain their reasoning to someone else.[45]

Learning to trust one's thinking and engaging in principled action begin to develop early and depend greatly on good teaching. Once again, we see clearly that learning and discipline are inseparable. In Chapter 7, encouraging children to explain how they got a given answer was suggested as a means of improving learning. Here it is discussed as a way of developing autonomy.

THE PROBLEM OF MOTIVATION

We turn now to the second most frequently mentioned classroom problem and perhaps the most neglected problem—motivating students to learn. In our technologically oriented society, we have searched for mechanical substitutes for motivation; behavior-modification systems have been proposed in much of the literature as a means of involving pupils in their work. But time and again we have found that students' attention is likely to be superficial and short-lived when they are untouched by the assigned work and there is no interest. There is no substitute for motivation—the real thing. (Teachers know this, for they rank motivation as a leading problem.)

Motivation is positive in its very essence. It is a moving and dynamic element in children that is sparked by (indeed, feeds upon) the positive attitudes and encouragement of adults. Teachers' interactions with students are crucial for motivation. In fact, part of teaching *is* motivation. The studies of Bloom on improving instruction suggest that teachers should "attempt to find something positive and encouraging in each student's response."[46] If observation of the teacher reveals that this quality of instruction is missing or needs improvement, the supervisor should point out its importance as a variable in student achievement.

In studying a teaching situation where motivation is a problem, the supervisor may find it helpful to begin by checking the factors under "Quality of Interactions with Students" on the troubleshooting guide (Table 7–1). Does the teacher give students equal opportunity for learning and convey positive expectations to all students rather than just the top few in the class? If these factors are not in evidence, this may be where the trouble lies. (However, any and all of the factors on the guide can increase student motivation, if given attention, such as by relating the subject matter to the life experiences of students and integrating students' contributions into the class discussion. Good teaching motivates students toward productive, self-impelled learning.)

Expectations and Motivation

The "expectancy phenomenon" has been treated previously and will be given only the briefest attention at this point. Essentially, the teacher's expectancy of pupils' academic achievement may be communicated to pupils, potentially influencing their self-evaluations of ability and, ultimately, their achievement.

It goes without saying that reduced expectations of children are unlikely to solve the problem of motivation (or any classroom problem, for that matter). Thus it is astonishing to find a writer in *Theory Into Practice* make the suggestion that teachers lower their expectations of students as a means of "stress management" on the ground that high expectations "are almost impossible to meet in today's classroom." He continues,

> It is ludicrous to suggest in our teacher preparation programs that teachers can expect to achieve the kinds of results achieved (yesteryear) when teachers had students who were highly motivated and when parents were highly supportive of schools and viewed the schools as bastions of opportunity for their children.[47]

The effect of such statements is destructive. The above statement perpetuates the myth of motivated students and supportive parents of yesteryear, in comparison to today's shortcomings. Moreover, many students today *are* highly motivated, often due to the work and expectations of their teachers, and many parents *are* highly supportive of schools. Furthermore, studies show that parents continue to place great faith in education and to view the schools as a ladder to higher social and economic positions for their children.[48] As noted in Chapter 1, parental demands for more and better educational opportunities for their children have, if anything, intensified. To propose that student teachers be led to believe otherwise and lower their expectations as a means of stress reduction is quackery.

"Surely, the teacher in a class of chronically unmotivated students must have different expectations as to what is possible than a teacher of the gifted," suggests the writer.[49] He might have added, "and pass them on to the students." What he is proposing flies in the face of research on teacher interaction with students in the classroom. Merely reading such proposals provides evidence of the need for supervisors to evaluate all proposals critically in terms of the entire body of research.

Enthusiasm: The God Within

"The Greeks have given us one of the most beautiful words of our language, *enthusiasm* which means, the god within."[50] So wrote René Dubos in his biography of Louis Pasteur. For Pasteur, the basic element in his success as an ardent and imaginative teacher and a brilliant scientist was his enthusiasm, in its literal meaning: He firmly believed that he was inspired by the god within.

The emphasis placed by Pasteur on enthusiasm as the best explanation for his success is pertinent here because researchers have found that enthusiastic teaching is indeed related to pupil achievement.[51] The reason seems clear. The teacher's strong excitement about a subject moves and motivates students, whereas the teacher's flat and listless presentation has a depressing effect. Often a lack of teacher enthusiasm lies at the heart of the motivation problem. As William James observed in 1899, in his *Talks to Teachers:* "It is useless for a dull and devitalized teacher to exhort her pupils to wake up and take an interest. She must first take one herself; then her example is effective as no exhortation can possibly be."[52] Yet despite its enormous importance as a motivating force, the word *enthusiasm* is rarely found in the index of educational psychology textbooks.

Components of Enthusiastic Teaching. Table 8–2 presents some teaching behaviors that relate to enthusiastic teaching and have been found by researchers to be related to student achievement. Any and all of these behaviors can be developed by a teacher if found not in evidence by the supervisor. The fact that a teacher can be motivated to teach either with or without enthusiasm, and with strikingly different results in either case, is shown clearly in an experiment conducted by Mastin in the 1960s.[53] Twenty teachers of sixth- and seventh-grade youngsters in Des Moines, Iowa, were asked to give two illustrated lectures to their classes, one dealing with ancient Egypt and the other with ancient Rome and Pompeii. The first lesson was given by the teacher "in such a manner as to convey to the group a feeling that he had an indifferent attitude toward the ideas and pictures being presented and the subject of the lesson." One week later the same teacher gave the second lesson, but this time, so "as to convey to his pupils the impression that he was enthusiastic about the ideas and illustrative materials of the lesson and the subject."[54] The pupils were given tests of knowledge and attitude toward the subject and the teacher after each lesson.

In nineteen out of twenty classes the class mean of the lesson which had been taught with enthusiasm was higher than the mean of the lesson taught with indifference. This was true whether it was taught first or second, or whether it was the Egyptian or the Roman lesson. A study of individual scores showed that nearly 80 percent of the students made higher scores on the test over the enthusiastically presented lesson, and more than two-thirds of the students gave the enthusiastic teacher higher scores on the attitude scale and indicated an interest in learning more about the subject. More important, perhaps, according to Rosenshine, studies of enthusiastic-surgent versus indifferent-dull teacher behavior provide "strikingly consistent results."[55]

Studies also indicate that the ideas in teacher's presentations are remembered more frequently when accompanied by gesture. In one study, high school students achieved higher scores when the speaker gestured, even when they only heard the speaker, which points to the importance of vocal inflection. (Gesturing is usually accompanied by variations in pitch and volume.[56]) In a review of the correlational research on teacher education and student achievement since Rosenshine's review, Bettencourt and his associates found that the research "has continued to yield positive results."[57]

Table 8–2.   Some Dimensions of Enthusiastic Teaching: Supervisor's Appraisal Guide

Dimension of Enthusiasm	In Evidence	Not in Evidence/ Needs Attention
1. The energy dimension		
(a) Teacher is energetic	_____	_____
(b) Teacher is enthusiastic	_____	_____
(c) Teacher asks varied questions, with emphasis on questions of interpretation and opinion as well as factual questions	_____	_____
(d) Teacher praises and encourages frequently	_____	_____
2. The animation dimension		
(a) Teacher is a fluent speaker	_____	_____
(b) Teacher is expressive (varies voice in pitch and volume)	_____	_____
(c) Teacher accompanies statements with gestures	_____	_____
(d) Teacher uses eye contact	_____	_____
(e) Teacher is mobile (moves about frequently) but is relaxed	_____	_____
3. The stimulation dimension		
(a) Teacher communicates a sense of excitement about the subject being taught	_____	_____
(b) Teacher is imaginative and creative in explaining ideas and concepts	_____	_____
(c) Students follow teacher's example and exhibit interest and involvement in the lesson	_____	_____

The Teachability of Enthusiasm. It is of interest and importance to supervisors that teacher enthusiasm has been increased experimentally. In an experiment with first-year elementary teachers, Bettencourt and his coworkers used microteaching techniques (the videotaping of teachers in action) to provide teachers with a mirror of what they were (or were not) doing, and the teachers increased their level of enthusiasm "in most cases substantially."[58] The pupils of teachers who received enthusiasm training were "substantially" more attentive than the pupils of control group teachers. It is of great interest that this was true whether they were doing independent seatwork or involved in a teacher-led activity. The enthusiasm continued to have a motivational effect even when the children were working by themselves. The researchers explain the effect this way: "Our examination of the videotaped lessons suggests that teachers' expression of enthusiasm conveys the message that they are eager for students to learn and will persist in helping them. Once students receive such a motivational message, they may not need to continue receiving it through exposure to constant teacher enthusiastic behavior."[59]

THE PROBLEM OF INDIVIDUAL DIFFERENCES

Teachers really want to gear the curriculum to the needs of individuals. We know this because of the high ranking they give to this problem. But individualized systems of teaching with their stress on step-by-step mastery should in no way be considered synonymous with meeting differences in pupil ability—not to mention their attitudes, interests, and talents. Our society is enriched by the diverse talents, interests, and skills of its people. The use of self-instructional "learning activity packages" does not help the school to cultivate this diversity and interdependence. Indeed, some educators believe that relying on individualized systems to deal with individual differences "may widen rather than narrow the gap between student needs and teacher responses."[60]

The development of individualized (mastery) systems in America was discussed in Chapter 2 and the reader may find it helpful to refer back to that discussion. In this section we first consider the research on individualized systems and then we will turn to ways that supervisors and teachers can provide for differences in learners.

Individualized Systems of Instruction: The Findings

Supervisors and teachers who look to individualized systems as a means of improving achievement of students in elementary and secondary schools will discover that the research findings are disappointing. In mathematics teaching, for example, Schoen found that results were strongly against systems of individualized instruction, at both the elementary and secondary school levels.[61] Although Bloom and his colleagues, Block and Burns, have stressed the effectiveness of mastery strategies at all levels of instruction and in a variety of subject areas,[62] some researchers have found methodological weaknesses in the research on mastery learning. For example, according to Bangert, Kulik, and Kulik, in the studies that Block and Burns cite in support of the effectiveness of mastery learning, both experimental and control groups used self-instructional materials; there was no control group taught by conventional classroom methods. (The reader has heard of a "no-win situation"; self-instructional materials were in a "no-lose situation.") Thus the studies by Block and Burns did not meet the criteria for experimental research.[63]

Bangert, Kulik, and Kulik reviewed experimental studies on individualized systems from grades 6 through 12. They report that a number of the studies that they located could not be included in their analysis because they were unacceptable as studies of comparative effectiveness. In one study, students in the experimental group were permitted to retake examinations in order to raise their scores, but students in the control group had to be content with their initial scores. In another, examinations were given to only a fifth of the experimental group (those who had reached a certain unit) but were given to all members of the control group.[64] This is a classic case in educational research of setting up the control group as a "wooden-legged competitor" in order to prove the superiority of the experimental group.

The results of the experimental studies analyzed by Bangert, Kulik, and Kulik show that "individualized systems at the secondary level yield results that are much the same as those from conventional teaching. In the typical individualized class, students do not gain more on achievement measures than they do in the typical conventional class. Nor do students gain more in critical thinking ability, in self-esteem, or in appreciation of the subject being studied." They add that "these conclusions will not be a surprise to those familiar with reviews of findings on individualized systems in mathematics education."[65] The point of importance is that whether they go under the label of individualized instruction or something else, teaching methods should not be adopted that clearly are not an improvement over existing methods. A critical aspect of supervision and leadership is to be able to resist the barrage of promotional claims about a new method and base one's conclusions about effectiveness on research evidence. Supervisors (and teachers) must, themselves, be at the level of autonomous thinking. They must also be critical consumers of research.

But of course there is an additional problem in the case of so-called individualized systems of instruction. As Gibbons observes, they "encourage teachers to claim to be individualizing while continuing mass teaching methods."[66] Yet one cannot in all fairness blame the teachers, who, as Veatch observes, "simply follow the precepts of the particular program they are inflicted with."[67] Mastery learning and other individualized systems have become a vast commercial enterprise and it is vitally important that supervisors recognize this as one of their leading problems in improving the work of teachers and the opportunities of students.

Dealing with Individual Differences

If a teacher had only one student, the problem of individual differences in that classroom would not exist. What we would have is one-to-one tutoring. As noted in Chapter 5, Bloom views the teacher's problem as one of teaching individuals in classes as well as they can be taught under good tutoring conditions. There is no magic program that can make this possible. Moreover, according to Talmadge, "To search for a perfect individualized program fitted to the needs of each person is a fantasy that diverts our attention from ways we can realistically respond to individual differences."[68]

The principle of individual differences has in education the status of one of the Ten Commandments in religion. Each child is an individual and the school should know him as an individual, provide for his learning rate, and help him when he is in trouble. The evolution of this principle is one of the great achievements of American education. The trouble is that it it tends to remain at the status of a lofty commandment—a "Thou shalt." (One can even find in the earlier literature references to the "*belief* in individualized instruction.")[69]

Much of the literature on individual differences approaches the problem from the standpoint of the psychologist and is concerned with how people differ in the rate, style, and quality of their learning. Often overlooked in the discussion of how individuals differ is that these differences cause problems for teachers. (Cronbach observed that individual differences used to be eliminated by eliminating the students; less successful learners dropped out.[70]) Differences are opportunities. Every class that helps a youngster develop his or her talents or interests is a celebration of possibility. But individual differences in learning are classroom problems and should be recognized as such by the supervisor.

Learning and Individual Differences: A Problem-Solving Approach. Supervisors and teachers need a systematic scheme for attacking the problems presented by the differences in ability, interest, and attitudes of individual students. Table 8–3 presents three factors that must be examined and shows how they are applicable in a teaching–learning situation. The factors are the *problem* (or symptoms of a problem) exhibited by the learner, the best data available concerning the *learner*, and the *curriculum*. On the surface, the teacher may see the problem as Susie's failure to complete her worksheets and other assignments, along with her lethargic attitude in the classroom. But this behavior is only symptomatic of a deeper problem. The teacher must examine insofar as practicable the possible conditions bearing on Susie's behavior, namely her ability, home environment, physical and emotional health, and peer relations. Finding these conditions to be favorable, the teacher examines Susie's behavior in connection with the classroom activities and assignments (the curriculum). The teacher observes that when Susie is given opportunities to read for pleasure or for ideas, she becomes attentive. When asked about her other classroom assignments, Susie says that the ditto worksheets are boring. Earlier, the teacher had rationalized that if other students do the worksheets without complaint, then the fault rests solely with Susie. However, the teacher observes that although the other youngsters complete the worksheets successfully, they exhibit little enthusiasm. A considerable portion of class time is devoted to these worksheets and other mechanical exercises and recitations. Realizing that Susie's behavior is symptomatic of a wider problem affecting all pupils, the teacher's hypothesis stemming from the classroom situation is that the assignments and other classroom activities (the curriculum) must be made more stimulating and challenging not only for Susie, but for all the youngsters. (Boredom has always been the greatest problem of school learning.)

As shown in Table 8–3, the right questions must be asked if the right solutions are to be found. Very often what may appear on the surface to be an individual problem is actually symptomatic of a much wider and deeper classroom problem. In proceeding to reconstruct the curriculum so as to make it idea oriented rather than skill-drill oriented, the teacher is addressing the curriculum problem in the light of the pupil-motivation problem. In this connection, skills are developed through meaningful application to concepts and ideas rather than in isolation.

Turning to factors other than the curriculum, it should be noted that if the teacher had found in Susie's case that the home was not supportive, then the teacher should have sought to address this variable. Nevertheless, since the curriculum is the variable most completely under the school's control, improving the instructional program for individual learners, as well as for the class as a whole, is where the school must direct its emphasis.

Supervisory Support: The Essential Ingredient. If teachers are to do a good job of solving the problems presented by individual students, they must have realistic conditions for doing so. Actually, these conditions are nothing more or less than supervisory support in its most concrete forms. The following are specific ways that supervisors and administrators can provide this support:

1. Assign teachers a reasonable number of students to teach. It is not uncommon in these days of burgeoning enrollments at the elementary school level, for

Table 8–3 Responding to Individual Learners

Problem Situation	Learner	Classroom Context and Curriculum	Problem	Hypotheses
Susie is lethargic, stares off into space; fails to complete worksheets; often gives wrong answers in recitations; appears bored.	Susie is exceptionally bright and well liked by peers. Parents are supportive and home environment is favorable. Recent medical examination by family physician reveals no organic or emotional problems. When asked about her classroom assignments, Susie says the worksheets and other exercises are boring.	Considerable portion of classroom time is devoted to worksheets and mechanical exercises. The teaching–learning repertoire can best be described as a series of skill-drill exercises and recitations focused on recall. Other students do the assignments, satisfactorily, for the most part, though the weaker pupils do not show much improvement. None of the pupils show any real enthusiasm or interest in their work.	How can the classroom work be made more challenging and interesting, not only for Susie but for all pupils?	Pupil motivation will be enhanced and learning will be improved through idea-oriented teaching instead of skill-drill teaching and rote learning. A richer variety of learning resources and activities are needed, giving emphasis to the development of skills through their applications in meaningful contexts.

first-grade teachers to find themselves facing classes with thirty or more students. If individualization is to be more than a farce of mass methods under that name, teachers must study students as individuals and work with them as individuals. This is impossible unless teachers have the time to do so.

2. Provide teachers with sufficient books and materials that they can get into students' hands. Individualization is impossible without appropriate materials.

3. Provide a central library. Students must have a library if they are to have access to the wide variety of books and other materials needed in widening and deepening their knowledge. No classroom library with books brought by the teacher can meet this requirement. In addition to using the library as needed (without a rigid schedule for class visits), students should be allowed to use it to read for recreation. The library should be open at all times of the school day and also before and after school.

4. Give teachers freedom in planning and conducting their work. As emphasized throughout this book, the teacher must be permitted (indeed, encouraged) to use her or his own judgment about materials and methods that will be most suitable for the students in her or his own class. Individualization is impossible without this freedom.

5. Provide teachers with time and the opportunity to improve their own work. This may take the form of meetings to discuss mutual problems in adapting instruction to individual differences in various curriculum areas. Those teachers who have been particularly successful can convey their ideas and methods to others. Or (as suggested earlier) teachers can visit other classes and other schools. A good professional library is also demanded by research developments in teaching and learning and the need for teachers to apply these new understandings in their work.

6. Give greater attention to the question, "How can children be helped to discover and develop their talents?" Creative people do not develop in a vacuum but in an environment that encourages the development of creativity. If children are provided only with a narrow set of experiences, their potential for creativity in writing, music, or art will never be realized. Creativity is a districtwide and schoolwide responsibility as well as the teacher's responsibility. Every school should have facilities and resources for a rich curriculum, including vocal and instrumental music, science, shopwork, the arts, and so on. Every school should have as its objective the early identification and encouragement of the creative potentialities of all children.

THE PROBLEM OF RELATIONSHIPS WITH PARENTS

The home is the most powerful ally of the school where children's learning is concerned. Yet in too many schools, teachers and supervisors have not looked clearly at this force and have not cultivated it as a means of improving pupil achievement. Parents and teachers are bound to each other by the common desire that the children do well. This is a more-than-sufficient basis for cooperation and mutual respect. But as the professionals who have the responsibility to do everything possible to help children learn, teachers and supervisors must take the lead in developing a strong partnership with parents. In many classrooms where lack of support from parents is a problem, teachers have not opened home–school communication early in the school year. Parents and teachers should get to know each other before they must communicate on a professional basis about the progress or lack of progress of students. Prevention is the best cure for poor home–school relationships.

The Home Environment and School Learning

Relationships with parents have to be understood by supervisors and teachers at two distinct levels. The first is a *social level:* People react more positively to individuals they know and like than to complete strangers. Teachers are more likely to get the support they need from parents if the school brings parents and teachers together to get acquainted and to talk informally. Although supervisors and teachers may see "open school nights" and coffee hours primarily as opportunities to acquaint parents with the educational goals of the school, the social purpose of such meetings is equally important. They can provide the opportunities to lay the foundations of mutual trust and support.

The second is an *educational level,* and is concerned with the realities of the home's influence on children's school achievement.

Effects of the Home Environment. There is a growing body of evidence that points to the importance of the home as an essential partner in the educational process. More important for supervisors and teachers, researchers have gone beyond looking at global environmental variables of income and social class to study dynamic process variables, that is, what parents do in their interactions with the child that is likely to promote the development of school learning. Preeminent of all researchers in investigating this problem is Benjamin Bloom. The following environmental processes, as described by Bloom, correlate highly with school achievement:

1. Work habits of the family—the degree of routine in the home management, the emphasis on regularity in the use of space and time, and the priority given to schoolwork over other more pleasurable activities.
2. Academic guidance and support—the availability and quality of the help and encouragement parents give the child for his or her schoolwork and the conditions they provide to support the child's schoolwork.
3. Stimulation in the home—the opportunity provided by the home to explore ideas, events and the larger environment.
4. Language development—opportunities in the home for the development of correct and effective language usage.
5. Academic aspirations and expectations—the parents' aspirations for the child, the standards they set for the child's school achievement, and their interests in and knowledge of the child's school experiences.[71]

It is important to note here that much of the research on the impact of the home on school success was generated in the War on Poverty of the 1960s and was addressed to the learning problems of low-income children. However, the research tended toward universally applicable principles.[72] Now all parents and teachers are seen as necessary partners, not just disadvantaged parents. (The literature on reading has been particularly influenced by research on the language deficiencies of poor children.[73])

The point of importance is that the parental role in school learning is now a part of the general literature on school learning. Bloom points this out on the very first page of his book, *Human Characteristics and School Learning:* "The home, especially in the age period of about two to ten, develops language, the ability to learn from adults, and some of the qualities of need achievement, work habits, and attention to tasks which are basic to the work of the schools" and *"it is possible that many homes which do it poorly could do much better if the parents were made more aware of the effects of their interactions with their children."*[74] What Bloom is saying is that an important part of the educational process must be carried on in the home. Children must understand the conversational pattern of a good lesson, for example, if they are to learn from their teacher. (This is what is meant by the ability to learn from an adult.)

Bloom is also suggesting the possibility of educating parents about their role, and changing conditions in the home that affect students' learning. We know that home environmental processes are crucial for school learning, but can they be altered, with positive effects on school achievement? This question is of enormous importance for supervisors. (Teachers complain that they lack the support of parents.)

Changing the Home Environment. A study conducted by Janhom (one of Bloom's students at the University of Chicago) offers useful insights to supervisors on approaches to changing home environments.[75] The study, which involved a control group and three experimental groups of parents, found that the most effective approach was for the group of parents to meet with a parent educator for about two hours twice a month for six months. The meetings began with a presentation made by the parent educator on one of the five home environmental processes listed above, and then the parents discussed what they did as well as what they planned to do to support their youngsters' school learning.

A second experimental approach included visits to each home by a parent educator twice a month for six months. The third experimental approach was to send newsletters about the home environment processes to the home twice a month for six months.

The four groups of parents were observed and interviewed at the beginning and the end of the six-month period. Although the three experimental approaches showed significantly greater changes in the home environment than the control group, the most effective method was the series of meetings with the parent educator. The changes in the home environment of this group were far greater than the changes in the other three groups of parents.

Standardized tests on reading and arithmetic were given to the fourth-grade children of all these parents at the beginning and the end of the six-month period. The children of the meeting group of parents had changed significantly in achievement in contrast to the control group. The average student in this group was above 84 percent of the students in the control group. In comparison, the parent educators' visit to each home was only half as effective. Thus the evidence suggests a parent education program which takes the form of parents meeting with a parent educator, focused on the home environment processes that appear to be strongly related to school achievement.

According to Bloom, "The methods of changing the home environments are relatively costly in terms of parent educators meeting with groups of parents in a series of semimonthly meetings, but the payoff of this approach is likely to be very great."[76] As the Nobel prize–winning economist Theodore Schultz points out, such costs should be viewed as "an investment in an important form of human capital."[77] Parent education has an economic value. The rates of return on investments in parent education, in terms of economic growth, are high. Their children can get better jobs, play a more productive role in society, and derive more satisfactions from their lives. We know that parent education can improve children's school learning and prospects, and it should be a high-priority expenditure (again, better viewed as an investment). As the professional leader of the school board, the administrator (whose goals are to improve the work of teachers and enhance the lives of students) must educate the board about the value of parent education.

SUMMARY

Troubleshooting can help teachers deal with their major classroom problems in the best possible way—by helping them to apply what we have learned from research on teaching and learning. Problems such as discipline, motivation, and individual differences lie at the heart of classroom teaching and are the persistent professional problems about which educational science continues to inform (and reform) our work. Problems such as insufficient materials and resources are of a different sort and are readily solvable as supervisors meet their responsibilities. Learning to view problems as opportunities is part of becoming a good principal or superintendent. The problem of relationships with parents is most usefully viewed as an opportunity for improving students' learning. Research on the effects of parent education on achievement strongly supports the development of parent education programs where groups of parents meet with a parent educator. The investment in parent education has a high return. Parent–school relations have a social dimension as well as an educational dimension. Positive relationships are built when parents are brought into the school on a social level, before problems occur.

Discipline—the teacher's leading problem—encompasses both the teacher's ability to control the class and the students' development toward self-direction. Many supervisors overlook the latter; yet only as children move from *basic* discipline (the ability to listen and follow directions) to *constructive* discipline (the ability to work with others on a common problem) can the school meet its responsibility in a democratic society. At the *generative* stage of discipline, students behave autonomously and are socially responsible. Teachers who encourage students to explain their thinking are developing the students' autonomy. Both students and teachers have responsibilities at each stage of discipline. A problem that many classroom teachers have is that they view teaching and class control as separate entities. Teaching and discipline are inseparable. One is "disciplining" when one gives directions, asks questions that stimulate student explanations, provides pupils with opportunities for responsible self-direction, and so on. Class control can be improved by increasing the participation of students in productive learning activities.

Any supervisor who would help teachers deal with motivation, which teachers identify as their second most serious problem, might begin by checking the factors in the troubleshooting guide (Table 7–1, "Quality of Interaction with Students"). The supervisor should also look to the teacher's enthusiasm, which generates the energy and provides the direction for pupils' work. (Table 8–2 presents some dimensions of enthusiastic teaching.) Although the preclassical and classical Greeks regarded enthusiasm (they have given us this beautiful word) as a gift of the gods, studies have shown that teacher enthusiasm can be increased through inservice education and that increased levels of enthusiasm have pervasive effects on children's motivation and achievement. (The effects continue when students are working by themselves.)

High on the list of teachers' problems is meeting the needs of individuals in a class. "Individualized systems" such as programmed instruction and mastery learning are really mass instruction and do not provide guidance and support leading to self-directed learning; only flesh-and-blood teachers can do that. Moreover, the research evidence does not favor individualized systems over traditional programs when effectiveness is measured by achievement, students' self-esteem, and attitudes toward the subject matter being taught. There is no shortcut to responding to individual learners. One must plan an attack on the problems presented by individuals which requires knowing the cause of their troubles, so that the condition can be improved. Often the cause is the curriculum. The responsibility for meeting individual differences has been placed on the teacher, but all of the teacher's good intentions are not enough without the conditions that only administrators and supervisors can provide: time for curriculum planning, a reasonable number of pupils to teach, sufficient and appropriate books and other curricular resources, a good central library, and opportunity for teachers to study their own problems (instead of someone else's vision of their problems) are absolutely essential.

Given these supporting conditions, most problems can be solved, if not prevented, through classroom supervision aimed at creating enthusiastic teachers and excited learners. There are profound differences between good management and leadership. Although both are necessary, it is leadership that helps new teachers to hold on to and realize their ideals by focusing on pupil potentials rather than limitations. "Increases in the acquired abilities of human beings are open-ended."[78]

PROBLEMS FOR STUDY AND DISCUSSION

1. Examine the inservice education program of a school system. What evidence do you find that the program is addressing the leading problems that all teachers have to face (and will as long as there are children to be taught)? If such evidence is lacking, how do you account for this?

2. In connection with the discussion of individualized instruction in this chapter, what is your assessment of the following argument for adopting the technique?:

There have been very few instances in which students in individualized classes have done less well than those receiving traditional instruction. The finding of "no difference" is often interpreted in a negative manner, but this isn't necessarily true. There are many potential benefits from individualization: the staff may be happier in their jobs, or students may be more positive about their educational experiences. These are worthwhile outcomes, and the evaluations argue that these can be obtained without sacrificing achievement.[79]

3. Do you agree that "idealistic teachers become frustrated. Frustration in turn leads to demoralization. Demoralization results in emotional exhaustion, apathy or cynicism"?[80] Justify your support or opposition to this statement.

4. How do you account for the tendency of many supervisors to overlook the developmental side of discipline in their evaluations of teachers' work and focus entirely on the teacher's ability to control the class?

5. In this chapter it was pointed out that experimental studies demonstrate that teacher enthusiasm is significantly related to pupil achievement. How would you instruct a group of teachers to increase their enthusiasm? (Indicate specifically what they need to do and why.)

6. In discussing the research on teaching effectiveness, N. L. Gage makes the following statement:

Changing teaching practices *causes* desirable changes in student achievement, attitude and conduct. And the changes in achievement are substantial, not trivial. Moreover, the changes are brought about not by revolutions in teaching practice or school organization but by relatively straightforward attempts to educate more teachers to do what the more effective teachers have already been observed to be doing.[81]

Give examples of teaching practices that have been found to favorably influence students' achievement, attitude, and behavior.

7. What are the implications of the statement in Problem 6 for developing inservice education programs?

8. As discussed in this chapter, the failure of beginning teachers is a serious problem in many secondary schools, yet many of the factors in failure are under the principal's control. It is in the best interests of both the new teacher and the school system to eliminate controllable causes of failure. Formulate a school district policy intended to provide the new teacher with a good beginning.

9. In his study of schooling, Goodlad found that "lacking at all levels were the kinds of activities and teacher behaviors one tends to associate with awareness of and attention to individuals as persons and learners."[82] In your opinion, what directions can supervisors and administrators take to improve this situation?

10. In 1957, it was observed in a publication of the American Association of School Administrators that

in the days when teaching emphasis was largely on memory work, pupil–teacher ratio was less important than it is today when the individual differences of pupils must be considered.[83]

Do you believe that this statement has applicability for today? Why or why not?

11. According to Goodlad, "The tracking practices of secondary schools appear more to sacrifice and penalize individuals than to cultivate their individuality."[84] Do you agree with this position? Why or why not? If you answered affirmatively, does your school put students in tracks, or does it have a diversified curriculum without tracking and aim for a deliberate mix of students in its general education program? Explain.

12. In your opinion, what are the attitudes and behaviors of supervisors in schools where teachers do not lose their ideals?

NOTES

1. Ralph W. Tyler, "A Guide to Educational Trouble-Shooting," *Educational Leadership*, Vol. 41 (May 1984), p. 30.
2. Simon Veenman, "Perceived Problems of Beginning Teachers," *Review of Educational Research*, Vol. 54 (Summer 1984), p. 153.
3. Ibid., p. 156.
4. William E. Stark, *Every Teacher's Problems* (New York: American Book, 1922), pp. 8–9.
5. Herbert T. Olander and Mary Elizabeth Farrell, "Professional Problems of Elementary Teachers," *The Journal of Teacher Education*, Vol. 21 (Summer 1970), p. 277.
6. Ibid., p. 280.
7. Veenman, op. cit., p. 143.
8. Ibid., p. 144.
9. Michael Rutter et al., *Fifteen Thousand Hours: Secondary Schools and Their Effects on Children* (Cambridge, Mass.: Harvard University Press, 1979).
10. See John Dewey, *The School and Society* (Chicago: University of Chicago Press, 1899), p. 7.
11. Veenman, op. cit., p. 146.
12. Kenneth M. Zeichner and B. Robert Tabachnick, "Are the Effects of University Teacher Education 'Washed Out' by School Experience?" *Journal of Teacher Education*, Vol. 32 (May–June 1981), p. 7.
13. Veenman, op. cit., p. 146.
14. Zeichner and Tabachnick, op. cit.
15. Homer Coker, Donald M. Medley, and Robert S. Soar, "How Valid Are Expert

Opinions About Effective Teaching?" *Phi Delta Kappan*, Vol. 62 (October 1980), p. 132.

16. See Daniel Tanner and Laurel N. Tanner, *Curriculum Development: Theory into Practice*, 2nd ed. (New York: Macmillan, 1980), pp. 372–374.

17. Veenman, op. cit., p. 158.

18. Janet C. McIntosh, "The First Year of Experience: Influence on Beginning Teachers" (doctoral dissertation, University of Toronto, 1976), *Dissertation Abstracts International*, Vol. 38, pp. 3192–3193.

19. Jack O. Vittetoe, "Why First-Year Teachers Fail," *Phi Delta Kappan*, Vol. 58 (January 1977), p. 429.

20. Veenman, op. cit., p. 158.

21. William H. Kurtz, "How the Principal Can Help Beginning Teachers," *NASSP Bulletin*, Vol. 67 (January 1983), pp. 43–45.

22. Ibid., pp. 42, 44.

23. Ibid., p. 43.

24. Ibid., pp. 43–45.

25. Veenman, op. cit., p. 159.

26. Donald Cichon and Robert H. Koff, "Stress and Teaching," *NASSP Bulletin*, Vol. 64 (March 1980), pp. 91–104.

27. Fred C. Feitler and Edward Tokar, "Getting a Handle on Teacher Stress: How Bad Is the Problem?" *Educational Leadership*, Vol. 39 (March 1982), pp. 456–457.

28. Ibid., p. 456.

29. Richard Kindsvatter, "The Dilemmas of Discipline," *Educational Leadership*, Vol. 39 (April 1982), p. 512.

30. Laurel N. Tanner, *Classroom Discipline for Effective Teaching and Learning* (New York: Holt, Rinehart and Winston, 1978), p. 13.

31. Jere E. Brophy and Joyce G. Putnam, "Classroom Management in the Elementary Grades," Chapter 6 in National Society for the Study of Education, *Classroom Management*, Seventy-eighth Yearbook, Part II (Chicago: University of Chicago Press, 1979), pp. 205–206.

32. Ibid., p. 207.

33. See Tanner, op. cit., pp. 5–16 for a discussion of the models of discipline; see also Brophy and Putnam, op. cit. pp. 207–213.

34. Tanner, op. cit., p. 160; see also Jacob S. Kounin, *Discipline and Group Management in Classrooms* (New York: Holt, Rinehart and Winston, 1970), p. 45.

35. William W. Wayson and Thomas J. Lasley, "Climates for Excellence: Schools That Foster Self-discipline," *Phi Delta Kappan*, Vol. 65 (February 1984), p. 419.

36. Ibid., pp. 419–421.

37. Cited in Regina S. Jones and Laurel N. Tanner, "Classroom Discipline: The Unclaimed Legacy," *Phi Delta Kappan*, Vol. 62 (March 1981), p. 496.

38. Jean Piaget, *The Moral Judgment of the Child* (London: Routledge & Kegan Paul, 1932); and *The Psychology of Intelligence* (New York: Harcourt Brace Jovanovich, 1950), pp. 87–158.

39. Constance Kamii, "Autonomy: The Aim of Education Envisioned by Piaget," *Phi Delta Kappan*, Vol. 65 (February 1984), p. 415.

40. Tanner, op. cit., p. 6.

41. Lee Owens and Jennifer Barnes, "The Relationship Between Cooperative, Competitive and Individualized Learning Procedures and Students' Preferences of Classroom Learning Atmosphere," *American Educational Research Journal*, Vol. 19 (Summer 1982), p. 198.

42. For additional illustrations of discipline-developing activities see Tanner, op. cit., pp. 139–153.

43. Robert J. Havighurst, *Developmental Tasks and Education,* 3rd ed. (New York: David McKay, 1972), p. 79.
44. Kamii, op. cit., p. 413.
45. Ibid.
46. Benjamin S. Bloom, "The 2 Sigma Problem: Search for Methods of Group Instruction as Effective as One-to-One Tutoring," *Educational Researcher,* Vol. 13 (June–July 1984), p. 11.
47. Anthony C. Riccio, "On Coping with the Stresses of Teaching," *Theory into Practice,* Vol. 22 (Winter 1983), pp. 43–44.
48. See, for example, Launor F. Carter, "The Sustaining Effects of Compensatory and Elementary Education," *Educational Researcher,* Vol. 13 (August–September 1984), p. 9.
49. Riccio, op. cit., p. 44.
50. René J. Dubos, *Louis Pasteur—Free Lance of Science* (Boston: Little, Brown, 1950), p. 392.
51. Barak Rosenshine, "Enthusiastic Teaching: A Research Review," *School Review,* Vol. 78 (August 1979), pp. 499–513. See also Edward M. Bettencourt et al., "Effects of Teacher Enthusiasm Training on Student On-Task Behavior and Achievement," *American Educational Research Journal,* Vol. 20 (Fall 1983), pp. 435–450.
52. William James, *Talks to Teachers* (New York: Henry Holt, 1899), p. 50.
53. Victor E. Mastin, "Teacher Enthusiasm," *The Journal of Educational Research,* Vol. 56 (March 1963), pp. 385–386.
54. Ibid., p. 385.
55. Rosenshine, op. cit., p. 506.
56. Ibid., p. 509.
57. Bettencourt et al., op. cit., p. 436.
58. Ibid., p. 440.
59. Ibid., p. 446.
60. Robert L. Bangert, James A. Kulik, and Chen-Lin C. Kulik, "Individualized Systems of Instruction in Secondary Schools," *Review of Educational Research,* Vol. 53 (Summer 1983), p. 143.
61. Harold L. Schoen, "Self-paced Instruction: How Effective Has It Been in Secondary and Post-secondary Schools?" *The Mathematics Teacher,* Vol. 69 (May 1976), pp. 352–357.
62. Benjamin S. Bloom, *Human Characteristics and School Learning* (New York: McGraw-Hill, 1976). See also James H. Block and R. B. Burns, "Mastery Learning," in Lee S. Shulman (ed.), *Review of Research in Education,* Vol. 4 (Itasca, Ill.: Peacock, 1976).
63. Bangert, Kulik, and Kulik, op. cit., p. 152.
64. Ibid.; see also Patricia P. Fernandez, "A Presentation and Evaluation of an Individualized Instruction Course in First Year Algebra" (unpublished doctoral dissertation, University of Utah, 1972); James H. Hanneman, "An Experimental Comparison of Independent Study and Conventional Instruction in Tenth Grade Geometry" (unpublished doctoral dissertation, University of Florida, 1971).
65. Ibid., p. 150.
66. Maurice Gibbons, *Individualized Instruction: A Descriptive Analysis* (New York: Teachers College Press, 1971), p. 9.
67. Jeannette Veatch, "Key Words and Other Ways to Teach Beginning Reading," Forty-sixth Yearbook of the Claremont Reading Conference (Claremont, Calif.: The Claremont Reading Conference, 1982), p. 55.
68. Harriet Talmadge, "What Is Individualization?" in Jan Jeter (ed.), *Approaches to Individualized Education* (Alexandria, Va.: The Association for Supervision and Curriculum Development, 1980), p. 21.

69. Guy L. Bond and Bertha Handlan, *Adapting Instruction in Reading to Individual Differences* (Minneapolis, Minn.: University of Minnesota Press, 1948), p. 2.
70. Lee J. Cronbach, "How Can Instruction Be Adapted to Individual Differences," in Robert M. Gagne (ed.), *Learning and Individual Differences* (Columbus, Ohio: Charles E. Merrill, 1967), p. 24.
71. Bloom, "The 2 Sigma Problem: The Search for Methods of Group Instruction as Effective as One-to-One Tutoring," op. cit., p. 10.
72. Burnett A. Hines, "Concomitant Effects of Parental Involvement in Federally Supported Early Childhood Programs" (unpublished doctoral dissertation, Temple University, 1983).
73. See, for example, Barbara Simmons and Paula Smith Lawrence, "Beginning Reading: Welcome Parents," *Childhood Education,* Vol. 57 (January–February 1981), pp. 156–158.
74. Bloom, *Human Characteristics and School Learning,* op. cit., p. 1.
75. S. Janhom, "Educating Parents to Educate Their Children" (unpublished doctoral dissertation, University of Chicago, 1983).
76. Bloom, "The 2 Sigma Problem: The Search for Methods of Group Instruction as Effective as One-to-One Tutoring," op. cit., p. 10.
77. Theodore W. Schultz, *Investing in People* (Berkeley, Calif.: University of California Press, 1980), p. 21.
78. Ibid., p. 140.
79. Conrad G. Katzenmeyer and Linda J. Ingison, "Evaluation of Individualization," *Approaches to Individualized Education* (Alexandria, Va.: Association for Supervision and Curriculum Development, 1980), p. 64.
80. Anthony C. Riccio, "On Coping with the Stresses of Teaching," *Theory into Practice,* Vol. 22 (Winter 1983), p. 44.
81. N. L. Gage, "What Do We Know About Teaching Effectiveness?" *Phi Delta Kappan,* Vol. 66 (October 1984), p. 91.
82. John I. Goodlad, "Individuality, Commonality, and Curricular Practice," Chapter 12 in *Individual Differences and the Common Curriculum,* Eighty-second Yearbook of the National Society for the Study of Education, Part I (Chicago: University of Chicago Press, 1983), p. 305.
83. American Association of School Administrators, *The Superintendent as Instructional Leader,* Thirty-fifth Yearbook of the American Association of School Administrators (Washington, D.C.: The Association, 1957), p. 63.
84. Goodlad, op. cit., p. 313.

SELECTED REFERENCES

Association for Supervision and Curriculum Development. *Improving Teaching,* 1986 Yearbook. Alexandria, Va: The Association, 1986.

Bloom, Benjamin S. *Human Characteristics and School Learning.* New York: McGraw-Hill Book Company, 1976.

Gage, N. L. *The Scientific Basis of the Art of Teaching.* New York: Teachers College Press, 1978.

Good, Thomas L. and Jere E. Brophy. *Looking in Classrooms,* 3rd ed. New York: Harper & Row, 1984.

Gagne, Robert M. (ed.). *Learning and Individual Differences.* Columbus, Ohio: Charles E. Merrill Books, Inc., 1967.

Gibbons, Maurice. *Individualized Instruction: A Descriptive Analysis.* New York: Teachers College Press, 1971.

Havighurst, Robert J. *Developmental Tasks and Education,* 3rd ed. New York: David McKay Company, Inc., 1972.

James, William. *Talks to Teachers.* New York: Henry Holt and Company, 1899.

Jeter, Jan (ed.). *Approaches to Individualized Education.* Alexandria, Va.: The Association for Supervision and Curriculum Development, 1980.

Joyce, Bruce and Marsha Weil. *Models of Teaching,* 2nd ed. Englewood Cliffs, N.J.: Prentice-Hall, 1980.

Kounin, Jacob S. *Discipline and Group Management in Classrooms.* New York: Holt, Rinehart and Winston, 1970.

Leichter, Hope J. *The Family as Educator.* New York: Teachers College Press, 1974.

Marjoribanks, Kevin (ed.). *Environments for Learning.* London: National Foundation for Educational Research, 1974.

National Society for the Study of Education. *Classroom Management,* Seventy-eighth Yearbook, Part II. Chicago: The University of Chicago Press, 1979.

———. *Individual Differences and the Common Curriculum,* Eighty-second Yearbook, Part I. Chicago: The University of Chicago Press, 1983.

———. *The Psychology of Teaching Methods,* Seventy-fifth Yearbook, Part I. Chicago: The University of Chicago Press, 1976.

Piaget, Jean. *The Moral Judgment of the Child.* London: Routledge & Kegan Paul Ltd., 1932.

———. *The Psychology of Intelligence.* New York: Harcourt Brace Jovanovich, Inc., 1950.

Rutter, Michael, et al. *Fifteen Thousand Hours: Secondary Schools and Their Effects on Children.* Cambridge, Mass.: Harvard University Press, 1979.

Schultz, Theodore W. *Investing in People.* Berkeley, Calif.: University of California Press, 1980.

Stark, William E. *Every Teacher's Problems.* New York: American Book Company, 1922.

Tanner, Daniel, and Laurel N. Tanner. *Curriculum Development: Theory into Practice,* 2nd ed. New York: Macmillan Publishing Company, 1980.

Tanner, Laurel N. *Classroom Discipline for Effective Teaching and Learning.* New York: Holt, Rinehart and Winston, 1978.

Wittrock, Merlin C. (ed.). *Handbook of Research on Teaching,* 3rd ed. New York: Macmillan Publishing Company, 1986.

Part IV

Sources and Forces
for Educational
Improvement

Chapter 9

Forces for Educational Improvement: Change and Conflict

The schools have been criticized variously for being overly conservative and resistant to change,[1] or for being all too amenable to adopting changes or innovations in responding to external influences.[2]

Although there are valid aspects to both sides of the issue, administrators, supervisors, and teachers must appreciate how the schools are affected by the following: (1) the shifting expectations and pressures in successive periods of social change; (2) the innumerable specialized and segmental reform projects promoted by external agencies, without due consideration by these agencies as to how the recommended reforms will interact in connection with the total program of the school; (3) the conflicting and contradictory external pressures and influences on schools from various special-interest groups; (4) the tendency of the schools to yield to the dominant external pressures or "trendiness" of the times in order to demonstrate responsiveness and openness to change; (5) the failure to subject proposed reforms to a well-developed philosophical outlook consonant with the principles of a free society and according to the best available research evidence; (6) the failure to develop reform measures from a sound research base; (7) the tendency to impose measures for change and reform from above, without any sense of commitment and recognized need by those most affected by the reform measures; (8) the tendency to derive proposed remedies from sources external to the educational situation; (9) the tendency to treat reform measures as ready-made solutions to be imposed on the educational situation, instead of treating them as proposals to be tested as possible solutions to problems stemming from the educational situation; (10) the advocacy of reform measures without revealing the complete agenda and valuations underlying such advocacy (the problem of the "hidden agenda"); and (11) the underly-

273

ing and faulty assumption, indigenous to our culture, that innovation and change are synonymous with improvement.

SOURCES OF INFLUENCE ON EDUCATIONAL POLICY AND PRACTICE

School administrators, supervisors, and teachers not only are under constant pressure and influence from various bodies representing conflicting interests, but find themselves shifting their priorities in successive epochs in accordance with the dominant wave of a particular period. Very often the reform shifts are a succession of reactions and counterreactions to excessive and misguided reform measures taken in an earlier period. Unfortunately, the sources of advocacy and influence for such misguided measures are rarely identified and held accountable. Accountability inevitably rests with the public schools. Compounding the problem is the vulnerability of the schools to the successive waves of reform by reaction and counterreaction, and the attendant failure of educators to reconstruct the situation in a comprehensive effort to find substantive problem solutions for educational improvement.

Consequently, it is of utmost importance for supervisors and administrators to: (1) be consciously aware of the sources of influence on educational policy and practice; (2) subject the motives and prescriptions of external sources to the most rigorous scrutiny in the light of the school district's philosophy and in the light of the research literature; (3) assess the likely interactions of the proposed measures with existing practices (rather than treating them segmentally); (4) anticipate, insofar as possible, the likely long-range implications and consequences of adopting the proposed measures; and (5) subject all adopted measures to continuous evaluation before they become institutionalized.

Participants, Power, and Processes in Educational Change

Unless supervisors and administrators are consciously aware of the various sources, forces, and processes for educational change, the schools will be vulnerable to whatever pressures or fashions are dominant at a particular time. A useful model for understanding change processes in education has been developed by Gordon N. Mackenzie. Although Mackenzie's analysis is focused on curricular change processes, it appears to be fully applicable to change processes affecting the broad spectrum of educational policy and practice—from school finance to statewide assessment of educational achievement; from federal legislation on equality of educational opportunity to the use of new instructional media; and so on.

As shown in Table 9–1, Mackenzie's analysis of change processes is made in the cultural context of (1) internal and external participants, (2) their sources of power and methods of influence, (3) the several phases in the process of change and the ways in which the participants relate to the change process, and (4) the ways in which the internal participants (and the schools) are affected. The focal points for such change are school administrators, supervisors, teachers, the curriculum, materials, facilities, and time.[3]

Table 9-1 Curriculum Change: Participants, Power, and Processes

Participants in ———→ Curricular Change	Having Control of Certain ———→ Sources of Power and Methods of Influence	Proceed Through Various ———→ Phases in a Process	To Influence the Determiners of the Curriculum
Internal participants	Advocacy and communication	Initiated by internal or external participants	Teachers
Students	Prestige	Criticism	Students
Teachers	Competence	Proposal of changes	Subject matter
Principals	Money or goods	Development and clarification of	Methods
Supervisors	Legal authority	proposals for change	Materials and facili-
Superintendents	Policy, precedent, custom	Evaluation, review and reformula-	ties
Boards of education	Cooperation and collaboration	tion of proposals	Time
Citizens in local communities		Comparison of proposals	
State legislatures		Initiated by internal participants:	
State departments of education		Action on proposals	
State and federal courts		Implementation of action deci-	
External participants		sions	
Noneducationists			
Foundations			
Academicians			
Business and industry			
Educationists			
National government			

Source: Reprinted by permission of the publisher from Gordon N. Mackenzie, "Curricular Change: Participants, Power, and Processes," in Matthew B. Miles (ed.), *Innovation in Education* (New York: Teachers College Press, © 1964 by Teachers College, Columbia University. All rights reserved), p. 401.

Power and Influence. One can gain considerable insight into the educational change processes by using Mackenzie's model (Table 9–1) to analyze how power and influence have been exercised by various internal and external participants. For example, one might trace the sources and forces of censorship of textbooks and other curricular materials by special-interest groups and individuals— contrasting the pressures directed at local school boards with those directed at state boards of education and state departments of education in connection with statewide textbook adoption. One might examine how the vast programs of private foundations, such as Ford and Carnegie, to promote the new technology in the schools during the 1950s and 1960s eventually became financed through federal funds. Or one might study the growth of the testing industry and the forces supporting this industry, along with the influence of achievement testing on the curriculum, including the testing program of the National Assessment of Educational Progress (NAEP) and the statewide minimum-competency testing movement. Or one might trace the sponsorship and influence of various national reports on educational reform, how they reflect the major sociopolitical currents in various periods, and how prescriptions for reform take contradictory shifts in accordance with the main currents of the times.

In each case the sources of power and methods of influence might be identified, such as (1) engaging the media for advocacy and communication; (2) using prestige for advocacy or support; (3) engaging competence; (4) buying change through funding or resource allocation; (5) exercising legal authority; (6) exercising the mechanisms of policy, precedent, or custom; and (7) engaging in cooperation, collaboration, and other forms of alliance (see Table 9–1). The other forms of alliance are made through *contracting* (agreements negotiated for future performance), *coopting* (acquiring or absorbing outside elements into an organization to enhance the organization's power and influence and/or to avert opposition or competition from the outside elements, and *coalescing* (combining with other organizations for mutual benefit and enhancement of influence).[4]

Unanticipated Consequences of Policies and Programs Promoted by External Participants.

Private foundations such as Ford and Carnegie have been successful in influencing educational policy and practice through the use of many of the mechanisms cited above. However, their programs for effecting educational improvement have produced very few long-term benefits when these foundations have proceeded to formulate programmatic prescriptions to be induced on the educational situation, rather than working with the internal participants in seeking problem solutions stemming from the educational situation.

Innumerable examples can be given to illustrate how external participants or organizations exert power and influence in public educational policy and practice, along with the various ways in which they engage in contracting, coopting, and coalescing. The National Assessment of Educational Progress, funded by the U.S. Department of Education, is administered under contract with the Educational Testing Service for the design and evaluation of the program. The Rand Corporation has been contracted by various federal agencies to evaluate the effectiveness of various federal educational programs. An example of coalescence was the formation in 1965 of the now defunct General Learning

Corporation by Time, Inc. and General Electric for the purpose of entering the promising market in educational technology as the result of the Elementary and Secondary Education Act of 1965, which provided federal funds for the new technology. General Learning Corporation proceeded to coopt the former U.S. Commissioner of Education as its president. As another example, the College Entrance Examination board engaged the U.S. Commissioner of Education as its president after the commissioner had launched a national program for career education during the early 1970s—a program endorsed by President Nixon on the ground that our schools had been giving too much emphasis to college entrance.

At various times certain federal agencies have virtually overshadowed the U.S. Office of Education (now the U.S. Department of Education) in exerting influence on public education or in sponsoring reform programs in public education. This has given rise to problems of duplication and uncoordination of effort, conflicting roles and functions, and disjointed treatments. The educational programs sponsored by the U.S. Office of Economic Opportunity (OEO) during the latter 1960s and early 1970s is a notable example. The OEO proceeded to promote education vouchers to provide public funds for alternative schools and private schools, and to create educational programs for disadvantaged children and youth without involving the schools as the primary agency for such programs.

Another notable example was the unprecedented national curriculum-reform program in school mathematics and science, funded by the National Science Foundation (NSF), in response to the alleged crisis of the Cold War and space race of the 1950s and 1960s—giving rise to curricular imbalance and priority for the academically talented at the expense of the wider student population. Ironically, where this effort was aimed at increasing our nation's pool of scientific and engineering talent, it actually resulted in a decline in the proportion of high school seniors taking physics and a decline in the number of college students majoring in physics at a time when the college enrollment was increasing by over 50 percent.[5] Similar results occurred in chemistry and engineering.[6] Belatedly, it was realized that adolescents do not respond well to externally imposed pressures in regard to career choices, and that the curriculum must take into account the nature of the adolescent learner rather than the narrow and abstract interests of the university scholar-specialist.[7]

As discussed later, in the wake of allegations during the early 1980s that our schools were responsible for our nation's declining position in global markets, NSF sought to regain its once-dominant role in elementary and secondary curricular reform in mathematics, science, and technology—without acknowledging its earlier failures in this domain.

There are innumerable examples of how the anticipated consequences of various programs to reform the schools have failed to materialize and how the disappointing outcomes should have been anticipated at the beginning. When reforms are promoted or imposed without seeking problem solutions stemming from the educational situation and without the direct involvement of those directly affected by the reforms, the reform projects or programs are not likely to succeed. When priority is given to a narrow segment of the educational enterprise without taking account of the interactions with other elements, imbalance and dissonance are bound to result. When a narrow "solution" is imposed at the expense of other needs, the consequence is conflict and the outbreak of other problems.

Unanticipated Consequences of Policies and Programs Imposed Within the School System. Very often the aforementioned problems arise *within* a school system for the reasons already indicated. This is particularly the case when decisions are imposed segmentally from above, without taking into account the best available evidence bearing on a problem and without the joint involvement of those who are most directly affected by the decisions.

A case in point occurred when the New York City Board of Education imposed a nonpromotion policy in 1980, requiring pupils to repeat the seventh grade when their reading scores were below grade level. The nonpromotion policy was imposed on the grounds that it would raise standards and would impel pupils to meet the higher standards. Advocates of the nonpromotion "solution" came from many quarters, including a noted education professor who contended that achievement would be raised and the schools would be improved by adopting the nonpromotion policy and by devoting the elementary curriculum to the "acquisition of basic skills."[8] Ironically, the schools had been under a back-to-basics retrenchment for several years prior to the adoption of the nonpromotion policy. In other words, the reductionist skill-drill curriculum was already in place and its negative effects were known. Soon after the nonpromotion policy was adopted, the prospects for a dropout epidemic were predicted and the limitations of the skill-drill approach to "basics" were cited. As an educator warned,

> Instead of diagnosing, treating and preventing learning problems, a simpleminded non-promotion policy is adopted. The inevitable consequence is the school "pushout."
>
> When adolescents are held back in classes with pupils one or two years younger, the older youths become embarrassed, alienated and defeated. Some of the proud ones become class bullies. Discipline problems are exacerbated. The answer is not nonpromotion or segregation in special classes. Constructive treatment is required, such as tutoring and curriculum redesign to reveal the applications of subject matter to life experience.
>
> The skill-drill approach to "basics" tends to be mechanical, error-oriented and devoid of meaning. Teaching must be idea-oriented, not error-oriented. The basic skills are not ends but means through which one develops working power—the power to learn more effectively by deriving wider and richer meanings from experience, and thereby to exercise more intelligent control over experience.
>
> "Get tough" prescriptions, such as non-promotion, have never worked because they are directed at symptoms rather than at causes of a problem. Such prescriptions are far worse than the disease.[9]

Within a few years, the press was carrying horror stories of many thousands of youngsters who were repeating the seventh grade, that almost 3,000 youngsters were repeating the seventh grade for the third time, and that nearly half the students in the school system were not completing high school.[10] Referring to this appalling dropout rate, the president of Hunter College in New York City called it "the shame of this city."[11] Not until great irreparable damage had been done did the central administration take constructive action to remedy the situation by allowing the students to enter high school, where they would receive more individualized attention as part of a dropout-prevention program. Nevertheless, the resources allocated for the program appeared inadequate to a situation that requires concerted effort throughout the years of schooling.

Obviously, the deleterious effects of the nonpromotion policy should have been anticipated, and a constructive program could have been implemented from the beginning to get at the causes of the problem. Instead, the simplistic "solution" of nonpromotion was directed at masking the symptoms of a far-deeper problem, which only served to exacerbate the problem and to give rise to a rash of related problems. The point is that when "solutions" are directed at the symptoms of a problem rather than its underlying causes, the problem not only will remain unsolved, but will grow worse while resulting in an outbreak of concomitant problems. Many "unanticipated" effects of a policy decision can be anticipated and avoided when those ultimately responsible for such decisions are committed to acting on the best available evidence, while also involving the key internal participants (principals, supervisors, teachers, counselors, curriculum coordinators) in the study of the problem and in the decision-making process.

The Dilemma of Educational Policy

Our schools have been particularly vulnerable to the influence of powerful external agencies in shaping educational policy and practice. In this section the focus is on the shifting and often contradictory platforms for educational reform, as promulgated by external agencies, during successive periods of sociopolitical change.

A seeming contradiction in the American educational scene is the absence of an educational policymaking body representing the public interest in the broadest spectrum while the nationalizing influences on American education have been pervasive, especially since midcentury. Education in the United States has been regarded as a state function, and the states have relegated most of the specific decision-making powers on policy and operations to the local school boards. The U.S. Department of Education has acted to induce educational change and reform in the same way as did its predecessor agency, the U.S. Office of Education—through "buying" change and reform through funds legislated by Congress in support of specific programs. At the same time, this agency has coupled such programmatic financial support with other agencies and mechanisms of power and influence (Table 9–1) to induce change where compliance cannot be mandated legally. As discussed later, this "strategy" has had mixed results, largely because the programs have been promoted in the absence of a base for systematic formative and summative evaluation giving evidence of effecting needed problem solutions, and because the innovative programs often are adopted only nominally by the schools or without the needed adaptation to local conditions and problems.

It is beyond our purview to analyze in detail how various individuals, groups, and agencies have sought to fill the vacuum created by the absence of a responsible and broadly representative national policymaking body for American education. Nevertheless, a brief discussion of some nationalizing influences in education will illustrate why it is incumbent on supervisors and administrators at the local level to assume responsibility for evaluating the various sources of power and influence affecting our schools, and why it is necessary for them to undertake such evaluation in the light of a coherent and comprehensive policy or outlook.

Filling the Vacuum. Addressing the problem of the lack of a responsible, broad-based, nationwide policymaking body for education, Conant proposed in 1964 that the fifty states enter into a compact for the creation of an "Interstate Commission for Planning a Nationwide Educational Policy."[12] For over two decades, Conant had served as a member of the Educational Policies Commission, established by the NEA in 1937 to function as an independent body of leading educators and lay citizens to address problems pertaining to American educational policy. From the time of its beginning to its demise during the post-*Sputnik* period, this body assumed a constructive and progressive stance on problems and issues affecting American education. With the issuance of over 100 pamphlets and books over the course of its history, the Educational Policies Commission sought to link educational policy to the principles of American democracy.[13]

Only two years after Conant's proposal in 1964 for the creation of an "Interstate Commission," the Education Commission of the States was established as a nationwide interstate compact to develop policies to improve public education. Eventually, all but two states became members. In retrospect, Conant's proposal may seem naive, given the record of the commission. Nevertheless, the vacuum in educational policy continues to leave the schools vulnerable to shifting sociopolitical tides and to the influence of special-interest groups.

Programs and Prescriptions: Neglect of the Wider Democratic Interest. For the most part, the Education Commission of the States (ECS) has been a political arm of the governors of the membership states. Specific programs have been sponsored by the commission and specific educational policy prescriptions have been issued, but Conant's vision that such a commission would represent the wider democratic interest in public education never materialized.

The most influential project sponsored by ECS is the National Assessment of Educational Progress (NAEP), a nationwide testing program (now administered by the Educational Testing Service), financed by the U.S. Department of Education, to assess the progress in educational achievement of pupils in our elementary and secondary schools. NAEP was originally promoted and financed by the Ford Foundation and the Carnegie Corporation on the ground that it would provide the nation with an index of "gross educational product" akin to gross national product, and that it would enable educational policymakers to determine "with greater certainty that investing so much—in terms of money or materials or teachers or time—to attack a particular problem will produce a given result."[14] No such outcomes were forthcoming, principally because test data were gathered in the absence of guiding multiple working hypotheses aimed at problem solving. Nevertheless, NAEP catalyzed a wave of statewide minimum-competency testing programs in the schools under the aegis of accountability.

As discussed later, during the 1980s the Education Commission of the States has sought to influence American educational policy and practice on a far broader scale by issuing recommendations for national educational reforms.

NATIONAL REPORTS FOR EDUCATIONAL REFORM: ADVOCACY, POWER, AND INFLUENCE

The call for major educational reforms tends to accompany or follow periods of social transition or periods of perceived crisis. Under these circumstances, external pressures are exerted on the schools to impose prescribed reforms, although at various times changes are bought through financial inducements by external agencies ranging from the state level up to the federal level. The private foundations also have sought to induce change by supporting specific projects for demonstration and promotion. Legislative mandates by the states and court decisions impose change by compliance.

A powerful means for inducing educational reform has been through advocacy, whereby a given agency external to the schools appoints a commission, panel, task force, or prestigious individual to undertake a "study" and to formulate recommendations based on the findings. This approach is commonly taken during periods of perceived crisis and, consequently, often commands wide media attention. The focus typically is on inducing pervasive changes in educational policy and practice rather than on promoting a specific innovation.

A major problem with this approach is that the commission, panel, task force, or authoritative individual can go on to other things once the report is issued. They do not have to suffer the consequences of misguided or ill-conceived remedies. Their appointment is temporary, and the schools can be left to bear the brunt of the consequences.

The sponsoring agency typically has a hidden agenda for reform. Clues to the agenda may be deduced by examining the "track record" of the sponsoring agency and its officials, and of the individuals designated to produce the report.

All of these external influences for educational change and reform are essentially different from the change and reform resulting when the internal participants (supervisors and administrators) of a school or school district seek change and reform to solve a recognized problem required for organizational self-renewal. This does not mean that any external forces for change are to be resisted or regarded as counter to the possibilities for self-renewal. If supervisors and administrators are consciously aware of the sources and forces for change, if they subject the various external proposals to systematic evaluation in connection with the perceived need for the self-renewal of the school or school district, and if the internal participants are involved in this evaluation process, constructive response is possible.

Shifting Tides in Policy and Priority

Table 9–2 presents a synopsis of some of the major reports issued during the twentieth century by various individuals, agencies, and organizations seeking to influence American educational policy and practice. The analysis presented is not intended to be exhaustive, simply to illustrate how the reports reflect vastly different and often conflicting points of focus according to different periods of sociopolitical change and sometimes within a given period.

For example, the *Cardinal Principles* report of 1918, the reports of the Educational Policies Commission around midcentury, and the Conant report of 1959 all supported the comprehensive high school in which comprehensive curricular offerings are provided for general education, vocational education, college preparation, and exploratory and enrichment education. Each of these reports recommended these comprehensive offerings without tracking students. And each of the reports stressed the vital role of the comprehensive high school for a democratic society.

The *Cardinal Principles* report was issued at a time of major social change following World War I, when the very structure of our school system was being decided. In the face of sharp opposition by those who favored our adoption of the traditional dual system of secondary schooling common in Europe, the Commission on the Reorganization of Secondary Education which produced the *Cardinal Principles* report opted for a unitary structure through the comprehensive high school—a unique American invention designed to offer a comprehensive and diversified curriculum for all youth regardless of background or destiny. However, this institution was to be threatened for its survival in each period of crisis—the Great Depression of the 1930s, the Cold War and space race of the 1950s and 1960s, the education retrenchment of the 1970s, and the emphasis on education for global economic competition in the early 1980s.

The Crisis of the Great Depression

As shown in Table 9–2, the crisis period of the Great Depression prompted the Educational Policies Commission of the NEA to issue a number of reports, most notably *The Structure and Administration of Education in American Democracy* (1938). The report criticized the federal education programs for being conducted by agencies outside the schools and called for such programs to be administered through the schools. This was a very serious problem in that a host of federal educational programs had been created to deal with the crisis conditions of the Great Depression, and many of these programs were being administered by federal agencies whose principal concern was not education. The result was the failure to meet the educational needs of youth involved in these programs; the neglect of the schools in attacking educational problems, including the problem of dropouts; and the proliferation of disjointed, uncoordinated, and conflicting programs. History was to repeat itself more than a quarter of a century later when the Office of Economic Opportunity, a federal antipoverty agency, sponsored a number of educational programs that failed to connect with, and often conflicted with, the schools. The consequence was a great deal of promotional rhetoric, but limited results.[15]

Other recommendations in the Educational Policies Commission Report of 1938 concerned the need for maintaining local and state autonomy in education while providing increased federal support without federal control, for the schools to reconstruct the curriculum in general education to meet the needs and interests of all children and youth, for the schools to address the problems of youth unemployment and disaffection through the expansion of vocational education within the comprehensive high school, for encompassing in the common school system the nursery school and/or kindergarten up through the junior college, for teachers to be involved in the formulation of educational policy, for curriculum development as the responsibility of the professional staff of the school and school district (and not that of external agencies or groups), for the consolidation of schools and reorganization of districts to provide for a more comprehensive curriculum and more adequate facilities and resources, and for the promotion of the public school as a secular school.

The Midcentury Turning Point of Postwar Reconstruction

At midcentury the schools were facing an impending crisis of a population explosion, a critical teacher shortage, and a critical need for new facilities and resources. Tax conservatives opposed the expansion of education and advocated a back-to-basics regimen. In sharp contrast, reports of the Educational Policies Commission toward the end of World War II envisioned the vast expansion of public education to meet the needs of a democratic society. The Commission's report of 1944, revised in 1952 (see Table 9–2), reaffirmed the role and function of the comprehensive high school, and made a daring proposal for curriculum integration for common learnings based on the needs of youth. Also recommended were diversified programs for vocational education and open-access higher education through the community college. However, the crisis of the Cold War and space race dealt a damaging blow to any efforts being made for curriculum synthesis for common learnings or general education, and for building the curriculum on youth needs. In fact, the Educational Policies Commission itself became a Cold War casualty.

The Crisis of the Cold War and Space Race

Soon after *Sputnik I,* at a time when the schools were under harsh criticism for the alleged U.S. lag behind Soviet space technology, and at a time when great pressures were being exerted to eliminate the comprehensive high school in favor of a dual system of secondary schooling along traditional European lines, James B. Conant was enlisted by John Gardner, then president of the Carnegie Corporation, to make a study of the American high school. Conant had served as chairman of the Educational Policies Commission at the time when it had published its report of 1952 on American secondary education.

In his study, *The American High School Today* (1959), Conant offered strong support for the comprehensive high school by showing from test data how such schools could serve all youth, while the most academically able students could perform at a level at least as high as that attained by students in select college-

Table 9–2 Some of the Major Policy Reports for American Educational Reform in the Twentieth Century

Report	Author and/or Sponsor	Sociopolitical Milieu	Major Recommendations
Cardinal Principles of Secondary Education (1918)	Commission on the Reorganization of Secondary Education (NEA)	Post–World War I vision of a democratic society	Provide universal secondary education Establish comprehensive high school Comprehensive curriculum (health, command of fundamental processes, worthy home membership, vocation, democratic citizenship, worthy use of leisure, ethical character) Unified studies for general education and curriculum variables for diversified needs Coeducation Extend access to public higher education
The Structure and Administration of Education in American Democracy (1938)	Educational Policies Commission (NEA)	Great Depression	Begin the common school with the nursery school or kindergarten and continue through the junior college Provide for heterogeneous grouping of pupils to promote social integration and growth for democratic citizenship Design the curriculum in general education to meet the interests and needs of children and youth Expand vocational education in the setting of the comprehensive high school Consolidate and locate the federally supported education programs for children and youth within the public schools Consolidate schools and reorganize districts to provide for a more comprehensive and diversified curriculum with more adequate facilities and resources Involve teachers in the formulation of educational policy Curriculum development should be the responsibility of the professional staff of the school and district, not that of external groups or agencies Provide federal support of public education while retaining local autonomy Promote the public school as a secular school

Document	Sponsor/Author	Era	Purposes/Recommendations
Education for ALL American Youth (1944, 1952)	Educational Policies Commission (NEA)	Post–World War II vision of a democratic society	Provide universal secondary education Strengthen the comprehensive high school Comprehensive curriculum based on needs of youth (salable skills, health, democratic citizenship, successful family life, consumer education, scientific thinking and significance of science in society, aesthetic appreciation, worthy use of leisure time, ethical values, reflective thinking) Develop integrated common learnings for general education, specialized studies for vocational education, and exploratory and enrichment studies Provide open-access higher education
The American High School Today (1959)	James B. Conant (Carnegie Corporation)	Cold War/post-*Sputnik* era	Provide universal secondary education Strengthen the comprehensive high school for a democratic society Develop academic studies for general education Provide diversified studies for vocational education Provide ability grouping without curriculum tracking, based on aptitude testing Establish programs for academically talented (advanced placement, academic inventory, counseling)
The Process of Education (1960)	Jerome S. Bruner, Chair. (National Academy of Sciences, National Science Foundation, U.S. Air Force, U.S. Office of Education, Rand Corporation)	Cold War/post-*Sputnik* era	Elementary and secondary curriculum focused on the intellectual aims of education through the structures of the academic disciplines; use of discovery methods, analytical and intuitive thinking for knowledge production in the academic disciplines, especially in science and mathematics Give emphasis to the academically talented and academic acceleration Use new instructional technology

Table 9–2 (Continued)

Report	Author and/or Sponsor	Sociopolitical Milieu	Major Recommendations
Crisis in the Classroom: The Remaking of American Education (1970)	Charles E. Silberman (Carnegie Corporation)	Child- and youth-centered concern in the wake of the discipline-centered curriculum reforms of the 1960s and the era of youth disaffection and disruption	Humanize the schools through the open classroom at the elementary level, and through a freer atmosphere in the secondary school with unscheduled time for independent study, electives, and other optional learning activity; emphasis in the high school on a liberal, humanizing education; reduce or eliminate vocational studies
The Reform of Secondary Education (1973)	National Commission on the Reform of Secondary Education (Kettering Foundation)	Education and social retrenchment; the "youth problem" (disaffection, disruption, unemployment)	Reduce school leaving age to 14 Replace comprehensive high school with specialized academic high schools, area vocational schools, and alternative schools Establish career education Curriculum based on performance criteria through accountability testing Stress citizenship responsibilities Stress mastery of basic academic skills
Youth: Transition to Adulthood (1974)	James S. Coleman, Chair, Panel on Youth (President's Science Advisory Committee)	Education and social retrenchment; the "youth problem" (disaffection, disruption, unemployment)	Replace comprehensive high school with alternative specialized schools Reduce the holding power of the high school by providing education through work organizations Reduce school time by delimiting school functions to academic studies and school-work alternation Use education vouchers and provide alternatives to schooling to develop skills

Document	Source	Problem	Recommendations
The Education of Adolescents (1976)	National Panel on High School and Adolescent Education (U.S. Office of Education)	Education and Social retrenchment; the "youth problem" (disaffection, disruption, unemployment)	Replace the comprehensive high school with academic high schools and part-time schools Reduce compulsory attendance to academic day of 2–4 hours Delimit the curriculum to essential academic skills for most adolescents
A Nation at Risk: The Imperative for Educational Reform (1983)	National Commission on Excellence in Education (U.S. Department of Education)	Competition for world leadership in science, technology, and industrial markets	Raise graduation requirements in the four academic "basics" and add the "new basic" of computer science Continue to provide electives for personal/vocational goals, but raise standards and reduce time for electives Begin foreign languages in elementary school Use nationwide standardized achievement tests to certify transition through levels of schooling Institute ability grouping Increase homework and consider longer school day and school year Upgrade teacher education Provide teacher merit pay Increase federal support of programs designed to promote the national interest
Action for Excellence: A Comprehensive Plan to Improve Our Nation's Schools (1983)	Task Force on Education for Economic Growth (Education Commission of the States)	Competition for world leadership in science, technology, and industrial markets	Develop statewide plans for educational improvement Establish partnerships between businesses and schools Strengthen state mandates Improve managerial efficiency of schools with help of business Increase academic learning time and emphasis on academic subjects/higher standards Eliminate nonessential subjects Provide basic academic skills for productive employment, including understanding of our basic economic system

Table 9–2 (Continued)

Report	Author and/or Sponsor	Sociopolitical Milieu	Major Recommendations
Action for Excellence (cont'd.)			Monitor student progress through periodic achievement testing Emphasize computer literacy Utilize instructional technology Provide teacher merit pay and establish higher standards for teaching
Educating Americans for the 21st Century (1983)	Commission on Precollege Education in Mathematics, Science and Technology (National Science Board of the National Science Foundation)	Competition for world leadership in science, technology, and industrial markets	Establish priority in school science, mathematics, and technology through massive federal funding Raise requirements in mathematics and science for college entrance Reestablish NSF leadership role in curriculum development in mathematics, science, and technology Establish Presidential National Educational Council to formulate national educational goals Foster partnerships between local schools, business, and academia Establish a federal mechanism for assessment of student achievement for national, state, and local evaluation and comparison Provide special financial incentives for teachers of mathematics, science, and technology; raise teaching standards
High School: A Report on Secondary Education in America (1983)	Ernest L. Boyer (Carnegie Foundation for the Advancement of Teaching)	Competition for world leadership in science, technology, and industrial markets	Increase federal support Establish clear educational goals Provide core of common learning of 14½ units required of all, consisting of English, foreign language, history, civics, science, mathematics, and a half-unit each in technology, health, work seminar, and senior independent project Require foreign language in elementary school Replace vocational studies with career exploration Expand guidance services Provide teacher merit pay

288

Report	Source	National concern	Recommendations
			Utilize instructional technology
			Provide programs for the gifted and establish a national network of residential academies in science and mathematics
			Develop school–corporate connection for improved school management and support
A Place Called School (1984)	John I. Goodlad (study funded by private foundations and federal grants)	Competition for world leadership in science, technology, and world industrial markets	Develop curricular balance and coherence in a common core of studies for general education, with 18% in literature and language, up to 18% in mathematics and science; and up to 15% in each of the other fields (social studies, arts, career exploration)
			Eliminate vocational programs
			Eliminate curriculum tracking and pupil ability grouping
			Engage pupils in greater decision making for their classroom learning
			Begin school at age 4 and end at age 16
Investing in Our Children (1985)	Committee for Economic Development	Competition for world leadership in science, technology and world industrial markets	Increase business involvement in local school policy-making process
			Establish statewide system of educational standards and for monitoring pupil achievement through testing; establish minimum state standards for the diploma
			Focus the curriculum on basic academic and behavioral skills for employability
			Improve managerial efficiency of schools with help of business
			Expand our vocational centers coupled with academic high schools to replace the comprehensive high school
			Institute teacher merit pay

preparatory schools. Conant made the case for the comprehensive high school as a key institution of American democracy. Although he supported general education, he viewed it as being properly provided through the standard academic subjects. He endorsed the practice of ability grouping in the academic studies on a subject-by-subject basis, and opposed the tracking of students through which college-bound students and vocational students are separated or streamed in all subjects. He recommended strong programs of vocational education for the development of marketable skills, and larger schools to provide the diversified curricula and facilities needed for a cosmopolitan student population. Conant gave special attention to the academically talented and devised an Academic Inventory through which school principals and counselors would be able to ensure that the most academically able boys and girls were enrolled in advanced classes in science and mathematics and in modern foreign languages.

As a former renowned scientist, president of Harvard, and U.S. ambassador to West Germany, Conant commanded great respect and exerted great prestige. His report was effectively addressed to local school boards throughout the nation. Despite the many conservative features of his report, Conant had almost singlehandedly saved the comprehensive high school. But by the latter 1960s and during the 1970s, the continuing problem of youth unemployment led to the establishment of many separate, specialized, area vocational schools through state and federal funding. Oddly, this occurred at a time when advanced democratic European nations were beginning to adopt the comprehensive high school as the needed model for advancing educational and social opportunity.[16]

The Cold War and space race were to exert their greatest impact on the schools through the national curriculum-reform projects in the sciences and mathematics, funded by the National Science Foundation and extending throughout the elementary and secondary levels. The key document providing the rationale for the discipline-centered reforms in the sciences and mathematics, and for the role of university scholar-specialists in creating the "new mathematics" and the "new science," was a conference report of 1960, *The Process of Education*, written by the Harvard psychologist Jerome Bruner. The Woods Hole Conference had been convened, as noted in Table 9–2, under the auspices of the National Academy of Sciences, National Science Foundation, U.S. Air Force, U.S Office of Education, and the Rand Corporation. The conference membership was dominated by scientists. At the outset, Bruner's report cited the "long-range crisis in national security" as the basis for redirecting the focus of the schools on "quality and intellectual aims," as he went on to fault the schools for neglecting the top quarter of students "from which we must draw intellectual leadership in the next generation."[17] Hundreds of millions of dollars were expended by the National Science Foundation in supporting university scholar-specialists in bringing the "new mathematics" and "new science" to the elementary and secondary schools. Although the impact on the school curriculum was far reaching, it was not long lasting. The discipline-centered approach had neglected the applications of knowledge to pervasive social problems (ecology, poverty, democratic citizenship, and so on) and had virtually ignored the nature of the learner.

Humanizing the Schools

The Cold War era of the national discipline-centered curriculum reforms was followed by a call for curriculum "relevance." During the period from the mid-1960s to the early 1970s, the colleges were buffeted by a wave of student protest and disruption, with the Vietnam War serving as the focal point. This disruption soon reached down into the high schools. The 1960s also witnessed a rash of riots in the ghetto areas of some of our leading cities, galvanizing a new concern for reordering our national priorities. At the same time, books were appearing on national best-seller lists, authored by radical romanticists who called for child-centered and adolescent-centered schools, curriculum "relevance," greater freedom for students, alternative schools, and open classrooms.[18] This new literary movement in radical romanticist criticism of our schools not only provided considerable fuel for debate, but resulted in a host of segmental changes in our schools—ranging from providing more free electives to establishing a wide assortment of alternative schools.

But it was Silberman's *Crisis in the Classroom: The Remaking of American Education* (1970) that exerted the greatest influence for school reform during the early 1970s. Unlike the romanticists who were offering radical prescriptions in a literary vein without any official sponsorship, Silberman's criticisms appeared more measured and constructive, and his study carried the influential sponsorship of the Carnegie Corporation. Moreover, his focus on the open classroom (allegedly patterned after the British open classroom) as the chief vehicle, if not the panacea, for humanizing the elementary and middle school appealed to educators as a concrete and workable institutional change. At the same time, Silberman's call for humanizing the schools gave support for more free electives in the secondary school and the establishment of alternative schools. Unfortunately, the open classroom was instituted by administrators and supervisors mainly as a structural rearrangement of the elementary school rather than for providing the needed curriculum synthesis in the elementary school.

Despite the liberalizing or humanizing tone of Silberman's report, he had virtually nothing to say in support of the comprehensive high school. In fact, he viewed the proper high school curriculum as emphasizing liberal education to the virtual exclusion of vocational education.

Educational Retrenchment

By the latter 1970s, a counterreaction against "humanizing" the schools had set in. Under the banner of back-to-basics, the schools were beset by a wave of retrenchment. Silberman disappeared from the educational scene. As a journalist, he was able to find "other fish to fry." Open classrooms, open schools, and alternative schools were no longer in vogue as the new retrenchment took hold.

As shown in Table 9–2, the 1970s witnessed a series of reports on the adolescent and the secondary school in which adolescence appeared to be regarded as a stage of pathology in human development. Of particular significance is that the "adolescent problem" was regarded as so severe and pervasive that it prompted the President's Science Advisory Committee to form the Panel on Youth and the U.S. Secretary of Education to form the National Panel on High School and Adolescent Education.

The problem of youth disaffection, unemployment, and disruption was seen by these national panels and by the National Commission on the Reform of Secondary Education (Kettering Foundation) as evidence that our schools were failing and that it was time to return the high school to its narrow academic mission—emphasis on basic academic skills. This was to be followed by work training and education in nonschool settings for the masses, and a higher-ordered academic program in the high school for the college bound. In essence, the reports called for the replacement of the comprehensive high school with an academic high school, the creation of alternative schools for those youngsters who did not fit into the academic setting, emphasis on the mastery of basic academic skills, reduction in the age of compulsory school attendance, the allocation of public funds to businesses and industries to support the training of adolescents for work, and other alternatives to schooling.

Teaching to Think. As in the case of previous eras of educational retrenchment when the call is for back-to-basics, idea-oriented teaching tends to suffer and there is an accompanying rise in the censorship of curricular materials. During the latter 1970s and early 1980s, the *Newsletter on Intellectual Freedom* of the American Library Association was replete with documentation of incidents revealing a marked rise in the censorship of school library books, textbooks, and other curricular materials. In the aftermath of the narrow-minded back-to-basics retrenchment, the schools came under criticism for a decline in pupil thinking abilities. A special section of *The New York Times* on education appearing in early 1983 was titled "Teaching to Think: A New Emphasis," and professional journals in education were featuring issues focused on the "new" emphasis on thinking abilities[19]—without giving recognition and making capital of the earlier efforts and achievements in this direction by experimentalist-progressive educators who viewed reflective thinking as a necessary foundation for an enlightened citizenry and a free society.[20]

However, in the wake of the new wave of attacks on the schools in connection with the drive for technoindustrial mobilization to regain our nation's dominant position in global markets, there was the impending danger that the "new" emphasis on teaching to think would be narrowly directed, as was the case with the discipline-centered curriculum projects stemming from the crisis of the Cold War and space race.

Education for National Technoindustrial Mobilization

By the 1980s the era of education retrenchment through back-to-basics came to be overshadowed by a new wave of national reports offering conflicting prescriptions for school reform in a period marked by alarming concern over the decline of U.S. preeminence in world industrial markets.[21]

Shifting Federal Educational Policy. "If an unfriendly foreign power had attempted to impose on America the mediocre educational performance that exists today, we might well have viewed it as an act of war," declared the National Commission on Excellence in Education in the opening page of its report issued in 1983.[22] Appointed by the U.S. Secretary of Education, the National Commission on Excellence found its report being given the widest media coverage and being treated as an official document on federal educational reform policy.

Reminiscent of the tone of urgency and emergency that characterized the criticisms leveled at our schools during the era of the Cold War and space race, the new nationalizing call was to redirect the mission of the schools toward regaining the nation's technological leadership and dominance in world industrial markets. "The citizen is dismayed at a steady 15-year decline in industrial productivity as one American industry after another falls to world competition,"[23] stated the report in fixing the blame on the schools rather than on government, industry, the scientific community, or the universities.

Once again our nation's schools were being called on to give priority to the academically talented and to specific curricular reforms—higher graduation standards, national standardized tests to certify levels of achievement at various transition points in schooling, lengthening the school day and school year, emphasizing the "new basics" of academic studies and including computer literacy and technology in the "new basics," increasing student homework, instituting foreign languages in the elementary school, establishing teacher merit pay, and increasing federal support of programs designed to promote the national interest.

A Nation at Risk was followed by renewed demands for increased federal support for education at a time when the executive branch was opposed to such initiatives. This situation impelled the U.S. Secretary of Education to have the staff of the National Commission on Excellence conduct a survey of the initiatives taken by the individual states. Scarcely seven months after the issuance of *A Nation at Risk,* the staff report was published with the following opening words: "Throughout the Nation, public and private actions by individuals and groups at local, state, and national levels are meeting the challenge to improve education."[24]

In examining the staff report, it was clear that such a swift and remarkable transformation of education was not taking place. Most of the state initiatives in the staff report were under way before the appearance of *A Nation at Risk.* As political bodies, state departments of education were all too eager to report their accomplishments when given the opportunity. Virtually no problems or deficiencies were reported.

Nevertheless, it was clear that *A Nation at Risk* had given impetus and legitimacy to the movement to raise academic requirements, to give special emphasis to science and mathematics, to employ achievement tests on a statewide basis to certify pupil transition through levels of schooling, to emphasize "computer literacy," to examine teacher education, to explore schemes for teacher merit pay, and to develop statewide plans for education in response to the national interest in the competition for world industrial markets.

The Bandwagon Effect.   Another example of a political document on educational reform is the report of the Task Force on Education for Economic Growth, *Action for Excellence: A Comprehensive Plan to Improve the Nation's Schools,* issued in 1983 barely more than a month after the appearance of *A Nation at Risk.* Sponsored by the Education Commission of the States, the task force was given the mandate to develop its "comprehensive plan" in response to the state of "emergency" relating to the nation's declining position in global economic competition. The membership of the task force was dominated by governors and chief executives of major U.S. corporations. In its report, the task force criticized the schools for the decline of U.S. dominance over world industrial markets and recommended that the schools be mobilized through a partnership with industry so as to develop the highly skilled human capital needed to regain our nation's preeminent position.

In essence, the task force echoed the sentiments of *A Nation at Risk.* However, it gave even greater emphasis to the business connection with the schools and recommended that school administrators improve their managerial efficiency and skills with the help of business and industry. The task force report, *Action for Excellence,* called for the redefinition of basic skills to encompass the skills needed in the technological workplace and the "mobilization" of our educational system to teach the new skills for the development of our nation's "human capital."[25]

Misplacing the Blame for Economic and Political Defects.   Neither *Action for Excellence* nor *A Nation at Risk* examined the shortcomings of institutions other than the schools in connection with our alleged state of emergency in global economic competition. Nor did they recognize the importance of the social studies in illuminating the sources and implications of our societal problems. Dewey's observation of 1922 appeared particularly apropos to the authors of *A Nation at Risk* and *Action for Excellence* when he wrote, "If the average boy and girl could be walled off from all ideas and information about social affairs save those acquired in school, they would enter upon the responsibilities of social membership in complete ignorance that there are any social problems, any political evils, any industrial defects."[26]

The call for a business–education partnership in various national reports on educational reform prompted an educator to observe that "the most notable change in the past year has been the increased involvement of businesses in education policy making," while going on to recommend that "education's best alternative seems to be to accept and work with business zestfully (lest business leaders misconstrue caution as delay and obfuscation)."[27] Oddly, no voices were being heard concerning the possible dangers of such alliances when a free society requires that the schools enable their students to gain insight into pervading social problems, political evils, and industrial defects. Ironically, this was a time when renewed attention was being given in the mass media and in leading business schools to evidences of a decline in ethical standards by corporate management.[28]

The report *Action for Excellence* listed the goal of "good citizenship" under "basic employment," while failing to mention *democratic* citizenship and what this means in terms of critically examining our pervading social problems and issues in the perspective of our historic experience. No mention was made of the importance of the arts, health, physical education, and recreation.

In 1985 the Committee for Economic Development (CED), an organization of business executives, issued a report, *Investing in Our Children: Business and the Public Schools*. As shown in Table 9–2, the CED report echoed the prescriptions for school reform that were advocated in *A Nation at Risk* and *Action for Excellence*. The CED report called for establishing statewide measures for educational standards and for monitoring pupil achievement; involving business in the policy-making process of the local schools; improving the managerial efficiency of schools with the help of business; concentrating the curriculum on basic academic and behavioral skills for employability; expanding area vocational centers coupled with academic high schools to replace the comprehensive high school; and instituting teacher merit pay. The CED report called upon the schools to transmit to students the traits of responsible citizenship as they are essential to success in the workplace, without mentioning the need for *democratic* citizenship.

The CED report appeared to cap the barrage of reports on school reform in the wake of the Japanese economic challenge of the 1980s. Whereas at midcentury the principal educational vehicle for a free society was envisioned in the form of the comprehensive high school, the policy prescriptions for the 1980s called for dismantling this unique American invention—born after great struggle against those who advocated our adoption of the divided school system of the Old World.

Finally, the work of school administrators and supervisors was seen as requiring a complete recasting along the lines of managerial efficiency modeled after the industrial sector.

Reestablishing the Curricular Priority for Mathematics, Science, and Technology.
The year 1983 also witnessed the issuance of a report by the National Science Foundation's National Science Board (NSB) Commission on Precollege Education in Mathematics, Science and Technology, entitled *Educating Americans for the 21st Century*. Dominated by college presidents, professors, and industrialists, the Commission faulted our schools and not our industrial–political–scientific establishments for the shortcomings in the quality of our nation's manufactured products and position in world trade. Reminiscent of the era of the Cold War and space race, the Commission stated the case for turning the mission of our schools to meeting narrow nationalistic interests in these words:

> Prepared citizens (especially in science, mathematics and technology as well as other basic academic and technical subjects) are required for the operation of the Nation's essential industries and services, the ability of those industries to compete internationally and for military security.
>
> Federal involvement is necessary when certain skills are extremely short or when there is a great need for an urgent program to produce vital talent (e.g., shortages of trained doctors or other medical personnel in wartime or the national response to Sputnik).[29]

In appallingly unscientific fashion, the NSB report proceeded to make the case for our nation's inferior position against other nations in school achievement by comparing test results for the mass of American 18-year-olds with the small elite of school compeers in other nations. The NSB report documented this alleged inferiority of our schools with a reference to an article that actually warned against making such misinterpretations. In this connection, the author of the article, Torsten Husén of Sweden, chairman of the International Assessment for the Evaluation of Educational Achievement, pointed out that the top U.S. students score at about the same level as the corresponding group in other nations—the difference being that in the selective school system of other nations, "the high standard of the elite is bought at the price of more limited opportunities for the majority of students."[30]

As summarized in Table 9–2, the NSB report called for the massive infusion of federal funds for the support of curriculum improvement in mathematics, science, and technology; minimum state-mandated requirements in these subjects for high school graduation; higher requirements in mathematics and science for college entrance; a federal mechanism for measuring student achievement in order to make national, state, and local comparisons; higher pay for teachers in the priority fields of mathematics, science, and technology; the creation of partnerships between local schools, business, and academia; and the establishment of national educational goals at the Presidential level.

The NSB Commission cited the National Assessment test scores in faulting the schools for the decline in student thinking abilities, but failed to acknowledge that the National Assessment staff had attributed the decline to the back-to-basics retrenchment and state minimum-competency testing imposed on the schools during the 1970s. The Commission called for a coherent curriculum in mathematics and science, but failed to address the need for a coherent curriculum for general education—including the need to broach the widespread misuses of science and technology, and the needed relationship between technology and vocational education.

Choosing to overlook the failures of the NSF-funded national curriculum reforms which produced the "new math" and the "new science" in response to the crisis of the Cold War and space race of the late fifties and decade of the sixties, the NSB Commission of NSF proceeded to make the following recommendation: "The National Science Foundation, which has the recognized expertise in leading curriculum development, should again take the leadership in promoting curriculum evaluation and development for mathematics, science and technology."[31]

The narrow, nationalistic, crisis-motivated prescriptions to be imposed on our schools, as conceived by the NSB Commission, raise far-ranging implications for the role and function of public education in a free society. There are incalculable dangers of adopting the same mechanisms employed by totalitarian nations, such as the USSR, in subordinating education to the narrow interests of the state. Dewey cited this same danger in 1916 when he traced the evolution of German nationalism, which turned the schools to serving the interests of the military and in the struggle for international supremacy in commerce. The consequence was that the "state" was substituted for humanity and cosmopolitanism was submerged by nationalism.[32]

Policy Reports Based on Studies of Schooling

In sharp contrast to the reports of the national commissions, panels, and task forces for educational reform issued during the 1970s and 1980s are the reports of two large-scale studies of schooling: *High School: A Report on Secondary Education in America* (1983) by Ernest L. Boyer of the Carnegie Foundation, and *A Place Called School* (1984) by John I. Goodlad. Both of these reports avoided the accusatory and condemnatory language characteristic of the other reports issued during the 1970s and 1980s. Both of these reports were based on the actual study of conditions in selected schools in different sections of the nation by teams of observers and data collectors. Both reports drew extensively from selected literature on education while going beyond such literature and data in formulating recommendations on educational policy and practice.

In connection with the findings and recommendations, many of which had a direct bearing on school supervision, these two studies pointed to the need to develop coherent programs of general education in the secondary school, although, as shown in Table 9–2, their prescriptions were very different. Both studies pointed to the need for classrooms to be more cooperative–collaborative in tone and climate, and for increased emphasis on reflective thinking rather than on rote learning and mechanical skills. Both called for the elimination of curricular tracking, while Goodlad made a powerful case against ability grouping in the elementary and secondary schools. Both studies warned of the dangers in the trend toward highly specific curricular mandates and interventions by the states. (It will be recalled that *A Nation at Risk, Action for Excellence,* and *Investing in Our Children* had recommended such state mandates and interventions.)

Although it appeared clear that neither the Boyer nor the Goodlad report was swept up in the sociopolitical tide of the times, when it was in vogue to attribute our threatened technological and industrial position in global competition to the shortcomings of our educational system, a number of their recommendations not only extended beyond their data base but were unsupported by the professional literature and ran counter to our historic traditions. For example, Boyer and Goodlad pointed to the importance of career education with work experience, but viewed this as a function of general education. In criticizing vocational education, they opted for the virtual elimination of the comprehensive high school in favor of a general academic high school. In this connection they not only struck a blow at the comprehensive high school, but they ignored the educational literature supporting this unitary school both from the standpoint of democratic philosophy and the standpoint of the research that supports the comprehensive concept.[33] Oddly, neither Boyer nor Goodlad leveled any criticisms at the separate, specialized area vocational schools that had been established since the late 1960s, nor did they examine the consequences for creating a dual system of education.

The lack of support for the comprehensive high school on the part of such educators as Boyer and Goodlad, and in the reports of the "national" commissions of the early 1980s, contrasts sharply against the abiding faith in this unique American institution by Conant. In 1970, Conant wrote:

I am an advocate of the comprehensive school, but I must admit that the future of this institution is far from certain in the United States. It is strange that the enthusiasm for an American invention is so limited in this country just at the time when other nations are beginning to explore application of the basic idea. . . . Are the high schools of the United States to be so designed as to be effective means of forwarding the idea of unity based on diversity in a democratic community, or is the comprehensive concept to be given at best only lip service? Far more than the nature of our schools is involved in the answer to this question. The entire structure of our nation may be at stake—possibly even its survival as an open society of free men.[34]

Strangely absent from the reports on educational reform during the early 1980s was any consideration of the social divisions created by a divided school system, such as those that were so prevalent in the Old World. In fact, the Boyer report went so far as to recommend the establishment of a national network of federally supported residential academies in science and mathematics for gifted and talented students, on the ground that the vital interests of the nation are at stake. Again, no consideration was given to the implications of segregating such adolescents from their peers, nor of the consequences in a democratic society when education is turned to serving narrow nationalistic interests.

Boyer also devoted an entire chapter of his report to extolling the benefits of building the "corporate connection" with the schools, without raising any precautions concerning the possible dangers raised by such connections.

Goodlad went so far as to call for the total restructuring of our school system. Instead of twelve years of schooling beginning at age 6 after kindergarten and ending at age 18, Goodlad recommended that schooling begin at age 4 and end at age 16. The problem of ending formal education at age 16 and finding productive employment for the majority of our youth who do not go on to college, along with the social consequences of such a scheme, was never examined in any detail. Many mechanisms and programs for accelerating the advancement of academically able youth into college have been attempted and continue to be available (early admission to college, advanced placement, diploma by examination, etc.), though such efforts at large have not resulted in reducing the years of schooling for the targeted population. Adolescents appear to prefer to remain in school with their own age group, and appear to feel that penalties are exacted through educational compression and acceleration.

EVALUATION: THE RESPONSIBILITY OF EDUCATORS AND THE SIGNIFICANCE OF PERSPECTIVE

The response to the reports on school reform of the early 1980s was focused mainly on intensifying state mandates for the curriculum—giving particular emphasis to science and mathematics, lengthening the school day, giving priority to the academically talented, devising mechanisms for teacher merit pay, and emphasizing "computer literacy." In essence, the adopted reform measures have been highly segmental and have not been subjected to systematic evaluation. School districts have proceeded to invest in microcomputers without carefully considering the lack of appropriate software for education and the failure of the efforts made with computer-assisted instruction and other new media (teaching machines, television, programmed instruction, etc.) during earlier periods.

As political documents, the reports of national commissions on school reform tend to reflect the dominant sociopolitical tides of the times. School administrators and supervisors are impelled to demonstrate their responsiveness to the times by following these tides. But as educators they are responsible for evaluating proposals for reform and educating their constituencies accordingly. As educators they must clearly discern the difference between political documents on school reform and actual studies of the schools in connection with evaluating the findings and prescriptions offered. This does not mean that political documents are to be discounted and that only research studies are to be taken seriously in formulating educational policy and practice. Our history is replete with political documents that have served us well in setting our course for social and educational improvement (ranging from the Bill of Rights down to the *Cardinal Principles* report of 1918).

Awareness of Underlying Valuations in Research

Supervisors and administrators need to realize that any significant piece of research affecting educational policy and practice is invariably undergirded by the valuations of the researcher, and often the findings and recommendations of a given piece of research are not consonant with the body of research literature.

Hence the supervisor and the administrator must make an independent assessment of the research and of political documents for educational reform in terms of their congruence or conflict with (1) the principles of American democracy (i.e., optimum educational opportunity for all), (2) the best available knowledge from the professional literature, (3) the historic experience with any similar reform measures, (4) our cultural traditions and commitments, and (5) the cosmopolitan and comprehensive needs of the constituencies to be served.

This means that those most affected by reform proposals need to be directly involved in the evaluation and implementation process, to be fully aware of the sponsorship and the valuations underlying the research and the proposals for reform, to consider the possible interactions of any given reform with existing practices and functions of the educational system, and to put even the most promising reform proposals to the test of systematic evaluation (pilot studies at the local level, reviews of the literature, consultation with researchers representing different sides or perspectives of the problem, observation study of practices in operation elsewhere, etc.). Above all, change, innovation, or reform per se must not be regarded as desirable, but must be explicitly directed at solving problems to effect educational improvement.

Evaluation: The Need for Perspective

Mention has been made of the need for administrators, curriculum directors, supervisors, and teachers to evaluate given reform proposals or innovations in the light of previous experience with similar measures. Otherwise, the schools become vulnerable to the repetitive cycles in which given reforms and innovations are promoted, adopted, and discarded like changing clothing fashions—not to mention the price to be paid as the result of misguided schemes.

As discussed earlier, among the key proposals issued during the early 1980s by the national commissions on educational reform was for our elementary and secondary schools to embark on a partnership with business, to make systematic use of the newer instructional technology, and to stress "computer literacy." A brief review of the previous cycle with the new instructional technology will illustrate the importance of evaluating the contemporary proposals in the perspective of the earlier experience. At the proposal stage in the promotion of an educational innovation or reform, there is the tendency of proponents to make unwarranted claims while neglecting to subject the proposed measure to the test of research and evaluation.

A Case in Point: The Promised Technological Revolution in Education. It will be recalled that during the 1950s, a veritable educational revolution was heralded as being imminent through the utilization of television for systematic instruction in the schools.[35] However, the revolution through television failed to materialize in the schools, although television did bring about profound changes in home life, political campaigning, the sports industry, mass communication of social and political events, and commercial advertising. Toward the end of the 1950s and through the decade of the 1960s, the promised educational revolution shifted away from television and to teaching machines and computer-assisted instruction. During that period, federal funds were made available through the National Defense Education Act (1958) for the use of the new instructional technology in the schools, while the private sector viewed instructional technology as a promising new growth industry. The great visions of a technological revolution and a new business–government thrust in education prompted Francis Keppel to leave his post as U.S. Commissioner of Education and to assume the presidency of the now defunct General Learning Corporation, a joint venture of Time, Inc. and General Electric, to develop and market the new hardware and software.

Second Thoughts. In 1966, Charles E. Silberman, then a senior editor of *Fortune*, authored a cover story in that publication, "Technology Is Knocking at the Schoolhouse Door." In that article, Silberman claimed that through the new instructional technology, "the new business–government thrust is likely to transform both the organization and content of education, and through it, the character and shape of American society itself," and he went on to express his anticipation of "a quantum jump in learning and in man's use of intellect."[36] Only four years later, in his report for the Carnegie Corporation—a national best-seller entitled *Crisis in the Classroom: The Remaking of American Education*—Silberman advocated the "humanizing" of our schools and criticized the "advocates and prophets" of computer-assisted instruction for having made "extravagant predictions of wonders to come."[37]

In 1967, an official publication of the U.S. Office of Education envisioned the time when schools would be replaced by home computers.[38]

In 1966, Patrick Suppes of Stanford University had claimed that "one can predict that in a few more years millions of school children will have access to what Philip of Macedon's son Alexander enjoyed as a royal prerogative: the personal services of a tutor (computer) as well-informed and responsive as Aristotle."[39] Eight years later, Suppes and his associates acknowledged that the research findings on computer-assisted instruction revealed no significant differences over conventional instruction and that the computer may find its use in small supplemental doses for elementary skill-drill practices.[40]

In 1973, Postman and Weingartner predicted that print will play only a secondary role in the classroom, with the major role being assumed by the new electronic technology.[41] But only six years later, Postman reversed himself in an attack on the new technology and in a defense of traditional classroom instruction.[42]

"The era that is in full bloom and about to fade is human-to-human instruction," predicted John Goodlad in 1968, as he went on to declare, "The era of instruction that will supersede the era of human-based instruction is that of man–machine interaction."[43] But by 1984 Goodlad criticized the sweeping claims being made for the new educational technology of the 1980s by pointing to the misguided and sweeping predictions that had been made in the 1960s. "Visions of such developments have led to excessive rhetoric regarding the replacement of teachers and even schools by machines," warned Goodlad.[44]

Contemporary Claims for Instructional Technology. Reminiscent of the sweeping claims made for the new electronic technology during the 1950s and 1960s are such recent statements from educators that "educators must recognize that outside the classroom, the 'Print Learning Age' is ending," that "the electronic revolution is here,"[45] and that "within twenty years, computers will have replaced the book as 'the major delivery device' in bringing education to students."[46]

Such sweeping claims do not appear to be warranted from our historic experience with technological advances, as noted in the following commentary:

> The demise of the stenographer was predicted with the invention of the Dictaphone, the demise of the theater with the invention of the talking motion picture, the demise of the concert hall with the invention of the phonograph, the demise of the motion picture with the invention of television and the demise of handwriting with the invention of the typewriter (albeit the ball-point pen has led to some very poor scripts).
>
> Aside from being easily portable and readable, in comparison to an electronic screen, and aside from its physical attractiveness, the book (with its pages) conveys a tactile quality and pleasure that no push-button circuitry can provide—even when one is only browsing or skimming through a book, or making marginal notations (preferably only on the pages of one's own books). Moreover, the book can be read while sitting, standing or lying down. It can even grace the walls of a home library or den when it is not being read.
>
> The physical attributes of a book and its printed pages are far more personal than the computer screen or printout, as indicated by the common practice of writing one's name in a book to designate valued ownership, or of writing an inscription when presenting a book as a gift to a friend.
>
> But the book is more than this. Its physical quality is intimately linked to the very evolution of human language and thought. We would do well to heed the

advice of Norbert Wiener, a pioneer of the new technology, who wrote in one of his books, "Render unto man the things which are man's and unto the computer the things which are the computer's."

Incidentally, if one should want to learn how to program or use a computer, there are many good books on the subject.[47]

The Need to Consider the Wider Implications. There is no question that the development of the microcomputer has effected an economic breakthrough, so that the cost factors connected with the computer technology of the 1960s have been overcome. Yet expenditures for basal texts and other curricular materials amount to well under 1 percent of the school budget.[48] In seeking to effect economies during times of retrenchment, school districts typically cut back on books and other curricular materials despite the fact that such materials constitute such an appallingly minute fraction of the school budget and despite the fact that such materials are at the heart of the curriculum.

In promoting computer technology as replacing the book (and other printed matter) as the dominant medium of instruction, there is an abiding failure to make the necessary distinctions between computerized instruction and learning through the use of books and other print media, and through social interaction.

Print Media and the New Technology: Qualitative Differences. The term "computer literacy" became a slogan in promoting the new educational technology in the 1980s. As discussed earlier, various national reports on educational reform listed "computer literacy" as one of the "new basics," and the competencies for "computer literacy" were described as "the ability to follow predetermined procedures" along with the ability to operate the computer devices for carrying out the necessary predetermined functions.[49]

In contrast, the act of reading a book or of writing a theme is not necessarily a matter of convergent learning as in following a predetermined procedure, but involves emergent learning. Hence the process of reading a book or writing a theme is qualitatively different from following a computer program. The latter cannot substitute for the former. Everyone has experienced disappointment, for example, in seeing a motion picture based on a novel that one had read previously. In reading the novel, the reader is engaged in creating the character and scenes through the "mind's eye." The author's depictions are intended to be sufficiently rich and open so as to stimulate the imagination of the reader. On the other hand, the computer program is a predetermined and literal representation of data, and the process of following the program is primarily a convergent one.

Of course, computers can be used in helping to solve emergent problems, and computers make it possible to process vast quantities of data that heretofore would have swamped the individual. But the computer program, nevertheless, has little tolerance for ambiguity. Even the textbook allows for sufficient ambiguity to leave both the student and instructor free to take issue with the author's treatment of problems and issues where alternative interpretations are possible. This accounts for the fact that books, including textbooks, and other print media are frequently targets of censorship in schools, whereas computer programs are not so targeted.

It is also noteworthy and ironic that the book has been the principal vehicle through which instruction in operating and programming the computer is provided. This phenomenon was unanticipated, as it had been assumed that the computer program would be the most efficient means of providing instruction in operating and programming the computer. Apparently, the book provides for a dimension of flexibility that is lacking even in the case where one is seeking to learn how to use the computer.

Indeed, the computer has made it possible to make calculations in the sciences, industry, and government that previously were beyond human capacity, including the storage and retrieval of data. However, the schools have proceeded to purchase microcomputers for instruction when the needed software for higher cognitive learning is not available. Now and in the future educators must differentiate between the appropriate uses of the computer in relation to other media for learning.

The claim that the computer will replace print media appears misguided in view of the fact that it has generated more and not less print material. The word processor is a remarkably valuable device, but it is the human learner who composes and interprets the material that goes into and comes out of the word processor. In the same vein, it is the computer that should work for the learner, not the other way around.

The Social Aspect of Learning. Finally, the social aspect of learning must not be underestimated. Human-to-human interaction is vital in the learning process because civilization itself is based on human cooperation. The significance of social interaction also becomes evident even when individuals are engaged in the most routine tasks. For example, during the early 1980s one of the largest American banks established a procedure whereby all routine bank transactions would be handled through automatic tellers, and that unless a depositor had a large account, he or she was required to deal with the machine teller. This arrangement was touted by the bank management as a great convenience for the depositor in that it would eliminate the long lines that were customary at lunchtime and at the end of the week, aside from the fact that the machine tellers were found to be far more economical for the bank. However, the depositors raised such a hue and cry against the new procedure, with many transferring their accounts to other banks, that the required procedure of dealing with the machine teller was dropped. Logic had indicated that the new procedure would be far more efficient, economical, and convenient. But the bank management had overlooked the possibility that people prefer choices and that they value face-to-face (social) communication even in some of the most routine and seemingly mechanical transactions.

The process of learning is infinitely more complex and the value of human interaction is of paramount significance because human beings model themselves after other human beings. Teachers, along with one's fellow pupils, serve as models for emulation, approval, disapproval, and so on. There is no substitute for the human equation.

The admonition offered by the late Norbert Wiener, father of cybernetics, to differentiate between what is appropriate for the computer and what is appropriate for the human being seems particularly apropos to the educator.[50]

STRATEGIES FOR CHANGE

Schools, or for that matter, any organization, cannot function without a sense of stability and continuity. This, in turn, serves as a buffer against haphazard or thoughtless change, or change that occurs as mainly a response to external pressures without considering the needs of the internal participants and those of the organization (school). The need for stability and continuity, however, does not justify blind resistance to change. Change is a condition of life. Yet change, in and of itself, as emphasized earlier, does not signify improvement. Improvement comes through problem solutions.

Change by Advocacy and Persuasion

A considerable portion of this chapter has been devoted to the efforts and influences of various external bodies to effect substantial change in educational policy and practice through advocacy or persuasion. Throughout the twentieth century, successions of national commissions have been created to exert influence on educators, school boards, politicians, and the general public for the purpose of bringing about educational reforms (see Table 9–2). Since midcentury, various federal agencies and certain leading private foundations have been particularly influential in using this strategy. This approach has also been widely used at the state level. The commissions or individuals assigned to undertake the "study" and to issue their findings and recommendations command credibility through their prestige and influence. Coupled with the fact that such reports tend to be issued at times of perceived crisis, the findings and recommendations command wide media attention. The sponsoring agencies are highly knowledgeable in gaining access to the mass media, and they command the resources for enlisting individuals of influence and competence and for the dissemination of the findings and recommendations.

As discussed earlier, school administrators, supervisors, and local boards of education often are eager to demonstrate their responsiveness to the crisis remedies for fear of not moving with the tide, or they may simply accede to the authoritative and prestigious sponsorship and authorship of the report, or they may find the diagnoses and prescriptions suited to the problems they perceive as extant in their own school district. In cases where the response is motivated by the "flock mentality" or by deference to external authoritative persuasion, the adopted changes or reforms are apt to take the form of superficial adaptation if only because substantive change or reform requires commitment on the part of the internal participants. Not infrequently, the "change" takes the form of an adopted label or slogan—such as "academic excellence," "standards," "mastery," "individualized learning," and so on. Even when the school board or administrator may perceive the externally proposed remedies as suited to the problems in their own district, unless the internal participants who are most affected by the change (supervisors and teachers) are involved in the decision making, the response to mandated change is likely to be that of mere acquiescence or compliance rather than commitment—and the effects are likely to be superficial rather than substantive.

Change by Mandate or Coercion

With education regarded as a state function, mandates for change are commonly made through state legislation and decisions of state boards of education—affecting everything from the length of the school year to specific curricular requirements such as the teaching of state history and U.S. history. The governor and the chief state school officer may issue executive orders for compliance to various legal requirements. The courts have exercised great power in mandating a wide range of compliances, such as those concerning school desegregation, teacher tenure and dismissal, the teaching of creationism versus evolution, school prayer, bilingual education, and student rights.

Traditionally, the states have allowed local districts great latitude regarding the curriculum. Although the states typically have required the teaching of state history and the U.S. Constitution, for example, the schools have been allowed to determine how this is to be done. As an illustration, the requirement could be met through the broad field of social studies rather than by specific courses in state and U.S. history. All too often, however, the schools have tended to add specific courses to comply with any new curricular mandates—in effect, making the curriculum fit the mandate rather than having the mandate fit the curriculum.

Although the increased legislation affecting education has produced an increase in judicial activity, Reutter points out that the courts have continued to allow the local district considerable latitude over matters concerning the curriculum.

> Probably in no area of school operation have the courts been more liberal in interpreting implied powers of local boards than in curricular matters. This statement applies not only to addition of specific curricular elements, but to determination of methods of carrying out both specific and general mandates.[51]

The most notable area in which the courts have acted consistently to negate the powers of the states and local school boards pertains to state laws and local mandates that violate the U.S. Constitution, such as the teaching of creationism, the prohibition of the teaching of evolution, bible reading, and prayer. In most other matters pertaining to the curriculum, local school boards and the professional staff exercise wide latitude.

The effectively functioning local board of education will rely on the expertise of its professional staff for the design, development, and evaluation of the curriculum. One of the most important responsibilities of the school superintendent, which typically receives inadequate attention, is that of educating the board members to recognize this professional expertise and not to impinge on it.

Although state legislatures and state boards of education have increased their activity in mandating specific curricular requirements over the past decade, the most pervasive influence on the curriculum has resulted from the mandated statewide competency-testing programs since the 1970s.

Power strategies have been used by minority groups, teachers unions, and other special-interest groups—ranging from teachers of bilingual classes to antievolutionists—seeking to influence legislation or to gain more effective representation in school decision making. In the area of civil rights and educational opportunity, such strategies have been notably effective. In other cases, the vested-interest group succeeds in its mission, but its mission is not conceived in the wider interest of effecting educational improvement. An example of this is the power-coercive strategies by special-interest groups to censor textbooks and other curricular materials.

School officials often respond to the more compelling power strategies of external groups making curricular demands by employing ad hoc or segmental adjustments. For example, the demand for black studies and humanizing the curriculum during the late 1960s and early 1970s led to the addition of courses in black studies and humanities, without effecting a needed reconstruction of the curriculum in social studies and general education. In many schools the division between black studies and humanities was reflected in racial division in the course enrollments.

Change by Financial Inducement and Sponsorship

The federal government typically has sought to induce educational change by funding specific programs and projects in conjunction with the states. Most of these programs and projects have been segmental and narrowly targeted.

Two of the most successful and enduring federal initiatives in education were the Morrill Act, signed by President Lincoln in 1862, which gave rise to the great land-grant universities, and the various vocational education acts since the time President Wilson signed the Smith-Hughes Act of 1917. Both of these acts were comprehensive in scope and effect. The land-grand universities, referred to early in their history as the "people's colleges," not only extended higher education to the general population while establishing coeducation on an unprecedented scale, but forged an inseparable link between the theoretical and practical studies. Until the Vocational Education Act of 1963, the joint federal/state-funded programs in vocational education of less-than-college grade were accommodated mostly within the structure of the comprehensive high school—in sharp contrast to the traditional European practice of administering vocational education through segregated, specialized schools. The federally supported vocational programs have endured because they have been directed at meeting a continuing need at the local level, because they have been implemented within the dominant (mainstream) structure of the educational system, and because they have received sustained financial and political support.

Segmental Reforms in Response to Shifting "Crises." Since midcentury, wide-ranging federal initiatives have been taken to induce educational change—such as those encompassed under the National Defense Education Act (NDEA) of 1958 and the Elementary and Secondary Education Act (ESEA) of 1965, administered by the U.S. Office of Education (later the U.S. Department of Education). As discussed earlier, programs to induce educational change have also been funded through other federal agencies, most notably the national curriculum-reform projects in school science and mathematics, sponsored by the

National Science Foundation during the 1950s and 1960s, and the various educational programs for children and adolescents conducted apart from the schools under the sponsorship of the Office of Economic Opportunity (OEO) during the 1960s and early 1970s.

Virtually all of the major programs under NDEA, ESEA, NSF, and OEO were widely heralded and gained wide participation. Nevertheless, most eventually were phased out for want of producing the promised impact. From the start, the educational programs of OEO could not have a substantive impact on the schools because they were administered outside the schools. The NSF-funded projects in school science and mathematics were segmental, stressed specialized and abstract knowledge to the neglect of general education and knowledge applications in the life of the learner, and failed to consider the nature of the learner in connection with the processes of growth and development. The crisis mentality and narrow curricular priorities of NDEA—focused on science, mathematics, and modern foreign languages—neglected the larger goals and functions of education in a free society.

Great store was placed in changing the schools through the financing of the new instructional technology under NDEA, with insufficient attention being given to the quality of the software and to the adequacy of the technology in delivering what was promised. ESEA produced a host of fragmented projects in compensatory education for the disadvantaged. Title III of ESEA provided funding in support of innovative projects in the schools under the premise that the schools, being inherently intransigent, needed stimulus for change, and that change or innovation, in and of itself, would pave the way for improvement. In short order, "innovation" became a code word in the schools.

The Persistent Need for Formative and Summative Evaluation. With few exceptions, the programs and projects under NDEA, ESEA, NSF, and OEO lacked commitment to carefully designed and independent formative and summative evaluation. When evaluations were mandated, the sponsoring agency and local district often sought to "prove the project" or else engaged in "little more than a ritualistic defense of program activities."[52] As one educator observed, "Perhaps the true mark of an advanced and forward-looking school is not the length of its list of innovations in progress, but rather the degree to which it continues to participate in the experimental testing of new ideas and postpone wholesale adoption until its own or other evidence becomes available."[53]

In belated response to the mounting questions concerning the effectiveness of the various "change-agent" programs under ESEA, the federal government enlisted the Rand Corporation to evaluate the programs in terms of ascertaining the factors connected with enhancing or impeding educational change or innovation. The evaluation, conducted between 1973 and 1978, found that change projects or innovations in the schools tended not to be implemented as originally proposed or intended, and that even those that were implemented according to the proposed plans expired when the funding was ended.[54]

Again, it is all too easy to rest the blame on the schools. However, the innovations were approved for funding despite a host of deficiencies that should have been seen from the start. In short, the innovations were: (1) highly segmental;

(2) not actually targeted at seeking solutions to significant problems; (3) lacking a substantive research base; (4) adopted in an additive or ad hoc manner, without attending to the needed interdependence between the specific innovation and the ongoing practices and functions of the school; (5) adopted without effective faculty participation, commitment, and inservice preparation; (6) lacking in any program for systematic, independent, formative, and summative evaluation; (7) not connected to a concerted program for school renewal by the internal participants; and (8) often conceived and implemented as a production device akin to a production operation in the commercial world.

Similar shortcomings were characteristic of the efforts by such private foundations as Ford, Carnegie, and Kettering to transform the schools during the 1950s and 1960s through the new instructional technology and the managerial devices of business and industry.[55] Although such programs were promoted on the basis of effecting improvements in the quality of teaching and learning, the hidden agenda often was production efficiency—processing more pupils, with fewer teachers, at less cost, with less space, and in less time. (It should be recalled that these programs were promoted initially during a period of an acute shortage of teachers, buildings, and facilities—in the wake of a booming school population.)

Efforts of the private foundations and the federal government to "buy" change have been largely unsuccessful mainly because the key factors in effecting educational improvement, as cited above, are neglected, sidetracked, or undermined.

Reform, Counterreform. External demands for certain innovations in a given era often are superseded by the counterdemands of the succeeding era. Open classrooms reappear during eras when learner-centered pedagogy is in vogue, whereas the call for "standards," "efficiency," and "discipline" is heard when subject-centered pedagogy is the fashion. In the latter case, the innovation has taken the form of competency and achievement testing, along with other measures to demonstrate accountability. When the schools adopt innovations merely in response to external pressures or fashions, the innovations tend to be implemented superficially and often become little more than slogans or labels. For example, the concept of "independent study" has been used in connection with the traditional study hall monitored by teacher aides; the concept of "individualized learning" has been a descriptor for classroom activity in which pupils are working on identically convergent programmed materials (albeit at a different pace and sequence) or for classroom activity where pupils are engaged in mechanical and convergent exercises in different workbooks, and so on. Despite the label of "independent" or "individualized," the activity is established-convergent rather than emergent.

Responsiveness of the Schools. Some investigators allege that the school's resistance to change, innovation, or reform stems from the immunity of the school to the conditions of the marketplace, on the ground that the school functions without market competition.[56] However, some simple calculations demonstrate readily how economic factors exert a compelling effect on maintaining traditional teaching–learning arrangements in the schools. Assuming that the teacher's salary is a munificent $30,000 annually and that the teacher works with a full-time equivalent of twenty-eight pupils over a 180-day school year for six hours per day, the per pupil cost would amount to barely $1 per pupil hour. This is indeed a low market price by any standard. Moreover, such costs include teacher-preparation time and certain out-of-class responsibilities on the part of the teacher. School boards and administrators tend to fall back on the traditional classroom configuration because it is adjudged to be the most manageable arrangement considering the economic constraints under which schools operate.

Innovations or reforms typically necessitate incremental costs over normal operations. When the financial inducements for given innovations expire, the innovations also tend to be discontinued. The schools tend not to absorb the incremental costs of the innovations unless the internal participants are so highly committed to the changes that they are able to override the enormous pressures for economy of operation. Consequently, induced innovations, changes, or reforms require long-term financial support, strong commitment by the internal participants, and must give evidence of effecting significant problem solutions.

Change Through Research, Development, and Dissemination: The Networking Model

The "Agricultural Model." In growing recognition of the wide chasm between educational research and school practice, along with the great fragmentation of research efforts, a number of educational researchers during the late 1950s and early 1960s were looking to the "agricultural model" as an appropriate technology of implemented change for education. Under the Cooperative Research Program of the U.S. Office of Education, initiated in the late 1950s, arrangements had been made with universities and state education agencies for research, surveys, and demonstrations in education. However, these efforts were uncoordinated and failed to exert a marked impact on school practice.

Among the proposals made for a system of implemented change in education, patterned after the agricultural model, was one offered by Guba and Clark encompassing the following principal processes:

Research.
Development.
  Invention.
  Design.
Diffusion.
  Dissemination.
  Demonstration.
Adoption.
  Trial.
  Installation.
  Institutionalization.[57]

The foregoing model may be faulted for its linearity, since practical problems have a way of not conforming to a logical sequence of processes toward solution.

Moreover, the model above starts with research at the university or research center, whereas the model for agriculture typically derives from a problem situation in the field. This is a critical point in that the problems of the internal participants become the focus of the research. At the same time, when the research derives from problem situations in the field, the solutions are not end points but feed back into the field, from where new problems are identified and attacked in a continuous process.

In effect, the agricultural model effectively bridges the gap between the internal participants and the external expertise of the land-grant university. In production agriculture, for example, the research findings are tested and developed in the field through the agricultural experiment station. The results of the field tests, which indicate the improvement of agricultural practice, are diffused through actual demonstrations on farms, and proven practices are disseminated to farmers through the university extension specialist, county agricultural agent, high school teacher of vocational agriculture, bulletins published by the Cooperative Extension Service of the land-grant university, the mass media, and conferences, short courses, and institutes sponsored by the land-grant university. Approved practices are tried out by farmers and, if successful, are adopted and become fully operational. Continuous evaluation, modification, and feedback are ensured at every stage.

The processes noted above are, of course, highly abbreviated and oversimplified. The knowledgeable university extension specialist, county agricultural agent, or agriculture teacher will seek to work through farmers who have considerable peer influence, as well as with the agricultural cooperatives and other farmer organizations, and commercial agricultural enterprises.

Seeking to Apply the Agricultural Model to Education. The Elementary and Secondary Education Act (ESEA) of 1965 provided for the creation of a technology of implemented change in education, presumably patterned after the agricultural model. Under Title IV of ESEA, Research and Development Centers were created in different sections of the country to conduct basic and applied research in education and to disseminate information. Regional Educational Laboratories were also established to conduct some research while focusing mainly on the development and demonstration of research findings and providing needed technical assistance. The laboratories were expected to work closely with state departments of education, school districts, and community agencies in further developing innovations, demonstrating improved practices, subjecting innovations and practices to field testing, and disseminating the needed information.

The Research and Development (R&D) Centers and the Regional Educational Laboratories were established with the intention that they would emulate the successes of the agricultural experiment stations and the Cooperative Extension Service of the land-grant university in bringing the fruits of research to bear on educational practice. However, where these agricultural agencies of the land-grant universities developed highly comprehensive and coordinated programs in attacking field problems in cooperation with farmers (through the systematic development, diffusion, and demonstration of research findings), the work of the R&D Centers and Regional Educational Laboratories tended to be disjointed and narrowly specialized. For example, one laboratory might be working on the technology of instruction for disadvantaged children while another would be working on quantitative-skills projects or on developing microteaching packages for the training of teachers in the techniques of verbal reinforcement. Although some of the centers and laboratories produced evidence of success in a variety of projects, the projects tended to be segmental rather than interdependent elements of a holistic program for school improvement.

Many of the problems addressed by the centers and laboratories tended to follow the dominant fashions of the times, or stemmed from the specialized interests of researchers, administrators, and staff members—rather than from the educational situation. A great deal of activity was directed at proving the project. Many of the innovations were treated as mere "products" or "techniques" to be developed, demonstrated, promoted, and adopted in piecemeal fashion. Insufficient attention was given to how the adoption of one set of innovations will relate to other innovations and to the total school program.

Moreover, from the start there was some confusion in differentiating the functions of the R&D Centers and the Regional Educational Laboratories. And where the agricultural experiment stations and Cooperative Extension Service are agencies of the public land-grant universities, some of the R&D Centers were located at private universities having no tradition of commitment to serving the people at large, while the Regional Educational Laboratories were established independently of the universities.[58] Nor were all the Regional Laboratories established as public agencies. For example, the Education Development Center— a private nonprofit corporation which had originated in 1958 as a contractor for the NSF-funded projects in the "new physics," "new mathematics," and so on— came to be designated as a Regional Education Laboratory.

In short, the agricultural model was never adopted in education as intended, and a comprehensive and coordinated problem-solving capacity for education never emerged from these efforts. These disappointing results led to the creation of the National Institute of Education (NIE) in 1972 to house most of the federal effort in research and development, including the work of the centers and laboratories.

The agricultural model has been described as an empirical-rational model or strategy for change, based on the scientific production and utilization of knowledge. Such descriptors are derived from the underlying assumption that as the scientific findings provide empirical evidence that new knowledge or practice is beneficial, one rationally expects such knowledge to be transformed into practice.[59] However, in full recognition that human behavior is not so simple, the land-grant universities make effective use of the media, conduct practical field demonstrations through farmers who are known to exert considerable influence on their peers, sponsor conferences and short courses, provide direct field consultation, and employ various other educative means for demonstrating and disseminating improved practices.

Elaborate and highly functional networks have been developed for this purpose—providing formal and informal linkages among the agencies and agents of the land-grant university and its agricultural experiment stations, the cooperative extension service, and so on—in addressing widely shared field problems and in working with farmers on problem solutions.

The Need for Networking in Attacking Widely Shared Problems. Although the "agricultural model" has never been applied to education other than on a rather feeble and piecemeal scale, some educators have pointed to the limitations of this approach in education as evidenced by the disappointing outcomes of the R&D Centers and Regional Educational Laboratories.[60] But these agencies have lacked the needed networking, linkages with practitioners, collaborative efforts in addressing widely shared problems, investment in resources, technical expertise, influential leadership, and other elements characteristic of the agricultural model.

The R&D Centers and Regional Laboratories have tended to focus their efforts on developing and promoting segmental instructional products and packages as though their adoption by the schools will lead to educational improvement. In the absence of a highly coordinated effort to address significant and widely shared problems in education, it is not surprising that the results of such segmental efforts at product development and delivery are disappointing.

Several principles have been identified in the creation of successful networks in agricultural research and development.[61] Couched in educational terms, the principles may be stated as follows:

1. The problems identified are widely shared in practice and by the agencies and agents acting on them.
2. The problems are clearly defined and a realistic research agenda is drawn up for application under practical, developmental conditions.
3. The researchers, research agencies, and practitioners in the field (school administrators, curriculum directors, supervisors, teachers) share a strong self-interest in the problem solutions, leading to the development of a working and systematic collaborative effort. (Such collaboration and cooperation cannot be effectively mandated.)
4. The cooperating agencies and their agents possess the technical and practical expertise required for effecting needed problem solutions.
5. The cooperating agencies and participants commit the needed facilities, personnel, and other resources for a systematic attack on the problems.
6. Sustained support is provided so that the agencies and participants will be encouraged to attack longer-range problems of considerable import, rather than merely seeking to demonstrate short-term success by treating symptoms and not the underlying causes of the problems.
7. The efforts are guided by a strong participatory leadership which provides recognition for individual and joint achievements.
8. Problem solutions and their practical applications are systematically and continuously evaluated in the field with the collaboration and cooperation of the practitioners who have an actual stake in the outcomes. Here the external and internal participants share in a common concern and venture.
9. The problem solutions and their practical applications are widely disseminated with the involvement of practitioners through both formal and informal communication networks.
10. The communication or dissemination process is akin to the educative process rather than taking the form of mere advocacy or promotion.

11. Continuous assessment and feedback are provided in the field for effective adaptation, modification, adjustment, and improvement. This, in turn, leads to the identification of further problems in the field that are widely shared and subsequently need to be acted on.

In short, the principles listed above undergird a process that is characterized as *developmental* rather than mechanical.

Problem Solving as a Developmental Process. Figure 9–1 portrays how the processes in the agricultural model might be summarized in a way that is applicable to education. The processes should not be regarded as linear but as functionally interdependent and continuous (developmental). They typically derive from problems in the field and relate to the solution of such problems. Field problems

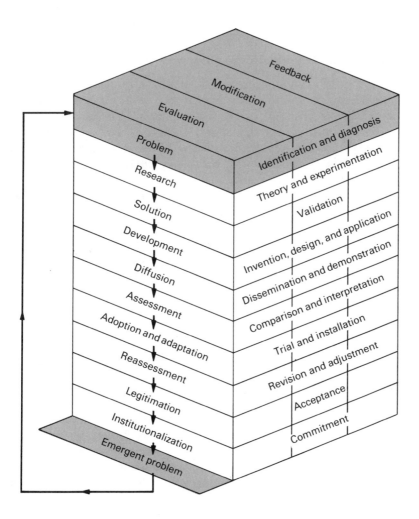

Figure 9–1. Educational problem solving as a continuous and integrated process.

and applied research are also common sources for basic research, which, in turn, can be fruitful to applied research.

As shown in Figure 9–1, all the processes require continuous evaluation, modification, and feedback. Successful adoption, adaptation, legitimation, and institutionalization of needed practices for educational improvement require not only acceptance, but *commitment* on the part of those who are most affected by the changes—namely the internal participants. Even more fundamental is the recognition of the significance of the problem by the internal participants and their desire to seek solutions.

The solution to a problem is not an end point but opens up insights and possibilities to solving other problems (Figure 9–1). The very idea of progress is based on the growth in the capability of people to exercise intelligent control over emergent conditions and thereby to improve these conditions. Hence problem solving must be treated as an ongoing *developmental* process as long as growth and improvement are expected to take place.

Change Through Organizational Renewal

In Chapter 5 it was shown how organizational self-improvement is more likely to occur in the democratic-participative system than in the other systems of organization, principally because the former type of system is characterized by an open pattern of communication, a thoroughly shared process of decision making based on the best available evidence and a widely shared responsibility for control and consequences. The focus is on solving substantive problems for continual organizational improvement.

However, because schools are continually buffeted by powerful and shifting external sociopolitical demands, administrators tend to follow the ad hoc or benevolent-authoritative system of organization under which they are readily able to demonstrate institutional responsiveness. It has been pointed out that in yielding to (or in embracing) whatever external forces for change are most dominant at a particular time, the changes or innovations tend to be adopted superficially—only to be discarded when the school is buffeted by a subsequent counterwave for change. Changes are adopted and discarded periodically without systematic evaluation or problem solving for educational improvement.

Needed Commitment to Problem Solving. Following a decade and a half of federally funded educational innovations, the National Institute of Education pointed to repeated research findings that innovations per se do not result in school improvement.[62]

It is puzzling as to how the architects of the federal legislation (Elementary and Secondary Education Act, Title III—Innovative Projects) came to assume in the first place that innovations per se would produce substantive improvements in our schools. Nevertheless, it was found that the schools that were able to effect significant improvements were characterized by a "problem-solving orientation" in which they utilized the federal funds to attack problems which they had identified earlier as in need of solution. It was further concluded that the problem of effecting improvement "is a problem of improving the organizational climate (problem-solving and decisionmaking structures, incentives to change, skills in managing collaborative planning and implementation, mutual support and communication . . .) in which people work," and that substantive improvement hinges on the capacity of schools and school systems "to engage in an active search for solutions to their own problems, to adapt solutions to the particulars of their own situation, and equally important, to adapt themselves as organizations to the requirements of the selected solutions."[63]

This does not imply that schools and school systems must work in isolation, or that they cannot benefit from external knowledge sources—such as through the consultative services of the university, the research literature, the experiences of other schools and school systems, and so on. Instead, it means that problems cannot be solved and improvements cannot be effected unless administrators, curriculum directors, supervisors, faculty, and other staff members are committed to problem solving and work in a more democratic-participative organizational system. It means that externally derived proposals for improvement cannot be effectively adopted on a piecemeal basis, but must be reconstructed to meet the unique conditions at the local level and in consideration of the possible interactions with existing practices. And it means that any implemented change must be evaluated both formatively (in process) and summatively (at the end of a given time period) in terms of the problem(s) to which it was directed. Such changes might well be tested on a pilot basis so as to gain some measure of any unanticipated outcomes, as well as to evaluate the potentials for effecting needed problem solutions.

Need for Aggregate Approach in Problem Solving. Unfortunately, when problem-solving strategies are employed in education they tend to be narrowly directed and confined to segmental elements or operations. For example, efforts to improve the teaching of a given subject matter (whether mathematics, science, social studies, English, the arts, etc.), without taking into account the necessary interdependence of all the studies comprising the curriculum in general education, are bound to produce fragmented and conflicting results. Not only do such efforts exacerbate the existing problem of curriculum isolation, but they give rise to the problem whereby gains in one area are sought at the expense of other areas of the curriculum. To confine "problem solving" to ad hoc and segmental elements or operations is self-defeating, for it only creates more problems than solutions. Unless problems are identified and addressed in recognition of the vital ecological relationships of the schooling enterprise, little progress can be made.

Proposals or prescriptions for change, no matter how forcefully they are presented, must be appraised in the light of the possible interactions with existing practice and the possible consequences of their implementation. Is there a sound research base for the proposal? Has the proposed change been implemented and evaluated elsewhere under conditions similar to those prevalent in this particular setting? What were the results, including the unanticipated consequences? Should the proposed change be tried out on a pilot basis at the local level where it can be evaluated under local conditions? How receptive are the teachers? These are some of the questions that might well be posed under the rubric of organizational renewal through problem solving.

Considerable knowledge/ability is required at all levels of the organization, and this knowledge/ability must be widely shared along with the responsibility for decision making. Organizational renewal cannot occur in a vacuum, just as it is impossible to lift oneself by one's bootstraps. The organizational leadership and membership must constantly seek to benefit from outside resources and must avoid inbreeding. At the same time they must be committed to the critical evaluation of externally advocated reform measures. By having a commitment to problem solving, they will be in a stronger position in making the case for proceeding with caution when confronted with external power-coercive mandates for reform that appear likely to be damaging to the mission of the organization.

Consonance with Philosophical Outlook. Proposed reforms also need to be assessed in terms of the professed philosophy of the school. If a school claims that the curriculum is designed to foster critical thinking, for example, but succumbs to external pressures for the censorship of curricular materials, or if the faculty suffers from self-imposed censorship, the school is not true to itself. The same applies to the school that claims critical thinking as a major curricular goal, but proceeds to evaluate pupil progress through tests that are delimited to the mere recall of factual information and exercises in narrow and mechanical skills that are devoid of intelligent and comprehensive application.

Institutional Networking. School and school-system renewal can be enhanced enormously through informal and formal networking with other schools and school systems, universities, Regional Educational Laboratories, and other agencies in gaining assistance with significant problems. Although it is not likely that the agricultural model will be developed for public education in the foreseeable future, the schools can contract with any or several of the existing agencies in seeking technical assistance with problems.

A widely held notion is that the schools are not often willing to cooperate in research studies. However, in a large-scale study on the longer-range effects of compensatory education at the elementary level, Carter reported that "our experience has been that the schools are willing to cooperate in research they believe will be of benefit."[64]

The next step, however, is for the schools to initiate efforts for technical assistance and conjoint action in attacking local problems that are perceived as persistent. It is not enough merely to cooperate with external agencies that are seeking to conduct research, since such research may not be directed at problems indigenous to the local conditions.

Problem Solving as an Educative Process. In essence, the problem-solving process is akin to the educative process. The administration, faculty, and staff of a school are themselves engaged in the educative process when they are seeking problem solutions through the use of the best available evidence. They must not wait for external prescriptions for "curing" indigenous problems, but must be continuously engaged in the identification and pursuit of problem solutions deriving from the educational situation in which they live.

Problem solving cannot be mandated or conveyed as an easy recipe. It requires wide participation, the free flow of ideas at all levels, a high degree of knowledge/ability, systematic planning, and the commitment of adequate material resources on an ongoing basis.

As in the case of all complex organizations, there is the tendency for schools and school systems to fall into the convenience of routines and to adhere to established practices that remain essentially intact regardless of the ad hoc changes or innovations that may be adopted periodically. The commitment to problem solving as an ongoing process of organizational renewal exposes such routines and established practices to continual scrutiny.

SUMMARY

Successive periods of social change invariably are accompanied by renewed demands and pressures being exerted on the schools by various external forces. Very often the demands and pressures for educational reform or change in a given period are directed at undoing the excesses of the reform measures taken by the schools in response to the demands and pressures of the predecessor period. The consequence is an incessant succession of waves for reform by reaction and counterreaction. Such shifting and contradictory tides for change represent much movement but little progress.

The contradictory shifts in priorities and demands in successive time periods find educators in a position resembling that of the inventor, described by Norbert Wiener, who, at one point, is given the task of creating the universal solvent which will dissolve any substance, and then, at another point, of inventing the universal container which will hold any liquid.[65] Under the circumstances, school administrators tend merely to follow the dominant tide of the times in order to demonstrate their responsiveness, even if the actions taken in one period serve only to cancel out those taken in the preceding period.

The easiest and quickest form of response is by the segmental adoption of "new" practices, projects, packages, or policies. Educational change, for the most part, may be characterized as a process of segmental incrementalism, coupled with shifts of priorities in response to external pressures and fashions. Little attention is given to the organic interaction of the adopted changes in the total program of the school. Moreover, in yielding to whatever external forces are most dominant, administrators tend to impose measures for change from above. The considerations of those most directly affected by such change, namely the teachers and students, tend to be overlooked or regarded as of secondary importance. Externally mandated or imposed changes are likely to be implemented by the internal participants through mere compliance rather than commitment, with the consequence that the anticipated results fail to materialize. The problem is further compounded by the unanticipated effects of externally imposed remedies. Unless solutions are sought to problems deriving from the educational situation, and with the full involvement of the internal participants, little progress can be made.

The more effective schools are characterized as having a professional staff with a problem-solving orientation and a democratic-participative organizational climate—with structures, resources, and incentives for collaboration, cooperative decision making, mutual support, and a continuing commitment to the active search for problem solutions. The process is developmental and education oriented rather than mechanical and end-product oriented.

The path to progress requires that problems stemming from the educational situation be addressed systematically and in consideration of the interdependence of elements in the educational situation. External forces cannot be ignored, but it is incumbent on supervisors and administrators to be fully aware of these forces and their modes of operation and influence.

In this chapter a model was offered for identifying and evaluating the various forces and sources of influence for educational change or reform. Emphasis was given to the obligation of educators to subject proposed remedies to systematic evaluation in the light of the best available research evidence bearing on the educational situation and in the perspective of previous experience. In the absence of sufficient evidence, promising proposals should be treated as hypotheses for testing under pilot conditions. Such proposals must also be evaluated so as to reveal the complete agenda and valuations underlying their sources of advocacy.

At various times of perceived "crisis" in society, documents calling for educational reform and changes in educational policy are issued by temporarily appointed "national" commissions, panels, and task forces under the auspices of private foundations, professional organizations, quasi-public agencies (e.g., Education Commission of the States), and public agencies (e.g., National Science Foundation, U.S. Department of Education, and state educational agencies). Many of these documents are political and need to be evaluated in terms of their consonance with the wider public interest, as opposed to narrow special interests. In times of perceived crisis, proposed remedies tend to be narrowly conceived and shortsighted. Proposals that serve to benefit one segment of the school population, at the expense of other children and youth, run counter to the ideals of a free society. Unless school professionals have a share in the wider social consciousness, the schools will be vulnerable to narrow and misguided interests.

PROBLEMS FOR STUDY AND DISCUSSION

1. How do you account for the vulnerability of the public schools to successive demands and pressures for reform by reaction and counterreaction? What is required to break this cycle?

2. Using Mackenzie's model on curriculum change (Table 9–1), trace the sources and influences connected with a particular program for educational change or reform. Was the program successful in meeting the anticipated goals? Why or why not? What were the unanticipated effects of the program? Were the undesirable effects avoidable? Explain.

3. Compare two "national" reports for educational reform issued during different eras in terms of (a) the problems addressed, (b) the allegations made,

(c) the evidence cited, and (d) the remedies proposed. In your opinion, were these reports well grounded in their diagnosis and prescriptions? Explain.

4. Curricular retrenchment through back-to-basics almost invariably accompanies periods of sociopolitical conservatism. How do you account for this? Why is it that in the aftermath of back-to-basics, educators find the schools under criticism for failing to develop the thinking abilities of pupils?

5. The report of the Woods Hole Conference (1959) blamed the post-*Sputnik* crisis in national security on our schools. Almost a quarter of a century later, in a report issued by the National Commission on Excellence in Education, our schools were blamed for our nation's declining position in global industrial markets and technological productivity. In neither report was any blame leveled at our political, scientific, industrial, and military leadership. How do you account for this?

6. In 1922, Dewey wrote, "If the average boy and girl could be walled off from all ideas and information about social affairs save those acquired in school, they would enter upon the responsibilities of social membership in complete ignorance that there are any social problems, any political evils, any industrial defects."[66] Do you believe that Dewey's criticism is valid today? Why or why not? A number of the "national" reports on education during the 1980s called for the establishment of a strong partnership between the schools and the business sector. Do you see any need for precaution regarding such a partnership?

7. What is your assessment of the proposals to restructure our schools, such as those offered by Goodlad and Boyer? How do you account for the lack of support in recent times for the comprehensive high school, in view of Conant's contention that this unique institution is vital to American democracy, and in view of the research revealing that nations with comprehensive secondary schools have the greatest educational yield?

8. How do you account for the fact that less than 1 percent of the school budget is allocated for books, including textbooks, and other curricular materials? Using your own school situation as a reference point, what would be the educational impact if the budget were tripled and if you and the teachers in your school were given full leeway in the selection of such materials? (What would you do with such a sudden "windfall"?)

9. What impact is computer technology likely to have on the use of books, including textbooks, in our schools? It has been noted that whereas books, including textbooks, are frequently targeted for censorship, the computer program is relatively immune from censorship. How do you account for this? Does this augur well for the book, including the textbook, as an invaluable educational instrument? Explain.

10. According to Reutter,

> Probably in no area of school operation have the courts been more liberal in interpreting implied powers of local boards than in curricular matters. This statement applies not only to addition of specific curricular elements, but to determination of methods of carrying out both specific and general mandates.[67]

> What are the statutory prescriptions relating to the curriculum in your state? How does your school meet these mandates? What alternative ways might be employed in meeting these mandates? Explain.

11. During the latter 1960s and through the decade of the 1970s, federal funds were provided under the Elementary and Secondary Education Act (ESEA) to support innovative projects in the schools. Why did this thrust for educational innovation, for the most part, fail to produce the promised improvements in education? What conditions and strategies are most likely to lead to sustained improvements in education? Are these conditions prevalent in your own school and school system? Explain.

12. Also under ESEA, funds were provided for the creation of a system for educational improvement through Regional Educational Laboratories and R&D Centers, allegedly patterned after the agricultural model. In what ways has this effort fallen short of the agricultural (networking) model, and how has the success of the effort been impeded as a result?

13. Compose a list of educational problems that are (or should be) widely shared by supervisors and teachers and that might serve as focal points of attack in seeking programmatic renewal in your school or school system. To what extent are these problems interrelated? What resources are, or should be, available in seeking the needed solutions? What procedures might be followed in the problem-solving process?

NOTES

1. Paul Woodring, *Investment in Innovation* (Boston: Little, Brown, 1970), pp. 267–268.
2. J. Lloyd Trump, *A School for Everyone* (Reston, Va.: National Association of Secondary School Principals, 1977), pp. 82–83.
3. Gordon N. Mackenzie, "Curricular Change: Participants, Power, and Processes," Chapter 17 in Matthew B. Miles (ed.), *Innovation in Education* (New York: Teachers College Press, 1964), pp. 399–424.
4. James D. Thompson, *Organizations in Action* (New York: McGraw-Hill, 1967), pp. 35–36.
5. Susanne D. Ellis, "Enrollment Trends," *Physics Today,* Vol. 20 (March 1967), p. 77.
6. Donivan J. Watley and Robert C. Nichols, *Career Choices of America's Most Able Youth* (Evanston, Ill.: National Merit Scholarship Corporation, 1968).
7. Philip H. Abelson, "Excessive Educational Pressures," *Science,* Vol. 156 (May 12, 1967), p. 741.
8. Diane Ravitch, "Yes, We Can Have Better Schools," *New York Daily News,* September 11, 1977, p. 75.

9. Daniel Tanner, "Disastrous School Non-promotion Policy," *The New York Times,* November 15, 1979, p. 23.
10. *The New York Times,* March 14, 1983, p. B 3.
11. *The New York Times,* October 30, 1984, p. B 4.
12. James B. Conant, *Shaping Educational Policy* (New York: McGraw-Hill, 1964), p. 123.
13. See, for example, Educational Policies Commission, *The Structure and Administration of Education in American Democracy* (Washington, D.C.: National Education Association, 1938).
14. *Carnegie Quarterly,* Vol. 14 (Spring 1966), pp. 2, 4.
15. Edward L. McDill, Mary S. McDill, and J. Timothy Sprehe, *Strategies for Success in Compensatory Education* (Baltimore: Johns Hopkins Press, 1969).
16. James B. Conant, "The Comprehensive High School," in Alvin C. Eurich (ed.), *High School 1980* (New York: Pitman, 1970), pp. 73, 80.
17. Jerome S. Bruner, *The Process of Education* (Cambridge, Mass.: Harvard University Press, 1960), pp. 1, 10.
18. See A. S. Neill, *Summerhill* (New York: Hart, 1960); John Holt, *How Children Fail* (New York: Dell, 1964), Paul Goodman, *Compulsory Mis-education* (New York: Horizon Press, 1964); Jonathan Kozol, *Death at an Early Age* (Boston: Houghton Mifflin, 1968); Neil Postman and Charles Weingartner, *Teaching as a Subversive Activity* (New York: Delacorte Press, 1969); Carl R. Rogers, *Freedom to Learn* (Columbus, Ohio: Charles E. Merrill, 1969); Herbert Kohl, *The Open Classroom* (New York: Random House, 1969).
19. "Teaching to Think: A New Emphasis," *The New York Times Winter Survey of Education,* January 9, 1983; *Educational Leadership,* Vol. 39 (October 1981), Vol. 42 (September 1984).
20. See John Dewey, *How We Think* (Boston: D. C. Heath, 1933); H. Gordon Hullfish and Philip G. Smith, *Reflective Thinking: The Method of Education* (New York: Dodd, Mead, 1961).
21. See Daniel Tanner, "The American High School at the Crossroads," *Educational Leadership,* Vol. 41 (March 1984), pp. 4–13.
22. National Commission on Excellence in Education, *A Nation at Risk: The Imperative for Educational Reform* (Washington, D.C.: U.S. Department of Education, 1983), p. 5.
23. Ibid., p. 18.
24. Report to the Secretary of Education by the Staff of the National Commission on Excellence in Education, *Meeting the Challenge* (Washington, D.C.: U.S. Department of Education, November 15, 1983), p. 1.
25. Task Force on Education for Economic Growth, *Action for Excellence* (Denver, Colo.: Education Commission of the States, 1983), pp. 9, 10, 15, 29, 40.
26. John Dewey, "Education as Politics," *The New Republic,* Vol. 32 (October 4, 1922), p. 140.
27. Michael Timpane, "Business Has Rediscovered the Public Schools," *Phi Delta Kappan,* Vol. 65 (February 1984), pp. 391, 392.
28. Ann Crittenden, "The Age of 'Me-First' Management: Losing Sight of Moral Standards," *The New York Times,* August 19, 1984, Sec. 3, pp. 1, 12–13.
29. National Science Board, *Educating Americans for the 21st Century* (Washington, D.C.: National Science Foundation, 1983), p. 65.
30. Torsten Husén, "Are Standards in U.S. Schools Really Lagging Behind Those in Other Countries?" *Phi Delta Kappan,* Vol. 64 (March 1983), pp. 458–460.
31. National Science Board, op. cit., p. 46.
32. John Dewey, *Democracy and Education* (New York: Macmillan, 1916), pp. 109–110.
33. Husén, op. cit., pp. 455–461.

34. Cited in Eurich, op. cit., pp. 73, 80.

35. Alexander J. Stoddard, *Schools for Tomorrow* (New York: Fund for the Advancement of Education, 1957).

36. Charles E. Silberman, "Technology Is Knocking at the Schoolhouse Door," *Fortune,* Vol. 74 (August 1966), pp. 122, 125.

37. Charles E. Silberman, *Crisis in the Classroom* (New York: Random House, 1970), p. 186.

38. U.S. Office of Education, *OE 100—Highlighting the Progress of American Education* (Washington, D.C.: U.S. Government Printing Office, 1967).

39. Patrick Suppes, "The Uses of Computers in Education," *Scientific American,* Vol. 215 (September 1966), p. 207.

40. Dean Jamison, Patrick Suppes, and Stuart Wells, "The Effectiveness of Alternative Instructional Media: A Survey," *Review of Educational Research,* Vol. 44 (Winter 1974), p. 56.

41. Neil Postman and Charles Weingartner, *The School Book* (New York: Delacorte Press, 1973), pp. 88–89.

42. Neil Postman, *Teaching as a Conserving Activity* (New York: Delacorte Press, 1979).

43. John I. Goodlad, *The Future of Learning and Teaching* (Washington, D.C.: National Education Association, 1968), pp. 9, 11.

44. John I. Goodlad, *A Place Called School* (New York: McGraw-Hill, 1984), p. 341.

45. *TC Today,* Vol. 10 (Fall 1981), p. 4.

46. Jack Magarrell, "Microcomputers Proliferate on College Campuses," *Chronicle of Higher Education,* Vol. 27 (April 6, 1983), p. 9.

47. Daniel Tanner, "What a Book Can Do That a Computer Can't," *The New York Times,* August 17, 1983, p. A 22.

48. National Commission on Excellence in Education, op. cit., p. 21.

49. Task Force on Education for Economic Growth, op. cit., pp. 15, 50.

50. Norbert Wiener, *God and Golem, Inc.* (Cambridge, Mass.: MIT Press, 1964), p. 73.

51. E. Edmund Reutter, Jr., *The Law of Public Education,* 3rd ed. (Mineola, N.Y.: Foundation Press, 1985), p. 149.

52. Milbrey W. McLaughlin, *Evaluation and Reform* (Cambridge, Mass.: Ballinger, 1975), p. ix.

53. Miriam L. Goldberg, "Evaluation of Innovations," Chapter 3 in Marcella R. Lawler (ed.), *Strategies for Planned Innovation* (New York: Teachers College Press, 1970), pp. 58–59.

54. Paul Berman and Milbrey W. McLaughlin, *Factors Affecting Implementation and Continuation,* Vol. 7, and *Implementing and Sustaining Innovations,* Vol. 8, of *Federal Programs Supporting Educational Change* (Santa Monica, Calif.: Rand Corporation, 1977, 1978).

55. See, for example, Woodring, op. cit.; Fund for the Advancement of Education, *Decade of Experiment* (New York: The Fund, 1961); Ford Foundation, *A Foundation Goes to School* (New York: The Foundation, 1972).

56. See Paul Berman et al., *Executive Summary,* Vol. 5 of *Federal Programs Supporting Educational Change* (Santa Monica, Calif.: Rand Corporation, 1975).

57. Egon G. Guba and David L. Clark, "Methodological Strategies for Educational Change," paper presented at the Conference on Strategies for Educational Change, Washington, D.C., November 8–10, 1965.

58. For example, the University of Wisconsin, a land-grant university, employs the motto "The State Is Our Campus" as indicative of its long commitment to serving all the people.

59. Robert G. Owens, *Organizational Behavior in Education,* 2nd ed. (Englewood Cliffs, N.J.: Prentice-Hall, 1981), p. 242.

60. Ibid., pp. 241–243.
61. Donald L. Plunknett and Nigel J. H. Smith, "Networking in International Agricultural Research," *Science,* Vol. 225 (September 7, 1984), p. 990.
62. Group on School Capacity for Problem Solving, *Program Plan* (Washington, D.C.: National Institute of Education, 1975), p. 1.
63. Ibid., pp. 4, 5.
64. Launor F. Carter, "The Sustaining Effects Study of Compensatory and Elementary Education," *Educational Researcher,* Vol. 13 (August–September 1984), p. 12.
65. Norbert Wiener, *The Human Use of Human Beings: Cybernetics and Society* (Garden City, N.Y.: Anchor books, Doubleday, 1954), p. 129.
66. Dewey, "Education as Politics," op. cit., p. 140.
67. Reutter, op. cit., p. 128.

SELECTED REFERENCES

Berman, Paul, and Milbrey W. McLaughlin. *Factors Affecting Implementation and Continuation,* Vol. 7, and *Implementing and Sustaining Innovations,* Vol. 8, of *Federal Programs Supporting Educational Change.* Santa Monica, Calif.: The Rand Corporation, 1977, 1978.

Berman, Paul, et al. *Executive Summary,* Vol. 5 of *Federal Programs Supporting Educational Change.* Santa Monica, Calif.: The Rand Corporation, 1975.

Boyer, Ernest L. *High School: A Report on Secondary Education in America.* New York: Harper & Row, Publishers, Inc., 1983.

Bruner, Jerome S. *The Process of Education.* Cambridge, Mass.: Harvard University Press, 1960.

Bunzel, John H. (ed.). *Challenge to America's Schools: The Case for Standards and Values.* New York: Oxford University Press, 1985.

Callahan, Raymond E. *Education and the Cult of Efficiency.* Chicago: The University of Chicago Press, 1962.

Caswell, Hollis L. (ed.). *The American High School: Its Responsibility and Opportunity,* Eighth Yearbook of the John Dewey Society. New York: Harper & Row, Publishers, Inc., 1946.

Commission on the Reorganization of Secondary Education. *Cardinal Principles of Secondary Education.* Washington, D.C.: U.S. Bureau of Education, 1918.

Committee for Economic Development. *Investing in Our Children: Business and the Public Schools.* New York: The Committee, 1985.

Conant, James B. *The American High School Today.* New York: McGraw-Hill Book Company, 1959.

———. *The Child, The Parent, and the State.* Cambridge, Mass.: Harvard University Press, 1959.

Educational Policies Commission. *Education for ALL American Youth—A Further Look.* Washington, D.C.: National Education Association, 1952.

———. *The Structure and Administration of Education in American Democracy.* Washington, D.C.: National Education Association, 1938.

Ford Foundation. *A Foundation Goes to School.* New York: The Foundation, 1972.

Fund for the Advancement of Education. *Decade of Experiment.* New York: The Fund, 1961.

Goodlad, John I. *The Dynamics of Educational Change.* New York: McGraw-Hill Book Company, 1975.

———. *The Future of Learning and Teaching.* Washington, D.C.: National Education Association, 1968.

————. *A Place Called School.* New York: McGraw-Hill Book Company, 1984.

Lawler, Marcella R. (ed.). *Strategies for Planned Innovation.* New York: Teachers College Press, 1970.

McDill, Edward L., Mary S. McDill, and J. Timothy Sprehe. *Strategies for Success in Compensatory Education.* Baltimore: Johns Hopkins Press, 1969.

Miles, Matthew B. (ed.). *Innovation in Education.* New York: Teachers College Press, 1964.

Myrdal, Gunnar. *Objectivity in Social Research.* New York: Pantheon Books, Inc., 1969.

National Commission on Excellence in Education. *A Nation at Risk: The Imperative for Educational Reform.* Washington, D.C.: U.S. Department of Education, 1983.

National Commission on the Reform of Secondary Education. *The Reform of Secondary Education.* New York: McGraw-Hill Book Company, 1973.

National Panel on High School and Adolescent Education. *The Education of Adolescents.* Washington, D.C.: U.S. Office of Education, 1976.

National Science Board. *Educating Americans for the 21st Century.* Washington, D.C.: National Science Foundation, 1983.

National Society for the Study of Education. *Policy Making in Education,* Eighty-first Yearbook, Part I. Chicago: The University of Chicago Press, 1982.

————. *Staff Development,* Eighty-second Yearbook, Part II. Chicago: The University of Chicago Press, 1983.

Oettinger, Anthony G. *Run, Computer, Run.* Cambridge, Mass.: Harvard University Press, 1969.

Owens, Robert G. *Organizational Behavior in Education,* 2nd ed. Englewood Cliffs, N.J.: Prentice-Hall, Inc., 1981.

Panel on Youth of the President's Science Advisory Committee. *Youth: Transition to Adulthood.* Chicago: The University of Chicago Press, 1974.

Postman, Neil. *Teaching as a Conserving Activity.* New York: Delacorte Press, 1979.

Postman, Neil, and Weingartner, Charles. *The School Book.* New York: Delacorte Press, 1973.

Powell, Arthur G., Eleanor Farrar, and David K. Cohen. *The Shopping Mall High School.* Boston: Houghton Mifflin Company, 1985.

Reutter, E. Edmund, Jr., *The Law of Public Education,* 3rd ed. Mineola, N.Y.: The Foundation Press, Inc., 1985.

Sarason, Seymour B. *The Culture of the School and the Problem of Change,* 2nd ed. Boston: Allyn and Bacon, Inc., 1982.

Schaffarzick, Jon, and Gary Sykes (eds.). *Value Conflicts and Curriculum Issues.* Berkeley, Calif.: McCutchan Publishing Corporation, 1979.

Silberman, Charles E. *Crisis in the Classroom: The Remaking of American Education.* New York: Random House, Inc., 1970.

Simon, Herbert A. *Administrative Behavior,* 3rd ed. New York: The Free Press, 1976.

Sizer, Theodore R. *Horace's Compromise: The Dilemma of the American High School.* Boston: Houghton Mifflin Company, 1984.

Stoddard, Alexander J. *Schools for Tomorrow.* New York: Fund for the Advancement of Education, 1957.

Tanner, Daniel. *Secondary Curriculum: Theory and Development.* New York: Macmillan Publishing Company, 1971.

Tanner, Daniel, and Laurel N. Tanner. *Curriculum Development: Theory into Practice,* 2nd ed. New York: Macmillan Publishing Company, 1980.

Task Force on Education for Economic Growth. *Action for Excellence.* Denver, Colo.: Education Commission of the States, 1983.

Task Force on Increased High School Graduation Requirements. *With Consequences for All.* Alexandria, Va.: Association for Supervision and Curriculum Development, 1985.

Thompson, James D. *Organizations in Action.* New York: McGraw-Hill Book Company, 1967.

Unruh, Glenys G., and William M. Alexander. *Innovations in Secondary Education,* 2nd ed. New York: Holt, Rinehart and Winston, 1974.

U.S. Office of Education. *OE 100—Highlighting the Progress of American Education.* Washington, D.C.: U.S. Government Printing Office, 1967.

Wiener, Norbert. *God and Golem, Inc.* Cambridge, Mass.: The MIT Press, 1964.

Wirt, Frederick M. and Michael W. Kirst. *The Political Web of American Schools.* Boston: Little, Brown and Company, 1972.

Woodring, Paul. *Investment in Innovation.* Boston: Little, Brown and Company, 1970.

Chapter 10

Sources of Educational Improvement

"It is ridiculous to suppose that we can save ourselves from drowning in information by installing faster printing [computer] devices," commented the Nobel laureate Herbert Simon as he went on to characterize this as "a touching faith in more water as an antidote to drowning!"[1]

Advances in computer technology have resulted in the generation of more, not less, data or factual information. But as Myrdal points out, "Facts do not organize themselves into concepts and theories just by being looked at; indeed, except within the framework of concepts and theories, there are no scientific facts but only chaos."[2] In other words, information is not synonymous with knowledge. People become knowledgeable to the extent that they are able to use information to solve problems, to gain insight into conditions bearing on their lives, and to develop increasingly intelligent control over these conditions so as to improve their lives. Answers to problems do not appear without intelligent questions for inquiry into problems.

Like people, organizations vary greatly in their knowledge/ability and capacity for renewal. The school or school system is no exception.

THE KNOWLEDGE/ABILITY FACTOR AND EDUCATIONAL IMPROVEMENT

Whatever technological breakthroughs may occur, the quality of life and effectiveness of an organization will be determined primarily by the problem-solving capability of the people who make up the organization. Technologies and administrative arrangements are designed presumably to serve people. Yet everyone has experienced the frustration and exasperation of having to subordinate themselves to an inflexible technology or bureaucratic requirement when common sense would dictate otherwise. Technological and bureaucratic arrangements and requirements are designed primarily to serve established-convergent situations, whereas the human factor is at its best in emergent-divergent-creative situations.

The capacity of an organization to engage in continual renewal depends on the capability of its members to cope intelligently with problems arising from emergent situations. Because schools are concerned with people (and their growth) rather than end products, the educative process is largely an emergent one. This requires a high degree of flexibility and knowledge/ability on the part of the professional staff and administration.

Seeking to "Satisfice" or to Optimize?

An unflattering description of "administrative man" is offered by Simon, who sees him as having the following two principal characteristics:

> First, because he satisfices rather than maximizes, administrative man can make his choices without first examining all possible behavior alternatives and without ascertaining that these *are* in fact all the alternatives. Second, because he treats the world as rather empty and ignores the interrelatedness of all things (so stupefying to thought and action), administrative man can make his decisions with relatively simple rules of thumb that do not make impossible demands upon his capacity for thought.[3]

Simon uses the term *satisfice* to describe any course of action that is satisfactory or sufficient to meet existing conditions.

The characterization of the administrator as seeking to satisfice rather than to optimize would appear to explain why so many school administrators either yield to the dominant tide of the times, or seek to demonstrate that they are following the tide—whether it is for curriculum retrenchment through back-to-basics, computer literacy, career education, open education, or establishing some priority in response to external pressures.[4] Shifts of priority are readily made in response to external pressures, such as the emphasis given to the disadvantaged in one epoch, only to be followed by a swing to the gifted and talented in a succeeding period. Instead of seeing the vital interrelatedness of the mission of the school, there is a tendency to see it segmentally.

The statewide-testing movement for *minimum* competencies is an example of the administrative mentality for seeking to satisfice. Another example is the establishment of "minimum standards" for promotion, graduation, and so on.

The Paradox of "Minimum Standards." Paradoxically, the establishment of "minimum standards" tends to follow in the wake of the demand for raising standards. The establishment of such minimums is a ready and easy way for administrators to demonstrate a concrete course of action to satisfice, but such a course necessarily falls short of the expectation that it will effect the needed improvements or problem solutions. Only the marginal students are affected directly by such "standards." In some respects, such standards may unwittingly serve to lower the achievement for other students when the minimum standards become a kind of "lowest common denominator." At the same time, the underlying conditions and causes of the low-achieving students remain untreated. The administrative quest for satisficing is met by having teachers teach-to-the test and by reducing the curriculum to the kinds of objectives and skills that are most easily inventoried and assessed by quantitative measures.

The Setting of Limits Versus the Opening of Possibilities. Although Simon contrasts the effort to satisfice against the quest to maximize, we prefer to use the term *optimize*. The latter term implies an outlook seeking not only the most from a situation, but the best possible choices and outcomes. Of course, complex situations do not lend themselves to revealing complete data. Emergent situations are complex, and conditions require that actions be taken without complete data on all factors bearing on the situation and on all the possible consequences of the actions. Hence such decisions or choices must be treated as hypotheses to be evaluated, and conclusions must be regarded as tentative. Optimizing is not an end point, but a process of effecting continual improvements by seeking and acting on the best available evidence.

The fact that the data are imperfect in emergent situations does not mean that the level of knowledge/ability is necessarily low. In fact, the level of knowledge/ability must be high if intelligent decisions are to be formulated and tested in the light of possible problem solutions. Certainly, the emergent situation demands a far higher and more sophisticated level of knowledge/ability than the established situation.

Satisficing is concerned with established parameters or limits. Optimizing is concerned with possibilities arising from emergent conditions. Satisficing is a regulative-mediative process, whereas optimizing is a generative-creative process.

Levels of Knowledge/Ability

The concept of *knowledge/ability* is proposed by the authors to denote the capacity to act on emergent situations so as to effect substantive improvements in the conditions bearing on such situations. It implies a capacity for utilizing the best available knowledge so as to effect solutions to emerging problems—thereby exercising increased control over the course of events rather than being controlled by them.[5]

Administrators, supervisors, curriculum directors, and teachers with a high level of knowledge/ability will seek to optimize rather than to satisfice in carrying out their work. They regard problems as opportunities for improvement rather than as barriers. They anticipate consequences rather than merely reacting to them. As a result, they are able to prevent problems from arising as well as being highly capable of utilizing the best available evidence in attacking emerging problems.

In contrast, those of relatively low knowledge/ability seek to avoid problems by maintaining existing conditions and routines as long as these are satisficing.

When problems arise, they tend to treat the symptoms rather than the underlying causes of the problems.

Table 10–1 presents three levels of knowledge/ability at which schools tend to function: (I) imitative-maintenance, (II) mediative-adaptive, and (III) generative-creative.[6] At Levels I and II the administrative goals and processes are directed at satisficing, whereas at Level III the emphasis is on optimizing the conditions and resources for continual improvement in the educative function of the school. The findings reported by Goodlad in "A Study of Schooling" indicate that most schools and school systems are functioning at Level I.[7]

The three levels are not sequential in that a school or school system does not rise to Level III by first moving through Levels I and II. The school or system that is functioning at Level I is likely to remain at Level I simply because the operations at this level are directed at maintaining the status quo and merely imitating or adopting whatever changes are in vogue at a particular time. Such changes tend to be superficial and transitory, though they may satisfice by creating the outward appearance of responsiveness. The saying that "the more things change, the more they remain the same" applies to the imitative-adoptive modus operandi of Level I. A brief examination of each of the three levels of knowledge/ability will reveal further their contrasting differences.

Level I: Imitative-Maintenance Level of Knowledge/Ability

As shown in Table 10–1, the administrative function at Level I is that of satisficing. The underlying administrative theme is "running a tight ship." The communication flow is top-down, and the system is largely authoritative and managerial rather than consultative. The locus of action is on the maintenance of established conditions, segmental operational units, and routine operations. When problems arise, they are treated segmentally and, as mentioned earlier, the treatment tends to be directed at the symptoms, or at the effects of the problem, rather than at the underlying causes. Serious problems are regarded as "crises" and the overriding concern is for "survival" rather than seeking problem solutions through the use of the best available evidence. Under such "crises," the response is one of reaction to symptoms with the hope of masking the problems.

Vulnerability to External Pressures and Fads. At the imitative-maintenance level, efforts are made to convey an image of dynamic activity by readily yielding to whatever demands or pressures are most powerful at a given time, or to whatever practices are the most trendy, but the changes tend to be superficially and segmentally adopted. Such changes are rarely substantive, tending instead to take the form of "quick fixes," slogans, and labels—such as "academic excellence," "standards," "individualized learning," "discipline," "minimum competencies," and so on. In the name of "standards," greater emphasis is given to the setting of limitations on learners rather than to developing their fullest potentials. As recommended by an influential educator, "Compulsory attendance in an educational institution should cease when a young citizen demonstrates mastery of the minima, and most young citizens should master the minima before senior high school."[8]

Table 10–1 Levels of Knowledge/Ability

Knowledge/ Ability Level	Controlling Function	Supervisory Mode	Administrative/ Supervisory Flow	Orientation	Mode of Functioning
I. Imitative-maintenance	Satisficing Reactive	Authoritative Inspectional-regulative Production-efficiency Adoptive	Top-down communication Decision making at top (mandates, directives)	Microcurriculum Established conditions Segmental Minimum standards Contingency-expediency	Rudimentary Routine Adoptive Maintenance of established practice Change induced as reaction to external pressures and dominant fashions Segmental treatment focused on symptoms and recipes
II. Mediative-adaptive	Satisficing Reactive Adaptive	Consultative Adaptive	Moderate lateral and upward communication, but reliance mainly on downward communication Some shared decision making	Microcurriculum Established conditions Segmental Awareness of emergent conditions and need for aggregate treatment Macrocurriculum Contingency-expediency	Interpretive Adaptive Modification/refinement of established practice in response to external pressures and dominant fashions
III. Generative-creative	Optimizing Interactive Self-actualizing Growth	Developmental Reconstructive Cooperative, democratic-participative	Full communication throughout Cooperative decision making on policy and practice	Macrocurriculum Emergent conditions Holistic Interdependent	Interpretive Adaptive Evaluative/developmental problem diagnosis, problem solving Reconstructive improvement of established practice (research based), search for improved practice (research based)

The "Cocoon Curriculum." At Level I: imitative-maintenance, the supervisory function is that of inspection and the educative function is that of production. Great stock is given to demonstrating "standards" through student scores on standardized-achievement tests. The teacher response is to teach-to-the-test.

The focus is on the microcurriculum. The basic skills are treated as separate subjects, an emphasis is given to mechanical drill exercises in workbooks and on ditto sheets. The so-called "academic subjects" are treated as insulated and isolated entities, leaving the school with a "cocoon curriculum."

No really systematic, facultywide effort is made toward attaining vertical curriculum articulation (relationships between and among grade levels in a given field of study). And even less effort is expended in developing horizontal curriculum articulation (interrelationships between and among the different fields of study). Not only are these macrocurricular concerns neglected, but no concerted attention is given to the design and implementation of a coherent program of general education, exploratory education, enrichment education, vocational education, and so on. Student activities are regarded as extracurricular rather than as integral elements of the school curriculum.

Compliance, Not Commitment. At Level I, curricular change is by segmental incrementalism until such time when external pressures or extant fashions augur for a more sweeping reform—in which case the sweeping reform is adopted by administrative mandate. The faculty response to such mandates is one of compliance rather than commitment. The faculty do not share a feeling of professional responsibility, and motivation tends to be low. Initiatives by faculty are largely behind the closed doors of individual classrooms. Hence there is relatively little upward and lateral communication.

"Success" Easily Demonstrated. At the imititative-maintenance level of knowledge/ability (Level I), it is easy for administrators to demonstrate quick "results" through mandated changes and by having teachers teach to-the-test. Since the curriculum is focused on skills that are most easily amenable to testing, the image conveyed to the public is that the emphasis is on high "standards" or the raising of "standards." The administration emphasizes tight controls, cost effectiveness, and efficiency of operations. Costs are kept relatively low through the reductionist, skill-drill curriculum and the limited demands that such a curriculum makes on facilities and resources. Because changes are segmentally adopted, the appearance of responsiveness and openness to innovation is readily given—but again, the concern is with image rather than substance, end product rather than the realization of potentials.

Wider Sense of Vision Lacking. With the focus on expediency, efficiency, and the demonstration of more immediate and "tangible" results, longer-term outcomes tend to be neglected under the imitative-maintenance level of knowledge/ability.

The contingency-expediency orientation of Level I mitigates against any shared commitment to a wider vision of the mission of the school in a free society and of how such a mission is to be realized through the curriculum and through faculty, administrative, and student cooperation. A statement of the school's philosophy is on file, but there is little relationship between the written philosophy and the curriculum along with the other day-to-day operations. For example, the statement of philosophy may include such terms as "democracy" and "critical thinking," but there is relatively little evidence of such goals being met through the curriculum and in the responsibilities given to the faculty and student body.

Reaction/Counterreaction. As mentioned, the impression given under the imitative-maintenance level of knowledge/ability is of considerable activity or movement as "quick fixes" are adopted in reaction to external demands or fashions. Eventually, as such reform measures fail to produce the claimed results, or as new external demands and pressures call for very different measures, new "quick fixes" are adopted to replace the old ones. Very often the previously adopted reform measures produce damaging effects, necessitating action to undo the damage. The sequence, then, is of repetitive reform by reaction and counterreaction, resulting in the appearance of considerable action when, in fact, there is little progress.

Figures 10–1 and 10–2 illustrate such cases of reform by reaction/counterreaction. In Figure 10–1, the sequence of events is traced in connection with the nonpromotion policy adopted by the New York City Board of Education during the late 1970s. It will be recalled from Chapter 9 that this policy was heralded as an action to "raise standards." In actuality, the policy was a reaction to the problem whereby a sizable population of pupils was performing below grade level on standardized achievement tests. However, instead of raising standards, the nonpromotion policy resulted in a marked increase in truancy, followed by a dropout rate of epidemic proportions—the legacy of an army of frustrated and resentful adolescents who found themselves unwanted in school and society.

With nearly half of the students failing to complete high school, the school system was faced with mounting criticisms. Moreover, the enrollment decline resulted in reductions in state aid to the district, requiring cutbacks in district-

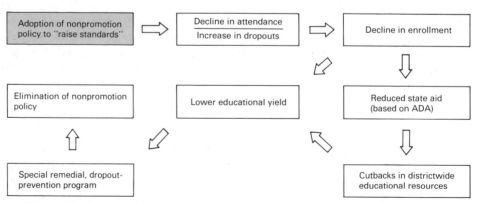

Figure 10–1. Unanticipated consequences of nonpromotion: an example of reform by reaction and counterreaction.

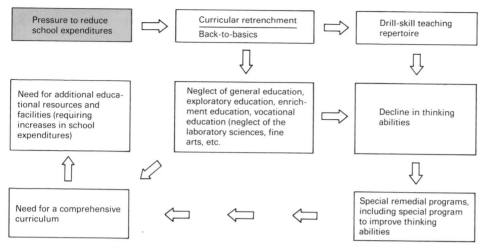

Figure 10–2. Unanticipated consequences of curricular retrenchment through back-to-basics: an example of reform by reaction and counterreaction.

wide educational resources. In effect, instead of raising standards, the consequence was a decline in educational yield (the level of school achievement of the total population of students of high school age).

As shown in Figure 10–1, the counterreaction to these consequences was the eventual establishment of a special remedial, dropout-prevention program and the elimination of the nonpromotion policy. Not only should the authorities have anticipated the deleterious effects of the nonpromotion policy at the time it was first proposed, but had the district been functioning at a high level of knowledge/ability the professional staff would have been enlisted to attack the roots of the problem of low achievement from the beginning. The nonpromotion measure was merely a reaction to the symptoms of a problem and, as a result, the prescription served to exacerbate the problem and to produce a host of related problems.

The entire situation can be evaluated not as a matter of "hindsight," but in terms of what should have been anticipated from the start. Over many decades, it has been known from the research literature that nonpromotion tends to result in lower performance on achievement tests than would be attained by comparable youngsters who are promoted. The damaging effects stem from the stigma of being held back and placed with younger pupils—the attendant poor morale, lowered self-esteem, and other psychosocial problems.[9] Moreover, the nonpromoted pupils are left to repeat the kinds of learning conditions that were ineffective and led to failure in the first place.

This is not to say that "social promotion" solves the problem of low achievement. A school system functioning at a high level of knowledge/ability would have an ongoing program in place for the prevention of failure and for the diagnosis and remedial treatment of learning problems.

Reductionist-Segmental Approach. Figure 10–2 illustrates how school systems functioning at the imitative-maintenance level of knowledge/ability respond in eras of sociopolitical retrenchment, when the call is for reducing educational expenditures through curricular retrenchment. The back-to-basics retrenchment is invariably accompanied by a reductionist teaching methodology focused on mechanical skills and drills. With skills being treated as ends, the opportunity for the application of skills is limited. At the same time the narrow focus on basic education, with the concomitant neglect of general education, denies the learners the opportunity to utilize their skills in the development of higher-ordered thinking abilities.

Interest in learning also declines when ideas, issues, and problems are neglected in the mechanical sterility of the drill-skill teaching repertoire. The neglect of a rich and diversified curriculum—encompassing the fine arts and industrial arts, laboratory sciences, vocational studies, and so on—also takes its toll on student motivation.

Eventually, as shown in Figure 10–2, the schools come under criticism for a decline in student thinking abilities and for the neglect of the laboratory sciences, the arts, vocational studies, and so on. The reaction of the schools is to devise special remedial programs to counter the decline in achievement and to improve thinking abilities. However, because such efforts tend to be segmental under the imitative-maintenance level of knowledge/ability, the results are bound to be disappointing. Instead of reflective thinking serving as a common function of the total curriculum, it is regarded as a special remedial skill. Similarly, special segmental efforts are made to adopt new curriculum packages in the sciences, mathematics, the arts, career education, and so on—without undertaking the needed curricular reconstruction to meet the comprehensive functions of general education, exploratory education, enrichment education, and vocational education.

Figures 10–1 and 10–2 illustrate how reforms by reaction/counterreaction carry the schools through a tortuous and misguided path through which they eventually wind back at "square one." The reader may find a redeeming feature in this process in that eventually, corrective action is taken and the damage is undone. But the fact remains that with each cycle of reform by reaction/ counterreaction, at least a generation of children and youth has been adversely affected. Moreover, by its very nature, reaction or counterreaction inevitably produces additional problems. For example, when special remediation programs are not related to the ongoing curriculum, the youngsters in such programs are unable to make the needed connections with the mainstream studies, and thereby overcome their deficiencies. If the special remedial program delimits the curriculum to mechanical skill-drill exercises, to the neglect of conceptual learning and the applications of skills in the life of the learner, the program will be self-defeating. When youngsters are segregated from their peers and from the mainstream studies through special remedial programs, serious psychosocial problems may emerge from their being stigmatized as "failures."

Even in the case where the school may seek to attack the problem of a decline in thinking abilities on the part of all students by instituting a special program to improve such abilities (Figure 10–2), such a segmental approach is unlikely to produce the intended results because the development of thinking abilities must be a function of the entire curriculum. At the imitative-maintenance level of

knowledge/ability, there is the tendency to react to each emerging problem segmentally or in isolation, with the result that the problem becomes compounded
further.

Instead of seeking to undo a misguided practice by means of reaction/
counterreaction, the need is to seek improvement continuously by attacking the
root causes of problems and by seeking to prevent problems from arising. When
problems do arise, they should be seen as opportunities for improvement and
not as impediments to progress.

Level II: Mediative-Adaptive Level of Knowledge/Ability

Although Level I and Level II have many attributes in common, the mediative-
adaptive level differs principally from the imitative-maintenance level of knowl-
edge/ability in that (1) changes or innovations stemming from external pressures
or influences are not simply adopted and tacked on to the existing operations,
but are adapted or modified to fit into the ongoing operations; (2) the supervisory and administrative mode is consultative rather than inspectional and regulative, thereby allowing for more shared decision making, although the reliance
on top-down communication and decision-making predominates—especially on
matters of policy; (3) the improved extent of lateral and upward communication
allows for somewhat greater opportunity for the spread of successful practices
by individual teachers, although the influence is largely through informal channels with the result that the spread of such practices tends to be segmental and
sporadic; (4) there is some awareness of the need to address macrocurricular
problems, such as the lack of curricular synthesis for general education, but this
is countered by an overriding concern to follow the easier path of segmental
treatment; (5) there is an awareness of the need for addressing emergent problems through aggregate treatment, but external pressures and influences are
allowed to take precedence for the sake of expediency and the desire to satisfice;
(6) teachers, supervisors, and administrators are consumers of professional literature on approved practices stemming from the best available research data and
are able to articulate such knowledge, but they are not committed to a concerted
effort toward curricular reconstruction for substantive problem solving; and (7)
the professional staff exhibits an awareness of sound theoretical ideas to guide
educational practice, but the linkage between theory and practice is wanting.

Segmental Adaptation. Despite the inherent advantage of adaptation of a new
practice or program to meet the conditions of particular situations, rather than
mere adoption, most situations are highly interactive. That is, even when adaptations are made to fit a given condition, the adaptations have ramifications
throughout a system. For example, the segmental adaptation of a given curriculum package in science to fit into the existing K–12 science curriculum still
does not provide for horizontal curriculum articulation, such as the needed
relationship between science and mathematics, or the need for a coherent curriculum in general education. Similarly, adaptations may be made in fitting a
new curriculum package into the existing program in social studies. But the
effects of such segmental adaptations will be limited without corresponding

attention being given to the need to revise the curriculum in literature and composition.

Although some informal efforts may be made for curriculum correlation, such as between English language arts and social studies, the courses offered in most areas have been developed segmentally and can be said to resemble a "cocoon curriculum."

As another example of segmental adaptation, a school may adapt certain approved practices, such as providing students with more extensive opportunities for theme writing on ideas of personal and social significance so as to enhance their language skills, enlarge their thinking abilities, and improve their motivation for learning. However, if such a program is targeted for gifted and talented students, while the others remain to fend with mechanical skill-drill exercises in workbooks and on ditto sheets, the benefits will be segmentally limited. Moreover, the implicit message conveyed to youngsters who are not adjudged to be gifted and talented is that they are not deserving or capable of engaging in more interesting and challenging learning experiences. But even where such a program is adapted to the English language arts curriculum so as to be made available to all students, the effects will be limiting to the extent that the curriculum in social studies remains focused on rote learning. This is the chief pitfall of the segmental approach characteristic of Levels I and II.

Short-Term Accommodation. Level II is a marked advance over Level I in that the professional staff is more aware of and better able to articulate problems and needs. Nevertheless, the segmental approach to educational improvement at Level II, along with the desire to accommodate and satisfice, yields disappointing results because the efforts fall short of the necessary reconstruction for substantive problem solving. This is especially apparent in connection with longer-term needs. In the short run, efforts to accommodate and satisfice may appear to be adequate in meeting contingencies or in responding to external pressures. But successions of short-term adaptations often turn out to be contradictory and self-canceling. What may be expedient to meet a contingency at a given time may well be totally inadequate in the long run. Moreover, the contingencies arising at a later time may result in accommodations that neutralize or run counter to the decisions and practices previously implemented.

Although at Level II there is some sense of vision as to the long-term needs and mission of the school in a free society, the professional staff is not actualized toward meeting these needs and fulfilling this mission.

Level III: Generative-Creative Level of Knowledge/Ability

As shown in Table 10–1, the generative-creative level of knowledge/ability is characterized by a concerted commitment to optimize conditions and outcomes through substantive problem solving. The professional staff is self-actualized for problem solving as the means to improvement. Instead of regarding problems as obstacles, they are seen as challenges for improvement. Instead of merely reacting to conditions, symptoms, or external pressures by taking the path of least resistance (as in the case of Level I), a reconstructive approach is taken in which the roots of problems are exposed and attacked. Mere adaptation, modification, or refinement of existing practices (as in the case of Level II) are regarded as insufficient for effecting far-reaching problem solutions.

Integrated Approach. Where the orientation at Levels I and II is primarily on established conditions, at Level III it is on emergent conditions in recognition that the environment is dynamic and that growth or progress derives from solving emergent problems.

Instead of treating the curriculum as a schedule of separate subjects, it is treated holistically and interdependently. Concerted attention is given not only to vertical curriculum articulation, but to horizontal articulation. There is an ongoing program of curriculum development in general education, enrichment education, exploratory education, and vocational education.

Approved practices based on the best available research evidence, as revealed in the professional literature, are widely utilized. Because there is a sound research base for such practices, and because there is ongoing evidence in support of such practices, they are not adopted and then later discarded merely to conform to misguided external pressures or trendy fads. Moreover, external pressures and trends are evaluated critically, so that there is no impetus to acquiesce to misguided influences or to yield to the temptation of moving with the flock. Promising new programs are evaluated formatively and summatively. When revealing evidence of success, they are integrated into the curriculum rather than being tacked on or plugged in.

Full Communication and Participation. The supervisory mode is developmental, reconstructive, and democratic-participative. There is full communication throughout the school and school system between and among the faculty, administration, supervisory staff, and supporting staff. As a result, the creative ideas and practices of individual faculty become widely shared both formally and informally. Decision making is cooperative not only on matters of practice but on the formulation and implementation of policy. The interschool articulation of educational programs within the district is ongoing.

Faculty are allocated time and material resources for curriculum development. A standing curriculum committee not only devotes its efforts to horizontal and vertical curriculum articulation, but to the development and evaluation of promising programs for educational improvement. Students are enlisted to work with the faculty and supervisory staff on curriculum improvement. When problems of censorship arise, they are channeled to the curriculum committee which is deemed by the administration and school board to have the professional expertise to handle such matters. As a result, the forces for censorship are effectively countered.

Follow-up studies are made of school graduates, transferees, and dropouts. Dropout prevention is given high priority, and provisions are made for continuation studies on a part-time basis for school leavers so that they may earn their high school diplomas.

University consultants are enlisted to work with the professional staff on a continuous basis and the professional staff is continually involved in inservice programs within the district and at the university. Special attention is given through inservice education to the beginning teacher as a developing professional. The district maintains an extensive professional library that is widely used by the professional staff. Each school also maintains a collection of teaching resource units and learning resource units in the school library. These resources are continually kept current and are widely used by faculty and students.

The professional staff shares a far-ranging sense of vision as to the needs and mission of the school in a free society and is actualized to meet these needs and fulfill this mission. This is clearly reflected in the curriculum, which is focused on the development of reflective-thinking abilities and the effective uses of knowledge in school and society.

Emphasis on Optimizing. The generative-creative level of knowledge/ability (Level III) should not be regarded as "ideal" or utopian in the sense of being impractical. It is "ideal" only in the sense that it is built on sound guiding *ideas*. Although most schools and school systems function at Levels I and II, these levels turn out to be impractical in the long run because of the propensity to satisfice rather than to optimize. The school district that is concerned with demonstrating the meeting of "minimum standards" by pupils (Level I) is reducing the function of education to the "lowest-common denominator." The modification, refinement, and adaptation of established practice in order to accommodate to certain emergent conditions or external pressures (Level II) still leaves the school or school district lacking in its capacity and commitment to seek solutions to substantive emergent problems. The strategy is one of response (reaction) rather than being reconstructive and self-actualizing.

Growth or progress requires the commitment and capability to solve emergent problems. The future becomes better than the past to the extent that such problems are being attacked here and now. The school or school system functioning at Level III is self-actualized to optimize its practices and outcomes to enable teachers and learners to become all that they are capable of becoming. The vision is on the possibilities rather than on the limitations of the educational situation. The concept is of growth and development rather than of end product. As a result, the generative-creative level of knowledge/ability turns out to be the most practical level of functioning in the long run.

Knowledge/Ability as the Key to Educational Improvement

Educational progress has been severely hindered by a faulty premise underlying educational policy, research, and practice—namely, that given inputs will yield equivalent effects in all schools or school systems. But because schools and school systems differ widely in level of knowledge/ability, they will differ widely in the effectiveness to which they are able to make use of their resources. Indeed, one can observe great differences in the level of knowledge/ability among teachers as one goes from classroom to classroom within the same school building.

In evaluating the effects of school expenditures on educational outcomes, researchers have ignored the knowledge/ability factor, with the result that they do not find a consistent and positive relationship between expenditures and outcomes. This has led them to the erroneous conclusion that increasing the investment in schooling will have inconsequential results for educational improvement. A notorious example of such research, and the endorsement given the findings by behavioral scientists and some politicians, was the study *Inequality* by Christoper Jencks and his associates.[10]

As discussed in greater detail later in this chapter, such research findings were used to justify a policy of educational retrenchment which took hold from the federal level on down to state and local levels during the decade of the 1970s and extending into the 1980s.

If increases in financial resources were tied to the improvement in the level of knowledge/ability of the professional staff so that they are better able to improve the internal life of the school, the results would be positive and powerful.[11] In other words, the variables connected with the level of knowledge/ability are the keys to educational improvement. When financial and other resources are directed at these variables, the investments in resources will yield improved outcomes. Under such circumstances, it becomes clear that our schools suffer from insufficient financial support to provide the resources needed to improve the quality of education.

SOURCES AND INFLUENCES FOR EDUCATIONAL IMPROVEMENT

Our discussion of the levels of knowledge/ability relates to the capacity of the professional staff to create an effective environment for learning and to bring about educational improvement. In this mission, the professional staff must draw on and respond to the following three principal sources and influences: (1) society (societal ideals and the social situation, stemming from the matured experience of the adult world), (2) the learner ("the immature, undeveloped being"), and (3) codified or systematized knowledge (for the selection and organization of subject matter and learning experiences).

Dewey was first to address these three fundamental factors (sources and influences) in the educative process when he warned in 1902 of the need to treat them as complementary rather than separately and antagonistically.[12] In earlier chapters it was shown how we have yet to learn this lesson, for in each epoch of educational reform (in reaction to some perceived crisis) there has been the tendency to advance one factor at the expense of the others. As discussed in Chapter 9, the succession of extremes taken in shifting the priority from one factor to another can be characterized as a succession of reactions and counterreactions in the name of educational reform.

The Learner, the Curriculum, and Societal Ideals

The role and function of the school cannot be shaped effectively without a shared vision of the good person leading the good life in the good society. A free society requires an enlightened citizenry having control over its own destiny. Hence the role and function of the school in a free society cannot be subordinated to narrow nationalistic interests if such a society is true to itself. Such subordination results in the fashioning of the curriculum so as to either ignore or distort the nature and needs of the learner. The reciprocal effect is curricular distortion and malfunction.

In the same vein, when codified, specialized knowledge (formulated as the product of adult scholarship) is conceived as the proper curriculum to be imposed on the immature learner, the nature and interests of the learner are ignored or distorted. Or when the learner is left largely to his or her own devices to determine the curriculum (in the name of "relevance"), the process becomes miseducative because the immature learner is not endowed with the knowledge and experience developed through the long evolution of humanity. In addressing the consequences of such oppositions for the educative process, Dewey warned that

> when this happens a really serious practical problem—that of interaction—is transformed into an unreal, and hence insoluble, theoretical problem. Instead of seeing the educative process steadily and as a whole, we see conflicting terms. We get the case of the child vs. the curriculum, of the individual nature vs. social culture. Below all other divisions in pedagogical opinion lies this opposition.[13]

Needed Interdependence. At various periods throughout the twentieth century, thoughtful educators have come to recognize the three fundamental factors or sources and the need to treat them as interdependent and complementary rather than as oppositional. A quarter of a century after Dewey had addressed this need, the Committee on Curriculum-Making of the National Society for the Study of Education, under the chairmanship of Harold Rugg, sought to develop a basis for consensus among professionals engaged in the newly emerging field of curriculum development. In their efforts, they sought resolution to the long-standing conflict concerning (1) the nature and interests of the learner, (2) the demands of adult life, and (3) the selection and organization of subject matter—in essence the three fundamental factors identified by Dewey. The committee acknowledged the importance of thoroughly systematized, codified, and specialized knowledge "developed through a long social evolution," but held that the curriculum should be developed "from the starting point of the learner, irrespective of the content and boundaries of existing subjects," and that "the ultimate test is the effectiveness with which subsequent situations are met by the individual so educated."[14] In other words, by devising the curriculum in appropriate recognition of the learner as a growing being, the learner will grow in the power to cope with the environment, thereby making for a better adult in a better society.[15] Through such an approach, there should be no conflict concerning the learner, society (demands of adult life), and the curriculum.

The same three sources were used in identifying and analyzing the process of curricular organization in the Eight-Year Study (1933–41)—the largest-scale longitudinal study ever undertaken in education, designed to free the high schools from college domination over the curriculum. The three factors or sources were analyzed in the Eight-Year Study in determining (1) the formulation of educational objectives, (2) selecting the means for attaining these objectives (curriculum), (3) organizing these means (methods), and (4) evaluating the outcomes.[16] The foregoing determinants in the process of curriculum development clearly corresponded with Dewey's essentials of reflection or inquiry for problem solving.

Curriculum Development as a Problem-Solving Process

Prior to midcentury, other curricularists were recognizing the needed harmony and interdependence of the three sources of data for curriculum development and educational improvement. For example, Taba pointed to the need to draw data from (1) studies of society, (2) studies of learners, and (3) studies of subject matter, in the process of curriculum development—which she viewed as a seven-step sequence:

Step 1: diagnosis of needs.
Step 2: formulation of objectives.
Step 3: selection of content.
Step 4: organization of content.
Step 5: selection of learning experiences.
Step 6: organization of learning experiences.
Step 7: determination of what to evaluate and the ways and means of doing it.[17]

Again, the process above bears a close correspondence to Dewey's essentials of reflection for problem solving. However, where the foregoing steps are in a linear order, Dewey had repeatedly cautioned that one does not start out with objectives, but with the educational situation from which problems are found.[18] Consequently, for example, evaluation is not the final step but is a continuous process beginning with the diagnosis of the problems stemming from the educational situation.

A PARADIGM FOR CURRICULUM DEVELOPMENT AND EDUCATIONAL IMPROVEMENT

In 1949, Ralph Tyler, who had served as research director for the Eight-Year Study, presented a systematic schema for the process of curriculum development. In this work, Tyler pointed to the need to draw on the three sources in their interdependence in seeking the answer to the following four questions:

1. What educational purposes should the school seek to attain?
2. What educational experiences can be provided that are likely to attain these purposes?
3. How can these educational experiences be effectively organized?
4. How can we determine whether these purposes are being attained?[19]

Although some curricularists have interpreted Tyler's questions as a four-step sequence,[20] Tyler had stated clearly that this is not to be the case, since the initial point of attack is determined by the nature of the problem(s) identified from the situation.[21]

In the process of answering the four questions in curriculum development, Tyler identified the following three sources of data: (1) studies of the learners themselves, (2) studies of contemporary life outside the school, and (3) suggestions from subject specialists.[22] Again, these sources of data correspond to those identified by Dewey in 1902, by the Committee on Curriculum Making of the National Society for the Study of Education in 1927, and in the Eight-Year Study, 1933–1941. In essence, what had evolved before midcentury were the necessary elements of a paradigm for curriculum development and educational improvement.

Some curricularists have interpreted Tyler's schema as one man's version of how a curriculum should be developed.[23] In so doing, they fail to recognize the evolution of thought in the curriculum field from which Tyler orchestrated the schema.

The third source, "suggestions from subject specialists," may be faulted for its narrowness—especially in consideration of the fact that educators must look beyond the specialized subjects in curriculum development. They must be concerned with the macrocurriculum and the interrelationships between and among the various subject fields. And they must draw on the wider world of organized knowledge to link the subject matters with the learner and society. Tyler recognized this in cautioning that subject specialists must be asked, "What can your subject contribute to the education of young people who are not going to be specialists in your field?"[24] He went on to discuss the need for differentiating between specialized education and general education, and the need for curricular structures other than the traditional subject divisions or disciplines.

The Curriculum and the Wider World of Knowledge

Figure 10–3 portrays the sources and influences as interdependent and complementary. It is seen that "subject matter" is not regarded as a discrete source but is derived from the wider world of organized knowledge, thereby providing linkages to society. In turn, this gives recognition to the responsibility of curriculum directors, supervisors, and teachers to draw from the wider world of knowledge in developing the subject matter. Hence the concept of curriculum is not merely synonymous with subject matter but encompasses the ways in which the subject matter (course of study) relates to the wider world of organized knowledge and to the life of the learner in school and society.

The concept of curriculum, then, is seen as that reconstruction of knowledge and experience, systematically developed under the auspices of the educational institution, to enable the learner to grow in gaining intelligent control over subsequent knowledge and experience.[25] This definition is consonant with Dewey's conception of education as "that reconstruction or reorganization of experience which increases ability to direct the course of subsequent experience."[26]

The Function of Philosophy

How these sources and influences are seen and acted on is determined by the philosophy of the professional staff. Here philosophy, as represented in Figure 10–3, is not to be regarded as some esoteric and self-serving exercise but as an outlook that serves as a compass or regulator to guide and test concrete practices.

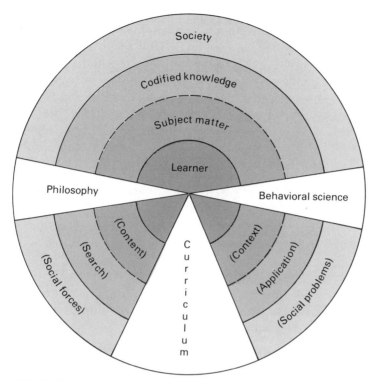

Figure 10–3. Curricular sources and influences.

[Adapted from Daniel Tanner and Laurel N. Tanner, *Curriculum Development: Theory into Practice*, 2nd ed. (New York: Macmillan, 1980), p. 89.]

One cannot conceive of democracy, for example, without reflective consideration of the good person leading a good life in a good society. In the words of Whitehead,

> There can be no successful democratic society till general education conveys a philosophic outlook.
>
> Philosophy is not a mere collection of noble sentiments. A deluge of such sentiments does more harm than good. . . . It is a survey of possibilities and their comparison with actualities. In philosophy, the fact, the theory, the alternatives, and the ideal, are weighed together. Its gifts are insight and foresight, and a sense of worth of life, in short, that sense of importance which nerves all civilized effort.[27]

"Theory is in the end," wrote Dewey, "the most practical of all things, because this widening of the range of attention beyond nearby purpose and desire eventually results in the creation of wider and farther-reaching purposes and enables us to use a much wider and deeper range of conditions and means than were expressed in the observation of primitive practical purposes."[28]

The philosophy one subscribes to determines the uses to which the behavioral sciences are put in connection with (1) the nature of the learner, (2) the nature of society, and (3) the design of the curriculum (including the learning activities). The essentialist, seeing the proper curriculum for the young learner as appropriately being concentrated on facts and skills, might opt for a behavioristic conception of the learner and for a mechanistic curriculum. The experimentalist, on the other hand, would see the learner as a growing organism in vital interaction with the environment—necessitating a holistic approach to the curriculum to enable the learner to grow as an autonomously thinking, socially responsible individual in the context of a free society. Moreover, the experimentalist gives considerable import to teacher–pupil planning, thereby seeing the learner as an influence as well as a source for determining the curriculum.

In other words, philosophy should enable supervisors and teachers to put each of the various conflicting psychologies of learning to the test of the wider vision—a vision that encompasses the fullest nature of the learner and the kinds of educative experience (curriculum) needed for the kind of society we want. Hence educational practice must provide the problems of inquiry rather than psychology, sociology, or some other behavioral science; and the use to which the behavioral sciences are put is regulated by philosophy.[29]

Emergence of a Paradigm for Curriculum Development and Educational Improvement

Seen interactively, the sources and influences portrayed in Figure 10–3 serve as a paradigm for seeking answers to such questions as: (1) "What are the ways by means of which the function of education in all its branches and phases— selection of material for the curriculum, methods of instruction and discipline, organization and administration of schools—can be conducted with systematic increase of intelligent control and understanding?"; (2) "What are the materials upon which we may—and should—draw in order that educational activities may become in a less degree products of routine, tradition, accident, and transitory influence?"; and (3) "From what sources shall we draw so that there shall be steady and cumulative growth of intelligent, communicable insight, and power of direction?"[30] Implied is that educational progress derives from drawing systematically on all the sources of data necessary to solve problems stemming from the educational situation.

Problem Solving. The evolution of the conception of educational improvement (and, more specifically, curriculum development) as a problem-solving process is shown in Table 10–2. Again, it should be stressed that the process is not linear. It does not begin with objectives, purposes, or preformulated needs that are superimposed on the educational situation. The process begins with the educational situation in which a significant problem arises. Objectives, purposes, or needs are determined and tested through the problem-solving process.

In their analysis of the process of curriculum development and evaluation in connection with the Eight-Year Study, Giles, McCutchen, and Zechiel portrayed the process not as a linear one, but as interactive. This is evident in their portrayal of the interaction of the determinants in curriculum development—

Table 10–2 Educational Improvement (and Curriculum Development) as a Problem-Solving Process

Dewey, 1916	Giles, McCutchen, and Zechiel, 1942	Taba, 1945, 1962	Tyler, 1949
Situation of significant experience	Identifying objectives	Diagnosis of needs	What educational purposes should be sought?
Identification of problem(s) deriving from situation	Selecting the means for attaining these objectives	Formulation of objectives	What educational experiences can be provided that are likely to attain these purposes?
Observations and information bearing on the problem(s)	Organizing these means	Selection of content	
	Evaluating the outcomes	Organization of content	
Formulations of suggested solutions (hypotheses)		Selection of learning experiences	How can these educational experiences be effectively organized?
Application and validation of suggested solutions		Organization of learning experiences	How can we determine whether these purposes are being attained?
		Evaluation	

Source: Daniel Tanner, "Curriculum History," in Harold E. Mitzel (ed.), *Encyclopedia of Educational Research*, 5th ed., Vol. 1 (New York: Free Press, 1982), p. 417.

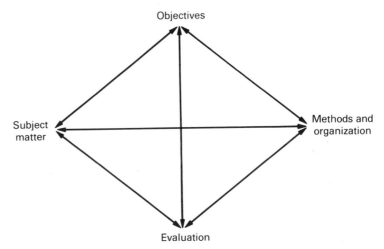

Figure 10–4. Interrelationship of determinants in curriculum development.
[From H. H. Giles, S. P. McCutchen, and A. N. Zechiel, *Exploring the Curriculum* (New York: Harper & Row, 1942), p. 2.]

objectives, means (subject matter), organization and methods, and evaluation— as shown in Figure 10–4.

Interaction of Determinants. Because the way in which the various determinants are conceived and applied is shaped by philosophy which, in turn, serves as a compass or regulator in drawing on the sources of data for educational improvement (Figure 10–3), the scheme in Figure 10–4 has been modified in Figure 10–5 to encompass philosophy. Figure 10–5 portrays these interactive determinants in the process of curriculum development. The strategies employed in formulating and applying these determinants are shaped by philosophy and derive from the educational situation.

Significance of the Paradigm. In essence, Figures 10–3, 10–4, and 10–5 and Table 10–2 reveal the sources, influences, and determinants as a paradigm for educational improvement and curriculum development. The concept of paradigm as explicated by Kuhn is a consensual model through which problem solutions are derived so as to enable the practitioners in a field to make progress.[31] As such, the paradigm is an economical, simplified, and persuasive model for dealing practicably with the complex process of educational improvement. It reveals the necessity of considering the sources and influences for education holistically and interactively.

As a simplified representation, there is always the danger that a paradigm will be interpreted as a mechanistic production model.[32] Indeed, it has been used in such a manner by behaviorists.[33] But it has also been used by experimentalists, such as in the Eight-Year Study, as a working structure for creating curricular balance and coherence, and for making the curriculum consonant with the nature and needs of the learner and with our highest social ideals.

As emphasized throughout this book, developmental supervision is a prob-

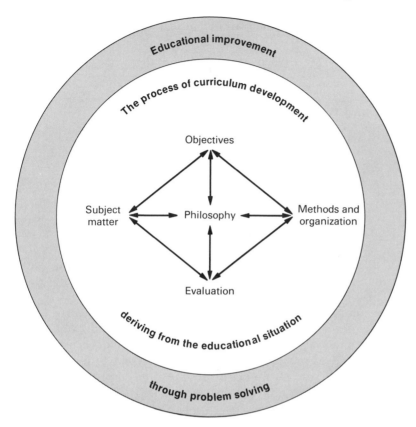

Figure 10–5. Interrelationship of determinants with philosophy in curriculum development.

[Adapted from Daniel Tanner and Laurel N. Tanner, *Curriculum Development: Theory into Practice,* 2nd ed. (New York: Macmillan, 1980), p. 88.]

lem-solving process, taking into account all of the determinants and their interactions in the educational situation to ensure that progress is continual.

RESEARCH INTO PRACTICE: THE PROSPECTS FOR PROGRESS

Gunnar Myrdal, a Nobel laureate in economics, was quoted in Chapter 5 in connection with his account of how he came to realize in his working life that the problems in the real world do not fit the disciplinary divisions of university scholarship but are complex and interdisciplinary. Myrdal went on to explain that in conducting research to solve practical problems, we must not limit ourselves to any single traditional discipline because such problems are not delimited to the boundaries of the discrete disciplines of organized scholarship.[34] Each specialized knowledge domain provides only a partial picture of reality. Compounding our difficulties is the tendency for the various social sciences to become arenas for competing schools of thought. Although such disputation is valuable and even vital to the advancement of knowledge, there is the danger that it will degenerate into self-serving divisions, specializations, and sects. When this happens, inquiry in the name of scholarship becomes isolated from and irrelevant to the pervasive and practical problems in the real world.

Valuations and Biases in Social Research

According to Myrdal, despite pronouncements that the social sciences are based on value-free inquiry, all significant inquiry requires a view, stemming from a viewpoint which, in turn, implies valuation. "Our whole literature [in the behavioral sciences] is permeated by value judgments, despite prefatory statements to the contrary," continues Myrdal, and "every study of a social problem, however limited in scope, is and must be determined by valuations." As a consequence, it is incumbent on social scientists to make their valuations conscious and explicit so as to avoid systematic biases in their work.[35] Clearly, then, in educational research, if one is looking for the limitations of schooling, the findings will be very different than if one is looking for the possibilities. The viewpoint determines the view that is obtained.

This does not mean that the social sciences are valueless because they are not value free. It means that the value premises should be exposed in the fullest light, and that alternative sets of value premises should be used as working hypotheses, insofar as practicable, within a given research investigation and in comparing different research studies bearing on a given problem.[36] In this way, there is protection against bias and the research provides a more powerful and compelling scientific basis for practical application.

The Problem of Systematic Bias in Social Research: Some Examples

"The great tradition in social science," observed Myrdal, has been for the social scientists to take a direct as well as an indirect responsibility for popular education. There is a recent trend, with which I must register my dissatisfaction, to abandon this great tradition."[37] Here Myrdal was referring to the predisposition of modern-day social scientists to look for the limitations rather than the possibilities and accomplishments of public education.

Earlier in this chapter it was noted that there has been a clear tendency for social science research to reflect the dominant shifts in the wider sociopolitical milieu. This is evident not only in the selection of problems that are addressed, but also in the shaping of the findings. Myrdal has noted that such shifts to follow the dominant tide are motivated by opportunism, and result in systematic research biases and distortions.[38] Moreover, it is far easier in social research to find no evidence, or limitations, than to find positive and constructive evidence toward solving a significant problem.

A brief review of one such study, which was used to justify a social policy of educational retrenchment, will illustrate this phenomenon and the resultant systematic bias in the research.

Looking for Limitations Rather than Possibilities. During the era of sociopolitical and educational retrenchment of the 1970s, university academicians not only were abandoning their traditional support of popular education, but were amassing data pointing to the limitations of popular education. Since the late 1960s, radical-revisionist historians of education had been waging an attack against the democratic-liberal tradition of population education.[39]

But it was the appearance in 1972 of a study on the limits of schooling that provided the "hard data" to justify a social policy for reducing our investment in schooling and abandoning the school as a key means for improving the lives of the disadvantaged. This study by Christopher Jencks and his associates, under the title *Inequality*, grew out of Jencks's work on "The Limits of Schooling" which had begun in the late 1960s.[40] As mentioned earlier, if a social scientist is looking for limits, then limits will be found. And this is what happened in the research by Jencks and his associates. In their research, they proceeded to show a low correlation between the level of formal educational attainment and subsequent adult income. From their findings, they concluded that there is little justification for increasing our investment in "marginal institutions like the school" since "the evidence suggests that equalizing educational opportunity would do little to make adults more equal"; that "the character of a school's output depends largely on a single input, namely the characteristics of the entering children"; and that "everything else" (regarding the characteristics of the school) "is either secondary or completely irrelevant."[41]

Almost immediately following the publication of these findings, leading social scientists proceeded to accept them as valid. The chairman of the sociology department of the University of California at Berkeley declared that the study "agrees almost exactly with my own," and Seymour Lipset of Harvard's government department stated, "Schools make no difference; families make the difference."[42] Oddly, neither Jencks nor any of the other social scientists who endorsed such conclusions proceeded to recommend a policy of massive parent education. In reviewing the data related to Jencks's study, for the President's Commission on School Finance, a report of the Rand Corporation proceeded to conclude that "there seem to be opportunities for significant redirection and in some cases reductions in educational expenditures, without deterioration in educational outcomes."[43] Referring to this report, Daniel Moynihan, a presidential adviser, who was on leave from Harvard, where he was a professor of education and social politics, observed that "with respect to school finance there is a strong possibility that we may already be spending too much."[44]

"Double Standard." Oddly, none of the social scientists recommended the reduction in public expenditures for higher education. Indeed, when examining the effects of higher education, university researchers invariably found pervasively positive results.[45] Yet the body of research on human growth and development tells us that if formal education in the years of young adulthood has positive effects on intellectual and attitudinal interests and capacities, then certainly the effect of earlier schooling should be even more powerful.[46]

Curiously, in depreciating the value of education, the social scientists, having garnered Ph.D.s for themselves, could be expected to seek the most and best schooling for their own children. (Such an assumption would seem reasonable in view of the census data showing, generation after generation, that college graduates seek the most further education possible for their own children.) It was clear that these social scientists were depreciating education for other people's children and not their own. This "double standard" not only augurs badly for a democratic society, but lends credence to Eric Hoffer's view that intellectuals are not awakened by their own education to the educational needs of the uneducated, but tend to take an aristocratic attitude toward the uneducated similar to that of a colonial functionary toward the natives.[47]

Opposite Conclusions from the Same Data Base. The study by Jencks and his associates was based largely on data from an earlier study by James Coleman, who had concluded from his data that "for those children whose family and neighborhood are educationally disadvantaged, it is important to replace this family environment as much as possible with an educational environment—by starting school at an earlier age, and by having a school which begins very early in the day and ends very late. . . . This implies new kinds of educational institutions with a vast increase in expenditures for education—not merely for the disadvantaged, but for all children."[48] Yet from essentially the same data, Jencks and his associates were able to draw the opposite conclusion regarding school expenditures and time in school.

The "Facts Kick." Eventually, attention was being called to a host of weaknesses in the Jencks study,[49] while subsequent studies were finding that schools do "make a difference."[50] The underlying premise of Jencks's study came under criticism as it was pointed out that the function of education is not to equalize income but to widen one's span of choices in life. For example, the income of a physician who chooses a career in public health cannot be expected to match that of one who chooses to practice plastic surgery in Beverly Hills. The same holds for the public defender in Los Angeles and the divorce lawyer in Beverly Hills. Moreover, Jencks had ignored some crucial variables, such as the age variable. The census data reveal that although the younger adult populations significantly exceed older adults in formal education, the older populations have significantly higher income simply because they have become more firmly established in their careers. Jencks also confounded the findings by lumping males and females together, although it is widely known that a high proportion of females earn less than males who have the same or even less formal education. Also ignored were the noncognitive effects of schooling, such as the positive influences on interests, attitudes, and values.

In the Jencks study, as in all similar studies, approximately 60 percent of the variance was beyond the measurement capability of the research instruments and methodology. In other words, most of the critical school variables, such as the quality of learning activities, were not accounted for. For example, the data on school library expenditures in the Coleman study, from which Jencks drew most of his data, reveal nothing about the quality of work assigned to students in the school library. The same holds true for all educational facilities and resources. The solution is not to reduce expenditures for school facilities, resources, and so on, but to improve the quality of the educative experience, and this usually will require increases in such expenditures. To make such increased investments pay off, the professional staff of the school must function at a high level of knowledge/ability.

Myrdal has observed that opportunistic distortions in social research eventually are corrected through subsequent studies which exert a power of self-healing as the "facts kick."[51] Subsequent studies both here and abroad eventually began to reveal what every parent knows—that schools do make a difference in the lives of children and youth. A large-scale study of secondary schools serving a high proportion of disadvantaged youth in inner London (England) found that "schools do indeed have an important impact on children's development and it does matter which school a child attends." The researchers also found that various qualitative factors, such as "good conditions for pupils, and the extent to which children were able to take responsibility were all significantly associated with outcome differences between schools"—and that "all of these factors were open to modification by the staff, rather than fixed by external constraints."[52]

These findings not only refuted the allegation by Jencks and his associates that the schools are only "marginal" institutions in the lives of children and that they have no really significant impact in countering the effects of disadvantaged homes, but also indicated that an administration and faculty functioning at a high level of knowledge/ability have the power to create a more effective environment for learning. Obviously, such an administration and staff, if provided with additional financial resources, would be better able to capitalize on such resources than would those functioning at a low level of knowledge/ability.

Analyzing data from fifty-four studies involving a population of 80,000 individuals, Hyman, Wright, and Reed sought to ascertain the endurance of the effects of education into the adult years. They found that "education produces large, pervasive, and enduring effects on knowledge and receptivity to knowledge." Addressing the attacks commonly leveled at the schools from many quarters of academe concerning noncognitive influences of schooling, the researchers noted that much of this criticism is polemic and is refuted by the evidence. "Surely the image of the school as stultifying the student, as destroying the natural passion for learning and the love of intellectual discovery, is not compatible with our finding that with more education there is more information seeking and more receptivity to new knowledge, implanted so well that they survive old age and other circumstances of life," concluded the researchers.[53]

Many educational sociologists, along with revisionist critics, have sought to show how our schools "create and reinforce patterns of social class" and other repressive inequalities of society.[54] Yet large-scale studies were revealing that social-class differences actually decline as an influence on educational goals as youth progress through high school, and that achievement, encouragement by the guidance counselor, and other school factors exert a greater influence on these goals than does social class. In other words, the schools may well serve to help overcome rather than to perpetuate social-class bias.[55]

Other researchers also were finding what parents already know—that "a good teacher shapes both the academic self-concept and achievement of the pupil so that an initial foundation yields cumulative benefits in later stages of life."[56] Virtually everyone can recall teachers and school experiences having significant bearings on their lives, and that such memorable instances are not vague reminiscences but are events that can be concretely and vividly described.

Educational Productivity. In earlier chapters it was noted that there have been many efforts to assess the productivity of education according to quantitative input–output production measures comparable to the manufacture of industrial products. Such efforts have failed largely because of the faulty underlying premise that education is comparable to the industrial manufacture of finished goods. Illustrative of such misguided thinking was the claim by the Carnegie Corporation, an original sponsor of the National Assessment of Educational Progress, that the national testing program would enable us to construct a kind of gross educational product comparable to the gross national product.[57] In an article, "The Schooling Industry as a Possibly Pathological Section of the American Economy," the economist Kenneth Boulding sought to demonstrate the "pathology" through quantitative measures for the "productivity of the schooling industry." His indicator of pathology was that "the school industry as a proportion of the total economy has risen much faster than its physical product [sic], suggesting that there has been a substantial increase in the 'real price' of education."[58] Not only does Boulding fail to recognize the intangible satisfactions that people get from formal education, for which no quantitative assessments can be made, but his conception of production derives from a simplistic index of school expenditure in relation to the number of school years completed.

In sharp contrast, the Nobel laureate Theodore Schultz has shown how over many years there has been a considerably higher yield from investing in "human capital" (i.e., schooling) than in physical capital in the American economy. From his detailed studies, Schultz finds that not enough has been spent on elementary and secondary schooling relative to expenditures on higher education, and that coupled with the problem of underinvestment is the neglect of quality in schooling. Here he points to the overemphasis on quantitative measures of schooling and the failure to recognize that significant improvements will come from addressing the problem of quality.[59]

At times of socioeconomic and educational retrenchment, the policymakers and many social researchers tend to look to human limitations rather than possibilities. At no time was this more evident than during the educational retrenchment period of the 1970s. Hence the work of Jencks was given great fanfare and credence, whereas that of Schultz was virtually ignored in redirecting educational policy.

Quantification Is Not Science but a Scientific Tool

No discipline in the social sciences is as subjected to the quantification of data and to the use of elaborate terminology as is economics. Myrdal regards much of this as a means of escapism—to avoid coming to grips with the need to identify the assumptions and valuations underlying the research. He also sees this as an effort to convey an air of scientific objectivity in such research. In Myrdal's words,

> The employment of algebraic formulas (however useful they may be for mastering complicated relationships), of Greek letters, and of other symbols facilitates

the escape from stating clearly implied assumptions and, in particular, from being aware of the valuation load of main concepts.

In the other social sciences as well, much of the very considerable attention devoted in recent decades to exuberant terminology is of the same character. It is to a great degree an elaborate attempt to "objectify" what is not, and cannot be, simply objective.[60]

The validity of this indictment becomes apparent when different economists of different sociopolitical persuasions employ elaborate statistical treatments in reaching very different policy prescriptions for attacking such problems as inflation, unemployment, national deficits, economic recession, and so on.

Educational research has been greatly affected by the propensity in the social sciences to create elaborate schemes for reducing complex phenomena to quantifiable data for manipulation. In such research there is a tendency to focus on those phenomena which are most amenable to quantification, with the result that significant aspects of a problem are ignored or distorted. Yet it would be a serious mistake to dismiss statistically based research as being of relatively little use, or to set nonstatistical research as preferable in studying complex phenomena. Nonstatistical research must also be protected against biases by identifying underlying valuations and by investigating alternative premises in investigating problems. Myrdal's criticisms are pointed at the need to expose statistical research to these precautionary measures, to direct such research at more significant problems through interdisciplinary approaches, and to recognize the limitations of reducing complex phenomena to quantitative measures.

The experimental method, which has enabled education and the social sciences to attack problems that heretofore were insoluble, relies on the tools of statistical mathematics. Similarly, survey research and cross-sectional studies on a vast scale have been made possible through advances in statistical mathematics.

The Quantitative/Qualitative Dualism. Unfortunately, some educators have identified a mode of research as "qualitative"—in distinction from quantitative research, leaving the impression that quantitative research is somehow devoid of qualitative ideas and values.[61] Although this may not be their intent, it is a case whereby the terminology or labels employed create a dangerous misconception.

At the same time, there are some educators who contend that many of our problems stem from the twentieth-century "belief in the potential of scientific inquiries as a means of informing and guiding educational practice."[62] In making this case, there is the tendency to portray scientific inquiry as scientism—focused on effecting greater efficiency and uniformity in education through set measures and procedures. In such a portrayal there is a failure to recognize science as an outlook which frees us from bias and dictate, enables us to understand and control events more intelligently, reveals new problems and the possibilities for their solution—thereby making for diversification and progress rather than conformity and uniformity.[63]

The very mode of hypothetical thinking that undergirds science requires the engagement of the imagination through which outcomes can be projected beyond the limitations of existing conditions, while being subjected to the responsibility of verification through application. In this way, knowledge and practice are advanced cumulatively and systematically.

The Educational Situation as the Source of Inquiry

Because educational problems are so complex, they must draw data from the various social sciences in an interdisciplinary way. To impose the tools of any single social science discipline on an educational problem is to restrict our perceptions, such as under the conditions described in the legend of the blind men and the elephant. Dewey warned that while there is no independent science of education, it would be unproductive to allow the various social science disciplines to determine the educational problems, objectives, and prescriptions. It is the *educational* situation from which problems are identified and educational ends are determined. "For education is itself a process of discovering what values are worth while and are to be pursued as objectives," commented Dewey.[64]

Each of the behavioral sciences has its own specialized techniques and perspectives of reality. Employed separately, we have the case of psychology being delimited to the study of the how of teaching and to the measurement of achievement without due consideration of the social bearings of what is to be learned and the kind of society that is to be created by education. Similar restrictions apply and distortions derive from failing to recognize that the social science disciplines are not educational science. They can serve as sources from which problems stemming from the educational situation can be addressed scientifically provided that they are utilized for interdisciplinary inquiry.

Research into Practice: Misplacing the Blame

"There is little in research that can be used to guide practice," contends Eisner in referring to experimental and other "conventional forms of educational research."[65] Such a criticism may well be warranted in cases where the research delimits to an insulated and isolated disciplinary domain or subspecialty of sociology, psychology, economics, political science, and so on. But to apply it as a blanket indictment of educational research is another matter. The gap between research and practice—the failure to make use of the best available evidence in improving practice and in solving practical problems—is a pervasive problem in society in general. For example, despite the long-standing and compelling research revealing the deleterious effects on children and youth from viewing violence on television, we continue to bring violence into the living room via television.[66]

In the same vein, one cannot dismiss medical research as offering "little to guide practice" simply because the best available knowledge is not fully realized in practice. Because more than 2.5 million children throughout the world die each year for lack of immunization against measles[67] is not reason to see the medical research that produced the measles vaccine as being of little practical value. Similarly, there is a great time lag in application between our research findings on infant nutrition and infant-food formulas, on highway design and highway safety, on automobile design and highway safety, on youth unemployment and antisocial behavior, on environmental pollution and human health, on nutrition and learning, on nutrition and cancer, and so on.

As research is amassed cumulatively and persuasively on a problem, it eventually becomes a basis for corrective action by professional practitioners. The great time lag between knowledge and practice may be appalling, but it is no reason for holding that the reseach is of little value because it produces no immediate and widespread effect on practice. Witness the great time lag in convincing physicians to wash their hands before examining the patient. Consider how Mendel's work in plant genetics, although published in 1865, was virtually ignored until the twentieth century. Or consider how the great impact of the environment on human development was not fully recognized until well into the twentieth century, despite the fact that it gave credence to the fundamental principle of human perfectibility in democratic theory as recognized by our forefathers.

In the public domain, research also becomes a basis for corrective action by public demand as the public becomes more informed and enlightened. Witness the growing public concern and demand for action in connection with environmental pollution. Until the late 1960s, few states maintained epidemiological data on the incidence of cancer in relation to area of residence and industrial location. In some states, the impetus for such research came from public demand and not from public officials or the scientific community.

The "Best Available Evidence" as the Key to Improved Practice

In education, considerable research has been amassed since the 1930s on the effects of the learning environment on human intelligence, on the ways and means of fostering the critical-thinking abilities of learners, on the relationship between attitudes and learning, and so on. Yet many of these findings are only beginning to gain some wide degree of recognition and application. Periods of sociopolitical retrenchment have produced setbacks for education, but one of the principal beliefs in a free society is that the method of intelligence wins out in the long run. That is, practices are continuously reassessed and redirected in accordance with the best available scientific evidence.

In his study of the research on teaching, Gage expresses his views concerning the value of research in comparison to "the alternative to scientific method" in these words:

> What are the alternatives to the effort to build a scientific basis for the art of teaching? For most of our history, the main alternative has been a combination of logic, clinical insight, raw experience, common sense, and the writings of persuasive prose stylists. . . .
>
> Since *Summerhill* appeared in 1960, we seem to have been more than ever at the mercy of powerful and passionate writers who shift educational thinking ever more erratically with their manifestos. The kind of research I have been describing is a plodding enterprise, the reports of which are seldom, I regret to say, as well written as the pronouncements of authors unburdened by scientific method. But, in the long run, the improvement of teaching—which is tantamount to the improvement of our children's lives—will come in large part from the continued search for a scientific basis for the art of teaching.[68]

No Easy Recipes. Here Gage alludes in part to the tendency to follow traditional routines and rule-of-thumb procedures, or to yield to the most persuasive rhetoric as a guide to reform, rather than to base practice on scientific evidence. "Nothing has brought pedagogical theory into greater disrepute than the belief that it is identified with handing out to teachers recipes and models to be followed in teaching," commented Dewey.[69] Ready-made recipes imply that a situation (the process of education) is static and convergent rather than dynamic and emergent, and that the teacher is not an inquirer. Ready-made recipes and rule-of-thumb procedures may be suited to mechanical situations but do not lead to the deeper insights and wider perceptions necessary to the progressive redirection of experience.

Compounding the Gap Between Research and Practice. The gap between research and approved practice, and indeed the resistance against research, is the result of many factors, including the forces of tradition, the tendency for individuals and organizations to seek the comfort of routines, the tendency for practitioners (supervisors and teachers) to seek recipes and to follow rule-of-thumb procedures, the seductiveness of inducing change by fad and fashion rather than by the best available evidence, the tendency to look to administrative dictate rather than authoritative evidence, the influence of vested interests as against the wider public interest, and sheer ignorance.

Compounding the problem, as discussed earlier, is the penchant for researchers to confine their work to specialized segments of a problem and to focus on those specific elements that are most amenable to quantification and manipulation.

We have also seen how many of the scientists and other specialized university scholars, who developed and promoted the national curriculum-reform packages in the wake of the Cold War and space race of the 1950s and 1960s, either avoided controlled research or manipulated the research conditions so as to prove the project.[70] Such limitations and distortions in research are damaging, of course, but corrections are eventually made as conflicting evidence emerges and as the problem is reconstructed in its holistic complexity. The point is that as long as there is an abiding commitment to the scientific evidence, the results are continually self-correcting.

Opposition to the best available evidence as a basis for illumined practice is manifested also by those who subscribe to a philosophy that does not regard such evidence as a basis for practice. Gage's reference to *Summerhill* alludes to the influence of A. S. Neill's best-selling book of the 1960s, which, along with other popular books by romantic naturalists, promulgated the view that the best pedagogy is laissez-faire. No research basis was offered for their romantic prescriptions. At the other end of the philosophic spectrum, the essentialists and perennialists, who seek a return to the fundamentals and who regard mind as a receptacle or muscle, choose not to draw their educational prescriptions from the best available research evidence. No amount of research will sway them from their convictions.

As discussed in the preceding chapter, many of the most persuasive and influential documents for educational reform are politically motivated rather than research based. But the mark of a profession is that practice is continually reconstructed and improved through the best available evidence (scientific inquiry).

The political orientation of a free society holds such inquiry as vital to social progress, because such inquiry is open, intolerant of bias, and committed to continuous self-correction.

The Teacher and the Supervisor as Investigators

Throughout this text, emphasis has been given to the vital role of the supervisor and the teacher in educational improvement. In this role the supervisor and teacher together are a key source for diagnosing classroom and schoolwide problems concerning the curriculum, learning, the educative environment, and the relationship between the school, home, and community. As professional practitioners, the supervisor and the teacher must be intelligently informed consumers of research and intelligent investigative participants. This has been borne out from the Eight-Year Study to the contemporary research findings on effective schools.[71] Some of the most elaborate, ambitious, and well-financed efforts to reform education—such as the Ford Foundation's Comprehensive School Improvement Program and the federally funded curriculum-reform projects of the 1960s—have gone awry for failure to regard the teacher and the supervisor as investigative participants.[72]

As Dewey observed, when teachers are regarded as merely "channels of reception and transmission," great deflection and distortion occur between research findings and practical applications. Moreover, the theory on which the research is based will lack vital connections with actual classroom practice.[73] When treated as "channels of reception and transmission," teachers are reduced to seeking and following recipes, prescriptions, and prepackaged formulations. Such devices tend to be implemented mechanically. Externally derived and imposed devices tend to be directed at treating the symptoms rather than the underlying causes of problems.

Dewey contended that the real or alleged incapacity of teachers to function as participative investigators stems in large part from the lack of opportunity and stimulation provided them for such a role. For without a sense of responsibility there can be no capacity. He concluded that "the contributions that might come from classroom teachers are a comparatively neglected field; or, to change the metaphor, an almost unworked mine."[74]

SUMMARY

The administrative concern for "satisficing" rather than for optimizing makes the school vulnerable to the repetitive cycles of "reform" by reaction and counterreaction. The concept of *knowledge/ability* has been used in this chapter to denote the capacity of an organization and its membership to utilize the best available evidence in effecting solutions to emergent problems, thereby effecting substantive improvements in their mission. Schools functioning at a relatively low level of knowledge/ability are concerned with satisficing, whereas those at a high level of knowledge/ability are concerned with optimizing. The former are concerned with operations within established parameters or limits, and change occurs mainly as a response to the prevailing tide or to dominant external pressures. The latter are concerned with possibilities arising from emergent conditions, and external tides and pressures are evaluated critically on the anvil of the "best available evidence." Three levels of knowledge/ability were identified in analyzing the differences in the functioning of our schools—namely, Level I: imitative-maintenance, Level II: mediative-adaptive, and Level III: generative-creative.

A paradigm for educational improvement was described. The paradigm addresses educational improvement as a problem-solving process in which pertinent data are drawn from three principal sources: (1) society (social ideals and the social situation), (2) the nature of the learner, and (3) codified or systematized knowledge (for the selection and organization of subject matter and learning experiences). Insoluble problems arise when any of these fundamental factors or sources are neglected or when any factor is emphasized at the expense of another. The vital interdependence of the three factors is crucial to educational progress. Otherwise, the result is conflict between our highest social ideals and the mission of the school, and between the learner and the curriculum. The philosophical outlook of the professional staff serves as a compass or regulator for guiding and testing concrete practices in relation to the aforementioned fundamental factors or sources. Hence democratic philosophy or theory would reject the notion of the learner as an organism to be conditioned and would regard education as a process whereby the learner gains in the ability to direct the course of experience with intelligence. Obviously, this has profound implications for the design and function of the curriculum. Unfortunately, in many schools, the statement of philosophy is a filed document rather than a functioning guide and regulator for testing actual practice.

In addressing educational problems, the professional staff of the school needs to draw data from the behavioral sciences. However, educational problems, objectives, and prescriptions must be developed from the educational situation, not from the behavioral sciences or any other external source. The behavioral sciences are highly specialized and diverse. Each discipline and subdiscipline presents only a partial picture of reality. Conflicting findings and prescriptions often are derived from the same data base as the result of the hidden valuations of the researcher, even in the case where quantitative data are used. Whether the researcher chooses to see the glass as half empty or as half full makes a critical difference in how the quantitative data are analyzed. Incomplete knowledge, like ignorance, can be used opportunistically to support biases. Underlying valuations of the researcher must be exposed and treated as hypothetical premises. In seeking to solve problems and to improve practice, educators need to draw data from the behavioral sciences through an interdisciplinary perspective, and they need to evaluate all pertinent sources of data to derive the best available evidence.

In far too many instances, educational research has been directed at those conditions that are most amenable to quantification. As a result, significant qualitative factors are overlooked or ignored. Precision takes precedence over vision. Technique determines the questions that are addressed, with the result that the questions are not always the most intelligent ones and the answers suffer accordingly. As such research is exposed to more complete data from alternative approaches, a fuller picture emerges and distortions are corrected. Progress depends on continual self-correction and continual reconstruction of the educational situation in the light of the best available evidence (through scientific inquiry as opposed to scientism).

Probably the most neglected source for inquiry into educational problems is the teacher. When the teacher is treated as a mere "channel of reception and transmission," the teacher then seeks ready recipes or prepackaged prescriptions—that is, if there are no mandated directives from above. The consequence is that practices become mechanical and great energy is directed at reacting to symptoms rather than getting at the underlying roots of problems. As a participative investigator, the teacher can serve as an intelligent source for diagnosing classroom and schoolwide problems and for waging an intelligent attack on these problems. If the teacher is treated as an educator, such efforts will not be directed at reacting to the most immediate symptoms but at the more profound problems of the educational situation.

PROBLEMS FOR STUDY AND DISCUSSION

1. The Nobel laureate Herbert Simon characterizes "administrative man" as being primarily concerned with seeking to satisfice rather than to maximize (optimize), and having a propensity for avoiding the complex inter-relatedness in situations so as to simplify the route to decisionmaking.[75] Would you say that Simon's characterization is applicable to the school administrator? Explain.

2. Minimum-competency testing has been promoted as a means for raising "standards." Do such testing programs represent an effort to satisfice or to optimize? Explain. Have these testing programs actually served to raise "standards"? Why or why not?

3. "Compulsory attendance in an educational institution should cease when a young citizen demonstrates mastery of the minima, and most young citizens should master the minima before senior high school," contends a leading school critic.[76] Do you agree? Why or why not? What is your assessment of the notion of "mastery of the minima" as the chief function of schooling for most people? How does this relate to the issue of satisficing or optimizing?

4. Using Table 10–1 as a reference point, at what level of knowledge/ability would you classify your school and school district? Justify your answer.

5. Is there a standing curriculum committee in your school? If not, do you see a need for such a commitee? Explain. If there is such a committee in your school, what is its membership, what functions does it perform, and what impact has it had for curriculum improvement? Would you describe it as focusing mainly on segmental concerns or on aggregate problems? Explain.

6. Are the levels of knowledge/ability hierarchical—that is, it it necessary to progress through Levels I and II in order to function at Level III? Why or why not?

7. The term "cocoon curriculum" has been used in this chapter to describe the courses of study in schools functioning at Level I and even to a considerable extent at Level II. What are the characteristics of such a curriculum? Would you say that the term "cocoon curriculum" is a valid descriptor of the course work required for the bachelor's degree at your college? Explain.

8. Using Figures 10–1 and 10–2 as guides, trace the unanticipated consequences of a segmentally adopted innovation or practice in your own school. Should these consequences have been foreseen? Explain.

9. How does the paradigm for curriculum development and educational improvement, as presented in this chapter, explain why the schools have been vulnerable to shifting waves of reform by reaction/counterreaction in successive epochs? Does the paradigm provide the clues needed to bring about a productive strategy for curriculum improvement and educational progress? Explain. What is the function of philosophy in the paradigm? How does this relate to the oft-quoted statement that "theory is in the end the most practical of all things"?

10. Is there a written statement of philosophy for your school? If such a statement exists, when was it written and by whom? To what extent is the statement made operational in terms of ongoing practices?

11. In the process of curriculum development or educational improvement, should one begin with a list of objectives, or is it better to begin with another strategy? Explain.

12. How do you explain the not uncommon phenomenon whereby different social researchers will derive conflicting conclusions and prescriptions from what is essentially the same data base? Does this mean that social research is of little value to the teacher, supervisor, curriculum director, or school administrator? Explain.

13. "The great tradition in social science," observed Gunnar Myrdal, "has been for the social scientists to take a direct as well as indirect responsibility for popular education. There is a recent trend, with which I must register my dissatisfaction, to abandon this great tradition."[77] How do you account for the tendency of so many social scientists to join the school blamers over the past two decades or so? Why do university researchers tend to find consistently positive effects when studying the impact of higher education on students, whereas they do not obtain similarly positive findings when they direct their research on schooling?

14. Early in this century, Dewey commented that the potential contributions of the teacher as a participative investigator into educational problems have been neglected to the extent that the teacher is almost an "unworked mine."[78] Is this observation pertinent to the contemporary educational situation? Why or why not?

NOTES

1. Herbert Simon, *Administrative Behavior*, 3rd ed. (New York: Free Press, 1976), p. 284.
2. Gunnar Myrdal, *Objectivity in Social Research* (New York: Pantheon Books, 1969), p. 9.
3. Simon, op. cit., Introduction.
4. See, for example, *Reducing the Curriculum* (Reston, Va.: National Association of Secondary School Principals, 1982).
5. Daniel Tanner and Laurel N. Tanner, *Curriculum Development: Theory into Practice*, 2nd ed. (New York: Macmillan, 1980), pp. 728–729.
6. Ibid., pp. 636–640.
7. John I. Goodlad, *A Place Called School* (New York: McGraw-Hill, 1984).
8. Theodore R. Sizer, *Horace's Compromise: The Dilemma of the American High School* (Boston: Houghton Mifflin, 1984), p. 88.
9. John I. Goodlad, "Research and Theory Regarding Promotion and Nonpromotion," *Elementary School Journal*, Vol. 53 (November 1952), pp. 150–155.
10. See Christopher Jencks et al., *Inequality* (New York: Basic Books, 1972); Arthur L. Stinchcombe, "The Social Determinants of Success," *Science*, Vol. 178 (November 10, 1972), pp. 603–604; Geodfry Hodgson, "Do Schools Make a Difference?" *Atlantic Monthly*, Vol. 231 (March 1973), pp. 35–46; Daniel P. Moynihan, "Equalizing Education: In Whose Benefit?" *The Public Interest*, Vol. 29 (Fall 1972), pp. 70–74.
11. Michael Rutter et al., *Fifteen Thousand Hours: Secondary Schools and Their Effects on Children* (Cambridge, Mass.: Harvard University Press, 1979), pp. 4–5; Theodore W. Schultz, *The Economic Value of Education* (New York: Columbia University Press, 1963).
12. John Dewey, *The Child and the Curriculum* (Chicago: University of Chicago Press, 1902), pp. 4–8.
13. Ibid., pp. 4–5.
14. National Society for the Study of Education, *The Foundations of Curriculum-Making*, Twenty-sixth Yearbook, Part II (Bloomington, Ill.: Public School Publishing Co., 1927), pp. 13, 22.
15. Ibid., p. 74.
16. H. H. Giles, S. P. McCutchen, and A. N. Zechiel, *Exploring the Curriculum* (New York: Harper & Row, 1942).
17. Hilda Taba, "General Techniques of Curriculum Planning," Chapter 5 in *American Education in the Postwar Period: Curriculum Reconstruction*, Forty-fourth Yearbook, Part I, National Society for the Study of Education (Chicago: University of Chicago Press, 1945), pp. 85–92.
18. John Dewey, *The Sources of a Science of Education* (New York: Liveright, 1929), pp. 33–34.
19. Ralph W. Tyler, *Basic Principles of Curriculum and Instruction* (Chicago: University of Chicago Press, 1949), p. 1.
20. Herbert M. Kliebard, "The Tyler Rationale," *School Review*, Vol. 78 (February 1970), p. 260.
21. Tyler, op. cit., p. 128.
22. Ibid., pp. 5–33.
23. Kliebard, op. cit., p. 270.
24. Tyler, op. cit., p. 26.
25. Tanner and Tanner, op. cit., p. 38.
26. John Dewey, *Democracy and Education* (New York: Macmillan, 1916), pp. 89–90.
27. Alfred North Whitehead, *Adventures of Ideas* (New York: Macmillan, 1933), p. 125.
28. *Sources of a Science of Education*, op. cit., p. 17.
29. Ibid., pp. 33, 56.
30. Ibid., pp. 9–10.

31. Thomas S. Kuhn, *The Structure of Scientific Revolutions,* 2nd ed. (Chicago: University of Chicago Press, 1970), pp. 11, 175, 182, 200, 204.

32. Kliebard, op. cit., p. 270.

33. W. James Popham and Eva L. Baker, *Systematic Instruction* (Englewood Cliffs, N.J.: Prentice-Hall, 1970), pp. 48–61.

34. Myrdal, op. cit., pp. 10–13.

35. Ibid., pp. 51–52, 55–56.

36. Ibid., p. 70.

37. Ibid., p. 41.

38. Ibid., p. 19.

39. See Diane Ravitch, *The Revisionists Revised: A Critique of the Radical Attack on the Schools* (New York: Basic Books, 1977).

40. Jencks et al., op. cit., p. v.

41. Ibid., pp. 255, 256, 265.

42. Stinchcombe, op. cit., p. 603; Seymour Lipset, as quoted by Geodfry Hodgson, "Do Schools Make a Difference?", op. cit., p. 35.

43. Rand Corporation, *How Effective Is Schooling?* (Santa Monica, Calif.: Rand Corporation, 1972), pp. x, xiii.

44. Moynihan, op. cit., p. 73.

45. See Kenneth A. Feldman and Theodore M. Newcomb, *The Impact of College on Students* (San Francisco: Jossey-Bass, 1969); Stephen B. Withey et al., *A Degree and What Else?* (New York: McGraw-Hill, 1971), pp. 128–129; Howard R. Bowen, *Investment in Learning* (San Francisco: Jossey-Bass, 1977); Alexander W. Astin, *Four Critical Years* (San Francisco: Jossey-Bass, 1977), pp. 211–221.

46. See Benjamin S. Bloom, *Stability and Change in Human Characteristics* (New York: Wiley, 1964).

47. Eric Hoffer, *The Ordeal of Change* (New York: Harper & Row, 1963), pp. 43, 53.

48. James S. Coleman, "Equal Schools or Equal Students?" *The Public Interest,* Vol. 4 (Summer 1966), p. 70. See also James S. Coleman et al., *Equality of Educational Opportunity* (Washington, D.C.: U.S. Office of Education, 1966).

49. Daniel Tanner, "The Retreat from Education—For Other People's Children," *Intellect,* Vol. 102 (January 1974), pp. 222–225.

50. Rutter et al., op. cit.

51. Myrdal, op. cit., p. 40.

52. Rutter et al., op. cit., pp. 1, 178.

53. Herbert H. Hyman, Charles R. Wright, and John S. Reed, *The Enduring Effects of Education* (Chicago: University of Chicago Press, 1975), pp. 109–111; see also Hyman and Wright, *Education's Lasting Influence on Values* (Chicago: University of Chicago Press, 1979).

54. Samuel Bowles and Herbert Gintis, *Schooling in Capitalist America* (New York: Basic Books, 1977), p. 11.

55. Richard A. Rehberg and Evelyn R. Rosenthal, *Class and Merit in the American High School* (New York: Longman, 1978), pp. 193, 252.

56. Egil Pedersen, Therese A. Faucher, and William W. Eaton, "A New Perspective on the Effects of First-Grade Teachers on Children's Adult Status," *Harvard Educational Review,* Vol. 48 (February 1978), p. 29.

57. *Carnegie Quarterly,* Vol. 14 (Spring 1966), p. 4.

58. Kenneth E. Boulding, "The Schooling Industry as a Possibly Pathological Section of the American Economy," *Review of Educational Research,* Vol. 42 (Winter 1972), pp. 135–136.

59. Theodore W. Schultz, *Human Resources* (New York: Columbia University Press, 1972), pp. 32, 33, 37.

60. Myrdal, op. cit., p. 59.
61. Robert C. Bodgan and Sari Biklen, *Qualitative Research for Education* (Boston: Allyn and Bacon, 1982).
62. Elliot W. Eisner, *The Educational Imagination*, 2nd ed. (New York: Macmillan, 1985), p. 10.
63. Dewey, *Sources of a Science of Education*, op. cit., pp. 8–9, 12.
64. Ibid., p. 74.
65. Eisner, op. cit., p. 358.
66. George A. Comstock, Eli A. Ruberstein, and John P. Murray (eds.), *Television and Social Behavior* (Washington, D.C.: National Institute of Mental Health, 1972); H. T. Himmelweit, A. N. Oppenheim, and P. Vince, *Television and the Child* (London: Oxford University Press, 1958).
67. *The New York Times*, December 20, 1984, p. A 12.
68. N. L. Gage, *The Scientific Basis of the Art of Teaching* (New York: Teachers College Press, 1978), p. 41.
69. *Democracy and Education*, op. cit., p. 199.
70. See Daniel Tanner, "Curriculum History," in Harold E. Mitzel (ed.), *Encyclopedia of Educational Research*, 5th ed., Vol. 1 (New York: Free Press, 1982), pp. 418–419.
71. See Wilford M. Aikin, *The Story of the Eight-Year Study* (New York: Harper & Row, 1942); Donald E. Mackenzie, "Research for School Improvement: An Appraisal of Some Recent Trends," *Educational Researcher*, Vol. 12 (April 1983), p. 5.
72. Ford Foundation, *A Foundation Goes to School* (New York: The Foundation, 1972), p. 18; Daniel Tanner, "Curriculum History," op. cit., p. 419.
73. Dewey, *Sources of a Science of Education*, op. cit., p. 47.
74. Ibid., p. 48.
75. Simon, op. cit.
76. Sizer, op. cit., p. 88.
77. Myrdal, op. cit., p. 41.
78. Dewey, *The Sources of a Science of Education*, op. cit., p. 48.

SELECTED REFERENCES

Aikin, Wilford M. *The Story of the Eight-Year Study.* New York: Harper & Row, Publishers, Inc., 1942.

Bloom, Benjamin S. *Stability and Change in Human Characteristics.* New York: John Wiley & Sons, Inc., 1964.

Bogdan, Robert C., and Sari Biklen. *Qualitative Research for Education.* Boston: Allyn and Bacon, Inc., 1982.

Dewey, John. *The Child and the Curriculum.* Chicago: The University of Chicago Press, 1902.

———. *Democracy and Education.* New York: Macmillan Publishing Company, 1916.

———. *The Sources of a Science of Education.* New York: Liveright, 1929.

Eisner, Elliot W. *The Educational Imagination,* 2nd ed. New York: Macmillan Publishing Company, 1985.

Ford Foundation. *A Foundation Goes to School.* New York: The Foundation, 1972.

Gage, N. L. *The Scientific Basis of the Art of Teaching.* New York: Teachers College Press, 1978.

Giles, H. H., S. P. McCutchen, and A. N. Zechiel. *Exploring the Curriculum.* New York: Harper & Row, Publishers, Inc., 1942.

Goodlad, John I. *A Place Called School.* New York: McGraw-Hill Book Company, 1984.

Hyman, Herbert H. and Charles R. Wright. *Education's Lasting Influence on Values.* Chicago: The University of Chicago Press, 1979.

Hyman, Herbert H., Charles R. Wright, and John S. Reed. *The Enduring Effects of Education.* Chicago: The University of Chicago Press, 1975.

Jencks, Christopher, et al. *Inequality.* New York: Basic Books, Inc., Publishers, 1972.

Myrdal, Gunnar. *Objectivity in Social Research.* New York: Pantheon Books, Inc., 1969.

National Society for the Study of Education. *American Education in the Postwar Period: Curriculum Reconstruction.* Chicago: The University of Chicago Press, 1945.

————. *The Foundations of Curriculum-Making,* Twenty-sixth Yearbook, Part II. Bloomington, Ill.: Public School Publishing Co., 1927.

Oakes, Jeannie. *Keeping Track: How High Schools Structure Inequality.* New Haven: Yale University Press, 1985.

Powell, Arthur G., Eleanor Farrar, and David Cohen. *The Shopping Mall High School.* Boston: Houghton Mifflin Company, 1985.

Rand Corporation. *How Effective Is Schooling?* Santa Monica, Calif.: The Rand Corporation, 1972.

Raven, John. *Competence in Modern Society.* London: H. K. Lewis & Co., Ltd., 1984.

Ravitch, Diane. *The Revisionists Revised: A Critique of the Radical Attack on the Schools.* New York: Basic Books, Inc., Publishers, 1977.

Rehberg, Richard A., and Evelyn R. Rosenthal. *Class and Merit in the American High School.* New York: Longman, Inc., 1978.

Rutter, Michael, et al. *Fifteen Thousand Hours: Secondary Schools and Their Effects on Children.* Cambridge, Mass.: Harvard University Press, 1979.

Schultz, Theodore W. *Human Resources.* New York: Columbia University Press, 1972.

Simon, Herbert. *Administrative Behavior,* 3rd ed. New York: The Free Press, 1976.

Sizer, Theodore R. *Horace's Compromise: The Dilemma of the American High School.* Boston: Houghton Mifflin Company, 1984.

Tanner, Daniel. "Curriculum History," in Harold E. Mitzel (ed.), *Encyclopedia of Educational Research,* 5th ed., Vol. 1. New York: The Free Press, 1982, pp. 412–420.

Tanner, Daniel, and Laurel N. Tanner. *Curriculum Development: Theory into Practice,* 2nd ed. New York: Macmillan Publishing Company, 1980.

Tyler, Ralph W. *Basic Principles of Curriculum and Instruction.* Chicago: The University of Chicago Press, 1949.

Whitehead, Alfred North. *Adventures of Ideas.* New York: Macmillan Publishing Company, 1933.

Wittrock, Merlin C. (ed.). *Handbook of Research on Teaching,* 3rd ed. New York: Macmillan Publishing Company, 1986.

Part V

Curriculum Design
and Development

Chapter 11

What the Supervisor Needs to Know About the Curriculum: Rationales and Functions

In Chapter 10 emphasis was given to the need for supervisors to see educational improvement (and curriculum development) as a problem-solving process. In this chapter the focus in on the conflicting rationales and contrasting functions of the curriculum.

"All other problems are solved when the problem of the curriculum is solved," maintained Mark Van Doren. Yet he contended that the problem of curriculum is not accepted as a real problem since "the curriculum is not something which it is fashionable to ponder."[1] If Van Doren is correct, it is indeed not surprising how such little attention is given to curriculum improvement in books on educational supervision and administration. As discussed earlier, a considerable portion of the literature in educational supervision relegates the problem of curriculum to educational policy—a matter that is seen as beyond the purview of the supervisor. The deleterious consequences of this stance were discussed earlier, especially in the artificial separation of curriculum and instruction and in delimiting the responsibility of the supervisor to improving the "delivery" of instruction by the teacher. This delimitation of the role of the supervisor is also artificial because the supervisor is constantly buffeted by the shifting demands and conflicting currents for curriculum reform and counterreform in successive epochs. Whether the supervisor likes it or not, he or she will have to grapple with the curriculum problem.

In being caught up with present-day demands and pressures for curriculum reform, supervisors may fail to recognize that the contemporary situation is linked to past events and that immediate concerns must be viewed in the larger perspective. Otherwise they will be vulnerable to the shifting tides of reform and counterreform, leading to successive epochs of curriculum expansion and curriculum retrenchment. Supervisors, administrators, and teachers need to recognize that the curriculum problem is an age-old problem reflecting the changing conceptions concerning the learner, knowledge, society, and the expectations imposed upon the school by society. "As things are," observed Aristotle, "mankind are by no means agreed about the things to be taught." Aristotle then added, "Again about the means there is no agreement."[2] This age-old problem continues to be of great disputation in modern times. The failure to address the curriculum problem adequately stems from the tendency to confine curriculum development largely within the insulated domains of the separate disciplines and subject fields—from the university down to the schools. The specialists within each domain vie for position of their domain over others in the hierarchy of studies that constitute that which we call "curriculum." Supervisors and secondary school teachers tend to see themselves as subject specialists, with the consequence that the vital interdependence of subject matters remains unrevealed to the learner.

Whitehead observed that there can be no vitality to the curriculum when it is seen and treated as a list of disconnected subjects. "The best that can be said of it is, that it is a rapid table of contents which a deity might run over in his mind while he was thinking of creating a world and had not yet determined how to put it together," wrote Whitehead.[3] In the natural world, knowledge cannot be confined to discrete disciplinary boundaries or subject fields. Consequently, if the subject matters in the school are to have meaning in the life of the learner and significance for the wider society, then the different domains of codified knowledge must be treated in their interdependence. Unfortunately, the problem of "the fatal disconnection of subjects," which Whitehead addressed, remains pervasive not only as the result of our age of knowledge specialism but also because skills are taught apart from ideas, and ideas are treated as remote from application.

The university scholar–specialist is concerned with the production of knowledge in his or her own domain or discipline. When the problem of *curriculum* is raised, the view of the specialist as specialist is to see the problem in terms of the preparation of budding knowledge specialists. But when the problem of *curriculum* is raised in terms of what knowledge/ability is needed for the educated person in a free society, we are placing ourselves outside the discrete, specialized knowledge domains or disciplines.[4] In so doing, we are compelled to give reflective consideration to the need to reconstruct knowledge in relation to our understanding of the nature of the learner and the kind of life the good person is to lead in the good society, to paraphrase Bode.[5] This task is compounded enormously by the conflicting views on the nature of the learner, the demands of society, and the needed design and function of the curriculum. It is no wonder, then, that "the curriculum is not something which it is fashionable to ponder."

The influence of progressive educators during the early decades of this century necessitated a profound change in the conception of curriculum to meet the changing conceptions of knowledge, changing conceptions of the learner as the result of advances in the behavioral sciences (particularly in connection with environmentalism), and changing expectations of the function of education in the light of democratic social theory. Nevertheless, to this day the conception and function of the curriculum remain a matter of great ferment, reflecting divisions in philosophical outlook and conflicting societal demands. When Van Doren contended that "all other problems are solved when the problem of curriculum is solved," he was referring to the fact that the function of the curriculum denotes the function of the school.

In this chapter the "problem of curriculum" is examined through four conflicting curriculum rationales and in the light of changing societal expectations. The conflicting curriculum rationales are represented as four controlling themes for the curriculum: (1) fundamental skills/literacy, (2) preservation and transmission of the cultural heritage, (3) knowledge production, and (4) individual and social growth. These rationales, in turn, correspond to the contrasting curriculum functions of (1) basic education, (2) liberal education, (3) specialized education (disciplinary), and (4) general education.

Supervisors need to have a perspective as to how these conflicting rationales and controlling themes have affected the curriculum over the years, if they are not to be caught up in the repetitive cycles of narrowly conceived measures for educational reform.

FUNDAMENTAL SKILLS/LITERACY

As discussed in Chapter 9, "back-to-basics"—the rallying cry of the essentialists—has been a recurrent demand during the twentieth century. The call for a return to the fundamentals tends to accompany periods of social and educational retrenchment. But basic education in the three R's gained great impetus as the result of the rising industrialism in England during the early nineteenth century. According to the late J. D. Bernal, a noted British scientist and science historian, "the new working class needed enough acquaintance with the three R's to do their jobs properly, and provision for teaching them was reluctantly provided on the cheapest possible basis. But there was all the more reason for seeing that the education of the masses did not go too far, and that it introduced no unsettling ideas."[6]

The situation in the United States was similar. However, the great waves of immigrants to these shores during the first three decades of the twentieth century gave further impetus to basic education for literacy and eventually for Americanization in the schools of our major cities where these millions of immigrants were concentrated.

Early on, American progressive educators warned of the impending danger in this country of adopting the Old World practice of providing a basic education for the masses, and a full and rich curriculum for the more privileged. In Dewey's words,

> He who is poorly acquainted with the history of the efforts to improve elementary education in our large cities does not know that the chief protest against progress is likely to come from successful business men. They have clamored for the three R's as the essential and exclusive material of primary education—knowing well enough that their own children would be able to get the things they protest against. Thus they have attacked as fads and frills every enrichment of the curriculum which did not lend itself to narrow economic ends. Let us stick to

business, to the essentials, has been their plea, and by business they meant enough of the routine skills in letters and figures to make those leaving the elementary school at about the fifth or sixth grade useful in *their* business, irrespective of whether pupils left school with an equipment for advance and with the ambition to try to secure better social and economic conditions for their children than they themselves had enjoyed.[7]

Essentialism in the Contemporary Scene

Dewey's concern is not a fading echo of history. As shown in Chapter 9, the 1970s and early 1980s were characterized by curriculum retrenchment through back-to-basics. The mandate to supervisors and teachers was clear: Teach for higher scores on the state minimum-competency tests. During the 1980s, business leaders were being called on to serve on a number of national panels to prescribe the needed reforms to serve our nation's industrial sector. In the wake of the shortcomings of the back-to-basics retrenchment of the 1970s, the call of the 1980s was for the "new basics."

The persistence of essentialism is reflected in a number of contemporary documents on educational reform. It will be recalled that the National Assessment of Educational Progress (NAEP), early on sponsored by the Education Commission of the States, triggered the individual states to establish statewide minimum-competency testing programs during the 1970s. By the early 1980s it was becoming evident through the testing program of the NAEP that the emphasis on minimum competencies through the back-to-basics movement had resulted in emphasis being given to narrow skills at the expense of thinking abilities.[8]

The "New Basics." In 1983 the Task Force on Education for Economic Growth of the Education Commission of the States, with a membership comprised mainly of chief executives of major corporations and governors, issued a report calling for a broadened conception of "basic education" so as to "upgrade the American labor force from top to bottom" in the wake of foreign competition for global markets.[9] In the words of the report,

> Over the years, our concept of *literacy,* for example, has undergone considerable revision, as technology has advanced in America and as the demand for knowledge has increased in the workplace. . . . Today, to most of us, basic literacy implies the ability to read, write and compute—at a rudimentary level to be sure, but at a level higher than was common among unskilled workers a century ago or even fifty years ago. . . .
>
> What we consider the basic skills today can be described fairly simply. In most states and communities that have established minimum competency requirements, "basic skills" are defined in minimal, rudimentary terms as follows:
>
> First, the ability to comprehend literally a simple written passage.
>
> Second, the ability to compute with whole numbers.
>
> Third, the mastery of writing mechanics.
>
> When state or local assessment projects test students for minimum competency it is these minimal skills that are examined. We expect our schools to impart much more than these basic skills; we demand that they impart no less. . . .

Beginning *now,* our definition of basic skills must expand to include more of the skills that will be demanded in tomorrow's technologically-sophisticated workplace. . . .

Competency in reading, for example, may well include not only the ability to literally decipher a simple written passage, but other skills as well: the ability to analyze and summarize, for example, and the ability to interpret passages inferentially as well as literally.

Basic minimal mathematical competency may well include, in the future, not just the ability to compute with whole numbers, but also . . . the ability to use arithmetic computations in solving practical problems.

Competency in writing may well comprise not just the ability to write a sentence or paragraph, but the ability to gather and organize information coherently.[10]

In envisioning the upgrading of the three R's so that they are related to knowledge applications and somewhat higher-ordered thinking skills, the task force avoided any mention of the need for students to examine problems and issues in the workplace, in government, in our economy, and in our society at large. Apparently, higher-ordered thinking skills are to be developed without examining extant social problems and issues.

"Mastery of the Minima" for the Masses. In essentialist fashion, Sizer sees the responsibility of the school being concerned with "mastery of the minima" for the masses, with compulsory attendance ceasing before senior high school, when such "mastery" is attained.[11] This view suffers from the questionable premise that there is such a set of "minima" to be "mastered," rather than recognizing that skills are not end points but are used as means to enhance growth in understanding and in the working power of intelligence. Also reflected in Sizer's view is the attitude that public education for the masses should be sharply delimited in scope and function, and that education beyond the eight years of schooling should be the province of a select and privileged population as it was during the early years of this century.

The Resurrected Doctrine of Mental Discipline

Essentialists and perennialists alike regard the traditional academic studies as preeminently suited for "developing mental powers," for "intellectual training," for the "discipline and furniture of the student's mind."[12] The doctrine of mental discipline, although long discredited through the pioneering research of Thorndike and Woodworth,[13] remains a basic tenet of essentialist and perennialist belief.

Built on the three R's of the elementary school are the fundamental academic disciplines of English (grammar, literature, and composition), mathematics, science, history, and foreign languages.[14] Other studies are regarded as nonessential or as "frills." Yet the curricular retrenchment through back-to-basics during the 1970s was so severe that even some essentialists began to have second thoughts. For example, the Council for Basic Education issued a bulletin defending the arts while acknowledging that the council's original canon did not include the arts in basic education.[15] For the essentialists, there appeared to be truth in the old aphorism, "Beware of what you want, for you might get it."

This clearly augurs for the responsibility of supervisors, curriculum directors, and administrators not to be taken in by narrow reductionist prescriptions by special-interest groups for curricular retrenchment. The curriculum must be treated holistically in its comprehensiveness.

College Dominance over the High School: The Academic–Nonacademic Dualism

The continuing powerful influence of the essentialist prescriptions for basic education is reflected in a report of the College Board issued in 1983 under the title *Academic Preparation for College*. "Improving preparation for college can help improve the quality of high school education overall, whether or not students intend to enter college," declared the report.[16]

The Bias for Basic Academics. Ignoring any consideration of the role and function of general education and the rich literature on general education in the secondary school and college, the report proceeded to reduce the curriculum to six "Basic Academic Competencies" necessary for "learning the Basic Academic Subjects."

In essentialist fashion, the report identified the "Basic Academic Competencies" as reading, writing, speaking and listening, mathematics [sic], reasoning, and studying; and the "Basic Academic Subjects" as English, the arts, mathematics, science, social studies (including history), and foreign language. In describing the arts among the Basic Academic Subjects, the report made no mention of the industrial arts, despite the fact that the fine arts evolved historically from the crafts.

The College Board report also recommended the inclusion of computer competency on the ground that it is an emerging "basic skill complementary to other competencies, such as reading, writing, mathematics, and reasoning."[17]

Failure to Recognize the Authentic Role of the School. As expected, *Academic Preparation for College* reflected the dominant influence of college professors who served as members of the project group that produced the report. In neglecting the authentic function of the secondary school in working with young adolescents and the need to develop a curriculum authentically suited to such a population, the report reasoned that preparation for college should be the principal function of the high school curriculum, and that such preparation will best serve all youth. Thus the function of the high school is seen as subordinate to the college, and taking steps to strengthen the college-preparatory curriculum is seen as the correct way to strengthen the curriculum for all youth. "Discussions with leaders of business and industry confirm," stated the report, "that much of the learning described here also can be valuable to students going directly into the world of work."[18]

The authors of the College Board report did not stop with the high school, but viewed the task of reordering the curriculum priorities of the high school as necessarily extending downward into the junior high school and elementary school. "Improving preparation for college will also involve strengthening elementary and junior high school curricula," declared the report.[19] Thus the junior high school and the elementary school are also to subordinate their curricula to the college, rather than providing curricula authentically suited to their pupil populations.

In short, the underlying premise of the College Board report is that "what students need to learn in high school is [to be] approached from the perspective of what is necessary for effective learning in college."[20] Following this logic, it can be held that what children need to learn in elementary school is to be approached from the perspective of what is necessary for effective learning in high school. That such premises fly in the face of what is known about child and adolescent growth and development would appear to be of no concern of those who see education as a "tooling-up" process.

Basic Education Versus General Education. As discussed later in this chapter, the view is widely shared among the professoriate that the elementary and secondary school curriculum should be concentrated on basic academic skills and basic academic subjects. Even some of the most fervent advocates of general education in the college choose to see the high school curriculum as properly being delimited to academic skills and to the traditional academic subjects. Where they choose to recognize the college experience as authentic in the lives of college students, they see the elementary and secondary school experience as preparation for some remote future.

An understanding of child and adolescent development would reveal that youngsters cannot put their needs and interests on a waiting list. Moreover, there is the persistent need in a free society to engage adolescents in the examination of the pervading problems and issues of our times. In effect, to postpone such study until the college years would be tantamount to denying the majority of our youth who do not go on to college their rights as citizens. The same consideration also applies to the denial of vocational studies in the high school, when in fact vocational education is part and parcel of a college education.

Failure to Build on the Body of Research Literature. It is reasonable to assume that in determining what is necessary for successful preparation for college, the College Board would draw from the rich body of research literature on the subject. However, such was not the case in the College Board report of 1983.

The monumental Eight-Year Study (1933–1941) revealed that the graduates of high schools that had developed experimental curricula which departed sharply from the traditional college-preparatory studies were more successful in college than their compeers who had followed the traditional curriculum to meet college-entrance requirements. Moreover, "the graduates of the most experimental schools were strikingly more successful than their matchees."[21] The matching of the students in the study and the comparisons of the matched pairs were done by the more than 300 colleges and universities that had waived their entrance requirements for the graduates of the experimental schools. The curriculum of the more experimental schools was characterized by interdisciplinary studies in general education focused on persistent problems in the lives of adolescents as members of a democratic society, giving emphasis to critical thinking and problem solving. Emphasis also was given to faculty–student participation in curriculum development and in improving the life of the school. The students from the experimental schools, most of whom were from public high schools that had participated in the study, not only outperformed their compeers academically, but were adjudged by the colleges as having a higher degree of intellectual curiosity and a more active concern for what was going on in the world. As the dean of Columbia College of Columbia University reported, "It looks as if the stimulus and the initiative which the less conventional approach to secondary school education affords sends on to college better human materials than we have obtained in the past."[22]

Looking back on the several volumes of reports on the Eight-Year Study, Cremin commented that "it is a pity they appeared in the middle of a war, for they never received the attention they deserve; even after two decades the challenge and excitement of the venture are apparent to the most casual reader."[23] There is a lesson here. Supervisors need to be aware of the heritage of research on the curriculum if they are to be able to assess proposals for educational reform critically, and if they are to be key agents for educational improvement.

Need for Diversified Studies Without Tracking. Subsequent studies have revealed that diversified studies in the high school can benefit college-bound students. For example, a study was made of 130 matched pairs of students enrolled in the University of Michigan and other Michigan colleges, comparing those who had freely elected business and industrial courses in high school, in addition to their academic studies, against students whose high school programs were delimited to academic, college-preparatory subjects. The findings revealed that the students who had taken the business and industrial courses in high school achieved significantly higher grade-point averages in college than did their matchees.[24] "Not only does there seem to be a point of 'no return on investment' in the college preparatory curriculum, but failure to recognize the value of so-called nonacademic programs may deprive many students of enriching experiences important to their success in college," concluded the researcher.[25]

Not only are typing and shorthand of great use in college, but the future engineer or scientist can benefit greatly from the industrial course work in high school. Furthermore, there is the great value in the industrial arts and fine arts in contributing to general education. The Harvard Report clearly recognized this, as expressed in the following statement concerning the industrial course work in high school:

> For those who intend to go into scientific or technological work, it [shop work] has special relevance. The manipulation of objects, the use of tools, and the construction of simple apparatus all are required for entry into the world of experimentation. Even the pure mathematician is greatly aided by shop experience; the forms, contours, and interrelations of three-dimensional objects provides a stimulus and satisfaction not to be achieved altogether within the limits of plane diagrams. The lack of shop training is at present a most serious deterrent to entry into all types of technological work and to college postgraduate training in science, medicine, and engineering.[26]

Turning to the value of the industrial arts in general education, the Harvard Report made these observations:

> Most students who expect to go to college are now offered an almost wholly verbal type of preparatory training, while hand training and the direct manipulation of objects are mainly reserved for the vocational fields. This is a serious mistake. . . . The direct contact with materials, the manipulation of simple tools, the capacity to create by hand from a concept in the mind—all these are indispensable aspects of the general education of everyone.[27]

Not only do many college educators today fail to recognize the benefits to be derived from such experience in the elementary and secondary school, but they regard the industrial arts, along with the technical vocational studies, as having little educative value.[28]

Similar attitudes toward the arts in the schools are widely prevalent even though the arts have gained a recognized place in the college curriculum. A study was conducted at Rutgers University comparing the college achievement of undergraduates who had taken a considerable number of courses in art and music in high school against those whose high school programs were confined almost exclusively to college-preparatory subjects. Initial differences in the population in aptitude and socioeconomic status were corrected by the analysis of covariance. All the students in the study were majoring in fields other than art and music in college. The findings revealed that both the male and female students who had taken a significantly higher proportion of nonacademic courses in high school (art and music) did at least as well in their academic performance in college than those whose programs in high school were predominantly concentrated on academic studies.[29]

The dualism between academic and nonacademic studies in the schools serves to deny youngsters the opportunity for learning experiences that can provide for enrichment and for the development of lifelong interests. This dualism also denies the contribution that the so-called nonacademic studies can make in general education.

PRESERVATION AND TRANSMISSION OF THE CULTURAL HERITAGE

The perennialist is concerned with the preservation and transmission of the cultural heritage and regards the great literary works of the Western world as the exemplars of this heritage. The higher literary education is the basis of liberal education, and liberal education is to be built on the basic education provided during the lower years of schooling. "The ideal education," wrote the late Robert Hutchins, "is not a utilitarian education. It is an education calculated to develop the mind." To this, added Hutchins, "I have old-fashioned prejudices in favor of the three R's and the liberal arts, in favor of trying to understand the greatest (literary) works that the human race has produced."[30]

Common Tenets of Perennialism and Essentialism

The perennialist shares with the essentialist many tenets, including the conception of mind as a muscle to be exercised by certain academic studies and the depreciation of the social studies, industrial arts, studio arts, vocational studies, and electives. Both condemn the place in the curriculum of studies dealing with contemporary problems and issues. Both share in the dualistic tenets of mind over body, academic over vocational, cultural over practical, thinking over doing, thinking over feeling.

Mental Discipline. To the perennialist and the essentialist, the best training for the mind, particularly in the elementary school, is through memory exercise or by filling the mind with facts and truths. "Elementary education can do nothing better for a child than store his memory with things deserving to be there," declared Mark Van Doren, and "he will be grateful for them when he grows up, even if he kicks now."[31] Or, in the words of Admiral Rickover, an essentialist: "For all children, the educational process must be one of collecting factual knowledge to the limit of their absorptive capacity. . . . To acquire such knowledge, fact upon fact, takes time and effort. Nothing can really make it 'fun.' "[32] Such views echo the perennialist dictum of Aristotle, that "youths are not to be instructed with a view to their amusement, for learning is no amusement, but is accompanied with pain."[33]

Literary Bias of Perennialism

Where the perennialist sees the Great Books as the repositories of "permanent truths" and "immutable values," the essentialist holds that intellectual excellence is derived through the systematic study of the logically organized, fundamental academic disciplines, including science. "Our erroneous notion of progress has thrown the classics and the liberal arts out of the curriculum, over-emphasized the empirical sciences, and made education the servant of any contemporary movements in society," argued Hutchins.[34] Although Hutchins was a great advocate of universal education and was on the same side as the progressivists as a staunch defender of academic freedom, his curriculum prescriptions were epitomized in the old literary tradition of liberal education. In this vein, he opposed vocational studies and electives at the secondary and undergraduate collegiate levels and held that the cultivation of the rational powers is derived through the liberal arts, capped by the Great Books, which, in the words of one of his disciples, "are a repository of knowledge and wisdom, a tradition of culture which must initiate each new generation."[35]

The Dualism Between the Cultural and Practical Studies. Dewey repeatedly challenged the dualistic tenets of perennialism and pointed to the dangers to democracy when the so-called "cultural" studies are held aloof from the studies that are socially serviceable, as though practical studies are not liberative of imagination and thinking power. "Only superstition makes us believe that the two are necessarily hostile so that a subject is illiberal because it is useful and cultural because it is useless."[36]

Ironically, although Hutchins was a severe critic of many aspects of American public education and was at odds with Dewey's experimentalist ideas, in his later years he became a staunch defender of our educational system while reappraising Dewey's ideas in a far more favorable light as the result of the rise of the child-centered radical romanticism during the late 1960s and early 1970s. In this regard, Hutchins proceeded to defend Dewey from misrepresentation by the advocates of rampant child-centered pedagogy.[37] Yet he never retreated from his staunch dualistic premise that the truly liberalizing studies are embodied in the great literary works of Western civilization, and that the practical and vocational studies are not truly educative.

Two Cultures: The Great Curriculum Divide

Although essentialism has exerted a more powerful influence over elementary and secondary education, perennialism continues to divide academia into "two cultures"—a problem addressed by Dewey and later by C. P. Snow.[38] The views of many contemporary perennialists on liberal education continue to carry an aristocratic invidium. Such an invidium is rooted historically in ancient Greece, where a liberal education was deemed the province of the freemen in their life of leisure, as opposed to the practical training for the slaves who do the work.

For example, in contending that the modern age of "mass man," with its emphasis on egalitarianism and the rejection of elitism, has brought about a decline in the quality of civilization, Barbara Tuchman dismisses the contributions of science and technology on the ground that "they belong to a different scheme of things from the creative components of civilized life."[39]

Humanities Versus Science. In holding the humanities aloof from the sciences, humanists ignore the very revolution wrought by science as a mode of thought in freeing humanity from ignorance, superstition, dogmatic authority, and blind dictate. This continuing bias against science on the part of perennialists, who see themselves as "humanists," stems from the ancient doctrine that the cultivation of the intellectual virtues is accomplished only through the "permanent" studies that constitute our intellectual inheritance. It is through such studies that the "permanent" truths are to be found. The notion of a priori, absolute, or permanent truths is inimical to science, for science sees the physical and biological universe as dynamic and evolving.

In extolling the study of the humanities, the perennialists or "humanists" regard the humanities as "the great human achievements" as exemplified by the masterworks of Western literature, arts, and philosophy. Hence by excluding science and technology from the "humanities," from "the great human achievements," the humanists help create a two-culture split. "Armed with all the powers, enjoying all the riches they owe to science," commented Jacques Monod, "our societies are still trying to live and to teach systems of values already blasted at the root by science itself."[40]

The Humanities: Looking Backward

As discussed later, general education, as contrasted against traditional liberal education, is conceived to bridge the great divide between the cultural heritage and the modern scientific studies in relation to the life of the learner in a free society. Yet the forces for traditional liberal education still persist. In response to the increasing knowledge specialism and the growing concern for career goals on the part of college students, the National Endowment for the Humanities issued a report by its chairman in 1984 entitled *To Reclaim a Legacy*, in which it was noted that "the humanities, and particularly the study of Western civilization, have lost their central place in the undergraduate curriculum."[41]

Definition of Humanities and Their Place in the College Curriculum. The report by William J. Bennett for the National Endowment for the Humanities defined the humanities as "the best that has been said, thought, written, and otherwise expressed about the human experience," and contended that "in order to tap the consciousness and memory of civilization, one must confront [sic] these texts and works of art." The report went on to describe the humanities as "a body of knowledge and a means of inquiry that convey serious truths, defensible judgments, and significant ideas. Properly taught, the humanities bring together the perennial questions of human life and the greatest works of history, literature, philosophy, and art."

The following areas of fundamental "knowledge in the humanities" were prescribed in the report as essential to a college education:

> Because our society is the product and we the inheritors of Western civilization, American students need an understanding of its origins and development, from its roots in antiquity to the present. . . .
>
> A careful reading of several masterworks of English, American, and European literature.
>
> An understanding of the most significant ideas and debates in the history of philosophy.
>
> Demonstrable proficiency in a foreign language (either modern or classical) and the ability to view that language as an avenue into another culture.[42]

In addition to the foregoing prescriptions, the report recommended the study of the history, literature, religion, and philosophy of at least one non-Western culture. And, almost as an afterthought, the report added the history of science and technology (but not the study of laboratory science). A list of specific authors of literary works and historical documents was offered for required reading, beginning with classical antiquity. Not a single scientist was on the list, and only four American writers were included.

Although the humanities were described in the report as "a body of knowledge and means of inquiry that convey serious truths, defensible judgments, and significant ideas," no mention was made of scientific inquiry as a contrasting mode of thought. And if the humanities are said to represent the great achievements of humanity, one must ask why the sciences are excluded. The answer is that in omitting the modern natural sciences and social sciences from its recommended core of common studies, the report of the National Endowment for the Humanities was revealing the perspective and bias of the perennialist tradition.

Figure 11–1 is extracted from the 1984 report, *To Reclaim a Legacy*, written by William J. Bennett, chairman of the National Endowment for the Humanities,

---

What Should be Read?

I am often asked what I believe to be the most significant works in the humanities. . . .

The works I mention virtually define the development of the Western mind. . . .

The works and authors I have in mind include, but are not limited to, the following:

From classical antiquity—Homer, Sophocles, Thucydides, Plato, Aristotle, and Virgil;

From medieval, Renaissance, and seventeenth-century Europe—Dante, Chaucer, Machiavelli, Montaigne, Shakespeare, Hobbes, Milton, and Locke;

From eighteenth-through twentieth-century Europe—Swift, Rousseau, Austen, Wordsworth, Toqueville, Dickens, George Eliot, Dostoyevsky, Marx, Nietzsche, Tolstoy, Mann, and T. S. Eliot;

From American literature and historical documents—the Declaration of Independence, the Federalist Papers, the Constitution, the Lincoln-Douglas Debates, Lincoln's Gettysburg Address, Martin Luther King, Jr.'s "Letter from Birmingham Jail" and "I have a dream . . ." speech, and such authors as Hawthorne, Melville, Twain, and Faulkner.

Finally, I must mention the Bible, which is the basis for so much subsequent history, literature, and philosophy.

Figure 11–1. "What should be read?" Suggested required readings for all undergraduates.

Source: [From William J. Bennett, Chair., Study Group on the State of Learning in the Humanities in Higher Education, *To Reclaim a Legacy*. Washington, D.C.: National Endowment for the Humanities, 1984, pp. 10–11.]

who became U.S. Secretary of Education in 1985. The list of works in Figure 11–1 was compiled by Bennett as illustrative of what all college students might be required to read "to receive an adequate education in the culture and civilization of which they are members." Bennett goes on to describe his list as comprising "the most significant works in the humanities"—works that "virtually define the development of the Western mind."[43] How the development of the Western mind can be "defined" without examining works in the sciences and social sciences is never explained. This illiberal attitude reveals the bias of traditional liberal education. Instead of creating the needed sense of unity, it sets the humanities apart from and above all other studies as though culture is something that is cultivated only from the exemplars of the past.

The Humanities in the High School. The list offered in Figure 11–1 for the college student has its counterpart for the high school student. Secretary Bennett's prescription for the college curriculum today reveals a serious bias that has a long tradition not only in the college, but in the high school. For example, Figure 11–2 contains the suggested "basic readings" for the ninth and twelfth

---

Suggestions for Basic Readings in High School Literature

THE 9TH GRADE

Classic Mythology (Bullfinch or Edith Hamilton), the *Odyssey* in a good prose translation, a book of the Bible in the King James version perhaps The Book of Ruth (to be taught strictly as literature). *Sir Gawain and the Green Knight* in a modernized version, some Malory, *Don Quixote, I,* a Shakespeare play complete (a minimum of one Shakespeare play should be read in each of the four years), *Robinson Crusoe, Great Expectations,* one of Tennyson's *Idylls,* and a modern novel like Lewis's *Arrowsmith.*

THE 12TH GRADE

Together with the study of Chaucer's English, readings should be assigned in *The Canterbury Tales* (the Prologue and a tale or two) in the original. Then could follow a study of Spencer's shorter poems, the fourth Shakespeare play, Milton's *Comus* and *Lycidas* and some prose, probably the *Areopagitica.* Johnson's *Preface to Shakespeare* and his *Life of Milton* could accompany these readings or follow upon them, and Pope's *Rape of the Lock* could be read together with Johnson's *Life of Pope. Tom Jones* would seem an appropriate eighteenth century novel. A carefully selected group of poems not previously studied from the five great romantic poets could provide the basis of a very intensive study of the short poem. A substantial Victorian novel like *Middlemarch* seems in order, along with the dramatic monologues of Browning and the lyrics of Tennyson. One of the great works of discursive prose should certainly be read, Mill's *On Liberty* or Ruskin's *Crown of Wild Olive,* for example. Then a Hardy novel, Conrad's *Heart of Darkness* or a longer novel, the poems of Hardy and Housman, and concluding considerations of the relations and distinctions between poetry and prose.

Figure 11–2. Suggested basic readings in high school literature, grades 9 and 12, San Francisco Curriculum Survey Committee, 1960.

Source: [From Report of the San Francisco Curriculum Survey Committee (San Francisco: Board of Education, 1960), pp. 33, 34.]

grades, extracted from a master list for each high school grade, as compiled by professors of English from the University of California, Berkeley, and Stanford University, in connection with the San Francisco Curriculum Survey of 1960. Not only is the bias toward classical authors evident, but it is clear that the professors failed to take into account the nature of the adolescent, the relationship of literature to contemporary social concerns, and the need to consider the effects of such readings on the adolescent's attitudes toward literature and how these attitudes are to be developed from such study.

This is not to deprecate the place of classical literature in the curriculum, but rather to point to the need to treat such literature as vitally related to the life of the learner and to the function of general education. As such, the literary works are not given a hallowed place in the curriculum, but share with the other studies the task of developing an enlightened citizenry for a free society. In the past, the humanists have treated the humanities as Holy Grail.

Turning to the contemporary scene, the 1984 report of the National Endowment for the Humanities criticized the secondary school for the decline in the study of the humanities over a period extending from the late 1960s to the 1980s, failing to acknowledge that the schools during this period were being buffeted by the back-to-basics wave of retrenchment and minimum-competency testing. Yet in also criticizing the high school for failing to prepare students in the essential skills of reading and writing, the report of the National Endowment for the Humanities neglected to acknowledge that such shortcomings were the result of the reductionist back-to-basics movement with its narrow emphasis on skill-drill mechanics, and the neglect of idea-oriented teaching and learning.

Moreover, the report of the National Endowment for the Humanities failed to mention the failures in connection with its early efforts to give the humanities a prominent place in the school curriculum. In the late 1960s and early 1970s, in reaction against the curriculum imbalance created by the priority given to the sciences and mathematics during the Cold War and space race, and aided by the creation of the National Endowment for the Humanities (1965), most of our larger high schools created courses in the humanities.

These courses were variously conceived and construed. Instead of reconstructing the curriculum in general education, humanities courses were introduced as electives. In many of our high schools, the humanities courses were elected mainly by college-bound students. In schools with large interracial populations, it was commonly seen that the racial lines were divided between students electing humanities courses and those electing courses in black studies.

The humanities courses never provided the needed curriculum synthesis for general education, for they not only were offered as another set of electives appealing to a special population, but served to exacerbate the divide with the sciences. As Harold Taylor pointed out in examining the humanities in the schools,

> I question the whole idea of the humanities as a special area of the curriculum designed to take care of human values which, presumably, the rest of the curriculum can then safely ignore while it goes on ladling out its generous supply of facts. The humanities are not culture-containers, or value-containers, or courses in the higher things. In one sense there is no such things as the humanities, unless we are willing to accept the idea that science is not a humanistic discipline and that facts have nothing to do with values.[44]

Unfortunately, the humanities were introduced as a reaction against the curriculum priorities and hierarchy created by the Cold War and space race, instead of serving as a vehicle for curriculum reconstruction and unity through general education. As we entered the era of curriculum retrenchment through back-to-basics during the 1970s, the humanities once again went out of vogue.

The prescriptions of the National Endowment for the Humanities to "reclaim the legacy" of the humanities during the 1980s were based on the literary and philosophic traditions that were dominant before secondary and higher education became universally accessible and before the modern scientific and vocational studies gained a place in the high school. The likely failure to "reclaim the legacy" of the humanities would appear to stem from the archaic piety that holds the humanities above, apart, and in opposition to the modern studies which have transformed our civilization. The needed sense of unity through diversity would have to be sought through general education, not through the traditional and illiberal role of "liberal education."

Liberal Education, General Education, and the Demands of Democracy

At midcentury, Conant contrasted the great divide in the curricular prescriptions of the adherents of liberal education, derived from the dominant literary and philosophic traditions as interpreted by literary scholars and connoisseurs before World War I, against the advocates of general education for *all* American youth in a democratic society. Conant went on to warn that we will have to discard the "cultural presuppositions" that undergirded education in an earlier era, in view of the demands of American democracy—a social setting vastly different from anything the world has ever seen before. Allies of the humanities must ruthlessly reexamine their premises and must make their studies "really relevant to the present scene," warned Conant.[45]

Opposition to the Comprehensive High School and the Comprehensive Curriculum. Contrary to Dewey and Conant, who both viewed the comprehensive high school as a vital institution for American democracy, perennialists and essentialists are unalterably opposed to a school that offers vocational studies along with general education, and exploratory and enrichment electives. They continue to see the school as properly and exclusively concentrated on the traditional academic subjects, with some concession given to the fine arts, especially the study of art as appreciation of the cultural heritage.

Efforts to Resurrect the Classical Languages in the Secondary School. Many perennialists recommend a revival of the classical languages in the schools on the ground that they are valuable for learning transfer, despite the compelling evidence to the contrary.[46] For example, a 1983 report of the College Board offered the following argument in favor of such languages for college-bound students:

> The classical languages and their literatures show the pervasive influence of Greek and Roman cultures on social and political institutions throughout Western history. Many of the words of English, Spanish, and the other major Western languages are present in English, particularly in law and medicine. . . .
> Latin and ancient Greek are generally taught not as spoken languages but as literary languages. Thus, the two principal outcomes are reading comprehension and some knowledge of Roman or Greek culture.[47]

Oddly, the statement above appeared in a publication produced through the College Board's Project Equality, which was organized "to ensure equality of opportunity for post-secondary education for all students."[48]

A Perennialist Manifesto for the Schools

Another widely read publication during the early 1980s was Mortimer Adler's *Paideia Proposal: An Educational Manifesto* (1982), calling for the reform of elementary and secondary education along traditionalist lines. Although Adler, like Hutchins before him, claims that his curricular prescriptions serve the interests of all children and youth and should be required of all, his curriculum is limited to the academic studies and fine arts.

In this connection, Adler and his "Paideia Group" prescribe a tripartite gradation of studies from grades 1 through 12 consisting of (1) the acquisition of organized knowledge in the academic studies and fine arts through didactic instruction; (2) the development of intellectual skills in the operations of reading, writing, speaking, listening, calculating, and exercising critical judgment through coaching, drilling, and practice exercises; and (3) the development of enlarged understanding of ideas and values by means of Socratic questioning and discussion of great literary works and other works of art.[49] No vocational studies or electives are allowed, except for the elective of a foreign language.

Exercising and Elevating the Mind. According to Adler, it is the third part of his tripartite gradation of studies which "aims at raising the mind up from a lesser or weaker understanding to a stronger and fuller one," and "the cooperative art of the teacher depends on the teacher's understanding of how the mind learns by the exercise of its own powers."[50]

The following definition, offered in parody by Ambrose Bierce, appears to portray accurately the conception of mind held by perennialists:

> MIND, n. A mysterious form of matter secreted by the brain. Its chief activity consists in the endeavor to ascertain its own nature, the futility of the attempt being due to the fact that it has nothing but itself to know itself with.[51]

Perennialists regard Socratic questioning and discussion of the great literary works as the highest form of intellective activity. But anyone who has experienced or witnessed such techniques to any intensive and extensive degree knows how easily a pliant class of students can be manipulated by a glib professional.

The conception of the curriculum as a storehouse of the exemplars of organized and recorded experience of humanity may well be regarded as out of touch with the modern world, but it nevertheless survives among many of those in academe who profess to being humanists.

The conception of mind as perpetuated by perennialists and essentialists may be totally at odds with our biological knowledge, but the heavy emphasis given to rote learning in the schools would indicate that such an archaic conception lives on in pedagogical practice.

KNOWLEDGE PRODUCTION

The university is concerned not only with the transmission of knowledge, but with the production of new knowledge through research. Research by university scholars has become increasingly specialized with the great expansion of knowledge and the explosion of information. The knowledge specialization of the university is reflected in the disciplines and subdisciplines of organized scholarship for research and teaching. The scholar-specialists within each of the disciplines and subdisciplines are concerned with advancing their own specialized research and scholarship, and preparing budding scholar-specialists who will carry on in this endeavor.

The Discipline-Oriented University and the Mission-Oriented Society

On the surface the role and function of the university as described above may appear clear and direct. However, as Alvin Weinberg, a noted nuclear physicist, points out, our society is mission oriented in that it must seek resolution of problems that cannot be confined within the discrete disciplines, whereas the university is discipline oriented in that the problems dealt with are largely generated and solved within the discrete disciplines.

The Student as Citizen. The great divide between specialized disciplinary knowledge and applied knowledge poses serious problems for society and for the student as a citizen.[52] Great problems arise in the undergraduate curriculum when the question is raised: "What is an educated person?" This question impels educators to look beyond the separate specialized disciplines because these disciplines are geared to prepare future scholar-specialists and because the educated person is more than this.

Furthermore, most of the students will not become university scholar-specialists but will enter a variety of professional careers in the wider society. Moreover, the professional schools of the university are concerned with preparing professional practitioners for society at large, as well as being concerned with research to advance professional knowledge and application. Although the professional schools draw from the specialized disciplines and subdisciplines, their task is more mission oriented than discipline oriented. For example, although medicine or engineering draws on certain basic sciences, the study of the basic sciences will not produce a physician or engineer. Moreover, research problems in medicine or engineering are not confined to the basic sciences, but require interdisciplinary investigation. Yet the graduate of the professional school is still a professional specialist. The point is that an educated person is more than a professional practitioner.

In an essay entitled "Dangers of Specialization," Whitehead warned that university knowledge specialism or professionalized disciplinary knowledge "produces minds in a groove" and

> each profession makes progress, but it is progress in its own groove. Now to be mentally in a groove is to live in contemplating a given set of abstractions. The groove prevents straying across country, and the abstraction abstracts from something to which no further attention is paid. But there is no groove of abstractions which is adequate for the comprehension of human life. Thus in the modern world, the celibacy of the medieval learned class has been replaced by a celibacy of the intellect which is divorced from the concrete contemplation of the

complete facts. Of course, no one is merely a mathematician, or merely a lawyer. People have lives outside their professions or their businesses. But the point is the restraint of serious thought within a groove. The remainder of life is treated superficially, with the imperfect categories of thought derived from one profession.

The dangers arising from this aspect of professionalism are great, particularly in our democratic societies. The directive force of reason is weakened. . . . The specialized functions of the community are performed better and more progressively, but the generalized direction lacks vision . . . so we are left with no expansion of wisdom and with greater need for it.[53]

Whitehead went on to contend that the solution lies in the recognition that general education requires a radically different approach to knowledge than that of specialized analytical knowledge so as to reveal concrete appreciations and provide for the full interplay of emergent and diverse values in society. But because the culture of the university rewards the knowledge specialist working within a discrete discipline or subdiscipline, the universities have tended to resist the radical restructuring of knowledge for general education. But even worse, at periodic intervals, the bias of the university scholar-specialist has been imposed on the curriculum of the elementary and secondary schools to the neglect of giving consideration to the nature of the learner and the need for general education for an enlightened citizenry in a free society.

The Disciplinary Doctrine and the School Curriculum

An extended discussion of the impact of the discipline-centered university on the school curriculum in connection with the national curriculum reforms in the schools during the 1950s and 1960s is provided in this chapter in view of (1) the continuing pressures to this day to subordinate the school curriculum to the narrow interests of university scholar-specialists, (2) the continuing pressures to subordinate the school curriculum to narrow nationalistic interests, (3) the lessons to be learned when there is failure to take account of the nature and needs of the learner and the wider social interest of a free society when reforming the school curriculum, (4) the need to recognize the necessary interdependence of studies in the school curriculum, (5) the need to recognize the vital role of the supervisor and teacher in curriculum development, and (6) the need to engage in formative (ongoing) and summative (total and concluding) curriculum evaluation when developing and implementing curriculum reforms, and to develop and test alternative models rather than adhering to a single doctrine.

The period from the mid-1950s through the 1960s was marked by a concerted effort on an unprecedented scale to impose the discipline-centered model, as conceived by university scholar-specialists, on the elementary and secondary schools. As discussed briefly in Chapter 9, this effort was supported through federal funds which were allocated largely through the National Science Foundation (NSF), giving priority to the sciences and mathematics as a response to the pressures of the Cold War and later to the space race.

The theoretical basis for these curricular reforms was explicated in a report of a conference, composed mainly of university scholar-specialists, convened by the

National Academy of Sciences less than a year following the launching of *Sputnik I*. The report, *The Process of Education,* written by psychologist Jerome Bruner, who chaired the conference, noted that the scholar-specialists "had been brought together to discuss the problems involved in teaching their various disciplines" and that wholesale reforms were required in the school curriculum to meet the "long-range crisis in national security."[54]

Structure of the Discipline. Bruner's report took note of the newly funded NSF projects in school physics and mathematics which were centered on the "structure" of these disciplines, and proceeded to advocate "mastery of the structure of the subject matter" as a principal premise for curriculum reform. Here the concept of "structure" was seen as the fundamental ideas undergirding inquiry within a discipline.[55] Oddly, it was assumed that the emphasis on structure would provide for knowledge applications and transfer of learning when, in fact, the model projects in the new physics and new mathematics, referred to in the report, were centered on theoretical knowledge to the exclusion of knowledge applications.

The Learner as a Miniature Scholar-Specialist. Bruner also advanced the questionable premises, in the light of what was known at the time concerning the developmental stages of the learner, that "intellectual activity anywhere is the same, whether at the frontier of knowledge or in a third-grade classroom," and that "there is a continuity between what a scholar does on the forefront of his discipline and what a child does in approaching it for the first time."[56] From these premises it was reasoned that "the schoolboy learning physics *is* a physicist and it is easier for him to learn physics behaving like a physicist than doing something else."[57]

Failure to See Intellective Development as Stages of Growth. Early in this century, Dewey had noted from observations in his laboratory school that young children think concretely rather than abstractly and

> there is no distinction between experimental science for little children and the work done in the carpenter shop. Such work as they can do in physics or chemistry is not for the purpose of making technical generalizations or even arriving at abstract truths. Children simply like to do things and watch to see what will happen.[58]

Nevertheless, Dewey pointed out that such activity is not merely to be allowed to go on at random, but can be directed in valuable ways through a rich and stimulating learning environment. He went on to stress that intellectual development is "a growing affair," hence "presenting distinctive phases of capacity and interests at different periods." He contrasted this modern view against the old notion of the "boy as a little man and his mind as a little mind," with the traditional course of study being based on the faulty premise that "the subject matter of the adult, logically organized facts and principles, is the natural 'study' of the child—simplified and made easier of course."[59] Dewey proceeded to describe the stages of intellective development, which decades later became a principal focus of Piaget's investigations.[60]

The fact that an older child or a young adolescent has reached the stage of formal operations (ability to think hypothetically) still does not answer the curriculum question of whether such thinking should be directed at and confined to specialized-disciplinary knowledge, or whether it should be energized through interdisciplinary knowledge for personal–social interest and development. There is a marked difference between the study of science to produce a scientist, and the study of science for general education and democratic citizenship. In crediting Dewey with the significance of inquiry–discovery as a teaching method, proponents of the discipline-centered curriculum reforms failed to realize that Dewey was making the case for such a method in illuminating social intelligence, not for advancing specialized-disciplinary knowledge.[61]

By failing to take into account the necessary interdependence of the fundamental factors in the curriculum paradigm, as discussed in detail in Chapter 10—namely, the organization of the curriculum in consonance with the nature of the learner and the conditions necessary for a democratic society—the disciplinary advocates were concerned with only a narrow and one-sided aspect of the curriculum, the learner, and society.

Imposing the Disciplinary Doctrine on the Schools

One might assume that educationists would be well aware of the dangers of seeing the curriculum only in terms of specialized-disciplinary knowledge, and of subordinating the curriculum to the narrow nationalistic interests of Cold War mobilization. But most educationists moved as a flock in endorsing the discipline-centered curriculum reforms and in perpetuating the disciplinary rationale as doctrine. In the words of Phenix, "All curriculum content should be drawn from the disciplines, or, to put it another way, *only* knowledge contained in the disciplines is appropriate to the curriculum," because "the disciplines reveal knowledge in its teachable forms" and "non-disciplined knowledge is unsuitable for teaching and learning."[62]

Phenix went on to contend that "there is no place in the curriculum for ideas which are regarded as suitable for teaching because of the supposed nature, needs, and interests of the learner, but which do not belong in the regular structure of the disciplines."[63] From this perspective, the curriculum is narrowly conceived as the *"guided recapitulation of the processes of inquiry which gave rise to the fruitful bodies of organized knowledge comprising the established disciplines."*[64]

Neglecting Interdisciplinary Knowledge and the Need to Bridge Knowledge and Experience. How disciplinary knowledge is solely appropriate for revealing knowledge in its "teachable forms" when it ignores the nature of the learner and the wider social interest was never explained by Phenix. As Whitehead had observed, "The craving for expansion, for activity, inherent in youth is disgusted by a dry imposition of disciplined knowledge. The discipline, when it comes, should satisfy a natural craving for the wisdom which adds value to bare experience."[65]

In the same vein as Phenix, Schwab warned educationists that unless they build the curriculum according to the structures of the disciplines, "our plans are likely to miscarry and our materials, to misteach" and "there will be failure of learning or gross mislearning by our students." He went on to contend that seeking conceptual schemes that cut across disciplines is a fruitless exercise.[66] Disciplinary advocates such as Schwab and Phenix also avoided consideration of how the different discrete disciplines are to be made to fit together as a coherent curriculum for learners who will not become scholar-specialists in each of the numerous disciplines (In fact, nobody becomes a knowledge specialist in every discipline.)

Inexplicably, Schwab's contention that it is fruitless to seek interdisciplinary conceptual schemes for inquiry and teaching was clearly at odds with developments in his own field of biology, in which advances in knowledge were requiring new fusions between and among the established disciplines, leading to such areas of interdisciplinary inquiry as biochemistry, biophysics, sociobiology, ecology, and so on. As the biologist Bentley Glass commented,

> It is well recognized that many, if not most, scientific breakthroughs come about when the techniques and concepts of quite different scientific fields are brought together in an original synthesis of insight and imagination. Yet it seems unavoidable that the increasing narrowness of specialization tends to reduce the possibility that this will happen.[67]

Albert Szent-Gyorgi, a biochemist and Nobel laureate in medicine, pointed out that the "unification of knowledge is the greatest achievement of science," and he went on to propose: "What I would like to see taught in school is this new subject—nature, not physics and chemistry."[68]

Avoidance of Controlled Research. The disciplinary doctrine became the basis for the national curriculum reform projects during the 1950s and 1960s, giving us the "new mathematics," the "new biology," the "new physics," and the "new chemistry." The practical applications of knowledge and relationships to the life of the learner and to problems in society were neglected in favor of puristic, specialized, theoretical knowledge. Ironically, for the most part, the scientists and mathematicians behind these projects avoided controlled research in developing, evaluating, and promoting their handiwork. When such research was conducted, it was designed to "prove the project," not to test the project against alternative approaches.[69] In effect, the university scholar-specialists were violating their own professed principles in the "search for truth."

"Teacher-proof" Curriculum Packages. Although inquiry–discovery was embraced as the method for teaching and learning, some of the leaders behind the discipline-centered curriculum packages were seeking "teacher-proof" courses of study.[70] In seeking to prevent teachers from "tampering" with the new curriculum packages, the advocates of "teacher-proof" curricula failed to recognize the inherent contradiction of how the learner is to become an inquirer if the teacher is to be prevented from evaluating and modifying the new curriculum packages in the light of the emergent conditions and problems in his or her own school and classroom. How the learner is to become an inquirer when the teacher is regarded by the supervisor as a low-grade technician was never ad-·dressed. Moreover, the learner as inquirer was to be limited to disciplinary inquiry, not to inquiry into problems of personal-social significance.

Unfortunately, the subject supervisors became a party to promoting these national curriculum packages in the schools. They failed to recognize that the function of the schools is not specialized knowledge production. Moreover, they tended to work in isolation from one another in accordance with their disciplinary specialties, thereby contributing to the problem of curriculum isolation and fragmentation.

The Flock Mentality in Academe. The disciplinary doctrine had become so pervasive in the national curriculum-reform projects in the sciences and mathematics during the 1960s that university scholar-specialists in the social sciences and even in English and the visual arts began to move as a flock in embracing this doctrine. With the bulk of the federal funds being allocated, largely through NSF, for the reform of school science and mathematics, it was only a matter of time before scholar-specialists in other fields were demanding support for similar efforts.

In 1962, Project Social Studies and Project English were established through the U.S. Office of Education to create new curricula for the schools in these neglected fields. Despite the modest level of funding in comparison to the NSF-funded projects in the sciences and mathematics, a rash of discipline-centered projects appeared in the separate social sciences, while the more amorphous field of English was being dissected and apportioned into myriad subspecialties along the lines of specialized university scholarship.

Neglect of the Needed Relationship Between Literature and the Social Studies. Although the research over several decades had revealed the desirability of correlating English and the social studies, the National Council of Teachers of English, which had long supported such correlation, proceeded to join with the College English Association and the Modern Language Association in criticizing such correlation and the practice of block-time classes in English and social studies.[71] John DeBoer, who had made a systematic review of the research on the teaching of English over many years, warned that "the sharp distinction between English and the social studies cannot possibly be defended."[72] But such warnings fell on deaf ears as the profession moved as a flock in seeking to embrace the disciplinary doctrine.

Today, any review of cases of the censorship of curricular materials, such as those reported in the *Newsletter on Intellectual Freedom*, will reveal that there are more incidents of the censorship of social ideas in literature than in the social studies. DeBoer's position on the necessary relationship between English (literature and composition) and the social studies would appear to be just as valid today.

Neglect of the Sociocivic Function of Education. Although a democratic society requires that the school curriculum come to grips with the sociocivic function of education, the social scientists promoting the discipline-centered curriculum reforms rejected this function on the ground that disciplinary inquiry in the social sciences is properly directed at advancing disciplinary knowledge. As a sociologist argued, "the plain fact is that many college and university teachers of sociology are not primarily interested in 'educating citizens'," and that the discipline of sociology is "undermined if the study of society is curbed [sic] and channeled by the demands of an ideology, even a democratic one."[73] Such a statement fails to address the consequences of curbing and channeling the study of society into sociology qua discipline, so that the sociocivic problems of democracy are ignored or avoided.

Endorsing the disciplines doctrine, an educational philosopher expressed his regard for the sociocivic function of the curriculum as "sociocivically repulsive."[74] Oddly, in seeking to protect the purity of their respective disciplines against contamination by the sociocivic function, the university scholar-specialists had no qualms about accepting federal funds to develop curricula to meet what Bruner had referred to as "the long-range crisis in national security."[75]

The Limits of Knowledge Purity and Abstraction

The concern for protecting the purity of disciplinary knowledge should have given curricularists and supervisors cause to pause and reflect on Dewey's criticism that those who seek to protect the "purity" of science (or of any discipline) are taking a stance on "the established tradition about 'purity,' which, like traditional feminine chastity, needed all kinds of external safeguards to hedge it about."[76]

It is puzzling that scholars in the social sciences and in English should have proceeded to seek the elemental factors that comprise the "structure" of their respective disciplines when such a monolithic concept was never demonstrated to exist in the sciences. For example, the Commission on Undergraduate Education of the American Institute of Biological Sciences sought to identify the common elements for an ideal core curriculum in college biology. In this effort, exhaustive analyses were made of the content of the undergraduate biology curriculum at universities generally regarded as having outstanding biology departments. The findings revealed that only 7 percent of the subject-matter information was shared in common.[77] This effort was then summarily abandoned. Obviously, the subject matter of biology will differ greatly depending on whether the orientation is chemical, molecular, ecological and social, and so on. Moreover, it will differ greatly when it is designed for the function of general education for the citizen in contrast to specialized education for the budding biologist.

Aftermath of the New Math and Other Disciplinary Curriculum Reforms

In the aftermath of the "new math," the "new science," and other discipline-centered curriculum reforms, educators began to have second thoughts as the research failed to support the sweeping claims made for these reform projects. For example, a large-scale longitudinal study revealed that youngsters exposed to the "new mathematics" of the School Mathematics Study Group did not measure up to their compeers who had been exposed to "conventional" math in being able to make computational applications.[78] The focus of the "new mathematics" on puristic and abstract concepts and processes, to the exclusion of mathematical applications, was clearly reflected in such evaluations. The mathematician Richard Courant held that the splitting of mathematics into a pure versus an applied orientation posed a most serious threat of one-sidedness to education, and he maintained that the relationships of mathematics to other areas of knowledge are necessary to keep mathematics from drying up into a dead skeleton.[79] Another mathematician writing in *Science,* the official journal of the American Association for the Advancement of Science, observed that "one can only conclude that much of modern mathematics is not related to science but rather appears to be more closely related to the famous scholastic arguing of the Middle Ages."[80]

Richard Feynman, Nobel laureate in theoretical physics, examined the textbooks for grades 1 through 8 in the "new mathematics" and criticized the material for being "an abstraction from the real world" and for being loaded with technical concepts "that are used by pure mathematicians in their most subtle and difficult analyses, and are used by nobody else." In condemning these texts for being "full of such nonsense," Feynman argued that "the utility of the subject and its relevance to the world must be made clear to the pupil."[81]

Similar criticisms were being leveled at the discipline-centered projects in school science. It had been claimed, for example, that the new physics would lead to a doubling of the proportion of students enrolled in high-school physics, producing also a marked increase in our nation's output of physicists.[82] Instead, the proportion of students taking high school physics underwent a significant decline. And during the five-year period from 1962 to 1967 when our nation's college population was increasing dramatically, the actual number of college majors in physics declined by over 15 percent.[83]

The editor of the journal *Science* expressed concern that these enrollment declines in physics were the result of the reaction of high school youth against the "new physics" course.[84] Similar criticisms were being leveled at the new high school chemistry projects. In addressing a national meeting of the American Chemical Society, a chemistry professor observed that the curriculum reforms in high school chemistry had pressured youngsters into doing "too much, too fast, too soon" and that in failing to consider the nature of the adolescent, educators had committed "a crime against a generation."[85]

Purity and Fragmentation Versus Application and Integration. An extensive and cogent criticism of the puristic orientation of the discipline-centered curriculum reforms was made by the scientist Alvin Weinberg, who warned of the dangers to society when the school curriculum is fragmented and made overly abstract, as he traced how "the professional purists, representing the spirit of the fragmented, research-oriented university, took over the curriculum reforms (in the schools) and by their diligence and aggressiveness, created puristic monsters."[86]

Why weren't such shortcomings and dangers foreseen at the time when the discipline-centered curriculum reforms were first proposed? The mathematician Morris Kline, one of the few who did warn of these shortcomings and dangers, explains that when the federal government turned to the universities to produce the national curriculum-reform projects for the schools, mission-oriented scholars were busily engaged in federally sponsored applied research. On the other hand, the puristic scholars were not so engaged, and were ready to seize the opportunity for grant monies from the prestigious National Science Foundation to work on school-curriculum reform. Kline also noted that these puristic professors were "presumptuous" in taking on "a task that calls for considerable pedagogical acumen," as he went on to stress that

> they [the professors] acted as though pedagogy was only a detail, whereas if they had really learned anything at all from their studies, they would have known that almost any problem involving human beings is enormously complex. The problems of pedagogy are indeed more difficult than the problems of mathematics, but the professors had extreme confidence in themselves.[87]

Opportunities and Fashion. Yet this does not explain why the pedagogues in the colleges of education were so quick to endorse the disciplinary doctrine. Myrdal has observed how university scholars are opportunistic and tend to move as a flock in following dominant trends and fashions.[88] This may explain why the educationists proceeded to follow the tide and to seek the grant monies available from the prestigious National Science Foundation for conducting institutes, workshops, and courses in promoting the new curriculum packages.

"Second Thoughts." In the aftermath of the discipline-centered curriculum reforms and in the wake of the exploding social problems and student protest movement of the latter 1960s, Bruner, Schwab, and Phenix retreated from their earlier stance on disciplinarity as the ruling construct for curriculum reform. Bruner called for a moratorium on curriculum reform based on the disciplinary rationale, acknowledging that it had caused much grief, and advocated that the curriculum be focused on the social problems that face us.[89] Schwab criticized the pervasive specialism in the curriculum, which creates in students the illusion that subject matters are the inevitable products of natural divisions, and he pointed to "the vicious diremptions created by the divisions." He then stressed the need to develop other modes of curriculum organization "by which the separated can be related and the ground laid for repair of diremptions."[90] Phenix called for the curriculum to give moral consideration to "concrete personal and social problems."[91]

However, the response to the demand for curriculum relevance by college and high school students during the late 1960s and early 1970s was to introduce more elective options and courses to meet special interests rather than to meet the function of general education.

Retrospective Assessment. In an effort to study the factors underlying the ultimate failure of the federally supported discipline-centered curriculum projects, the National Institute of Education established a Curriculum Development Task

Force in 1975. Summarizing the findings of the Task Force, an NIE official pointed to the forces of censorship as a chief factor in the collapse of these projects, capped by a congressional attack on one of these projects in 1975.[92]

However, these projects were already in a state of decline by the late 1960s. And although the new biology projects were attacked in some quarters by anti-evolutionists, high school biology textbooks have been attacked by antievolutionists since the time of the infamous Scopes trial in Tennessee in 1925.

By the late 1960s the discipline-centered projects were being criticized for neglecting knowledge applications and social problems, with the narrow emphasis given to abstract and specialized knowledge. As discussed earlier, educators were having second thoughts about these projects as the research failed to support the extravagant claims that had been made in promoting the new curricula, and as leading scholars challenged the appropriateness of the materials for children and youth.

Curricularists and supervisors had failed to foresee the problem of curricular congestion inherent in the disciplines doctrine. Eventually, these projects began to collapse from their own weight as they competed with each other for a place in the school curriculum. For example, to be true to the disciplinary doctrine, the broad field of social studies would have to be divided up into a myriad of disciplines from the elementary school up—to include the separate study of anthropology, economics, geography, political science, psychology, and sociology, along with history. The failure to develop the projects within a holistic and coherent curriculum framework applied not only to the social sciences but also to the natural sciences. Disciplinary knowledge as the single ruling doctrine for curriculum design and development came to be challenged as to its efficacy in view of the need for alternative interdisciplinary approaches in the light of the wider social interest.

In summary, these projects could not live up to the claims made for them because they had failed to take account of the necessary interdependence of the fundamental factors in the educative process—namely, the organization of a balanced and coherent curriculum that is consonant with the nature and needs of the learner and with the wider interests of a democratic society.[93] Another lesson to be learned is that subject supervisors need to work together to build a coherent curriculum through horizontal as well as vertical articulation—helping teachers reveal to students the interdependence of studies.

Purity and Priority

Lest one assume that the disciplinary doctrine is an artifact of a bygone era, one only has to examine the curricula in the various departments of the university and even in some departments of the high school, such as mathematics, to see that puristic and abstract knowledge compartmentalization lives on.

But the great irony is that a report of the National Science Board, issued in 1983 in response to the alleged threat to our nation's long-held preeminent position in technology and global industrial markets, should offer the following prescription for meeting this latest crisis: "The National Science Foundation, which has the recognized expertise in leading curriculum development, should again take the leadership role in promoting curriculum evaluation and development for mathematics, science and technology."[94]

INDIVIDUAL GROWTH AND SOCIAL GROWTH

During the first half of the twentieth century, increasing recognition was being given to the shortcomings of basic education for the masses and liberal education for the privileged. The narrowness of the traditional academic studies in the high school and of the traditional liberal arts in the college had relegated the modern utilitarian studies to such inferior status that it gave cause for the Harvard Committee on General Education in a Free Society, appointed by President Conant in 1943, to comment that "it is a strange state of affairs in an industrial democracy when those very subjects are held in disrepute which are at the heart of the national economy and those students by implication condemned who will become its operators."[95]

The Theory and Function of General Education

Stressing the vital significance of general education and specialized education in a free society, the Harvard Committee described general education as "that part of a student's whole education which looks first of all to his life as a responsible human being and citizen" and specialized education as "that part which looks to the student's competence in some occupation." The Harvard Committee went on to conclude that "the aim of education should be to prepare an individual to become an expert both in some particular vocation or art and in the general art of the free man and the citizen. Thus the two kinds of education once given separately to different social classes must be given together to all alike."[96]

Thus general education may be defined as "that part of the curriculum that is designed to provide for a common universe of discourse, understanding, and competence" for the purpose of developing "autonomously thinking, socially responsible citizens of a free society."[97] This requires an outlook on knowledge that is essentially different from that of specialized education, as well as a different organization and treatment of knowledge. The necessary interdependence of studies and the relationship of the studies to the life of the learner in the wider society are revealed through general education.

Although general education requires an outlook on knowledge and an organization of knowledge essentially different than specialized education, general education is not an isolated part of the curriculum. To use the metaphors of the Harvard Committee, "General education can be compared to the trunk of a tree from which branches, representing specialism, go off at different heights," or "general education at high school is like the palm of a hand, the five fingers of which are as many kinds of special interest—mathematics and science, literature and language, society and social studies, the arts, the vocations."[98] The trunk of a tree or palm of the hand represents the common core of studies and the necessary interdependence of studies from which the learner develops the working power for specialized studies, enrichment studies, and special-interest studies.

Unity Through Diversity. Giving recognition to the need for a diversified curriculum to meet the vocational, enrichment, and exploratory needs of students in the high school and college, the Harvard Committee also criticized the parceling and atomization of the curriculum, which divides student from student. The Committee viewed general education as the means for providing the needed sense of unity built on diversity. Moreover, general education and vocational education should function not in opposition, but in reciprocal illumination in the cosmopolitan (comprehensive) high school and college.

Early in the century, Dewey had laid the theoretical and operational groundwork for the necessary interdependence of general education and vocational education in the secondary school and college in a free society.[99] But the forces for division and opposition have persisted to this day. Dewey also viewed the function of education not as mere preparation for some remote adult life, but as a process of growth for social power and insight.

Education as Growth. To Dewey, the traditional conception of the function of the curriculum was preparation for adulthood, with the consequence that the child and adolescent were treated as probationary candidates for a remote future when they might qualify as full members of society.[100] "The best thing that can be said about any special process of education," wrote Dewey, "is that it renders its subject capable of further education." Regarding the curriculum, Dewey pointed out that "acquisition of skill, possession of knowledge, attainment of culture are not ends; they are marks of growth and means to its continuing." And the moral meaning of the institutions of democracy, and especially of the school, lies in "the contribution they make to the all-around growth of every member of society."[101]

As discussed later, the conception of education as growth called for a rejection of the traditional conception of curriculum as the subjects comprising the formal course of study.

General Education in a Free Society

From the time of the establishment of our land-grant universities, it had become apparent in many quarters that the traditional function of liberal education was illiberal in that it was conceived for a select population, and that its attendant bias against the modern studies in a scientific and technological age made it inadequate to the task of developing a sense of unity through diversity in a modern democracy. As noted by the Harvard Committee, science as a mode of thought based on testable evidence, as opposed to dogmatic authority, is of particular significance in the development of citizens for a free society.[102]

General Education in School and College. It was not until we were approaching mid-twentieth century when leading colleges and universities were using the term *general education* instead of liberal education. Progressive-experimentalist educators were envisioning general education in the secondary school as the means through which the common need for democratic citizenship among students of diverse backgrounds and destinations would be met[103] Pioneering ef-

forts had been made in experimenting with curriculum synthesis through problem-focused core studies in the schools participating in the Eight-Year Study
before midcentury.[104] Although such efforts were largely overshadowed by
World War II, the postwar era witnessed a notable number of secondary schools
instituting block-time and core courses for general education to the extent that
the U.S. Office of Education was making periodic surveys of such practices.[105]

During a period extending from the 1930s to midcentury, there was concerted activity in curriculum reconstruction in general education in our colleges
and universities. Notable programs were developed at such diverse institutions
as Amherst, Brooklyn, Columbia, and Harvard in the east; Chicago, Minnesota,
Michigan State, and Wisconsin in the midwest; and San Francisco State and
Stanford in the west.[106] Although the colleges and universities were not working
conjointly with the secondary schools, the Report of the Harvard Committee on
General Education (1945) did examine the function of general education in the
secondary school and college as a unitary mission. Such was the extent of concern and activity in curriculum reconstruction in general education that at midcentury the dean of the College of the University of Chicago could declare, "In
the nation, 'general education' is at last in vogue. Its principles bid fair to become
the operative educational theory of the remainder of this century."[107]

However, such great expectations went unrealized as general education became neglected and even overpowered as the result of the forces of specialism
and special interests over a period spanning the ensuing three decades. Knowledge specialism won out in higher education, and the university scholar-
specialists proceeded to impose their discipline-centered bias on the elementary
and secondary schools through the federally supported national curriculum-
reform projects of the 1950s and 1960s.

Rediscovery of General Education

The resulting fragmentation of the undergraduate curriculum eventually led to
the rediscovery of general education in higher education. During the latter part
of the 1970s the problem of general education was being addressed once again
not only in the professional literature but in the popular press. The *Report on the
Core Curriculum* issued to the Harvard faculty in arts and sciences by the dean in
1978 actually made front-page news,[108] and led an educator to opine in an article
in a national magazine that if the proposed curriculum reforms at Harvard are
successful, "they will exert a powerful influence on higher education for the
balance of the century."[109]

However, where the 1945 Harvard Report had examined general education
in the American college and high school as a common concern, the 1978 report
was focused exclusively on undergraduate education at Harvard. Nevertheless,
it did serve to galvanize a reawakening of interest in general education in higher
education. The 1978 report attacked the fragmentation created by distribution
(elective) requirements. Although the new plan continued the practice of meeting the requirements for general education through distribution electives, the
courses were sharply reduced to a core selection, taken together to meet the
function of general education as expressed by the following criteria for an

educated person: (1) ability to think and write clearly and effectively; (2) critical appreciation of the ways in which we gain knowledge and understanding of the universe, of society, and of ourselves; (3) understanding of other cultures and times; and (4) understanding and experience in thinking about moral and ethical problems.[110] In addition to the requirements in general education, each student would meet concentration requirements in a major field (specialization) and would have free electives for exploratory, enrichment, and special-interest education. Although the new plan lacked the curricular coherence characteristic of certain other colleges that were known for their pioneering work in general education, it nevertheless signaled a reawakening of concern in the nation for the function of general education in higher education.

General Education and Liberal Education in the College. Many colleges have continued to use the term *liberal education* to describe programs that are more appropriately conceived to function as general education. In such cases the use of the term *liberal education* may carry a prestigious flavor, but it behooves educators to recognize that such a flavor is derived from a long tradition of educational privilege and exclusivity, and that it denotes a past-oriented perspective of the curriculum.

The difference between liberal education and general education is not merely semantic, but marks a major turning point in educational outlook stemming from the need to make knowledge accessible and relevant to the shared life of all members of a free society. A recent report of the National Institute of Education fails to make this distinction and utilizes the term *liberal education* in describing the prescriptions it offers for the improvement of general education in the college.[111]

The Humanities in the Schools. Earlier in this chapter, some discussion was given to the efforts during the late 1960s and early 1970s to give the humanities a central place in the school curriculum. These efforts developed as a reaction against the fragmentation and imbalance of the curriculum brought on during the 1950s and 1960s with the discipline-centered reforms and the curriculum priorities and hierarchies created during that period. It was pointed out that the humanities were introduced as a segmental part of the curriculum and were pursued by a segmental population of the student body. Moreover, the humanities were treated apart from the sciences and other studies. Consequently, the humanities failed to provide for the unitary function of general education.

A 1980 report by the Commission on the Humanities of the Rockefeller Foundation called for establishing the humanities as a priority in the school curriculum, and pointed to the educational strictures wrought by an era of back-to-basics and statewide minimum-competency testing which resulted in "education built on principles of management and quantitative measurement." The report related the study of the humanities to the function of general education in the school and college, and acknowledged the need to fashion the study of the humanities in support of "the historic purposes of elementary and secondary education—discerning citizenship and personal growth."[112] However, while the report gained the attention of college educators, it had virtually no impact on the schools, which were still in the throes of the back-to-basics retrenchment, minimum-competency testing, and "minimum standards."

In another effort to revivify the humanities in the schools, the National Society for the Study of Education issued a yearbook in 1984 titled *The Humanities in Precollegiate Education*.[113] In addition to the unfortunate choice of title, which implies that the humanities in the schools are to be treated as something coming prior to, or in preparation for, college and not for general education, is the puzzling absence in the yearbook of any concerted examination of why previous similar efforts to revivify the humanities in the schools failed. Even more disturbing is that the term *general education* does not even appear in the index of the yearbook. Unless the humanities are so conceived and designed to provide for the needed curriculum unity and coherence, and this is questionable in view of their traditional divorce from the sciences and other modern studies, the humanities will be treated as another segmental part of the curriculum. And they will be construed to serve only a special population, such as the college bound.

The elevating of William Bennett, chairman of the National Endowment for the Humanities, to the cabinet post of U.S. Secretary of Education in 1985 may augur to some that at least the humanities will gain a central place in the school curriculum. But Bennett's position, as expressed in the report *To Reclaim a Legacy* (1984), issued under his chairmanship of the National Endowment, was steeped in the old tradition, which set the humanities above and apart from the sciences, the social sciences, the studio arts, and other modern studies. Such a position neglects to give needed consideration to the idea and practice of general education in the schools of a free society. Such a hallowed view of the humanities only serves to exacerbate the great curriculum divide which reflects the great social divisions.

Yet there is compelling evidence of a widespread and continuing interest on the part of the general public in the needed unity of the sciences, arts, and humanities—as indicated by the appearance of such books as *Science and Human Values* (1956) and *The Ascent of Man* (1974), both by the late Jacob Bronowski, on national lists of best-sellers. (The latter book was based on a widely popular television series created by Bronowski.) Interestingly, the material could not be regarded as a watered-down treatment, but represented a synthesis of knowledge to reveal that the sciences, arts, and humanities do not belong to different worlds. Unfortunately, the school curriculum—marked by fragmentation, division, and isolation—treats such knowledge as belonging to separate worlds. The need for curriculum unity and coherence through general education has been long submerged by narrow interests. At times, the humanities have been promoted as another special interest instead of being seen in the light of the need for general education.

General Education in the Schools. The long neglect of the need for general education in the secondary schools is reflected in the 1976 yearbook of the National Society for the Study of Education, *Issues in Secondary Education*, which devoted less than two pages to general education.[114] During the late 1970s, the reawakened concern and activity in reconstructing the undergraduate curriculum so as to provide for general education appeared to signal that the secondary schools would follow in this trend. Unfortunately, such efforts in the secondary schools were all too sporadic and were no match for the counterforces to general education.

In 1980, the Association for Supervision and Curriculum Development formed a network of seventeen high schools that were engaged in efforts to develop programs in general education. However, these efforts were highly diverse and few attempts were made to develop a coherent curriculum in general education among the network schools. Moreover, there was no plan for the systematic evaluation of the efforts of the network schools. It also became apparent that the network schools were beginning to pay more attention to the barrage of national reports being issued during the early 1980s, calling for the "new basics," rather than to their mission as members of the network to develop coherent programs in general education.[115]

The 1983 yearbook of the National Society for the Study of Education was devoted to individual student differences and the common curriculum.[116] Indeed, the title of the yearbook gave promise that the contributors would focus on the need to reconstruct the school curriculum so as to build a sense of unity from diversity—the principal task of general education. Such a focus appeared long overdue following an extended period in which the curriculum of the elementary schools had been reduced mainly to the basic skills, while the theme "back-to-basics" permeated the secondary schools. From the turn of the century through midcentury, progressive educators had sought to develop the elementary curriculum beyond basic education and to relate the curriculum to the life of the growing learner in relation to the life of the wider society. In the same vein, notable curriculum designs were developed for the articulation of studies to meet the function of general education in the secondary school.[117]

However, the 1983 yearbook *Individual Differences and the Common Curriculum* gave scant attention to revealing the interdependence of the various subject fields comprising the "common curriculum." Some contributors to the yearbook even advocated abandoning the idea of a common core, and recommended that science, for example, be studied as *different* sciences—such as in the case of the NSF-sponsored disciplinary projects of the 1950s and 1960s.[118] No concerted examination was made of the necessary interrelationships between literature and the social studies. The proposed "heart of the curriculum" in English for the 1980s was described as a "mastery curriculum"—"composed of all the skills and concepts which need to be sequenced, which teachers can be held accountable for teaching, which can be packaged in mastery learning units, and which will determine the selection of instructional materials."[119] The arts were approached mainly from the standpoint of aesthetics and connoisseurship—with artistic exemplars being regarded as "the chief targets of instruction, especially in grades seven to twelve."[120] The arts as a means of expression was regarded as being appropriate only in the common curriculum of the elementary school. The relationship of such activity to general education for the worthy use of leisure time, and the relationship of the arts to the human-made environment went unexamined. In short, the yearbook failed to come to grips with the need for

revealing the interdependence of studies through horizontal curriculum articulation and the need to meet the function of general education in a free society.

Amidst the barrage of reports on the high school during the early 1980s, two
studies gave attention to the need for general education or common learnings—
namely, Boyer's *High School: A Report on Secondary Education in America* (1983)
and Goodlad's *A Place Called School* (1984). Nevertheless, as discussed in Chapter
9, the proposals for general education by Boyer and Goodlad were relatively
modest. Moreover, both opted for the elimination of vocational education and
thereby, the elimination of the comprehensive high school. In effect, this would
leave us with a college preparatory/general academic high school, with vocational
education being provided in a segregated, specialized vocational school.

The "New Basics" Versus General Education in the Schools

The foray of reports on school reform during the early 1980s—issued by various
national commissions, panels, and task forces (see Chapter 9)—garnered most of
the attention of state and local school officials. This was especially the case for the
report of the National Commission on Excellence in Education, *A Nation at Risk*
(1983), issued at the behest of the U.S. Secretary of Education. This report came
to be regarded by state and local school officials as an official document on
American educational policy and reform.

The Commission, dominated by college administrators and professors, called
for the "New Basics" in the high school and not general education. The consequence was that general education in the secondary school was to be neglected
for yet another era, despite the rediscovery of the importance of general education in the college. In effect, the college educators were viewing the high school
primarily in terms of "tooling-up" for college or for some other future rather
than as an authentic educational institution with a curriculum designed to meet
the needs of adolescents in a free society.

Elitism of the College. It is not uncommon for leading proponents of general
education in higher education to see basic education as the chief function of the
secondary school. In so doing, they fail to recognize the inherent elitism in their
position, whereby the majority of adolescents who do not go on to college are to
be denied the kinds of learning experiences that are necessary for an enlightened citizenry in a free society. Hence Daniel Bell, a leading advocate of general
education in college, could proceed to describe the college experience through
general education as "the testing years—the testing of oneself and one's values,"
with the college being an environment "of broad intellectual adventure,"
whereas the function of the secondary school is that of "concentrating on facts
and skills."[121]

Through such a demarcation, the majority of adolescents are to be denied the
testing of their values and the broad intellectual adventure of general education.
The implication is that the noncollege-bound adolescent is incapable of fully
assuming the rights and responsibilities of productive citizenship in a free society. Even for those who are college bound, the curriculum of the high school is to

be merely a "tooling-up" as they find themselves on a waiting list for the broad intellectual adventure of the college years.

General Education Is Not a Curriculum Track. The long neglect of general education in the secondary school has resulted in the tendency for many school administrators to confuse general education with the general-curriculum track, whereby students who are not in the college-bound track or the vocational track are relegated to the nebulous general track. Even a former U.S. Commissioner of Education revealed this confusion in an address in 1971 before the National Association of Secondary School Principals, as he used the term *general education* when he was actually leveling an attack against the general-curriculum track.[122]

In the practice of tracking, students in the vocational track remain separated from others even in their course work in English, history, social studies, mathematics, and science. The college-bound students pursue the standard academic studies, while the general-track students are left to fend with watered-down academic studies and some shop or business classes that do not meet the standards for federal–state reimbursement as vocational studies. Graduation requirements are met through distributed electives whereby the noncollege-bound student selects general academic courses from lists under the departmental categories. The college-bound student pursues the standard academic program. Except for free electives, physical education, and student activities (varsity athletics, band, chorus, clubs, etc.), the tracked students are not heterogeneously grouped in their work. In essence there is no curriculum in general education or common learnings whereby a sense of shared learning experiences is provided with the intent of creating unity through diversity. This problem of isolation and division is exacerbated further by the area vocational school and the resultant debilitation of the comprehensive high school.

Distribution Requirements

Instead of embarking on the needed reconstruction of the curriculum in general education to provide for unity and coherence, the predominant practice in the secondary schools and colleges is to have students meet distribution requirements (courses to be elected from the various "academic" departments). This approach is variously referred to as the "Chinese-menu" curriculum, the "cafeteria" curriculum, or the "junkyard" curriculum. The latter term is not to imply that the courses in the distribution requirements are "junk" but rather that the student is expected to seek out a disjointed selection of odd parts and to build for himself a working assemblage of some kind.[123]

Distribution requirements tend to be a curriculum of default, since they typically make no demands on the separate departmental faculties to work conjointly in revealing to the student the necessary interdependence of knowledge in the shared life of a free society. The established departmental demands and responsibilities are placed on the administration of the school or college. As discussed earlier, this problem can be countered somewhat by implementing criteria through which the courses under distribution requirements must be designed to meet the function of general education. However, when the course listings under the various distribution categories are large, there is the tendency for the courses to be so selected that they divide students acording to special interests.

Various approaches to designing the curriculum in general education, other than distribution requirements, are discussed in the next chapter.

GENERAL EDUCATION: THE UNIFYING FUNCTION OF THE CURRICULUM

Table 11–1 contrasts the four controlling rationales for the curriculum that were discussed in this chapter, along with their contrasting orientations toward the subject matter in the curriculum. It should be reiterated that the interdisciplinary orientation toward subject matter to meet the function of general education does not imply that the basic skills are ignored. However, such skills are not regarded as ends in themselves, or as means toward mental discipline, but as instrumental to the development of wider and deeper understandings and applications of knowledge in the life of the learner. Nor does general education neglect the cultural heritage, but treats the human race experience in its relevance to the contemporary human condition. Yet general education is not a point of compromise with the traditionalist functions of the curriculum.

Heritage and Progress

Although general education provides for the resolution of the conflict between heritage and progress, there are those who adhere to the old traditions so steadfastly that they see basic education as appropriate for the masses, whereas liberal education is a form of privilege. There are even those who see general education as belonging in the province of the college, whereas the secondary and elementary schools are to be delimited to basic education and academic preparation. The basic argument about general education, as Conant pointed out, turns on the degree to which the old traditions dominate in determining the basis for the education of "*all* American youth." Accordingly,

> The watershed between two fundamentally opposed positions can be located by raising the question: For what purpose do we have a system of public education? If the answer is to develop effective citizens of a free democratic country, then we seem to be facing in one direction. If the answer is to develop the student's rational powers and immerse him in the stream of our cultural heritage, then we appear to be facing in an opposite direction.[124]

The inescapable demands for specialism in the postindustrial age point yet in another direction. General education serves as the core function of the curriculum in providing the needed sense of unity and interdependence in the face of such specialism. In addition to the function of general education and specialized education, the school and college curriculum encompasses such functions as exploratory education, enrichment education, and special-interest education—as provided through free electives, distributed electives, and student activities. All of these curriculum functions, along with the function of specialized educa-

Table 11–1　Four Curriculum Rationales

Controlling Theme	Function	Subject-Matter Orientation
Transmission and preservation of the cultural inheritance	Liberal education	Classical studies built upon academic fundamentals
Fundamental skills/literacy	Basic education	Fundamental academic skills and academic studies
Knowledge production	Specialized education	Disciplinary
Individual and social growth	General education[a]	Interdisciplinary

[a] As core for other curriculum functions—namely, specialized education, special-interest education, enrichment education, and exploratory education.

tion, draw on and branch out from general education. The nature of these curriculum functions and their necessary interdependence with general education, along with alternative approaches to curriculum organization and design, are examined in the next chapter.

The Search for Unity and Relevance

It has been pointed out that general education requires a different outlook, method, and organization of subject matter than does basic education, liberal education, or specialized education. Figures 11–3 and 11–4 contrast the treatment of subject matter from two distinctly different vantage points. The subject matter in Figure 11–3 represents specialized knowledge and is extracted from a high school physics textbook produced as an outgrowth of the Physical Science Study Committee, which was the "flagship" project for the discipline-centered curriculum reforms supported by the National Science Foundation. The material is specialized and technical, and is apparently designed for the preparation of the future physicist who will be engaged in specialized knowledge production.

Even though such specialized-technical material may be deemed as appropriate for the preparation of the future physicist, the knowledge specialist must take into account the nature of the adolescent in selecting and organizing the subject matter. For the treatment of the subject matter may either serve to impel an adolescent toward a career as a physicist, or may repel him or her away from such a career. Moreover, the fact that an adolescent is seeking to become a physicist, biologist, or chemist does not mean that the curriculum in science for that adolescent should be entirely from the vantage point of specialized-technical knowledge. The future scientist, as well as the future factory worker or salesperson, needs to understand the relationship of science to society.

Figure 11–4 contrasts sharply against Figure 11–3 in the selection and treatment of subject matter. The material in Figure 11–4 is from a college textbook in the interdisciplinary field of ecology. The material is nontechnical and focused on a major problem shared by all concerned and enlightened citizens. It is obviously designed for the function of general education. Although the text was written for the college level, it is widely used in the high schools with heterogeneous classes of college-bound students and students who will be entering the

On the Derivation of the Formulas for v'_1 and v'_2

For a head-on collision, in which the motions are along a straight line (as in Section 7–3), we can determine the final velocities v'_1 and v'_2 from the equations

$$-\Delta E_{K_1} = \Delta E_{K_2} \quad \text{and} \quad -\Delta p_1 = \Delta p_2.$$

(For vectors along a line, we drop the arrow and use the + or − sign to indicate direction, as in Chapter 3.) Writing ΔE_K as the difference between final and initial kinetic energies, we have

$$-(\tfrac{1}{2}m_1 v'^2_1 - \tfrac{1}{2}m_1 v_1^2) = (\tfrac{1}{2}m_2 v'^2_2 - 0).$$

We can factor this equation to give

$$-(m_1 v'_1 - m_1 v_1)\left(\frac{v'_1 + v_1}{2}\right) = (m_2 v'_2 - 0)\left(\frac{v'_2 - 0}{2}\right).$$

We see that each side of this energy equation is the product of the momentum change of one mass times the average of the initial and final velocities of that mass. Because we now that the momentum changes are equal and opposite, we can cancel $-\Delta p_1 = -(m_1 v'_1 - m_1 v_1)$ on the left with $\Delta p_2 = (m_2 v'_2 - 0)$ on the right. We therefore obtain the additional information that

$$v'_1 + v_1 = v'_2.$$

On substituting v'_2 from this equation into the equation of the conservation of momentum

$$-(m_1 v'_1 - m_1 v_1) = m_2 v'_2$$

we find

$$v'_1 = \frac{(m_1 - m_2)}{m_1 + m_2}\, v_1.$$

The energy and momentum relations thus lead to a specific prediction for the final velocity of m_1 when its initial velocity is given. Furthermore, by putting this value of v'_1 into $v'_2 = v'_1 + v_1$, we get

$$v'_2 = \frac{2m_1}{m_1 + m_2}\, v_1$$

which tells us the final velocity of the second mass.

Actually in getting this answer for the final velocities, we have put in quite a bit of information. Most of this information was introduced when we assumed that the collision was head on so that the bodies move only along the x axis. If we had allowed one body to approach the other off center (Fig. 7–5), the problem would be more complicated to handle, and we would have to put in the information representing the distance off center in order to get the answer. We also specified that m_2 is initially at rest. These equations do not apply if m_2 is in motion at the start of the interaction. The more general equations that apply then are derived by the same method.

Furthermore, we should note that we made a tacit assumption in finding v'_1 and v'_2. We assumed that there *was* a change in momentum in the interaction. It is possible even in our head-on collision to get another answer: if $v'_1 = v_1$ and $v'_2 = 0$, the momentum is unchanged and no energy transfers from one body to the other over the complete interaction. We shall not worry about this possible answer too much, however, because m_1 must pass right through m_2 in this case.

Figure 11–3. An example of subject matter for specialized education, from a high school physics text.
Source: [From Uri Haber-Schaim, John H. Dodge, and James A. Walter, *PSSC Physics*, 6th ed. (Lexington, Mass.: D. C. Heath, 1986), pp. 146–147.]

world of work after high school. The material in Figure 11–4 is from a chapter focused on the problem of the extinction of species as a result of the assault by human beings. Some of the other problems investigated in the text are food production and world population, water supply, the house as an environment, the urban–suburban environment, environmental pollution and human health, the quest for energy, the waste explosion, land-use planning and environmental restoration, the population explosion and population control, and so on. Obviously, such problems lend themselves to rich sources of readings beyond the textbook and the study of local community conditions. The study of ecology requires a synthesis of the natural sciences with the social studies, since environmental problems and social policy are interrelated. As such, ecology can serve as part of the common core of studies to meet the function of general education.

Another example of textual material that is used successfully with both college students and high school students is the report *State of the Environment* (1985), issued by the Conservation Foundation.

The successful use of such "college-level" material with mixed classes in the high school reveals that the future salesperson, homemaker, physician, lawyer, mechanic, farmer, chemist, politician, and office worker all have something to say to one another. They have certain concerns that they can share in common as members of a free society.

The material in Figure 11–4 reveals that when subject matter is appropriately developed for the function of general education, it is so centered on universal concerns that it is adaptable to widely ranging age groups and ability levels. The ideas, problems, and issues are of such common interest and concern that the supervisor and the teacher can discard the readability formulas and the usual procedures for assigning textbooks to specific grade levels and ability groups. This phenomenon has even been demonstrated with slower-learning high school students who were found to have made significant gains in critical thinking and in their interest in social issues when engaged in the study of common social problems and issues, as compared with compeers who pursued the traditional remedial drill work.[125]

Ideas, problems, and issues of common concern give meaning to the curriculum and generate the development of thinking skills. Traditionally, it has been assumed that one must first "master" the skills before one engages in

Some Endangered Animals in the United States*

Animal	Number in Coterminous United States
Timber wolf	1300 (12,000 with Alaska)
Grizzly bear	1000 (12,000 with Alaska)
Black-footed ferret	Unknown, but rare
Southern sea otter†	1200
Florida panther	50-100
Guadalupe fur seal	1000
Florida manatee or sea cow	1000
Key deer	600
California condor	40
Florida Everglades kite	120
Southern bald eagle	700
American peregrine falcon	150 (500 with Alaska and Canada)
Attwater's greater praire chicken	2200
Masked bobwhite	0 (some reintroduction now being tried in Arizona)
Whooping crane	80 (in the wild)
Eskimo curfew	Extremely rare
Puerto Rican parrot	20
Ivory-billed woodpecker	Unknown, but rare
Kirtland's warbler	400
Ipswich sparrow	4000
Pine barrens tree frog	500

*Source: *Threatened wildlife of the United States, 1973.* Bureau of Sport Fisheries and Wildlife, Resource Publication No. 114.
†threatened status

At times it seems that we are bent on reducing the thousands of species of birds and mammals to a few dozen we consider desirable; the rest are viewed as expendable. Our attacks on the organisms of the world have varied from outright assault to insidious nibblings, with the same destructive result. In this chapter we will look in greater detail at the negative impact we have had on our fellow organisms.

EXTINCTION BY DIRECT ASSAULT

Many animals have disappeared simply because they were edible. Others have become extinct because they became fashionable in our eyes. A few examples of more recent extinctions are discussed here.

THE PASSENGER PIGEON

Half as large again as the mourning dove and at least as savory, the passenger pigeon was probably the most abundant bird we have ever encountered, yet in a few decades it was hunted to extinction. In 1810 the ornithologist Alexander Wilson saw a flock of pigeons in Kentucky which he calculated to be 240 miles long and a mile wide. Wilson estimated the flock to contain 2.23 billion birds! Unlike geese or ducks, which flock only during migration and never in such numbers, passenger pigeons were gregarious throughout the year. Nesting was erratic, depending upon the availability of food. Usually, when beechnuts were plentiful, the birds nested in Michigan and Pennsylvania; when acorns were abundant, Wisconsin and Minnesota were favored. In 1871 one of the largest nestings ever observed took place in Wisconsin. The pigeons nested in almost every available tree over a strip seventy-five by fifteen miles covering over 850 square miles. Anywhere from five to a hundred nests were built in each tree. Such a nesting naturally attracted hunters from all over the country. One conservative estimate placed the number of pigeons in that nesting area at about 136 million.

The males and females sat on the nest alternately. The males left at daybreak, returning at midmorning to relieve the females, who fed until early afternoon, returning to allow the males a final afternoon feeding. This traffic to and from the nesting area presented a unique opportunity for hunters. One eyewitness gives this account of the proceedings:

> And now arose a roar, compared with which all previous noises ever heard, are but lullabys, and which caused more than one of the expectant and excited party to drop their guns, and seek shelter behind and beneath the nearest trees. . . . Imagine a thousand threshing machines running under full headway, accompanied by as many steamboats groaning off steam, with an equal quota of R.R. trains passing through covered bridges—imagine these massed into a single flock, and you possibly have a faint conception of the terrific roar following the monstrous black cloud of pigeons as they passed in rapid flight in the gray light of morning, a few feet before our faces. . . . The unearthly roar continued, and as flock after flock, in almost endless line, succeeded each other, nearly on a level with muzzle of our guns, the contents of a score of double barrels was poured into their dense midst. Hundreds, yes thousands, dropped into the open fields below. Not infrequently a hunter would discharge his piece and load and fire the third and fourth time into the same flock. The slaughter was terrible beyond any description. Our guns became so hot by rapid discharges, we were afraid to load them. Then while waiting for them to cool, lying on the damp leaves, we used, those of us who had [them], pistols, while others threw clubs, seldom if ever, failing to bring down some of the passing flock.[1]

Hunting was not limited to birds on the wing; birds were attacked on the nest with sticks, woods were set afire, and trees were chopped down. After a few more years of this kind of hunting, people began to wonder where the pigeons had gone; some said Canada, others Australia. But there was no escape from the unremitting pressure of the hunter. Why was the passenger pigeon not saved from extinction? Surely a few thousand birds of all those billions could have been preserved.

---

[1]Schorger, A. W., 1937. "The great Wisconsin passenger pigeon nesting of 1871." *Proc. Linn. Soc. N.Y.*, 48, pp. 1–26.

Figure 11–4. An example of subject matter for general education, from a college text in ecology.

Source: [From Richard H. Wagner, *Environment and Man*, 3rd ed. (New York: W. W. Norton, 1978), p. 187.]

meaningful learning. The result is that skills are treated mechanically and are devoid of meaning. To the learner, they remain merely mechanical.

TOWARD A MODERN CONCEPTION OF CURRICULUM

Traditionally, the term *curriculum* has been used synonymously with the course of study or subject matter. In a similar vein, it has been used to denote the systematic group of courses and course sequences to qualify the student for graduation or certification. Perennialists regard the curriculum as the cumulative tradition of organized knowledge representing the cultural inheritance. However, the changing world of knowledge, the changing demands of a free society, the changing conceptions of the learner, the extension of educational opportunity, and the increasingly comprehensive function of the school all served to require a more comprehensive and functional conception of curriculum. Nevertheless, to this day the curriculum is treated in too many schools as though it is so much subject matter as encapsulated in the subjects to be studied; and the chief curriculum problems are textbook selection, teaching for statewide competency tests, scheduling of classes in the secondary school, and the periodic need to examine the curriculum in the school accreditation process.

The School as a Specially Designed Learning Environment

During the 1930s, progressive educators were recognizing the significance of the school as a specially designed environment for learning and the need for a more dynamic conception of curriculum. A report on the Eight-Year Study published in 1942 stated that "the curriculum is now seen as the total experience with which the school deals in educating young people."[126] Many variations of this definition have been offered since that time. For example, Tyler viewed curriculum as "all of the learning of students which is planned by and directed by the school to attain its educational goals."[127]

Student Activities. This modern conception of curriculum also gave recognition to what was once regarded as "extracurricular" or "cocurricular"—in the form of student government, clubs, publications, orchestra, band, chorus, plays, athletics, and other activities—as integral aspects of the curriculum. The terms *student activities* and *extraclass activities* began to replace the earlier terms, which had regarded such activities as outside of or alongside the curriculum.

Over the years, the research findings have revealed that such activities in school and college, with the possible exception of varsity athletics and fraternity or sorority membership, have a positive influence on academic achievement. Moreover, participation in activity programs has a positive influence on receptiveness toward others of different backgrounds, self-confidence, attitudes toward learning, and political attitudes.[128] School administrators are aware of the power of participation in such activities in preventing dropouts. Court decisions right up to the U.S. Supreme Court have established the academic freedom of students to criticize public officials and policies and to examine controversial issues in student publications.[129] Such examination and expression may indeed exert a more powerful educative influence than the course in civics that is focused mainly on facts.

Resolving the Dualisms

The definitions of curriculum as seen in the Eight-Year Study and by Tyler and other experimentalists not only give recognition to the school as a learning environment, but carry the implication that objectives, subject matter, and the teaching–learning process are interdependent elements of curriculum. Such definitions resolve the problem of discontinuity between ends and means, and between knowledge and the ways through which knowledge is developed and utilized. Because students are systematically involved in the appraisal of their progress, the appraisal or evaluation process is integral to their educative experience and is encompassed by this modern conception of curriculum.

In addition to the traditional definitions of curriculum, the *Dictionary of Education* states that curriculum may refer to "what was actualized for the learner, as in actual treatment of all experiences of the learner under the direction of the school."[130]

The Curriculum–Instruction Dualism. As discussed in earlier chapters, the nature of specialized university scholarship has resulted in the identification of instruction as a process apart from curriculum. In this view, curriculum is regarded as a plan for instruction, whereas instruction is seen as "the pupil–teacher interaction situation."[131] In other words, curriculum is seen as ends (the intentions of what is to be learned), whereas instruction is seen as means.[132] This separation of ends and means is like having the learner engage in the act of reading apart from the material through which the act is to derive meaning. (We have all observed children reading aloud in class, but who are unable to explain what they have read. But is such a mechanical act really the act of reading?) In other words, the meanings to be derived from reading denote the significance of the act. Hence the materials and methods, the content and the process, the ends and means, are inseparable.

The separation of curriculum and instruction reveals the failure to recognize that any subject matter or realm of knowledge is inseparable from the processes of inquiry through which such knowledge is generated and utilized. It is just so much "subject matter" until it is transformed into working power for the learner in adding meaning to experience and in enabling the learner to control experience intelligently.

Put another way, the dualism between curriculum and instruction, between ends and means, is like separating science from the methods of scientific inquiry. The methods of science, or science as a mode of thought, reveal the authentic quality of science.

The consequence of the separation of curriculum and instruction is that the study of teaching is relegated to one group of specialists, the assessment of learning outcomes to another group of specialists, the determination of what should be taught to the educational policymakers external to the school, and the delivery of instruction to the teacher. Such jurisdictional separations serve to reduce the professional role of the teacher and supervisor, and lead to mechanical prescriptions.

In the same vein as the progressivists who saw the need for a unitary conception of curriculum, Doll defines curriculum as "the formal and informal content and process by which learners gain knowledge and understanding, develop skills, and alter attitudes, appreciations, and values under the auspices of [the] school."[133] Yet despite the inclusiveness of such modern definitions, they do not reveal the unique function of the school (or college) which sets it apart from other educative institutions in purpose and in the way in which knowledge is organized and treated. Doll's definition also raises serious questions as to whether the school is to "alter" attitudes, appreciations, and values—or whether it is to enlighten the learner.

The Unique Function of the School

It has been observed that virtually every institution of society has a curriculum—the family, church, business, industry, library, military, museum, newspaper, and radio and television (including the commercials "which teach people to want").[134] Nevertheless, the school (or college) is uniquely endowed with the responsibility for the systematic reconstruction of the knowledge paradigms and skills of the culture for the growth of the rising generation in working power to improve their lives and to improve society. "The scheme of a curriculum," wrote Dewey, "must select with the intention of improving the life we live in common so that the future shall be better than the past."[135] Thus the school as an environment for learning is uniquely different from that of any other institution. For these reasons, and as expressed in Chapter 10, curriculum is seen as *that reconstruction of knowledge and experience, systematically developed under the auspices of the school (or college/university), to enable the learner to grow in gaining intelligent control of subsequent knowledge and experience.* This definition is consonant with the conception of education as growth and of knowledge as intelligent working power "to enable us to adapt the environment to our needs."[136] Hence the learner is seen as developing the working power to grow in the capability of controlling circumstances rather than being controlled by them. This marks the difference between a free society and a closed society.

SUMMARY

Changing conceptions of knowledge, changing conceptions of the learner, and the great expectations for the power of education for a free society all served to reveal the inadequacies of the traditional conceptions and functions of the curriculum. As long as knowledge was regarded as static and as long as education was regarded as the province of a privileged elite, the controlling rationale for the curriculum was the preservation and transmission of the cultural heritage. The rising industrialism of the nineteenth century required training of the masses in the fundamental skills and for basic literacy, but this, too, served to reinforce social divisions.

In sharp contrast, the twentieth century witnessed the growing recognition of the need for the curriculum to be directed at individual and social growth. The old liberal education and the delimited basic education were inadequate to this task. Moreover, the old divisions between liberal education and vocational education, between culture and work, between thought and action, were no longer tenable. The new call was for general education—a curriculum of shared experience of and for a free society. General education was then conceived as a common ground that specialized and special-interest education would feed on and from which it would branch out. General education was not conceived as the antidote to specialism, but as that part of the curriculum which provides for a common universe of discourse, understanding, and competence necessary for a free society in an age of specialism and diversity.

The idea and practice of general education called for horizontal curriculum articulation to create a sense of unity, instead of what Whitehead criticized as "the fatal disconnection of subjects which kills the vitality of the modern curriculum." General education also required that the curriculum be made relevant to the life of the learner and to the life of the wider society. Notable efforts were made in developing such articulation for general education in the secondary school and college over an extended period leading up to midcentury. But the forces for specialized knowledge production in the university led to the neglect of general education and gave great impetus to the discipline-centered curriculum in the college and secondary school since midcentury.

Although in recent years there has been evidence of the rediscovery of the need for general education in the college, the attitude on the part of many college educators is that the school curriculum should be geared to basic education and the study of the standard academic subjects in preparation for college.

Statewide testing programs for minimum competencies, state mandates for specific subjects in the school curriculum, and periodic pressures for curriculum retrenchment have served to undermine general education and have distracted the schools from the need to develop curriculum articulation. These influences have also reduced the professional role of the teacher and supervisor, who are seen as having delimited responsibilities for curriculum development. Compounding the problem is the periodic pressure to establish curriculum hierarchies and priorities to meet narrow nationalistic interests under the battle cry of "crisis." The National Science Foundation calls for curriculum priority in the sciences, mathematics, and computer literacy. The National Endowment for the Humanities sees the humanities as the needed antidote to the sciences. The National Endowment for the Arts seeks a recognized place in the curriculum for the studio arts and performing arts. The vocational studies are relegated to the specialized vocational school, where youth are separated institutionally.

The need for supervisors and teachers to look at the curriculum holistically to reveal the necessary interdependence of studies remains neglected as the result of competing special interests. In yielding to these competing special interests and to the narrowly conceived pressures for reform in shifting epochs, teachers, supervisors, curriculum directors, and administrators take a segmental perspective of the curriculum. Curriculum development is then seen as a matter of adopting a new course of study or textbook in a given subject, monitoring basic-skills achievement, tightening requirements for graduation, changing the schedule of classes, grouping and tracking students according to ability levels and curriculum destinations—along with a host of other segmental administrative operations.

Yet the need for curriculum balance, coherence, and interdependence cannot be denied indefinitely. (Various curriculum designs for meeting this need are discussed in the next chapter.) Nor can the need for general education be denied indefinitely as long as a free society seeks to make its ideals executive.

PROBLEMS FOR STUDY AND DISCUSSION

1. How do you acount for the changing conceptions of curriculum during the twentieth century?

2. What major issues are connected with the four different controlling rationales for the curriculum? Which rationale seems to be predominant in public education today? Explain.

3. Describe the program of supervision in your school and school district as related to curriculum development. What shortcomings are in evidence and what steps need to be taken to provide for curriculum articulation?

4. In examining the curriculum of your school, can you find evidence of concerted attention being given to curriculum articulation to meet the function of general education? Explain. If such evidence is lacking, how do you account for this?

5. Examine the undergraduate curriculum of your own college in terms of the questions raised in problem 4. What conclusions do you reach?

6. As cited in this chapter, a 1984 report issued by the National Endowment for the Humanities advocates that the humanities be restored to their rightful legacy of having a central place in the undergraduate curriculum. What factors led to the decline of the humanities from their dominant place in the undergraduate curriculum? What, in your opinion, are the prospects for the restoration of the humanities as called for in the report? How do you account for the failure of the humanities to meet the function of general education in the high school and college?

7. In this chapter it was noted that the reported incidents of school censorship are more frequent in the study of literature than in the social studies. How do you account for this? Also in this chapter, an educator was quoted as warning that "the sharp distinction between English and the social studies cannot possibly be defended." Do you agree? Why or why not?

8. Is there a necessary difference in the selection and treatment of the subject matter when the course work in science in the school or college is intended to prepare the future scientist in comparison to the citizen? Explain.

9. What lessons can be learned from the failure of the national discipline-centered curriculum reforms of the 1950s and 1960s to accomplish what was intended and claimed? How do you account for the failure of the university scholar-specialists who developed the discipline-centered curricula to submit their handiwork to independent scientific evaluation?

10. Do you agree with the College Board that what students need to learn in high school should be approached from the perspective of what is necessary for effective learning in college? Why or why not? Following the same logic, one would maintain that what children need to learn in elementary school should be approached from the perspective of what is necessary for effective learning in high school. What is your assessment of the validity of such a position?

11. Examine some teacher-made tests in your school. To what extent are the test items centered on the recall of factual information and the performance of specific skills? To what extent are the test items centered on critical thinking abilities (comprehension, analysis, application, evaluation, etc.)? To what extent do the test items cross subject-matter boundaries?

12. It has been contended that many of our social institutions other than the school and college have a curriculum. Is there anything unique in the function of the school or college that gives special meaning to the term *curriculum*? Explain.

NOTES

1. Mark Van Doren, *Liberal Education* (Boston: Beacon Press, 1959; originally published 1943), p. 108.
2. *The Works of Aristotle, Politics,* Vol. VIII, trans. Benjamin Jowett, Vol X (Oxford: Clarendon Press, 1921), p. 1338.
3. Alfred North Whitehead, *The Aims of Education* (New York: Macmillan, 1929), pp. 10–11.
4. Boyd H. Bode, *Modern Educational Theories* (New York: Macmillan, 1927), pp. 338–339.
5. Boyd H. Bode, "Education at the Crossroads," *Progressive Education,* Vol. 8 (November 1931), p. 548.
6. J. D. Bernal, *Science in History,* Vol. 4 (Cambridge, Mass.: MIT Press, 1971), p. 1149.
7. John Dewey, "Learning to Earn," *School and Society,* Vol. 5 (March 24, 1917), p. 332.
8. *NAEP Newsletter,* Vol. 16 (Winter 1983, Spring 1983).
9. Task Force on Education for Economic Growth, *Action for Excellence* (Denver, Colo.: Education Commission of the States, 1983), pp. 9, 17.
10. Ibid., pp. 15, 17.
11. Theodore R. Sizer, *Horace's Compromise: The Dilemma of the American High School* (Boston: Houghton Mifflin, 1984), p. 88.
12. Ibid., pp. 85, 89.
13. Edward L. Thorndike and Robert S. Woodworth, "The Influence of Improvement in One Mental Function upon Efficiency of Other Functions," *Psychological Review,* Vol. 8 (May, July, November 1901), pp. 247–261, 384–395, 553–564.

14. Arthur Bestor, *The Restoration of Learning* (New York: Alfred A. Knopf, 1956), pp. 48–49.

15. Jacques Barzun and Robert J. Saunders, *Art in Basic Education* (Washington, D.C.: Council for Basic Education, 1979).

16. College Entrance Examination Board, *Academic Preparation for College* (New York: The Board, 1983), p. 34.

17. Ibid., p. 11.

18. Ibid., p. 3.

19. Ibid., p. 31.

20. Ibid., p. 3.

21. Wilford M. Aikin, *The Story of the Eight-Year Study* (New York: Harper & Row, 1942), p. 113. See also Dean Chamberlain, *Did They Succeed in College?* (New York: Harper & Row, 1942).

22. Ibid., p. 150.

23. Lawrence A. Cremin, *The Transformation of the School* (New York: Alfred A. Knopf, 1961), p. 254.

24. Robert W. Young, "The Relationship Between Business and Industrial Courses in High School with Academic Achievement in the First Year of College" (unpublished doctoral dissertation, University of Michigan, 1966).

25. Robert W. Young, "The Irrational Curriculum," *National Association of Secondary School Principals Bulletin*, Vol. 51 (September 1967), p. 47.

26. Report of the Harvard Committee, *General Education in a Free Society* (Cambridge, Mass.: Harvard University Press, 1945), p. 160.

27. Ibid., p. 175.

28. Sizer, op. cit., pp. 134–135.

29. Scott Whitener, "Patterns of High School Studies and College Achievement" (unpublished doctoral dissertation, Rutgers University, 1974).

30. Robert M. Hutchins, *On Education* (Santa Barbara, Calif.: Center for the Study of Democratic Institutions, 1963), p. 18.

31. Van Doren, op. cit., p. 94.

32. Hyman G. Rickover, "European Vs. American Secondary Schools," *Phi Delta Kappan*, Vol. 40 (November 1958), p. 61.

33. Aristotle, *Politics, Great Books of the Western World*, Vol. 9 (Chicago: Encyclopaedia Britannica, 1952), p. 544.

34. Robert M. Hutchins, *The Higher Learning in America* (New York: Yale University Press, 1936), p. 65.

35. Mortimer J. Adler, "The Crisis in Contemporary Education," *The Social Frontier*, Vol. 5 (February 1939), pp. 62–63.

36. John Dewey, *Democracy and Education* (New York: Macmillan, 1916), p. 302.

37. Robert M. Hutchins, "The Schools Must Stay," *The Center Magazine*, Vol. 6 (January–February 1973), pp. 12–13.

38. John Dewey, *Individualism Old and New* (New York: Capricorn, 1962; originally published 1939), pp. 51–64; C. P. Snow, *Two Cultures and the Scientific Revolution* (New York: Cambridge University Press, 1959). See also Daniel Tanner, "Knowledge Divided Against Itself," *Bulletin of the Atomic Scientists*, Vol. 39 (March 1983), pp. 34–38.

39. Barbara Tuchman, "The Decline of Quality," *The New York Times Magazine*, November 2, 1980, pp. 38–41, 104.

40. Jacques Monod, *Chance and Necessity* (New York: Vintage Books, 1972), p. 171.

41. William J. Bennett, *To Reclaim a Legacy, A Report on the Humanities in Higher Education* (Washington, D.C.: National Endowment for the Humanities, 1984), p. 1.

42. Ibid., p. 9.

43. Ibid., p. 10.

44. Harold E. Taylor (ed.), *The Humanities in the Schools* (New York: Citation Press, 1968), p. 21.

45. James B. Conant, *Education in a Divided World* (Cambridge, Mass.: Harvard University Press, 1949), pp. 74–75, 79, 83, 92.

46. Thorndike and Woodworth, op. cit.

47. *Academic Preparation for College,* op. cit., pp. 28, 29.

48. Ibid., Foreword, n.p.

49. Mortimer Adler, *The Paideia Proposal: An Educational Manifesto* (New York: Macmillan, 1982), pp. 21–36.

50. Ibid., pp. 53, 61.

51. Ambrose Bierce, *The Enlarged Devil's Dictionary,* Ernest L. Hopkins, ed. (Garden City, N.Y.; Doubleday, 1967; originally published 1906), p. 196.

52. Alvin M. Weinberg, *Reflections on Big Science* (Cambridge, Mass.: MIT Press, 1967), pp. 145–146.

53. Alfred North Whitehead, "Dangers of Specialization," in *Specialists and Generalists* (Washington, D.C.: U.S. Senate Committee on Government Operations, 1968), pp. 47–48; from *Science and the Modern World* (New York: Free Press, 1925).

54. Jerome S. Bruner, *The Process of Education* (Cambridge, Mass.: Harvard University Press, 1960), pp. ix, 1.

55. Ibid., pp. 8, 18.

56. Ibid., pp. 14, 28.

57. Ibid., p. 14.

58. John Dewey, *The School and Society* (Chicago: University of Chicago Press, 1943; originally published 1900), p. 44.

59. Ibid., p. 103.

60. Jean Piaget, *The Psychology of Intelligence* (New York: Harcourt Brace Jovanovich, 1950), pp. 87–158.

61. Bentley Glass, *The Timely and the Timeless* (New York: Basic Books, 1970), p. 38.

62. Philip H. Phenix in A. Harry Passow (ed.), *Curriculum Crossroads* (New York: Teachers College Press, 1962), pp. 57–58.

63. Ibid., p. 64.

64. Ibid., p. 64.

65. Whitehead, *Aims of Education,* op. cit., p. 50.

66. Joseph J. Schwab, "The Concept of the Structure of a Discipline," *The Educational Record,* Vol. 43 (July 1962), pp. 197, 203.

67. Glass, op. cit., p. 72.

68. Albert Szent-Gyorgi, "Interdisciplinary Science Education: A Position Paper," *The Science Teacher,* Supplement, Vol. 37 (November 1970), p. 3.

69. See Daniel Tanner, *Secondary Curriculum: Theory and Development* (New York: Macmillan, 1971), Chaps. 3, 4.

70. See William D. Romey, "The Curriculum-Proof Teacher," *Phi Delta Kappan,* Vol. 54 (February 1973), p. 407.

71. Modern Language Association, *The Basic Issues in the Teaching of English* (New York: The Association, 1959), p. 9.

72. John J. DeBoer, "The New English," *The Educational Forum,* Vol. 32 (May 1968), p. 401.

73. Gresham Sykes, "Sociology," in American Council of Learned Societies and the National Council for the Social Studies, *The Social Studies and the Social Sciences* (New York: Harcourt Brace Jovanovich, 1962), p. 158.

74. Michael Scriven, "The Structure of the Social Studies," in G. W. Ford and Lawrence Pugno (eds.), *The Structure of Knowledge and the Curriculum* (Chicago: Rand McNally, 1964), p. 101.

75. Bruner, op. cit., p. 1.

76. John Dewey, *Freedom and Culture* (New York: Putnam, 1939), p. 152.

77. Commission on Undergraduate Education in the Biological Sciences, *Content of the Core Curricula in Biology* (Washington, D.C.: The Commission, 1967), pp. 1, 26, 28.

78. Edward G. Begle and James W. Wilson, "Evaluation of Mathematics Programs," Chapter 10 in National Society for the Study of Education, *Mathematics Education*, Sixty-ninth Yearbook, Part I (Chicago: University of Chicago Press, 1970), p. 402.

79. Richard Courant, in George F. Carrier et al., "Applied Mathematics: What Is Needed in Research and Education," *SIAM Review*, Vol. 4 (October 1962), pp. 297–320.

80. R. W. Hemming, "Numerical Analysis Versus Mathematics," *Science*, Vol. 148 (April 1965), p. 474.

81. Richard P. Feynman, "New Textbooks for the New Mathematics," *Engineering and Science*, Vol. 28 (March 1965), pp. 13, 15.

82. American Institute of Physics, *Physics in Your High School* (New York: McGraw-Hill, 1960), pp. 17–18.

83. *Carnegie Quarterly*, Vol. 18 (Fall 1970), p. 5; Susanne D. Ellis, "Enrollment Trends," *Physics Today*, Vol. 20 (March 1967), p. 77.

84. Philip H. Abelson, "Excessive Educational Pressures," *Science*, Vol. 156 (May 12, 1967), p. 741.

85. L. Carroll King, in "High Student Failure Rate Serious Problem," *Chemical and Engineering News*, Vol. 45 (February 20, 1967), p. 44.

86. Weinberg, op. cit., pp. 153–154.

87. Morris Kline, *Why Johnny Can't Add* (New York: St. Martin's Press, 1973), pp. 129, 135.

88. Gunnar Myrdal, *Objectivity in Social Research* (New York: Pantheon Books, 1969), pp. 43, 53.

89. Jerome S. Bruner, "The Process of Education Revisited," *Phi Delta Kappan*, Vol. 53 (September 1971), p. 21.

90. Joseph J. Schwab, *College Curriculum and Student Protest* (Chicago: University of Chicago Press, 1969), p. 24.

91. Philip H. Phenix, "The Moral Imperative in Contemporary Education," *Perspectives on Education*, Vol. 2 (Winter 1969), p. 11.

92. Jon Schaffarzick, "Federal Curriculum Reform" in Jon Schaffarzick and Gary Sykes (eds.), *Value Conflict and Curriculum Issues* (Berkeley, Calif.: McCutchan, 1979), pp. 7–12.

93. See Daniel Tanner, "Curriculum History" in Harold E. Mitzel (ed.), *Encyclopedia of Educational Research*, 5th ed., Vol. 1 (New York: Free Press, 1982), p. 418.

94. National Science Board, *Educating American for the 21st Century* (Washington, D.C.: National Science Foundation, 1983), p. 46.

95. Report of the Harvard Committee, op. cit, p. 27.

96. Ibid., pp. 51, 54.

97. Daniel Tanner and Laurel N. Tanner, *Curriculum Development: Theory into Practice*, 2nd ed. (New York: Macmillan, 1980), p. 445.

98. Report of the Harvard Committee, op. cit., p. 102.

99. Dewey, *Democracy and Education*, op. cit., pp. 358–374.

100. Ibid., p. 63.

101. John Dewey, *Reconstruction in Philosophy* (Boston: Beacon Press, 1957; originally published 1920 by Henry Holt), pp. 184–186.

102. Report of the Harvard Committee, op. cit., p. 50.

103. See Educational Policies Commission, *Education for ALL American Youth* (Washington, D.C.: The Commission, 1944).

104. H. H. Giles, S. P. McCutchen, and A. N. Zechiel, *Exploring the Curriculum* (New York: Harper & Row, 1942).

105. Surveys conducted by Grace S. Wright were reported in the following publications of the U.S. Office of Education: *Core Curriculum in Public High Schools: An Inquiry Into Practice, 1949* (1950); *Core Curriculum Development: Problems and Practices* (1952); *Block-Time Classes and the Core Program in the Junior High School* (1958).

106. National Society for the Study of Education, *General Education in the American College,* Thirty-eighth Yearbook, Part II (Chicago: University of Chicago Press, 1939); *General Education,* Fifty-first Yearbook, Part I (Chicago: University of Chicago Press, 1952).

107. F. Champion Ward et al., *The Idea and Practice of General Education* (Chicago: University of Chicago Press, 1960), p. v.

108. *The New York Times,* February 26, 1978, p. 1.

109. Susan Schiefelbein, "Confusion at Harvard: What Makes an 'Educated Man'?" *Saturday Review,* Vol. 5 (April 1, 1978), p. 12.

110. Henry Rosovsky, *Report on the Core Curriculum* (Cambridge, Mass.: Harvard University Press, 1978), pp. 2–5.

111. Study Group on Higher Education, *Involvement in Learning: Realizing the Potential of American Higher Education* (Washington, D.C.: National Institute of Education, 1984).

112. Commission on Humanities of the Rockefeller Foundation, *The Humanities in American Life* (Berkeley, Calif.: University of California Press, 1980), pp. 4, 31, 33.

113. National Society for the Study of Education, *The Humanities in Precollegiate Education,* Eighty-third Yearbook, Part II (Chicago: University of Chicago Press, 1984).

114. National Society for the Study of Education, *Issues in Secondary Education,* Seventy-fifth Yearbook, Part II (Chicago: University of Chicago Press, 1976), pp. 145–146.

115. See Arthur D. Roberts, "The ASCD High School Network," *Educational Leadership,* Vol. 41 (March 1984), p. 47.

116. National Society for the Study of Education, *Individual Differences and the Common Curriculum,* Eighty-second Yearbook, Part I (Chicago: University of Chicago Press, 1983).

117. John Dewey, *The Child and the Curriculum/The School and Society* (Chicago: University of Chicago Press, 1902, 1915; combined edition, 1956); Hollis L. Caswell, *Education in the Elementary School* (New York: American Book, 1942); Harold B. Alberty and Elsie J. Alberty, *Reorganizing the High School Curriculum,* 3rd ed. (New York: Macmillan, 1962).

118. *Individual Differences and the Common Curriculum,* op. cit., pp. 162, 181–182.

119. Ibid., p. 204.

120. Ibid., p. 242.

121. Daniel Bell, *The Reforming of General Education* (New York: Anchor Books, Doubleday, 1968), p. 181.

122. Sidney P. Marland, Jr., "Career Education Now," Address before the Annual Meeting of the National Association of Secondary School Principals, Houston, January 23, 1971.

123. Arthur W. Chickering, *Education and Identity* (San Francisco: Jossey-Bass, 1969), pp. 204–206.

124. Conant, op. cit., pp. 74–75.
125. Charles K. Curtis and James P. Shaver, "Slow Learners and the Study of Contemporary Problems," *Social Education,* Vol. 44 (April 1980), pp. 302–309.
126. Giles et al., op. cit., p. 293.
127. Ralph W. Tyler, "The Curriculum—Then and Now," in *Proceedings of the 1956 Invitational Conference on Testing Problems* (Princeton, N.J.: Educational Testing Service, 1957), p. 79.
128. William G. Spady, "Status, Achievement, and Motivation in the American High School," *School Review,* Vol. 79 (May 1971), pp. 384–385; Alexander W. Astin, *Four Critical Years* (San Francisco: Jossey-Bass, 1977), pp. 115–122; Kenneth A. Feldman and Theodore M. Newcomb, *The Impact of College on Students* (San Francisco: Jossey-Bass, 1969), p. 266; Catherine Cornbleth, "Citizenship Education," in Harold E. Mitzel (ed.), *Encyclopedia of Educational Research,* 5th ed., Vol. 1 (New York: Free Press, 1982), p. 263.
129. Louis Fischer, "Academic Freedom," in Mitzel, op. cit., p. 5.
130. Carter V. Good, *Dictionary of Education,* 3rd ed. (New York: McGraw-Hill, 1973), p. 157.
131. James B. Macdonald, "Educational Models in Instruction," in James B. Macdonald and Robert R. Leeper (eds.), *Theories of Instruction* (Washington, D.C.: Association for Supervision and Curriculum Development, 1965), p. 6.
132. W. James Popham and Eva I. Baker, *Systematic Instruction* (Englewood Cliffs, N.J.: Prentice-Hall, 1970), p. 48.
133. Ronald C. Doll, *Curriculum Improvement: Decision Making and Process,* 5th ed. (Boston: Allyn and Bacon, 1982), p. 282.
134. Lawrence A. Cremin, *Public Education* (New York: Basic Books, 1976), p. 22.
135. Dewey, *Democracy and Education,* op. cit., p. 225.
136. Ibid., p. 400.

SELECTED REFERENCES

Adler, Mortimer J. *The Paideia Proposal: An Educational Manifesto.* New York: Macmillan Publishing Company, 1982.

Aikin, Wilford M. *The Story of the Eight-Year Study.* New York: Harper & Row, Publishers, Inc., 1942.

Alberty, Harold B., and Elsie J. Alberty. *Reorgnizing the High School Curriculum,* 3rd ed. New York: Macmillan Publishing Company, 1962.

American Council of Learned Societies and the National Council for the Social Studies. *The Social Studies and the Social Sciences.* New York: Harcourt Brace Jovanovich, Inc., 1962.

Bell, Daniel. *The Reforming of General Education.* Garden City, N.Y.: New York: Anchor Books, Doubleday, 1968.

Bennett, William J., *To Reclaim a Legacy: A Report on the Humanities in Higher Education.* Washington, D.C.: National Endowment for the Humanities, 1984.

Bestor, Arthur. *The Restoration of Learning.* New York: Alfred A. Knopf, Inc., 1956.

Bode, Boyd H. *Modern Educational Theories.* New York: Macmillan Publishing Company, 1927.

Boyer, Ernest L. *High School: A Report on Secondary Education in America.* New York: Harper & Row, Publishers, Inc., 1983.

Bruner, Jerome S. *The Process of Education.* Cambridge, Mass.: Harvard University Press, 1960.

Chamberlain, Dean, et al. *Did They Succeed in College?* New York: Harper & Row, Publishers, Inc., 1942.

College Entrance Examination Board. *Academic Preparation for College.* New York: The Board, 1983.

Commission on Humanities of the Rockefeller Foundation. *The Humanities in American Life.* Berkeley, Calif.: University of California Press, 1980.

Conant, James B. *Education in a Divided World.* Cambridge, Mass.: Harvard University Press, 1949.

Cremin, Lawrence A. *Public Education.* New York: Basic Books, Inc., Publishers, 1976.

Dewey, John. *The Child and the Curriculum/The School and Society.* Chicago: The University of Chicago Press, 1902, 1915; combined edition, 1956.

————. *Democracy and Education.* New York: Macmillan Publishing Company, 1916.

————. *Freedom and Culture.* New York: G. P. Putnam's Sons, 1939.

Educational Policies Commission. *Education for ALL American Youth–A Further Look.* Washington, D.C.: The Commission, 1952.

Giles, H. H., S. P. McCutchen, and A. N. Zechiel. *Exploring the Curriculum.* New York: Harper & Row, Publishers, Inc., 1942.

Glass, Bentley. *The Timely and the Timeless.* New York: Basic Books, Inc., Publishers, 1970.

Goodlad, John I. *A Place Called School.* New York: McGraw-Hill Book Company, 1984.

Hutchins, Robert M. *The Higher Learning in America.* New Haven, Conn.: Yale University Press, 1936.

Kline, Morris. *Why Johnny Can't Add: The Failure of the New Math.* New York: St. Martin's Press, Inc., 1973.

National Commission on Excellence in Education. *A Nation at Risk: The Imperative for Educational Reform.* Washington, D.C.: U.S. Department of Education, 1983.

National Science Board. *Educating Americans for the 21st Century.* Washington, D.C: National Science Foundation, 1983.

National Society for the Study of Education. *General Education,* Fifty-first Yearbook, Part I. Chicago: The University of Chicago Press, 1952.

————. *General Education in the American College,* Thirty-sixth Yearbook, Part II. Chicago: The University of Chicago Press, 1939.

————. *The Humanities in Precollegiate Education,* Eighty-third Yearbook, Part II. Chicago: The University of Chicago Press, 1984.

————. *Individual Differences and the Common Curriculum,* Eighty-second Yearbook, Part I. Chicago: The University of Chicago Press, 1983.

Report of the Harvard Committee. *General Education in a Free Society.* Cambridge, Mass.: Harvard University Press, 1945.

Sizer, Theodore R. *Horace's Compromise: The Dilemma of the American High School.* Boston: Houghton Mifflin Company, 1984.

Snow, C. P. *Two Cultures and the Scientific Revolution.* New York: Cambridge University Press, 1959.

Study Group on Higher Education. *Involvement in Learning: Realizing the Potential of American Higher Education.* Washington, D.C.: National Institute of Education, 1984.

Tanner, Daniel. "Curriculum History," in Harold E. Mitzel (ed.), *Encyclopedia of Educational Research,* 5th ed., Vol. 1. New York: The Free Press, 1982.

————. *Secondary Curriculum: Theory and Development.* New York: Macmillan Publishing Company, 1971.

Tanner, Daniel, and Laurel N. Tanner. *Curriculum Development: Theory into Practice,* 2nd ed. New York: Macmillan Publishing Company, 1980.

Taylor, Harold E. (ed.). *The Humanities in the Schools.* New York: Citation Press, 1968.

Thomas, Russell. *The Search for a Common Learning.* New York: McGraw-Hill Book Company, 1962.

U.S. Senate Committee on Government Operations. *Specialists and Generalists.* Washington, D.C.: U.S. Government Printing Office, 1968.

Van Doren, Mark. *Liberal Education.* Boston: Beacon Press, 1959; originally published 1943.

Ward, F. Champion, et al. *The Idea and Practice of General Education.* Chicago: The University of Chicago Press, 1960.

Weinberg, Alvin M. *Reflections on Big Science.* Cambridge, Mass.: The MIT Press, 1967.

Whitehead, Alfred North. *The Aims of Education.* New York: Macmillan Publishing Company, 1929.

Chapter 12

What the Supervisor
Needs to Know
About the Curriculum:
Design and Development

It was noted in the preceding chapter that curriculum change occurs mainly through the processes of accretion, deletion, compression, injection, and modification of subject matter in the course of study. This activity, coupled with the periodic adoption of textbooks or of new course-of-study packages and with the scheduling of subjects to be studied, is taken for curriculum development by many school administrators, supervisors, and teachers.

Curriculum reorganization and reform are undertaken mainly in response to the dominant external tides and pressures imposed on the school—whether it be "back-to-basics," emphasizing the "new basics," reemphasizing the traditional academic disciplines, giving new priority to the sciences and mathematics, adding computer literacy to the curriculum priorities, seeking to regain a place for the humanities, finding a place for the arts, recognizing the importance of the vocational studies, or instituting some other segmental change. "The whole is lost," observed Whitehead, in our fragmented approach to the curriculum.[1]

The need for the professional staff to engage in curriculum development as a central responsibility and as a continuous process also becomes evident when one considers that the curriculum is always in danger of being loaded down by the sheer bulk of compounded subject-matter being added on to the inherited subject matter. The problem is not solved by simple deletion and accretion. The subject matter must be alive and dynamic if it is to become the working power of intelligence.

"Knowledge does not keep any better than fish," commented Whitehead.[2] Here again, the problem is not merely one of updating the subject matter, but of continually building the curriculum as a vital synthesis of knowledge having direct bearings on the life and growth of the learner.

THE MACROCURRICULUM AND THE MICROCURRICULUM

The problem of curriculum fragmentation, imbalance, and isolation of studies reflects the failure of the professional staff to see the curriculum as a whole. When attention is given to the curriculum, it is directed at segmental elements within the separate subjects, or the revision of a given subject or course of study without due consideration to the relationships with other subjects, or the establishment of priority for certain subjects at the expense of others, or the adoption of certain segmental managerial practices in response to external demands, pressures, or fashions. The focus is on the microcurriculum, as the relationship of the parts to the whole is neglected.

When educators are engaged in efforts to improve curriculum articulation, especially horizontal articulation (the relationships among the various studies or scope of the curriculum), they are dealing with the macrocurriculum. The function of general education, as discussed in the preceding chapter, necessitates such articulation and represents a macrocurricular concern. Problems of the macrocurriculum are revealed when consideration is given to the necessary interdependence between general education and specialized education, or when critical thinking becomes a major theme in all subjects in the curriculum, or when such activities as reading and the writing of themes are regarded as a shared responsibility of all teachers (not just the teachers of English), or when efforts are made to correlate or develop some synthesis between literature and social studies, science and social studies, mathematics and science, and so on.

Neglect of the Macrocurriculum in School and College

The considerations noted above, which relate to the macrocurriculum, seldom receive concerted attention by the professional staff. Addressing this problem in higher education, Schwab wrote: "As far as students are allowed to see, the curriculum is not a subject of thought; it merely is. In many cases, indeed, thinking about curriculum is not merely invisible; it barely occurs."[3]

From the student's perspective in high school and college, the curriculum is seen in terms of courses to meet program requirements relative to career goals and graduation and courses to be elected. In the elementary school, unless the teachers make a concerted effort to develop horizontal curriculum articulation through integrated learning activities, the pupils see the curriculum simply as separate subject skills—with each day being parceled into so many minutes for reading, spelling, composition, social studies, arithmetic, science, and so on.

The segmental subject approach in the traditional elementary school is exacerbated greatly in the secondary school, where the faculty and the subject matters are divided into insulated departmental domains in imitation of the college. The problem is not departmentalization per se; rather, relatively little attention is given to interdepartmental coordination for horizontal curriculum articulation. The consequence is curriculum isolation and fragmentation.

Neglect of the Macrocurriculum in the Education of Teachers

The neglect of the macrocurriculum may be attributed to several combined factors. In their preservice preparation and certification, teachers, supervisors, school administrators, and even curriculum directors rarely are required to make any study of the macrocurriculum. The preparation and certification of teachers provide for some study of the curriculum and teaching methods, but such work is confined to the discrete subject fields.

For the prospective secondary school teacher, the professional course work in curriculum and methods is delimited to his or her major teaching field. Although the students preparing for a teaching career at the secondary level take certain professional courses in common, such as educational psychology and foundations of education, rarely do they work together in the systematic study of the macrocurriculum of the secondary school. When they are assigned to observe classes in the secondary school preliminary to student teaching, they are typically assigned to classes in their teaching fields.

Knowledge Specialism and Compartmentalization. As "products" of the discipline-centered university, prospective secondary school teachers see themselves as specialists when they enter student teaching and when they subsequently go on to their first teaching position where they become a member of a department. Their sense of departmental affiliation denotes their subject-matter domain. Their sense of schoolwide faculty affiliation is not derived from macrocurricular concerns and responsibilities, but rather from common interests relating to administrative policies, courses assigned, teacher benefits, and the like.

In meeting their requirements for a teaching major, prospective secondary school teachers pursue course work with scholar-specialists in a discipline-centered department. These university scholar-specialists are not concerned with the relationship of their specialized scholarship to the curriculum of the secondary school and to the needs of the prospective teacher, but tend to treat their subject as preparation for further specialization, as though the students were all on their way to the Ph.D. Conant's description of the problem a quarter of a century ago appears to be valid to this day. In Conant's words,

> I have found institution after institution in which most, if not all, the members of a subject-matter department (English or chemistry, for example) were totally unfamiliar with what was going on in the schools and couldn't care less. Academic faculties almost invariably specify the courses to be taken in a field of concentration in such a way that their graduates can proceed in the same field to graduate study leading to a Ph.D. More often than not, such a pattern of studies is *not* suitable for a future high school teacher.[4]

The task of making the specialized course work in the major field relevant to the curriculum of the school and to the needs of the future teacher is left to a single course in the professional sequence (a methods course in the teaching of social studies, science, English, etc.). It is no small wonder, then, when college students are frustrated by the enormous task of bridging their college studies to the demands of the school classroom.

As discussed in Chapter 6, a number of colleges have attacked this problem with notable success by treating teacher education as an all-college responsibility, in which the faculties in education and in arts and sciences work conjointly in program design and in the supervision of student teaching. But such efforts have been the exception rather than the rule. Moreover, any systematic study of the macrocurriculum of the school remains virtually nonexistent in the preservice program of teacher education.

Considering that the professional course sequence, including student teaching, constitutes only a very small fraction of the certification requirements for high school teaching, it is puzzling that it is the professional course work, not the bulk of the undergraduate studies (course work in the major field and the distribution requirements in arts and sciences), that is the target of so much criticism. But this may be explained by the fact that the very difficult problem of connecting the college studies to the school falls on the very limited professional sequence in education. Providing more opportunity for "laboratory" experience in directed observation of classes and in demonstration teaching, coupled with supervised extraclass work with youth in the school, is sorely needed. Such experience should also be designed to engage the prospective high school teacher in the study of how his or her teaching field interacts with the total curriculum of the school.

Prospective elementary and secondary teachers, supervisors, and principals are much more likely to see the necessary interdependence of the subjects that comprise the total school curriculum when they themselves are exposed to a coherent curriculum in general education in their own college studies.

Segmental Studies for Elementary Teaching. The prospective elementary teacher typically engages in course work in curriculum and methods in the several subject fields that comprise the curriculum of the elementary school, but such work for the most part is treated segmentally through separate courses for each field. The study of reading traditionally has been undertaken as though reading is a separate skill subject, not a process of thinking that extends through all subject matters in the curriculum. The fact that the elementary teacher is in a self-contained classroom may indicate a setting in which the teacher can give concerted attention to horizontal curriculum articulation, but such a setting in and of itself does not necessarily impel the teacher to address such concerns. The traditional practice even in the self-contained classroom has been to follow a segmental schedule of studies in which arithmetic, reading, spelling, writing, social studies, science, and so on, are taught as separate subjects. Where specialist teachers are provided in the elementary school in music, art, physical education, and science, insufficient attention is given to the articulation of these areas taken together with the studies in the self-contained classroom.

The trend in some states toward requiring a specialized "academic" major for prospective elementary teachers also has mitigated against horizontal curriculum articulation in the elementary school. Moreover, such a requirement has resulted in most prospective elementary teachers pursuing a major in English or social science, while only rarely does one find mathematics or science chosen as the major.

The specialized disciplines in the college are not designed in consideration of the teacher's work in reorganizing the material so as to make it appropriate to the intellectual and social development of children. It is not a matter of the teacher proceeding to "water down" such material. The teacher must make the material authentically suited to the cognitive and social development of the child.

The trend in some states toward requiring an "academic" undergraduate major for elementary teachers also serves to discriminate against the arts, which are such an important area of activity in the education of children. Where the college has a strong and coherent curriculum in general education, the requirement of an undergraduate major for elementary teachers may prove to have some positive benefits provided that the professional work in teacher education is so designed as to reveal the necessary connections in the total school curriculum. However, relatively few colleges have developed a strong, coherent curriculum in general education.

Curriculum Development as a Continuous Responsibility of the Professional Staff

In the preceding three chapters, considerable discussion was devoted to the school curriculum as the target of incessant criticism and pressure from sources external to the school. It was shown how so many of these external sources represent special interests rather than the wider public interest. Very often these criticisms have enormous implications for the macrocurriculum. Contributing to the problem is the tendency of these external sources to regard curriculum determination as a matter of policy, and to hold that such determination is beyond the province of the teacher. Further compounding the problem is the tendency for many educational researchers to treat curriculum and instruction as separate arenas. The consequence is to regard the teacher as being responsible mainly for the "delivery of instruction." Under such circumstances, teachers may see their responsibility for curriculum development mainly in their having a say in the adoption of textbooks or of segmental curriculum packages, and occasionally helping to write a particular syllabus for a course of study.

The Problem of Segmental Treatment. At the secondary school level, much of the activity in curriculum change is by the accretion and deletion of courses within departments, the adoption of new course packages and textbooks, and the revision of departmental syllabi in accordance with textbook changes. The focus is on the microcurriculum. As a result, the nature and direction of the total school curriculum suffers by default.

The school board and administration may mandate various requirements, such as for promotion and graduation, and the supervisor may seek to institute a new curriculum package, or sequence of studies K–12, in science or language arts, but the real test of the curriculum is determined by the learning experience of the pupils. And it is the teacher who plays the key role in developing the curriculum as a designed learning experience. If teachers treat the designed learning experience as encapsulated in so many segmental subjects, the result is the fragmentation, isolation, and congestion of studies. And the school becomes more vulnerable to external demands for segmental changes in the curriculum.

Teachers, supervisors, and administrators need to assume direct responsibility for curriculum development as a continuous schoolwide and districtwide process, giving attention to building the vital interrelationships among the studies. Obviously, teachers need released time and expertise for such responsibility.

Who Should Decide? In view of the problems just discussed, it should not be surprising that only 33 percent of teachers in a nationwide poll indicated that teachers should have the greatest influence in deciding what is taught in the public schools of their communities, and that 26 percent of the teachers had no opinion on the subject. Yet 79 percent of the teachers felt that teachers should have the most influence in the selection of books for use in school classrooms and school libraries.[5] Obviously, the determination of the curriculum and the selection of the source materials for the curriculum cannot be so easily dichotomized.

In recent years the various state departments of education have extended their role in specifying certain curricular guidelines and mandates, particularly with regard to high school graduation requirements, and have exerted an influence on the curriculum through statewide assessment testing. Nevertheless, the curricular mandates tend to be very broad—such as specifying the number of units in English, mathematics, science, and so on, for graduation.[6] The schools remain free to determine how the curriculum is to be designed and implemented. For example, schools can meet such broad state mandates in an infinite variety of ways—ranging from distribution-elective requirements to a common core of interdisciplinary studies. In other words, from a functional standpoint, curriculum design and development inevitably rests with the local school and school district.

There is no question that since midcentury the schools have been targeted by a variety of shifting nationalizing influences on the curriculum—ranging from federal priorities being given to the sciences and mathematics, to the disadvantaged learner, to career education, and so on. But again, the actual design and implementation of the curriculum fall back on the local level. As professionals, the school faculty and administration, together with the central-office staff, must assume the responsibility for interpreting and assessing state mandates and guidelines, along with the various federal programs or initiatives.

The real curriculum is determined by what goes on in the school and classroom, and it is the school faculty, supervisory staff, administration, and students who, whether by intention or default, make the curriculum. When the faculty, supervisory staff, and administration do not assume the responsibility for curriculum determination and development, the curriculum becomes vulnerable to the special interests of external groups or agencies and even of individual school board members. The responsibility of the faculty, supervisory staff, and administration is to see to it that the curriculum is so conceived and implemented as to best serve children and youth in view of the wider public interest, not the vested interests of special groups.

All Roads Lead to the Curriculum. Teachers are so immersed and loaded down with the day-to-day functions and demands of the classroom that they focus much of their concern on classroom management, failing to recognize that problems of student interest and discipline (or motivation) often reflect the inadequacies of the curriculum. This is compounded by the paucity of curriculum materials and resources available to the teacher, and the lack of time available for curriculum development.

The 1984 Gallup poll on education revealed that when asked to indicate the biggest problems with which the public schools in their community must deal, the problem of "poor curriculum/poor standards" was identified by only 7 percent of teachers as compared with 15 percent of the public in general. Unfortunately, the item in the polling instrument had lumped together "poor curriculum and poor standards," with the result that teachers may understandably have reacted to the item as critical of their work.

The four biggest problems as seen by teachers in order of frequencies of response were: parents' lack of interest/support (31 percent), lack of proper financial support (21 percent), pupils' lack of interest/truancy (20 percent), and lack of discipline (19 percent).[7] The last two items relate to pupil motivation toward learning and have a direct and profound bearing on the curriculum. Moreover, the problem of financial support relates directly to the facilities and resources bearing on the curriculum among other needs. When the lack of pupil motivation and discipline are treated apart from the curriculum, the tendency is to make antagonists of the pupil and the curriculum. And the consequence is miseducation.

STRUCTURE AND FUNCTION OF THE CURRICULUM

One of the oldest principles in biological science is that structure is related to function. This principle has profound implications for curriculum design and development.

In the preceding chapter, it was pointed out that the function of general education requires a very different organization and selection of subject matter and learning experiences than the function of specialized education (specialized knowledge production in the professions, or specialized work in the vocations). In the same vein, the organization of subject matter and learning experiences will differ markedly if the curriculum function is general education, as contrasted with traditional liberal education, or basic education.

Yet the relationship between structure and function has not been given the needed consideration by the professional staff of the school when engaged in efforts to revise the curriculum. Inherited labels to designate the various courses of study are used with little conscious effort to reveal the interrelationships of the parts to the whole curriculum. Moreover, there is a general lack of awareness of the alternative ways in which the curriculum might be organized to fulfill its expected functions.

Five Complementary Functions of the Macrocurriculum

The macrocurriculum may be seen as encompassing five functions: (1) general education (traditionalists would opt to see this as basic education in the school and liberal education in college), (2) specialized education, (3) exploratory education, (4) enrichment education, and (5) special-interest education. Figure 12–1 shows these five macrocurricular functions as interdependent, with general education serving as the common ground.

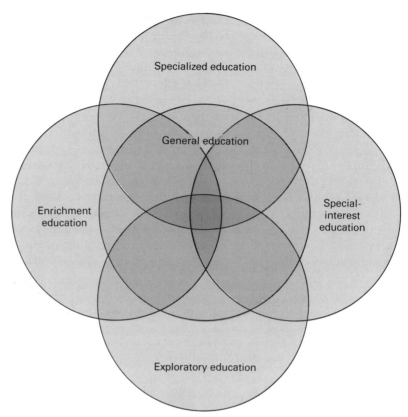

FIGURE 12–1. The five complementary functions of the macrocurriculum.

Source: Adapted from Daniel Tanner, *Secondary Education: Perspectives and Prospects* (New York: Macmillan, 1972, p. 319.

General Education

In the preceding chapter, general education was defined as that aspect of the curriculum designed to provide for a common universe of discourse, understanding, and competence which must be shared by all members of a free society. It is represented by the core of common learnings from which all other studies emanate.

Need for a "Grand Design." As discussed in the preceding chapter, general education in school and college has suffered from neglect since midcentury. Although some of our leading colleges have given evidence of rediscovering general education in recent years, the trend toward knowledge specialism and special-interest education continues.

A 1985 report by a committee of the Association of American Colleges referred to the undergraduate curriculum as being in a state of disarray and pointed out that this condition in the colleges has filtered down into the secondary schools, where there is a lack of curriculum structure and coherence in general education. The collapse of structure in the curriculum has led to the introduction of all kinds of special-interest studies in the colleges "without concern for the criteria of self-discovery, critical thinking, and exploration of values that were for so long central to the baccalaureate program," contended the report, and "one consequence of the abandonment of structure by the colleges has been the abandonment of structure in the schools."[8]

The report rested much of the problem with the professors whose allegiance to the academic disciplines is stronger than their commitment to the education of undergraduates for "a vision of the good life, a life of responsible citizenship and human decency." It went on to call on college administrators "to revive the responsibility of the faculty *as a whole* for the curriculum *as a whole*."[9] Here the report pointed out that although every college has a faculty curriculum committee, the work of the committee only rarely gives systematic consideration of the curriculum structure as a whole and of the function of the curriculum in meeting socially healthy goals for the student.

The 1985 report of the Association of American Colleges went on to describe the work of a model faculty curriculum committee as being engaged in "the grand design of the curriculum" and in emphasizing "the quality of teaching."[10]

The failure of the college faculty "as a whole" to take responsibility for the "grand design of the curriculum as a whole" also applies to the faculty of the elementary school and of the secondary school. Such a responsibility requires a working faculty curriculum committee supported by appropriate resources and allocated sufficient released time on a continuing basis.

Later in this chapter, the various structural frameworks for organizing knowledge for general education are examined in some detail.

Specialized Education

A second macrocurricular function is that of specialized education. Specialized education is represented as that aspect of the curriculum designed for preprofessional, professional, prevocational, and vocational preparation.

At the high school level, the student who aspires to become a scientist will ordinarily be advised to take a concentration of course work in the sciences and mathematics, including advanced-placement courses in these fields. The student who opts for vocational studies in the high school may enroll in such programs as (1) agricultural education, (2) distributive education (distribution and marketing), (3) health occupations education, (4) home economics education, (5) office occupations education, (6) trade and industrial education, and (7) pretechnical education (electronics, computer programming, machine tools). The student may proceed to enter the world of work in one of these areas after graduation from high school, or may go on to college to prepare for a career in agriculture, home economics, nursing, machine-tool design, and so on.

The vocational studies in the high school should be designed as broad career clusters—in view of the need of adolescents to explore widely and in consideration of the fact that adolescents undergo marked shifts in their interests and aspirations as they mature. Yet because the majority of adolescents do not go on to college, they will be severely handicapped in the world of work without a foundation for a career in a skilled occupation.

At the college or university level, specialized education is represented by the student's major field or professional program of studies. In recent years, the various professional schools have moved away from requiring specific preprofessional courses and sequences for admission, in recognition of the importance of general education at the undergraduate level. Nevertheless, the aspiring physician will seek sufficient preparation in the basic sciences in view of the emphasis given to the sciences on the science subtests of the Medical College Admission Test, for example.[11]

The aspiring physicist, chemist, biologist, mathematician, economist, sociologist, and so on, will pursue a major in the given discipline beginning at the undergraduate level and extending into the more specialized subdisciplines at the graduate level.

Dominance of the College over the School. Although discipline-centered studies are associated with specialized education at the college level, the national curriculum reforms of the 1950s and 1960s sought to impose the disciplinary model on the schools, beginning with the first grade and extending through the high school. As discussed in earlier chapters, this effort resulted not only in the neglect of general education, but in the failure to give needed consideration to the unique nature of the growing learner, the neglect of the relationship of the curriculum to the wider problems of society, and to curriculum congestion as each discipline was made to compete for discrete recognition. Even at the college level, the disciplinary model is inadequate for the function of general education because it is focused on specialized knowledge production.

Lack of Coherence in Departmental Specialization. The 1985 report of the Association of American Colleges, cited earlier, not only attacked the colleges for neglecting their responsibility for developing a coherent curriculum in general education and for yielding to the vested interests of departmentalized knowledge specialism, but pointed out that even the departmental concentration lacks coherence. The typical practice is merely to have students select from an array of proliferating and disjointed courses representing the special interests of the various faculty members of the major department.[12]

This problem, on a smaller scale, also applies to the high school, where courses are added to departmental offerings without consideration of the need for curriculum reconstruction at the macro level. Not only is consideration of interdepartmental responsibility for general education found wanting, but insufficient consideration is given to building curriculum coherence among the course offerings within each of the departments—whether it be the social studies, English language arts, sciences, fine arts, or the vocational areas. The college-preparatory program tends to be a traditional list of academic courses topped off by advanced-placement courses, reflecting little or no consideration of developing the curriculum to meet the authentic needs of the adolescent.

Exploratory Education

In the secondary school and college, the typical practice is to require students to distribute their electives among several fields beyond the common core of studies for general education and beyond the areas of concentration or specialization. The purpose of such distribution-elective requirements is to encourage the student to explore a range of fields. However, in many schools and colleges where little or no concerted attention has been given to designing a coherent curriculum in general education, distribution-elective requirements are expected to serve the function of general education. But because each student elects a different pattern of courses within the designated subject fields, and because the individual courses are not designed for general education, this approach fails to serve its intended function. The required sampling of courses in a variety of fields may lead the student to explore areas that he or she might otherwise neglect, but this is no substitute for general education, regardless of the breadth of the sampling.

In the high school or college, a student may elect courses in science with the intention of deciding whether to pursue a career in science. The exploratory experience may impel the student toward a scientific career or away from such a career.

At the elementary level, the exploratory function is met through a range of activities and projects extending from within the common core of studies. For example, a social studies unit on occupations will lead some children into the reading of different source material on given occupations, including simple biographical material; others may be engaged in surveying the different occupations in the community; and some may be working on a class mural depicting the different occupations in society. Although different youngsters are exploring the concept of occupations and the concept of society in a wide range of ways, the extent to which the exploratory activities by individuals and groups is made to relate to the common learnings in social studies will have bearings for general education. In other words, as shown in Figure 12–1, the various functions of the curriculum should be interdependent.

Enrichment Education

This function of the curriculum is intended to supplement and deepen one's educative experience beyond those connected with general education, specialized education, and exploratory education. As in the case of exploratory education, the enrichment function may be met in the secondary school and college through controlled or required electives, or through free electives.

In the secondary school, students who have completed the core courses in English language arts, for example, may be required to elect a course in literature to enrich their learning experiences beyond the required core studies in English.

At the elementary level, the enrichment function typically is provided not through course options, but through activities growing out of the common learnings. Thus the children who are working on a class mural depicting the various occupations in society, or the major historical epochs as part of a unit in the social studies, are gaining enrichment experiences in the visual arts.

Special-Interest Education

This function of the curriculum in the secondary school and college is typically met through free electives. Because college students would otherwise tend to pursue such electives in their major field, the college may require that the free electives be taken outside the major. The mathematics major in college may have developed a special interest in music theory, for example, and may pursue course work in music theory to meet such an interest. The high school student in ornamental horticulture may have developed a special interest in instrumental music or vocal music, and may elect music courses while also participating in the school band, orchestra, or chorus. The student intending to become a lawyer may have developed a special interest in hydroponics (the growing of plants in nutrient solutions instead of in soil) as the result of having elected a course in horticulture in high school. (The authors know of a student who developed a special interest in beekeeping as the result of taking a course in agriculture in high school, and who met all of his college expenses by producing and marketing honey under a private label while he was in college. Yet his chosen career was not at all related to this special interest.)

At the secondary school and college levels, special-interest education is provided not only through formal course work, but also through organized student activities such as clubs, publications, community service, and so on. Many student organizations in high school and college are oriented toward career goals as well as toward special interests.

The fifth-grader may have a special interest in photography or crafts, and may be involved in contributing his or her talents to the class work in social studies and science. The sixth grader may have developed a special interest in writing poetry as the result of the study of poetry in language arts, or he or she may have developed a special interest in trains as the result of a social studies unit on transportation.

Obviously, special-interest and enrichment education are not necessarily sharply demarcated, except that the former is more highly focused and concentrated.

ALTERNATIVE CURRICULUM DESIGNS

From the foregoing, it is seen that the five functions of the macrocurriculum must be treated in ecological relationship. This requires that the curriculum be so organized that it provides for the needed horizontal as well as vertical articulation of studies (scope and sequence).

The concept of the spiral curriculum relates not only to the deepening of studies as the learner progresses through school (vertical articulation), but to the widening of studies so as to reveal the vital interdependence of the various areas of knowledge and learning activities (horizontal articulation).

Despite the pervasive need for such articulation, only rarely are conscious efforts made to redesign the curriculum so as to create the needed coherence and unity. New courses and programs of study are introduced from time to time, while old courses and programs remain or are compressed or deleted. The approach is largely segmental, as each course and program of study is treated in isolation.

Few supervisors and teachers are consciously aware of the alternatives open to them in designing the curriculum. The prevailing segmental mind set is inherited from a tradition that sees curriculum development mainly as revising or updating the material in the standard subjects, adding new course-of-study packages and courses to replace the old, and tacking-on new material to the existing material in a given subject. Under these circumstances, the role of the supervisor is largely delimited to helping teachers improve their "delivery" of instruction and classroom management, while the problem of curriculum design and development remains neglected. Where subject supervisors are available, they tend to work within their separate subject fields. The consequence is the "cocoon curriculum."

Traditionally, the curriculum at the elementary level was organized according to the fundamental skill subjects of reading, grammar, spelling, writing, and calculating. Other subjects were added as recognition was given to the needed widening functions of elementary education.

The movement for general education during the twentieth century led to the realization that alternative designs of structures were required for organizing the curriculum. The major alternative designs for the subject curriculum are (1) disciplinary, (2) lamination, (3) correlation, (4) fusion, and (5) broad fields. In addition to these five contrasting approaches to the subject curriculum, the curriculum can be organized according to pervasive problems, themes, or activities that transcend the traditional subject boundaries. In other words, the extent of curriculum synthesis can be such that the learning experiences are no longer identified within the traditional subject compartments or fields.

A number of schools in the Eight-Year Study experimented with various approaches toward curriculum synthesis in general education by organizing the curriculum according to the pervasive problems and concerns of adolescents in the contemporary society.[13] This approach was commonly referred to as the core curriculum—in contradistinction to the traditional subject curriculum. However, over the years, the term *core* has been used in secondary and higher education to denote those studies that are required of all students to meet the function of general education—regardless of whether the common studies are organized according to disciplines, broad-fields subjects, interdisciplinary problems, or any other form of organization.

If the principle that structure is related to function applies to the curriculum, it behooves supervisors and teachers to examine systematically the alternative approaches to curriculum structure or design, and to seek to so structure the curriculum as to build the needed coherence and unity for optimum learning.

The Discipline-Centered Curriculum

The discipline-centered approach is the purest form of organizing knowledge in the subject curriculum. As discussed in earlier chapters, the disciplinary construct derives from the specialized knowledge domains of university scholarship. For almost two decades, a period extending from the 1950s through the 1960s, the disciplinary rationale of university scholar-specialists dominated the curriculum reforms at the elementary and secondary levels.

Although inquiry/discovery was embraced as the mode of teaching and learning in the discipline-centered curriculum reforms, it was confined to specialized, disciplinary knowledge. Thus the study of mathematics, physics, or economics in the school was so construed as to represent and treat the subject matter within the discrete disciplinary domains of the university scholar-specialist. The approach taken was as though each youngster was on his or her way toward the Ph.D. in each discipline. Thus a disciplinary advocate in the social sciences held that the needed approach is to "bring the frontiers of social science knowledge into the curriculum by respecting and protecting the integrity of each discipline," and he saw the central problem of curriculum reform being properly addressed by this question: "How can we identify those analytical tools of the various social sciences which can then be related to the students' experience at all levels from grade one to the Ph.D.?"[14]

Disciplinary Knowledge and General Education. One of the puzzling aspects of the whole disciplinary movement at the elementary and secondary levels was the fact that even college educators had long recognized the inadequacy of discipline-centered studies to meet the function of general education in higher education.[15] Yet the university scholar-specialists had no hesitancy in imposing this model of curriculum organization on the elementary and secondary schools.

Nevertheless, it should be noted that the latter 1950s and the decade of the 1960s were marked by the neglect of general education at the college level, as disciplinary knowledge specialization ruled the roost in academe. Instead of designing a coherent curriculum in general education, elective-distribution requirements were established. The undergraduate majoring in history, who sought to meet the distribution requirements in science by electing an introductory course in chemistry, for example, often found that the chemistry course was designed as the first course on the way to the Ph.D. in chemistry. The chemistry major who had elected an introductory course in economics to meet the distribution requirement in social science might have found the subject matter designed more appropriately as the first course toward the Ph.D. in economics, and so on.

The needed interrelationships of knowledge to broach the pervasive concerns of an enlightened citizenry were shunted aside as the disciplinary doctrine of the university was pushed down into the elementary and secondary schools.

The Disciplines and the Problem of Curriculum Congestion and Isolation. As shown in Figure 12–2, the disciplinary doctrine created a congestion of the curriculum as each disciplinary subject was made to compete for a recognized place in the curriculum. In seeking to protect the purity of each discipline, the

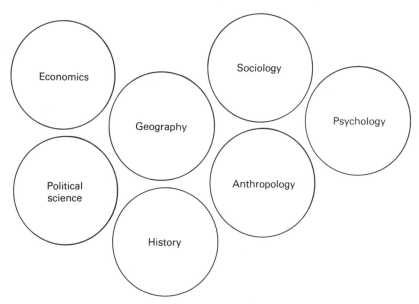

Figure 12–2. The social science disciplines and history.

social sciences, for example, were to be represented in the curriculum by a host of discrete disciplines, including anthropology, economics, geography, political science, psychology, and sociology—in addition to the study of U.S. history, state history, world history, and so on.

Added to the problem of curriculum congestion is the failure of the learner, from the elementary school to the university, to make the needed interconnections between and among the autonomous and insulated domains of disciplinary knowledge. Referring to the study of the sciences in the university, the late J. D. Bernal described the problem in these words:

> For the most part science subjects are taught separately and out of relation with one another. . . . Each subject is conceived of as a more or less closed body of knowledge preserving its purity not only from the world of practice but from other subjects. This results in a very considerable fossilization of the separate curricula, a process much assisted, of course, by the rigidity of the examination system.[16]

Neglect of Practical Application. To the extent that the purity and integrity of a discipline is protected and preserved, the more it is removed from the world of practice. For as soon as a discipline is made relevant to the world of practice, it loses its isolated character and identity, and acquires interdisciplinary connections.

In the real world, economic problems are not confined to economics, but to social and political policy, world resources, and so on. Psychology is not only a social science but also a branch of medicine. Geography encompasses not only the surface physical features of the earth, but the relationship of the physical features, climate, and natural resources to the economic development of nations and regions, among other things. In essence, the knowledge edifices known as disciplines are human-made creations to advance specialized knowledge in the university. In life, these separate thought edifices break down as knowledge becomes necessarily interconnected.

Examining the place of history as an independent realm of scholarship, the philosopher John H. Randall, Jr., commented:

> I have long been convinced that there is no such thing as "history," and for some time I have been coming to doubt whether there are any social sciences. . . . I am really in the same boat with the historians and the social scientists—there is no such thing as "philosophy" either. . . . There is no such thing as "history" in general, nor are there any men who are just "historians." Every history is *the* history of something, and every historian is trying to trace *the* past *of* something.[17]

Thus we have the study of the history of civilization, art history, the history of science and technology, and so on. In effect, history is a mode of inquiry rather than a specific subject matter.

Even in the biological and physical sciences, the disciplinary lines of separation lose their distinctions as new interconnections are required in solving significant problems. Thus, for example, such fields as biochemistry and biophysics have emerged.

Children and adolescents are vitally interested in the applications of knowledge to their own lives. When the purity of a discipline is so protected as to deny the learner the opportunity to connect the subject matter to life experience, the subject matter is seen as remote and artificial. Moreover, the concept of general education requires that the subject matter reveal the interconnections of codified knowledge to the life of the wider society. Here, too, specialized disciplinary knowledge is inadequate to the task of building a coherent curriculum for general education.

Curriculum Lamination

Various efforts have been made to bring together into a single subject certain subject matters that otherwise would be treated as separate subjects. However, when each of the subject matters is allowed to retain its separate identity, the effect is to layer or to laminate the various subject matters rather than to provide for synthesis.

The subject of general science in the elementary school, middle school, and junior high school traditionally has encompassed an admixture of topics and activities in physical science, earth science, astronomy, botany, and zoology. Under these circumstances, the subject matters are not really integrated into a broad field which general science is intended to represent.

In the high school and college, the humanities may be so organized that music and the visual arts are treated separately from literature, even though they are brought together under the rubric of a single course or course sequence. History and philosophy may also be separated. Thus, instead of the subject matters being truly integrated as a broad field of humanities, they are layered or laminated together without revealing their interconnections.

The industrial arts course in the junior high school may be organized around units of work and projects in such areas as woods, metals, plastics, graphic arts, and electricity. The goal is to expose students to a range of learning experiences in different areas of the industrial arts. However, unless a systematic effort is made to reveal the interrelationships among the various areas, they are treated as a series of laminated units of activity. The same may hold for the visual arts course in the high school, which provides for a range of separate activities in a variety of media—drawing, painting, sculpting, photography, motion pictures, and so on.

Curriculum Correlation

In recognizing the need to reveal the relationships between or among two or more subjects, teachers may seek to correlate certain subject matters and activities while retaining the identities of the separate subjects (Figure 12–3).

The elementary school teacher may proceed to engage pupils in the use of mathematics in the study of science or even in social studies. Geography and history might also be correlated, although they are taught as separate subjects. At the upper elementary level, the teacher may correlate the reading of certain literary works and the writing of compositions with work in the social studies and history.

Block-Time Teaching and Team Teaching. A common practice in the junior high school is block-time teaching, whereby a given teacher is responsible for teaching English and social studies in combined periods. The two subjects may be treated so as to retain their separate identities; yet the study of literature is correlated with the study of history, or the work in composition involves the writing of themes on topics of social concern. If the block-time teacher makes no concerted effort to correlate the two subjects, such as English and social studies, the two subjects are simply laminated into a single block of time.

In some cases, classes are combined in team-teaching arrangements to provide for curriculum correlation. The two teachers work as a team with their combined classes in English and social studies in an effort to correlate the two subjects.

Interdepartmental Correlation. The faculties of two departments in the high school, such as in English and social studies, may agree to organize the study of

Figure 12–3. Correlation.

American literature with the chronological study of U.S. history, although American literature and U.S. history continue to be taught as separate classes.

Or instead of seeking to correlate the separate subjects through a chronological-historical approach, a thematic approach may be followed in which the teacher of English and the teacher of social studies correlate the two subjects through such common themes as "man's inhumanity to man" or "self-identity in an age of mass-technological society." Yet each subject is taught separately.

Literature may be correlated with art and music through broad themes that have evolved historically, representing the major parallel movements from traditional forms to modern forms of expression.

Physical science and mathematics also lend themselves to correlation, though the possibilities for such correlation are seldom exploited. The same holds true for the social studies and statistics.

Because the subjects and subject fields retain their separate identities, correlation does not provide for true curriculum synthesis. Nevertheless, it represents a notable effort toward articulating subjects that otherwise would be studied as isolated entities.

Curriculum Fusion

It has been seen that although correlation is undertaken to reveal the relationships between two or more subjects or subject fields, the subjects or subject fields nevertheless remain intact. Each subject or subject field retains its identity. In contrast, fusion involves the merging of related subjects to the extent that a new subject is created.

Although fusion more commonly involves subjects within the same field, it may also involve the merger of subjects from two or more different fields. An example of the former is the combining of various history courses into the single subject of world history. The newer earth science course emerged from a fusion of certain areas of physical science and geography—two fields that traditionally had been treated in the curriculum as though they were virtually unrelated (Figure 12–4).

As early as 1912, Whitehead proposed the fusion of modern history with statistical mathematics in the secondary school, to provide for the quantitative study of social forces.[18] Today, our colleges commonly offer courses bearing such titles as "Computers in Society" and "Mathematical Sociology." Economic history is another example of fusion.

The emergence of sociobiology attracted widespread public interest during the 1970s as systematic study was being undertaken of the influence of human biology on human social behavior.[19]

From Fusion to Broad Field. The case of biology as a high school subject reveals a notable transformation. Before the turn of the century, separate courses in the high school were offered in botany, zoology, anatomy, and physiology. The Committee of Ten in 1894 listed these separate courses along with other sciences as examples of "good" secondary school programs of studies.[20] Over the early decades of the twentieth century, these separate subjects were fused into the

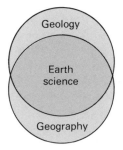 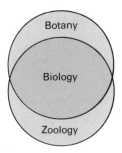

Figure 12–4. Fusion.

single subject of biology. Nevertheless, for many years biology was divided into a semester's study of botany, followed by a semester of zoology—representing a kind of lamination rather than fusion. Eventually, the subject matter was fused as a unitary course in biology and became a general education subject in the high school (see Figure 12–4).

Modern biology represents such an encompassing treatment of the variegated and interactive life sciences that it has now emerged as a broad field of study rather than merely the fusion of different subjects from related areas. (As discussed later, a broad field represents a synthesis of an entire branch of knowledge, or of two or more entire branches of knowledge.)

Because knowledge in the real world recognizes no sharp boundaries or divisions, disciplines and broad fields are fused together in the university, leading to the emergence of such subjects as biochemistry, biophysics, bioengineering, and biostatistics.

The Broad-Fields Curriculum

When the various subject matters from an entire branch of knowledge, or from two or more branches of knowledge, are treated as a more or less unified whole, the new subject becomes a broad field. The broad-fields approach represents a more advanced effort toward curriculum synthesis than fusion.

Broad-fields subjects representing some degree of synthesis of subject matters from given branches of knowledge may be variously designated as social studies, social science, American studies, general science, physical science, English language arts, fine arts, industrial arts, and so on. However, these designations often serve as a mere label or rubric for disjointed or laminated studies. Thus the English language arts may be treated in the curriculum not as a unitary broad field, but as separate subjects in grammar, composition, and literature.

The curriculum in the elementary school typically is organized according to the broad fields of language arts, social studies, science, and visual arts, along with mathematics, music, and so on. However, for many years the more progressive teachers have organized the learning activities so that the fields are treated interrelatedly, such as through the study of geography or by organizing the learning experiences around certain comprehensive concepts and centers of interest—such as occupations, transportation, or "Where does our food come

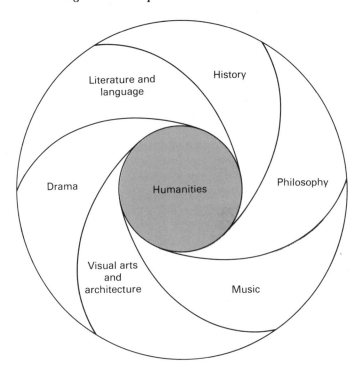

Figure 12–5. The broad field of humanities.

from?" Skills in the fundamental processes are developed functionally in connection with such studies. At the other extreme, the subject matter in the elementary classroom is reduced to skill-drill exercises in reading, spelling, grammar, writing, reciting, and calculating (the old back-to-basics emphasis on the "three R's").

A number of colleges have developed broad-fields courses for general education in which an interdisciplinary approach is taken in a course sequence over an entire academic year in each of several broad fields, such as social science, biological science, physical science, humanities, and so on.

The Humanities and the Dualism Between Appreciation and Performance. The humanities course in the high school and college represents an effort at revealing the interrelationships among several branches of knowledge—representing the accomplishments of humanity throughout history in literature (drama, poetry, novel), the fine arts (music, painting, sculpture, architecture, and related arts), dance, and philosophy (Figure 12–5).

Paradoxically, although the humanities encompass the visual arts, drama, and music, the tendency is to treat these studies as "nonacademic" subjects in the school, whereas the humanities are regarded as an "academic" subject. This dualism stems from the perennialist tradition, which holds that studying *about* a subject, particularly through literary works and historical treatment, is more intellective than putting knowledge into action through performance—whether in the studio, theater, or laboratory. Thus the fine arts are studied historically in the humanities, leaving the creation of art and artistic performance to the "nonacademic" side of the curriculum. This unfortunate dichotomy separates "appreciation" from "doing." Yet there can be only incomplete appreciation without the act of "doing." This dichotomy is also reflected in the creation by the federal government of two separate and competing agencies in 1965—the National Endowment for the Humanities and the National Endowment for the Arts.

The fine arts and performing arts have not been effectively developed as a broad field in the school curriculum, but have been treated mainly as separate subjects and areas of activity—music (instrumental and vocal), graphic arts, painting, sculpture, crafts, photography, drama, motion pictures, television, costume and fashion design, industrial design, and so on. Moreover the fine arts as a broad field have not been correlated in the curriculum with the broad field of the industrial arts.

Toward Synthesis. Turning to the sciences, the broad-fields course(s) in natural science, developed by a number of colleges to meet the function of general education, represents the synthesis of two entire branches of science—physical science and biological science.

Ecology is a newly emergent broad field. Biology may be studied from an ecological perspective. However, ecology as a broad field may represent a synthesis of knowledge drawn from a host of fields—the biological sciences, physical sciences, social sciences, agriculture, engineering, urban planning, health, and recreation (Figure 12–6). Such a synthesis becomes necessary when the study of ecology is organized so as to address pervading societal and global problems—ranging from the extinction of wildlife to the effects of the environment on human health. So treated, ecology is no longer a broad-fields subject, but an interdisciplinary, problem-focused approach to the curriculum. The subject-matter lines or boundaries that define the broad field have become so indistinct that the treatment is no longer subject centered, but problems centered. We shall return to the problem-focused curriculum in general education later in this chapter.

The broad-fields approach is not a mere sampling of disparate subject matters within a laminated framework. Instead, subject matters that otherwise would be treated separately are brought together to reveal their interdependence in such a way that a new subject field emerges. The broad-fields approach represents a notable effort toward overcoming such pervasive problems as curriculum fragmentation, congestion, isolation, and specialization—problems that take their toll in ineffective learning. Moreover, efforts toward curriculum synthesis also reveal the interdependence of knowledge and its applications.

As discussed later, the ultimate synthesis occurs when the curriculum in general education is no longer centered on subjects, even broad-fields subjects, but on transdisciplinary problems or issues of common concern to all members of a free society.

Amherst College is noted for having developed broad-fields courses early in this century in efforts to unify the curriculum for general education. Columbia College of Columbia University also pioneered in efforts to develop a coherent

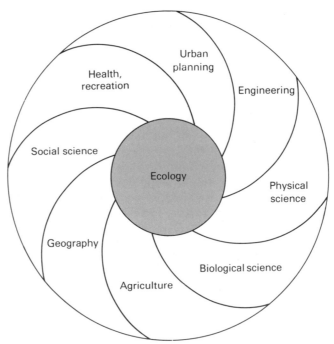

Figure 12–6. The broad field of ecology.

curriculum in general education. At Columbia, what was to become a two-year course sequence in Contemporary Civilization in 1929 actually had its origins in course work on "War Issues" and "Peace Issues" during and following World War I. Over several decades the two-year sequence in Contemporary Civilization and the two-year sequence in the Humanities course served as the core of identity which gave Columbia its distinction in general education. From the start, the Contemporary Civilization course was more of a social-issues course than a broad-fields course. In 1959, the common second year of Contemporary Civilization was dropped in view of the more specialized interests of the various departments in the social sciences.[21] Nevertheless, the issues-centered approach was continued in the year-long Contemporary Civilization course.

Since the 1940s, such differing types of institutions as the University of Chicago and Michigan State University developed unified, sequential broad-fields courses to serve the function of general education, carrying such designations as Social Science, Natural Science, and Humanities. A key theme of the curriculum in general education at Michigan State was "critical thinking," and systematic evaluations were conducted over many years to study student growth in critical thinking.[22] Although the curriculum in general education at both of these universities has undergone significant change over the years, the broad-fields approach remains a dominant mode of curriculum organization. Today, at the University of Chicago, students may opt to pursue from among several variants in the sequence of studies within each broad field, such as in social science, but each variant is unified under a theme (e.g., "Freedom and the

Political Order"). At Michigan State, a three-term sequence in natural science not only integrates the biological and physical sciences in classroom and laboratory work, but the social implications of science are explored. Students may also meet the science requirement in general education by pursuing studies in certain interdisciplinary, problem-focused courses.

Combined Fields. Mention has been made of block-time classes in an effort to correlate the studies in two different fields, such as English and social studies. In some schools offering block-time classes, the curriculum is so reconstructed that it goes beyond correlation by interrelating the learning activities in such a way that the subject-field boundaries become less and less distinct. Thus the broad fields of English language arts and social studies become combined fields. Despite the promising possibilities, combined-field studies have not been widely implemented. The paucity of appropriate curriculum materials, the departmental structure of the secondary school, and the preparation of secondary school teachers and supervisors as subject specialists in the discipline-oriented university, have mitigated against the combined-fields approach. In some schools, team teaching has been employed to bridge the English language arts and social studies, but the effort may result only in correlation if each teacher regards himself or herself as a subject specialist.

The Problem-Focused Core Curriculum

Several alternative designs have been examined for organizing the subject curriculum. An alternative to the subject curriculum for purposes of general education is the problem-focused core based directly on the common concerns of youth in contemporary society. This approach has been described as a "quantum leap" beyond the subject curriculum.[23]

Although the problem-focused core draws on organized subject matter, such subject matter is not treated as material "to be covered," but as instrumental in attacking the persistent or common problems faced by youth as members of an open society of free people. As discussed in Chapter 11, the problem-focused core curriculum was developed in the most experimental and successful schools in the Eight-Year Study. It was also proposed in the model curriculum developed in connection with the report of the Educational Policies Commission in 1952.[24] However, only a small number of secondary schools actually implemented a problem-focused core curriculum. The major thrust during the era after midcentury was away from general education and toward discipline-centered studies in the wake of the Cold War and later the space race. A major problem from the time of the inception of the problem-focused core curriculum was the resistance against controversial ideas in the curriculum. Although the censorship of curricular materials continues to this day, it was particularly rampant from the 1930s extending into the period of McCarthyism during the 1950s. Other factors mitigating against the problem-focused core curriculum were the scarcity of needed curricular materials, the enormous demands placed on the faculty and the supervisory staff to develop the curriculum, and the traditional preparation of secondary school teachers as subject specialists.

In those schools that had developed a problem-focused core curriculum in general education, the common practice was to offer it in block-time classes encompassing at least two subjects that otherwise would be scheduled as separate periods. The block time typically included the homeroom, so that the block-time teacher also served in a guidance capacity. The problems to be studied typically were preplanned by the faculty through comprehensive teaching-resource units, but required considerable teacher–pupil planning in the implementation of the curriculum. In most such schools, the problem-focused core was supplemented by certain subject-centered courses for general education, such as mathematics.[25]

The Persistent-Life-Situations Proposal. A variation of the problem-focused curriculum was developed by Florence Stratemeyer and her associates around midcentury, in which the curriculum from early childhood to adulthood is based on "persistent life situations."[26] However, many of the "situations" identified by Stratemeyer and her associates were not broadly integrative problems of personal–social significance, but were activities related to a wide range of learning experiences.

Moreover, whereas the proponents of the problem-focused core curriculum viewed critical thinking as the unifying method in the curriculum, Stratemeyer separated the learning activities so that those activities relating to "intellectual power" came under a different category than the other activities, such as those relating to maintaining health, developing aesthetic appreciation and expression, growing in effective social participation, and so on. In other words, the proponents of the problem-focused core curriculum held that one should be engaged in the use and growth of intelligence in all significant life activities— whether in dealing with problems of maintaining good health, in learning responsible social participation in a free society, or in developing wider and richer aesthetic appreciations and expression.

The persistent-life-situations curriculum more closely resembles the activity curriculum, discussed later, than a problem-focused curriculum—since most of the situational activities identified by Stratemeyer and her associates do not require systematic inquiry for problem solutions.

Recent Efforts Toward Curriculum Synthesis. The rediscovery of general education during the late 1970s and early 1980s led to a number of proposals for greater curriculum synthesis through problem-focused studies. For example, Project Synthesis was initiated in 1979 by the National Science Teachers Association with funds from the National Science Foundation to develop a curriculum framework in which the study of science and technology relates to the life of the individual, reveals significant societal issues, and relates to the many kinds of work that people do in society.[27]

Twenty years after the inception of the Biological Sciences Curriculum Study (BSCS)—one of the leading national curriculum-reform projects of the post-*Sputnik* era—Bentley Glass, the first chairman of BSCS, acknowledged a change of perspective in these words: "More and more, during these two decades, I have come to realize the necessity of applying our biology to areas of human values and social needs, of rational guidance through times of shattering change impelled by scientific discovery and technological application." Glass concluded his remarks with this quote written by John Dewey in 1903: "Any scene of action which is social is also cosmic or physical. It is also biological. Hence the absolute impossibility of ruling out the physical and biological sciences from bearing upon ethical science."[28]

Also taking stock on the twentieth anniversary of BSCS, the current BSCS director stressed the change in perspective that had occurred in recognizing the need to bridge science with the life of the learner and with the life of the wider society. Yet he acknowledged that some of the newer BSCS curricular materials for the elementary, middle, and junior high school were developed in module form so that any material found to be controversial or objectionable by a school constituency could easily be removed without rejecting the entire BSCS program. The director also acknowledged that certain controversial material was avoided altogether in view of the current climate.

> In the 1960s we had no difficulty defining the parameters of biology and remaining within them. As the social climate changed and our attitudes developed with experience, we began to realize that biology impinged on almost every facet of human endeavor; so we started broadening our activities on a more transdisciplinary base. The BSCS program that most extensively reflects this broadened interpretation of biology is the Human Sciences Program, involving not only the natural sciences but the social sciences and humanities as well, integrating multidisciplinary content in such a way as to deal with a given point, such as ecology or population. . . .
>
> We have, in the absence of data to the contrary, refrained from full explication of certain social matters that are still contentious within the population in order that students may not be disadvantaged by community refusals to use BSCS materials.[29]

The fact that the developers of curriculum materials today will avoid certain controversial subject matter, despite its appropriateness in the curriculum for children and adolescents, provides a clue of what the conditions may have been like a half a century ago when the idea of the problem-focused core curriculum was being introduced. Yet the need for the treatment of social problems and issues in the curriculum in general education remains persistent. In his study of the high school, Boyer made the following proposal in 1983 under the heading "From Courses to Coherence":

> We must bring a new interdisciplinary vision into the classroom and the total program of the school. The content of the core curriculum must extend beyond the specialties to touch larger, more transcendent issues.
>
> Teachers must play a key role in making these connections between the disciplines. They must view the curriculum in a more coherent way. We cannot expect students to see relationships that teachers do not see. Teachers also should work together collaboratively. . . .
>
> Specifically, we recommend that all students during their senior year, complete what we choose to call the Senior Independent Project, a written report that focuses on a significant contemporary issue one (sic) that draws upon the various fields of academic study that have made up the student's program. This assignment is part of core requirements. Students will receive one-half unit credit.[30]

A puzzling aspect of Boyer's proposal is how such a half-unit project in the senior year of high school could possibly provide for the synthesis of a curriculum core that is otherwise comprised of the usual separate courses in English, history, civics, science, mathematics, and so on. The idea of a year-long problems-of-democracy course in the twelfth grade was first proposed early in this century[31] and came to be widely adopted, although such a single course could not possibly build coherence into an otherwise segmented curriculum. Yet in 1959, Conant revivified the idea of a year-long, heterogeneously grouped problems-of-democracy course in the twelfth grade that would meet the following great expectations:

> This course should develop not only an understanding of the American form of government and of the economic basis of our free society, but also mutual respect and understanding between different types of students. Current topics should be included; free discussion of controversial issues should be encouraged. This approach is one significant way in which our schools distinguish themselves from those in totalitarian nations. This course, as well as well-organized homerooms and certain student activities, can contribute a great deal to the development of future citizens of our democracy who will be intelligent voters, stand firm under trying national conditions, and not be beguiled by the oratory of those who appeal to special interests.[32]

The lesson to be learned after looking back on all this is that the functions of the senior-year course described by Conant should pervade the entire curriculum in general education if they are to be achieved. The fact that the need for problem-focused studies of personal and social significance for adolescents is rediscovered periodically is testimony to a great unmet need in general education.

At the elementary and middle school levels, there is a persistent need to relate the curriculum to the personal and social development of the learner. The BSCS Human Sciences Program is an activity-centered curriculum for the period of transition from childhood to early adolescence, and includes the study of such problems as "Extending the Senses," "Making Sense," "Growing Bigger," "Growing Older," "Growing Different," "Learning and School," "Making Rules," "Where Do I Fit?," "Seeing Things Differently," "What's Going on Inside [My Body]?," and others.[33] Such questions or problems may be ignored in the school curriculum, but they cannot be ignored by the child and will be dealt with in one way or another. Such problems do not go away by "benign neglect" and too often result in misinformation and distortion in the absence of planned educative experiences.

In recent years, many colleges have developed transdisciplinary problem-focused courses designed to extend and enrich the students' learning experiences beyond the regular course sequence in general education. For example, Michigan State University has developed many such transdisciplinary courses, a few of which are listed as follows: *Science and Pseudoscience; Technology, Society and Public Policy; Issues in Science and Religion; The Bioecology of Health; Engineering and Public Policy; Interdisciplinary Issues in Aging; Our Place in Nature; American and*

World Problems; Casualties of Contemporary Society; Cultures in Crisis, World Urbaniza-tion: Cultures and Common Issues; Freedom and Justice; and *Energy Consumption and Environmental Quality.*

Nevertheless, the persistent need and challenge in secondary and under-graduate education is to provide for the treatment of pervading problems and issues of significance to the learner and to the wider society within the framework of the core studies in general education. Otherwise, the curriculum becomes fragmented into a host of courses on special topics of special interest to different subpopulations of the student body, rather than serving the common interest.

Special interests are served through various elective options and through specialized studies. But problems of common concern can serve as the unifying basis for general education in the secondary school and college.

One of the most notable recent efforts to build an entire college curriculum, including the curriculum in general education, around transdisciplinary prob-lems rather than traditional disciplines was undertaken in the planning of the University of Wisconsin–Green Bay before it opened its doors on a newly con-structed campus in 1969.

The organizing framework for the entire curriculum of the University of Wisconsin–Green Bay is ecology. The core curriculum for general education begins with freshman-year seminars focused on such problems as the human condition in world perspective, technology and human values, resource utiliza-tion, crises in communication, and contemporary moral problems. During the sophomore and junior years, the students extend their seminar studies to com-munity and regional projects. In the senior year, the seminars are devoted to integrative themes, such as culture, community, and environment.

Each student's major or area of concentration may be in any broad field or discipline, but the studies are integrated around a broad problem area con-nected with the environment. The entire undergraduate curriculum is based on three themes: (1) social responsibility, (2) the applications of knowledge to the solution of real problems, and (3) integrative education.

After having visited the campus soon after its opening, a former editor-in-chief of *Harper's Magazine* wrote, "If I were about to start to college, it would be my first choice—ahead of anything in the Ivy League."[34]

The Activity Curriculum

Giving recognition to children's propensities to do things with materials and see what happens, to share experiences, and to express themselves artistically, pro-gressive educators early in this century sought to treat learning as an active process. The curriculum in early-childhood education was organized around centers of activity and interest that transcended the traditional subject bound-aries. The fundamental processes or basic skills were taught through the centers of activity and interest, rather than being taught as separate skill subjects. Some educators were using the terms *experience curriculum* and *activity curriculum* inter-changeably.

Although the activity or experience curriculum was intended to provide for curriculum synthesis, it was not necessarily grounded in a deliberate social rationale as in the case of the problem-focused core curriculum.

The Open Classroom. The activity curriculum also came to be implemented on a fairly wide scale in the primary schools in England. In England, it came to be called the "integrated day," "integrated curriculum," or "open classroom."

In 1963 the Central Advisory Council for Education (England) was commissioned by the minister of education to study primary education and the transition to secondary education. The council's report was issued in 1967 and almost immediately attracted international attention. One of the practices enthusiastically endorsed in the council's report was the "integrated curriculum" or "open classroom" in the primary school—a revolutionary departure from the traditional subject curriculum. "Throughout our discussion of the curriculum," stated the council's report, "we stress that children's learning does not fit into the subject categories."[35] Although the council's report noted that subject divisions may be expected in the curriculum for older children, it warned that "experience in secondary schools has shown that teaching of rigidly defined subjects, often by specialist teachers, is far from suitable."[36]

The council's report went on to review the various ways of integrating the curriculum—through centers of interest, projects, and use of the environment. In essence, much of what the council recommended as desired educational practice bore an uncanny resemblance to the American progressive educational reforms of the 1920s and 1930s.

By the late 1960s a counterreaction had set in against the discipline-centered curriculum reforms in the United States. The new call was to "humanize" the schools. The journalist Charles E. Silberman, who earlier had heralded the discipline-centered curriculum reforms,[37] did an "about face" in 1970 when he authored a report for the Carnegie Corporation in which he criticized the discipline-centered reforms and called for the humanizing of our schools by adopting the British open classroom.[38] Silberman's report immediately became a national best-seller, and the open classroom and open school ("schools without walls") became widely promoted and implemented in this country. Unfortunately, little systematic effort was made to provide for curriculum synthesis. In many open classrooms, the learning activities were divided into different sections of the room where pupils were assigned traditional work on skills in mathematics in one corner, reading in another corner, and so on. In many cases, the open classroom and open school were instituted mainly as a vehicle for economizing on space utilization and the deployment of staff rather than for curriculum synthesis and the improvement of learning.

The open classroom and open school also was transmogrified by radical romanticists into a laissez-faire setting of spontaneous activity based on children's immediate felt interests. The radical romanticists denigrated the planned curriculum. In the words of a leading advocate of this kind of open classroom, "the things that work best for him [the teacher] are the unplanned ones, the ones that arise spontaneously because of a student's suggestion or sudden perception."[39]

In 1902, Dewey had warned of the emptiness of appealing to interest through mere excitation and without the educative medium (the curriculum). Such an approach is just as bad as the continued repression of initiative in order to gain conformity to some external and arbitrary power of authority, contended Dewey.[40]

In short, what was originally intended as an effort to integrate the curriculum and make it consonant with the nature of the developing learner through centers of activity and open-classroom arrangements came to be so variously interpreted in the late 1960s and early 1970s (just as it was so variously interpreted in Dewey's day) that the original purposes became lost.

The Project Method. The confusion that beset the open classroom during the 1960s and 1970s, and the failure to carry out its intended purpose of unifying the curriculum in connection with the life of the child, reduced the open-classroom concept to a slogan or label. A similar fate befell a very different approach toward curriculum synthesis early in this century, namely the project method, as proposed by William Kilpatrick.[41]

The project method was being developed systematically early in this century in high school classes in vocational agriculture, in which students applied the principles of scientific agriculture to actual field projects under the teacher's supervision. Each student was required to make systematic plans and maintain detailed records of the projects, showing how the various approved practices learned in the classroom were being transformed into actual practice. In this way, the project method was being employed in a manner consistent with Dewey's problem method.

As discussed earlier in this book, Kilpatrick viewed the project method as a universal method from the elementary school upward to create continuity between ideas and practice, and to create curriculum synthesis. Eventually, Kilpatrick and his followers began to label almost any activity as a project, just so long as it could be seen as a "purposeful" act and was engaged in "wholeheartedly." As a result, almost any activity came to be labeled a "project," with the consequence that the concept lost its vital bearings for problem solving and for revealing the interrelationships and applications of knowledge.[42]

Nevertheless, the activity and project approaches remain feasible to this day—from the elementary school through the high school and into the college. For example, the project method continues to be integral to the curriculum in vocational agriculture in the high school since the time of its inception—early in this century. Many leading colleges or schools of engineering incorporate student projects in the curriculum. Over many years, California Polytechnic University has required students to engage in field projects as an integral part of the agricultural curriculum. As discussed earlier, projects on the environment are integral to the core curriculum at the University of Wisconsin–Green Bay.

Mention was made in Chapter 4 of the *Foxfire* books, which have sold some 7 million copies over a period spanning two decades and which grew out of an activity or project curriculum in a tenth-grade class in a rural school in Georgia. Under the leadership of an imaginative teacher, students gathered and published a wide range of materials about their community in the form of a magazine, which later came to be published as a national best-selling book series of eight volumes.[43] The *Foxfire* books incorporate such diverse material as folktales, local crafts, interviews and photographs of local "characters," and various accounts termed "affairs of plain living." Remarkably, what at first blush was taken as material of only local interest in an Appalachian community came to gain universal interest for adolescents and adults alike in every section of the country. In 1984, *Foxfire* was made into a successful Broadway musical.

Similar approaches to the curriculum (project methods) were undertaken by progressive teachers over many years. For example, during the 1950s a French motion picture, *Passion for Life,* gained wide international popularity as a commercial or entertainment film; yet it was also sponsored by UNESCO as an educational film—giving a true account of a progressive teacher in a rural school after World War II who integrated the curriculum through projects and activities. One of the projects depicted in the film was the creation by the students of a "Foxfire" book which they illustrated and printed. The film related how the publication of the book caused great controversy in the community, but also how the progressive approach to the curriculum led to the improvement of student motivation and to unprecedented student success with the external examinations. (The film is still distributed as an educational film for college classes in teacher education.)

Such techniques also had been developed by progressive teachers in this country, who engaged students in the writing of stories in the English class, illustrating the stories in the art class, and printing and binding the books in the industrial arts class. Over a period of a school year, an individual class would produce a series of books that were subsequently read and discussed by students in other classes in English.

As another example of earlier uses of the activity or project approach, there is a published account of how a sixth-grade class at the Lincoln School in 1930–1931 engaged in a variety of projects in connection with a unit of work on architecture and the city. One of the projects that unexpectedly grew out of the unit of work was the creation of a cooperative store to supply the pupils with architectural drawings and photographs for their notebooks. Projects in the industrial arts were undertaken in connection with the study of architecture in history.[44]

Thus it should be recognized that the activity or project approach not only has a long history, but continues in various forms to this day at virtually every level of schooling and into the college. However, this approach has gone awry whenever its enthusiasts have promoted it as an all-encompassing scheme for curriculum synthesis, rather than as one of many approaches to building a more lifelike and coherent curriculum.

As pointed out in various sections of this text, educational history is replete with instances whereby promising and successful practices are subsequently seized upon only as a slogan or as a panacea, with the result that they come to be adopted only superficially or in forms that bear little resemblance to the original concept. This has been the case with the open classroom, the project method, and the activity curriculum. In many instances, what was called an "activity curriculum" was little more than a laissez-faire classroom lacking systematic curriculum planning by the teacher, with classroom activities being based on the spontaneous or felt needs of the children. In the absence of preplanning by the teacher, spontaneous activity has no place to go.

THE MACROCURRICULUM: A FURTHER LOOK

One of the great contradictions in academe is the widespread bias on the part of many university academicians against the vocational studies, fine arts, and industrial arts in the schools—with these areas of the curriculum being commonly referred to as "nonacademic," whereas in the college or university no distinction is made between "academic" and "nonacademic" studies. Paradoxically, mutual tolerance, if not respect, for the various and diverse areas of study is integral to the value system of the university professoriate. In fact, the very concept of university implies a sense of interdependence and unity among the different areas of inquiry.

In reality, the college or university is engaged in vocational education as well as general education, special-interest education, exploratory education, and enrichment education. The attitude in the university that gives recognition to the need for a comprehensive and diversified curriculum is juxtaposed by an attitude that would delimit the schools to the traditional academic subjects and fundamentals. This dualistic bias poses serious problems for the school and society.

Throughout this chapter and the preceding chapter, emphasis has been given to the need for the professional staff of the school to give concerted attention to the functions of the macrocurriculum so that the various studies are treated as vitally interdependent. The neglect of the macrocurriculum not only has led to curriculum isolation, but to antagonism. We have the case of the academic versus the vocational side of the curriculum, the essentials versus the nonessentials or "frills," the intellective studies versus the practical studies, and so on. Such dualisms and antagonisms can be resolved only by treating the various diversified studies and functions of the curriculum as mutually enhancing.

The Bias Against the Comprehensive Secondary School

Although virtually every student in the college or university is concerned with preparation for a vocation, the legitimacy of vocational education in the high school is repeatedly brought into question not only by traditionalists, but also by those who are generally regarded as "moderates" or "liberals." For example, as noted in Chapter 9, both Boyer and Goodlad contend in their studies of the schools that vocational studies are "irrelevant or inadequate" in view of the outmoded equipment and facilities available in the high schools and in view of the rapid technological changes in the workplace.[45] Yet, although Boyer and Goodlad found gross deficiencies in the academic side of the curriculum, they did not recommend that the academic studies be eliminated on the ground that they are "irrelevant or inadequate" as they are presently treated in the curriculum. Just as facilities and resources can be upgraded and modernized in the sciences and other academic areas of the curriculum, so too can they be upgraded and modernized in the vocational areas.

Dangers of a Dual System.   The danger of a double standard for determining the legitimacy of a particular curriculum function is that a dual educational structure will be created, as James Conant had feared.[46] Because a majority of adolescents do not go on to college, where they can prepare for a vocation, the high school is their only opportunity for such preparation outside the workplace.

No advanced industrial society has been able to rely on the workplace as the means for vocational education for the majority of the youth population. Business and industry provide for specialized on-the-job training for those who already occupy a place in the organization and who already have a relatively high level of work skills. But advanced industrial societies must choose between vocational education being provided in the setting of the comprehensive high school or in the separate, specialized vocational school. The advantages of the comprehensive high school setting for such educational preparation in a democratic society have been well documented over the course of our history and in a wide variety of sources.[47]

Comprehensive Goals.   The goal of vocational education in the high school is not to prepare each student for a highly specific job, but to enhance the function of education in general to "help young people to move horizontally to other occupations, and vertically to higher responsibilities, as future opportunities occur," noted Myrdal.[48] In the setting of the comprehensive high school, the lines between and among the areas of study can be made more fluid than in the specialized vocational school, and youth from different backgrounds and career destinations can share in the common concerns as members of a joint culture.

Broadly conceived, vocational education should enable the adolescent to find roots in the reality of the human community. As Freud pointed out in his analysis of the significance of work in the conduct of life, "No other technique for the conduct of life attaches the individual so firmly to reality as laying emphasis on work; for his work at least gives him a secure place in a portion of reality, in the human community."[49]

It is no wonder, then, that our society has been beset by rampant social dislocation and disaffection among large segments of the youth population when so many are denied the opportunity to gain the needed preparation for a productive place in the world of work.

Obsolescence: The Specious Argument.   The contention that vocational education becomes readily outmoded or obsolescent applies only to the narrowest kinds of training. At the time of the widespread introduction of the Dictaphone, Hutchins predicted that the stenographer would become obsolete.[50] No such thing happened. The demand for secretary-stenographers became ever greater. Moreover, this attitude denies the educative possibilities of vocational preparation and the continuing educability of the skilled worker in making the needed transformation as new technologies are developed. The aircraft industry grew out of the automobile industry. The mechanics who had worked on horse-drawn coaches became the automobile mechanics. The mechanics who had worked on aircraft piston engines learned how to service and repair jet engines (which are far simpler than piston engines). Just as the physician, teacher, physicist, and dietitian must keep abreast of their fields, so too must the farmer, mechanic, and computer technician.

An effective curriculum in vocational education would reveal to the learner the many problems and shortcomings of the business and industrial sectors of the economy in serving the wider public interest. It would help reveal the possibilities for corrective measures against shoddy products, lack of pride in workmanship and service, misleading advertising, and disaffection in the workplace. Such a curriculum would greatly illumine the social studies and general education. Students could be engaged in the writing of logs in which observations concerning their cooperative work experience are recorded, including the diagnosis of problems encountered on the job. They could also be engaged in a wide range of field projects that extend and enrich their school studies. The development of critical-thinking abilities is not delimited to the traditional academic studies, but can extend throughout the curriculum.

The university has managed to find a recognized place for a diversified and comprehensive curriculum—including the studio arts, performing arts, agriculture, engineering, home economics, sciences, humanities, and so on. Yet the opposition to a comprehensive curriculum in the secondary school persists in the face of the fact that the secondary school population has diverse as well as common needs.

The Macrocurriculum and the Development of the Learner

In this chapter, five functions of the macrocurriculum have been examined along with alternative curriculum designs. The problems and possibilities connected with various approaches to organizing the subject matter have been explored in some detail. It has been noted that the particular *form* or structural arrangement for organizing the curriculum will have profound bearings on the *function* of the curriculum. A knowledgeable professional staff will utilize designs that are appropriate to the function of the curriculum and in consideration of the nature of the learner.

Figure 12–7 illustrates how the various macrocurricular functions might be apportioned as the learners progress from the elementary through the secondary phase of schooling. Again, it should be stressed that the lines between the curricular functions are not hard and fast, since the functions are necessarily complementary. In the discussion that follows, an attempt is made to illustrate how the curriculum at each phase of schooling might be organized in consideration of the growth and development of children and youth, and in view of their common and special needs and interests. The needed curriculum reconstruction obviously will require a conjoint effort on the part of the curriculum director, principal, supervisors, and teachers.

From the Elementary Through the Middle Phase. At the primary level, virtually the entire curriculum is devoted to common learnings (general education) and enrichment education. In designing the curriculum for younger children, the knowledgeable professional staff will recognize that these children are not ready for formal operations or formal hypothetical thinking. The learning activities

Grades

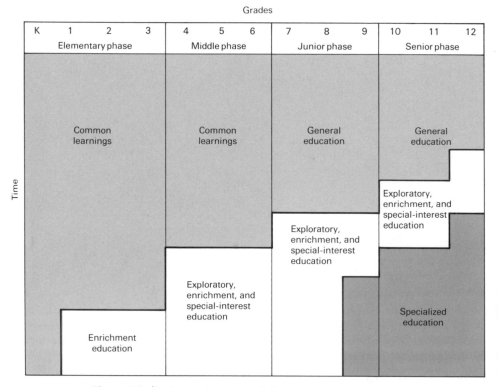

Figure 12–7. Apportionment of the macrocurriculum, K–12.

must be so organized as to stimulate children to develop deeper and wider concepts from experience so that they can make perceptual and intuitive judgments, and so that they can learn to solve physical problems by anticipating consequences perceptually.[51] Skills in reading, writing, calculating, and communicating orally are not treated mechanically as ends in themselves, but are developed through broadly integrative concepts, areas of interest, activities, and projects—such as those concerning community, growing and developing as a person, making things, enjoying art and music, working with others, and so on. Emphasis is given to the relationship of cognitive development to social and physical development, including the fostering of desirable attitudes toward learning. The curriculum is not segmented into rigidly isolated subject-matter compartments or isolated skills.

At the upper elementary and middle school level, the curriculum continues to be focused mainly on common learnings (general education) and enrichment education, with some options provided for exploratory education. In connection with a class unit on transportation, for example, some youngsters may choose to work on a mural depicting the history of transportation, while others are building a scale model of a community in the industrial arts showing the various modes of transportation. Or in the area of nature study, one group of youngsters may choose to make a survey of the wildlife in their area, while others choose to investigate the different kinds of trees that are found in and around their community. The work of the various groups of pupils is shared through written and oral reports so as to reveal, for example, the necessary relationships of plantlife to wildlife. Increasing use is made of the school library and community library in conjunction with classroom activities and for recreational reading.

At the upper-elementary and middle phase of schooling, the learning activities are designed to provide for the development of the capability to think hypothetically through formal operations. Yet the problems that are investigated are not technical and specialized, but broadly conceived so as to relate to the life of the learner and the wider society. For example, the problem of "What's going on inside my body?" would be approached not only biologically, but also psychologically and socially.

Although the organization of studies may begin to resemble a broad-fields curriculum, systematic efforts could be made through team teaching to devise problems and units of work that interconnect the broad fields and that engage students in the development of skills, concepts, and abilities that cross through the various broad fields. For example, more advanced mathematical abilities could be developed through the use of mathematics in the investigation of problems in the broad fields of natural science and social studies, such as in the study of population changes and trends in the community, region, state, nation, and world. Projects in the visual arts could be related to the social studies and nature study. Pupils might be engaged in the writing of reports on problems in natural science and social studies and in connection with their reading of literature. Poetry might be correlated with music. In the words of the composer, Virgil Thomson, "Poetry and music are two sides of the coin of vocal expression" and "a revision of the study of poetic literature as well as that of music is indicated, which would take account of the coin between the two faces."[52] In the same vein, the industrial arts and fine arts could be interrelated and brought together in the dramatic arts through the design of stage sets, costume design, and so on.

At the middle school and junior high school level, some elective options are provided to engage students in the exploration of areas of learning outside the common core—such as electives in the industrial arts, fine arts, homemaking, typing, and so on—coupled with a wide range of student club activities.

The Secondary Phase. Throughout the secondary school level, the core in general education might be organized through block-time teaching, incorporating the homeroom, in which the focus is on the systematic investigation of significant problems of youth in a free society—such as the wise use of our natural resources, the world population explosion and the problem of hunger, human rights, social criticism in literature, the social implications of science and technology, censorship of ideas, career goals, and so on. In addition to the problem-focused studies in the block-time classes, the core in general education might include the correlated study of mathematics and physical science, of the industrial arts and fine arts, and of the sciences and humanities. The tenth-grade course in biology would be designed for general education and would follow an ecological approach. The program in physical education and recreation would be designed to develop wholesome lifelong recreational interests, rather than being limited to team sports.

As the student progresses through the high school, the elective options are expanded to provide for specialized education (vocational and college-preparatory studies), exploratory education, enrichment education, and special-interest education. The college-bound student may pursue certain disciplinary courses—such as in chemistry, physics, and advanced mathematics—but attention is given to the correlation of these studies.

Although the curriculum is highly diversified into a variety of programs, the students are not tracked. The classes in general education are heterogeneously grouped, whereas the students divide themselves "naturalistically" through the specialized studies and in their electives for exploratory education, enrichment education, and special-interest education. The summer session is not limited to remedial studies, but provides for acceleration and enrichment education as well.

Much can be done to overcome the constraints imposed upon the curriculum by the class schedule. A modified form of the modular-flexible scheduling proposal could be developed to allow for block-time or double-period classes in the problem-focused core, in certain laboratory-science classes, in vocational studies, and in physical education. The original schemes for modular-flexible scheduling in the high school often tended to be unnecessarily complicated.[53] But under a modified scheduling arrangement, certain features of modular-flexible scheduling could be adopted so as to overcome the traditional lockstep schedule. Not all double-period classes would need to meet daily. The double-period class in physical education might meet twice or three times weekly. The biology class might meet four days per week as a single period, with a double period for classroom and laboratory work on one day each week. The class in fine arts might meet twice weekly in a double period, and so on. All students would be scheduled for time blocks for independent study in which they could decide whether to use this time on a given day for work in the library, learning-resource center, laboratory, or music studio. In conclusion, the schedule should be fashioned to serve the curriculum, rather than the curriculum being made to conform to the schedule.

SUMMARY

Curriculum development is not simply a matter of course-of-study revision, accretion, and deletion. Treated holistically rather than segmentally, the curriculum reveals the interrelationships of studies along with their vital bearings on the life of the learner and on the life of the wider society. This requires continual reconstruction of the curriculum not only to accommodate new knowledge but to transform knowledge through the educative process so that it becomes the working power of intelligence.

Not only is there the tendency to treat knowledge compartmentally in the traditional subject curriculum, but in different epochs there has been the tendency to set the different studies against one another in the school curriculum rather than seeing them as mutually enhancing and interdependent. Hence we have the case of the "academic" versus the "nonacademic" side of the curriculum, the divorce between theory and practice, and the divide between the sciences and humanities.

Only rarely does the professional staff of the school and school district give systematic attention to the macrocurriculum—the scope and sequence of studies for general education, specialized education (college-preparatory, prevocational, and vocational education), exploratory education, enrichment education, and special-interest education. As a result, the nature and direction of the total school curriculum suffers by default.

Certain curriculum requirements may be mandated by state departments of education and school boards, but *how* the curriculum is to be designed, structured, and implemented (including the actual selection of the topics, problems, concepts, materials, and learning activities) is the responsibility of the professional staff of the local school and district. Teachers need released time and consultant expertise on a continual basis if they are to meet this responsibility. As professionals, teachers cannot be treated as mere technicians to "deliver" instruction while the curriculum is determined by sources external to the actual educational situation.

There is an old, established principle in the biological sciences that structure is related to function. This principle is of great significance for the curriculum. For example, the function of general education requires a different structure or framework than that of specialized education. Economics, mathematics, or chemistry for the future economist, mathematician, or chemist may be organized as discipline-centered subjects. But citizenship requires the applications of knowledge to problems of personal and social significance that transcend the specialized disciplines. Thus the organization of studies for general education must be more encompassing than that of specialized education. This will require a framework or structure for the subject matters very different from that which is employed for specialized education.

Although the organization and treatment of subject matters for specialized education for the vocations and professions are necessarily focused on knowledge applications, the applications are made within the context of specialized practice and are not regarded as within the purview of the citizen who is not a specialist in the given vocation or profession.

To many teachers, supervisors, and school administrators, the curriculum is seen simply as a body of different subjects to be studied. To paraphrase Gertrude Stein, "A subject is a subject is a subject." But subjects are variously organized as (1) fundamental skills, (2) disciplinary studies, (3) laminated studies, (4) fused studies, (5) correlated studies, and (6) broad-fields studies. Or the curriculum may be organized not as subjects in the usual sense, but according to areas of interest, themes, problems of personal and social significance, and activities that transcend the traditional subject divisions. Moreover, the entire curriculum in general education may be articulated around a focal emphasis, such as critical thinking.

Various structures or frameworks typically are used simultaneously in different combinations in the curriculum of the school and college. But only rarely does a faculty give conscious and concerted attention to the need for developing the appropriate structure or framework for the subject matters in view of the function of the curriculum—whether it be the function of general education, specialized education, exploratory education, enrichment education, or special-interest education. Moreover, by giving appropriate attention to the macrocurriculum, the problems of curriculum congestion and fragmentation can be countered. Seen as a continuously widening and deepening spiral, the curriculum reveals the interrelationships among the various studies (scope or horizontal articulation) and also provides for a coherent sequence of studies (vertical articulation).

Paradoxically, the great divide between the so-called "academic" and "nonacademic" studies is found in the schools but not in higher education. This divide is rooted in the ancient tradition which holds that literary and abstract studies are of greater intellective value than knowledge gained through useful application. For example, the study of the fine arts through history and connoisseurship in the subject of humanities is considered an academic endeavor, whereas in the studio the arts become nonacademic subjects. Consequently, the interrelationships between appreciation and performance are neglected. This also applies to the division between the academic and vocational studies, with the consequence that the studies are not mutually enriching. The ancient divorce between thinking and doing, theory and practice, knowledge and action, intellectual and useful, ornamental and practical, continues to plague the school curriculum. Such divisions in the curriculum lead to divisions in the wider social life, where mutual respect for different callings is lacking, where work is regarded only as a means of making a living, and where leisure is regarded as a form of escape rather than a productive and enriching activity.

PROBLEMS FOR STUDY AND DISCUSSION

1. In his proposal for reforming our schools, Goodlad states that "whereas the primary phase [as conceived in the proposal] emphasized the acquisition of academic, social, and physical skills, the elementary phase emphasizes their use."[54] Do you see Goodlad's separation between skill "acquisition" and the "use" of skills as valid? Explain.

2. From his observations of grouping practices in the schools, Goodlad found that heterogeneous classes reflect a more productive learning atmosphere than do homogeneously grouped classes. Consequently, he recommends that in the common core of studies at all levels of schooling, students should be assigned to classes randomly in a way that assures heterogeneity.[55] Considering the intended function of general education, what is the underlying rationale for heterogeneous grouping? Do you agree with Goodlad? Explain.

3. How do you account for the failure of so many school and college faculties to give needed attention to the structure of the curriculum in relation to the function of general education? What are the shortcomings of the discipline-centered subject curriculum in meeting the function of general education?

What alternatives are there in the organization of subject matter and learning experiences for general education, other than through the separate disciplines?

4. How do you account for the division of the school curriculum into "academic" and "nonacademic" subjects, whereas no such division exists in the college or university? What are the educational and social consequences of such a curriculum division in the schools?

5. Examine the curriculum in a junior and senior high school in your own school district and the curriculum in your own college or university. Is there a common core of studies for general education? To what extent are students allowed to meet the requirements in general education through distributed electives? It is widely conceded that the function of general education is not served through distribution-elective requirements. Yet this practice continues in our secondary schools and colleges. How do you account for this?

6. In your own school district, do students attend a separate area vocational school for their vocational classes on a shared-time or full-time basis? Or can they pursue vocational studies within the setting of their home high school (a comprehensive high school)? Are the vocational students tracked together in their "academic" classes either by design or because of scheduling constraints? What is the proportion of the vocational students who participate in extraclass activities in comparison to the college-bound students? If there is a discrepancy in such participation between the two populations, how do you account for the difference?

7. How do you account for the long-standing and widespread bias against vocational education for those youth in high school who are not college bound, whereas college-bound youth are accorded the opportunity to prepare for a vocation in college?

8. How do you account for the spectacular popularity of the open classroom during the late 1960s and early 1970s, followed by its rapid decline? Do you see the open classroom being reinvented in a modified form in the future? Explain.

9. To what extent are the professional staff in the schools of your district engaged in ongoing efforts to improve the articulation among the various subjects in the curriculum? Is there a standing faculty curriculum committee in your school? If so, how often does the committee meet, and what kinds of curricular problems are addressed? What roles are played by the supervisors and the principal toward improving such curriculum articulation?

10. If you were asked to submit a plan for redesigning the curriculum for your school, what would be the major features and recommendations in your plan? What arguments would you offer in support of your plan?

NOTES

1. Alfred North Whitehead, "Dangers of Specialization," in *Specialists and Generalists* (Washington, D.C.: U.S. Senate Committee on Government Operations, 1968), p. 48; from *Science and the Modern World* (New York: Free Press, 1925).
2. Alfred North Whitehead, *The Aims of Education* (New York: Macmillan, 1959; originally published in 1929), p. 147.
3. Joseph J. Schwab, *College Curriculum and Student Protest* (Chicago: University of Chicago Press, 1969), p. 246.
4. James B. Conant, *The Education of American Teachers* (New York: McGraw-Hill, 1963), pp. 169–170.
5. Alec Gallup, "The Gallup Poll of Teachers' Attitudes Toward the Public Schools," *Phi Delta Kappan*, Vol. 66 (January 1985), pp. 329–330.
6. See National Commission on Excellence in Education, *Meeting the Challenge* (Washington, D.C.: U.S. Department of Education, 1983).
7. Alec Gallup, "The Gallup Poll of Teachers' Attitudes Toward the Public Schools," *Phi Delta Kappan*, Vol. 66 (October 1984), p. 104.
8. Association of American Colleges, *Integrity in the College Curriculum* (Washington, D.C.: The Association, 1985), p. 3.
9. Ibid., pp. 6, 9.
10. Ibid., p. 11.
11. Report of the Panel on the General Professional Education of the Physician, *Physicians for the Twenty-first Century* (Washington, D.C.: Association of American Medical Colleges, 1984), p. 4.
12. Association of American Colleges, op. cit., p. 28.
13. Wilford M. Aikin, *The Story of the Eight-Year Study* (New York: Harper & Row, 1942).
14. Lawrence Senesh, "Orchestration of the Social Sciences in the Curriculum," in Irving Morrisett and W. Williams Stevens, Jr. (eds.), *Social Science in the Schools* (New York: Holt, Rinehart and Winston, 1971), p. 126.
15. Russell Thomas, *The Search for a Common Learning: General Education, 1800–1960* (New York: McGraw-Hill, 1962).
16. J. D. Bernal, *The Social Function of Science* (Cambridge, Mass.: MIT Press, 1967; originally published in 1939), p. 78.
17. John H. Randall, Jr., "History and the Social Sciences," in Salo W. Baron, Ernest Nagel, and Koppel S. Pinson (eds.), *Freedom and Reason* (New York: Free Press, 1951), pp. 287, 292.
18. Alfred North Whitehead, *Essays in Science and Philosophy* (New York: Philosophical Library, 1947), pp. 183–184.
19. Edward O. Wilson, *Sociobiology: The New Synthesis* (Cambridge, Mass.: Harvard University Press, 1975).
20. National Education Association, *Report of the Committee of Ten on Secondary School Studies* (New York: American Book, 1894), pp. 41, 46–47.
21. See Daniel Bell, *The Reforming of General Education* (Garden City, N.Y.: Anchor Books, Doubleday, 1968).
22. See Paul L. Dressell and Irwin J. Lehmann, "The Impact of Higher Education on Student Attitudes, Values, and Critical Thinking Abilities," in Ohmer Milton and Edward J. Shoben (eds.), *Learning and the Professors* (Athens, Ohio: Ohio University Press, 1968), pp. 118–123.
23. J. Lloyd Trump and Gordon F. Vars, "How Should Learning Be Organized?" Chapter 9 in National Society for the Study of Education, *Issues in Secondary Education*, Seventy-fifth Yearbook, Part II (Chicago: University of Chicago Press, 1976), p. 223.

24. Educational Policies Commission, *Education for ALL American Youth—A Further Look* (Washington, D.C.: The Commission, 1952).

25. See Grace S. Wright, *Block-Time Classes and the Core Program in the Junior High School* (Washington, D.C.: U.S. Office of Education, 1958).

26. Florence B. Stratemeyer et al., *Developing a Curriculum for Modern Living*, 2nd ed. (New York: Teachers College Press, 1957).

27. National Science Teachers Association, *Science–Technology–Society: Science Education in the 1980s* (Washington, D.C.: The Association, 1982).

28. Bentley Glass, "The BSCS—Retrospect and Prospect," *BSCS Journal*, Vol. 1 (November 1978), pp. 3, 4; the Dewey quote is from "Logical Conditions of a Scientific Treatment of Morality" (Chicago: University of Chicago Press, 1903).

29. William V. Mayer, "The BSCS Past," *BSCS Journal*, Vol. 1 (November 1978), p. 9.

30. Ernest L. Boyer, *High School: A Report on Secondary Education in America* (New York: Harper & Row, 1983), p. 115.

31. Commission on the Reorganization of Secondary Education, *The Social Studies in Secondary Education* (Washington, D.C.: U.S. Bureau of Education, 1916), pp. 53–54.

32. James B. Conant, *The American High School Today* (New York: McGraw-Hill, 1959), pp. 75–76.

33. *BSCS Journal*, Vol. 3 (April 1980), p. 3.

34. John Fischer, "The Easy Chair," *Harper's Magazine*, Vol. 242 (February 1971), p. 20.

35. Report of the Central Advisory Council for Education (England), *Children and Their Primary Schools* (London: Her Majesty's Stationery Office, 1967), p. 203.

36. Ibid., p. 198.

37. Charles E. Silberman, "The Remaking of American Education," *Fortune*, Vol. 63 (April 1961), pp. 125–131.

38. Charles E. Silberman, *Crisis in the Classroom: The Remaking of American Education* (New York: Random House, 1970).

39. Herbert R. Kohl, *The Open Classroom* (New York: Random House, 1969), pp. 40–41.

40. John Dewey, *The Child and the Curriculum* (Chicago: University of Chicago Press, 1902), p. 16.

41. William H. Kilpatrick, "The Project Method," *Teachers College Record*, Vol. 19 (September 1918), pp. 319–335.

42. See John Dewey, *The Way Out of the Educational Confusion* (Cambridge, Mass.: Harvard University Press, 1931).

43. See Elliot Wigginton and Margie Bennett, *Foxfire Eight* (Garden City, N.Y.: Anchor Books, Doubleday, 1984).

44. Emily Ann Barnes and Bess M. Young, *Children and Architecture* (New York: Teachers College Press, 1932).

45. Boyer, op. cit., p. 123; John I. Goodlad, *A Place Called School* (New York: McGraw-Hill, 1984), p. 344.

46. James B. Conant, *My Several Lives* (New York: Harper & Row, 1970), pp. 665–670.

47. Ibid. See also Torsten Husén, "Are Standards in U.S. Schools Really Lagging Behind Those in Other Countries?" *Phi Delta Kappan*, Vol. 64 (March 1983), pp. 455–461.

48. Gunnar Myrdal, *Challenge to Affluence* (New York: Vintage Books, 1965), p. 33.

49. Sigmund Freud, *Civilization and Its Discontents* (New York: W. W. Norton, 1962), p. 27.

50. Robert M. Hutchins, *Education for Freedom* (Baton Rouge, La.: Louisiana State University Press, 1943), p. 51.

51. Jean Piaget, *Science of Education and Psychology of the Child* (New York: Orion, 1970), pp. 159–160.

52. Virgil Thomson, in Ruth M. Weeks (ed.), *A Correlated Curriculum*, Report of the

National Council of Teachers of English (New York: Appleton-Century-Crofts, 1938), p. 310.

53. See J. Lloyd Trump and Delmas F. Miller, *Secondary School Curriculum Improvement*, 3rd ed. (Boston: Allyn and Bacon, 1979), pp. 396–408; Robert N. Bush and Dwight W. Allen, *A New Design for High School Education* (New York: McGraw-Hill, 1964).

54. Goodlad, op. cit., p. 335.

55. Ibid., pp. 297–298.

SELECTED REFERENCES

Aikin, Wilford M. *The Story of the Eight-Year Study*. New York: Harper & Row, Publishers, Inc., 1942.

Alberty, Harold B., and Elsie J. Alberty. *Reorganizing the High School Curriculum*, 3rd ed. New York: Macmillan Publishing Company, 1962.

Association of American Colleges. *Integrity in the College Curriculum*. Washington, D.C.: The Association, 1985.

Bell, Daniel. *The Reforming of General Education*. Garden City, N.Y.: Anchor Books, Doubleday, 1968.

Bennett, William J. *To Reclaim a Legacy: A Report on the Humanities in Higher Education*. Washington, D.C.: National Endowment for the Humanities, 1984.

Bernal, J. D. *The Social Function of Science*. Cambridge, Mass.: The MIT Press, 1967.

Boyer, Ernest L. *High School: A Report on Secondary Education in America*. New York: Harper & Row, Publishers, Inc., 1983.

Chamberlain, Dean, et al. *Did They Succeed in College?* New York: Harper & Row, Publishers, Inc., 1942.

College Entrance Examination Board. *Academic Preparation for College*. New York: The Board, 1983.

Commission on Humanities of the Rockefeller Foundation. *The Humanities in American Life*. Berkeley, Calif.: University of California Press, 1980.

Committee for Economic Development. *Investing in Our Children: Business and the Public Schools*. New York: The Committee, 1985.

Conant, James B. *The American High School Today*. New York: McGraw-Hill Book Company, 1959.

Dewey, John. *The Child and the Curriculum/The School and Society*. Chicago: The University of Chicago Press, 1902, 1915; combined edition, 1956.

Educational Policies Commission. *Education for ALL American Youth—A Further Look*. Washington, D.C.: The Commission, 1952.

Goodlad, John I. *A Place Called School*. New York: McGraw-Hill Book Company, 1984.

National Science Board. *Educating Americans for the 21st Century*. Washington, D.C.: National Science Foundation, 1983.

National Society for the Study of Education. *General Education*, Fifty-first Yearbook, Part I. Chicago: The University of Chicago Press, 1952.

Report of the Harvard Committee. *General Education in a Free Society*. Cambridge, Mass.: Harvard University Press, 1945.

Silberman, Charles E. *Crisis in the Classroom: The Remaking of American Education*. New York: Random House, Inc., 1970.

Study Group on Higher Education. *Involvement in Learning: Realizing the Potential of American Higher Education*. Washington, D.C.: National Institute of Education, 1984.

Tanner, Daniel. *Secondary Curriculum: Theory and Development*. New York: Macmillan Publishing Company, 1971.

Tanner, Daniel, and Laurel N. Tanner. *Curriculum Development: Theory into Practice,* 2nd ed. New York: Macmillan Publishing Company, 1980.

Taylor, Harold E. (ed.). *The Humanities in the Schools.* New York: Citation Press, 1968.

Thomas, Russell. *The Search for a Common Learning.* New York: McGraw-Hill Book Company, 1962.

Weinberg, Alvin M. *Reflections on Big Science.* Cambridge, Mass.: The MIT Press, 1967.

Whitehead, Alfred North. *The Aims of Education.* New York: Macmillan Publishing Company, 1929.

Wigginton, Elliot. *Sometimes a Shining Moment: The Foxfire Experience.* Garden City, N.Y.: Anchor Books, Doubleday, 1985.

Part VI

Faculty Development and School Improvement

Chapter 13

Establishing and Administering the Inservice Education Program

This chapter will present some ways of getting an inservice education program started, and will discuss in detail some of the activities that are generally included in inservice (or staff development or personnel development) programs. Let it be said at the outset, however, that there is no single best way of starting an inservice education program, nor is there one best inservice education activity. The approach taken in an individual school must fit its particular situation and should emerge from the problems of primary concern to the teachers and principal, as well as the supervisors in the school system. A few moments' conversation in the lunchroom between teachers and the principal, or among teachers, can contribute more to the solution of critical educational problems than a formal inservice education activity (a lecture, for example) that is outside the mainstream of teachers' concerns.

Previous chapters have discussed the responsibilities of supervisors for improving education and have presented specific ways that supervisors can help teachers overcome difficulties and make improvements. But methods and activities do not a program make; inservice education must be planned as a professional improvement program. As a prelude to this chapter it may be well, then, to begin with a brief summary of some of the basic functions of inservice education that have evolved with the professional status of teaching.

SOME BASIC FUNCTIONS OF INSERVICE EDUCATION

A general perspective of the relation between preservice education and inservice education is needed in order to see clearly the functions of inservice education. Preservice education is professional preparation and is related to that of preparing lawyers, doctors, and engineers. As Tyler has pointed out (based on his work with schools of medicine, engineering, nursing, agriculture, and education), "A profession is an occupation that assumes responsibility for some tasks too complex to be guided by specific rules. Professionals perform these tasks by artistic adaptation of general principles."[1] In order to perform their responsibilities competently, professionals must understand the objectives underlying these responsibilities. They must, further, be able to apply the principles that are relevant to a particular situation, to develop courses of action, and to follow them in accord with the principles of their profession. Whether we are talking about doctors or teachers, "professionals must learn how to work out appropriate answers for individual situations."[2]

Time is simply not available in the preservice program to learn all of the principles that teachers can use in their profession. As Tyler tells us, "The primary function of teacher education is to help individuals develop a rough cognitive map of the phenomena of learning, teaching and professional ethics so that they can get the feel of professionalism."[3] The best theory also insists that the preservice education of teachers requires an understanding of how the whole educational enterprise, and teaching in particular, relates to the values and commitments of a democratic society. (As pointed out in Chapter 1, the function of supervision in a democratic society is to improve the educational opportunities of children and youth, and all professional workers should have this outlook in common.)

Two major factors contribute to the importance of inservice education. First, professional knowledge is continually evolving; some of the things a professional needs are not realized or have not been developed at the time he or she enters the profession. Thus a program of professional education is lifelong. A second factor is that teachers have only begun to develop as teachers by the time of graduation; in no sense is any new teacher handed over to the school as a finished product. (This is true no matter how skilled the teacher may be in managing a group of children; teaching is far more than management.) Preservice teacher education programs must make clear to their students that what they are learning is only a beginning, and that the principles and practices of teaching are matters for continuing inquiry. Supervisors in school systems must also emphasize this view.

Given the primary purpose of preservice education, there are at least four basic functions of inservice education: (1) developing the ability to solve classroom problems, (2) improving the curriculum, (3) helping individuals learn what they need to know to reach their own professional goals, and (4) providing the stimulation for continuous learning needed to grow professionally and to prevent boredom and burnout. These functions rest on the fundamental assumption that inservice education is developmental. Unfortunately, however, inservice education still has a deficit orientation. Tyler, for example, identifies "remediation" (remedial programs for teachers) as a basic function of inservice education.[4] (This is at odds with his conception of preservice education.) As Burrello and Orbaugh advise, "Inservice education must move from a deficit orientation to a developmental orientation, that is, from making up for shortcomings in preservice education to helping participants further their professional development."[5] Our knowledge about inservice education points to the developmental view as the only possible view. As Dale Mann has written: "The key to professional behavior is through treating teachers as professionals."[6] But it is Dewey who provides the reason why all teachers, even the most poorly prepared and least effective, must be involved in truly professional activities: "Only by sharing in some responsible task does there come a fitness to share it."[7]

The four functions of inservice education should serve as the basis for planning programs of inservice education.

ORGANIZING THE INSERVICE EDUCATION PROGRAM

Research has shown that inservice programs in which teachers participate as planners are more successful than are programs organized without teacher involvement. The findings of the Rand study on federally funded programs designed to introduce new practices in public schools are of great interest here.[8] Top-down strategies where plans were made in the central office and announced to teachers resulted in disappointing programs because the plans were the administrators' and did not emerge from the problems and needs of particular classrooms and teachers.

Yet teacher initiation of inservice programs without supervisory support did not fare much better. It is difficult for teachers to maintain enthusiasm when there is little evidence that supervisors also care. More important, perhaps, if recommendations from problem-solving efforts are actually to be implemented, principals and central office personnel *have* to be included from the start. Teacher-initiated programs dried up as quickly and as completely as did top-down programs. The most useful programs in terms of increasing the effectiveness of the school in dealing with its serious problems were the programs characterized by collaborative planning. As McLaughlin and Marsh conclude in an analysis of the Rand findings: "Teachers become better teachers and students benefit" when programs "appeal to a teacher's sense of professionalism."[9] Neither being left out of the planning process nor left on their own (to develop programs that are peripheral to the inservice education program of the school system) appeal to teachers' sense of professionalism. The second approach is almost as demeaning as the first, although it is the top-down approach that tends to characterize (and thus doom) inservice education. Indeed, one still finds in the supervisory literature recommendations that teachers should be "receivers of information" in inservice sessions dominated by a leader because teacher involvement in problem-solving activities is "an unproductive inservice activity."[10] As Sparks points out, such conclusions are incongruent both with our experience and the body of research on supervision.[11] We would add that they threaten to turn back the clock.

Research clearly supports a broad-based institutional approach to inservice education. Teachers must be given an opportunity to suggest what to do, and how to do it, and they must decide whether the activity has been effective. Supervisors must provide leadership in problem identification, and they must see that there are resources available and opportunities to work together. Granted that teachers must participate, the principal's role is crucial. As discussed earlier, research shows that differences in achievement can be attributed to qualitative differences in principals' leadership styles. The principal must take the initiative in unleashing a faculty's potential for professional development and responsibility. Because what the principal does makes such a difference, the principal must make time for what is most important. As one principal said, "When we decide that improving instruction is the most important matter we can attend to, it will get done."[12] (The problem of time for educational leadership was discussed in Chapter 1.)

However, it is one thing to make the decision to commit time and attention to inservice education, and quite another to make it operational. Implementing the decision may require inservice education for the principal. Until recently, little attention has been paid to the need for persons in leadership positions to develop educational-leadership skills. According to Donaldson, principals want practical help "in transforming their role from manager to that of instructional leader," and summer institutes and professional workshops can help principals "restructure their roles to make more time for classroom visits and conferences with teachers."[13] Principals must visit classrooms frequently if they are to identify schoolwide problems and help individual teachers to solve their problems and perform their professional responsibilities more effectively.

Setting the Stage: Effective Strategies

Principals must set the stage for inservice education by communicating their involvement in curriculum improvement to the faculty, and their belief in them as professionals. The following strategies have been found effective by principals.

Schedule Regular Classroom Observations. Nancy Sievert, a principal, has found that "a systematic plan of classroom observations that is consistently followed is solid evidence of a principal's interest in what and how children are learning." As a means of keeping other activities from interfering, she suggests that principals block out one morning a week on their calendars and have their secretary guard the time.[14]

As pointed out in Chapter 7, the factors for educational troubleshooting provide a checklist of specific things to look for. Whether or not it is this particular list, criteria must be used and teachers must know what is being looked for. They also must understand that the purpose of the observation is to offer help and support. Each observation should be followed up with a conference to discuss the lesson's strengths and areas that need attention. In the conference, plans should be cooperatively developed by the teacher and principal for strengthening weak factors. As discussed, these plans should be viewed as tentative solutions for classroom problems.

Descriptions of effective principals indicate that principals might enhance their effectiveness by asking teachers to provide them with written plans on the changes they intend to make.[15] Principals (or central office supervisors) can use them as a guide in their next observation and conference.

It is absolutely essential that observations of elementary teachers include more than one subject area or activity.[16] As shown in the checklist in Chapter 7 (Table 7–1), teaching methods should be determined by purposes and the subject matter, along with consideration of the nature of the learners. Thus, methods are impossible to assess if only social studies lessons or only mathematics lessons are observed.

Secondary school teachers should also be observed in more than one class or kind of activity.

The success of an inservice program depends greatly on getting the problems of teachers out in the open. If teachers are evaluated on their willingness to disclose problems, their problems will be brought out in the open. Principals should jot down the problems as they are mentioned by individuals (or the faculty, at meetings). Over a period of months and years this procedure can be very helpful in planning the inservice program. But it should be used continuously, not just when trying to find problems in order to initiate an inservice program. The point is that the supervisor does not have to contrive methods to get teachers to disclose their problems when this is a basis for teacher evaluation. Stated as a principle: The inservice education program should be consistent with the bases for teacher evaluation.

Focus Attention on Educational Goals. Educational goals must be kept in mind or they tend to be forgotten (even by those who participated in their development). Referring to goals at faculty meetings and in the weekly bulletin and asking for opinions on various aspects of the educational program communicates the principal's interest and involvement to the staff. (The opinions can be reported on at faculty meetings.) Inservice education should be tied directly to the goals of the school. This is another principle for the organization of a sound inservice education program.

Involve the Faculty in Making Decisions. The literature on leadership is conclusive about the importance of involving people in the decisions that affect them. In a school characterized by collaborative decision making the principal meets with teachers and establishes committees with responsibility for study of a particular problem and for making recommendations to the entire faculty. The principal then organizes the faculty to act on the recommendations, obtain resources, and assist in implementation and evaluation of results. Participatory decision making communicates the principal's confidence in teachers as professionals. In an environment where shared decision-making techniques are used, teachers make curricular decisions, select materials, and experiment with new educational approaches.

Support Teachers Against Unfounded Criticisms. Professional growth depends on a positive school climate, one that strengthens teachers' sense of their professional contributions. A school climate is improved when a principal finds it utterly necessary to insulate teachers from unjustifiable criticism within the community. A principal explains:

> A prevalent complaint voiced by classroom teachers is that principals are at times reluctant to support teachers against unfounded criticisms lodged against them by parents, students or community members. When a problem arises, teachers contend that some principals will compromise a teacher's position to alleviate an

uncomfortable situation. The end result is that teachers feel isolated and deserted.[17]

Principals should recognize that ill-considered and unfounded criticism can create such anxieties in teachers that their effectiveness is impaired. To alleviate teachers' anxieties, the principal must discuss with the teacher alternative ways of dealing with the criticism. Solutions should be acceptable to all involved. As the principal in the foregoing example cautions, "the entire process should not impair a teacher's dignity and self-respect."[18] The point of importance here, however, is that the principal is in a position to insulate teachers from unfounded criticism. This is real leadership and can have a positive (and lasting) impact on the faculty. For example, when Senator Joseph McCarthy attacked the professors of Teachers College, Columbia University, for being subversive, Dwight D. Eisenhower, who was then president of Columbia University, insulated the professors from the unfounded criticism by responding that there were no subversives among his faculty. Eisenhower was a strong and loyal administrator. (One usually thinks of loyalty as flowing upward from the staff to the administrator, but it also has a downward flow.) Interestingly, Eisenhower's insulation of the faculty from attack during the witch hunts and infringements on academic freedom of the early 1950s is what they seem to remember best about him more than three decades later.[19]

In our own time, there have been demands by legislators and administrators across the nation that teachers take competency examinations in mathematics, reading, and language. Although the motive is to improve the performance of teachers, the method is (to say the least) based on a deficit orientation rather than a professional development orientation and cannot help but convey to teachers that they do not possess the ability to educate students effectively. Thus it is more important than ever that principals maintain an atmosphere that contributes to teachers' sense of making a professional contribution to education.

Recognize Effective Teaching. The kind of leader who inspires teachers acknowledges their significant contributions. Looking for the strengths is basic to the development of an inservice program. For example, a teacher with superior abilities in teaching remedial mathematics may share his or her methods with other teachers at a meeting held for that purpose. In observing this teacher, the principal should seek to determine just what it is that the teacher does well that makes him or her so effective. Principals and supervisors must also be lifelong students of education.

Certainly, teachers should be recognized for using the kinds of practices that the principal wants to encourage in all faculty. Recognition can come in many forms: a verbal compliment, a note to the teacher, acknowledgements at faculty meetings, inviting the curriculum director or coordinator to observe and confer with the teacher, or inviting the teacher to participate in a conference—all convey the principal's awareness and appreciation to teachers.

The foregoing should not lead supervisors to the unfortunate conclusion that ineffective teachers should be ignored. Ineffective teachers are simply teachers with classroom problems. They need and want the support of a principal who will help them in their efforts to deal with problems and thus become more effective. The inservice education program must give each teacher the maximum opportunity for growth.

One School, or One School System?
Building a Comprehensive Program

It has already been pointed out that an inservice program based entirely on local effort would be inadequate. The resources of the central office staff must be available to every building. (Small school systems may find it helpful to join together in obtaining consultant services.) Although principals are responsible for initiating inservice programs at their school, the inservice program of the school system is the responsibility of the assistant superintendent for curriculum and instruction, who works with the elementary curriculum coordinator, the secondary curriculum coordinator, and the coordinator of the various subject fields (see Chapter 4).

In some school systems, supervisors from the central office do not initiate programs but work with principals in organizing activities that seem to be addressed to teachers' problems. Whenever similar problems are found in several schools, systemwide activities are planned by supervisors and principals. These common problems are often discovered by principals at their meetings, or they may be identified by supervisors in their discussions with teachers. Districtwide committees are formed for consideration of such problems as the development of a sequential program for the teaching of English, health education, or parent education. Subject-field or grade-level meetings are planned when desirable, and outside consultants are hired if local personnel do not have the expertise (or time) to assist with the problem under consideration.

In other school systems, principals do not originate the inservice program but are inescapably its facilitator. In such cases principals must work closely with their colleagues and offer support and encouragement to teachers. Robert S. Gilchrist and his associates pointed out some years ago that "initiating activities at the local school level will help to insure that the program is centered on problems significant to teachers."[20] John Goodlad and others have built their work on this principle as it continues to be valid.[21] Nevertheless, as Gilchrist and his associates warned, "The superintendent who emphasizes the autonomy of the individual school in inservice education does not thus relieve the central office of responsibility."[22] There are some things that the central office is simply in a better position to do and provide than the local school.

Take, for example, helping teachers arrange programs of intraschool visits. Central office supervisors are in a better position than principals to know about the new developments and promising methods being used in various classrooms throughout the school system. The supervisor is also better able than most principals to provide curriculum materials for experimental purposes. Supervisors are usually more able than principals to make available significant research findings to teachers. (This does not, of course, relieve principals and teachers of the responsibility for reviewing the research for themselves.) Central office personnel are usually better able than an individual school principal to develop cooperative programs with universities, and they are more likely to help teachers to become involved in professional association activities (Association for Supervision and Curriculum Development, for example). This is because curriculum development is their special function.

The point is that central office supervisors have much to contribute to a teacher's professional development. The principal whose working philosophy includes drawing on the best available resources will have no difficulty in working closely with supervisors.

Program Coordination. Returning to the problem of coordination, whoever has the responsibility in the school system for coordinating the educational program should be responsible for coordinating inservice education activities. Unfortunately, inservice education activities frequently are rather badly coordinated. As Howey and Vaughan point out, "Little continuity and coordination exists between or among staff development offerings and it is difficult if not impossible for participants to see how apparently unrelated inservice activities will in any basic way allow them to do a more effective job of helping their students learn."[23] The problem is one of unmet administrative responsibilities, but there are two additional factors that merit examination. First, much (if not, most) current inservice education did not emerge from attempts to help teachers more effectively deal with their problems as they perceive them.

Second, as Howey and Vaughan report, inservice education still follows "a largely deficit, undifferentiated group approach."[24] The individual's skills or knowledge are not considered in planning the program, which is often mandated. Just what is mandated may shift drastically from one year to the next (in one year it may be "affective education" and the next, classroom management), creating a fragmented, disjointed program. One can say without fear of contradiction that inservice education responds more to educational fads than to teachers' individual needs. But this is not because we lack adequate principles of inservice education, but only because we do not use them to guide our efforts.

Curriculum Development and Professional Development. Since a major purpose of inservice education is curriculum development, the curriculum council of the school system should be the agency that coordinates inservice education with curriculum development. As indicated in Chapter 3, the assistant superintendent for curriculum and instruction chairs this group, at least initially. Curriculum development and inservice education may seem indistinguishable, but professional growth does not automatically occur by engaging teachers in a curriculum development project for the purpose of improving the curriculum. For professional development to take place, it should be included as an objective of the project.

It should also be noted that involvement in a curriculum development project should lead to other professional growth activities, such as graduate course work, professional reading, and school visitations. Thus what may seem at first glance to be a fragmented and disjointed set of professional activities may simply be that one activity has led to another. This is desirable; as Dewey tells us, "the educational process has no end beyond itself; it is its own end" and "the adult uses his powers to transform his environment, thereby occasioning new stimuli which redirect his powers and keep them developing."[25] Thus the coherence in professional growth activities may be there, but unapparent. (Each person's development leads to his or her own program.)

Finally, an inservice program that offers teachers a variety of opportunities for professional growth is diversified and comprehensive, not fragmented. As such, it is more likely to meet all four purposes of inservice education than is a program that locks teachers into the one activity mandated by the central office.

PROFESSIONAL ORIENTATION FOR NEW TEACHERS

The orientation of new teachers is an important administrative and supervisory function; how a new faculty member is introduced to his or her assignment can greatly influence the contributions that the teacher will eventually make to the school system. Moreover, the newly appointed teacher must quickly be made to *feel* like a growing, contributing professional, as well as a member of the particular school faculty. Future growth depends on one's view of oneself, which, in turn, depends largely on the view and treatment by others. Orientation activities must be carefully planned by the school system, but the orientation program must be a seamless part of the inservice education program. Otherwise, the new teacher is set apart. (The objective is professional integration, not segregation.)

Assuming, as do the authors of this book, that orientation is a very important aspect of inservice education, one properly might expect to find it included in discussions of inservice education. However, astonishing though it may seem, orientation is not generally considered a part of the inservice education or staff development program by writers on teacher development. ("Orientation" is not even mentioned in the index of *Staff Development,* the Eighty-second Yearbook of the National Society for the Study of Education. Yet the editor for the society presents the book as a "basis for considering *in depth*" the problems of inservice education.")[26] Giving attention to the new teacher is a sound investment because it can improve the quality of learning. Moreover, well-planned orientation programs can do much toward preventing the failure of new teachers. (Chapter 8 presented a number of strategies that administrators and supervisors can use to prevent the failure of first-year teachers.)

Categories of "New" Teachers

Not all new teachers are fresh from the college or university. It is particularly important to recognize that there are at least four groups of new teachers, with special needs:

1. Inexperienced teachers.
2. Teachers from another school system.
3. Teachers from another school in the same school system.
4. Experienced teachers who return to teaching.[27]

Moreover, the educational literature also singles out the special needs of two other groups of new teachers: teachers new to inner-city schools, and teachers transferred to other schools in their district as a result of desegregation policies or changing enrollments.[28]

Perhaps the most serious criticism that can be leveled against orientation programs today is that they tend to treat "new" teachers as a gross commodity, ignoring the differences in their special needs. Most school districts define "new" as being new to the system, and systemwide orientation programs for new teachers usually lump beginning teachers and experienced teachers together in one, undifferentiated group.[29] There are other problems with orientation programs that will be discussed shortly, and suggestions will be made for their improvement. (Most programs are too brief and too intensive, for example.) But let us turn now to the new teachers actually faced by supervisors and their particular needs.

Inexperienced Teachers. What principals and the central office staff do to meet the needs of neophyte teachers is crucial for developing and retaining competent teachers. We have far too little solid knowledge relating to induction procedures. Hall points out that researchers have given little attention to the strategies to assist teachers in the "induction phase" (the first three years of teaching), and "the research that has been done tends to be descriptive of the experiences of teachers and their trial by fire."[30]

Granted this, as pointed out in Chapter 8, not all beginning teachers suffer; there are remarkable differences in the quality of the support and assistance given the novice, leading to remarkably different experiences from school system to school system. As indicated in Chapter 3, some teachers have a sense of growing professional power while others feel diminished, and the latter often cite as the reason a lack of support from their administrators and supervisors. Although it is certainly true that we need more knowledge from research about what helps beginning teachers, it is also true that we have, largely, failed to base our orientation programs on what we know about organizational development and effective leadership.

For example, we know that "administrative support, especially by principals, is essential" for organization development in schools.[31] It is apparent that the implications of this principle include orientation, which is vital for organization development and renewal. Some researchers take the position that urban school systems are characterized by "adversarial relations" rather than by a "positive orientation to communication and collaboration."[32] Be that as it may, communication between supervisors and beginning teachers is an absolutely essential part of orientation in all school systems. No one suffers ill effects from too much communication; everyone suffers from too little communication. A study conducted by Heichberger and Young on teachers' perceptions of supervision supports this view. The teachers indicated that "the most important link between a teacher and his supervisor is effective communication," and further, that "the principal must set the stage for open communication."[33]

Actually, orientation (of both neophytes and experienced teachers) begins when the teacher is interviewed for the position; the first contact with the school system establishes the tone for future relations. The candidate should be made to feel at ease and should be given sufficient information about the educational program and plans for its improvement so that he or she can raise relevant questions. It is vitally important for the school system to know how the candidate feels about the kind of curriculum in operational use and teaching and learning in general.

If the candidate seems interested in the position and the school system is impressed with the candidate's potential, she (or he) should be invited to visit the school where she will be assigned. Arrangements should be made for the candidate to visit classes (ideally, the grade or classes she will teach). Opportunities should also be provided to examine instructional resources and pose questions concerning working conditions and whether all students are served well (in the high school, students who are not college bound as well as those with a desire to go to college). The purpose of the visit is to help the visitor to acquire an honest picture of the school under the most normal circumstances possible.

The inexperienced teacher whose student-teaching experience was under a supervisor who saw little value in cooperative learning experiences may feel a jolt of fear when visiting classes where youngsters are productively engaged in group problem-solving activities. The candidate may wonder if she can possibly fit into the educational program, and may need to hear that the necessary help will be forthcoming.

If a contract is signed, the beginning teacher should immediately be assigned a "buddy" who, in the first year of the teacher's service, will help in integrating the neophyte into the life of the school. Colleagues are an important professional resource.[34] The "buddy" plan has proven effective in the schools where it has been implemented. Its effectiveness hinges both on the selection of buddies with good interpersonal skills and on the leadership style of the principal. For the principal must instill in the faculty the feeling that it is a team and that they have a responsibility for the success of new team members.

As noted above, teachers value early and open communication with supervisors. A number of scholars have suggested the importance of a letter from the principal as a startup device. Indeed, this form of early communication, which is actually no more than a simple courtesy, has long been recognized as an approved practice in personnel development. For example, in their classic book on personnel administration, Elsbree and Reutter suggested:

> A friendly letter from the principal in whose building the teacher has been assigned, if written early, can contribute considerably to the "settling down" phase of induction. Such a letter might well contain, in addition to the usual note of welcome, bits of information about the teacher's assignment that will enable the newcomer to do some preliminary planning and encourage him to ask questions. This step could easily lead to a series of exchanges of considerable significance for everyone concerned.[35]

The advice remains fresh and extremely helpful. (The letter should, of course, be sent to all newly appointed teachers, but it is particularly important to give attention to the beginner.)

The Experienced Teacher. The new teacher who is older, at least in terms of years of experience, must also become integrated into life in the new school.

Since administrative procedures differ from school to school, the buddy system may be helpful to this teacher as well. What is important here, however, is that the changed environment be a stimulus for improving teaching. For example, if a summer workshop in curriculum improvement has been planned, thought should be devoted to how the new teachers can be involved. Moreover, new teachers should be viewed as a potential source of many useful suggestions for dealing with the problems being worked on by the faculty in educational improvement efforts.

In the case of experienced teachers who have returned to the profession or who have been assigned to a new level of teaching, it might be in the interest of the school system to pay their tuition for courses selected to prepare them for working at this level. School visitations and reading to keep abreast of the developments that have occurred in the field should be strongly advised. New teachers should also be given an opportunity to participate in the selection of the curricular materials that they will be using in their classes.

Finally, as in the case of inexperienced teachers, experienced teachers who have returned to education should be favored in terms of providing optimum teaching conditions that will improve their chances to succeed. Certainly, their assignments should be no more difficult than those given to teachers who are not new to the school.

Teachers Who Are Transferred. The Supreme Court has dealt with the matter of faculty desegregation, stating that segregated faculties deny minority students equality of educational opportunity and ordering that teacher desegregation plans be put into effect.[36] The orientation of teachers who have been transferred to meet federal faculty desegregation guidelines is an important problem for administrators in the school systems involved. Of considerable interest here is Wilkerson's study of the attitudes of elementary school teachers in Philadelphia with respect to faculty desegregation. The study, which compared the attitudes of teachers who were involuntarily transferred for desegregation reasons with those who were not, found that both groups were supportive of school desegregation (student and faculty desegregation) in principle.[37]

And the research bears them out. Braddock, Crain, and McPartland reviewed the research on the effects of desegregation and found that blacks educated in desegregated elementary and secondary schools are more successful as adults than are blacks from segregated schools.[38] Not only do the test scores of minority students go up after desegregation, but "desegregation enables minorities to join other Americans in becoming well-educated, economically successful, and socially well-adjusted adults."[39]

Of even greater import here, however, is Wilkerson's finding that urban teachers are basically progressive and believe that desegregated schools are better places than segregated schools for educating children. The problem for supervision is to build on and further develop their sense of professional responsibility by involving them together in inservice activities designed to help all children achieve success. School success encompasses social development as well as cognitive growth.

How can the curriculum enrich the common experience of majorities and minorities instead of dividing them from one another? This is a question that should be the concern of the faculty in desegregated schools. The superintendent of schools has a major role in directing attention to this problem. However, the principal must involve newly transferred teachers into the life of the school immediately, and the principal must arrange for the faculty to sit down together with the express purpose of examining the opportunities of desegregation for improving the program of the school.

A technique of great potential value in this regard is for the faculty group to develop the answers to the following four questions which are germane to any effort for school improvement:

1. What are the characteristics of the best school that we can describe?
2. What are the areas of strength and of weakness in our school?
3. How can we change our weak qualities into those of the best school perceived?
4. How can we determine whether progress is being made in making these changes?

Step 3 involves establishing objectives which are required for determining progress or change. As progress is made, the objectives should change.[40] The changing objectives are a stimulus for teachers' continuing professional growth. There are no end points to the inextricably interrelated processes of educational improvement and professional growth, only turning points.

The foregoing discussion on the orientation of desegregated faculty does not imply that the question of *how* faculty are desegregated has ceased to exist. A study of the Houston schools, which were placed under court-ordered faculty desegregation, found that the achievement of black students was negatively related to the extent that their teachers were racially isolated, but that achievement was also lower for black youngsters who were assigned teachers who were transferred involuntarily for faculty desegregation purposes.[41] The achievement of black, white, and Hispanic students was positively associated with teacher experience and negatively related to teacher turnover. The youngest and least experienced white teachers were involuntarily placed in minority schools and the teacher turnover in those schools often increased several times over. It is well known that faculty turnover lowers student achievement. Nor does the solution lie with the involuntary placement of experienced teachers in a cross-race setting, for they often express great dissatisfaction about involuntary placement in unfamiliar surroundings.[42] Tyler reports a successful strategy used in Detroit: Volunteers were requested among experienced teachers to transfer to inner-city schools. There were many voluntary teacher transfers.[43] The point of importance here is that, as was found in Houston, "poorly planned desegregation policies can have undesirable consequences."[44] Moreover, voluntary (cooperative) engagement is more apt to lead to the resolution of a problem; coercive mandates tend to create all kinds of residual problems.

The Orientation Program

Many school systems have designed formal orientation programs to acquaint teachers new to the school system with members of the staff and the board of education, operational policies and regulations, and the community. Beginning teachers usually anticipate that they will be allocated sufficient time and resources for setting up a classroom for the first time. According to those who have studied orientation programs, the reality is often quite different. Houston and Felder characterize it as "a series of ceremonial welcomes, one meeting after another, a barrage of instructions"[45] (with little time being left to plan or set up a classroom). Kowalski conducted a survey of 349 school systems to determine the nature of formal orientation programs for new teachers and reported that although the educational literature indicates "that new teachers are primarily interested in problems affecting human relations in the classroom and in the school building, many school district programs focus on inspirational addresses, minor administrative duties of teachers, social get-togethers, and tours of buildings and communities."[46]

Are administrators so naive as to believe that the general school district orientation program really helps the neophyte begin teaching with success? More than three decades ago, Elsbree and Reutter reported that school superintendents "rate the much-heralded general faculty meeting held at the beginning of the year as relatively low among common practices used to promote the effectiveness of newly appointed teachers."[47] Elsbree and Reutter continue: "There can be no doubt that the problems of the beginner are unique and require much closer supervisory attention than that provided through general faculty meetings."[48]

Then why do school districts go on year after year, having general faculty meetings, teas, and luncheons? Probably because these affairs are not merely ceremonial but have a function: They offer new teachers contact with the officials of the school system. Lest we forget, school systems are frequently criticized for lack of communication between organizational levels (see Chapter 3). According to Elsbree and Reutter, "Pride in belonging to a school system is contingent upon acquaintance with those who play a responsible part in its affairs. Therefore, new teachers should be introduced to the whole staff, so that the latter will recognize and greet them when their paths cross in the future."[49] Some new teachers' comments about orientation programs are in line with this assessment. "Made us feel that the people 'upstairs' were human" and "Nice to meet the people at the top" are examples.[50]

One is led to conclude with Elsbree and Reutter that "to the degree that these occasions are organized, so as to create a feeling of 'at homeness,' they are desirable features of an orientation program. Otherwise they contribute little."[51]

The social and ceremonial function of orientation does not substitute for the professional function. A new teacher commented about the orientation program in her district: "I wish we could have gotten together with other teachers in our department or teaching area." And another said about the building-level orientation, "No time spent with me—first year teacher—just a general meeting for all teachers."[52]

The function of orientation programs is to help the teacher make a successful adjustment and keep on growing. Experts on induction recommend that the orientation program be continuous rather than an intensive "crash course," and be a permanent part of the inservice education program.[53]

Present Weaknesses. Many school systems tend to rely on "buddies" and on fellow teachers not formally designated as buddies to assist new teachers. As we have indicated, experienced colleagues can and should be very helpful, but they should not be expected to serve as a total support system for new teachers. There are at least three reasons for this: (1) colleagues have other professional responsibilities and are not freely available to assist in planning lessons and locating materials, (2) beginners hesitate to ask for assistance and experienced teachers hesitate to offer it,[54] and (3) the advice given by colleagues is not always professionally sound.

An adequate support system encourages beginning teachers to ask for the help they frequently require and provides the needed assistance. It also helps them become better acquainted socially with other beginning teachers and with more experienced colleagues. (Beginning teachers have an emotional bond and find security in each other's company.)

Promising Procedures. A number of school systems have begun to develop support systems for their new teachers. A simple but promising procedure being used in the Arlington, Texas, schools is to ask new teachers to report several days before other teachers. Its advantages have been described thusly: "Beginners are provided the time and assistance they so desperately need to plan and prepare for the beginning of school. They work in their own rooms, unpack and organize materials, plan instruction, and make bulletin boards. They learn to travel from home to school and become more familiar with their school's neighborhood. By the time school begins, street names and landmarks are familiar, and the school itself is less threatening."[55]

Houston schools provide a well-organized support system for beginning teachers throughout their first year. Teacher facilitators are assigned to work with the new teachers and to help them in every possible way. They visit the new teacher's classroom and teach model lessons, and they assist in planning lessons and overcoming classroom discipline problems. "In the process, they build a bond of confidence and trust that fosters open communication and encourages new teachers to ask for the help they often need."[56]

When asked to evaluate their new teacher orientation programs, new teachers in a Wisconsin school district ranked "assistance given by other staff members" as the most helpful orientation activity.[57] An increasing number of voices have begun to say that the help should come in the form of a facilitator, whose full-time job it is to assist new teachers.

Preparing School Building Orientation Programs. Central offices frequently issue suggestions to principals to assist them in preparing school building orientation programs. Presented below are the guidelines provided the principals in the Hartford County, Maryland, schools, which include a list of suggested topics of concern to new teachers. Curiously, curriculum development is not specifically identified among the topics. Nevertheless, the idea for such a guide is universally useful.

Orientation of New Teachers

Teachers who are new to the school need considerable orientation in order that they may make an easy adjustment to their situation. This process should begin promptly after a teacher has been assigned to the school. During the spring and summer months, the principal may profitably introduce the new teacher to his teaching assignment, the policies and practices of the school, the materials of instruction to be used, the expectations which are held for teachers, and other relevancies.

Orientation for new teachers should also be provided during the preschool meetings. However, it is impractical to attempt more than a rudimentary introduction to the job during this period. The principal will need to extend and expand opportunities for work with his new staff members as the school year progresses.

Much of the work with new teachers may need to be done on an individual basis, although some areas lend themselves well to group enterprise. Particularly in the larger schools, where there are many new faculty members, the principal will find it economical in terms of time to plan meetings for the entire group.

The individual school situation and the backgrounds of the teachers involved will determine the areas in which help needs to be provided. It is a good idea to include the teachers in the planning of any series of meetings since they will be in the process of identifying problems as they work in the classrooms. The principal should, however, plan adequately to provide help in those areas where he sees the need.

As with all faculty meetings, those with new teachers should be scheduled well in advance so that there will be an opportunity for preparation. Some duplicated agenda or discussion guides may be helpful in most cases. These meetings should be scheduled so that new teachers will not be overburdened with this type of activity.

The following topics are of a general nature and may have application for most new teacher groups:

1. Classroom management.
2. Good housekeeping.
3. Teacher pre-planning.
4. Classroom discipline.
5. Teacher–parent relationships.
6. Reporting to parents.
7. Guidance in the classroom.
8. Professional ethics.
9. Use of bulletin boards.
10. Use of audio-visual aids.
11. Supervisory services.
12. Teacher evaluation.
13. Interpreting school records.
14. Teacher–teacher relationships.
15. Teacher–pupil planning.
16. Grouping for instruction.[58]

School–University Programs. Another promising orientation idea is for the school system to collaborate with a nearby school of education in offering programs for new teachers to help them get off to a successful start. For example, University of Houston's College of Education coordinated a workshop entitled "Begin Teaching with Success" for new teachers coming to the Houston metropolitan area. Teachers from several school systems worked with the new teachers to help prepare for the beginning of school. The program was collaboratively designed by university faculty and school district personnel, and was attended voluntarily by new teachers.[59]

Last, but certainly not least, informal social gatherings can help in alleviating the worries of new teachers. Teacher unions in some cities sponsor such socials and also provide assistance in personal matters such as locating a place to live and shopping. Orientation involves personal adjustment as well as professional adjustment and the two are intertwined.

CONDUCTING WORKSHOPS, CONFERENCES, AND INSTITUTES

In a very real sense, the professional lives of teachers are a continuing workshop. Teachers identify their problems and deal with them with varying degrees of effectiveness, often without realizing that they are engaged in problem solving, and almost always with complete (or nearly complete) autonomy. The teachers in Goodlad's "Study of Schooling" said that they had virtually complete decision-making power in their classrooms.[60] They also indicated that they seldom attended workshops or other inservice activities that bring teachers together from different schools. Such professional development activities were not popular, but why should they be? For the teachers also reported "very infrequent contacts with their principals on such substantive matters as discipline, curriculum, instruction, interactions with parents, and staff relations," and further that they had themselves initiated the infrequent discussions that had occurred.[61] It is clear that principals were not knowledgeable about teachers' problems and were therefore not in a position to take the leadership in the development of inservice activities of value to teachers. Indeed, the principals were reinforcing the isolation and professional stagnation of their teachers.

A workshop is a situation (or setting) for solving problems. To ensure a successful workshop, the workshop situation should arise from the problems of the participants. The workshop given by the Houston schools for beginning teachers is an excellent illustration. It cannot be overdrawn that the administrator or supervisor must take the initiative in creating open communication to provide a valid basis for workshops or for any inservice programs. In addition to classroom visits, the educational leader can keep the channels of communication open in two other ways: by making himself or herself available to teachers, and by listening to their problems as *they* perceive them. The manner of things in classroom observations is that the supervisor's (or principal's) assessment comes first (is given first priority); it is the supervisor, after all, who is assessing the teaching situation. There is a very real danger that the teacher will never have an opportunity to discuss the problems of primary concern to him or her unless the principal listens as well as talks, and creates a climate of acceptance.

Faculty Participation

As discussed in Chapter 4, the principal is in a better position than anyone else in the school to make observations of problems that are common to several faculty members or the entire school, and which could (or should) be addressed in workshops or other inservice sessions. For example, the principal may see very clearly the need for the revision of a curriculum area. Nevertheless, faculty must make inservice education valuable for themselves and should participate in the selection of the problems that they feel require attention. A way of affording teachers the opportunity to have a direct impact on the inservice education program is to create an inservice education committee for the school.

Williamson and Elfman have given attention to this problem, and they conceive of the committee as being composed of interested faculty and the principal. Teachers may be elected or appointed to the committee through their professional organization or union, and since it is important to have the confidence of the entire faculty, one teacher should be included from each grade level or subject area. The committee identifies the needs of the school and constructs a questionnaire that permits faculty members to rank the problems on the list in order of importance. The committee selects those problems the faculty indicates as needing immediate attention.[62]

Many teachers will not, willingly, attend inservice programs, nor will educational problems be solved until teachers can have an impact on their inservice programs. Moreover, if teachers rank their problems, they must think about them; this has value in and of itself. Often, however, the machinery already exists in the school for principals and teachers to identify a problem and attack it together. If the school has a curriculum council, the faculty should think carefully before deciding to form another inservice committee. Duplication of effort can only result in a weak and fragmented professional development program. The important point is that faculty should identify their needs through a single committee at the building level.

Conducting Workshops

The term "workshop" has been grievously misused. A real workshop gives the participant an opportunity to make an intensive study of a problem that has arisen out of his or her experience as a teacher. A real workshop brings people together with common problems and purposes, and has a competent staff who are available to any workshop member who needs and wants their help. A real workshop requires time and is probably best conducted in the summer when teachers can get insights and experience and be free from other responsibilities. (It will be recalled from the discussion in Chapter 2 that the first workshop was conducted at Ohio State University in 1936 in an eight-week summer session.) Some school districts employ teachers on a twelve-month basis (the Los Angeles Unified School District is an example), and the teachers are free at times throughout the year.

As described in Chapter 2, some school systems have made appropriations for substitutes so that teachers can be released from teaching to work on professional problems during the school year. Gilchrist observed from his experience as a school superintendent that this "may cause the teaching staff to develop an entirely different outlook on the inservice program. They know then that the program has importance and dignity."[63] Nevertheless, the teachers are still under the strain of teaching, and the summer seems like an optimum time for workshops. There is some evidence that teachers feel this way, too. When asked to rank inservice education activities in order of their usefulness, a representative sample of public school teachers in South Dakota ranked "workshop-block of time set aside in the summer for intensive study of a problem in your school" as "very useful," but "workshop-block of time set aside during the school year for intensive study of a problem in your school," as "not useful."[64]

Good workshops have results; the participants actually do something about what they have learned when they get back to the classroom. They may be helped in this regard by the workshop staff, who go to the school on invitation from individual teachers. (Workshop staff members can be hired to provide assistance to the faculty beyond the period of the workshop.) It will be recalled from the discussion on the Eight-Year Study that those schools that made most use of consultants made the most effective changes (in terms of student outcomes).

Phases of the Workshop. Table 13–1 is presented to help supervisors organize and conduct a summer workshop. Obviously, the phases described would apply to any good workshop, whatever the time or season. As seen in Table 13–1, the five phases in workshops are the *problem-identification stage*, the *administrative-planning stage*, the *workshop-planning stage*, the *workshop stage*, and the *implementation-evaluation stage*.

An enormously important part of the problem-identification stage is for supervisors to identify schools with the same problem. It is better, for both educational and economic reasons, if more than one school is involved in the workshop. (As mentioned, school staff tend to look inward instead of outward, and this tendency needs to be countered.) It should also be noted that teachers are involved in each stage. As Table 13–1 shows, in the workshop-planning stage they have an opportunity to relate workshop activities more closely to their own particular needs.

Although not actually indicated in the table, teachers should also participate in locating appropriate workshop staff members and consultants. Some teachers are knowledgeable about the resources available through the university and elsewhere, and can make valuable suggestions. Joyce and McKibbin conducted an inquiry into the nature of the professional growth of teachers and found great differences in the extent to which teachers exploit opportunities for professional growth.[65] More about this shortly. The point of importance here is that some teachers actively seek out the professional development opportunities that are available to them and are an excellent source of ideas about possible workshop faculty. Inservice committees (or curriculum councils) at the building level should make their ideas about workshop staff known to the district-level curriculum council. In fact, the district-level curriculum council should solicit suggestions.

Table 13–1   Phases in Conducting a Summer Workshop

Months	Phase	Work to Do
September October November	Problem-identification stage	Identify local problems; present findings to curriculum council and assistant superintendent for curriculum and instruction
December January	Administrative-planning stage	Meet with curriculum council to determine priorities for summer workshop; obtain workshop budget approval; disseminate information to administrators and supervisors
February March April May	Workshop-planning stage	Select workshop staff members and consultants; appoint or elect coordinators; select workshop center; arrange adequate secretarial services; select learning resources that will be needed; survey teachers for ideas and suggestions for the workshop; publicize the workshop; decide on applicants; arrange for housing and meals (if the workshop is away from home)
June July August	Workshop stage	Establish workshop policies with participants; clarify problem or purpose of workshop; set up workshop committees; develop a system of working individually and in groups; visit libraries, examine research and new materials; use problem-solving processes; establish plan for formative and summative evaluation
September–	Implementation-evaluation stage	Implement practices (problem solutions) in classroom/school; evaluate outcomes; modify treatments as needed; provide follow-up assistance for implementation and evaluation of practices (problem solutions)

A competent workshop staff should be selected, comprised of people who know the problems of the participants, who enjoy serving in a resource-person role rather than in a lecturing-directing role, who work well in a team situation, and who have full time for the workshop. The value of consultative help cannot be overstressed. The presence of consultants at the workshop staff's side will help the participants to grow professionally and will probably lead to production of work of a higher quality than if they were not present (such as in the development of curriculum materials). The hallmark of a good workshop is that it provides expert assistance.

The success of a workshop depends greatly on planning—both preplanning and continuous assessment and planning during the workshop. The workshop program should be evaluated weekly by the planning committee and the following week's schedule planned accordingly. In a good workshop, teachers are advised by people who, in addition to being knowledgeable about the problem under consideration, are friendly and responsive personalities. Association with fellow workshop members from other schools and backgrounds contributes to the teacher's thinking about his or her specific problems and broadens his or her professional orientation. Experience in studying a given problem should improve the teacher's ability to solve other professional problems in the future.

Conferences and Institutes

It will be remembered that the teachers' institutes, which developed in the late 1840s and 1850s, were gatherings of teachers for the purpose of improving teaching. They had to take the place of normal schools for many teachers, and at the same time they afforded teachers the opportunity to hear lectures by prominent educators. Since their purpose was to develop initial teaching competency and stimulate teachers to go on learning, the distinction between their preservice and inservice functions was blurred. With the expansion of teacher training facilities, institutes lost their function of providing initial training.

The institutes of the nineteenth century are of more than purely archaeological interest because many school districts still hold institutes and conferences that are pale replicas of the institutes of bygone days. All too often the conference programs consist of presentations that are someone else's idea of what teachers need to hear, are unrelated to the problems that concern teachers most, and all too often have a deficit orientation in the tradition of the first institutes. Conditions have surely changed. Many teachers are at least as well, if not better, prepared professionally than their supervisors, but the institute remains much as it was—a dinosaur that refuses to die.

Robert Perrin, a university professor, offers this reminiscence of the teachers' institutes that he attended as a high school English teacher.

> I remember the coffee was always too strong and the doughnuts were always good. I remember we always enjoyed going out for lunch. I remember thinking I would have had a better time teaching than sitting through session after session, listening to people who had little to tell me that would work in my classrooms. My memories of high school teachers' institutes as a high school teacher were not good ones.[66]

Things did not seem much better from the other side of the podium. As a university presenter, Perrin remembered that the teachers leafed through the handouts that he had prepared "as though they were random pages in a telephone book," and remembered "women knitting rather than listening."[67] These experiences led Perrin to conduct a survey of English teachers in Illinois to find out what kinds of conference activities they preferred. The teachers' clear preference was for sessions presented by fellow teachers to help them make their teaching more effective. As Perrin concluded, "they want to know about the methods that work from teachers currently working in similar circumstances and against similar odds."[68]

The question of why conferences are not addressing teachers' needs quickly enters the picture. Three major reasons offered by Perrin are: (1) the structure of the school system does not encourage teachers to become involved in conferences as presenters; (2) many supervisors decide for their teachers, without asking them what *they* prefer; and (3) teachers are not making their feelings known and must "insist on having specific kinds of presentations and presenters at conferences."[69] Certainly, if teachers are able to make their feelings known through their inservice committees or curriculum councils, and have the kinds of presentations they prefer, what Sarason called "existing regularities"[70] will be changed; schools must give teachers the time off to address other teachers at another district's institute, for example.

What is indeed fascinating, and of particular importance to us here, is that the teachers in Perrin's analysis were calling for a collaborative professional growth model where teachers share their knowledge and problems. According to Mohlman, Kierstead, and Gundlach, who pilot-tested this type of inservice education program, "teachers thrive in such a professional development setting."[71]

Conferences and institutes should be part of ongoing problem-solving activities. As groups of teachers work together to study their problems, there is no reason why they should not share the outcomes with teachers from other school districts (and every reason why they should). In the collaborative approach to problem solving, teachers draw on the expertise of supervisors and university consultants. Of interest, in this regard, is that the teachers in Perrin's study cited university professors as their second choice for presenters. But he cautions that such presentations are unlikely to be valuable unless they are addressed to teacher's needs as the teachers themselves perceive them.[72] As in the case of workshops, one starts with the problem, not the institute or conference. (The institute should not be a useless appendage to problem solving, conducted in the name of tradition.) Workshops, conferences, and institutes should also serve as a source of promising ideas and practices for consideration and implementation locally in solving local problems. Finally, the school systems that involve teacher representatives in planning conferences are operating in accord with the findings of research on effective inservice education practices. The necessity for using teachers' suggestions, and for having teachers as presenters is well documented.

FOSTERING THE PROFESSIONAL GROWTH OF TEACHERS

It will be remembered that in addition to developing teachers' ability to deal with problems and improving the curriculum, inservice education has two other functions: helping teachers to reach their own professional goals, and providing the stimulation needed to grow professionally and to prevent boredom and burnout. A good inservice education program focuses on school needs and on teacher needs. Actually, the two types of needs are inseparable; as teachers learn more about educational problems and how to solve them, they are improving the school's effectiveness, and they gain such satisfactions as knowing that they have helped students to learn things they have not learned before. (Seeing the results of one's work gratifies certain needs of the individual that are associated with his or her work.) The practical assistance given beginning teachers helps them to gain increased professional competence, and, thus, meets their needs for respect and a sense of competence.[73]

The trouble is that after the probationary stage, teachers are all too often left on their own. This is terribly unfortunate because the school benefits and teachers benefit when teachers continually aspire to better performance. They are more likely to do so in a stimulating school environment, as will be discussed shortly. Inservice education programs must be planned to meet the developing professional needs of teachers throughout their careers, which includes helping teachers obtain a credential or prepare for a new role (that of school counselor, for example). Not only do teachers believe that this is an important function of inservice education,[74] but school systems benefit from the upward professional mobility of teachers. As Tyler explains, teachers have to prepare for the jobs they see on the horizon and, in so doing, they develop new insights which they bring to the school system. "This counteracts the tendency toward limited views and sterile performance."[75]

Differences in Teacher Involvement in Professional Growth Activities

Teachers are individuals like anyone else. In a large study of the professional growth of teachers in California, Joyce and McKibbin found tremendous differences "in the extent to which teachers pull growth-producing experiences from their environment and exploit personal and professional activities."[76] Some teachers are close to their principals and use them for much assistance. They seek out supervisors and other teachers, belong to professional groups, attend conferences, and use ideas from workshops. They read widely, travel, and are intensely involved in a great variety of activities that enrich their personal and professional lives. They are actively involved in attempting to improve the schools in which they teach. As Joyce and McKibbin write, "They simply will not be denied. . . . They do not spend energy complaining about colleagues, administration, poor presenters at workshops, and so on. They simply take what they can where they can get it, which does not mean they are indiscriminate—their energy is simply oriented toward their growth rather than toward impediments to it."[77]

Just as there are teachers who operate at the psychological level described by Maslow as self-actualizing, so are there teachers who seem to operate at the bottom of Maslow's hierarchy of needs (the survival level). They will rarely take courses without a material benefit like a salary increment. Any possibility of changing the school's curriculum tends to be viewed suspiciously. "Change to them means they are not doing a good job and therefore are threatened. When in that state they may see themselves as one of the best teachers of the school." Their survival orientation causes them to try to squelch ideas for improving current practices, and if they have a strong position in the school's social system, they succeed. In addition to actively opposing, they use their power in the informal system of the school to cut down or ridicule ideas suggested by others. In the process of protecting themselves, they insulate the whole school from efforts to improve. As Joyce and McKibbin point out, "the informal social system is a powerful determining factor in whether inservice education activities will be sustained or even initiated."[78]

The problem is not confined to education. For example, if young doctors go into clinics where the older and apparently successful doctors use shortcuts instead of careful diagnosis and are derisive of the "impractical theories" of medical schools, they tend to lose much of their desire to become master diagnosticians. They are, instead, much tempted to emulate their older, experienced colleagues and be swept along with the stream. One is led to recall Andrew Manson, the young doctor in A. J. Cronin's novel *The Citadel*, who, for a time, abandons his ideals to become a "practical physician" in the example of his experienced, successful, but ignorant colleagues. He rationalizes his shortcuts by calling his earlier training and interest in research "a lot of hot air . . . all theories."[79] The very great change in his personality attests to the remarkable power of the informal social system in medicine—or in any field.

In one of the schools studied by Joyce and McKibbin, the principal seemed to have excellent rapport with the faculty—they laughed and talked together on the way to the faculty meeting. But at the meeting, ideas suggested by faculty members were ridiculed by the leader of the school's social system. This made several of the teachers very uncomfortable (the ideas of their friends were being held up for ridicule), but they said nothing, perhaps because the principal also said nothing, and simply allowed the ideas to become diminished. As Joyce and McKibbin observed, he "was not very skilled in handling the faculty as a group," despite his pleasant dyadic interactions with them.[80]

Clearly, the informal system of the school was impinging on the formal system and the principal was not functioning as a leader. If he had supported and encouraged the teachers who had come back from workshops with new ideas, he probably would have been supported by the other teachers, who were distressed by the treatment of their colleagues. (Perhaps he was afraid of the leader of the school's informal social system.)

In addition to self-actualized teachers and resistant teachers, Joyce and McKibbin found teachers who are simply withdrawn and are, therefore, hard to involve; they seldom take workshops or university courses or draw upon supervision, and they rarely participate in the informal interactions in the school in which they work.

Implications for Supervisors. Obviously, supervisors can expect to find that some teachers will exploit the positive opportunities created for them and others will not. Supervisors must create many opportunities for the self-actualizing teachers who are stimulated by emerging environments and who add to the stimulation; the objective is to activate the constructive energies of other teachers and to make the faculty self-actualizing in a collective sense, so that they can deal as a faculty with the problems of the school. Attention must, of course, be given to the school social system. Many of the ideas that we have discussed in this book were generated by specialists in organizational development and are concerned with improving the school's social system. It will be remembered, for example, that by asking teachers to serve on committees that will report back to the faculty on various matters, the principal is taking a step toward creating a formal inservice education program. If the principal selects leaders in the school's social system who are self-actualizing individuals, the principal is also improving the social system (making it more affirmative).

Much can be done toward creating a new social system by following the suggestions given earlier in this chapter for initiating an inservice program, such as recognizing effective teaching and, of course, supporting individuals as they bring ideas from outside the school for consideration by the faculty. And as Joyce and McKibbin point out, "strong interchange between teachers and principal and teachers and teachers" is a characteristic of an affirmative social system.[81] An open informal system requires open communication.

Volunteers. The self-actualizing people described above who use every professional development activity that is available to them are usually the individuals who volunteer to try out new inservice education programs or participate in experiments concerned with changing teaching practices to improve student achievement. N. L. Gage observed in a Phi Delta Kappa Award Lecture that using volunteers in these experiments "often arouses doubts as to the meaning of the results for teachers in general. Volunteers may have a higher motivation to improve. . . . So it is argued that what is learned from volunteers may not apply to the teachers who do not volunteer."[82] Gage takes issue with this argument, for two reasons: "research workers have no other alternative," and (more important for us here) "as results with volunteers become more promising more and more teachers will volunteer."[83] In a school with an open social system the volunteers will be likely to share their new ideas and concepts with other teachers and the principal.

The important point here is that the excitement of self-actualizing teachers about what they learn is contagious. The wise principal will hope that it grows to epidemic proportions and will do everything possible to spread the contagion. As is perfectly obvious, administrators should actively seek out the self-actualizers when recruiting new faculty—and provide an environment where they can flourish.

Avoiding Boredom and Burnout

After a certain point in time, which varies across individuals but is generally within seven to ten years of graduation, the majority of teachers, doctors, or members of any profession reach a plateau of development. Tyler tells us that "interviews with graduates indicate that if they do not participate in some form of continuing education experience they find their work routine and boring after a while."[84] Professionals who experience the suffering of boredom will decline in effectiveness. The reason is simple, yet profound: People have to have new challenges—they are not machines to be kept running; they need to be problem solvers. Sarason has described the effects of boredom and routine on teachers, including departure from the profession, and he observed that "if teaching becomes neither terribly interesting nor exciting to many teachers, how can one expect them to make learning interesting or exciting to children?"[85]

Work Satisfaction. How individuals respond to their work has long been a focus of research in the fields of industrial and organizational psychology. Originally, those who studied job satisfaction tried to relate it to productivity, and the research often had industrial sponsors.[86] Now we have come to understand that how people react to their jobs is of importance to society. As Hopkins, an organizational psychologist, points out, because of rapid technological changes and the growing size of organizations, alienation in the work place has become common. Indeed, as she observes, "Alienation and its effect on the quality of life [is] among our society's most pressing problems."[87] Thus research on job satisfaction has an urgent purpose—improvement in the quality of worklife, in ways that are defined by individual workers. Enhancing teachers' job satisfaction is important both for increasing the school's effectiveness and for dealing with a social problem—alienated workers in both the private and public sectors.

Research on job satisfaction has found that among the strong predictors of job satisfaction are variety, planning, freedom, decision making, and learning new things.[88] In industry, incorporating these elements in the job requires job redesign; it will be remembered from our discussion earlier that corporations in Sweden, Japan, and West Germany (and much less commonly, in the United States) have redesigned jobs in accord with these predictors. As Hopkins points out, "As the job redesign movement has discovered in the industrial world, it is not easy to redesign job characteristics given the nature of the task requirements of varying industrial and commercial enterprises."[89]

But a school is not a factory or department store, and it is not a large corporation office or a governmental office in a state capital. It is not part of the routine job world where employees sit at a workstation for eight hours a day. Education as a profession should offer teachers variety, freedom, full participation in decision making, and the opportunity to learn new things. In fact, teachers *must* learn many new things, if they are to draw on the best available knowledge in dealing with their professional responsibilities. Because the utilization of new knowledge is indispensable for performing effectively, practicing teachers should be required to take university courses for continued certification, just like practicing physicians (see Chapter 4).

Teaching, unlike an industrial or commercial enterprise, does not require total job redesign to incorporate the elements of job satisfaction. One can find all of the foregoing predictors of job satisfaction in the literature of education, and they are not new; they have been there for decades. Take variety, for example. Fibkins points out that teachers "must be afforded opportunities for change and growth," including opportunities for research and writing.[90] The action-research movement of the 1950s was predicated on the idea that inservice education programs ought to furnish teachers with opportunities to improve the curriculum by investigating their classroom problems.[91] (Fibkins also suggests providing teachers with opportunities to teach at different grade levels and to be engaged in team teaching.)

Similarly, Schneider explored the question of to what extent teachers should be involved in the decision-making process, and she found that the teachers in her survey who perceived themselves as highly involved in decision making had a "significantly higher level of job satisfaction" than teachers with medium or low involvement. She concluded that "administrators should provide, to the greatest extent possible, opportunities for teachers who are affected by a decision, interested in the decision, and/or knowledgeable about the decision to be involved in making the decision."[92] Teachers in her study reported high levels of interest in such problems as selecting textbooks and other instructional materials, developing procedures for reporting student progress to parents, establishing and revising school goals, and hiring new faculty members to teach in their subject departments or teams (units). The importance of her findings is not diminished by the fact that participatory decision making has long been a principle of educational administration.[93]

Research on job satisfaction indicates that a job has both depth and scope, and is most likely to be satisfying, if it "requires that you learn new things, requires that you do a lot of planning ahead, allows a lot of freedom as to how you do your work, allows you to make a lot of decisions on your own, allows you to do a variety of things, and requires a great deal of skill."[94] Teaching requires all these things (or should). Where some inservice programs are weak is in providing the stimulation to go on learning and in meeting teachers' needs for variety. It must be cautioned, however, that the aforementioned qualities (freedom, for example) are not enough to make teaching satisfying or effective. Teachers need supervisory support (called "job resources" in industry) to do the job.

Burnout. The term "burnout" was originally coined by Freudenberger to describe the exhaustion—both mental and physical—of staff members of health care institutions.[95] In the late 1970s and early 1980s professional organizations and teacher education institutions directed special attention to "teacher burnout," which, according to Farber, manifests itself in anger, depression, fatigue, boredom, and cynicism. He states more specifically that teachers who are burned out may devote less attention to planning classes, may expect less from their students and less satisfaction from their jobs, may be unsympathetic toward students, may frequently feel exhausted, and "may fantasize or actually plan on leaving the profession."[96]

A qualification should be introduced in any discussion of teacher burnout; as Farber points out, "No study has systematically investigated the process or dimensions of teacher burnout."[97] Most of the literature bearing on the subject consists of research on teacher stress, a related but not identical concept. Yet, as Harrison pointed out at a conference on stress and burnout held at Teachers College, Columbia University, in 1982, stress often leads to exhaustion, apathy, despair, and the feeling of being victimized. Stress is so similar a concept that one need not invoke the "burnout" label[98] (and one is on safer and surer theoretical ground).

Yet whether or not one chooses to call it burnout, it is clear that many teachers are not finding satisfaction in their profession. In a National Education Association (NEA) poll, one-third of the teachers surveyed said that if they were beginning their careers all over again they would not become teachers.[99] These teachers were feeling the pain of wasted possibilities and unused talents. They felt that their capacities were not being utilized optimally. This is indeed tragic under the conditions of our existence: only one life per person.

The most important point about burnout where we are concerned is that not all individuals experience it. In the foreword to the collection of papers presented at the Teachers College conference on burnout, Sarason reminds us "that in the same society not all people who do the same work, even in the same work setting, experience burnout."[100] Obviously, individuals differ in their tolerance for and responses to stress. But there is also considerable agreement among psychologists that a teacher's loss of motivation and hope for doing well are attributable to alterable factors or conditions within the school. As Farber points out, when teachers have opportunities for collaboration and support, they are less likely to burn out than when they lack these opportunities. The sense of isolation that many teachers feel magnifies their classroom problems and contributes to stress (as well as leaving the problems unsolved). They then begin to feel that their professional efforts do not matter, so why try? Continuous collaboration among teachers is needed not just to solve educational problems but so that teachers feel part of a profession. It is of interest and importance that psychologists believe that the best way to prevent burnout is to provide an environment that is "a growth-producing, motivating one for teachers."[101] How this can be done has been the focus of this book.

SUMMARY

A good inservice education program accomplishes two purposes: It improves the effectiveness of the school and fosters the (individual) teacher's professional–personal development. For most individuals, work is one of the main elements in their lives. The way we react to our work environment alters our self-perceptions and self-esteem. A significant proportion of teachers feel that their talents have been wasted and would not choose teaching if they were beginning their careers all over again. Doubtlessly, teachers have been hurt by public criticism but part of the problem lies within the teacher's work environment, which often fails to supply the nutrients for positive self-esteem as a teacher. Many teachers have few opportunities to feel part of a profession and to develop their capacities optimally. Inservice education is intimately concerned with this problem, and a sound program provides teachers with opportunity for collaborative problem solving, curriculum development, sharing new knowledge, planning and participating in inservice activities, experimentation, writing, and preparing for a new role. Education, unlike industry, does not have to be redesigned to incorporate the features of job satisfaction. (Teaching, for example, allows a great deal of freedom as to how one does one's work.) But special attention should be given to affording teachers with opportunities for change, such as teaching at different grade levels and engaging in research and writing. Teachers must see their work as developmental—as contributing to what Dewey called an "expanding and enriched life."[102] For a teacher's (or a supervisor's) work to be satisfying it must be rewarding at both a developmental and a social level. (Teachers must see that their efforts make a difference to children's lives, and their own lives must be enriched in the process.) In accord with this principle, inservice education has four functions: solving classroom problems, improving the curriculum, helping individuals reach their own professional goals, and providing the stimulation for the continuous learning needed to ensure professional growth and prevent boredom and burnout.

A deficit approach to inservice education runs counter to the concept of professionalism (a professional's education is lifelong), counter to our experience in the field of supervision, and counter to the body of research on organization development. Workshops and conferences should begin as efforts to deal with problems that have been cooperatively identified by teachers and supervisors, not be disembodied adjuncts to such efforts. School faculties tend to look inward rather than outward, and workshops that involve teachers from several schools or school systems can counter this tendency. The workshop should serve as a source of promising ideas and practices for solving local problems. Workshops are best conducted in the summer, when teachers are not teaching. A good workshop provides teachers with expert assistance in problem solving and has results; teachers actually do something about what they have learned when they get back to the classroom.

Although it is true that teachers must be involved as problem identifiers, planners, and participants, supervisors must take the lead in initiating and coordinating the program. (Much of the recent literature has conveyed the misconception that teachers can do this alone; studies show that teacher-initiated inservice programs tend to dry up.) Startup strategies include classroom observation, focusing attention on educational goals and asking the faculty for their opinions on various aspects of the educational program, involving the faculty in the decisions that affect them, providing a climate that contributes to teachers' sense of making a professional contribution, and recognizing and building on the strengths of effective teachers. Principals should jot down problems as they are mentioned by individuals or the faculty at meetings. (Over a period of months and years, this procedure can be enormously helpful in planning inservice activities.)

The orientation of new teachers should be regarded as part of the inservice program. Not all new teachers are neophytes; experienced teachers who are returning to teaching also have special needs. The orientation of teachers who are involuntarily transferred presents special problems (and opportunities) for supervisors. Wherever possible, involuntary transfer should be avoided. In any case, the question of *how* faculty are acculturated in the new school setting is of primary importance, both for pupil progress and teacher satisfaction. "Buddy" teachers can be helpful to new teachers, but experienced colleagues are not an adequate support system for beginning teachers. A well-organized support system provides continuous supervisory assistance to beginners in curriculum planning and in overcoming discipline problems, and encourages them to ask for the help they need.

Inservice programs must be planned, to meet the developing needs of teachers throughout their careers. The informal social system of the school can either facilitate or impede curriculum improvement. Principals can develop more affirmative social systems by putting self-actualizing teachers in leadership positions on faculty committees, and encouraging them to share new ideas. Self-actualizing teachers thrive in an environment with a great variety of activities and can activate the energies of individuals who are at relatively low levels of professional development.

PROBLEMS FOR STUDY AND DISCUSSION

1. As discussed in this chapter, a well-planned orientation program assists the beginning teacher in becoming a problem solver. According to Burke and Schmidt, school districts should "arrange for an experienced teacher to be assigned as a mentor for the beginning teacher. The entry-year teachers may then approach their mentor for advice, information, suggestions, or confidential discussions."[103] What is your assessment of this recommendation?

2. Do you believe that there is a clear distinction between teachers' psychological needs and their professional needs? Explain.

3. Organization development *interventions* are activities designed to improve the organization's functioning. The following steps (or measures) were used by organization development specialists to build a sense of comradeship and cohesion in a municipal government organization:
   1. Get the *right people* together for
   2. A *large block of uninterrupted time*
   3. To work on *high priority problems or opportunities that*
   4. *They have identified* and that are worked on
   5. In *ways that are structured* to enhance the likelihood of
   6. *Realistic solutions and action plans* that are
   7. *Implemented* enthusiastically and
   8. *Followed up* to assess actual versus expected results.[104]
   Do you believe that this intervention would be useful for principals in building an affirmative social system in their school? Explain.

4. Organization development consultants assist the client organization in the way it goes about solving problems. The consultant observes the way a group works together—patterns of interaction, for example. (Organization development is organization improvement through problem solving.) Examine the inservice education program of a local school. What evidence do you find of the faculty working as a group to solve problems? If such evidence is lacking, how do you account for this?

5. In a survey of professors of supervision and supervisors in school systems, three-fourths of the professors agreed with the statement that "the school is the most appropriate unit of change, not the district or the individual." However, only half of the supervisors agreed with it.[105] How do you account for the difference in their response? Do you agree or disagree with the statement? Why or why not?

6. In discussing the limitations of school-based programs of inservice education, W. Robert Houston observed that they "often emphasize only practical ideas, tricks, and ideas that can be implemented simply, immediately, and with little effort," thus producing a weak program. (Professionals must understand and draw on theoretical principles.) Moreover, "the trend toward inbreeding becomes a problem when the primary input comes from within the district . . . the recommended practices tend to become local and parochial."[106] In your opinion, how can supervisors avoid these weaknesses in planning professional development programs?

7. As discussed in this chapter, an NEA poll found that a significant proportion of teachers are dissatisfied or demoralized. Do you view this as a major problem in the field of supervision? Why? What are the implications of this finding for planning inservice education?

8. Do you believe that inservice education should be concerned with meeting the professional needs of teachers past the age of 55? Explain.

9. As pointed out, the initial purpose of those who studied job satisfaction was to relate it to productivity. Recently, however, researchers in industrial and organizational psychology have been seeking "to improve the quality of workers' lives by increasing job satisfaction."[107] In your opinion, has the field of educational supervision reflected this change in focus, or is it still production oriented? Explain.

10. Do you believe that supporting teachers against unfounded criticism influences the success of professional development? Why or why not?

11. Warwick has contended that inservice education has been "a series of *ad hoc* arrangements which carry the institution along on a hand-to-mouth basis."[108] Draw up a set of principles or guidelines that a supervisor can follow to develop an inservice program that is cohesive, coherent, coordinated, and continuous.

NOTES

1. Ralph W. Tyler, "Accountability and Teacher Performance: Self-directed and External-directed Professional Improvement," in Louis Rubin (ed.), *The In-Service Education of Teachers* (Boston: Allyn and Bacon, 1978), p. 135.
2. Ibid.
3. Ibid., p. 135.
4. Ibid., p. 142.
5. Leonard C. Burrello and Tim Orbaugh, "Reducing the Discrepancy Between the Known and the Unknown in Inservice Education," *Phi Delta Kappan*, Vol. 63 (February 1982), p. 386.
6. Dale Mann, "Impact II and the Problem of Staff Development," *Educational Leadership*, Vol. 42 (December 1984–January 1985), p. 44.
7. John Dewey, "Democracy for the Teacher," *Progressive Education*, Vol. 8 (March 1931), p. 217.
8. See Paul Berman and Milbrey W. McLaughlin, *Federal Programs Supporting Educational Change*, Vol. VII: *Factors Affecting Implementation and Continuation* (Santa Monica, Calif.: Rand Corporation, April 1977).
9. Milbrey W. McLaughlin and David D. Marsh, "Staff Development and School Change," in Ann Lieberman and Lynne Miller (eds.), *Staff Development: New Demands, New Realities, New Perspectives* (New York: Teachers College Press, 1978), p. 75.
10. Ruth K. Wade, "What Makes A Difference in Inservice Education? A Meta-analysis of Research," *Educational Leadership*, Vol. 42 (December 1984–January 1985), pp. 48–54.
11. Georgea M. Sparks, "The Trees or the Forest? A Response to Ruth Wade," *Educational Leadership*, Vol. 42 (December 1984–January 1985), pp. 55–58.
12. Nancy Sievert, "Staff Development: The Principal's Role," *Thrust*, Vol. 13 (November–December 1983), p. 19.
13. Gordon A. Donaldson, "Rx For School Leadership: The Maine Principals' Academy," *Phi Delta Kappan*, Vol. 63 (February 1982), pp. 400–401.
14. Sievert, op. cit., p. 20.
15. *R&DCTE Review: The Newsletter of the Research and Development Center for Teacher Education*, Vol. 2 (January 1984), p. 2.

16. See Susan S. Stodolsky, "Teacher Evaluation: The Limits of Looking," *Educational Researcher,* Vol. 13 (November 1984), pp. 11–17.

17. John Cruz, "The Principal: Key to Staff Motivation," *Thrust,* Vol. 13 (November–December 1983), p. 21.

18. Ibid.

19. Gordon N. Mackenzie, in a conference with the authors of this text, September 29, 1984.

20. Robert S. Gilchrist et al., "Organization of Programs of In-Service Education," Chapter 12 in *In-Service Education,* Fifty-sixth Yearbook of the National Society for the Study of Education, Part I (Chicago: University of Chicago Press, 1957), p. 288.

21. See John I. Goodlad, "The School as a Workplace," Chapter 3 in *Staff Development,* Eighty-second Yearbook of the National Society for the Study of Education, Part II (Chicago: University of Chicago Press, 1983), pp. 36–61; see also Ann Lieberman and Lynne Miller, "The Social Realities of Teaching," in Lieberman and Miller, op. cit., pp. 34–68.

22. Gilchrist et al., op. cit.

23. Kenneth R. Howey and Joseph C. Vaughan, "Current Patterns of Staff Development," Chapter 5 in *Staff Development,* op. cit., p. 98.

24. Ibid., p. 99.

25. John Dewey, *Democracy and Education* (New York: Macmillan, 1916), p. 59.

26. Kenneth J. Rehage, "Acknowledgement," *Staff Development,* Eighty-second Yearbook of the National Society for the Study of Education, op. cit., p. ix.

27. Joan P. Kowalski, *Orientation Programs for New Teachers* (Arlington, Va.: Educational Research Service, Inc., 1977), p. 2.

28. Ibid.

29. Ibid., p. 4.

30. Gene Hall, "Induction: The Missing Link," *Journal of Teacher Education,* Vol. 33 (May–June 1982), p. 53.

31. Michael Fullan, Matthew B. Miles, and Gil Taylor, "Organization Development in Schools: The State of the Art," *Review of Educational Research,* Vol. 50 (Spring 1980), p. 139.

32. Ibid.

33. Robert L. Heichberger and James M. Young, Jr., "Teacher Perceptions of Supervision and Evaluation," *Phi Delta Kappan,* Vol. 57 (November 1975), p. 210.

34. Robert J. Alfonso and Lee Goldsberry, "Colleagueship in Supervision," Chapter 7 in *Supervision of Teaching,* 1982 Yearbook of the Association for Supervision and Curriculum Development (Alexandria, Va.: The Association, 1982), p. 94.

35. Willard S. Elsbree and E. Edmund Reutter, Jr., *Staff Personnel in the Public Schools* (Englewood Cliffs, N.J.: Prentice-Hall, 1954), p. 112.

36. E. Edmund Reutter, Jr., *The Supreme Court's Impact on Public Education* (Phi Delta Kappa and National Organization on Legal Problems of Education, 1982), pp. 69–70.

37. Elvedine Wilkerson, "A Comparative Study of Teacher Attitudes Regarding Forced Desegregation of Urban Elementary School Faculties" (unpublished doctoral dissertation, Temple University, 1979).

38. Henry B. Jomills, Robert L. Crain and James M. McPartland, "A Long-Term View of School Desegregation: Some Recent Studies of Graduates as Adults," *Phi Delta Kappan,* Vol. 66 (December 1984), pp. 260–264.

39. Ibid., p. 260.

40. Benjamin S. Bloom, J. Thomas Hastings, and George F. Madaus, *Handbook on Formative and Summative Evaluation of Student Learning* (New York: McGraw-Hill, 1971).

41. Jimy M. Sanders, "Faculty Desegregation and Student Achievement," *American Educational Research Journal*, Vol. 21 (Fall 1984), pp. 605–616.
42. Ibid., p. 606.
43. Ralph Tyler, in a discussion with the authors of this book, January 7, 1985.
44. Sanders, op. cit., p. 605.
45. W. Robert Houston and B. Dell Felder, "Break Horses, Not Teachers," *Phi Delta Kappan*, Vol. 63 (March 1982), p. 457.
46. Kowalski, op. cit., p. 1.
47. Elsbree and Reutter, op. cit., p. 118.
48. Ibid.
49. Ibid., p. 114.
50. Kowalski, op. cit., pp. 65–66.
51. Elsbree and Reutter, op. cit., p. 114.
52. Kowalski, op. cit., p. 66.
53. Ibid., p. 2.
54. Nathalie Gehrke, "Teachers' Role Conflicts: A Grounded Theory-in-Process," *Journal of Teacher Education*, Vol. 33 (January–February 1982), pp. 41–46. See also Janet M. Newberry, "The Barrier Between Beginning and Experienced Teachers," *Journal of Educational Administration*, Vol. 16 (May 1978), pp. 46–56.
55. Houston and Felder, op. cit., p. 459.
56. Ibid.
57. Kowalski, op. cit., p. 65.
58. Ibid., p. 77.
59. Houston and Felder, op. cit., p. 459.
60. As cited in Kenneth A. Tye and Barbara B. Tye, "Teacher Isolation and School Reform," *Phi Delta Kappan*, Vol. 65 (January 1984), p. 320.
61. Ibid., p. 321.
62. Peter A. Williamson and Julia A. Elfman, "A Commonsense Approach to Teacher Inservice Training," *Phi Delta Kappan*, Vol. 63 (February 1982), p. 401.
63. Gilchrist et al., op. cit., p. 302.
64. Patricia Zigarmi, Loren Betz, and Darrell Jensen, "Teachers' Preferences in and Perceptions of In-Service Education," *Educational Leadership*, Vol. 34 (April 1977), pp. 545, 547–551.
65. Bruce Joyce and Michael McKibbin, "Teacher Growth States and School Environments," *Educational Leadership*, Vol. 40 (November 1982), pp. 36–41.
66. Robert Perrin, "Teachers' Institutes: Are Teachers Getting What They Want?" *English Journal*, Vol. 72 (April 1983), p. 33.
67. Ibid.
68. Ibid., p. 34.
69. Ibid., p. 35.
70. See Seymour B. Sarason, *The Culture of the School and the Problem of Change*, 2nd ed. (Boston: Allyn and Bacon, 1982), pp. 95–117.
71. Georgea G. Mohlman, Janet Kierstead, and Mae Gundlach, "A Research-Based Inservice Model for Secondary Teachers," *Educational Leadership*, Vol. 40 (October 1982), p. 19.
72. Perrin, op. cit., p. 35.
73. Gehrke, op. cit., pp. 41–46.
74. Kenneth R. Howey, "In-Service Teacher Education: A Study of the Perceptions of Teachers, Professors, and Parents About Current and Projected Practice," paper presented at the annual meeting of the American Educational Research Association, Toronto, March 1978.
75. Tyler, op. cit., p. 147.

76. Joyce and McKibbin, op. cit., p. 36.

77. Ibid., p. 37.

78. Ibid., pp. 40–41.

79. A. J. Cronin, *The Citadel* (Boston: Little, Brown, 1965; originally published in 1937), p. 154.

80. Joyce and McKibbin, op. cit., p. 41.

81. Ibid., p. 41.

82. N. L. Gage, *Hard Gains in the Soft Sciences: The Case of Pedagogy* (Bloomington, Ind.: Phi Delta Kappa Center on Evaluation, Development and Research, 1985), p. 22.

83. Ibid., pp. 22–23.

84. Tyler, op. cit., p. 148.

85. Sarason, op. cit., pp. 195–200.

86. Anne H. Hopkins, *Work and Job Satisfaction in the Public Sector* (Totowa, N.J.: Rowman & Allanheld, 1983), p. 3.

87. Ibid., p. 5.

88. Ibid., p. 124.

89. Ibid.

90. William L. Fibkins, "Organizing Helping Settings to Reduce Burnout," in Barry A. Farber (ed.), *Stress and Burnout in the Human Service Professions* (New York: Pergamon Press, 1983), p. 177.

91. See Association for Supervision and Curriculum Development, *Research for Curriculum Improvement* (Washington, D.C.: The Association, 1957).

92. Gail T. Schneider, "Teacher Involvement in Decision Making: Zones of Acceptance, Decision Conditions and Job Satisfaction," *Journal of Research and Development in Education,* Vol. 18 (Fall 1984), pp. 29, 31.

93. See for example Clyde M. Campbell, *Practical Applications of Democratic Administration* (New York: Harper & Row, 1952).

94. Hopkins, op. cit., p. 43.

95. Herbert J. Freudenberger, "Staff Burn-Out," *Journal of Social Issues,* Vol. 30, No. 1 (1974), pp. 159–164.

96. Barry A. Farber, "Teacher Burnout: A Psychoeducational Perspective," *Teachers College Record,* Vol. 83 (Winter 1981), p. 237.

97. Ibid., p. 236.

98. W. David Harrison, "A Social Competence Model of Burnout," in Farber, *Stress and Burnout in the Human Service Professions,* op. cit., p. 29.

99. Willard H. McGuire, "Teacher Burnout," *Today's Education,* Vol. 68 (November–December 1979), pp. 5–7.

100. Seymour Sarason, "Foreword," in Farber, *Stress and Burnout in the Human Service Professions,* op. cit., p. vii.

101. Farber, "Teacher Burnout: A Psychological Perspective," op. cit., p. 240.

102. John Dewey, *Art as Experience* (New York: Minton, Balach, 1934), p. 27.

103. Peter S. Burke and William S. Schmidt, "Entry Year Assistance: A Promising Practice," *Action in Teacher Education,* Vol. 6 (Spring–Summer 1984), p. 72.

104. Wendell L. French and Cecil H. Bell, Jr., *Organization Development: Behavioral Science Interventions for Organization Improvement,* 2nd ed. (Englewood Cliffs, N.J.: Prentice-Hall, 1978), p. 123.

105. Fred H. Wood, Frank O. McQuarrie, Jr., and Steven R. Thompson, "Practitioners and Professors Agree on Effective Staff Development Practices," *Educational Leadership,* Vol. 40 (October 1982), pp. 28–31.

106. W. Robert Houston, "Emerging Roles of the School-Based Teacher Educator," in Karl Massanari, William H. Drummond, and W. Robert Houston, *Emerging Profes-*

sional Roles for Teacher Educators (Washington, D.C.: American Association of Colleges for Teacher Education and the ERIC Clearinghouse on Teacher Education, 1978), p. 56.
107. Hopkins, op. cit., p. 3.
108. David Warwick, *School-Based In-Service Education* (Edinburgh: Oliver & Boyd, 1975), p. 8.

SELECTED REFERENCES

Association for Supervision and Curriculum Development. *Research for Curriculum Improvement*, 1957 Yearbook. Washington, D.C.: The Association, 1957.
————. *Supervision of Teaching*, 1982 Yearbook. Alexandria, Va.: The Association, 1982.
Bloom, Benjamin S., J. Thomas Hastings, and George F. Madaus. *Handbook on Formative and Summative Evaluation of Student Learning.* New York: McGraw-Hill Book Company, 1971.
Campbell, Clyde M. *Practical Applications of Democratic Administration.* New York: Harper & Row, Publishers, Inc., 1952.
Cronin, A. J. *The Citadel.* Boston: Little, Brown and Company, 1965; originally published in 1937.
Dewey, John. *Art as Experience.* New York: Minton Balsch, 1934.
————. *Democracy and Education.* New York: Macmillan Publishing Company, 1916.
Elsbree, Willard S., and E. Edmund Reutter, Jr. *Staff Personnel in the Public Schools.* Englewood Cliffs, N.J.: Prentice-Hall, Inc., 1954.
Farber, Barry A. (ed.). *Stress and Burnout in the Human Service Professions.* Elmsford, N.Y.: Pergamon Press, Inc., 1983.
Gage, N. L. *Hard Gains in the Soft Sciences: The Case of Pedagogy.* Bloomington, Ind.: Phi Delta Kappa Center on Evaluation, Development and Research, 1985.
Goodlad, John I. *A Place Called School.* New York: McGraw-Hill Book Company, 1984.
Hopkins, Anne H. *Work and Job Satisfaction in the Public Sector.* Totowa, N.J.: Rowman & Allanheld, Publishers, 1983.
Kowalski, Joan P. *Orientation Programs for New Teachers.* Arlington, Va.: Educational Research Service, Inc., 1977.
Lehming, Rolf, and Michael Kane. *Improving Schools: Using What We Know.* Beverly Hills, Calif.: Sage Publications, Inc., 1981.
Lieberman, Ann, and Lynne Miller (eds.). *Staff Development: New Demands, New Realities, New Perspectives.* New York: Teachers College Press, 1978.
National Society for the Study of Education. *In-Service Education*, Fifty-sixth Yearbook, Part I. Chicago: The University of Chicago Press, 1957.
————. *Staff Development*, Eighty-second Yearbook, Part II. Chicago: The University of Chicago Press, 1983.
Reutter, E. Edmund, Jr. *The Supreme Court's Impact on Public Education.* Phi Delta Kappa and National Organization on Legal Problems of Education, 1982.
Rubin, Louis (ed.). *The Inservice Education of Teachers.* Boston: Allyn and Bacon, Inc., 1978.
Sarason, Seymour. *The Culture of the School and the Problem of Change*, 2nd ed. Boston: Allyn and Bacon, Inc., 1982.
Warwick, David. *School-Based In-Service Education.* Edinburgh: Oliver & Boyd, 1975.
Wittrock, Merlin C., ed. *Handbook of Research on Teaching*, 3rd ed. New York: Macmillan Publishing Company, 1986.

Chapter 14

How to Judge a School: Developmental Criteria

The idea of evaluating or judging a school often is regarded by the professional staff as a matter of external imposition. Indeed, this attitude is warranted when the evaluation or judging of a school is conducted hierarchically and when the focus is on conformance to externally mandated practices.

Early in this century, Whitehead commented that "the first requisite for educational reform is the school as a unit, with its approved curriculum based on its own needs, and evolved by its own staff."[1] In 1984, Goodlad stressed the need to view *"the school as the unit for improvement."*[2]

Neither Whitehead nor Goodlad was contending that the individual school should function in isolation from other schools in the district. Whitehead was objecting to the external constraints imposed on schools which prevent their staffs from engaging in curriculum development to meet the needs of their learners. Indeed, Goodlad held that "we are close to the time when each unit (school) in a network would be connected to all the others."[3] Obviously, district-wide support services and resources must be provided. The communication flow from school to school within the district should be open and full to ensure districtwide articulation of efforts to improve education. The flow should be not only from the top-down, but should be upward from the individual school and laterally from school to school within the district.

Both Whitehead and Goodlad were also attacking the tendency to treat various aspects of the school—its curriculum, instructional practices and resources, and so on, as isolated entities. Indeed, the various subject matters in the curriculum tend to be treated in their separateness rather than connectedness. The result is that the school as an entity is poorly understood, and segmental efforts toward improvement have limited effects.[4] "Improving schools does not mean improving the quality only of teachers, principals, teaching, administering, curricula, and materials as though they were separate entities," wrote Goodlad, but rather that "it means improving all of these together."[5]

From his "Study of Schooling," Goodlad found that "inquiry into problems and issues cutting across the entire school is not normal activity for teachers and principals."[6]

The hypothesis that the road to school improvement lies in treating the school in a unitary way requires that all aspects of the school be seen in vital organic interdependence rather than as isolated parts. Otherwise, the professional staff (teachers, supervisors, and administrators) will be working in isolation or at cross purposes with each other and with the students, the climate of the school will not be productive, the various studies will be treated in isolation, and the truly educative function of the school will suffer.

Substantive educational improvement requires the identification, diagnosis, and search for problem solutions through the concerted engagement of the professional staff of the school as a unit.

Moreover, externally imposed mandates or pressures not only tend to suffer from segmentation and imbalance, but tend to result in compliance rather than in commitment. The net effect is the concealing rather than the revealing and solving of problems by the professional staff, and the staff will exercise great energy and ingenuity in such "protective" measures. The same applies to the students.

As noted in Chapter 11, the incessant forays of conflicting demands and prescriptions for reform leveled at our schools from external sources impel many school administrators to demonstrate that their schools are in conformance with whatever tide for reform is dominant at a particular time. Such a response is largely political and results in great educational waste as the tides of reform shift in a countervening direction. At the same time, the expertise of the professional staff of the school and school district is allowed to go untapped, or is even curtailed or diverted to demonstrate compliance with external demands or mandates. Problem solutions require commitment and expertise on the part of the professional staff, along with time and supporting resources. The problem-solving capabilities of the professional staff remain a virtually untapped mine of talent and energy.

Of course, it is far easier and less threatening to seek to demonstrate successful compliance than it is to engage in the diagnosis of problems and the search for problem solutions. But the former approach tends to lead to mechanical, segmental, and superficial change; the latter approach is developmental and focused on improvement or progress.

CRITERIA FOR SCHOOL EVALUATION AND RENEWAL

Throughout this text, emphasis has been given to the concept of developmental supervision as a problem-solving process, with the school as the fundamental unit for educational improvement in conjunction with districtwide educational improvement. In this chapter, various developmental criteria are drawn together to illustrate in summary fashion how they may be applied by the professional staff in evaluating their own school so as to bring about continuous educational improvement.

The illustrative criteria presented in this chapter are documented in various chapters throughout this text. Many of the criteria are research based. Others pertain to conditions and practices that are regarded in the literature as necessary for the professionalization of teaching, while a number are derived from the various professional education organizations as recommended conditions, approved practices, or principles for guiding educational practice.

The criteria are not complete in any sense, but are intended to illustrate the scope of concerns, conditions, and practices encompassed in a school self-study. The professional staff of a school will need to modify and add to many of the criteria presented in this chapter to fit local conditions and needs. In this process they will need to draw from the work of the various professional education associations in identifying the more specific approved practices and recommended conditions pertaining to specialized concerns. Reference is made to a number of these organizations in connection with some of the criteria discussed in this concluding chapter.

Checklists of criteria are presented in this chapter to illustrate how an appropriate instrument might be utilized for the school self-study. The criteria to be rated are organized into the following categories: (1) Philosophy of the School; (2) Administrative Policy and Practice; (3) Innovations and Reforms: Policy and Practice; (4) The Climate for Supervision; (5) Supervisory Roles and Functions; (6) Teacher Effectiveness and Classroom Climate; (7) Curriculum Development; (8) Inservice Education/Staff Development; and (9) Teaching–Learning Resources, Facilities, and Services.

Obviously, the categories are interdependent and, consequently, a number of the criteria are necessarily overlapping. In this connection, the professional staff of the school will be able to make cross-comparisons as to the consistency of how certain of these criteria are being met in different aspects of the educational program. For example, if the program of inservice education is adjudged to be developmental in orientation (focused on improvement through problem solving) rather than deficit oriented, while innovations and reforms are not so focused or oriented, but are imposed administratively from above or are adopted segmentally simply to be *au courant*, then the professional staff and the administration will need to give concerted attention to this contradiction.

At the same time, the checklists should be used to compare the responses of the supervisory staff and the faculty. Not only will this help the supervisory staff identify specific areas in need of improvement, but will reveal any differences in perceptions and attitudes between the supervisory staff and the faculty. Thus the rating scales can be used as a basis for the supervisory staff and the faculty to work conjointly to reconcile differences through full communication and problem solving.

Through the use of the Checklist of Developmental Criteria for School Improvement, as presented in the pages which follow, the professional staff will be able to identify the areas of needed improvement in their school and school system. By comparing the responses on the Checklist rating scale by administrators, supervisors, and teachers, discrepancies can be identified so as to enhance communication, resolve conflict, and marshal the constructive energies of the entire professional staff through democratic-participative decision making for educational improvement. There can be no better basis for a staff-development program than working cooperatively on the identified problems and areas of need in the school as a whole.

Efforts to improve school effectiveness have tended to be focused on inducing segmental changes confined within only one or two of the nine categories encompassed in the Checklist of Developmental Criteria for School Improvement. There is a common failure to recognize and treat the school as an ecological system. The consequence is that not only do segmental changes fail to deliver the promised results, but they give rise to unanticipated problems. The Checklist of Developmental Criteria is designed to enable the professional staff to see the school as an ecological system and to identify possibilities for renewal through problem solving.

When school administrators and supervisors seek merely to "satisfice" rather than to optimize, they tend to meet external attacks and mandates by adopting slogans, fads, or currently popular innovations while failing to bring about the claimed improvements in conditions and practice. In this vein, they are apt to formulate or seize upon recommended practice segmentally and superficially. For example, a recent report from the U.S. Department of Education advances a number of recommended school practices that are presumably based upon the body of research on teaching and learning. In the report *What Works: Research About Teaching and Learning,* teachers are advised to be effective "time managers." The report goes on to state that "How much time students are actively engaged in learning contributes strongly to their achievement."[7] But as discussed in this text, the research actually reveals that the determining factor is not time alone but the *quality* of the use of time (time devoted to productive learning). Taken superficially, administrators and supervisors may seek to impose procedures for inventorying time-on-task in classrooms, rather than seeking to engage teachers in developing ways of devoting more classroom time to generative learning activity.

The Checklist of Developmental Criteria for School Improvement is designed to enable the professional staff of the school and school system to function at the generative-creative level of knowledge/ability (Level III) rather than at the imitative-maintenance level (Level I) or the mediative-adaptive level (Level II) of knowledge/ability (see Chapter 10). In using the Checklist as an instrument for the cooperative and continuous evaluation of the school and school system (involving all members of the professional staff), substantive problems will be revealed rather than concealed, and problems will be seen as opportunities for improvement. Through the cooperative engagement of the professional staff in self-study, administrators and supervisors can avoid the problem that plagues most ineffective schools—namely, overt compliance and covert resistance by the staff. Effective schools are marked by a commitment on the part of the professional staff to ongoing improvement.

The entire process of self-study, using the Checklist of Developmental Criteria, should be seen as an educative process for the professional staff in which individual and collective energies are marshaled for continual growth and renewal.

CHECKLIST OF DEVELOPMENTAL CRITERIA
FOR SCHOOL IMPROVEMENT*

Circle the number that best expresses your evaluation of the extent to which each criterion, condition, or practice is in evidence in your school/district.

> 1 = Strongly in evidence
> 2 = Some evidence
> 3 = Little or no evidence
> 4 = Evidence to the contrary

A. PHILOSOPHY OF THE SCHOOL

1. The philosophy of the school is a working document, not a filed document, developed by the entire professional staff. It is used as a compass and regulator to identify possibilities, to make comparisons with actualities, and to actualize the professional staff toward the attainment of possibilities. The curriculum is the test of the philosophy in operation.   1 2 3 4

2. The professional staff shares a sense of vision and a commitment to the needs and mission of the school in a free society, and is actualized to meet these needs and fulfill this mission. This is reflected in the protection of the academic freedom of teachers and students, and in the curriculum, which fosters the development of independent thinking and democratic social responsibility.   1 2 3 4

3. The professional staff shares a vision of future possibilities for the school and is working toward the attainment of longer-range goals, as well as meeting immediate needs. Immediate needs are consonant with long-range goals.   1 2 3 4

B. ADMINISTRATIVE POLICY AND PRACTICE

1. The local school board sets broad educational policies through full consultation with the administration, which, in turn, engages in full consultation with the professional staff.   1 2 3 4

2. The board of education relies on the expertise of the professional staff for the design, development, and evaluation of the educational program. The superintendent serves to "educate" the board on these matters and exercises the leadership needed for districtwide educational improvement.   1 2 3 4

3. The school board has a written policy that protects the academic freedom of teachers and students. The statement clearly places the responsibility for the selection and use of curricular materials with the professional staff. The statement meets the guidelines developed by the American Library Association, National Council of Teachers of English, National Council for the Social Studies, and National Science Teachers Association.   1 2 3 4

4. The principal and supervisory staff support the faculty against unfounded criticism.   1 2 3 4

5. A standing curriculum committee is in operation in the school, devoting its efforts to curriculum articulation and to the development of promising programs for educational improvement. The committee is provided with the needed time and resources to perform its functions effectively.   1 2 3 4

6. External complaints concerning curricular materials or instructional practices, or any efforts to censor curricular materials, are referred to the standing curriculum committee for review and action.   1 2 3 4

7. A districtwide curriculum council works on districtwide curriculum articulation. Membership includes district supervisors and faculty representatives from the curriculum committee of each school. The council is chaired by the Associate Superintendent of Curriculum/Instruction or the Director of Curriculum.   1 2 3 4

8. Communication is maintained with other schools in the district and in other districts to share ideas and practices relating to common concerns through formal and informal contacts, jointly sponsored workshops and projects, and interschool faculty visitation. The schools in the district function as a network, not in isolation.   1 2 3 4

9. The school network serves to facilitate the extension of successful programs and practices throughout the district. Care is taken to transform the programs and practices to meet the conditions of each individual school unit.   1 2 3 4

10. It is recognized that successful programs and practices in one school cannot simply be transplanted to or superimposed on another school, but require transformation through inservice education and commitment on the part of the faculty of each school.   1 2 3 4

11. Teachers are free to initiate requests for assistance from supervisors without first having to go through the principal for permission.   1 2 3 4

CHECKLIST OF DEVELOPMENTAL CRITERIA
FOR SCHOOL IMPROVEMENT (Cont'd.)

Circle the number that best expresses your evaluation of the extent to which each criterion, condition, or practice is in evidence in your school/district.

1 = Strongly in evidence
2 = Some evidence
3 = Little or no evidence
4 = Evidence to the contrary

B. ADMINISTRATIVE POLICY AND PRACTICE (Cont'd.)

12. The administrative structure of the school district and school is reviewed periodically to ensure that it is fully functional.   1 2 3 4

13. The organizational structure of the educational program of the school is reviewed periodically to ensure that it is fully functional. Alternative designs are evaluated carefully—such as the "school-within-a-school," nongraded classes/continuous progress, modular-flexible scheduling, and so on.   1 2 3 4

14. The home is recognized and treated as a potentially powerful ally of the school, and systematic efforts are made by the professional staff to foster home–school cooperation. Parents are informed by the professional staff (teachers, counselors) on how they can contribute to the success of their children in school. Group conferences for parents are conducted on a regular basis by the professional staff.   1 2 3 4

15. Educational problems as well as accomplishments are communicated to parents and the wider community to enlist support toward the solution of problems.   1 2 3 4

16. The effectiveness of the school is determined not by any single measure, or narrow set of measures, but by the capacity and commitment of the professional staff (teachers, supervisors, administrators) to identify, diagnose, and solve emergent problems. The evaluation program is comprehensive and continuous.   1 2 3 4

C. INNOVATIONS AND REFORMS: POLICY AND PRACTICE

1. Proposals for reform—whether generated at national, state, or local levels—are evaluated carefully by examining the research literature and reviewing previous experiences with   1 2 3 4

similar reform measures. (It is recognized that reform measures have a way of being reinvented and discarded at periodic intervals without educators seeking to learn from the lessons of the past.)

2. Reform measures are not adopted segmentally, but are instituted in organic relationship to the total educational program. The process is not one of adoption, but of adaptation and transformation to meet local conditions and needs. The improvement of curriculum and instruction is seen as originating in efforts to solve a problem, not in adopting an innovation.   1 2 3 4

3. Reforms or innovations are implemented to benefit the entire learning community of the school, not to benefit one group at the expense of another (e.g., the gifted and talented over the disadvantaged), or one area of the curriculum at the expense of another (e.g., the sciences and mathematics at the expense of the arts and humanities).   1 2 3 4

4. Externally promoted educational reforms are evaluated critically by the professional staff in the light of the best available research evidence for effecting educational improvement, the philosophy of the school, the unique conditions of the local school, and the possible interactions of the reform measures with existing practices.   1 2 3 4

5. Reforms or innovations are adopted to improve the educational program, rather than to demonstrate acquiescence to external pressures or eagerness to follow the latest tide of fashion.   1 2 3 4

6. Those who are most affected by reform proposals (e.g., the teachers) are directly involved in their evaluation (determining the efficacy of the proposals for improving the educational program of the school) and in the decision making (adoption, adaptation, transformation, or rejection).   1 2 3 4

7. Reform measures or innovations are not adopted segmentally, but are transformed by the professional staff to meet local conditions, and the transformation is effected through a sense of commitment rather than compliance or imposition.   1 2 3 4

8. Reform measures and innovations are treated as hypotheses for testing through formative evaluation (in progress) and summative evaluation (at the end of a given time period), before they become institutionalized. Pilot programs are developed for evaluating the reform measures or innovations. The expertise of the university is tapped as needed in the evaluation process.   1 2 3 4

CHECKLIST OF DEVELOPMENTAL CRITERIA
FOR SCHOOL IMPROVEMENT (Cont'd.)

Circle the number that best expresses your evaluation of the extent to which each criterion, condition, or practice is in evidence in your school/district.

1 = Strongly in evidence
2 = Some evidence
3 = Little or no evidence
4 = Evidence to the contrary

C. INNOVATIONS AND REFORMS (Cont'd.)

---

9. Sufficient favorable evidence is available before reform measures or innovations are implemented on a wide scale. 1 2 3 4

10. Reform measures and innovations are adequately financed, but not at the expense of another ongoing program that is operating successfully or that is in equal need of attention. 1 2 3 4

D. THE CLIMATE FOR SUPERVISION

---

1. The school functions as a democratic-participative organizational system in which decisions are collaboratively developed by the entire professional staff and with the students. 1 2 3 4

2. The school climate is that of a community of belongingness, service, mutual respect and support; responsibility for productive learning is shared by the administration, faculty, and student body. 1 2 3 4

3. Communication is open and free-flowing rather than hierarchically downward. 1 2 3 4

4. The talents and motives for responsibility and self-direction on the part of the professional staff and students are fully tapped. 1 2 3 4

5. Support is provided for individual initiative by teachers as a means of catalyzing the spread of fresh ideas and practices. 1 2 3 4

6. Constructive ideas and suggestions are highly valued, widely shared, constantly elicited, and continuously implemented wherever practicable. 1 2 3 4

7. The motivational needs of teachers and students are productively expressed (belonging, self-esteem, competence, self-actualization, enlightenment, and creative engagement). 1 2 3 4

8. Education is seen as a developmental-emergent process, rather than an established-production process. The emphasis is on growth and optimizing human potentials, rather than on setting limits on people. 1 2 3 4

9. Concerted efforts are made to create optimal conditions for the school as a productive learning environment, rather than aiming at meeting minimal conditions. 1 2 3 4

10. Teachers readily communicate their problems and needs to the principal and supervisors. 1 2 3 4

11. Teachers and students are seen as the key sources for effecting educational improvement. They are not treated by the administration and supervisory staff as mere "channels of reception, transmission, or imposition" of policy and practice. 1 2 3 4

12. Student discipline is developed through responsible self-control, self-direction, and respect for others, rather than being a matter of authoritarian rule and imposition. 1 2 3 4

13. Teachers have professional autonomy to exercise initiative and responsible self-direction in the context of full collaboration with fellow faculty and other members of the professional staff of the school and school district. It is recognized that teacher isolation is not synonymous with teacher autonomy, and that decision making in the individual classroom does not add up to the decision making required for schoolwide and districtwide problem solving. 1 2 3 4

E. SUPERVISORY ROLES AND FUNCTIONS

1. The supervisory process is developmental (educative) rather than deficit-oriented (fault-finding). 1 2 3 4

2. The professional staff functions at Level III of knowledge/ability (the generative-creative level, rather than Level II (the mediative-adaptive level), or Level I (the imitative-maintenance level), as evidenced by the criteria in Table 10–1. The administration serves to support supervisors and teachers in effecting improvements in the educational program, rather than seeking the maintenance of established practice ("running a tight ship"). 1 2 3 4

3. The supervisor is an educational leader charged with the responsibility of working with the faculty, individually and collectively, on a collaborative basis in identifying, diagnosing, and solving classroom, schoolwide, and districtwide curriculum-instruction problems. 1 2 3 4

CHECKLIST OF DEVELOPMENTAL CRITERIA
FOR SCHOOL IMPROVEMENT (Cont'd.)

Circle the number that best expresses your evaluation of the extent to which each criterion, condition, or practice is in evidence in your school/district.

> 1 = Strongly in evidence
> 2 = Some evidence
> 3 = Little or no evidence
> 4 = Evidence to the contrary

E. SUPERVISORY ROLES AND FUNCTIONS (Cont'd.)

---

4. The principal functions as an expert generalist who sees the school as a whole and gives such direction to the school that it is consonant with the needs of the community and the wider society.　　1　2　3　4

5. The expertise of the supervisor extends beyond a specialized subject field and encompasses the relationship of his or her specialty to the school curriculum as a whole.　　1　2　3　4

6. A key qualification in the selection of supervisors is that they have expertise in curriculum development as a schoolwide and districtwide process, providing not only for curriculum articulation vertically (within a given subject field, grade level by grade level), but horizontally (between and among the various fields that comprise the total school curriculum).　　1　2　3　4

7. A key qualification in the selection of teachers is that they are able to see the interdependence of the various studies, regardless of their particular specializations or levels of assignment, and are committed to the full articulation of the school curriculum.　　1　2　3　4

8. The supervisor–teacher relationship is best described as one of collegial collaboration, and the entire professional staff functions as a collegial team.　　1　2　3　4

9. The district is well staffed with qualified supervisors.　　1　2　3　4

10. The principal and supervisors are highly knowledgeable concerning teachers' problems and assist teachers in solving problems.　　1　2　3　4

11. The supervisory process is focused on the growth in the ability of teachers to identify, diagnose, and solve emergent problems in the classroom and school.　　1　2　3　4

12. The faculty exhibits a strong collaborative commitment to problem solving as the key to school improvement.　　1　2　3　4

13. Teachers, supervisors, and administrators seek to reveal problems, rather than to conceal them, so that action may be taken toward their solution.   1 2 3 4

14. The problems to be solved are derived from the educational situation, not from an external special-interest group or from individual promoters of special remedies.   1 2 3 4

15. The key focus of the supervisory program is on improving the curriculum, teaching, and learning.   1 2 3 4

16. The faculty together with the supervisory staff seek to identify (a) the qualities that make for the best school possible, (b) the strengths of the school and areas in need of improvement, (c) the ways and means of creating the kind of school that is envisioned, and (d) the ways and means of gauging the progress toward creating the best school possible.   1 2 3 4

17. The principal delegates routine detail work effectively so that the principal's time, talent, and energies can be devoted to the improvement of the educational program.   1 2 3 4

18. The principal works collaboratively with the professional staff on budgetary allocations for educational improvement.   1 2 3 4

19. Teachers are provided with the needed supportive technical assistance and material resources for problem solving.   1 2 3 4

20. The professional staff identifies short-term needs in consonance with long-term needs. It is recognized that when problems are masked by treating symptoms for the short term, the result is the compounding of problems in the long term (e.g., teaching-to-the-test may raise test scores in the short run, but this is done at the expense of important educational goals).   1 2 3 4

21. Working for student success (and the prevention of student failure) is a function of the entire professional staff. The approach is developmental in orientation (focused on student potentials), rather than deficiency oriented (focused on student limitations).   1 2 3 4

22. The principal and supervisors make frequent visits to classrooms to see the educational program in action and to elicit from teachers the kinds of help needed in solving problems.   1 2 3 4

23. Teachers often initiate contacts with the principal and supervisors in seeking help with educational problems.   1 2 3 4

24. The principal and supervisors provide continual assistance to teachers in response to problems identified by teachers, while helping teachers to identify problems for diagnosis and treatment.   1 2 3 4

CHECKLIST OF DEVELOPMENTAL CRITERIA
FOR SCHOOL IMPROVEMENT (Cont'd.)

Circle the number that best expresses your evaluation of the extent to which each criterion, condition, or practice is in evidence in your school/district.

1 = Strongly in evidence
2 = Some evidence
3 = Little or no evidence
4 = Evidence to the contrary

E. SUPERVISORY ROLES AND FUNCTIONS (Cont'd.)

---

25. The principal's role is that of an educational leader, rather than a school manager, whose major function is to marshal all of the resources of the school and school district to improve the educational program.   1 2 3 4

26. Teachers receive written periodic evaluations from supervisors. The evaluations are developed cooperatively between the teacher and supervisor.   1 2 3 4

F. TEACHER EFFECTIVENESS AND CLASSROOM CLIMATE

---

1. The classroom functions as a participative-group system revealing a spirit of cooperation and mutual respect between teacher and students and among students.   1 2 3 4

2. The ways of teaching are congruent with the goal of developing the powers of students for independent thinking and democratic social responsibility.   1 2 3 4

3. Students share with the teacher the responsibility for the success of the class as a whole. More advanced students help others. The success of one student is not gained at the expense of another student.   1 2 3 4

4. The teacher works for student success and the prevention of failure. The teacher's approach is developmental in orientation (focused on student potentials) rather than deficiency oriented (focused on student limitations). The focus is on the development of optimal competencies rather than minimal competencies.   1 2 3 4

5. Communication is open—upward from student to teacher and laterally from student to student(s), as well as downward from teacher to student(s).   1 2 3 4

6. Students are learning to assume the responsibility for initiating and directing many of their learning activities, rather than depending on the teacher to tell them what they must do.   1 2 3 4

7. The social motive for productive learning is developed along with individual autonomy. Assignments include group projects and individual projects to enable students to learn how to work together for the common good, as well as how to work independently.   1 2 3 4

8. Learning activities are appropriately varied to meet individual differences without creating student isolation. The work of subgroups is shared by the entire class; such work is not delimited to mechanical exercises but involves collaborative investigation.   1 2 3 4

9. The teacher is genuinely enthusiastic about the classroom work, and students share the enthusiasm and exhibit a genuine sense of interest and commitment to the learning activities.   1 2 3 4

10. The teacher gives explanations or rationales for his or her decisions or actions to students. The decisions or actions by teachers are not seen by students as arbitrary because explanations and rationales are provided and, insofar as possible, students are involved in the decision making that affects them directly.   1 2 3 4

11. Learning activities are designed to foster cognitive growth in conjunction with affective and social growth. Efforts are made to foster desirable attitudes toward learning in recognition that such attitudes are fundamental to cognitive growth and development.   1 2 3 4

12. The teaching–learning process is idea oriented rather than error oriented. Facts and skills are not treated as ends but as the means and resources for the development of higher-ordered thinking abilities and the intelligent application of knowledge in the life of the learner.   1 2 3 4

13. Class discussion is catalyzed by thought questions initiated by students as well as teachers.   1 2 3 4

14. There is full class participation. Students are not reluctant to participate for fear of revealing their lack of knowledge or understanding. The classroom is not dominated by teacher "telling" or didactic instruction.   1 2 3 4

CHECKLIST OF DEVELOPMENTAL CRITERIA
FOR SCHOOL IMPROVEMENT (Cont'd.)

Circle the number that best expresses your evaluation of the extent to which each criterion, condition, or practice is in evidence in your school/district.

1 = Strongly in evidence
2 = Some evidence
3 = Little or no evidence
4 = Evidence to the contrary

F. TEACHER EFFECTIVENESS (Cont'd.)

---

15. Teachers give explanations and stimulate explanations from students in connection with classroom work. Teachers do not merely seek to elicit correct answers from students, but engage students in explaining how they derived their answers. When errors are made, teachers engage students in open inquiry in diagnosing the source of the error. Students are not reluctant to reveal their need for assistance and not embarrassed or penalized for revealing such need. Their willingness and capability in reporting their need for explanation or assistance is regarded positively rather than negatively by the teacher. Mistakes are treated as opportunities for improvement and for collateral learning. 1 2 3 4

16. Constructive and instructive suggestions, rather than negative criticisms, are offered by the teacher to students and by students to their peers. Such suggestions encourage and help students succeed in their work. This also applies to the teacher's evaluation of students' written work. 1 2 3 4

17. Individual variation in the classroom is recognized by providing sufficient time for the completion of given individual learning activities, and by selecting and assigning activities in recognition of individual differences without isolating individuals. 1 2 3 4

18. The teacher recognizes opportunities for collateral learning and capitalizes on such opportunities so as to motivate learners to go beyond what is required in the classroom (e.g., in studying about disease and health, the student becomes interested in the life of a particular scientist, and the teacher helps the student locate a biography of that scientist). 1 2 3 4

19. Time allocation for classroom activities is flexible, so that when students are productively engaged in an unanticipated emergent learning situation, the teacher will not ter- 1 2 3 4

minate the event in order to shift to another learning activity that may be less productive.

20. Students are allowed sufficient time to gather their thoughts   1 2 3 4
    and to express them vocally and in writing.

21. Discipline is seen as integral to the educative process—as   1 2 3 4
    growth in purposive self-control and self-direction on the
    part of each student in the context of social responsibility,
    rather than a matter of external imposition or authoritarian
    control by the teacher. Motivation is seen as a key factor in
    preventing discipline problems, and concerted and continu-
    ous efforts are made to stimulate genuine student motiva-
    tion for learning.

22. Where problems of student motivation and discipline are in   1 2 3 4
    evidence, they are treated as curricular problems, rather
    than being treated in isolation. Growth in self-discipline is
    seen as an educational function, in contrast to the treatment
    of discipline as a matter of external, authoritarian impo-
    sition.

23. Students are grouped in classrooms not for the purpose of   1 2 3 4
    exacting uniformity, but to capitalize on the powerful edu-
    cative bearings of a cosmopolitan group. Classroom learn-
    ing activities are designed to enable students to learn from
    one another. Individual variation is seen as essential to the
    growth and vitality of the group, not as a negative factor.

24. The physical environment of the classroom is attractive and   1 2 3 4
    conducive to a productive psychosocial climate for learning.

G. CURRICULUM DEVELOPMENT

1. The school is recognized outside the district for its success-   1 2 3 4
   ful programs and practices, and attracts educators from
   neighboring districts who seek to gain new ideas for school
   improvement.

2. Curriculum development is treated as a problem-solving   1 2 3 4
   process involving the entire professional staff of the school
   and school district (see Table 10–2).

3. The responsibility for the curriculum, including the selec-   1 2 3 4
   tion and use of curricular materials, resides with the professional staff, not with any external source or special-interest
   group.

CHECKLIST OF DEVELOPMENTAL CRITERIA
FOR SCHOOL IMPROVEMENT (Cont'd.)

Circle the number that best expresses your evaluation of the extent to which each criterion, condition, or practice is in evidence in your school/district.

1 = Strongly in evidence
2 = Some evidence
3 = Little or no evidence
4 = Evidence to the contrary

G. CURRICULUM DEVELOPMENT (Cont'd.)

---

4. Teachers and supervisors, under the leadership of the director of curriculum, are engaged in continuous and systematic curriculum development to articulate the curriculum throughout the district as well as within the school. Curriculum articulation is developed horizontally (between and among subject fields) and vertically (from grade level to grade level and from school to school within the district).   1 2 3 4

5. The curriculum is treated as an ecological system rather than an amalgamation of separate parts. Efforts to improve the teaching of a given subject matter are undertaken in relation to its interdependence with all subjects in the curriculum and with the wider functions of the curriculum (the macrocurriculum), such as the function of general education. The professional staff gives concerted attention to the "grand design" of the school curriculum.   1 2 3 4

6. The curriculum is conceived and developed as a whole, with the various studies treated as interdependent through correlation and synthesis. Transdisciplinary approaches enable students to become engaged in the study of problems of personal and social significance. (For example, the social studies, literature, and composition are treated interrelatedly; mathematics is related to the sciences and social studies; the relationships between science and society, and between the arts and society, are revealed; and so on.)   1 2 3 4

7. Teachers and supervisors are engaged in continuous and systematic curriculum development across the entire curriculum as well as within the subject fields. Supervisors do not work in isolation according to their fields of specialization.   1 2 3 4

8. Students work with the professional staff on curriculum improvement.   1 2 3 4

9. The curriculum is attuned to the nature of the learner (e.g., developmental stages and motivational needs) and to the qualities that make for democratic citizenship (individual autonomy in the context of social responsibility).   1 2 3 4

10. Instructional improvement is seen as integral to curriculum improvement and to the improvement of learning. The supervisory program treats curriculum, instruction, and learning as interdependent.   1 2 3 4

11. Statements of educational objectives give emphasis to the development of higher thinking abilities in which facts and skills are put to meaningful use, rather than being treated as ends in themselves.   1 2 3 4

12. The units of study are organized according to concepts, ideas, themes, problems, and projects of personal–social significance which stimulate inquiry—rather than being organized according to topics. The units are interconnected, rather than being treated in isolation, so that students can derive deeper and wider understandings, appreciations, and capabilities as they progress from unit to unit.   1 2 3 4

13. Learning skills are developed through growth in the use of concepts, ideas, and understandings that give richer meaning to experience—rather than being treated mechanically and as isolated ends in themselves. Skills are developed through the curriculum, rather than being treated as separate subjects. (It is recognized that although general education encompasses basic education and much more, basic education is not a substitute for general education.)   1 2 3 4

14. Classroom activities and assignments are designed to stimulate students to seek and interpret relevant knowledge from a wide variety of subjects and sources, revealing the interdependence of knowledge.   1 2 3 4

15. The balance and coherence of the curriculum is maintained in the face of any special priorities that may be established for the school (e.g., priority given to science and math is not at the expense of the arts and humanities).   1 2 3 4

16. The responsibility for the actual design and development of the curriculum resides with the professional staff of the school district and school. State curricular mandates are not seen as an excuse for avoiding this responsibility. (For example, the state may mandate specific subjects for high school graduation, but does not mandate how the subjects are to be organized and treated in the curriculum.)   1 2 3 4

CHECKLIST OF DEVELOPMENTAL CRITERIA
FOR SCHOOL IMPROVEMENT (Cont'd.)

Circle the number that best expresses your evaluation of the extent to which each criterion, condition, or practice is in evidence in your school/district.

> 1 = Strongly in evidence
> 2 = Some evidence
> 3 = Little or no evidence
> 4 = Evidence to the contrary

G. CURRICULUM DEVELOPMENT (Cont'd.)

---

17. Individualized learning provides for student self-direction and responsibility and derives from systematic teacher–student planning. Individualized learning is not regarded as synonymous with the convergent-mechanical exercises characteristic of workbooks, programmed instruction, and ditto sheets.   1　2　3　4

18. The secondary school curriculum is not dominated by the college-preparatory function, but is comprehensive to meet the diversified needs of a cosmopolitan student population through vocational, college-preparatory, enrichment, and exploratory studies.   1　2　3　4

19. Students are not segregated into program tracks in the high school.   1　2　3　4

20. In the secondary school, there is a coherent curriculum in general education, rather than distribution-elective requirements.   1　2　3　4

21. A coherent program of general education provides for those learnings that all citizens in a free society share in common, with opportunities to examine pervasive problems and issues of personal–social significance.   1　2　3　4

22. Teachers are free from external constraints and pressures that may lead to the censorship of the curriculum or of curricular materials, or to teacher self-imposed censorship.   1　2　3　4

23. At the secondary level, the curriculum in general education is designed to meet the needs of a heterogeneous student population and to capitalize on the positive attributes of a cosmopolitan class group. The elective options for exploratory, enrichment, and special-interest studies allow for multiage/multigrade groupings of students   1　2　3　4

24. Block-time classes are offered in the junior high school to enable students to identify with a core teacher and to foster curriculum correlation and synthesis, especially in English language arts and social studies. Team-teaching arrangements may be provided. Social concerns and problems are examined through the reading of literary works and historical documents, the writing of themes, participation in panel discussions, and work on a variety of individual and group projects.   1 2 3 4

25. Interdepartmental cooperation and planning are in evidence in the junior and senior high school to provide for horizontal curriculum articulation and for a coherent program of general education.   1 2 3 4

26. Standardized tests are used appropriately and do not mitigate against a balanced and rich curriculum (e.g., students engage in writing across the curriculum, in working on projects in the fine arts and industrial arts, and so on—despite the fact that the learning outcomes from such activities are not evaluated vis-à-vis standardized tests).   1 2 3 4

27. Standardized tests are used for diagnostic purposes, not for purposes of determining student grades or for segregating students into different classes. (It is recognized that standardized aptitude tests are not valid predictors of student achievement, and that ability grouping into separate classes does not, in itself, produce higher achievement.)   1 2 3 4

28. Teacher-made tests are focused on student growth in higher-ordered thinking through comprehension, analysis, application, and problem solving.   1 2 3 4

29. Teacher-made tests are used by the teacher to evaluate the teacher's success in effecting student growth in achievement.   1 2 3 4

30. The evaluation of student achievement is based on comprehensive criteria, rather than being based primarily on test results.   1 2 3 4

31. The school schedule is designed to facilitate the educational program, rather than to constrain it. (For example, classes in physical education/recreation are scheduled block-time two days per week, rather than as a single period daily, to allow a greater proportion of time devoted to productive activity in relation to the time taken in the locker room and for warm-up routines.)   1 2 3 4

CHECKLIST OF DEVELOPMENTAL CRITERIA
FOR SCHOOL IMPROVEMENT (Cont'd.)

Circle the number that best expresses your evaluation of the extent to which each criterion, condition, or practice is in evidence in your school/district.

> 1 = Strongly in evidence
> 2 = Some evidence
> 3 = Little or no evidence
> 4 = Evidence to the contrary

G. CURRICULUM DEVELOPMENT (Cont'd.)

---

32. Scheduling considerations do not result in the tracking of students in their course work in the secondary school. The schedule is designed to provide students with opportunity to pursue a full and rich program of studies and to participate in student activities.   1 2 3 4

33. The curriculum is not treated as a schedule of segmental subjects.   1 2 3 4

34. The fullest opportunity is provided for coeducational learning activities throughout the curriculum.   1 2 3 4

35. Teachers have the deciding voice in the selection of textbooks and other curricular materials, with care taken to ensure that adequate attention is given to the scope and sequence of the total school curriculum.   1 2 3 4

36. The textbook does not determine the course of study, but is used along with a rich variety of curricular materials, resources, and activities for productive learning.   1 2 3 4

37. Students are free to take their books and other curricular materials home with them.   1 2 3 4

38. Textbooks and other curricular materials are plentiful and up to date.   1 2 3 4

39. In the secondary school, the homeroom is heterogeneously grouped and functions as a significant social unit, rather than serving as a routine daily session for attendance and announcements.   1 2 3 4

40. The homeroom teacher functions in a guidance capacity and arranges for special help for those students whose achievement is below capacity.   1 2 3 4

41. Homework is meaningfully directed through assignments that enhance school achievement and stimulate student interest in the subject matter. It is not mechanical drudgery.   1 2 3 4

42. Teachers read and comment on all homework from a proficiency rather than a deficiency orientation.   1 2 3 4

43. A full range of advanced-placement courses is offered in the high school. The teachers do not seek to imitate the college professor in lecture methods, but utilize a wide variety of approaches appropriate for adolescents in stimulating their interest in advanced study (e.g., through panel discussions, theme writing, projects, and so on).   1 2 3 4

44. A comprehensive program of extraclass activities is provided, enabling students to assume responsibilities through self-directed learning. All students have opportunities for wide participation. Emphasis is given to the development of wholesome, lifelong, recreational interests. Such activities are recognized by the professional staff as integral to, not apart from, the total school curriculum. These activities provide for multigrade/multiage grouping of students.   1 2 3 4

45. The student council is actively engaged in identifying and addressing schoolwide student concerns and problems, and works collaboratively with the faculty and administration on school improvement. The range and nature of student concerns and problems to be addressed are not delimited by the administration and faculty.   1 2 3 4

46. Students are widely engaged in community-service activities of an educative nature, and these activities grow out of and feed back into the curriculum (e.g., children at the primary level may be planting seeds to beautify the school grounds; adolescents may be engaged in a reading project for the blind; and so on).   1 2 3 4

47. A full-time kindergarten is an integral part of the total educational program of the elementary school.   1 2 3 4

48. The summer school program encompasses a comprehensive range of course offerings and activities for enrichment, acceleration, and recreation—rather than being confined mainly to remedial or makeup work.   1 2 3 4

49. Periodic student surveys are conducted to elicit suggestions for curriculum improvement. The students are informed of the findings and are enlisted to work with the professional staff on curriculum improvement.   1 2 3 4

50. The school district conducts a diversified program of adult classes and activities to meet community needs.   1 2 3 4

CHECKLIST OF DEVELOPMENTAL CRITERIA
FOR SCHOOL IMPROVEMENT (Cont'd.)

Circle the number that best expresses your evaluation of the extent to which each criterion, condition, or practice is in evidence in your school/district.

1 = Strongly in evidence
2 = Some evidence
3 = Little or no evidence
4 = Evidence to the contrary

H. INSERVICE EDUCATION/STAFF DEVELOPMENT

---

1. Teacher development is a districtwide responsibility, as well as a responsibility of the principal and faculty in the individual school.　　1　2　3　4

2. The entire professional staff of the school and district is engaged in a systematic program of inservice education to enhance continuous professional growth. The program is planned, conducted, and evaluated cooperatively.　　1　2　3　4

3. The principal, director of curriculum, and supervisors exercise leadership in coordinating the inservice program in full collaboration with the faculty, and ensure that adequate material resources are provided to help teachers grow professionally.　　1　2　3　4

4. Inservice education is an ongoing program for school improvement, guided by well-understood and agreed-upon goals. The program is developmental in orientation rather than deficit oriented.　　1　2　3　4

5. Inservice education is integral to the overall program of curriculum development.　　1　2　3　4

6. The needs of the school, the teachers, and the students are treated as mutually interdependent.　　1　2　3　4

7. The inservice program is designed to enhance teacher motivation and capability for problem solving, to stimulate deeper insights and wider perspectives for educational improvement. The program is not concentrated on narrow convergent training, such as in the adoption and implementation of a prepackaged, segmental instructional program.　　1　2　3　4

8. Teachers are major decision makers in planning the inservice program and in identifying and diagnosing the needs and problems to be addressed.　　1　2　3　4

9. The inservice education program provides teachers with sufficient time to reflect on their work and to develop the means for improving their effectiveness.   1 2 3 4

10. The inservice education program provides for (a) a regular schedule for classroom visitation with each teacher by the principal and supervisors, (b) a conference with the teacher following each visit for collaborative evaluation and planning, and (c) a sufficient number of visits with each teacher to observe a variety of teaching–learning situations.   1 2 3 4

11. The goals and functions of the inservice program are consonant with the goals of the educational program of the school.   1 2 3 4

12. Full opportunity is provided for "grass-roots" initiation to ensure that the inservice program is directed at problems and concerns of greatest significance to teachers.   1 2 3 4

13. The functions of teacher evaluation and inservice education (staff development) are seen as mutually enhancing, rather than conflicting, because teachers are evaluated on their awareness of problems, willingness to expose problems, and efforts in seeking help in solving problems.   1 2 3 4

14. Strong incentives are provided supervisors and teachers for working on problem solutions.   1 2 3 4

15. The reward system favors the revealing rather than the concealing of problems.   1 2 3 4

16. The teacher sees classroom problems as within his or her capability of control and solution.   1 2 3 4

17. When problems are beyond the teacher's capability, rather than resting the blame with some external causation, the teacher seeks and receives the needed help from the supervisor, and/or administrator, and from fellow teachers.   1 2 3 4

18. The evaluation of teaching effectiveness is based on comprehensive criteria, rather than being narrowly focused on those classroom activities and student outcomes that are most easily amenable to quantifiable measurement. Teaching is understood as a complex process and it is recognized that there are many ways of teaching effectively, just as there are many ways of learning effectively.   1 2 3 4

19. Faculty morale is high as the result of a democratic-participation system of organization in which full support is provided by the administration for faculty development and educational improvement.   1 2 3 4

CHECKLIST OF DEVELOPMENTAL CRITERIA
FOR SCHOOL IMPROVEMENT (Cont'd.)

Circle the number that best expresses your evaluation of the extent to which each criterion, condition, or practice is in evidence in your school/district.

1 = Strongly in evidence
2 = Some evidence
3 = Little or no evidence
4 = Evidence to the contrary

H. INSERVICE EDUCATION/STAFF DEVELOPMENT (Cont'd.)

---

20. Teachers seek help from supervisors in solving substantive educational problems, rather than looking for ready recipes.   1 2 3 4

21. The faculty is actualized to seek educational improvement on a continuing basis, and the efforts yield demonstrable results.   1 2 3 4

22. Teachers eagerly share their successful ideas and materials through faculty meetings, inservice education projects, teacher centers, scheduled interclass visitation–observation, and informal contacts.   1 2 3 4

23. Recognition is given to individual and joint achievements of teachers in improving the educational program, and the successful practices are widely disseminated throughout the school, district, and the schools of neighboring districts.   1 2 3 4

24. Outstanding teachers are enlisted in helping other teachers.   1 2 3 4

25. Faculty meetings are devoted mainly to the improvement of the educational program; teachers, supervisors, and administrators cooperatively plan the agenda. The meetings are not dominated by the principal.   1 2 3 4

26. The inservice program is well supported; sufficient provisions are made for released time for teachers, outside expertise, and material resources.   1 2 3 4

27. Inservice workshops are planned cooperatively with the faculty and are focused on problem solutions. The workshops are evaluated in terms of the progress made in solving problems. The entire professional staff is involved in the evaluation process.   1 2 3 4

28. Inservice workshops are followed up with the needed support services and material resources to enable teachers to   1 2 3 4

bring about the targeted improvements in the educational program.

29. Workshops, institutes, and other inservice sessions sponsored by the school and school district are not treated in substitution for advanced university study.   1 2 3 4

30. Teachers participate widely in advanced university study to improve their professional capabilities and to develop collegial relationships with teachers from widely differing schools and school systems.   1 2 3 4

31. All teachers are fully certified and most have completed the master's degree or are actively engaged in pursuing the master's degree.   1 2 3 4

32. An interschool visitation program provides for wide faculty participation in observing promising programs and practices in other schools in the district, area, and state.   1 2 3 4

33. Major aspects of the inservice program are evaluated formatively and summatively.   1 2 3 4

34. The orientation of new teachers is an integral function of the inservice program. The orientation takes account of the differences among beginning teachers and among experienced teachers from other schools in the same system as well as those from other systems. Special assistance is provided for those teachers who have been transferred to meet school desegregation guidelines or changes in enrollment patterns.   1 2 3 4

35. A year-long inservice program is conducted for beginning teachers in which their problems and concerns are shared openly, and through which appropriate support is provided—including the supply of material resources.   1 2 3 4

36. Special supervisory assistance is provided beginning teachers to help them in the successful transition from preservice education to professional teaching, and to ensure their professional growth (through appropriate assignments, plentiful resource materials, adequate facilities, and measures to prevent teacher isolation).   1 2 3 4

37. Beginning teachers are not assigned to courses (or students) "rejected" by veteran teachers, or to facilities that are regarded as less desirable by veteran teachers.   1 2 3 4

38. The support system for new teachers encourages them to seek assistance with problems, and the needed help is readily provided.   1 2 3 4

39. New teachers participate in the selection of curricular materials that they will be using in their classes.   1 2 3 4

CHECKLIST OF DEVELOPMENTAL CRITERIA
FOR SCHOOL IMPROVEMENT (Cont'd.)

Circle the number that best expresses your evaluation of the extent to which each criterion, condition, or practice is in evidence in your school/district.

1 = Strongly in evidence
2 = Some evidence
3 = Little or no evidence
4 = Evidence to the contrary

H. INSERVICE EDUCATION/STAFF DEVELOPMENT (Cont'd.)

40. The working climate not only provides opportunities for beginning teachers and newly transferred teachers to express their ideas for improving the educational program, but their ideas are openly solicited and valued by the entire professional staff.   1 2 3 4

41. Experienced teachers who are new to the school are viewed as potential sources of ideas and suggestions, and are enlisted in working on existing problems with their new colleagues. The principal works to involve all new teachers immediately in the total life of the school.   1 2 3 4

42. In focusing on problem solving, the continuing inservice education program stimulates teachers to grow professionally, rather than to settle into dull routines.   1 2 3 4

43. Consultants are engaged on a regular basis to work with the professional staff on problem solutions on both a short-term and a long-term basis. The consultants are responsible for the follow-up of their own work.   1 2 3 4

44. The professional staff works with the university in seeking to solve school and school-district problems. A cooperative, ongoing school–university program is in operation for this purpose.   1 2 3 4

45. The number of teacher preparations is never excessive, and teachers are provided with at least one period daily for preparation, individual conferences with colleagues, and for occasional visitation–observation in other classes.   1 2 3 4

46. Alternative patterns of staffing are explored and implemented to reduce teacher load and to improve the educational program.   1 2 3 4

47. If the school is located within reasonable proximity to a college or university, the school serves as a center for stu-   1 2 3 4

dent teaching or internship. A core of cooperating teachers works conjointly with the college supervisor in designing and evaluating the program.

48. A problem-solving approach is followed by the cooperating teacher and student teacher/intern to ensure that the experience is directed at professional growth rather than adjustment and compliance.　　1　2　3　4

49. The cooperating teacher shares with the student teacher/intern all of the available material resources, without requiring that they be used. The student/intern is encouraged to develop his or her own resources and repertoire.　　1　2　3　4

50. The supervisory staff and most members of the faculty hold membership in one or more of the leading professional educational associations noted for work on curriculum development (e.g., Amercian Vocational Association, Association for Supervision and Curriculum Development, International Reading Association, National Art Education Association, National Council of Teachers of English, National Council of Teachers of Mathematics, National Council for the Social Studies, National Science Teachers Association, and so on).　　1　2　3　4

51. Supervisors and teachers are effective consumers of research and are engaged concertedly and continually in applying the best available evidence to the improvement of practice in the school and classroom. Where the evidence is incomplete, practices are treated as hypotheses for further testing.　　1　2　3　4

52. A high proportion of the faculty answer affirmatively to the question, "If you were to begin your career over again, would you become a teacher?"　　1　2　3　4

I. TEACHING–LEARNING RESOURCES, FACILITIES, AND SERVICES

1. The school plant is physically attractive, functional, in harmony with community development patterns and needs, and is located with ready access to community recreational resources. (Ideally, the school site is adjacent to park land.) The site is adequate for possible future expansion/modification of buildings and facilities. The outdoor recreational facilities are ample not only for student use, but for community use.　　1　2　3　4

2. The school site and physical facilities are so arranged that learning activities are not impeded by outside noise, or by inside noise from the gym, shops, music studios, and so on.　　1　2　3　4

CHECKLIST OF DEVELOPMENTAL CRITERIA
FOR SCHOOL IMPROVEMENT (Cont'd.)

Circle the number that best expresses your evaluation of the extent to which each criterion, condition, or practice is in evidence in your school/district.

> 1 = Strongly in evidence
> 2 = Some evidence
> 3 = Little or no evidence
> 4 = Evidence to the contrary

I. RESOURCES AND SERVICES (Cont'd.)

---

3. The school is of sufficient size to provide the professional staff, facilities, and resources required for a rich curriculum to meet the needs of a cosmopolitan pupil population. Yet the school is so organized that students and the professional staff are engaged in close working relationships.   1 2 3 4

4. In the case of the high school where a large enrollment is required in order to warrant the investment in the required specialized facilities and resources for a diversified curriculum, the school is organized under a "house plan" so that students are able to identify with a core professional staff affiliated with the "house."   1 2 3 4

5. The facilities, equipment, and resources in all areas of the curriculum meet the standards set by the appropriate professional organization (laboratories, shops, studios, resource centers, gymnasium, athletic fields, auditorium)   1 2 3 4

6. There is a districtwide media program which is well coordinated, staffed, and financed. (See the current edition of *Media Programs*, published by the American Library Association.)   1 2 3 4

7. The school has a media program under the direction of a media professional who participates in curriculum development. The media program is integral to the curriculum, not merely an ancillary service.   1 2 3 4

8. The facilities, staffing, and resources of the school media center meet the guidelines of the American Association of School Librarians. [See the current edition of *Media Programs*, published by the American Library Association (e.g., the basic collection for a school with 500 or fewer users includes at least 8,000 to 12,000 books, or 16 to 24 books per user, with access to 60,000 titles to ensure satisfaction of 90 percent of initial requests, and 50 to 175 periodical/   1 2 3 4

newspaper titles). See also the standards for other media resources, including those for the computer-learning laboratory.]

9. The school media center is attractive, functional, and serves as a true center for responsible, self-directed, learning activity.   1 2 3 4

10. The school media center is open to students for individual and group use throughout the school day, including the lunch period, and before and after regular school hours.   1 2 3 4

11. Class assignments engage each student in the use of the media center for investigative work and for the preparation of reports.   1 2 3 4

12. Students are encouraged to use the media center for recreational reading and browsing, and to use the equipment for viewing and listening.   1 2 3 4

13. The media center is never used as a study hall or for purposes other than for which it is intended.   1 2 3 4

14. Teachers receive help in preparing multimedia learning resources and are encouraged to draw upon the staff of the media center for assistance.   1 2 3 4

15. The entire professional staff collaborates fully on budgetary allocations for learning resources; the principal and teachers are provided discretionary funds for the purchase of special learning materials that are needed to improve the curriculum.   1 2 3 4

16. Students are surveyed periodically to ascertain their needs for learning resources and to elicit their suggestions for improving the facilities, resources, and services.   1 2 3 4

17. Students and teachers in the secondary school have ready access to typewriters, word processors, and other equipment.   1 2 3 4

18. A rich collection of teaching resource units (for teachers) and learning resource units (for students) is maintained in the school media center and is used extensively by teachers and students.   1 2 3 4

19. Teachers are assigned rooms of their own in which they conduct most of their classes, have their own desks and files, can store their instructional materials, and have shelf space for classroom libraries.   1 2 3 4

CHECKLIST OF DEVELOPMENTAL CRITERIA FOR SCHOOL IMPROVEMENT (Cont'd.)

Circle the number that best expresses your evaluation of the extent to which each criterion, condition, or practice is in evidence in your school/district.

1 = Strongly in evidence
2 = Some evidence
3 = Little or no evidence
4 = Evidence to the contrary

I. RESOURCES AND SERVICES (Cont'd.)

20. Students are provided with adequate work space. The classroom furniture is functional and movable for varied teaching–learning activities. Classroom storage space meets instructional needs. Students are provided with adequate locker space for their books and private belongings.   1 2 3 4

21. Teachers are provided with needed clerical–technical assistance and resources for the preparation of curricular materials through the school media center, and avail themselves of such services and resources.   1 2 3 4

22. The district maintains an extensive professional library that is widely used by the professional staff.   1 2 3 4

23. The ratio of professional staff to students is no greater than 1:20. Class size is adjusted appropriately to age/grade level and to the nature of the learning activity. There are no overcrowded classrooms.   1 2 3 4

24. In the secondary school, each teacher has no more than 140 students in all classes combined on a daily basis.   1 2 3 4

25. The guidance and counseling program is well articulated districtwide from the elementary school through the high school. Each counselor is responsible for no more than 250 to 300 students in the secondary school. The facilities are attractive and afford privacy.   1 2 3 4

26. Students in the secondary school feel free to initiate contacts with their counselor for help with personal, social, and academic problems. An ongoing program is in place to assist students with employment, and to provide for career counseling.   1 2 3 4

27. The guidance staff works closely with parents and with the faculty to improve the work of the teacher as a guidance person in the classroom.   1 2 3 4

28. An effective dropout-prevention program is maintained by the high school.   1   2   3   4

29. The high school operates a continuation program to enable students to earn their diplomas on a part-time basis.   1   2   3   4

30. Annual follow-up studies are conducted of graduates, trans- ferees, and dropouts; the findings are widely shared by the professional staff for curriculum improvement and the im- provement of the guidance and counseling program.   1   2   3   4

31. Transfer students receive special assistance to ensure suc- cessful adjustment—academically, psychologically, and socially.   1   2   3   4

32. In the secondary school, the physical facilities and the or- ganization of the schedule allow each student free time to work independently in the school library, resource center, shop, laboratory, or studio. There are no study halls.   1   2   3   4

33. The schedule of courses is sufficiently flexible so that stu- dents do not have to make forced choices because of sched- ule constraints.   1   2   3   4

34. Remedial programs are provided without isolating and stig- matizing students. The programs are designed to correct any inadequacies in the ongoing instructional program of the school, as well as to provide the needed individual re- mediation.   1   2   3   4

35. Handicapped students and students with special needs are provided with special support services without being isolated from other students.   1   2   3   4

36. Health facilities and services are fully adequate. Provisions are made for regular medical examination, referral, and follow-up.   1   2   3   4

37. The school serves as a center for community activities.   1   2   3   4

SUMMARY

School improvement requires that teachers, supervisors, and administrators in- quire into problems and issues that cut across the entire school. All aspects of the educational program need to be recognized and treated in their interdepen- dence, and this requires that the professional staff works collaboratively in iden- tifying, diagnosing, and solving schoolwide problems. In this way, the productive energies and talents of the professional staff are fully tapped. Problems can be solved only when they are revealed, not when they are concealed.

The criteria presented in this chapter for evaluating the school are intended to illustrate the range and kinds of concerns, conditions, and practices that the professional staff might consider in a cooperative and continuous process of school improvement. The process should be one of self-study for self-renewal.

The success of a school cannot be measured by its past accomplishments; its success is determined by the commitment and capacity of the professional staff to effect problem solutions. The school, like the learners themselves, must be undergoing constant growth and development if it is to do more than survive. The rationale for developmental supervision is based on this dynamic of growth and self-renewal.

PROBLEMS FOR STUDY AND DISCUSSION

1. After reviewing the various criteria for school improvement presented in this chapter, indicate those criteria that you would modify and show how and why you would want them to be modified.

2. What criteria of your own devising would you add to the lists, and why?

3. Make a study of your own school using your revised lists of developmental criteria. What problems, needs, and concerns are revealed? If you were the principal, how would you proceed with the professional staff in addressing these problems, needs, and concerns?

4. Devise a brief instrument that might be administered to students to elicit their suggestions for the improvement of their school. Include a sufficiently diverse assortment of items so as to sample broadly the conditions that relate to the school as a living environment—such as the adequacy of the school library, the cafeteria menu, the curriculum/course offerings, and so on. Administer the instrument to your own class, making certain that the responses are kept anonymous. How did the findings compare with your expectations? Any surprises? Make the findings available to your class and use the results as a basis for class discussion. What additional findings are revealed from the class discussion?

5. Do you agree with Whitehead that "primarily it is the schools and not the scholars (students) which should be inspected"?[8] Explain.

6. Examine the statement of philosophy developed by the professional staff of your own school. Do you adjudge it to be a *living* document? Why or why not?

7. Examine a variety of student assignments and teacher-made tests in different areas of the curriculum. To what extent are the items designed to stimulate students to engage in interpretation, evaluation, and application of knowledge?

8. In his "Study of Schooling," Goodlad found that "teachers perceived that they and their colleagues were not deeply involved in resolving schoolwide

problems—a finding that agreed with our findings on their inservice educa-tion activities."[9] How do you account for the finding that inservice programs tend to be segmental and give insufficient attention to schoolwide problems?

9. Goodlad also found in his study that student participation was far less in evidence in their academic classes than in the arts and vocational classes. "And it appears that participation in extracurricular activities such as stu-dent government, the yearbook, clubs, and so on assures some opportunities for making decisions, exercising creativity, and assuming responsibility—something not as often provided in academic classes."[10] How do you account for the general lack of decision-making responsibility and creativity on the part of students in their academic classes, as contrasted with other classes and extraclass activities?

10. Over the years, progressive educators have pointed to the desirable learning experiences to be derived from a rich curriculum, including the fine arts, performing arts, shop classes, and extraclass activities. Research studies have supported the value of such work not only in terms of enriching school life and engaging students in responsible decision making, but such experience in school appears to have a positive effect on student achievement later in college.[11]

Despite these findings, many school critics tend to look askance at so-called nonacademic studies and extraclass activities. In 1985, the Texas legis-lature passed a law barring any student who fails to attain a grade of 70 in any course from participation in extraclass activities over the subsequent grading period. The unanticipated consequence was that students were be-ing barred not only from sports, but from participation in science clubs, band and orchestra, government, drama, debate, and other educative activi-ties. Soon it was reported that the law would have to be rescinded or drasti-cally modified.[12] How do you account for the persistent bias against the so-called nonacademic studies and extraclass activities? Should extraclass activities be regarded as integral to the school curriculum? Why or why not?

NOTES

1. Alfred North Whitehead, *The Aims of Education* (New York: Macmillan, 1957; origi-nally published in 1929), p. 21.
2. John I. Goodlad, *A Place Called School* (New York: McGraw-Hill, 1984), p. 31.
3. Ibid., p. 301.
4. Ibid, pp. 17, 28.
5. John I. Goodlad, "The School as Workplace," Chapter 3 in National Society for the Study of Education, *Staff Development*, Eighty-second Yearbook, Part II (Chicago: University of Chicago Press, 1983), p. 39.
6. Ibid., p. 38.
7. U.S. Department of Education. *What Works: Research about Teaching and Learning* (Washington, D.C.: The Department, 1986), p. 34.
8. Whitehead, op. cit., p. 21.
9. Goodlad, *A Place Called School*, op. cit., p. 188.

10. John I. Goodlad, "Rethinking What Schools Can Do Best," Chapter 2 in National Society for the Study of Education, *Education in School and Nonschool Settings,* Eighty-fourth Yearbook, Part I (Chicago: University of Chicago Press, 1985), p. 38.

11. William G. Spady, "Status, Achievement, and Motivation in the American High School," *School Review,* Vol. 79 (May 1971), pp. 384–385; Scott Whitener, "Patterns of High School Studies and College Achievement" (unpublished doctoral dissertation, Rutgers University, 1974); Robert W. Young, "The Relationship of Business and Industrial Courses in High School with Academic Achievement in the First Year of College" (unpublished doctoral dissertation, University of Michigan, 1966).

12. *The New York Times,* April 28, 1985, pp. 1, 32.

SELECTED REFERENCES

American Association of School Librarians. *Media Programs: District and School.* Chicago: American Library Association, 1975.

Association for Supervision and Curriculum Development. *Staff Development/Organization Development,* 1981 Yearbook. Alexandria, Va.: The Association, 1981.

———. *Supervision of Teaching,* 1982 Yearbook. Alexandria, Va.: The Association, 1982.

———. *Using What We Know About Teaching,* 1984 Yearbook. Alexandria, Va.: The Association, 1984.

Bowers, David G. *Systems of Organization.* Ann Arbor, Mich.: The University of Michigan Press, 1976.

Boyer, Ernest L. *High School: A Report on Secondary Education in America.* New York: Harper & Row, Publishers, Inc. 1983.

Brookover, Wilbur, et al. *School Systems and Student Achievement: Schools Can Make a Difference.* New York: Praeger Publishers, 1979.

Conant, James B. *The American High School Today.* New York: McGraw-Hill Book Company, 1959.

———. *The Comprehensive High School.* New York: McGraw-Hill Book Company, 1967.

Good, Thomas L., and Jere E. Brophy. *Looking in Classrooms,* 3rd ed. New York: Harper & Row, Publishers, Inc., 1984.

Goodlad, John I. *A Place Called School.* New York: McGraw-Hill Book Company, 1984.

Havighurst, Robert J. *Developmental Tasks and Education,* 3rd ed. New York: David McKay Company, Inc., 1972.

Hummell, Dean L., and Charles W. Humes. *Pupil Services: Development, Coordination, Administration.* New York: Macmillan Publishing Company, 1984.

Joyce, Bruce, and Marsha Weil. *Models of Teaching,* 2nd ed. Englewood Cliffs, N.J.: Prentice-Hall, Inc., 1980.

National Society for the Study of Education. *Classroom Management,* Seventy-eighth Yearbook, Part II. Chicago: The University of Chicago Press, 1979.

———. *Education in School and Nonschool Settings,* Eighty-fourth Yearbook, Part I. Chicago: The University of Chicago Press, 1985.

———. *Individual Differences and the Common Curriculum,* Eighty-second Yearbook, Part I. Chicago: The University of Chicago Press, 1983.

———. *Staff Development,* Eighty-second Yearbook, Part II. Chicago: The University of Chicago Press, 1983.

Sarason, Seymour B. *The Culture of the School and the Problem of Change,* 2nd ed. Boston: Allyn and Bacon, Inc., 1982.

Tanner, Daniel, and Laurel N. Tanner. *Curriculum Development: Theory into Practice,* 2nd ed. New York: Macmillan Publishing Company, 1980.

Tanner, Laurel N. *Classroom Discipline for Effective Teaching and Learning.* New York: Holt, Rinehart and Winston, 1978.

U.S. Department of Education, *What Works: Research about Teaching and Learning.* Washington, D.C.: The Department, 1986.

Wirth, Arthur G. *Productive Work—In Industry and Schools.* Lanham, Md.: University Press of America, Inc., 1983.

Wittrock, Merlin C., ed. *Handbook of Research on Teaching,* 3rd ed. New York: Macmillan Publishing Company, 1986.

Name Index

Subject Index